The food and cooking of

MEXICO

South America and the Caribbean

The food and cooking of

MEXICO

South America and the Caribbean

Explore the vibrant and exotic ingredients, techniques and culinary traditions, with over 350 sensational step-by-step recipes with over 1450 photographs

Jane Milton, Jenni Fleetwood and Marina Filippelli

LORENZ BOOKS

This edition is published by Lorenz Books
Lorenz Books is an imprint of Anness Publishing Ltd
Hermes House, 88–89 Blackfriars Road, London SE1 8HA
tel. 020 7401 2077; fax 020 7633 9499; www.lorenzbooks.com; info@anness.com

UK distributor: Book Trade Services; tel. 0116 2759086; fax 0116 2759090;
uksales@booktradeservices.com; exportsales@booktradeservices.com
North American distributor: National Book Network; tel. 301 459 3366; fax 301 429 5746;
www.nbnbooks.com
Australian distributor: Pan Macmillan Australia; tel. 1300 135 113; fax 1300 135 103;
customer.service@macmillan.com.au
New Zealand distributor: David Bateman Ltd; tel. (09) 415 7664; fax (09) 415 8892

A CIP catalogue record for this book is available from the British Library.

Publisher: Joanna Lorenz
Editorial Director: Judith Simons
Editors: Jennifer Mussett, Joanne Rippin
Photographers: Nicki Dowey, Will Heap, Patrick McLeavey, Simon Smith and Janine Hosegood
Home Economists: Caroline Barty, Fergal Connolly, Joanne Craig, Annabel Ford, Tonia George and Lucy McKelvie
Stylist: Helen Trent
Designer: Nigel Partridge
Additional recipes: Rosamund Grant, Elisabeth Lambert Ortiz, Maggie Mayhew, Kate Whiteman

ETHICAL TRADING POLICY
Because of our ongoing ecological investment programme, you, as our customer, can have the pleasure and reassurance of knowing that a tree is being cultivated on your behalf to naturally replace the materials used to make the book you are holding. For further information about this scheme, go to www.annesspublishing.com/trees

Previously published in two separate volumes, *The Food and Cooking of the Caribbean, Central and South America* and *The Food and Cooking of Mexico*

10 9 8 7 6 5 4 3 2 1

NOTES

Bracketed terms are intended for American readers.

For all recipes, quantities are given in both metric and imperial measures and, where appropriate, measures are also given in standard cups and spoons. Follow one set, not a mixture, because they are not interchangeable.

Standard spoon and cup measures are level. 1 tsp = 5ml, 1 tbsp = 15ml, 1 cup = 250ml/8fl oz

Australian standard tablespoons are 20ml. Australian readers should use 3 tsp in place of 1 tbsp for measuring small quantities of gelatine, flour, salt etc.

Medium (US large) eggs are used unless otherwise stated.

ACKNOWLEDGEMENTS

Jane Milton would like to thank her mother for typing the recipes and her father for proof-reading them. She would also like to thank Tom Estes from Cafe Pacifico for sharing his knowledge of tequila and much more.

Jenni Fleetwood would like to pay tribute to Elisabeth Lambert Ortiz, Elisabeth Luard and Judy Bastyra, experts on the food and drink of Latin America and the Caribbean. She would also like to thank Jane Raphaely, and the 107ers for decades of support.

Marina Filippelli would like to thank her friends and family who were always present with suggestions, advice and a healthy appetite, especially Lizzie and Nick. Special mention also goes to her parents who instilled in her a love for the food and culture of Brazil.

Additional picture material provided by South American Pictures: pages 7–31.

CONTENTS

INTRODUCTION: A BRIEF HISTORY

Latin America and the Caribbean is a vast area comprising a large number of individual countries, each with diverse ways of preparing and serving food. The only thing they have in common is that they have all been subject to a Spanish or Portuguese influence, even if only, as is the case with some Caribbean islands, by way of exposure to their neighbours.

The events that led to the domination of the continent by two European powers began when Christopher Columbus petitioned for support for a voyage of discovery across the Atlantic in search of a sea route to India. At first he was turned down, but King Ferdinand and Queen Isabella of Spain eventually agreed to his request, largely out of a desire to find a new source for the spices the people of southern Spain had learned to love when under the control of the recently expelled Moors.

Columbus set sail on 3 August 1492, and in October of that year he reached Watling Island in the Caribbean. Convinced he had reached the Indies, he continued to Cuba and Hispaniola (now Haiti and the Dominican Republic). In 1500 the Portuguese explorer Pedro Cabral landed on the coast of Brazil, and two years later Columbus reached the South American mainland. The early explorers were not interested in conquest, but individuals such as Hernán Cortés and Francisco Pizarro were dedicated to it. During the 16th century they invaded Mexico and Peru respectively, while other parts of Latin America fell to other conquistadors. In the process, great civilizations were overthrown and the stage was set for the total take-over of the continent by Spain and Portugal.

It was Napoleon III, the 19th-century French emperor, who coined the term "Latin America" and applied it to those countries on the American continent where Spanish and Portuguese were spoken, including the Spanish-speaking Caribbean islands and Mexico. The term is now used to include all the islands.

The term "Latin America" suggests that nothing of value existed before the conquest, and it does not acknowledge the indigenous peoples nor the great civilizations – Maya, Aztec and Inca – they spawned. However, the term has value, if only as shorthand, in giving some indication as to the major cultural and culinary influences in this part of the world in the post-Columbian era.

NEW SETTLERS

When the first conquistadors landed in Latin America, they found many foreign ingredients. The most important of these was corn, which the indigenous peoples called *maïs*. Like wheat, corn could be used to make bread, but it was more versatile. The husks could be used as wrappers; the stalks for training beans; and the silks as ties. The cobs could be eaten fresh or stored for the winter.

Where corn and beans grew, so did squash. This remarkable food also kept well and yielded delicious seeds. Tomatoes were another important find, as were chillies. When Columbus first tasted a dish made using these fiery red and green pods, he assumed its heat came from black pepper and named the pods peppers.

The ships that brought the invaders sailed back to Spain laden with produce, then returned with settlers who brought their own bounty – cattle, pigs, sheep, wheat, sugar cane and nuts.

Below: The Caribbean islands and Central America have a vast coastline and fish and shellfish play an enormous part in their cuisines.

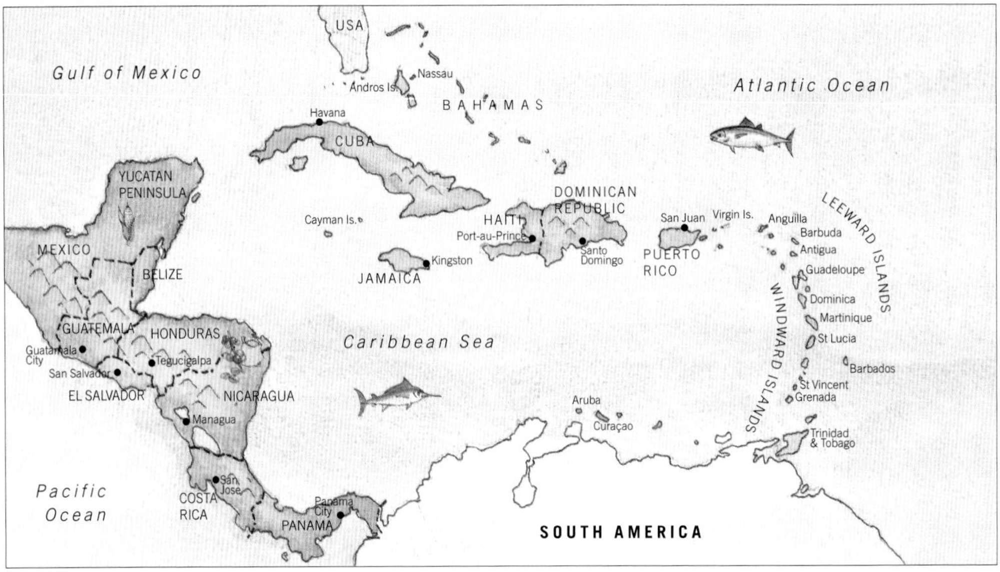

Priests came to Latin America too. Their aim was to convert the native population, but they also had valuable horticultural skills to pass on. The South American wine-making industries were started by priests who needed a ready supply of communion wine.

Lands were settled and crops were planted, but such activities required labour. At first the native population gave their assistance, but they soon rebelled. The situation grew worse with the *encomienda* system, which gave Spanish individuals land rights. The indigenous peoples were forced to work for no payment other than Spanish lessons and religious instruction. They were shockingly exploited and the work was hard, especially for those already weakened by disease. They died in their thousands.

SLAVES AND SETTLERS

The colonists responded by importing African slaves to work the burgeoning sugar plantations. The Africans made a huge contribution to the regional cuisines, especially in Brazil. The climate was similar to their homeland, so the many vegetables and fruits they brought with them flourished.

Below: Native South American ingredients are sold daily at a busy traditional vegetable market in Peru.

Above: Although the cuisines of Latin America differ from country to country, there are some common ingredients.

The Spanish and Portuguese settlers intermarried freely with indigenous and African women and, as a result, the *mestizo* ("mixed") population grew.

The food became *mestizo* too. Many of the cooks were either indigenous or African women, and they prepared a mixture of their own recipes plus the dishes their employers wanted. Spanish ingredients – such as onions, garlic and rice – were incorporated, and Spanish dishes were adapted to include chillies, tomatoes and even cocoa. This two-way trade led to a vibrant Latino cuisine, bursting with colour and flavour,

Other nations made a valuable contribution too. Indentured labourers from India, South-east Asia and the Far East have all contributed their own styles of cooking, and some Caribbean islands are, in culinary terms, forever England, France, Denmark or Holland, depending on their settlers.

Latin America is a turbulent part of the globe where the only certain thing is change; this is as true of the cuisine as anything else. Immigrants continue to introduce new dishes, and tourists take away memories of delicious meals they hope to recreate at home. This time the trade is between Latin America and the world. While pizza becomes commonplace in Brazil, ceviche is enjoyed in Canada, and Californian chefs hanker for *huitlacoche* (corn truffles).

Latin America still has secrets to divulge. In the jungles and hidden Andean valleys there are undoubtedly new ingredients waiting to be discovered. These will add another layer to a cuisine that is as exciting as it is extraordinary, and keeps on evolving.

MEXICO

Food is a very important aspect of the Mexican way of life. Producing and purchasing the raw materials, preparing food and eating it account for a large part of each day, and wonderful dishes are created to mark special occasions and celebrations.

SOME HISTORICAL INFLUENCES ON THE MEXICAN DIET

In pre-Columbian Mexico there was already an established pattern of agriculture. Foods such as corn (maize), beans, chillies and peppers were widely cultivated, along with avocados, tomatoes, sweet potatoes, guavas and pineapples. Vegetables such as *jicama*, *chayote* and *sapote* were also grown.

During the Mayan era, the priests, who were the ruling class, allocated land for the growing of crops. They also arranged for the storage of seed and the distribution of surplus food. The warlike Aztecs, who came to power in the 15th century, were less inclined to share. Their rulers appropriated food for themselves, including chocolate, which was made into a frothy drink, believed to be an aphrodisiac.

The Aztecs inherited a rich culinary tradition. The central market in Tenochtitlan was famous for its fabulous array of foods and it is reported that Montezuma often required of his servants that they prepare more than two dozen dishes daily for his delectation. The emperor would then stroll among the groaning tables, discussing the ingredients with his chefs, before making his selection. During the subsequent meal, young women, chosen for their beauty, would bring him hot tortillas and gold cups filled with frothy chocolate.

COLUMBUS COMES TO MEXICO

When the Spaniards first arrived in Mexico in 1492, they had few cooks with them, and so local people were hired to prepare food. Dishes made with corn, chillies, beans, tomatoes and chocolate were prepared and the Spaniards became particularly fond of chillies, chocolate and vanilla. With the Spanish came livestock, which was warmly welcomed. Until this time, the native turkeys and the occasional wild boar were the only source of meat.

The introduction of the domestic pig was significant not merely for its meat, but also for the lard, which was used for frying and became a staple ingredient in Mexican kitchens. Frying had not been possible before, due to the absence of animal fats and oils. The Spaniards began to adapt their own recipes to the local ingredients, and the local people in turn adapted their cooking to include meat, which had been such a rarity in the past. The fusion began.

Above: Corn cultivation in Mexico's pre-Columbian era. Mural by Diego Rivera.

Below: A modern mural by Diego Rivera showing pre-Columbian corn sellers.

In 1519 the Spanish adventurer Hernando Cortés landed near the site of present day Veracruz. Within three years he had conquered Mexico, and the country was ruled as a viceroyalty of Spain for the next three hundred years. Cortés portrayed himself as the liberator of the tribes oppressed by the Aztecs and used his fanatical missionary zeal to justify his own exploitation of the Mexicans. Monks and nuns were sent from Spain to convert the pagan Mexicans to Catholicism. When they reached the New World, these religious missionaries had more than missals in their luggage; they also brought seeds, and soon citrus fruit, wheat, rice and onions augmented the supplies that served the Mexican kitchen.

TEXAS IS LOST TO THE USA

Mexican independence from Spain was finally gained in 1821, after a lengthy war. Three years later, on the death of General Iturbide, a new republic was established. At that time Mexico possessed large tracts of land in what is

Above: Hernando Cortés, the Spanish conqueror of Mexico.

now the United States, including Texas. In 1836 Texas formed an independent republic, joining the USA some nine years later. This triggered the Mexican Civil War, as a result of which Mexico ceded to the United States all territories north of the Rio Grande. From a culinary perspective, this is significant, as it helps to explain the historic links between Mexico and the "Lone Star" State, and the origin of the Tex-Mex style of cooking. It also accounts for the popularity of the Mexican style of cooking in California and New Mexico.

FRENCH OCCUPATION OF MEXICO

The Civil War proved costly in financial terms, and put the country greatly in debt to France, England and Spain. When they could no longer repay the debt to France, that country seized the opportunity to take control of Mexico. Austrian-born Maximilian Hapsburg, a relative of Napoleon, was put in charge of the French occupation. The French met with considerable resistance and the *Cinco de Mayo* (5th May) holiday commemorates a famous Mexican victory over their forces. However, this success was short-lived, and France installed Maximilian as Emperor of Mexico in 1864. The French occupation lasted only three years, but left a lasting legacy in the beautiful breads and pastries for which Mexican cooking is now renowned. Following Maximilian's execution in 1867, Mexico experienced another period of unrest, but since 1920 has been more stable.

OTHER INFLUENCES

The Mexican culture is often described as "*mestizo*". The word means "a mixture" and was originally applied only to the offspring of ethnic peoples and Spanish invaders. Today it reflects many culinary influences from beyond its borders, such as the introduction of brewing by German settlers. The Germans also introduced a cheese, now called *queso de Chihuahua* after the town in northern Mexico where the settlers lived. The presence of many sweet-and-sour dishes in the Mexican cuisine reflects an Oriental influence, as does the Mexican classification of foods as "hot" or "cold". This has nothing to do with the temperature at which these foods are served, but relates instead to the effect they have on the body. "Hot" foods are considered to be easily digested and warming, whereas foods designated as "cold" are held to be difficult to digest and likely to lower body heat. Examples of hot foods are coffee, honey and rice, while fish, limes and boiled eggs would all be regarded as cold. A proper balance between hot and cold foods is believed to be vital for good health.

Mexican cuisine is sure to continue to evolve, adapt and embrace foreign influences. It is also likely to become more homogenous as regional recipes are absorbed in the national repertoire. Like its language, the food and eating habits of a country are never static.

Below: Maya Indians in traditional dress perform the dance of the Mestizos.

Regional Cooking in Mexico

Mexico has not one single cuisine, but many. It is a vast country, the third largest in Latin America, with a wide diversity of landscapes, from snow-capped mountains to citrus groves, and a distinct range of climatic zones. These geographical factors have helped to shape a variety of different styles of cooking within the same country. The extremely mountainous nature of the landscape led in the days before the Spanish Conquest to the development of a large number of isolated and completely distinct Indian communities, each with its own style of cooking. When the Spanish invaded, they certainly had a considerable impact on the cuisine in the areas where they were most active, but parts of the country remained impervious to their influence, and the people there continued to cook in much the same way as their parents and grandparents had done before them.

Above: Bananas and mangoes on sale in a street market in Chihuahua.

Even today, when tourism has introduced new ingredients and ideas, there remain pockets of Mexico where contact with the outside world is limited, and where old dishes, some of which hark back to Aztec times, are preserved.

The altitude, rather than the latitude, determines the climate in Mexico. The coastal region below 914m/3000ft is *tierra caliente* – the hot zone. Here the climate is sub-tropical, and mangoes, pineapples and avocados flourish. Next comes *tierra templada,* the temperate zone, which rises to 1800m/6000ft.

CULINARY REGIONS

Even in present-day Mexico, regional foods are still very apparent. This is due in some measure to the different climates, which mean certain things cannot grow in every area, or to favourable geographic locations: in Vera Cruz, a coastal area, fish dishes are prevalent. In the coming years this is likely to be eroded more as improved transportation allows products from the different regions to be transported more easily and quickly between areas.

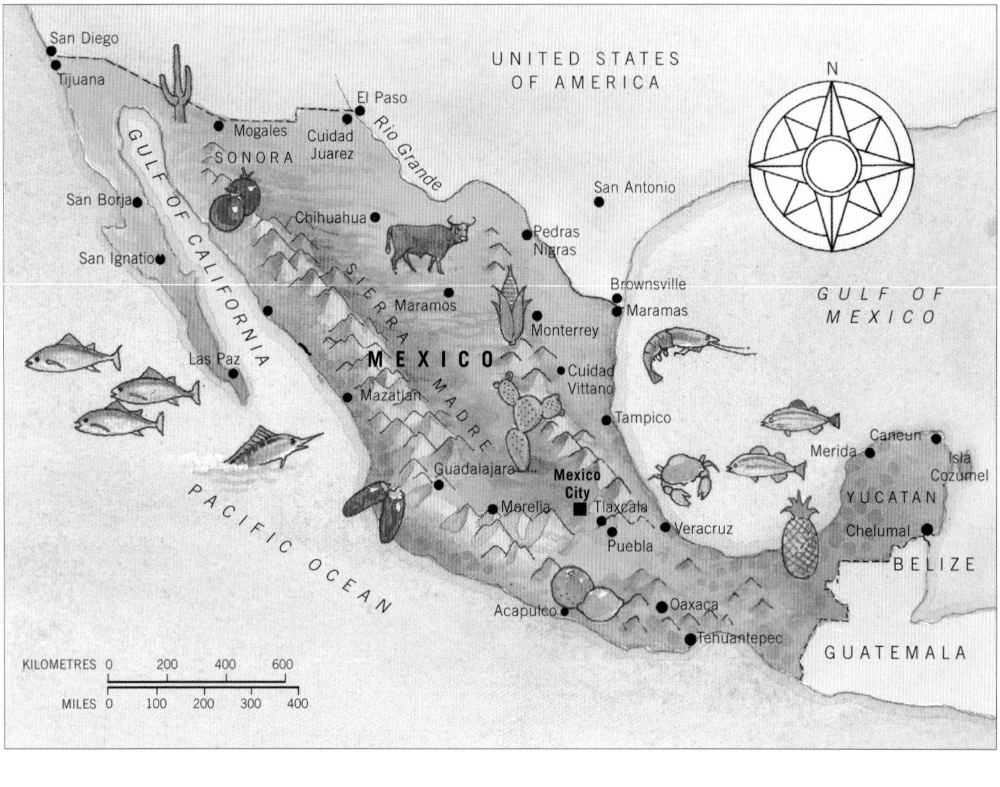

Above: Cooking tortillas in a Mexican street-cafe.

Many familiar vegetables and fruits are grown in Mexico, including green beans, peppers, tomatoes, cabbages, cauliflowers, onions, aubergines and courgettes. At the greatest altitude lies the cold zone (*tierra fria*).

These areas of Mexico are all very different from each other, and when it is considered that the rainfall varies from as little as 5cm/2in a year in the north-west to over 300cm/120in in parts of the south-west, it is easy to comprehend how so many diverse styles of cooking came to evolve. Better infrastructure may mean that the regionality of the cuisine will be eroded in time, but at the moment each region has a strong individual identity.

THE NORTH

The northern area of Mexico, stretching from Sonora, near the Gulf of California, to Monterrey in Nuevo León, has some striking contrasts. The mountain areas are sparsely populated and life here is very tough. Sonora and Chihuahua are the cattle rearing parts of Mexico. Good grazing encouraged the Spanish to establish herds of their hardy longhorns here, and specialities of the region include a beef stew called *Caldiddo* and the famous dried beef or *carne seca*. This is produced by first salting the beef, then drying it and finally treating it with lemon juice and pepper.

The ubiquitous beans are as popular in the north as they are elsewhere. A favourite dish of the local *charros* or cowboys is *frijoles* (beans), cooked with scraps of meat, chillies, herbs and spices over an open fire. So well loved is the dish that it is often served in homes and restaurants.

Monterrey is the industrial heart of the region. Brewing employs a large percentage of the population, and this is the home of *frijoles borrachos*, a dish that consists of beans cooked in beer with onion, spices and garlic. The flavour of the beer permeates the beans, earning them their name, which translates as "drunken beans".

The north of Mexico is also the main cheese-producing region. Cheese was introduced by monks who travelled with the Spanish conquerors. Chihuahua is known for *chiles con queso* – melted cheese with chilli strips.The greatest treasure of the north is the soft flour tortilla, produced here because this is the only part of Mexico where wheat is grown. Burritos, portable parcels of meat, beans and rice wrapped in wheat flour tortillas, are typical of this region.

Baja California is a peninsula in the north-western corner of the country, bordering the Pacific and the Gulf of California. It is the oldest continuously producing wine-making region of Mexico. In recent years the region's wines, particularly the whites, have won international acclaim.

THE COASTAL REGIONS

The northern Pacific coast has some magnificent beaches. The sea is well stocked with fish, especially bass, tuna and swordfish. *Ceviche*, that delicious dish made of raw fish "cooked" by the action of lime juice, is very popular in the region. It is often made from prawns or other local shellfish.

This area generally has good soil, and grains of various types are widely cultivated, as well as chillies and other vegetables. So famous are the tomatoes produced in this region that the state basketball team is called *Tomateros* (the tomato growers). There are a number of coconut plantations along the coast, and dishes such as coconut soup are popular. Further south is the state of Jalisco, the home of tequila. Red snapper are caught on this part of the coast and cooked over open fires.

Below: Maguey, *growing here in the Oaxaca valley, is used in tequila.*

Above: Strings of chillies drying in the sun on the Pacific coast of Mexico.

Inland is the colonial town of Guadalajara, famous for *pozole*, a pork stew thickened with hominy – yellow or white corn which has been dried and has had the husk and germ removed, and which has been eaten by the Indians in Mexico for centuries. Another speciality is *birria*, a stew made from lamb or kid.

Down the coast is Acapulco, a very cosmopolitan city with Latin, Oriental and indigenous Indian influences. The cuisine of this area – Oaxaca – has strong Spanish influences, but is also home to some of the most traditional Mexican dishes, such as the *moles* – gloriously rich meat stews which incorporate nuts and chocolate. This is orange country, too, and citrus fruit features strongly in the recipes of the region. *Asadero*, a supple curd cheese similar to the Italian cheese, *Provolone*, originated in Oaxaca.

Chiapas, the southernmost state bordering Guatemala, exhibits some influences from that country. Chillies are commonly served alongside dishes, as accompaniments, rather than as integral ingredients.

The eastern seaboard, lapped by the Caribbean Sea, is known as the Gulf Coast. The climate here is tropical, and this is reflected in the food. Bananas, vanilla, avocados, coffee and coconuts grow on the coast, mangoes and pineapples in the south, and to the north are orchards of apples and pears.

The Gulf Coast has abundant fish stocks. The southern state of Tabasco, on the isthmus of Tehuantepec, is particularly famous for its fish. The catch includes sea bass, striped bass, crabs, lobsters and prawns. The port of Veracruz has a famous fish market, with red snapper the local speciality. The cuisine in this area is rich, and many of the towns have lent their names to dishes or ingredients.

Below: A palm tree in Chetumal with coconuts ready for harvesting.

Above: Prickly pear cactus growing at Santa Bulalia.

In this part of Mexico, *tamales* (little filled parcels) are rolled in banana leaves, rather than the corn husks which are used elsewhere. Another local speciality is *jicama*, a crisp vegetable, which is served raw with a sprinkling of lime juice and ground chillies.

THE BAJIO, CENTRAL MEXICO AND MEXICO CITY

To the north of Mexico City is the Bajio, a fertile area bordered by mountains. This is sometimes referred to as Colonial Mexico, and many of the local specialities are distinctly Spanish in origin, such as stuffed tongues and rich beef stews. Traditional Mexican foods are to be found here too, especially *nopales* (cactus paddles) and prickly pears (cactus fruit). *Pulque* – the drink made from the juice of the agave (or century) plant – is popular in this area. Pork is the favourite meat, often served as *Carnitas*. These are pieces of pork which are cooked in lard flavoured with orange, until the outside of each piece is crisp, while the inside is beautifully tender and succulent.

Central Mexico, a land-locked area, lies to the south of Mexico City, and includes the towns of Puebla and Tlaxcala. Puebla is the home of the classic dish, *Chiles en Nogada*, which

consists of stuffed chillies dipped in batter, then fried and served with a walnut sauce. Puebla is also associated with the famous *Mole Poblano*, which was said to have been invented by nuns in a local convent. *Mole Poblano* is a wonderfully complex dish in which turkey or chicken is cooked in a paste made by mixing crushed dried chillies, cinnamon and cloves, with sesame seeds and ground nuts, as well as onion, garlic and sometimes tomatillos.

Tlaxcala, which means "the place of many tortillas" is a town renowned for its food. Chicken stuffed with fruit and nuts is one popular dish, while another consists of lamb cooked in agave leaves. Both are usually washed down with the local *pulque*.

Vast, sprawling and vibrant, Mexico City is one of the most cosmopolitan places on earth, a fact that is reflected in its food. It is often said that Mexicans love to eat and would eat all day if they could, and in Mexico City there is nothing to stop them. The streets are filled with vendors selling all sorts of snacks. Some offer tortas and tortillas filled with various meats (including the chorizo for which nearby Toluca is famous), cheeses, beans and chillies. Others sell *tamales*, *sopes* and tacos to the commuters who rush past on their way to work. Another item available on market stalls is *cuitlacoche*, a corn fungus which tastes like a flavoursome mushroom. This has been regarded as a delicacy since pre-Columban times. *Cuitlacoche* is cooked and used to fill *crepas* (crepes), which the Mexicans adopted into their cuisine after the French occupation in the 19th century.

Above: Dried chillies and other fruit for sale on the streets of Mexico City.

Below: Thick tortillas are served here with cooked meats, chillies and beans.

THE SOUTH

Although there are differences between all the regions of Mexico, it is in the Yucatán that these are most marked. This is partly due to the isolation of the area, which was for centuries cut off from the rest of the country by dense jungle and swampland. The Maya lived here before the conquistadors came to Mexico, and their influence on the cooking can still be seen, particularly in *pibil*-style dishes, which got their name from the *pib* or pit in which they were steamed in Mayan times.

Although the poor soil does not readily support agriculture, corn is grown in areas where the vegetation has been cut and burned, and is ground to make meal, *masa harina*, which is used for corn tortillas and a host of other Mexican dishes. The pungent herb *epazote* is used in the cooking of this region, imparting a distinctive flavour.

Good fish, squid and shellfish, including the large prawns for which the area is well known, are available all along the coast. *Ceviche* is a popular dish, and is made from several different types of fish and shellfish, either singly or in combination.

Huevos Motuleños, a dish of eggs with refried beans and tomato sauce, is a well known Yucatec dish. Also typical of the area are dry spice pastes, called *recados*. These are mixtures of dried spices and vinegar or citrus juice, which are rubbed on to meat before it is cooked. *Recados* are made throughout the country, but they are particularly popular in the Yucatán. Some include ground achiote seed (annatto powder), which is valued for the earthy flavour and bright yellow colour it imparts. Another hallmark of Yucatec cooking is the habañero, a fiery chilli which is grown exclusively in the region.

Below: A field of corn on the cob drying on the plants.

MEXICAN MEAL PATTERNS

Many of the traditional Mexican dishes are very labour-intensive, reflecting the old society where the women worked all day long collecting the food required and then preparing it. Today, despite industrialization, the traditional meal patterns are still observed, especially in rural areas. Most Mexicans still eat their main meal in the middle of the day, and follow it by a siesta. Even in the cities, where meals are beginning to conform to the international pattern of breakfast, lunch and dinner, the biggest meal of the day is still eaten at lunchtime.

Above: Women prepare the main family meal in a rural Mexican kitchen.

DESAYUNO

This is a light meal eaten first thing in the morning, soon after waking. It usually consists of a cup of coffee and a bread or pastry – perhaps *churros* or *pan dulce* (sweetened bread).

ALMUERZO

Having started work very early in the morning, most Mexicans are ready for something fairly substantial by about 11am. Almuerzo is more brunch than breakfast, and usually includes an egg dish such as *Huevos Rancheros* or scrambled eggs with salsa and cheese. Tortillas are served, and coffee, milk or fruit juice washes everything down.

Above: Prickly chayote, *used in Mexican salads and vegetable dishes.*

Below: Green chillies for sale in a Mexican market.

COMIDA

This is the main meal of the day, generally eaten at a leisurely pace from about 3pm. The meal is made up of several courses. Soup is almost always served, and this is followed by a rice or pasta dish. The aptly named *platillo fuerte* – the phrase means "heavy dish" – is the main attraction. This dish is accompanied by tortillas, salad and pot beans or Refried Beans. The clay pot used to cook the pot beans – *Frijoles de Olla* – adds flavour to them. Garlic, coriander, onion and stock with chillies are additional ingredients, and cream or cheese is stirred in just before serving. The meal closes with *postre* (dessert) and an after-dinner coffee.

MERIENDA

A light supper, this is often made up from the leftovers of the lunchtime *comida* dishes, which are wrapped in a tortilla to make a burrito. If a more substantial meal is required, a stew or *mole* might be served, with *Cafe con Leche* or hot chocolate to follow the food. *Merienda* is usually eaten between 8 and 9pm.

CENA

This more elaborate meal – dinner – is served when entertaining guests in the evening or on special occasions. It replaces the *merienda* and is made up of two or three courses served any time between 8pm and midnight.

THE MAIN EVENT

Comida – the main meal of the day – provides the perfect opportunity for relaxing with family or friends. Here are some suggestions of suitable dishes to serve at this time:

SOPA

A hearty soup would not be appropriate, as this is the prelude to a large meal. *Thalpeno*, a thin soup with chicken and avocado, would be ideal, as would a cold coconut soup.

SOPA SECA

Translating as "dry soup" this is actually a rice or pasta dish, served after the conventional soup and before the main course. Rice or vermicelli is cooked in a little oil and then simmered in a broth with onions, garlic, tomatoes and other vegetables. Most of the liquid used is

absorbed by the rice or pasta, hence the name. The rice dishes vary – peas are sometimes added to the basic recipe, and coriander and chillies are used to make the popular "Green Rice". In another variation, yellow rice is flavoured and coloured with achiote (annatto), a golden colouring made from the ground seeds of a flowering tree.

PESCADO Y LEGUMBRES

Sometimes a fish course is served before the main dish. Typically this would be *Ceviche* – raw fish "cooked" by the action of lime juice. Alternatively, a vegetable dish might be offered; perhaps a native vegetable such as *jicama*, served as a salad with a chilli and lime dressing. Plantains are also popular, and either these or courgettes might be fried along with cheese and green chillies.

PLATILLO FUERTO

The "heavy dish" is typically a stew, served with corn tortillas and a salad. Meatballs in a tomato and chilli sauce is one option; pork with green cactus sauce another. A fisherman's stew of mussels, prawns and cod would also be suitable. For the accompaniment, a cactus or *chayote* salad would be ideal, or a fresh-tasting salsa of *rajas con limon* – strips of chilli and lime.

Above: A family eating their main meal in an open-air restaurant in Mexico City.

FRIJOLES

Cooked dried beans are an inevitable – and important – part of the main meal. Traditionally, they formed a very big part of the staple diet of the indigenous people, so the number and variety of bean dishes is exhaustive. Most people, if asked to name a Mexican bean dish, suggest Refried Beans, which is all too often a flavourless mush of badly seasoned pinto beans. The home-cooked equivalent couldn't be more different: tender beans deliciously flavoured with bay leaves, garlic and chillies. Equally delicious are pot beans, *Frijoles de Olla* – dry pinto beans put into a pot and cooked very slowly with water and a little lard until they melt in the mouth. These are traditionally served with Guacamole, salsa, soured cream and crumbled fresh cheese.

POSTRE Y CAFE

After such a heavy meal, the dessert often consists of a fruit platter or a simple, refreshing *Flan* – similar to a crème caramel. A cake made from ground pecan nuts and honey is another favourite. *Comida* traditionally concludes with a drink of coarsely ground coffee sweetened with *piloncillo* (the unrefined dark brown cane sugar typical of Mexico) and stirred with a cinnamon stick. A delicious alternative, which packs rather more punch, is coffee with a shot of Kahlúa or tequila.

SNACK FOODS

Mexicans love to snack. Street food is very popular throughout the country. In towns, stalls equipped with steamers sell *tamales* – little corn husk parcels filled with spiced meat or cheese – from first thing in the morning, so that shift workers can still have their *almuerzo* even if they cannot get home. Later in the day, the stalls sell corn soup or *menudo*, a soup made with tripe. Still more stalls are set up at lunchtime by women who serve home-made food to the workforce. The food is very similar to what would be eaten at home: soup, rice or pasta dishes, stews with tortillas or bread, and desserts. In the evening, the stalls sell *quesadillas*, enchiladas and *antojitos* (little whims or nibbles). On the coast, traders sell prawns on skewers, *Ceviche* (marinated raw fish) threaded on sticks or *elotes* – tender cobs of cooked corn dipped in cream and sprinkled generously with well-flavoured crumbly cheese.

Below: Corn on the cob is cooked and sold as a snack in street stalls.

MEXICAN FEASTS AND FESTIVALS

Long before Christianity came to Mexico, the Indians worshipped gods whom they believed provided their food. The Aztecs were convinced that the world would come to an end unless the gods were constantly propitiated with prayers, sacrifices and rituals. Corn (maize) was regarded as a divine gift – a miraculous staple food which grew in all climates and soils.

Feast days, when people cooked particular dishes or brought specific foods as offerings to the gods, were frequent events. When Christianity spread through Mexico many of these days were appropriated by the Church and either assigned as saints' days or linked to celebrations marking important days in the religious calendar.

JANUARY 6TH – *DÍA DE LOS SANTOS REYES*

As the culmination of two weeks of Christmas festivities, January 6th marks the meeting between the Magi – the Three Kings – and the infant Jesus. Mexicans commemorate that exchange of gifts with ceremonies of their own, and this is the day on which Christmas presents are given and received. Central to the celebration is King's Day Bread, a yeasted sweet bread ring filled with crystallized fruit, covered with icing and decorated with candied fruit jewels.

Right: Maya Indians in traditional dress perform a bottle dance.

Below: A Mexican dancer wearing a Spanish-influenced traditional dress.

FEBRUARY – CARNIVAL

The weekend before the beginning of Lent sees the beginning of a five-day carnival, a final fling before the period of self-denial. Processions of brightly coloured floats, dancing in the street and feasting are all characteristic of this celebration.

APRIL – *SEMANA SANTA*

Holy week – the period leading up to Easter Day – is an important time in the Mexican calendar, particularly for the many Catholics in the country. One custom peculiar to Mexico is the breaking of confetti-filled eggs over the heads of friends and family.

MAY 5TH – *CINCO DE MAYO*

This day commemorates the defeat of the French army at the Battle of Puebla in 1862. After the defeat Napoleon sent 30,000 soldiers into the country, and after a year the French had taken power. *Cinco de Mayo* is of particular importance in the state of Puebla, but is celebrated in other parts of the country and in some American states with large Mexican populations such as southern central California and Texas. Nowadays the holiday is a celebration of Mexican culture, drink and music.

Above: Sugar skulls on sale for the celebration of one of Mexico's most important festivals, The Day of the Dead.

SEPTEMBER 16TH – MEXICAN INDEPENDENCE DAY

A holiday to mark the day in 1810 when the revolt against Spanish rule began. Outside Mexico, the festival is often promoted by commercial outlets, such as Mexican restaurants and bars.

NOVEMBER 1 & 2 – *LOS DÍAS DE LOS MUERTES*

Commonly called The Day of the Dead, this is in fact a two-day festival, that combines in one both the ancient Aztec tradition of worship of the dead and the Christian festival of All Saints' Day.

The festival originally came about because of a widely held belief that the souls of the dead are permitted to spend a brief period on earth every year – like a holiday – to give their families a chance to spend time with them. Family members gather at the graveside, bringing the favourite foods of the deceased person, as well as other symbolic dishes that are traditionally eaten on this day. The foods include a sweet pumpkin dessert and *tamales*. At the grave candles are lit, incense is burned, special prayers are said and the food and drink are eaten in a party atmosphere. Although the festival commemorates the dead, it is seen by everyone as a joyous occasion. The Mexican attitude is that life is to be lived to the full, and death is simply a part of the cycle.

DECEMBER 25TH – *NAVIDAD*

For 12 days before Christmas Day, the festival is heralded by processions – called "*posadas*" – depicting Joseph, with Mary on the donkey, searching for a room at the inn. Christmas Day sees the start of a two-week family holiday for most Mexicans. On the afternoon of the day itself families share a special meal. This traditionally starts with the sharing of the *rosca* – a sweet ring-shaped loaf with a small ceramic doll representing the infant Jesus baked inside it. Whoever finds the doll in their slice of cake must host a party on February 2nd, *Día de Candelaria* (Candlemas). The high point of the Christmas feast is the main course, when *Mole Poblano*, a rich turkey dish made with chillies, nuts, tomatoes, garlic, cinnamon and chocolate is served. It is accompanied by *tamales blancos* – corn husk parcels filled with a flavoured mixture that is based on white cornmeal.

Below: A shop window advertises "bread of the dead" for the festival.

MEXICAN WEDDINGS

These almost always take place in church. It is traditional for the bride and groom to be united during the ceremony with a *lazo* – a large rosary which is wrapped around them both. Gold or silver coins, a Bible and a rosary are given to the couple during the service by the "*padrinos*", a man and woman especially chosen by the bride and groom for this task. The coins symbolize prosperity. Mexican wedding cookies are served at the subsequent feast. Made from almonds and butter, baked and then sprinkled with icing sugar, these have a shortbread-like texture.

THE CARIBBEAN

A culinary cruise around the Caribbean is richly rewarding, enjoying the ubiquitous fresh fish. Having feasted your eyes on sparkling turquoise seas, palm-fringed beaches, green velvet mountains and exquisite gardens, you can dine on dishes that are as diverse as the islands themselves. These islands offer some of the best seafood in the world, plus fragrant stews, spicy side dishes, unusual salads and sweet treats such as coconut ice cream and luxurious Caribbean fruit and rum cake.

EARLY HISTORY

The earliest inhabitants of the Caribbean islands were the Ciboney, hunter-gatherers who had themselves migrated from northern South America. They were supplanted by the Taino, Arawak-speaking fishermen and farmers, who in turn were harried by the warlike Caribs in a pattern that would be repeated again and again down the centuries as nation after nation fought for control of the islands.

The Taino were peace-loving people who lived in small communities and grew cassava, corn, squash, (bell) peppers, beans, sweet potatoes and yams – crops that remain the mainstay of the Latin American diet. Those who lived on the coast caught fish, which they often ate raw, and their diet was supplemented with ducks, turtles, snakes and small rodents.

The arrival of Christopher Columbus in 1492 spelled the beginning of the end for the Taino. Many of them succumbed to diseases, such as measles and smallpox, never before seen on the islands. Others died in the service of Spanish settlers who worked them cruelly on the land and digging for gold. The Caribs fared a little better. Most of them were now confined to the more eastern islands, and their fierce reputation and remote location acted as a deterrent to would-be settlers. However, by the end of the 16th century, only a handful of the former inhabitants of the islands remained.

In their place came Spanish, English, French and Dutch settlers, the latter occupying the islands that Christopher Columbus had overlooked: Aruba, Curaçao and Bonaire. These islands, which would eventually become part of the Dutch Antilles, were "discovered" in 1499 by Alonso de Ojeda, one of Amerigo Vespucci's henchmen, and settled first by the Spanish and then by Dutch traders in the first half of the 17th century. The British and French, meanwhile, were becoming solidly entrenched in the Caribbean. Having already taken St Christopher (St Kitts) in 1623, the British quickly set up colonies on the islands of Nevis, Barbados, Antigua and Montserrat, while the French settled in Guadeloupe, Martinique and St Lucia.

Below: The Caribbean islands are very beautiful, lush and fertile.

Above: A local woman inspects the produce at a Caribbean street market.

SPANISH POSSESSIONS

The Spanish continued to dominate the most strategically important islands of Cuba, Jamaica, Puerto Rico and Hispaniola (modern-day Haiti and the Dominican Republic).

During the next 200 years, the islands of the Caribbean became pawns in the hands of the European powers. They sometimes changed hands so frequently that would-be settlers set sail from home in the belief that they would be ruled by their compatriots, only to discover on reaching their destination that it was now under the control of someone else. The island of St Martin, for instance, was tossed between Holland, Great Britain and France more than a dozen times, the shortest period of occupation being just 10 days. The island is still half Dutch and half French, which explains why it is today known by two separate names: Sint Maarten and Saint Martin.

Today, most of the islands have achieved autonomy from their European conquerors and have banded together to form Caricom, the Caribbean Community and Common Market.

Creole cooking

This term is used to describe many traditional Caribbean recipes. It generally refers to dishes that have their roots in both Europe and Africa, and is also used in Louisiana and some other southern states of the USA. There, Creole cooking has French, Spanish and African influences, whereas in the Caribbean, the Spanish and African influences are dominant. The expression *cocina criolla* is loosely applied throughout Latin America as a catch-all term for the native cuisine.

FOOD AND DRINK

The turmoil of the early years meant that recipes tended to do the rounds. The Spanish dish *pescado en escabeche* became known as eschovished fish, caveached fish or *escovitch. Callaloo*, a soup made from the leaves of a plant similar to spinach, is another successful migrant, being known variously as *le calalou, callilu, callau* and *calaloo.*

The French brought *bouillabaisse* to the islands, even though the fish used in the Caribbean version is very different from that found off the coast of Brittany. On Dominica and Montserrat they found frogs so large that their local name – mountain chicken – does not seem inappropriate. These French settlers wasted no time in teaching local cooks how to prepare frog's legs.

The Danes contributed recipes such as herring gundy, a dish of salt herring with potatoes, peppers and onion, and *croustadas*, which resemble savoury waffles. From the Dutch came *erwensoep* – a hearty pea soup – and the utterly delicious stew cooked within a whole cheese, *keshy yena.*

Made from fermented sugar cane, some of the world's best rums are still produced in the Caribbean, and rum cocktails are always a popular choice.

Below: Hard-working Caribbean fishermen bring the daily catch ashore, ready to be sold at market.

Above: Sugar cane is a major export for the region; the annual harvest in Cuba is exhausting but rewarding work.

NEW CROPS

It is widely believed that Columbus planted the first sugar cane on the Caribbean islands. By the start of the 17th century, the crop's huge potential was being fully appreciated, and large sugar-cane plantations had been established, together with plantations of other crops new to the islands, such as bananas, plantains, coffee, coconuts and oranges.

Growing all of these new crops required a large amount of labour, and since the indigenous population had been largely wiped out, this led to the importation of slaves on a massive scale. They arrived in their thousands, enduring dreadful journeys by sea and harsh lives after reaching their destination. The slaves often had to subsist on dried fish or meat alone, since they were forbidden from raising cattle and denied the opportunity to catch fresh fish. The many traditional Caribbean dishes based on salt cod, such as Jamaican salt fish and ackee, originated during this period. The slaves, who came mainly from West Africa, introduced ingredients such as yams and okra, which were quickly incorporated into the Caribbean cuisine. They improved their bland diet even further by the imaginative use of spices, laying the foundation for the hot pepper sauces that would become synonymous with the islands in years to come.

When slavery was eventually abolished in the 1830s, indentured labourers from the Middle East, India and the Far East were brought to the islands; these labourers introduced yet more ingredients to the melange that is Caribbean cooking. Spicy curries and dishes such as lamb pelau entered the repertoire, along with *roti* and *dhal puri*, large flat breads filled with curried meat, fish or potatoes.

Today it is mainly tourism that drives the economy of the Caribbean islands. Although this has had some negative effects on the local cuisine, mainly due to the introduction of the "international menu" that some travellers demand, it has also stimulated interest in regional specialities. The more dynamic Caribbean chefs are revelling in the wonderful ingredients that are at their disposal, especially the superb seafood on offer all year round. New and exciting dishes continue to emerge alongside old favourites.

STREET FOOD AND SNACKS

Snacking is a popular pastime on the Caribbean islands, which goes some way towards explaining the abundance of food available from roadside stalls and bars, or beach vendors. In fact, street food accounts for 20–30 per cent of urban household expenditure on the islands. Whatever the time of day, wherever you are, tasty morsels can be found to satisfy your hunger pangs.

Among the items traditionally offered by street vendors are deliciously light fritters, made from conch, salt cod or perhaps split peas, with spring onions (scallions) or chillies for extra flavour. Barbecued jerk chicken is another favourite, and for easy eating and instant gratification you cannot beat a bowl of crispy plantain and sweet potato chips or lightly cooked coconut king prawns, served with a glass of ice cold beer or one of the rum cocktails for which the islands are famous.

The quintessential Caribbean fast food, enjoyed by locals and tourists alike, is *roti*, a large flat bread with a tasty curried filling such as conch, goat or a selection of vegetables. Plantain dumplings are also a popular choice.

Below: In Havana, Cuba, a street vendor prepares sausages, delicious stuffed pastries and fried potatoes.

Above: The "Day of Kings" festival, which celebrates African gods, is a time for partying on the streets of Cuba.

FEASTS AND FESTIVALS

Carnival is the highlight of the year on the Caribbean islands. The build-up begins with the calypso season, which starts in January, then as Ash Wednesday approaches, signalling a period of sobriety and self-control, the streets ring to the sound of steel bands. In Aruba and Trinidad and Tobago, Carnival is a particularly extravagant affair. Local festivals are also held throughout the year. Puerto Rico commemorates the island's African-American heritage every June, and Jamaica has a popular reggae festival in July. Saints' days are always a good excuse for a celebration too, and they inevitably offer the opportunity to sample local food.

Special occasions are often marked by the roasting of a suckling pig. Slow roasting and regular basting ensures that the meat is beautifully tender, but the best part for many diners is the stuffing. This varies from island to island and from cook to cook, often being made to a recipe that is a closely guarded secret. It may be hot and spicy, fresh and fruity or made from offal, with the heart, liver and kidneys of the pig mixed with sausage, onions and herbs. Rum or brandy is often added to give an extra kick.

No festival would be complete without food, and traditional Caribbean festival fare, available from street vendors, includes fish cakes, Jamaican saltfish fritters ("stamp and go"), and rice and peas. More adventurous regional delicacies include *griot* (hot Haitian fried pork), jerked chicken and curried goat. Street-side food vendors can often be seen serving up more exotic foods, including fresh catfish and red snapper, Thai noodles or Mexican empanadas. In addition, hot dogs, sweets (candy), fresh fruit smoothies, soft drinks, ice-cold beer and rum cocktails are always popular.

The rum tradition

Not much goes on in the Caribbean that doesn't involve rum. It was developed in the 16th century by colonists who distilled molasses to trade for slaves in Africa. From here it was sent north to European markets, where a Spanish wine merchant, Facundo Bacardi, developed a process of charcoal filtering, to make rum taste better. Bacardi is now the leading brand of white rum and the best-selling spirit worldwide. Aged rum is darker, taking on the colour of the barrel in which it ages. It has a mellower taste that makes it perfect for sipping. Not all dark rums are aged, however – some have colour and flavour additives. There are dozens of rum cocktails available throughout the Caribbean. Three favourites are the daiquiri, the mojito and the pina colada.

BRAZIL

Whether it is because it is the largest country in South America or because of its rich cultural and racial diversity, Brazil is a place that celebrates excess. The Brazilian people love to eat, love to drink and love to dance. A trip to this, the only Portuguese-speaking country in South America, is a glorious assault on of the senses, and never more so than during Carnival, when the streets throb with the sounds of samba music and the vibrant colours of the costumes fizz like the fireworks that explode overhead. The food is just as exciting. Sample delicious seafood in Rio de Janeiro, unusual pork dishes in Minas Gerais, tender beef in Rio Grande or the spicy specialities of Bahia, where Africa meets South America in an explosion of unusual and fiery spices.

Below: The Amazon river and rainforest cover much of Brazil and are home to many unusual species and crops.

EARLY HISTORY

Some 50,000 years ago primitive peoples crossed from Asia to America by way of the Bering Strait land bridge and began the long trek south. Nobody knows for certain quite when they reached South America, but hunter-gatherers were certainly enjoying the fruits of the Amazon basin by 8000BC. Fish, manatees, turtles, game animals and birds were plentiful, and they supplemented their diet with cassava (*manioc*), nuts and fruits that grew in the area. Some migrated to the coast and survived mainly on shellfish, as is evident from the huge shell mounds that they left behind.

Above: Coffee berries are picked by hand when ripe, then exported around the globe in huge quantities.

Brazil did not have the great civilizations that evolved in Central America and the west of the continent. Instead, as the indigenous people abandoned their nomadic lifestyle for farming, settled communities or chiefdoms were established. As well as cassava, corn, sweet potatoes and squash were grown, often on the shell mounds left by their predecessors. The existence of these early settlers was not as peaceful as it sounds, however. At least one of the tribes, the Tupinambá, were cannibals who not only ate their enemies, but fattened them up first.

PEDRO CABRAL

In 1500, the Portuguese explorer, Pedro Cabral, claimed Brazil for Portugal, but he only stayed long enough to erect a cross, say a few prayers and take on board his ship some unusual wood that yielded a red dye – *pao Brasil*. His compatriots at home were not very excited about this new territory, but Portuguese merchants considered that the wood might be worth exploiting, and a few expeditions were mounted to cut down the trees. Trading stations were gradually set up along the coast to the north and south of Salvador de Bahia, and the country came to be known by the same name as the wood, Brazil.

In the beginning, these Portuguese settlers and the indigenous peoples co-existed amicably enough, but when what had been a minor timber operation began to escalate into a mass export operation, the natives began to withdraw their labour. They were even less enthusiastic about working on the many sugar plantations that had been established from the middle of the 16th century onwards. The Portuguese settlers tried to force the native South Americans by enslaving them, but so many died from exhaustion or disease that the plantation owners began to import African slaves instead.

SUGAR AND THE SLAVE TRADE

By the time slavery was finally abolished in Brazil towards the end of the 19th century, around four million African slaves had made the terrible journey from their native land to Brazil. Many did not even survive the long crossing, and many others died shortly after their arrival on the plantations (*engenhos*) where sugar was grown and processed.

A few successfully escaped to form their own secret communities, known as *quilombos*, while others survived their bondage by focusing on keeping alive their music, culture and religion, and cooking food similar to that which they enjoyed at home. It was the Africans who originally introduced ingredients such as black-eyed beans (peas), okra and yams to Latin America, and these thrived in a climate that was quite similar to that of West Africa. Food was used for purposes of ritual as well as sustenance, and some of the recipes cooked throughout Brazil today evolved from the foods prepared by African priestesses to offer to their gods.

Dendê oil

African slaves transported to Brazil initially missed one of their favourite ingredients, dendê oil, which comes from the fruit of the African oil palm and is valued for its rich orange-red colour. Fortunately, they soon discovered that a similar colour could be obtained by adding crushed annatto (achiote) seeds to ordinary oil. Dendê oil is now widely used in Brazilian cooking, especially in Bahia, where the African influence is strongest.

Above: In more cosmopolitan cities such as Rio, every imaginable cuisine from around the world is available.

GOLD RUSH

In the late 17th century, Brazilian explorers, known as *bandeirantes*, began to find gold in the mountain streams to the north of Rio de Janeiro. The ensuing gold rush led to a boom time in Brazil. Despite the relative inaccessibility of the main goldfields, new towns quickly began to spring up in the area that would later come to be known as Minas Gerais (which translates as "general mines").

Prospectors travelled to this area from all over Europe, hoping to make their fortune. Many of the country's sugar-cane planters also joined the gold rush, taking their slaves with them.

Several years later, around 1720, diamonds were also discovered in the region, and for about a century, Brazil became the world's major supplier of both gold and diamonds. To this day, Minas Gerais remains one of the richest areas in the country.

THE ROYAL COURT

In 1808, after the occupation of Portugal by the French, the Portuguese royal court decamped to Rio de Janeiro, making the city the new capital of their empire. When King Dom João VI finally returned to Spain in 1821, he left his son Dom Pedro I behind to rule Brazil. Dom Pedro I was subsequently recalled to Portugal, but he defied his father and the Portuguese government and declared Brazil's independence in 1822, with himself as Emperor.

GERMAN FARMERS

Dom Pedro's wife, Empress Dona Leopoldina, conceived the idea of peopling the vast area of southern Brazil with European farmers to work the land. Thousands of German colonists arrived and settled in the state of Rio Grande do Sul. In places such as Novo Hamburgo and Blumenau, their culinary contribution is evident and remains today, with sauerkraut, sausages, spätzle and delicious sweet pastries.

COFFEE – THE NEW CROP

In the century following independence, coffee replaced sugar as Brazil's premier export product. Further foreign immigration was encouraged for the purpose of having enough labour to work on the coffee plantations. Immigrants, especially Italians, quickly followed by Japanese, Spanish and Portuguese, flocked to cities such as Sao Paulo. Coffee was the major source of income for Brazil in the 1870s and the 1880s, and in 1889 the powerful coffee producers helped to bring about a military coup after which Brazil became a republic.

Below: Large freshwater catfish are displayed for sale at the busy Ver o Peso *market in the Amazon.*

Above: The traditional Brazilian Saturday lunch is feijoada completa, *a meal of meats, rice, beans, greens and farofa.*

FOOD AND DRINK

There is a wide variety of food on offer throughout Brazil. In the coastal belt, where the majority of the population lives, cosmopolitan cities such as Rio de Janeiro, Salvador and Sao Paulo have every type of restaurant imaginable to choose from, including those that specialize in regional cuisine.

Among the specialities is *feijoada completa*, not so much a dish as a lavish feast. A huge platter of fresh and smoked meats, including pig's tongue, is flanked by black beans, rice, spring greens, farofa (flavoured toasted cassava flour), orange slices and several sauces, all washed down with *caipirinha*, which is a mixture of *cachaça*, sugar and lime. Although they have a burgeoning wine industry in the temperate south, Brazilians prefer to drink iced beer or *cachaça*, which is often mixed with fruit juice or milk.

Rice is grown in Brazil and is the most widely used accompaniment, along with the ubiquitous farofa. In coastal areas, fine seafood is on offer.

REGIONAL CUISINES

There are four main regional cuisines in Brazil, plus the cooking of the Amazon region, where roasted game, exotic freshwater fish and unusual fruits can be encountered.

Comida Mineira is the cuisine of Minas Gerais. For over a century Minas Gerais was the wealthiest part of Brazil, and it is still rich in minerals. Farming is also important there. Crops include corn, beans, coffee and fruit, and there are large herds of beef and dairy cattle. Pork is the favourite meat, especially *lombo*, pork fillet or tenderloin. Bean dishes are also typical of the region, a favourite being *tutu*, which consists of black beans cooked with cubes of bacon and cassava flour and served with meat. Minas Gerais is also well known for its cheeses.

The well-travelled chilli

When African slaves introduced the malagueta chilli to Brazil, few people realized it was a returning immigrant. It originated in Central America, was taken to the northern hemisphere by the Spanish and eventually found its way to West Africa, finally returning to the continent of its birth in the baggage of slaves bound for Brazil.

Comida Baiana is perhaps the best known style of cooking in Brazil, celebrating that province's connection with Africa. Popular ingredients here include okra, dendê oil, dried shrimp, coriander (cilantro), coconut milk and lots of fresh seafood. A popular snack is *acarajés*, tasty bean patties or fritters, split and filled with various sauces. *Moqueca* is an aromatic dish of seafood, tomatoes, (bell) peppers, fresh coriander (cilantro) and dendê oil, invariably served with farofa to soak up the delicious coconut sauce. Brazilians like to finish a meal with fresh fruit. Desserts tend to be very sweet and are often based on custards in the Portuguese style. Avocado is often served as a mousse or ice cream.
Comida do Sertão is the cuisine of the vast plateau in the north-east of Brazil and can be sampled in the country's capital, the purpose-built city of Brasília. Dried salted meat – *carne seca* – comes from this region and beans are used in hearty meat dishes. Pumpkins, peppers and corn also feature, along with exotic fruits such as guavas, mangoes and carambolas. Favourite sweetmeats of the region include candied orange peel and candied figs.

Below: A Bahiana street vendor prepares local delicacies for passers-by, including acarajés, *delicious fried bean fritters.*

Comida Gaúcha means meat and plenty of it. This describes the cooking style of the vast Brazilian cattle country down south. A big feature of this area are the popular *churrascarias* – restaurants where you can sample almost every cut of meat imaginable, including all types of offal and a wide variety of delicious sausages.

Above: Brazil is renowned for its spectacular Mardi Gras carnival, when everyone takes to the streets to party.

STREET FOOD AND SNACKS

Brazilians like to be able to eat wherever and whenever the whim takes them, so street food is always on offer. This ranges from simple hot dogs, hamburgers and toasted cheese sandwiches to the filled bean or cheese patties known as *acarajés*. Pastries on offer include *pastels, esfihas* and *empadinhas*, which are baby empanadas stuffed with a variety of delectable fillings, such as fresh palm hearts in a tasty savoury sauce.

FEASTS AND FESTIVALS

The main celebration of the year throughout Brazil is *Carnaval*. Rio de Janeiro is the city usually associated with this extravaganza, but Brazilians often prefer to celebrate by taking part in the less touristy but equally electric spectacles in cities such as Salvador, Recife and Olinda. The build-up to *Carnaval* begins soon after Christmas and reaches its peak as Lent begins.

ARGENTINA, URUGUAY AND PARAGUAY

The cuisines of these three countries have one major ingredient in common – beef. Argentines eat a great deal of it and Uruguayans eat even more. It is less popular in Paraguay, but even there you will often find barbecues piled high with tender steaks, ribs and parts of animals that you never knew existed. Few ethnic dishes survive in these countries, except in Paraguay, where the indigenous Guaraní once lived. Their traditional crops – cassava, corn and sweet potatoes – are still staples.

EARLY HISTORY

Although this part of South America was claimed by Spain in the early part of the 16th century, there was no rush to colonize the territory. The first of the explorers to come ashore, Juan Días de Solís, was attacked by hostile natives and – according to some records – eaten. This was a powerful deterrent, although it did not prevent one of the survivors of the expedition from pressing on to Paraguay and then Bolivia. Here he acquired some silver, which was discovered after his death on the return journey. This sparked a rumour that Spain's recent acquisition might hold riches. The country was christened Argentina, meaning "place of silver", but when reality failed to match rumour the Spanish lost interest. In any event, by 1531 they were preoccupied with Peru, where gold and silver was being "liberated" from the Inca Empire by Francisco Pizarro.

The first permanent settlements in Argentina were in the Andean valleys close to the border. Santiago del Estero, Tucumán and Córdoba were established in 1535. A year later, Pedro de Mendoza set up camp close to the Rio de la Plata, on a site that would one day become Buenos Aires. His hopes of founding a city were dashed, however, when natives attacked and he was forced to decamp to Uruguay.

Until the arrival of the Spanish, this part of South America was peopled by various tribes of hunter-gatherers turned farmers, growing crops such as corn, cassava, sweet potatoes, beans and peppers. Coastal peoples supplemented their diet with food from the sea – fish, shellfish and even seals. There were no great civilizations in this area, like those that existed in Peru or Central America. Pottery, stone carvings and rock paintings survive, but few of the inhabitants themselves withstood the arrival of the Europeans. War and disease quickly decimated their numbers, and by the end of the 19th century, very few of the early people remained.

Below: Gauchos on an Argentine cattle ranch demonstrate their riding skills for Dia de la Tradicion.

Above: The different varieties of corn display many striking colours – here they have been left to dry in the sun.

THE PAMPAS

In 1581 the Spanish made a second attempt to establish a settlement on the banks of the Rio de la Plata in Argentina, and this time they succeeded. The extensive plains, or pampas, surrounding the place they called Buenos Aires proved to be incredibly fertile, and agriculture was rapidly established.

Cattle and horses that had escaped the original settlement had bred freely, and vast herds of animals now roamed across the pampas. This unexpected bounty was exploited by gauchos, or cowboys, who broke the horses and corralled the cattle. At first the animals were mainly killed for their hides, but when large salting plants were established in the early 19th century, the beef industry burgeoned. The pampas were fenced off and huge estates, *estancias*, were quickly established. Only the very rich could afford to buy these estates and soon the landed class became the most powerful people in Argentina.

In 1816 the country, for the first time, became independent. During the second half of the 19th century, demand for cheap food in Europe led to further expansion of the beef industry and immigrants poured in. Meat processing factories, including the famous Fray Bentos plant just across the river in Uruguay, were built. At the same time sheep farming was becoming established in Patagonia and by the early part of the 20th century, Argentina was a major exporter of beef and lamb, wheat and wool. These remain important today, although now much of the pampas is given over to grain and oil seed farming.

AN ARGENTINE ASADO

The traditional way of cooking meat in Argentina is *al asador* – on the spit. The meat is impaled on metal rods, which are stuck into the ground at an angle to prevent the meat juices from dripping on to the fire. Whole carcasses or sections of carcasses are cooked this way, and the meat is sliced off and served after guests have enjoyed the traditional appetizers – kidneys, morcilla and chorizo sausages, livers and *chinchulin* (loops of stuffed intestine).

Below: The herbal tea drink, yerba maté, *is drunk throughout Argentina, and is often served in a dried, decorated gourd.*

Above: In Buenos Aires, Argentina, a chef prepares large pieces of meat to be grilled at a traditional asado.

FOOD AND DRINK

With so much good quality beef at their disposal, it is not surprising that meals revolve mainly around meat, which is usually served with a piquant sauce, *chimichurri*. Fish is not as popular as meat, despite being in plentiful supply, and vegetables are not much in evidence either. Meat consumption is lower in Paraguay, which, along with northern Argentina, is the only area where ethnic cuisine is still widely served. Corn meal is used to make delicious spoonbreads and puddings. Cassava, which Paraguayans call *mandioca*, is baked with cheese and eggs or transformed into flat breads that resemble tortillas. The influence of indigenous cooks is also evident in Argentine dishes such as *carbonada criolla*, a stew served in a pumpkin; and *humitas*, a puréed corn mixture which is often steamed in corn husks.

Immigrants have exerted considerable influence on the food of Argentina and Uruguay. The pasta and pizzas in Buenos Aires and Montevideo are said to be as good as any in Italy, and the Italians also inspired an Argentine dish in which pork is baked in milk. The Spanish influence remains strong, but Middle Eastern, Chinese, Japanese and Korean settlers have also made their mark. In the beautiful Lake District, where the Andes provide a towering backdrop to towns that look more European than South American, visitors can sample delicious fondues, sweet pastries or the local chocolate.

Yerba maté, a type of herbal tea, is the drink of choice in Argentina, Uruguay and Paraguay, along with wine, beer and *caña*, a cane spirit.

STREET FOOD AND SNACKS

Empanadas with various fillings are popular, as are tiny cheese and ham sandwiches. Pastries are often very sweet, especially the ones that incorporate *dulce de leche* (caramelized milk). Churros, the Spanish answer to doughnuts, are enjoyed with hot drinks.

FEASTS AND FESTIVALS

The most interesting festivals in this area are those that focus on the gaucho tradition. These include demonstrations of riding skills and the opportunity to sample a traditional *asado*. In Montevideo, the summer *Carnaval* is famous for the African drumming that accompanies *candombe* dance troupes.

PERU, BOLIVIA AND ECUADOR

Many of the world's most popular foods come from the arable Andean highlands of Peru, Bolivia and Ecuador. Potatoes originated in this region, as did tomatoes, squashes, pine nuts, quinoa, tamarillos, sweet potatoes and several types of bean. All of these foods were cultivated by some of the most fascinating civilizations the world has ever seen.

EARLY HISTORY

Unlike Brazil and Argentina, where no major civilizations were based, this part of South America has been home to a succession of highly developed cultures. Among these were the Nasca of Southern Peru, who etched the soil with elaborate geoglyphs so large that their shapes – patterns, birds and animals – can only be fully appreciated from the air. In the north of the country, the Mochica people built impressive pyramids, while the Tiahuanuco established an empire that ruled Peru, Bolivia, Chile and Argentina for over 1,000 years. Shortly after their collapse towards the end of the 12th century, a Quechua tribe, one of many in the mountains, began to establish a power base in the area around Cuzco. Their leader, known as the Inca, was Manco Capac. Within 300 years the Inca empire stretched from Colombia to northern Chile and ruled over more than 15 million subjects. Aside from their military might, skilled governance and prodigious building skills, the Incas also improved farming by introducing terracing and irrigation, cultivating new crops such as cassava and peanuts, and elevating the already high status of corn by declaring that only the Supreme Inca himself could plant the first seed of the new season.

The Inca civilization endured until 1533, when Cuzco fell to the Spanish conquistador, Francisco Pizarro. Along with Ecuador and Bolivia, Peru (which at that time included the northern part of present-day Chile) became part of the Viceroyalty of Peru, administered first from Lima and then from Quito. A period of Spanish colonial rule followed, coming to an end when Peru declared its independence in 1821. Ecuador did the same thing a year later, and Bolivia followed in 1825.

Below: Corn grows in abundance on the Incan agricultural terraces in the Peruvian highlands.

FOOD AND DRINK

Their shared history, first as part of the great Inca empire and later under Spain, means that the countries of Peru, Ecuador and Bolivia share similar cuisines, though each country has its own specialities. The Spanish influence is most noticeable on the coast, while in the high Andes, Quechua people fought to preserve their customs, eschewing Spanish ingredients and cooking methods. Away from the big cities it is still possible to come across dishes that have changed little for centuries.

Potatoes are eaten extensively throughout this region. Cooks are fortunate in having a wide variety of potatoes to choose from, and they take great care in selecting the right type for the dish. The yellow Papa Amarilla, for instance, tastes great in *causa*, a Peruvian speciality, which has an infinite number of variations. One way of preparing it is to layer cooked potatoes with flaked fish, chopped tomatoes and avocado; another variation tops the potato with an onion sauce before garnishing it with hard-boiled eggs, lettuce, peppers and olives. Equally delicious is *ocopa arequipena*, in which cooked potatoes are covered in a spicy cheese and walnut sauce.

A typical Peruvian dish is *carapulcra*. Dried potatoes, a throwback to Inca days when potatoes were freeze-dried on top of the high mountains, then squeezed dry and placed in the sun until hard, are traditionally used for this dish, although fresh potatoes can be substituted if the dried variety are unavailable. Potato and cheese rissoles are extremely popular in Ecuador, while in Bolivia potatoes are often simply mashed with a little oil and lemon juice, then served with chopped cassava, locally known as *yuca*, and corn, both of which are staple foods.

One of the most fascinating Peruvian ingredients is quinoa, known as the "mother grain" by the Incas. The tiny grains have a mild, slightly bitter taste and firm texture, and should be cooked in the same way as rice. Quinoa is an excellent source of protein and can be added to stews, bakes or salads.

Above: At an Ecuadorian market in Otavalo, women in traditional costume buy fresh fruit and vegetables.

FISH AND MEAT

Bolivia is one of only two landlocked countries in Latin America. As a result, the inhabitants do not eat as much sea fish as their neighbours, but fresh fish in the form of trout from Lake Titicaca is very popular. Peruvians enjoy a wide variety of fish and are especially fond of corvina or striped bass. They also have access to excellent seafood. The Pacific seaboard is noted for its delicious ceviche, the dish famous for "cooking" the fish by marinating it in fresh citrus juices. Lime juice is usually used in ceviche but in Ecuador the juice of bitter oranges is preferred.

Although Peruvians produce beef and pork and enjoy both, they are particularly partial to duck and chicken and also like to eat *cuyes* (guinea pigs). These vegetarian animals are raised in much the same way as rabbits or hens, and smallholders will often let them range freely around their homes. *Cuyes* are also raised commercially, on farms. Popular ways of cooking *cuyes* include stewing in a rich sauce and grilling over an open fire. Other exotic meats can be sampled in the jungles of Ecuador, where animals such as wild boar and monkey are often eaten.

Because mountain-bred animals are often tough, their meat is usually chopped into very small pieces, then stewed with corn and the rocoto or mirasol chillies that are widely used in this part of Latin America. This helps to tenderize the meat.

Many fruits are grown in this region, including pineapples, cherimoyas, mangoes, guavas and passion fruit. Bananas and plantains are also widely cultivated, especially in Ecuador. Other important ingredients are walnuts, pine nuts and peanuts, which are often ground to make rich sauces.

A favourite drink is *pisco*, a grape brandy that is common to Peru and Chile. *Chicha*, a type of beer made from fermented corn, is also drunk.

STREET FOOD AND SNACKS

A popular snack is *anticuchos* (ox heart kebabs). The meat is trimmed, marinated in spiced vinegar and speared on lengths of sugar cane before being grilled with a spicy basting sauce. Other street foods include empanadas or *pastelos* (pastries stuffed with a variety of tasty fillings) and *humitas* (fresh corn dough with a savoury or sweet filling, steamed in a corn husk parcel). Crisp plantain chips are an Ecuadorian speciality, while Bolivians like to snack on caramel-coated popcorn called *pasacaya*.

FEASTS AND FESTIVALS

Easter is celebrated in style in all three countries. The best-known Quechua festival is Inti Raymi (the festival of the sun), which celebrates the winter solstice on 24 June each year. This huge celebration often continues for days. In Ecuador, the self-proclaimed banana capital of the world, there is a banana festival every September.

Below: In La Paz, Bolivia, a market trader displays just some of the many varieties of potato grown in the region.

CHILE

A slender ribbon of a country, Chile is dominated by the Andes mountain range and measures some 4,830km/3,000 miles from north to south, but is never much more than 160km/100 miles wide. In the north is the strangely beautiful Atacama Desert; in the south, beyond the Continental ice field, lies a rugged land of glaciers and fjords. Between these extremes is a temperate, fertile zone where fruits and vegetables grow abundantly. The waters off the coast of Chile provide superb seafood.

EARLY HISTORY

The north of Chile was once ruled by the Incas, but before they came to prominence in the early 13th century, the land played host to a succession of tribal groups. The first of these is believed to have settled in the south of the country as early as 14,000 years ago. More recent inhabitants were the Aymara, who cultivated corn and potatoes in the far north, trading these foods for guano, a rich fertilizer gathered by coastal tribes. Also occupying the northern region were the Atacameño, whose descendants still uphold some of their tribal traditions. Another important group, the Mapuche, were fierce warriors who successfully kept the Inca and Spanish invaders at bay for centuries.

The Spanish finally gained a foothold in Chile in 1541, when Pedro de Valdivia founded Santiago. The town was almost lost six months later when natives attacked, but the community survived and less than 20 years later the Spanish were firmly entrenched.

The colonists quickly began to establish large estates or haciendas over much of the country. These were initially worked by native South Americans who were little more than slaves, but when the spread of European diseases virtually annihilated the native population, tenant farmers of mixed blood (*mestizos*) took their place.

Until the 18th century, Chile remained a largely agrarian country. As the Audiencia de Chile, linked for administrative purposes to the Vice-royalty of Peru, it was ruled from Lima, and was only permitted to trade with the mother country. All goods destined for Spain therefore had to go via Lima.

Chile was ripe for change when Napoleon's invasion of Spain in the early 19th century signalled the beginning of the end of that country's dominance in Latin America. When Napoleon placed his brother on the Spanish throne, the citizens of Santiago who were loyal to the deposed King Ferdinand VII refused to acknowledge the usurper, and declared on 18 September 1810 that they would rule Chile themselves until the French were ousted from Spain. This independence was short-lived, however, as troops from Peru soon re-established control. Independence would only be formally declared in 1818, after José de San Martin's liberation army had crossed from Argentina into Chile.

Below: Chile's ice fields, such as Torres del Paine, Patagonia, lie to the south of a more temperate, fertile area.

Above: Garlands of dried shellfish hang from market stalls in Puerto Montt, Chile, a town known for its seafood.

After initial turmoil, the country became relatively stable. Agriculture and mining prospered, and were bolstered by the arrival of settlers from Ireland, England, Germany, France, Italy, Croatia and the Middle East. All of these immigrants had an influence on the Chilean cuisine, but the national diet still has strong links with its origins, and traditional ingredients such as corn, squash, beans and potatoes are widely used.

FOOD AND DRINK

Any discussion about food in Chile inevitably centres on the extent, excellence and variety of seafood available. The plankton-rich Humboldt current is responsible for the largesse, which includes crabs, clams, mussels, abalone, razor clams, sea urchins, squid, octopus, scallops and lobsters. Some or all of these types of seafood, plus less identifiable specialities such as *picorocco* (giant barnacles), are likely to be among the treats on offer at that most Chilean of feasts, the *curanto*, a massive cookout that involves a carefully constructed pit, hot rocks and leaves to seal in the steam.

Fish is equally abundant. Popular varieties include congrio, a slender fish that resembles an eel; corvina, a type of bass; swordfish and the Patagonian toothfish. Chile is also one of the world's biggest exporters of salmon.

Corn features widely in many recipes, from soups and breads to the delicious *pastel de choclo*, which is a traditional stew topped with a corn crust. Meat is not as central to the diet as it is in neighbouring Argentina, but Chile produces some fine beef, pork and lamb nevertheless.

Chilean desserts are similar to those served elsewhere on the continent, mainly taking their inspiration from Spain and making great use of the thick, sweet caramelized milk called *dulce de leche*. The central valleys produce excellent fresh fruit throughout the year, and deliciously sweet cakes and pastries are also available, courtesy of German settlers.

Chileans enjoy a good bottle of wine and are extremely proud of their vineyards, which are rapidly gaining worldwide recognition. Also popular is draft beer, known locally as *schop*, and the delicious grape brandy, *pisco*.

A curanto on Chiloé

The beautiful archipelago of Chiloé, situated off Puerto Montt, is famous for its fine seafood, wooden churches and laid-back atmosphere. This is a great place to sample the *curanto* – a full-scale Chilean seafood feast.

STREET FOOD AND SNACKS

For munching on the move, Chileans tuck into meat, seafood, empanadas, *humitas* and sandwiches, from steak with all the trimmings to *ave-palta* (chicken and avocado).

FEASTS AND FESTIVALS

Independence Day on 18 September is celebrated with music, dancing, eating and drinking, and marks the start of summer. The rodeo season also starts in September, with the major event, the National Rodeo, taking place in March. Ngillatun is an ancient Mapuche festival celebrating harvest and fertility.

Below: An impressive array of fresh fruit and vegetables are on offer at a market in Valdivia in Chile's Lake District.

COLOMBIA AND VENEZUELA

At the upper end of South America lie two countries that are as mysterious as they are magnificent. Colombia and Venezuela have some of the most rugged terrain on the continent. From the tropical rainforest of the coast, the land rises to range after range of high mountains, the cordilleras of the Andes. Ravines, mighty rivers and dense vegetation make exploration difficult, and communities have historically been isolated. Until the first settlers arrived there was, therefore, no universal style of eating, and the Spanish were able to establish theirs as the core cuisine in both countries.

EARLY HISTORY

Columbus discovered the mouth of the Orinoco River in 1498. The first Spanish settlement in Venezuela was established in 1521 and in Colombia four years later. In the early 19th century both countries united with Ecuador and Panama to form the union of Gran Colombia, after their independence was won by Simon Bolivar. Venezuela left the union to become a separate state in 1830, as did Ecuador, and Panama eventually left the union in 1903.

FOOD AND DRINK

Both Colombia and Venezuela have lowland plains, temperate zones above 900m/3,000ft and highlands leading to alpine-style meadows. At sea level, sugar, cacao, coconuts, bananas and rice are cultivated. Higher up are the coffee plantations and corn fields, and above these cereal crops, potatoes and temperate fruits are all grown. This huge diversity of landscape means that both countries have a wide range of foods available to them, from the traditional ingredients such as cassava, squash, beans and corn to a dazzling array of fruits.

Favourite Venezuelan dishes include delicacies such as *mondongo* (tripe with vegetables, corn and potatoes), *sancocho* (fish stew) and *parrillado* (barbecued meats), while Colombian specialities include rabbit in coconut milk, chicken hotpot with three different types of potato, and a delicious pineapple custard. Colombia has the benefit of a coastline on both the Caribbean Sea and the Pacific Ocean, so it has a wonderful selection of fish and seafood readily available. *Arepas* (flat corn breads) are a very popular snack. Both countries produce lots of coffee and it is one of their major exports; Colombian coffee is reckoned to be among the finest in the world.

Above: Roadside vendors are a common sight in Colombia, selling fruits such as bananas, melons and pineapples.

A seasonal speciality and a great delicacy in the lowland regions are flying ants, which are toasted and served like peanuts. In Venezuela a delicious spicy sauce, *katara*, is made from the heads of leaf-cutter ants.

The lure of El Dorado

The rumour of a land where gold was so plentiful that people powdered themselves with gold dust lured many 16th-century adventurers to the countries now known as Guyana, Surinam and French Guiana. The glut of gold never materialized but the Spanish, Dutch, English and French all thought that the land was worth fighting for.

The English eventually triumphed in Guyana, but only after many years of Dutch settlement. Surinam went to the Dutch and French Guiana became first a French penal colony and then an overseas department of France. Still heavily subsidized by France, French Guiana has a distinctly Gallic atmosphere, with pavement cafes and food with a distinctly French flavour. In Guyana and Surinam, where African slaves and indentured labourers from India, China and the East Indies were imported to work the sugar plantations, the cooking is more eclectic. Javanese noodle dishes and Chinese stir-fries are sold alongside native South American Indian dishes like pepperpot – a stew with meat tenderized by cassareep (cassava extract). Seafood is popular, especially prawns (shrimp), and plantains, bananas, cassava, beans, peanuts and squash are also widely used. The area is famous for its superb fruit, and for unusual vegetables like *pom*, a large yellow root that closely resembles cassava.

CENTRAL AMERICA

The land that connects Mexico with the rest of South America consists of seven countries, Guatemala, Belize, El Salvador, Honduras, Nicaragua, Costa Rica and Panama. Beans and rice are the staple foods in all these countries, but there is also fine fish to be had, thanks to the proximity of the Pacific Ocean and the Caribbean Sea.

EARLY HISTORY

The empire of the Maya extended to Honduras. When they disappeared from Central America around AD900 they not only left behind ruined cities like Tikal in Guatemala, but also new foods and sophisticated farming techniques, some of which were adopted by natives.

Columbus reached the shores of Honduras and then Costa Rica in 1502, but the area was not settled until some 20 years later, after troops led by Pedro de Alvarado came south from Mexico. Alvarado took Guatemala, Honduras and El Salvador. By 1530 there were Spanish colonists in most of Central America. Government was a haphazard affair, but in 1535 Guatemala, Honduras, El Salvador, Nicaragua and Costa Rica were incorporated into the Viceroyalty of New Spain, headquartered in Mexico City.

Below: Corn fields flourish alongside impressive mountains at the south-east tip of Lake Atitlan in Guatemala.

In 1821, the quintet opted out and two years later formed a federal republic, known as the United Provinces of Central America. The states were all autonomous, however. Belize became British, largely by default. Although the area was technically Spanish, British buccaneers established bases there and were later joined by British soldiers from Jamaica. In 1798 the British connection was formalized, and the link was only broken in 1981 when Belize became independent. Panama, meanwhile, looked to the south and was part of the Union of Gran Colombia until 1903. The building of the Panama Canal brought affluence to the area, and Panama is still one of the wealthier countries in Central America.

FOOD AND DRINK

The food of Central America is not as exciting as the surroundings, but competing against orchid-clad forests, volcanoes, waterfalls, barrier reefs and beautiful beaches would be a tall order. Dishes based on rice and beans are everywhere, but there are plenty of alternatives. Fish is universally popular. Varieties include tuna, mackerel, snapper, pompano, swordfish and mahi-mahi. The fish is often cooked simply and served whole, but there are also plenty of rich fish soups and stews. Lobsters, clams, prawns (shrimp) and other types of seafood are also widely available. Chicken is always on the menu, alongside specialities such as *mondongo* (tripe stew) and *cecina* (beef marinated in citrus juices). There is a strong Mexican influence in Guatemala and Belize; Panama takes inspiration from Colombia; and Creole dishes are found on the Caribbean coast. Coffee is grown in Costa Rica, El Salvador and Guatemala and is enjoyed by everyone, from the very young to the very old.

Above: In Costa Rica, a worker spreads out coffee beans to dry in the sun.

Fabulous fruits

Central America is blessed with bountiful fruit. Markets throughout the region are filled with bananas, cherimoyas, mangoes, papayas, pineapples and guavas, plus many more varieties that are local to each country. Delicious fruit drinks are a popular choice. *Refrescos* or *frescos* are milk- or water-based, while *batidas* sometimes contain rum or a similar spirit. Also refreshing are *pipas*, large green coconuts that stallholders cut open on request so that thirsty purchasers can sip the cool liquid inside.

The Mexican, South American and Caribbean Kitchen

Mexican, South American and Caribbean cuisine is founded on simple ingredients of excellent quality. Fresh seafood, quality cuts of meat and locally grown fruits and vegetables are abundant. Each country has developed its own specialities, with common flavourings and techniques.

EQUIPMENT

Latin American cooks are endlessly inventive, not only in the way they cook, but also in their approach to kitchen equipment. While the items featured here could give your cooking a more authentic touch, few are essential. If you intend making your own tortillas, a press and *comal* will be extremely useful, but for most purposes, it is perfectly possible to improvise.

METATE

Made from a sloping piece of volcanic rock and looking rather like a three-legged stone stool, this grinding stone is used to make *masa* dough from skinned, cooked corn kernels. It can also be used to grind cocoa and *piloncillo* (unrefined cane sugar). The grinding is done with the aid of a stone roller, a *muller*, which is made from the same stone as the *metate*. Before a new *metate* can be used, it must be tempered. A mixture of dry rice and salt is placed on the grinding surface, and the *muller* is rocked back and forth to press the mixture into the surface and remove any loose pieces of sand or grit. These are fairly difficult to obtain outside South America, but they are available by mail order.

Below: A metate *is a traditional grinding stone made from volcanic rock. The design has not changed for many centuries.*

MOLCAJETE AND TEJOLOTE

The Mexican mortar, the *molcajete*, is traditionally made from volcanic rock and must be tempered in the same way as the *metate*. The short, stubby pestle used to grind ingredients is called a *tejolote*. The best *molcajetes* are heavy and not too porous. Before purchasing, grind the *molcajete* briefly with the *tejolote*. If the stone seems soft and a lot of dust is formed, it is probably too porous. Similar to the Thai equivalent, which it closely resembles, it is ideal for grinding herbs, garlic, chillies and other spices such as achiote (annatto), as well as nuts and seeds for making *mole poblano*, for example. Fresh salsas, such as guacamole, are often made with a *molcajete* and *tejolote*. The flavours of the ingredients are crushed out, which gives a rustic texture and flavour. However, grinding spices or pounding chillies with a *molcajete* and *tejolote* is hard work so many Mexican cooks use a food processor or a blender instead.

Above: A mortar and pestle, or molcajete e tejolote, *is an essential tool for grinding spices and chillies.*

TORTILLA PRESS

In Mexico and other parts of Latin America where tortillas and similar griddle cakes are made, the *masa* dough was traditionally shaped by hand. Skilled women were able to make an astonishing number of perfectly shaped tortillas in a very short time, but this is something of a dying art. Today, most people use tortilla presses, and in tortilla bakeries or *tortillerias* the whole process is mechanized. The most effective tortilla presses are made from cast iron, but because these must be seasoned (oiled) before use, and carefully maintained, many people prefer steel presses. Tortilla presses consist of two round metal plates, hinged together. They come in various sizes and are heavy, in order to limit the leverage needed to work them. The dough is placed between the plates, which are then squeezed together with the aid of a lever. Placing thin sheets of plastic on the plates or covering them with plastic bags before making the tortillas will ensure that they are easy to remove once they are pressed. Tortilla presses are sold in good speciality kitchen shops and are also widely available by mail order.

Below: Perfect tortillas can be easily pressed with a heavy steel or cast-iron tortilla press.

COMAL

This is a thin circular griddle, traditionally used over an open fire to cook tortillas. They were placed among the hot coals and pulled out with long sticks. Clay *comals* take longer to heat up, but they do not require oiling before use, unlike metal ones. If you cannot find a *comal*, a cast-iron griddle or large frying pan will do the job equally well.

FARINHERRA

This is a traditional shaker used mainly in Brazil for sprinkling *farinha de mandioca* (cassava flour) over meat or fish dishes, such as *feijoada*, to mop up the sauce and juices.

CUSCUZEIRO

This looks a bit like a metal colander supported on a frame, and it is used as a mould for the popular Brazilian dish *cuscuz paulista*. The *cuscuzeiro* is lined with a variety of foods that will look decorative when the dish is turned out, for example, slices of tomato, hard-boiled eggs or slices of pepper, with perhaps a few fresh prawns (shrimp). A moist corn meal mixture is then packed on top of these ingredients. More layers are added until the container is full, and it is then covered and steamed. When turned out the layers of the *cuscuz* look pretty and it tastes delicious. The name suggests that *cuscuz* evolved from couscous, and the method of preparation certainly calls to mind the North African dish.

EARTHENWARE DISHES

The Spanish influence on the region's cuisine is clearly visible in the clay pots (*ollas*) that are traditionally used for cooking stews and sauces throughout Latin America. Often beautifully hand-painted and decorated, they give food a unique earthy flavour, but are seldom found outside the region, as their fragility means that they do not travel well and are rarely exported. Sadly, modern materials and designs have made them relatively rare in Latin America itself. Flat earthenware dishes decorated around the edge are more easily found, and these are often used as serving dishes. Traditional Spanish *cazuelas* (shallow terracotta dishes) and casseroles also make excellent alternatives.

Above: For slow-cooking rich stews and sauces, Latin American cooks often use ollas, *traditional hand-decorated Spanish clay pots, which give an authentic flavour.*

Left: Available as metal or clay varieties, a comal *is the traditional griddle pan used for cooking tortillas.*

CORN

The Aztecs called it "first mother and father, the source of life". Corn was equally highly revered in Peru, first by the indigenous South Americans, who worshipped the corn goddess, and then by the Incas, who decreed that corn could only be planted after the Supreme Inca had turned the first sod with a golden plough reserved for this purpose.

Corn was a sacred food, of huge significance. Not only was it a vital source of sustenance, but it also provided shelter, fencing and even clothing. Every part of the plant was used, even the silks surrounding the kernels, which became ties for tamales. When corn was cooked, whoever added it to the pot had first to breathe on it to rid it of its fear of dying and accustom it to the heat.

Some corn was eaten fresh, but most was dried and stored, then processed to make a type of porridge called *atole*. This was a lengthy chore, made easier by the discovery that the skins came off much more easily if the kernels were heated in a lime solution. When boiled in fresh water, the skinned kernels made a mash (*pozole*), versions of which were eaten by the indigenous peoples of Central and South America.

The cooked skinned kernels were also the basis for *masa*, a dough made by crushing the corn. The dough was then transformed into tortillas or similar flat breads, using techniques that are much the same today.

Corn is a valuable carbohydrate food but it is deficient in the amino acids lysine and tryptophan. If corn is the sole food source, as in some parts of Africa, diseases such as kwashiorkor and pellagra result. The problem has not arisen in South America or the Caribbean, however, because the basic diet also includes beans and squash, which compensate for the nutritional deficiencies of corn.

History

Corn evolved in Central America but its precise origin is not known. No wild forms have ever been found, and its ancestor may have been a type of grass with tiny kernels, each embedded in a cob no bigger than a haricot bean. How the grass evolved into the much larger plant with rows of kernels growing side by side on a substantial cob is not known, but the indigenous farmers were highly efficient plant breeders.

Corn was already widely grown throughout South America when Columbus first encountered it on the island of Cuba. The tall, leafy plant was called *maïs*, and in many parts of the globe it is still known as maize. The alternative name arose because Columbus and his crew saw it as a staple food equivalent to the corn they grew back home, and dubbed it native corn.

Above: White Andean corn is ground and used to make masa *dough.*

Below: South American corn comes in many colours, including vibrant red.

Varieties

There are five main varieties of corn. Dent corn is the most widely grown globally, and is mainly used for animal feeds and oil. Other varieties are popcorn, flint corn, flour corn and sweet corn, which is the type used in cooking. Baby sweet corn cobs are often picked before they are mature, then cooked and eaten whole. Yellow corn kernels are the most common, but the corn grown in South America comes in other colours too, including red, blue, purple and the pale white that is typical of the Andean region. There are even variegated types available, which have sweet white, red and purple kernels on the same cob. For flavour, one of the most highly prized varieties is Peru's purple corn, *maiz morado*, which has a subtle citrus flavour and is used to make *mazamorra*, a delicious pudding, or the unusual drink, *chicha morrada*.

Buying and storing

If possible, corn should be cooked within 24 hours of being picked. This is because the sugar in the kernels starts to turn into starch as soon as the cobs are cut. Look for husks that are clean, shiny and well filled. If you are not sure whether the corn is ripe or not, take a look at the tassels, which should be golden brown. Unless you are planning to cook the corn the minute you get home, do not part the green husks to check out the contents; once the kernels have been exposed to the air, they will quickly begin to dry out.

Preparing corn

Corn can be cooked in many different ways, but when served as an accompaniment it is usually simply boiled.

1 Strip off the green husks surrounding the cobs.

2 If only the kernels are required, lift the cob slightly and slice downwards using a sharp knife to remove a few rows at a time.

3 Whether using whole cobs, slices or just the kernels, plunge the corn into lightly salted boiling water for 4–5 minutes, until tender. Drain and serve with a knob of butter.

Huitlacoche

During times of drought, corn kernels are sometimes infected by a fungus, which turns them grey and causes them to swell to many times their original size. Far from being a disaster, this is seen as a boon, because the "corn truffles" as they are sometimes known, have a delicious, earthy flavour when cooked and are regarded as a delicacy around the world.

Cooking

Corn remains a staple ingredient in modern Latin America. Young, tender corn cobs are first stripped of their husks and then either steamed or cooked whole on a brazier or barbecue as a delicious fast-food snack. The puréed kernels also make an excellent soup. In Argentina, corn is often added to stews, such as the popular meat stew, *carbonada criolla*, while in Ecuador the kernels are mixed with salt cod and other vegetables to make the traditional dish, *fanesca*.

CORN MEAL

Also known as maize flour, corn meal remains slightly gritty when cooked, giving a characteristic texture to the flat breads for which it is most often used. The product known as cornflour in the UK and cornstarch in the US is a pure starch extracted from the grain. When mixed with regular wheat flour in a cake, it produces a lighter result. *Masa harina* is sometimes known as tortilla flour, which indicates its purpose. Although Latin cooks will often make *masa* (tortilla dough) from cooked corn kernels, the flour is an easier option. It comes in various grades, depending on what sort of corn it is made from. *Masarepa* is a similar product, used for making *arepas*, the flat griddle cakes that are popular in Venezuela and Colombia.

Right: Wet corn is ground to make masa harina, *which can then be used to make corn tortillas.*

Above: Dried corn husks should be soaked in cold water before use.

DRIED CORN HUSKS

These make handy wrappers for Mexican tamales and Peruvian *humitas*. They are fairly brittle, so should be soaked in water for about 30 minutes before being used to wrap ingredients. Dried corn husks are not always easy to obtain outside Latin America, so baking parchment can be used instead.

CORN TORTILLAS

Have ready a tortilla press and two clean plastic bags, slit if necessary so that they will lie flat. Tortillas are more traditionally cooked on a special griddle called a *comal*, but a cast-iron griddle or large heavy-based frying pan will work just as well.

MAKES 12 × 15CM/6IN TORTILLAS

INGREDIENTS
- 275g/10oz/2 cups *masa harina*
- pinch of salt
- 250ml/8fl oz/1 cup warm water

1 Place the *masa harina*, salt and water in a large bowl and mix together using a wooden spoon until it forms a dough.

2 Turn out the dough on to a lightly floured surface and knead well for 3–4 minutes until firm, smooth and no longer sticky. Cover the bowl with clear film and leave the dough to stand at room temperature for 1 hour.

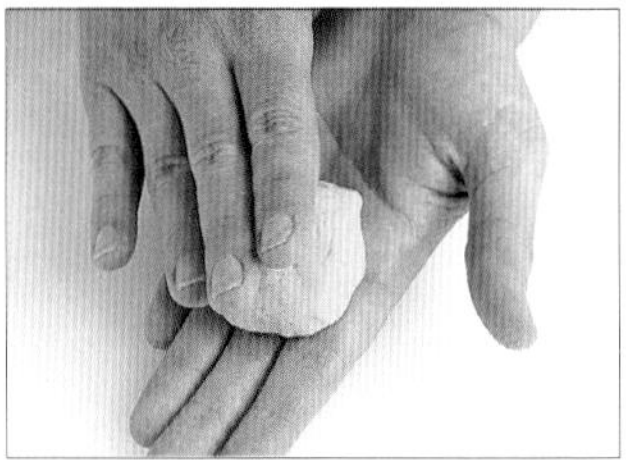

3 Pinch off 12 pieces of dough of equal size and roll each piece into a ball. Work with one piece of dough at a time, keeping the rest of the pieces of dough covered with clear film (plastic wrap) so that they do not dry out.

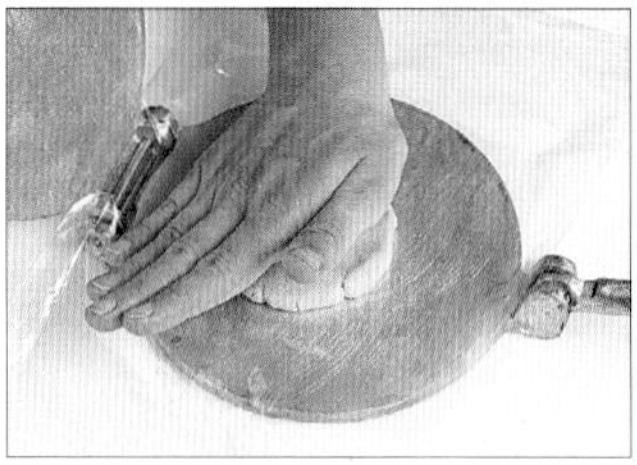

4 Open the tortilla press and place a plastic bag on the base. Put a dough ball on top and press with the palm of your hand to flatten slightly.

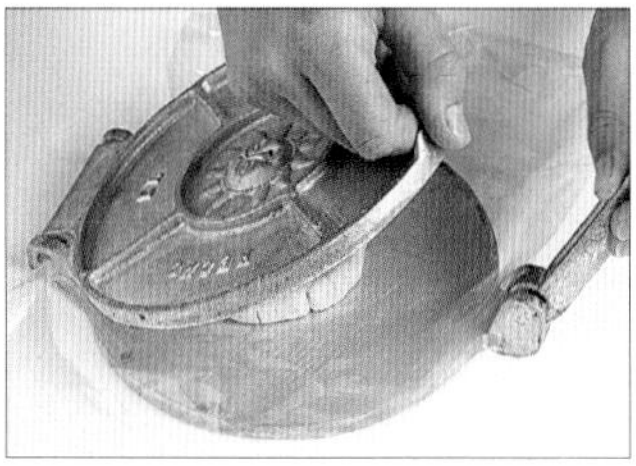

5 Lay a second plastic bag on top of the round of dough and close the press. Press down firmly several times to flatten the dough into a thin round.

6 Place a large frying pan or griddle over a moderate heat. Open the press and lift out the tortilla, keeping it sandwiched between the plastic bags. Carefully peel off the first bag, then gently turn the tortilla over on to the palm of your hand. Carefully peel off the second plastic bag. It can help if you peel the plastic off smoothly with a firm, yet not too forceful, hand. Pull back towards your wrist.

7 Flip the tortilla on to the hot frying pan or griddle and cook for about 1 minute or until the lower surface is blistered and is just beginning to turn golden brown. Turn over using a palette knife and keep warm until ready to serve.

8 Place a clean dish towel in a large ovenproof dish. Transfer the cooked tortilla to the dish, wrap the dish towel over the top and cover with a lid. Keep warm while you cook the remaining tortillas in the same way.

COOK'S TIP

If you do not have a tortilla press, you can improvise by placing the dough between two clean plastic bags and rolling it out with a rolling pin.

Basic *masa*

Traditionally, tortillas are made with *masa*. *Masa* is made by mixing dried white corn with food grade calcium oxide, although this is difficult to locate in small quantities. For making tortillas, most cooks, even in Mexico, find it easier to use *masa harina*, which is the flour made when *masa* is dried and ground. *Masa harina* should not be confused with cornmeal, polenta or maize meal, all of which are made from corn, but without being soaked or cooked with lime. The taste of tortillas made with *masa harina* is slightly different from that of tortillas made from fresh *masa*, but the flour is much easier to cook with and does away with the need for a *metate*.

FLOUR TORTILLAS

Wheat-flour tortillas are more common than corn tortillas in the north of Mexico, especially in the areas around Sonora and Chihuahua, where wheat is grown. Flour tortillas differ from corn tortillas in that they include lard, which gives them more pliability and elasticity. For best results, make sure you use a good-quality plain (all-purpose) flour.

MAKES ABOUT 12 × 25CM/10IN TORTILLAS

INGREDIENTS

- 500g/1¼ lb/5 cups plain (all-purpose) flour, sifted
- 2.5ml/½ tsp baking powder
- pinch of salt
- 100g/3¾ oz/scant ½ cup lard
- about 120ml/4fl oz/½ cup water

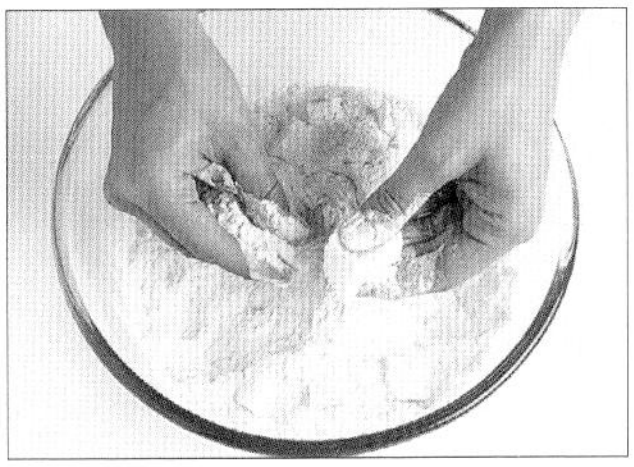

1 Mix the flour, baking powder and salt in a large bowl. Rub in the lard, then gradually add enough water to draw the flour together into a stiff dough.

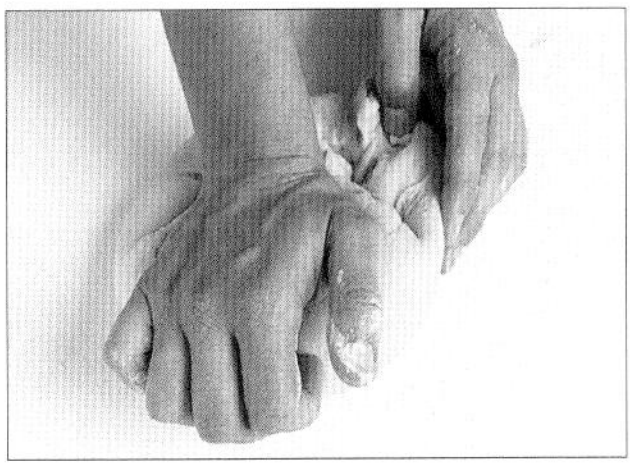

2 Turn out the dough on to a lightly floured work surface and knead it for 10–15 minutes, until it is elastic. Use the heel of your hand, using your other hand to steady the dough, preventing it from shifting position on the board.

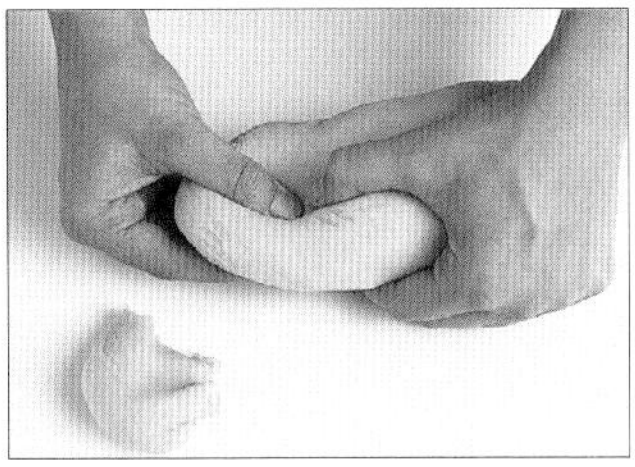

3 Divide the dough into 12 even-size pieces and roll into balls using the palms of your hand. Cover the pieces with clear film (plastic wrap) while you are working to stop them drying out.

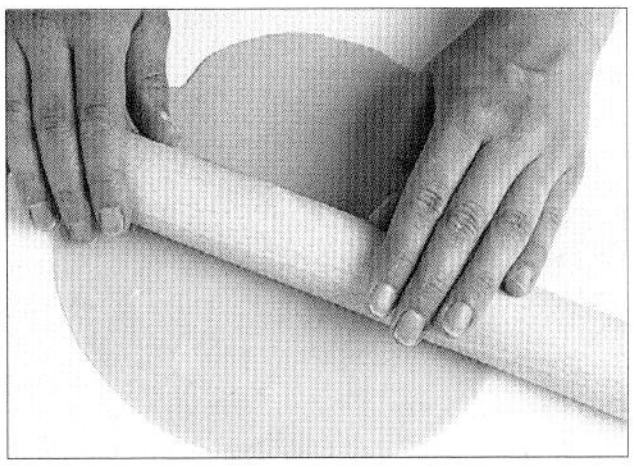

4 Roll out each ball on a lightly floured surface. Give the dough a quarter turn after each roll to keep the round even. Keep rolling until the round is about 30cm/12in across.

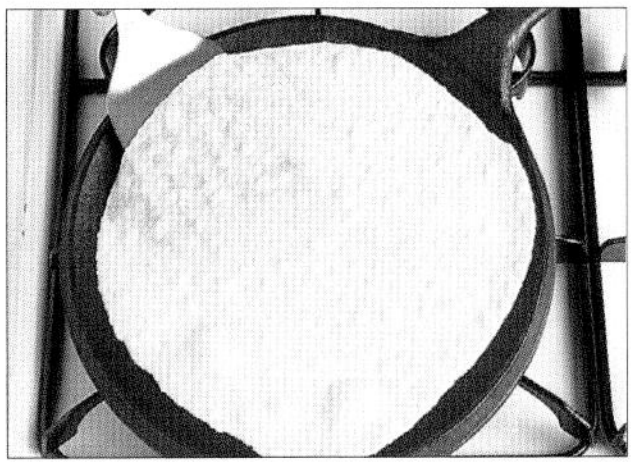

5 Warm a large heavy-based frying pan or griddle over a medium heat. Cook one tortilla at a time, placing each one in the ungreased pan or on the griddle and cooking it for 45 seconds–1 minute or until the lower surface begins to blister and brown. Lift the edge with a knife to check. Turn over and cook the other side for about 1 minute.

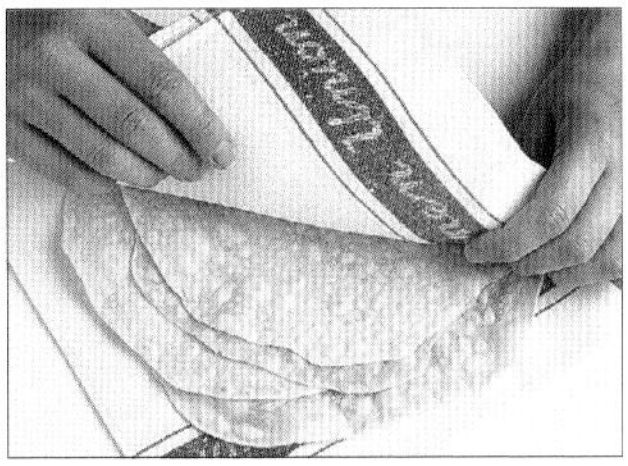

6 Wrap the cooked tortillas in a clean, dry dish towel to keep them soft and warm while you make the rest.

COOK'S TIPS

- If the corn tortillas crack when they are pressed, remove the dough from the press, return it to the bowl and add a little extra water.
- To reheat cold tortillas, sprinkle them with a few drops of water, wrap them in foil and place in an oven preheated to 140°C/275°F/Gas 1 for 10 minutes. Alternatively, wrap them in clear film and microwave on maximum power for about 20 seconds.

Quick and easy tortilla fillings

- Cut a skinned chicken breast into thin slices and stir fry with slices of red and yellow pepper. When the chicken is cooked add the juice of a lime and some fresh oregano, add salt and pepper to taste then use the mixture to fill freshly warmed tortillas. Add some grated cheese if you wish and a spoonful of sour cream.
- If you have some rice and refried beans left from the previous day, mix them together and reheat in a frying pan with a little oil. When the mixture is thoroughly heated spoon into the tortillas with some grated cheese, slices of tomato and spring onions (scallions).
- Stir fry some mushrooms with plenty of black pepper. Add a dash of soy sauce and a little double (heavy) cream, season to taste then spoon into the tortillas.

FOLDING AND COOKING TORTILLAS

Many Mexican dishes are made with tortillas. The difference lies in the filling, folding and cooking.

BURRITOS

These are flour tortilla envelopes enclosing various fillings and then folded into the classic shape and the edges sealed with flour and water.

CHIMICHANGAS

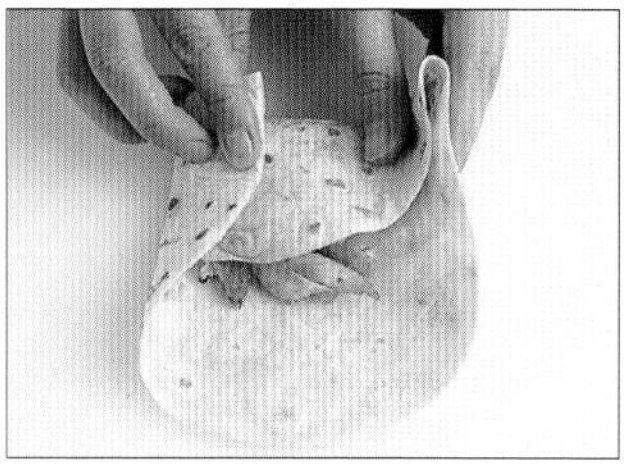

A chimichanga is a burrito that has been folded, chilled to allow the edges to seal and then deep fried in hot oil until crisp and golden.

CHALUPAS

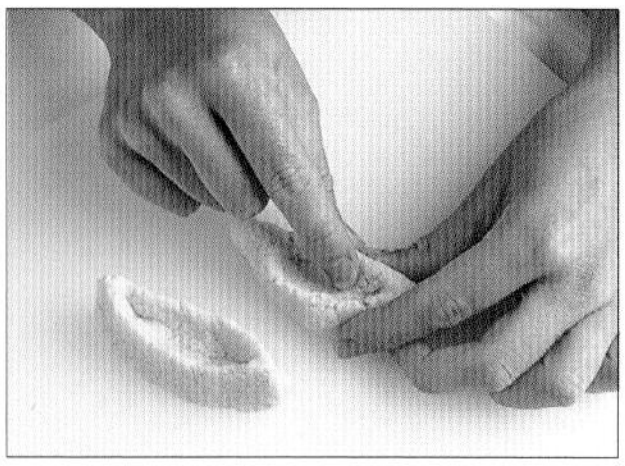

Chalupas are pieces of *masa* shaped to resemble canoes or boats and fried until opaque and golden. They are topped with beans, salsa and cheese.

ENCHILADAS

These can be made from either corn or wheat tortillas. A little filling is laid down the centre of a tortilla, which is then rolled to make a tube, rather like cannelloni. Filled tortillas are laid side by side in a baking dish before being topped with a sauce and baked in the oven or finished under the grill.

FAJITAS

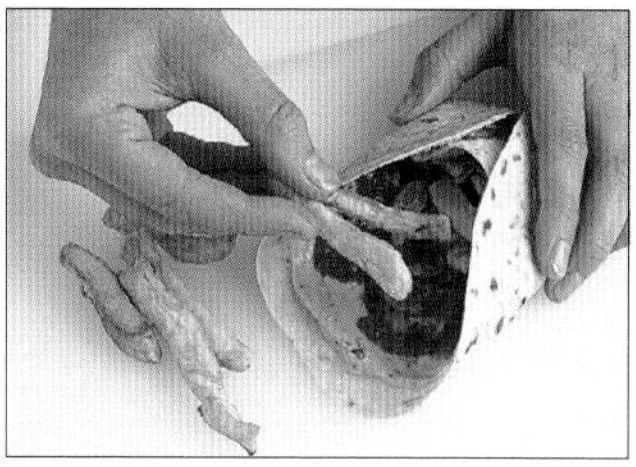

These are ideal for informal dinner parties, as various fillings are placed on the table with the hot tortillas, and guests fill and roll their own. The tortilla is then folded to form a pocket around the filling.

FLAUTAS

Corn tortillas are filled with a pork or chicken mixture, rolled tightly into flute shapes, then fried until crisp.

QUESADILLAS

These tasty treats are made by placing a corn or flour tortilla in a warm frying pan and spreading one half lightly with salsa. A little chicken or a few prawns (shrimp) are sometimes added, and fresh cheese is sprinkled on top. The other half of the tortilla is then folded over, and the quesadilla is cooked for 1–2 minutes, turning once.

TACOS

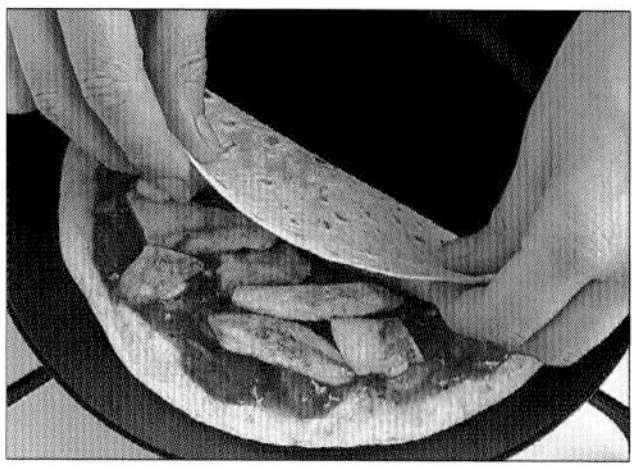

The crisp tortilla shells which are often sold in supermarkets as tacos are in fact a Tex-Mex invention. True Mexican tacos are corn tortillas that have been filled and folded in half; they remain soft. *Taquitos* are miniature tacos – ideal for picnics or parties.

TOSTADAS

These are individual corn tortillas fried until crisp and then topped with shredded meat, refried beans, salsa, guacamole, soured cream and a little fresh cheese. The finger-food versions are called *tostaditas*.

TOTOPOS

Triangles of corn tortilla, fried until crisp, are called *totopos*. Serve them with a salsa – they are delicious served while still warm.

Above: Blue and yellow tortilla chips. Plain, lightly salted chips are best for dipping with salsa.

READY-MADE TORTILLAS

Making Mexican meals is much easier than it once was, thanks to the availability of ready-made tortillas and tortilla chips.

CORN TORTILLAS

Many supermarkets stock 15cm/6in fresh corn tortillas. Look for them in the bread section. They are ideal for making tacos, tostadas, *totopos* and enchiladas. They do not have a very long shelf life but they do freeze well. Follow the manufacturer's instructions for warming them as methods vary.

FLOUR TORTILLAS

These are available in 15cm/6in, 20cm/8in and 25cm/10in sizes, and the packaging is usually marked in inches rather than centimetres. The smallest ones are perfect for fajitas or flour tortilla quesadillas, while the 20cm/8in tortillas are a good size for large quesadillas (to share). Use the largest tortillas for burritos and chimichangas as they allow more room for the filling. Like corn tortillas, fresh flour tortillas are sold in the bread section of supermarkets or in vacuum packs beside the ethnic food ingredients. The longer-life products tend to be a bit drier and less pliable than the fresh variety, which can be frozen. Flour tortillas sold in shops often contain lard, which makes them softer than the ones that use vegetable oil or fat.

Above: Corn tortillas

TACO SHELLS

A Tex-Mex invention, these are so awkward to eat that they are responsible for putting many people off eating Mexican food. They are, however, an excellent substitute for *chalupas*, if making your own seems too much like hard work. Fill them with salsa, beans and fresh, crumbly cheese.

Below: Taco shells are difficult to eat but do have their uses.

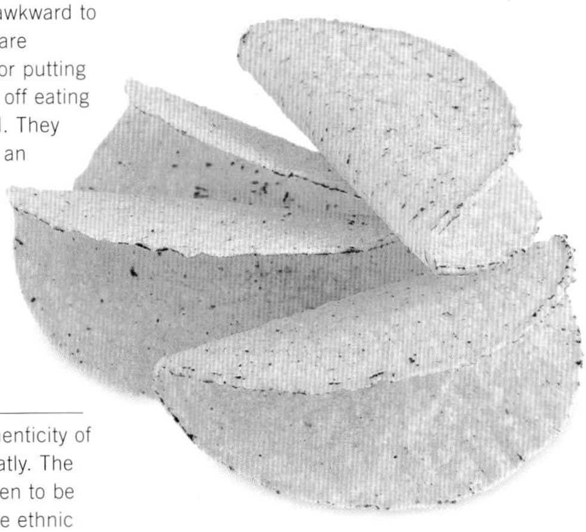

Below: Wheat-flour tortillas

TORTILLA CHIPS

The quality and authenticity of these vary greatly. The best are often to be found in the ethnic food sections of supermarkets rather than with the crisps and snacks. Many of the ones sold in the snack food section have added flavourings, some of which are not remotely Mexican. Plain, lightly salted chips are best for dipping with salsa. Many specialist food stores and health food stores sell organic corn chips and naturally coloured red and blue corn chips (made from coloured corn kernels). These look especially good mixed with yellow corn chips in a dish. Warm them in a low oven or microwave before serving.

RICE

After its introduction to Latin America and the Caribbean by the Spanish in the 16th century, rice rapidly became a staple food crop. Large tracts of wetlands are given over to rice production, especially in Brazil, which grows as much rice as Japan. Rice is an important source of protein and carbohydrates for the poorest sector of the population, especially in urban areas where individuals spend 15 per cent of their income on white rice.

In Brazil, rice is an essential accompaniment to almost all main meals, particularly the national dish, *feijoada*, and is often layered in a mould with many other ingredients. Rice is also an extremely important ingredient in Caribbean cooking. In Peru, Colombia and Ecuador, where cooked rice is served quite dry, its granular texture earns it the name *arroz graneado*. Rice is also used to make drinks, such as the Mexican *horchata* and Ecuador's fermented rice drink, *arroz fermentado*.

Varieties

White long-grain rice is the variety grown throughout the region, although the influence of immigrants means that other varieties are imported. White rice has been fully milled to remove the outer husk from the inner kernel, leaving a white grain with a delicate fragrance and slightly nutty flavour.

Left: White long-grain rice is served as an accompaniment throughout Latin America and the Caribbean.

Buying and storing

Buy good quality rice in packets and store it in a cool, dry place. Rice keeps well, but once opened, it should be transferred to an airtight container. If cooked rice is cooled quickly, it can be stored for up to 24 hours in the refrigerator. Make sure it is piping hot before it is served next time. Don't reheat rice more than once, and never keep it warm for long periods because there is a risk of food poisoning.

Quinoa
Indigenous to Peru, quinoa is a complete protein, possessing all eight essential amino acids. Low in saturated fat and high in fibre, it is a good source of calcium, potassium, zinc, iron, magnesium and B vitamins. Cooked like rice, the grain becomes soft and creamy, but the germ stays crunchy.

Preparing rice
White long grain rice is fluffy and absorbent when cooked, and makes the perfect accompaniment to soups, stews and sauces. It may also be cooked with other ingredients to make a composite dish. If serving rice as an accompaniment:

1 Add 15ml/1 tbsp oil to a pan, heat gently, then add 1 clove of crushed garlic.

2 Add the rice to the pan and roast the grains for a few minutes until they begin to turn golden.

3 Transfer the rice to a pan full of lightly salted water. Bring to the boil, then add a tight-fitting lid and simmer gently until all of the liquid has been absorbed.

If the rice is to be mixed with other ingredients, for example in the Mexican dish, *sopa seca*, try the following method. It encourages the rice to absorb other flavours and reduces the final cooking time.

1 In a pan or heatproof bowl, soak the rice in freshly boiled water for 10 minutes.

2 Drain thoroughly before adding the other ingredients.

This fairly unusual method of cooking rice is very popular throughout the region, especially in Colombia, and is particularly delicious served with seafood.

1 Add 50ml/2fl oz/¼ cup coconut milk to a pan with a pinch of brown sugar.

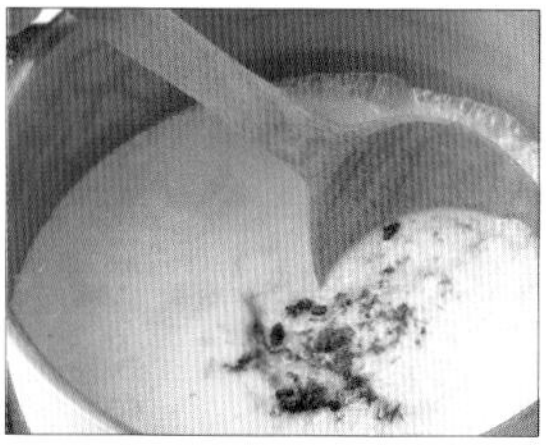

2 Add the rice, bring to the boil and simmer gently for 10–15 minutes, or until tender.

POTATOES

The potato is native to South America and was discovered by pre-Inca peoples in the foothills of the Andes. Archaeological digs in Peru and Bolivia have uncovered evidence that it was used as a food as long ago as 400BC. In Peru, the potato had religious significance, and the potato goddess was depicted with a potato plant in either hand. Potato designs were found in Nazca and Chimu pottery. One of the ways the South American Indians had of measuring time was to gauge how long it took to cook potatoes to certain consistencies. The Incas perfected the art of freeze-drying potatoes 2,000 years ago by leaving them out on lofty mountain tops to produce the early convenience food, *chuno*. In an entirely natural process, the night air froze the potatoes and the sun completed the lengthy dehydration process.

When the Inca empire was invaded by Francisco Pizarro in the 16th century, potatoes were among the plunder that the Conquistadors took back to Spain with them. Cultivation quickly spread throughout Europe via explorers such as Sir Francis Drake. Today there are up to 4,000 varieties worldwide. The potato is the staple food for two-thirds of the world's population and our third most important food crop.

Under the skin

Most of the nutrients in potatoes are either in or just beneath the skin, so it is best to avoid peeling potatoes if at all possible.

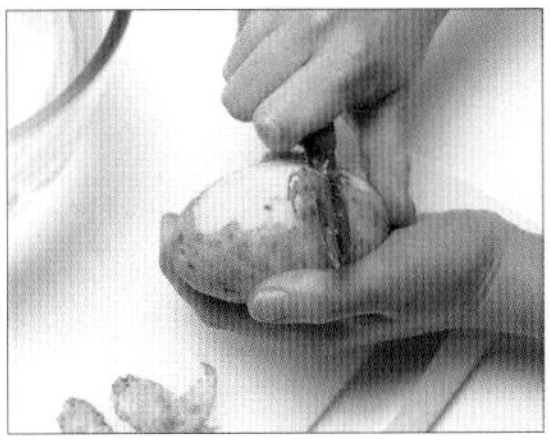

If you need to peel them, use a potato peeler that removes only the very top surface.

Potatoes are one of the best all-round sources of nutrition known to man. A valuable carbohydrate food, they also contain fairly high levels of protein. They are a very good source of vitamin C, a fact that was of huge value to early seafarers, who discovered that feeding potatoes to their crews helped to prevent scurvy. Potatoes also contain potassium, iron and vitamin B.

Above: Grown in Uruguay and Venezuela, the Red Pontiac has dark red skin and white waxy flesh.

Varieties

In the UK, only about 15 varieties of potato are on general sale, but in Peruvian markets it is claimed that you can buy up to 100 different types, ranging in size from tiny potatoes to large ovals. Worldwide there are thought to be around 4,000 varieties. The colours are equally diverse, including red, black, yellow, brown, purple and black. Most are known only by their local names, but some are beginning to reach markets in the northern hemisphere. Look out for the Purple Peruvian, with its earthy, slightly nutty-tasting lavender flesh. Also prized, particularly for mashing, is the buttery Papa Amarilla, or yellow potato. Among the varieties with dark skins and dazzling white flesh are the Yanaimilla and the Compis. Potatoes will grow anywhere from sea level to 4,300m/14,000ft, so it is not surprising that so many different varieties continue to be cultivated in their place of origin.

Buying and storing

When buying potatoes, it is important to choose a variety that will give you the right results for the cooking method you intend to use. Check the labels or ask for advice from the seller. Store potatoes in a dark, cool, dry place. Paper sacks are better than plastic bags, which create humid conditions and hasten deterioration.

Preparing and cooking

In Latin America, potatoes are usually either boiled in the minimum of water, as in the Peruvian speciality, *ocopa arequipena*, or diced and fried, which is a popular method in Mexico. Chillies are frequently added. Purple Peruvian potatoes are excellent in salads and they require less cooking than white or yellow potatoes.

Below: With striking dark skin and white flesh, Compis potatoes are grown by farmers in the Andean highlands.

BEANS

Along with corn and rice, beans are an extremely important food throughout the Caribbean and Latin America. The inhabitants of Mexico and Central America eat around six times as many beans as are consumed in Britain every year, and in Chile, where meat can be relatively scarce, they are a vital source of protein. Beans are served, in one form or another, at most meals.

Several varieties of bean are indigenous to this part of the world. They were traditionally planted with corn and squash, the idea being that the corn stalks would support the growing beans, while the squash plants spread out to suffocate encroaching weeds. This ancient method of cultivation also ensured that the beans enriched the soil depleted by the corn. The beans were served fresh in season, but vast amounts were dried to furnish versatile and nutritious dishes all year round. In the Caribbean, beans are often referred to as "peas".

Beans are a good source of protein and carbohydrate and supply vitamins A, B1 and B2. They also contribute valuable amounts of minerals such as potassium and iron to the diet.

Below: Black beans are an essential ingredient in the extravagant Brazilian national dish, feijoada.

Above: Versatile white beans, a type of haricot (navy) bean, are plump and soft with a delicious floury texture.

Varieties

Black beans These small, shiny, kidney-shaped beans, sometimes known as black turtle beans, are particularly popular in Mexico, the Caribbean and Brazil. They are highly valued for their creamy white flesh and delicate earthy flavour, reminiscent of mushrooms. Their skins remain bright and shiny after cooking, so they look dramatic when combined with rice or other ingredients. Black beans are often used in salsas and soups, and are eaten as an accompaniment to Brazil's national dish, *feijoada*. In Costa Rica they are often fried with white rice to make the traditional breakfast dish, *gallo pinto*.

White beans A type of haricot (navy) bean, these vary in size but are always the same plump oval shape. When cooked, they have an earthy, rather floury flavour, and a fairly soft texture, but they retain their shape well. White beans are an extremely versatile ingredient and can be substituted for most other varieties when a recipe calls for dried beans.

Pinto beans A smaller, paler version of the borlotti bean, the pinto has an attractive orange-pink skin speckled with rust-coloured flecks. One of the many relatives of the kidney bean, pinto beans are native to Latin America. They feature extensively in Mexican cooking as well as the cuisines of most other Spanish-speaking countries. The skins soften on cooking, which makes them easy to mash, so they are the perfect ingredient for the popular Mexican dish, *frijoles refritos* (refried beans).

Red kidney beans The shiny, dark red skin of these beans hides a

pale interior. They retain their shape and colour when cooked and have a soft, mealy texture. Red kidney beans are particularly popular in Brazil, Mexico and some parts of the Caribbean, where they are used to make a delicious red bean chilli and the Jamaican speciality, rice and peas. They can also be used instead of the traditional pinto beans to make a variation on refried beans.

Lima beans These beans originated in Peru and are named after that country's capital city. Cream-coloured and tender, with soft flesh, these hold their shape well when cooked. Lima beans have a delicate flavour, similar to that of walnuts. Fresh lima beans are delicious. One variety of lima bean is the large white butter bean, which is familiar throughout Europe. Be careful not to overcook lima beans as they become pulpy and mushy in texture.

Black-eyed beans/peas Small and white, with a distinctive black mark, these beans were introduced to the Caribbean from West Africa. They need not be soaked before use because they rapidly become tender when cooked. They taste slightly sweet and readily absorb other flavours, especially in stews and curries. Add black-eyed beans to soups and salads for extra flavour.

Gungo peas Also known as pigeon peas, these are approximately the size of a garden pea. They have a sweetish, slightly acrid flavour, and are used fresh, canned or dried.

Chickpeas Also known as garbanzo beans, robust and hearty chickpeas resemble shelled hazelnuts and have a delicious nutty flavour and creamy texture, although they require lengthy cooking. Spanish migrants first introduced chickpeas to Latin America, and although they have never been as important or popular as native beans, they are now naturalized throughout the region. When fresh, they can be eaten raw or cooked, but they are more commonly available dried. The skin on chickpeas can be tough and you may like to remove it. Do this once the chickpeas are fully cooked and cooled.

Above: Chickpeas were first introduced to Latin America by Spanish settlers, but quickly became a popular ingredient.

Buying and storing

When buying fresh beans, buy young ones with bright, firm skins because the pods of older beans are likely to be slightly tough. Be sure to use fresh beans as soon as possible after purchase because they do not store well. Most fresh beans need little preparation other than trimming the ends, but older beans may need stringing.

When buying dried beans, look for plump, shiny beans with smooth, unbroken skins. Beans toughen with age and will take longer to cook the older they are, so although they will keep for up to a year in a cool, dark place, it is best to buy them in small quantities from a store with a regular turnover of stock. Avoid beans that look dusty or dirty, and store them in an airtight container in a cool, dark, dry place.

Canned beans are a useful standby as they require no soaking or lengthy cooking. Choose canned beans that do not have any added sugar or salt, and be sure to drain and rinse well before use. Canned beans still contain a reasonable amount of nutrients.

Preparing dried beans

Dried beans must be soaked before cooking.

1 Tip the beans into a colander or sieve (strainer) and pick them over to remove any grit or damaged beans.

2 Rinse the beans under cold running water and then drain.

3 Soak in cold water overnight, changing the water once.

4 Drain the soaked beans, rinse them, then place in a large pan with plenty of cold water.

5 Bring to the boil and boil vigorously for 10 minutes to remove natural toxins (this is particularly important with lima beans or red kidney beans).

6 Reduce the heat and simmer until the beans are tender.

COOK'S TIP

If you don't have time to soak dried beans overnight, put them in a pan with water to cover, bring them to the boil, then remove from the heat and leave to soak for about 1 hour.

CHILLIES AND SWEET PEPPERS

Chillies and their mild-mannered cousins, the sweet (bell) peppers, are without doubt Latin America's greatest contribution to the global kitchen. Full of flavour, colourful, nutritious and versatile, they are now so widely used in many different cuisines that it is difficult to imagine a world without them.

FRESH CHILLIES

The first chillies were tiny wild berries that grew in the South American jungle thousands of years ago. The plants gradually spread northwards from central South America through Central America and the Caribbean to south-western North America, evolving over the centuries into the wide range of shapes and sizes we encounter today.

It was Christopher Columbus who introduced chillies to the rest of the world. When he tasted a highly spiced dish on San Salvador, he assumed that its heat came from black pepper. He named the plant pimiento (pepper), and this name endured long after he realized his mistake. Columbus took chilli plants back with him when he returned to Europe, and by the 16th century they were widely distributed. Today the chilli is the most extensively cultivated and most commonly used spice in the world.

There are as many as 200 different varieties of chilli, varying enormously in shape, size, colour, flavour and, most of all, in the amount of heat they deliver.

Below: Poblanas, popular in Mexico, are often roasted to intensify their flavour.

Above: Scotch bonnet chillies are popular throughout the Caribbean and are used to make hot pepper sauce.

The fiery sensation from chillies is caused by capsaicin, an alkaloid that not only causes a burning sensation in the mouth, but also triggers the brain to release endorphins, natural painkillers that promote a sense of wellbeing and stimulation; this is why eating chillies can become quite addictive. Capsaicin is concentrated in the seeds and membrane of the pods, so removing these parts before eating will reduce the fieriness of a chilli considerably. Chillies are an excellent source of vitamin C and also yield valuable quantities of beta-carotene, folate, potassium and vitamin E. They stimulate the appetite, help improve circulation, and can also be used as a powerful decongestant.

Varieties

Of the vast range of chillies grown in Latin America and the Caribbean, the following are the most popular. They have been rated on a scale of one to ten for heat and are listed in order of potency, mildest first. Be careful: the heat can vary widely, even with chillies from the same plant, so use these ratings as a guide only.

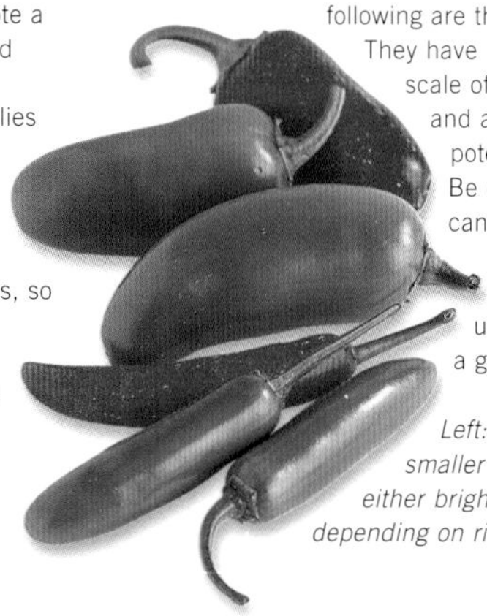

Left: Jalapeños and the smaller serrano chillies are either bright green or red, depending on ripeness.

Poblano These mild to medium-hot chillies (heat scale 3) are very popular in Mexico. Big and beautiful, poblanos are about 7.5cm/3in long, with thick flesh and a rich, earthy flavour. They start off dark green with a purple-black tinge and ripen to dark red. Green poblanos are always used cooked, and roasting gives them a more intense flavour. They are perfect for stuffed dishes such as *chillies rellenos* and taste good in traditional mole sauces. Dried poblanos are called anchos.

Jalapeño Well known and widely used the world over, jalapeños are medium-hot (heat scale 4–7). Plump and glossy, they are used in stews, salsas, breads, sauces and dips. Green jalapeños have a fresh, grassy flavour; red ones are slightly sweeter. Smoke-dried jalapeños are known as chipotle chillies.

Fresno Plump and cylindrical, these chillies are usually sold when red. They have thick flesh and a hot, sweet flavour (heat scale 5). Fresnos are excellent in salsas, ceviche, stuffings, bread and pickles. Roasting brings out their delicious sweetness.

Serrano Thin-skinned and quite slender, serranos are the classic Mexican green chilli (*chiles verdes*) and are always used in guacamole. Although they are quite fiery (heat scale 7), they have a clean, biting heat, matched by a high acidity. Both red and green serranos are frequently added to cooked dishes. They can also be pickled.

Measuring the heat
The heat level of a chilli is often measured in Scoville units on a scale where 0 is the rating for a sweet (bell) pepper and 557,000 relates to the hottest chilli grown in Latin America, the habañero. The simpler system used in this book rates the chillies on a scale of one to ten, with one indicating the mildest and ten the hottest.

Left: Sweet, juicy fresnos are perfect for fresh salsas or pickles.

Aji mirasol Extensively used in Peruvian cooking, these chillies are narrow and tapered, with a tropical fruit flavour, yet they are decidedly hot (heat scale 6–7). Fresh yellow ones are particularly prized for salsas and ceviche. They are also used in cooked dishes, such as soups or stews, and are sometimes made into a paste, which is mixed with oil to make a hot dipping sauce.

Brazilian malagueta These very hot chillies (heat scale 8) are believed to be a wild form of tabasco. Very small, only about 2cm/¾in long, they have thin flesh and a fresh yet fiery taste. Malaguetas are often added to marinades and vinegars.

Jamaican hot, Scotch bonnet and habañero These chillies are closely related and are all intensely fiery (heat scale 10). The Jamaican hot is bright red and has a sweet hot flavour. It goes well with tropical fruits and is also used in fresh salsas, Caribbean fish stews, curries and spicy chutneys. The Scotch bonnet is an essential ingredient in many Caribbean dishes, especially curries and jerk sauce, and is used to make Jamaican hot pepper sauce.

Below: Chilli powder is a good alternative when fresh chillies are not available.

Preparing Fresh Chillies
Take great care when handling chillies, as the capsaicin they contain is an extremely powerful irritant. Wear rubber gloves while preparing chillies or wash your hands in soapy water afterwards. If you touch your skin by mistake, splash the affected area with cold water. Avoid scratching or rubbing inflamed skin because this could aggravate the problem.

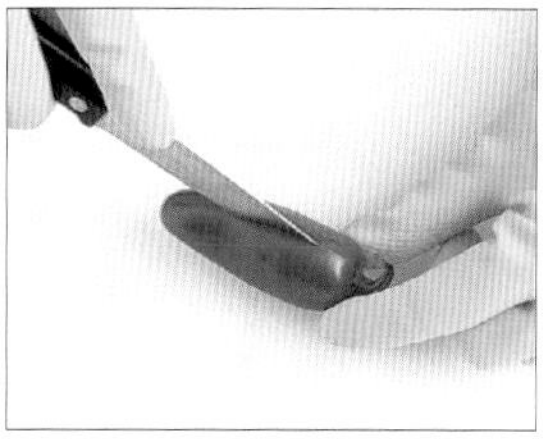

1 Cut the chilli in half lengthways, cut off the stalk and carefully scrape out the seeds (unless you wish to leave them in for extra heat).

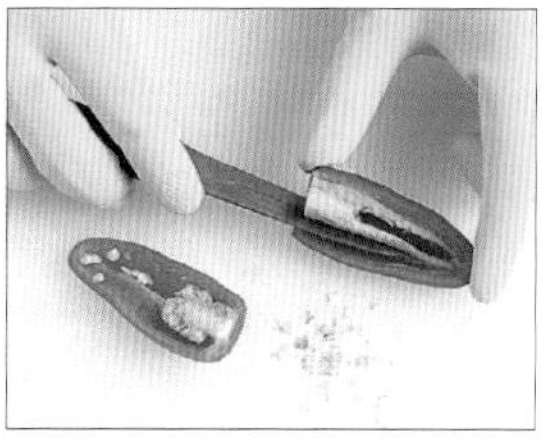

2 Remove the remaining core and any white membrane.

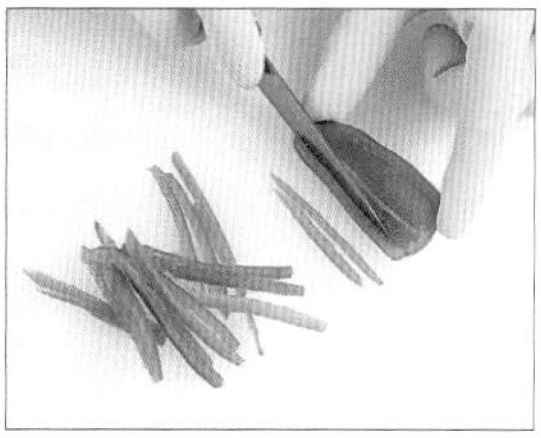

3 Finely slice or chop each piece, depending on use.

SWEET PEPPERS

Sometimes known as capsicums, sweet (bell) peppers are native to Mexico and Central America and were widely grown there in pre-Columbian times. Pepper seeds were carried to Spain in 1493 and from there spread rapidly throughout Europe. They also spread rapidly throughout South America and were a staple food of the Incas in Peru. They contribute colour and flavour to a huge variety of dishes, including salsas, stews and spicy meat fillings, as well as fish dishes, vegetable accompaniments and salads. Sweet peppers come in many unusual shapes and sizes, from chilli-size rounds to slender drops, bells and even hearts. Colours range from bright green, through yellow and orange to vibrant red, and there is even a dark purple variety (but this does turn green when cooked). Mild and sweet in flavour, with crisp, juicy flesh when ripe, they can be eaten either raw in salads or cooked. A popular way of serving peppers is to stuff and bake them.

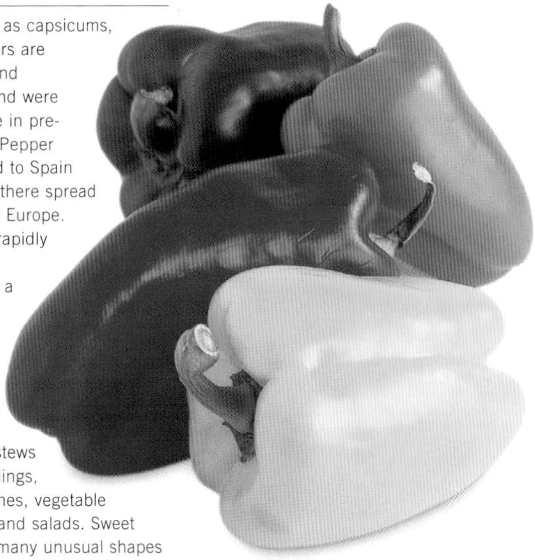

Above: Delicious either cooked or raw, sweet peppers should look glossy, feel firm and have a crisp, juicy bite. Avoid those that are wrinkled.

Buying and storing

Whether you are buying hot chillies or mild sweet peppers, look for firm, shiny specimens with unblemished skins. Avoid peppers that are limp, that wrinkle when touched or that have "blistered" areas on the skin. Green peppers should be purchased before they change colour, but should not be too dark as this indicates immaturity and lack of flavour. Avoid red peppers with dark patches on the skin, as this could be a sign that they have begun to rot inside. Store peppers in the vegetable crisper in the refrigerator. Sweet peppers will keep well for up to a week and chillies up to three weeks.

Preparing sweet peppers

Depending on use, the core and seeds should usually be removed before cooking sweet peppers.

1 Halve or quarter the peppers, then, using a small, sharp knife, carefully cut out the core, any white membrane and the seeds.

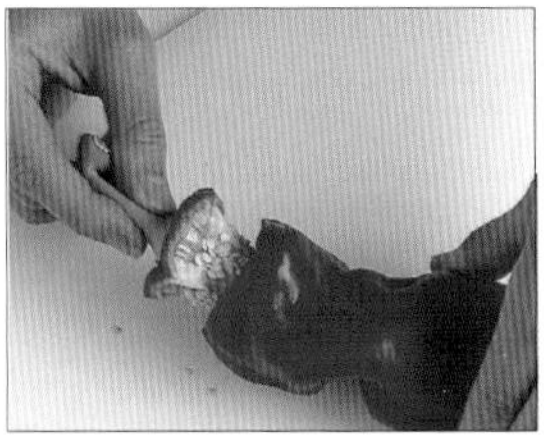

2 If the peppers are being used whole, for example to be stuffed, cut around the stem and pull out the seeds like a plug.

Roasting peppers and chillies

To really bring out the delicious, sweet flavour of fresh peppers and chillies, try roasting them.

1 Place them under a hot grill (broiler) and turn occasionally until the skins blister and char.

2 Alternatively, dry-fry them in a frying pan or griddle until the skins are scorched.

3 Place them in a strong plastic bag and tie the top tightly, or place them in a bowl and cover with cling film (plastic wrap).

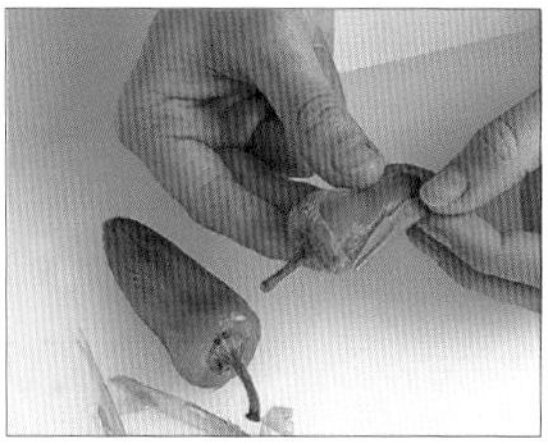

4 After approximately 20 minutes, remove the skins, then slit each pepper or chilli. Remove the seeds and membrane, and tear or slice the flesh into pieces.

DRIED CHILLIES

Left: Cascabels have a delicious, slightly nutty flavour.

Travel through Latin America and you will frequently see bunches of colourful chillies dangling from hooks on the walls of houses. In the bright sunshine they soon dehydrate and can be packed away until needed. When rehydrated, the chillies will not taste the same as before. In many cases they will have acquired a new intensity and richness of flavour, which is one of the reasons why Mexicans really value dried chillies and view them as distinct from the fresh, often giving them completely different names. Each variety has unique characteristics, and cooks will often blend several types to get exactly the results they require.

Varieties

The following are the most widely used varieties of dried chilli.

Ancho These dried red poblanos have a rich deep colour and mild fruity flavour (heat scale 3). Anchos can be stuffed and are often used in mole sauces.

Mulato Related to the ancho and with the same level of heat, mulatos taste smoky rather than fruity.

Guajillo These large dried chillies, orange-red in colour, have a slightly acidic flavour (heat scale 3–4).

Pasada Roasted, peeled and dried, these chillies have a toasty flavour (heat scale 3–4), with apple, liquorice and cherry notes.

Cascabel The name means "little rattle" and refers to the sound the seeds make when the chillies are shaken. Thick-skinned and smooth, cascabels have a rich, woody flavour (heat scale 4).

Pasilla Long, slender and very dark, the flavour of pasillas is rich with hints of berries and liquorice (heat scale 4).

Chipotle Smoke-dried jalapeños, these have wrinkled dark red skin and thick flesh. Chipotles need long, slow cooking to soften them and bring out their full, smoky taste (heat scale 6–10).

Aji mirasol The dried version of Peru's favourite chilli is deep yellowish red with a berry-like fruit flavour (heat scale 6–7).

Pequin These small chillies are pale orange-red in colour, with a light, sweet, smoky flavour suggestive of corn and nuts (heat scale 8–9). They are excellent in sauces, salsas and soups and can be crushed over food as a condiment.

Habañero Used in moderation, these have a wonderful tropical fruit flavour (heat scale 10). Like dried Scotch bonnets, they are often used to make classic hot pepper sauces, particularly in the Caribbean, and are also good when added to fish stews and salsas.

Right: Habañeros are used for chilli sauces.

Below: Anchos are delicious stuffed or added to stews.

Above: Pasadas are often used in sauces for meat or fish, or in rich spicy stews.

Buying and storing

Dried chillies should be flexible. Avoid any that smell musty or have powdery skins, as this could indicate insect infestation. Store for up to 1 year in an airtight container in a cool, dry place.

Preparing dried chillies

To appreciate their full flavour, dried chillies should be soaked before use. Toasting dried chillies before soaking will give a lovely smoky flavour. If the chillies are to be used in a slow-cooked stew, soaking is not necessary.

1 Lightly dry-fry or toast the dried chillies in a frying pan or griddle for a couple of minutes.

2 Seed large chillies and tear into pieces, then soak in warm water until soft. Soak smaller chillies before cutting into pieces.

Caribbean hot sauces

Most islands have their own recipe for hot chilli sauce. Based on the fiery habañero or Scotch bonnet chilli pepper, they should be used sparingly by the uninitiated.

Other Vegetables

A visit to a market in any Latin American country is a real feast for the eyes. Fruit and vegetables are laid on mats or heaped high on tables, strings of chillies hang overhead and everywhere there are people bustling or bargaining. The colours are glorious, the aromas are unfamiliar and there will usually be several local specialities on sale.

CHAYOTES

Also known as christophenes or chokos these pale green gourds are particularly popular in the Caribbean, where they are used in soups, salads and stews. Raw chayote is crisp and clean-tasting, rather like water chestnut. The cooked vegetable has a rather bland flavour, so needs plenty of seasoning. Cholesterol-free and low in calories, chayotes are a good source of fibre and vitamin C.

Buying and storing

Choose smooth, unwrinkled chayotes and store in the refrigerator. They keep well but are best used as soon as possible after purchase.

SQUASH

Cultivated in Latin America long before Columbus sailed, squash is an important food. Many different types are eaten in Latin America, from courgettes (zucchini) to huge hard-skinned pumpkins. Squash are eaten in both savoury and sweet dishes, often with brown sugar. Pumpkin and prawns (shrimp) is an unusual but delicious combination. A hollowed-out pumpkin makes a good container for cooking and serving, as in the Argentine stew, *carbonada criolla*. A good source of fibre and carbohydrate, pumpkins are low in calories. Varieties with bright flesh are high in vitamin A.

Buying and storing

If buying courgettes or other summer squash, the general rule is that the smaller the specimen, the better the flavour. Store courgettes in the refrigerator and use as soon as possible. Due to their hard skins, unbruised pumpkins and other winter squash keep well. Cut pumpkin should be wrapped in clear film (plastic wrap) and stored in the refrigerator.

Below: Halved chayotes can be baked for a simple yet delicious side dish.

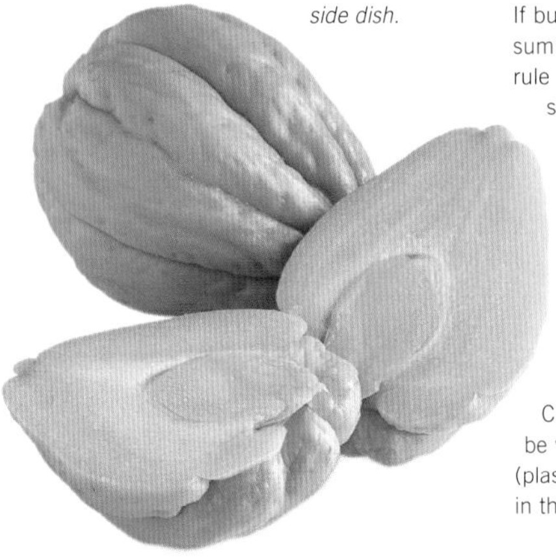

Preparing chayotes

Chayotes can be peeled, chopped and cooked in soups or stews, or cut in half and baked.

1 Preheat the oven to 190°C/375°F/Gas 5. Cut the chayotes in half, place them skin side down on a shallow baking tray and brush with a little olive oil.

2 Bake for approximately 25 minutes or until tender.

Roasting squash

Instead of roasting, pieces of squash could be lightly boiled or steamed and added to stews.

1 Preheat the oven to 190°C/375°F/Gas 5. Cut the squash into wedges, remove the skin and seeds.

2 Place the wedges in a large roasting pan with a little olive oil and roast for approximately 45 minutes or until tender.

Below: Pumpkins can be easily stored over the long winter months, making them a popular ingredient all year round in many Latin American countries.

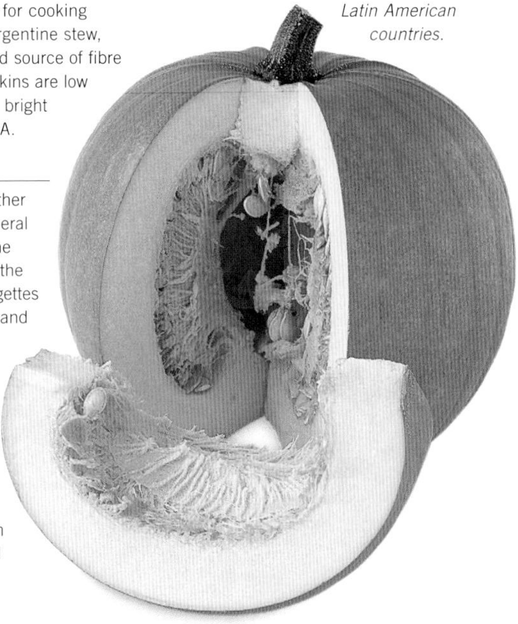

Above: *Thin slices of sweet potato are fried to make chips, a popular street snack throughout Latin America.*

SWEET POTATOES AND YAMS

These root vegetables are not related, although the American habit of calling red sweet potatoes yams can lead to confusion and the two are sometimes mixed up. Sweet potatoes have been grown in South America for centuries. In pre-Inca times, sun-dried sweet potato slices were a popular treat and Mayan cooks also used the vegetable to provide a sweet note in many savoury meat and fish dishes. Yams were brought to South America by African slaves and are widely used throughout the Caribbean and Brazil. Both of these vegetables provide some vitamin C, while orange-fleshed sweet potatoes also contain beta-carotene.

Varieties

There are hundreds of varieties of both sweet potatoes and yams. In Latin American cooking, the red-skinned sweet potato with white flesh is best known. The most commonly used yam is brown, with moist cream-coloured flesh that becomes dry when cooked.

Buying and storing

Buy vegetables that are firm and dry, with no soft areas. Store loose or in a brown paper bag in a cool, dry place, but do not put them in the refrigerator.

Preparing and cooking

Like regular potatoes, sweet potatoes can be scrubbed and baked in their skins, or peeled and sliced, then boiled or fried. They are delicious mashed or creamed, and make very good chips. Yams must be thickly peeled and should be washed well before and after slicing; this helps to remove any toxins that may be present in the raw tuber. Always cook yams very thoroughly.

CASSAVA

Also known as *manioc, mandioc* or *yuca* (in Peru), this starchy tuber looks like a long, fat sausage with dark, rough outer skin. Native to Brazil, it is also a popular ingredient in West Indian cooking. It is important to distinguish between sweet and bitter cassava: the root and leaves of the former can safely be eaten, but bitter cassava contains cyanide. Although bitter cassava is used for making beer, tapioca and cassava flour – *farinha de mandioca* – it must be detoxified first. Sweet cassava is a carbohydrate food with a high fibre content, and the leaves are a valuable source of protein. *Cassareep* is a delicious syrup made from cassava and flavoured with cinnamon and cloves. It is an essential ingredient in the traditional Jamaican pepperpot stew. Cassava is fairly bland so it is best served with a sauce or dressing such as the traditional Cuban *mojo*, which is a mixture of oil, citrus juices and garlic.

Below: Sweet cassava is a native root vegetable high in fibre and nutrients.

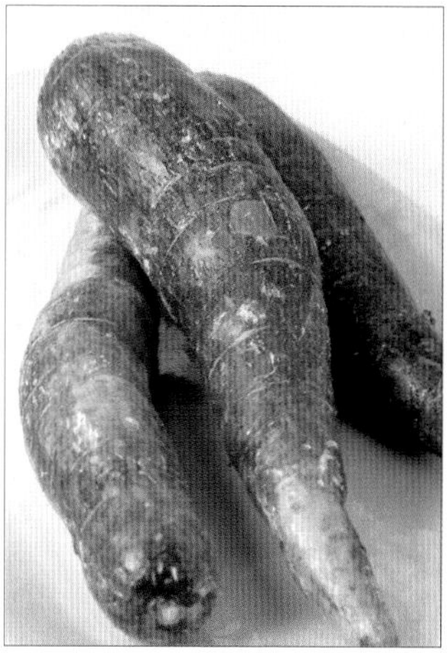

Buying and storing

Most cassava that is exported around the world is first coated in a layer of wax to keep it fresh. When buying sweet cassava, look for roots that are fairly firm, dry and odour-free.

Preparing cassava

An extremely versatile vegetable, sweet cassava can be cooked in a number of ways.

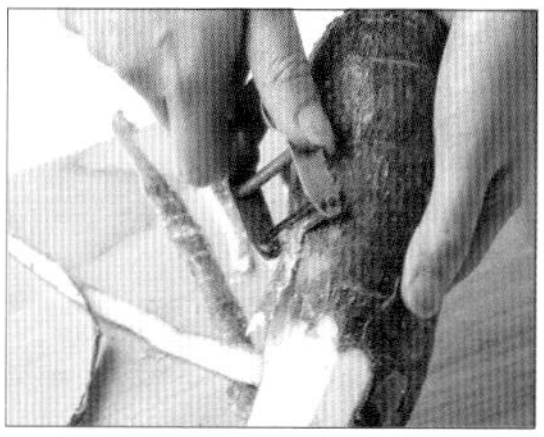

1 Scrub the root, peel, then cut into fairly large pieces, removing the fibrous core.

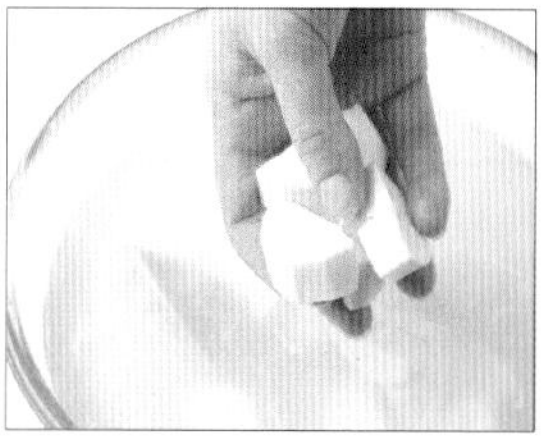

2 Drop the pieces into a bowl of acidulated water to prevent discoloration.

3 Boil, steam, bake or fry the cassava pieces until tender.

PALM HEARTS

The terminal bud of the Acai or cabbage palm has long been considered a regional delicacy. Native to South America, this fast-growing palm is now widely cultivated in vast plantations, mainly in Brazil and Costa Rica. Fresh palm hearts make very good eating, but are rarely available outside the country of origin. Canned palm hearts have a slightly different texture to fresh, but are still delicious and make a good alternative. Low in saturated fat and cholesterol, palm hearts are a valuable source of vitamin C.

Buying and storing

Fresh palm hearts should be pale, moist and evenly coloured. To enjoy them at their best, use as soon as possible after purchase. Canned hearts are much more readily available.

Preparing and cooking

To prepare fresh palm hearts, simply strip off the outer layers. Eat them raw or roast or steam in the same way as asparagus. Canned palm hearts are delicious in soups, salads and pies.

Below: Canned palm hearts make a good alternative if fresh ones are unavailable.

Above: Look for okra pods that are firm, plump and smooth, but not too big.

OKRA

Also known as ladies' fingers, these pods ooze a sticky liquid when cut, which acts as a thickener in sauces. Okra was introduced to Latin America by African slaves and is an important ingredient in Brazilian and Caribbean cooking. A source of vitamin C, fibre-rich okra also contains folate, thiamin and calcium.

Buying and storing

Okra should be a fresh, pale green colour. Buy smaller pods and avoid any that are flabby, shrivelled or bruised. Store in the refrigerator and use as soon as possible after purchase.

Preparing and cooking

If cooking whole, trim the top of each pod. If destined for a composite dish, where the viscous liquid will act as a thickener, cut the pods into slices. Otherwise, leave whole. Okra can be steamed, boiled or fried. Try it Brazilian-style, with chicken and chillies. The Barbadian speciality, Cou-cou, combines okra with corn meal.

LEAFY GREEN VEGETABLES

A number of leafy green vegetables are on sale in Latin American markets, and many are available only in certain areas. The young tops of cassava and sweet potatoes are regularly eaten, as is amaranth, a chard-like vegetable esteemed by the Aztecs. *Callaloo* is the name given to the leaves of two related tubers that are used for a popular Caribbean soup. *Nopales* are the edible leaves of the prickly pear cactus, while bottled *nopales*, commonly known as *nopalitos*, can be found in specialist food stores.

Unusual tubers

Jicama is indigenous to Mexico but has achieved widespread popularity thanks to its crisp, juicy flesh. Also known as yam bean or Chinese turnip, it can be eaten raw with orange juice and chilli powder, or cooked, and is especially good in salsas.

Oca looks like a short, fat wrinkled carrot. There are several varieties available, including white, yellow, red and purple. Its sharp taste is moderated by sun-drying the tubers before cooking.

Yacón, related to the Jerusalem artichoke, is highly valued in Peru and Bolivia for its sweet, crunchy flesh. It can be eaten either raw or cooked.

Añu is a white or yellow tuber from a nasturtium-like plant with edible leaves and flowers. It is an important crop in Ecuador, Peru, Bolivia, Colombia and Venezuela.

Jicama *has crisp, juicy flesh, similar to green apples or water chestnuts.*

FRUIT VEGETABLES

Neither savoury nor sweet, these are popular throughout Latin America.

TOMATOES

Along with chillies and corn, tomatoes are one of Latin America's most important contributions to the global cooking pot. Although they originated in the lands to the west of the Andes, both the Mayas and the Aztecs grew the little cherry-sized fruit vegetables and the Spanish introduced them to Europe. Largely composed of water, tomatoes are a good source of vitamins A and C. Raw ones contain useful amounts of vitamin E. Tomatoes also contribute the powerful antioxidant, lycopene, which may help to lower the risk of cancer.

Varieties

There are hundreds of varieties ot tomato. Cherry tomatoes, the closest in size to their Peruvian ancestors, are delicious in salads, juicy plum tomatoes make excellent sauces and beefsteak tomatoes are great for stuffing. Tomatillos (literally translated as "little tomatoes") are covered in brown papery husks. The fruit itself is green, with a clean, slightly acidic flavour.

Buying and storing

For the best flavour, buy tomatoes straight from the grower and store them at room temperature. Chilling tomatoes dulls their taste. Fresh tomatillos are difficult to obtain outside Latin America, but canned ones make a perfectly acceptable substitute.

Below: Fresh tomatillos are a tasty addition to spicy Mexican salsas.

Above: Tomatoes were enjoyed by the Mayas and Aztecs in ancient times.

Preparing and cooking

When adding to salsas and sauces, tomatoes should ideally have the skin removed. To skin tomatoes, cut a cross on the base, put them in a heatproof bowl and pour over boiling water. Leave for 30–60 seconds, then remove the remaining skin with a sharp knife. In Mexico, tomatillos are used fresh and raw, mostly in salsas, but they also taste great cooked.

AVOCADOS

The most nutritious of all the fruit vegetables, the avocado is native to Mexico, where it is called *acuacate*. In Brazil it is known as *abacate*, and in the US, alligator pear.

Nutrition

Despite the hefty calorie content – half an avocado delivers around 143kcals – the fat they contain is mostly mono-unsaturated and is a valuable source of energy. Avocados are protein-rich and also contain vitamins E, C and B_6, plus copper and iron.

Varieties

Among the many varieties, some with soft, smooth skins, others encased in dark, wrinkled shells, the avocado with the best flavour is the hass, a dark avocado with buttery, golden yellow flesh.

Buying and storing

Obtaining the perfect avocado can be a tricky business. Some supermarkets package the fruits with a "ready to eat" label, which is helpful if the avocados are hard-skinned. To test if a soft-skinned avocado is ripe, press the top end gently – it should just give. Ripe avocados can be stored in the refrigerator; unripe ones should be put in a paper bag with a banana to soften.

Preparation and cooking

Avocados soon discolour when cut, but sprinkling the cut surface with lemon juice will help prevent this. To halve an avocado, run a knife lengthways around the fruit, cutting in to the stone (pit), then ease the halves apart. Remove the stone and peel the halves before chopping the flesh. The most common use for avocados is in guacamole, but they also taste wonderful in soups and mousses. Avocados are seldom cooked, but in Latin America slices are often added to soups or stews just before serving. In Brazil, avocado is served as a creamy dessert, *creme de abacate*.

Below: Although high in calories, avocados contain healthy fats and plenty of vitamins and minerals.

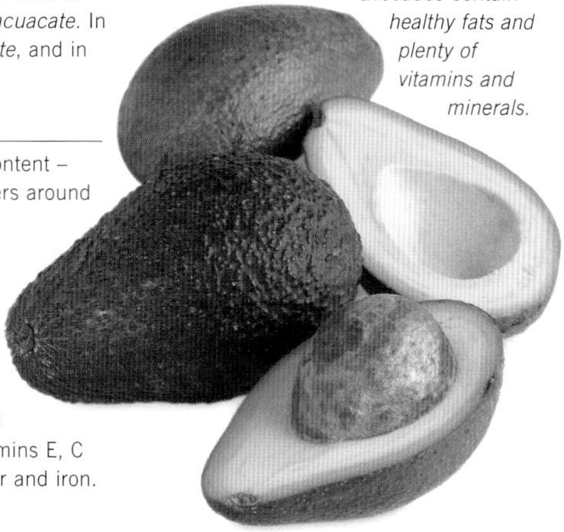

GUACAMOLE

Guacamole originated in Mexico, but has become one of the world's most popular dishes. Mashed avocado is the main ingredient, but other items, such as onion, garlic, diced tomato, chopped chillies, lime or lemon juice and seasonings are added. The smooth, buttery taste of the avocado gives this dip a creamy texture, yet it contains no saturated fat. Guacamole is often served with tortilla chips as a simple dip. It is an essential accompaniment to fajitas, is used in *tortas*, and is served alongside meat and fish dishes.

Simple Guacamole

1 Cut two avocados in half. Remove the stones (pits) and scoop out the flesh. Place in a blender and process until almost smooth. Transfer into a bowl and add the juice of half a lime.

2 Add one-quarter of a small onion, chopped finely, a crushed garlic clove and a handful of fresh coriander, also chopped finely.

3 Add salt and other seasoning to taste and serve immediately, with tortilla chips for dipping. The guacamole will keep in the fridge for 2–3 days if it is kept in an airtight container.

VARIATION

Try adding chopped fresh tomatoes and fresh chilli to give your guacamole added flavour, texture and fire.

Preparing avocado

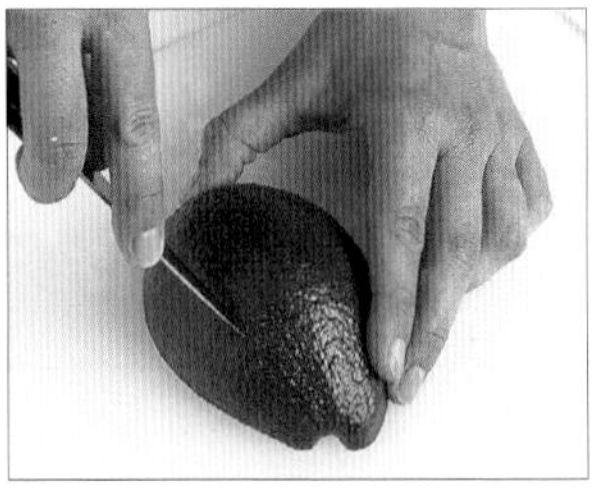

1 If a recipe calls for avocado halves or mashed avocado, run a small, sharp knife all the way around the fruit, cutting right in until the knife touches the stone (pit).

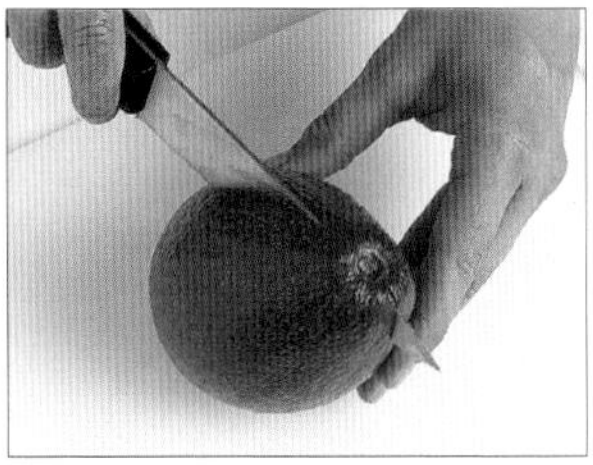

2 Gently prise the two halves apart with the knife.

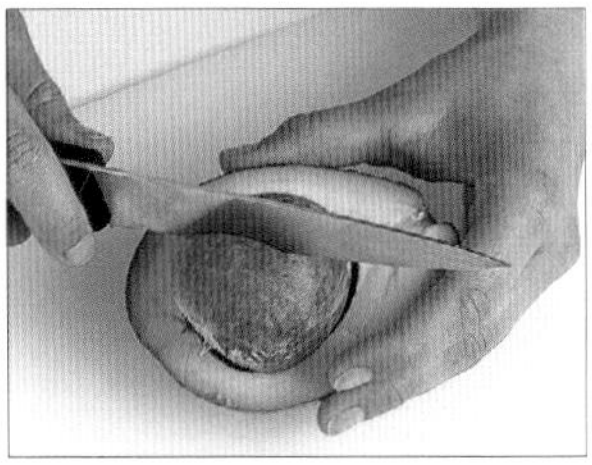

3 Push the knife blade into the stone, then lift it away. If any of the brown skin from the stone remains on the avocado flesh, remove it. The avocado halves can be served with vinaigrette, filled with prawns or topped with thin slices of ham. Alternatively, the flesh can be scooped into a bowl and mashed.

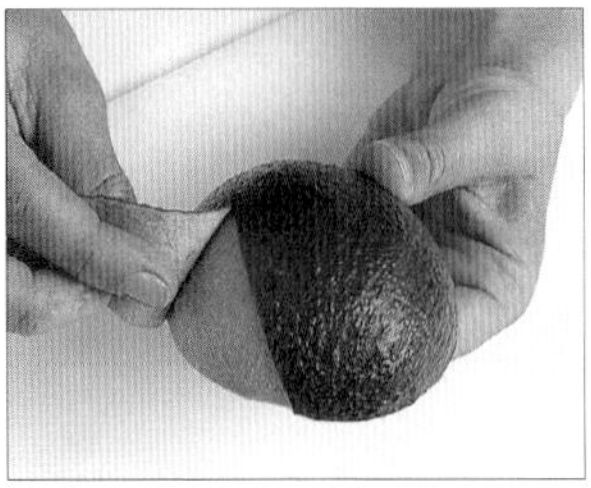

1 For avocado slices, cut the fruit in half, remove the stone, then nick the skin at the top of each half and ease it away until you can peel away the skin completely; if the avocado is ripe, it will come away cleanly and easily.

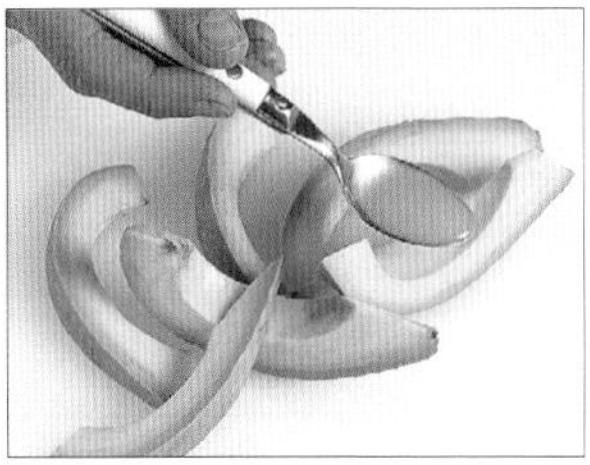

2 Cut the peeled avocado halves into slices, leaving them attached at one end if you want to fan them on the plate. Sprinkle them with lemon or lime juice to stop them from discolouring too quickly.

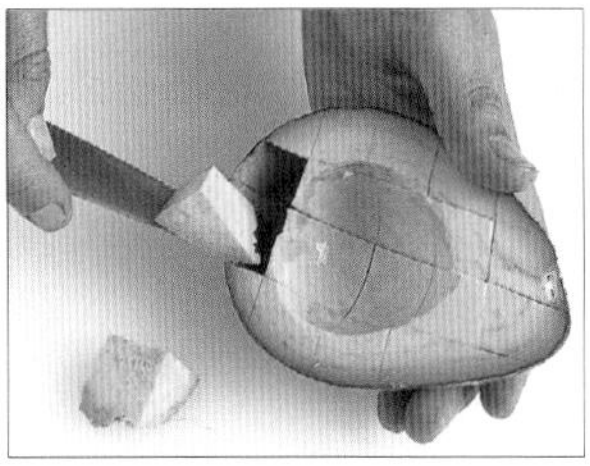

1 For cubes of avocado, score the half of avocado and then with the tip of the knife gently lift each cube out one by one.

Left: Tomatillos with husks

TOMATILLOS/TOMATE VERDE

Despite the name by which we know them – and the fact that they are sometimes referred to as Mexican green tomatoes – tomatillos are not members of the tomato family. Instead, they are related to physalis, those pretty little orange fruit surrounded by papery lanterns, which are so popular for garnishing. They have been grown in Mexico since Aztec times, when they were known as *miltomatl*. Mexicans seldom use the term "tomatillo", preferring to call these fruit by one of their many local names, which include *fresadilla* and *tomate milpero*.

Description

Ranging in colour from yellowish green to lime, tomatillos are firm, round fruit, about the size of a small tomato but lighter in weight, as they are not juicy. Fresh ones usually have the brown papery husk attached to them at the stem end. The flavour resembles that of tart apples with a hint of lemon, and is enhanced by cooking, although a *salsa cruda* of raw tomatillos has a very pleasant, clean taste.

Buying and Storing

Fresh tomatillos are difficult to come by outside Mexico, but some specialist stores sell them, and they are also available by mail order in season. They can also be grown from seed, a most worthwhile enterprise for anyone who loves their clean, slightly acidic flavour. If you do locate a supply of fresh tomatillos, look for firm fruit with tight-fitting husks, and store them in the fridge for up to one week.

In the same way that canned carrots bear little resemblance to fresh ones, canned tomatillos are softer and not as tasty as fresh, but they are more readily available and preferable to missing out on this great flavour completely. When buying canned tomatillos, be sure to take account of the loss of weight when the liquid is drained off – it can be as much as a third of the total.

Main Uses and Cooking Tips

Tomatillos are used in table salsas and in the sauce (*tomate verde salsa*) which is poured over enchiladas before they are cooked. They can also be used instead of tomatoes in guacamole, giving a piquant flavour to the sauce. To cook fresh tomatillos, remove the husks and dry fry them in a heavy-based frying pan until the skins have begun to char and the flesh has softened. Alternatively, put them in a pan with water to cover, bring to the boil, then simmer them until they soften and begin to break down. If the dish in which they are used requires stock, use the cooking liquid.

Above: Canned tomatillos

Salsa cruda de tomatillo

1 To make a rough-textured salsa with tomatillos, process 450g/1lb raw tomatillos in a food processor or chop them finely, then mix with one chopped small onion and one crushed garlic clove. Add two seeded and chopped jalapeño chillies and salt to taste.

2 Finely chop a small bunch of fresh coriander (cilantro) and add it to the tomatillo mixture.

3 Stir well, spoon into a clean bowl and serve at once with freshly made corn tortilla chips.

FRUIT

Some of the world's most colourful, exotic and intensely flavoured fruits are to be found throughout Latin America and the Caribbean.

PINEAPPLES

The taste of a freshly picked ripe pineapple is incomparable. Their aroma is so intense that a single pineapple can perfume the entire house, and the flesh is so sweet that it is unnecessary to add sugar or any other sweetener. Cultivated in Central America and the Caribbean long before the arrival of Columbus, this majestic fruit has become popular the world over. Costa Rica and the Dominican Republic are the major producers. Pineapples are used in both sweet and savoury dishes and make refreshing drinks. In Venezuela and Columbia, pineapple is a popular flavouring for sweet custard desserts. Rich in vitamin C and a valuable source of fibre, pineapples also contain bromelain, a protein-digesting enzyme that soothes digestive complaints.

Varieties

There are hundreds of varieties of pineapple, ranging in size from the small "baby pineapples" to specimens 30cm/12in long. Some turn a deep golden yellow as they ripen, while others remain a bronze-green colour. The latest varieties to be cultivated are deliciously sweet and juicy.

Below: Papaya is a popular addition to Latin American fruit salads.

Above: Pineapples can be used to make a delicious refresco or fruit drink.

Buying and storing

Choose firm, ripe fruit with no bruising. The leaves should be glossy and fresh, and there should be a distinctive pineapple aroma. One test of ripeness is to gently pull a leaf from the bottom of the plume; if it comes away easily, the pineapple is ripe. Store whole pineapples in a cool place, but not the refrigerator, and use them as quickly as possible. Slices or cubes of pineapple should be stored in an airtight container and chilled in the refrigerator, where they will keep for up to three days.

PAPAYAS

These Latin American natives were slow to gain popularity in Europe. Before careful packaging techniques and speedy air travel ensured that the fruit reached its destination in good condition, the papayas on sale throughout Europe were far from their best – hard and unappetizing or soft and squashy. Today, the situation has improved considerably and more and more people are now beginning to appreciate the sweet, scented flesh of this delicious fruit. Papayas are extremely easy to digest, thanks to an enzyme called papain, which they contain. Papain is a natural tenderizer, a fact that was well known to the pre-Colombian Indians who often marinated their meat in papaya juice to improve the quality. Amply stocked with vitamins A and C, and calcium, papayas are also a valuable source of fibre.

Preparing pineapple

The fruit is usually served fresh and raw, but cooking brings out the sweet flavour still more and pineapple tastes particularly good in hot, spicy dishes. Avoid using fresh pineapple in gelatine-based desserts, as the bromelain will prevent it from setting.

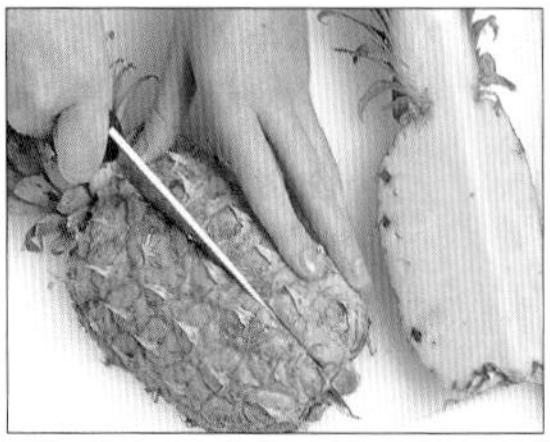

1 To grill (broil) pineapple, cut the fruit into quarters, remove the core from each piece, then loosen the flesh by running a sharp knife between the flesh and the skin, as when preparing melon.

2 Douse liberally with rum, sprinkle with brown sugar and place under a hot grill (broiler) until caramelized.

3 To cube pineapples, quarter the fruit, then remove the core and skin from each quarter, taking care to cut out the peppery "eyes". Cube the wedges or cut them into sticks.

Preparing mangoes

Ripe mangoes are juicy and can be messy to eat. For convenience, cut the fruit into cubes or strips.

1 Cut a broad slice from either side of the mango, removing the "cheeks" or plump sides.

2 For long pieces, peel the skin from each cheek, slice the flesh lengthways, then cut off any flesh still sticking to the stone (pit).

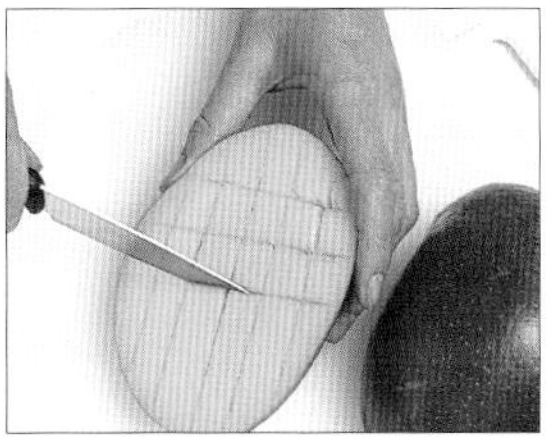

3 To dice mango, leave the flesh on the skin and use a sharp knife to mark it into neat squares.

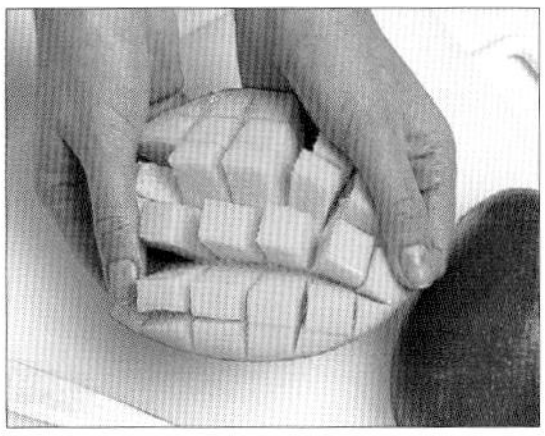

4 Gently press the mango cheek back on itself so that the pieces stand proud. Either eat straight from the skin with a spoon or use a sharp knife to slice off the chunks.

Below: A Caribbean native, Julie, one of more than 300 varieties of mango has sweet, tender flesh and an intense perfumed fragrance.

Varieties

All papayas are pear-shaped, but the size varies considerably, with some weighing up to 5kg/11lb or more. The skin starts off green, before ripening to a bright yellow or red. The sweet, scented flesh can be either pink or yellow. A hybrid form of papaya is the *babaco* from Ecuador, a fruit that can be served fresh or cooked. Stewed *babaco* tastes particularly good with roast meats.

Buying and storing

Look for small, soft papayas with undamaged, yellow skins. Handle them gently and use them as soon as possible. Store ripe papayas in the refrigerator; unripe papayas will continue to ripen at room temperature.

Preparing and serving

Cut the fruit in half and scoop out the seeds. The flavour of papaya is often improved with a squirt of fresh lime juice. Papaya can be combined with coconut milk to make a soothing drink, while in the Caribbean, the unripe fruit is used in savoury dishes.

MANGOES

While many exotic native fruits have been transported from Latin America to European countries, mangoes made the journey in the opposite direction. These delectable fruits originated in Asia, but were enthusiastically embraced by Caribbean and Central American farmers as soon as they were introduced. The meltingly tender flesh, with its unique fragrance and flavour, makes mangoes a popular choice for drinks, desserts and even some savoury dishes. Ripe mangoes are a good source of fibre and they contain generous amounts of vitamin C. The vibrant orange flesh also makes them a valuable source of beta-carotene.

Varieties

Over 300 varieties of mango are commercially cultivated, with many more being grown in tropical gardens. One of the most popular varieties imported into Europe from the Caribbean is Julie. This medium-sized mango, slightly flattened on one side, comes mainly from the islands of Jamaica and Trinidad and Tobago. It contains only a small amount of fibre and is particularly noted for its fine flavour. Two other favourites are the kidney-shaped Madame Francis, which originated in Haiti, and the Brazilian Itamarica. Of the fibreless varieties, the Jamaican Bombay Green is highly regarded, as is Brazil's Mango de Ubá.

Buying and storing

Not all mangoes turn yellow or become rosy-cheeked when ripe, so colour is not necessarily a clear indication of ripeness. Avoid fruit with dark patches on the skin as this is a sign that the fruit is past its best. A perfect mango will have an intense sweet aroma and will yield when lightly pressed. Unripe mangoes will quickly ripen if placed in a paper bag with a banana.

Above: Guavas are used to make the delicious sweetmeat dulce de guayaba.

GUAVAS

Native to Central and South America, guavas were introduced to Europe by the Conquistadors. Brazil remains a major producer of these highly perfumed fruit, known as *guayabas* in Mexico. Guavas are usually used in desserts, but their flavour is such that they are equally good in savoury dishes, especially with fish. Guavas are an excellent source of vitamin C, better than most citrus fruits. They also contain vitamins A and B_6.

Varieties

The fruits can be oval or round, with shiny skin that turns pale yellow when ripe. Some varieties have creamy white flesh, while others have pink or even purple flesh. Guava flesh has a clean, sweet, slightly acidic flavour, and a rather musky scent, but this disappears when the fruit is cooked.

Buying and storing

Look for firm, fairly small fruit that has ripened to a uniform yellow. Avoid any that are bruised or pockmarked. Wrap them well to avoid contaminating other foods with their musky odour, and store them in the refrigerator.

Preparing and serving

If the guavas are young there is no need to peel them. Just wash the fruit, then slice it, removing the larger seeds. Older fruit will need to be skinned and seeded. Guavas can be eaten raw with a little sugar to bring out their flavour, or cooked. In Latin America, sweetened guava pulp is used to make *dulce de guayaba*, which is similar to *membrillo*, the Spanish quince "cheese".

CITRUS FRUITS

The only citrus fruit that originated in Latin America is the grapefruit. A descendant of the Polynesian pomelo or shaddock, it is said to have been cultivated on Barbados. Grapefruit is thought to be useful in helping to lower cholesterol. Oranges came from China and India, and were introduced to the Caribbean by early traders. Seville oranges are particularly popular in the islands – although too bitter to eat raw, they are widely used in poultry and meat dishes. Limes were also an early import, hugely valued because they helped to prevent scurvy. Limes grow well in Latin America and their juice is widely used. Its most famous function is as a marinade for raw fish; the

Below: Grapefruits are native to Latin America.

Dulce de guayaba

This sweet guava paste, popular throughout Latin America, is delicious served with a hard cheese such as Manchego.

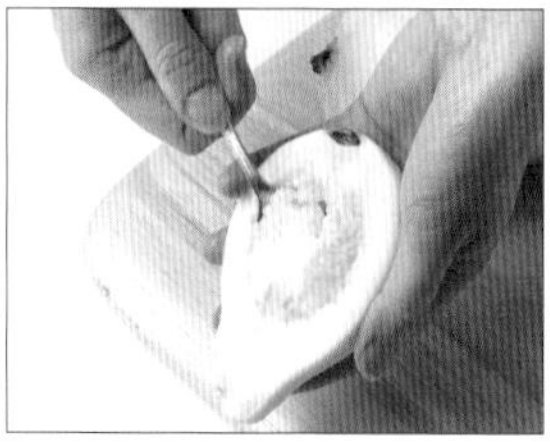

1 Peel 1kg/2¼lb guavas, then half each guava and scoop the seeds into a bowl. Add 200ml/7fl oz/ scant 1 cup water and set aside.

2 Chop the guavas and put them in a large, heavy pan. Pour over water to cover, bring to the boil, then cover and simmer, stirring frequently, for about 2 hours. Strain in the juice from the guava seeds and stir well.

3 Purée the mixture in a food processor, then press through a sieve into a bowl. Using a cup measure, scoop it into a heavy pan, noting the number of cups. Add an equal number of cups of sugar and stir in 30ml/2 tbsp lime juice.

4 Stir over a low heat until the mixture reddens and becomes very thick. Pour into a shallow pan and smooth the surface. Dry out in a barely warm oven and serve in small squares.

Above: Limes are a popular ingredient, especially in Mexican dishes.

action of the acid on the protein cooks the fish. Lemons are used in Latin American cooking, but are secondary to limes. All forms of citrus fruit are low in calories and are good sources of fibre and vitamin C.

Varieties

Grapefruit may be white, pink or ruby. There is also a green-skinned variety with sweet flesh. Oranges are either sweet or bitter. There are many varieties of sweet oranges, including Valencias, which are juicy and seedless. Of the bitter oranges, Sevilles are the best known. In addition to being used in cooking, bitter oranges are the basis for several Caribbean liqueurs, including curaçao. There are three main types of lime – Tahitian, Mexican and Key Limes. Mexican limes are fairly small but have a strong and aromatic flavour.

Buying and storing

The juiciest fruits are those that feel fairly heavy for their size. Choose those with firm skin, avoiding any that are damaged or wrinkled. This advice is especially relevant to limes because they perish more quickly than other forms of citrus fruits. Choose bright green limes with shiny skins that are unmarked by brown patches. Grapefruit, lemons and limes should be stored in a cool place or the refrigerator for up to 1 week; oranges have a slightly longer shelf-life and will keep well for up to 2 weeks at cool room temperature.

BANANAS

Introduced to South America from Portugal in the 16th century, bananas rapidly became naturalized and are today a very important food crop in the region. In some areas, such as the Windward Islands in the Caribbean, they are practically the only crop. A large proportion of the world's organic bananas come from this area, as well as from the Dominican Republic and Mexico. Bananas are convenient, nutritious, tasty and so easy to digest that they can be eaten by everyone, old or young. With high levels of potassium, bananas also contribute vitamins C and B_6. The carbohydrate they contain boosts flagging energy levels. Banana leaves are used as a wrapper for *pastelles*, the corn meal and meat parcels that are a speciality on Trinidad and Tobago, and similar wrapped dishes.

Varieties

There are hundreds of different varieties of banana, though few are identified by name. Most familiar in our stores are the common yellow curved bananas, but it is sometimes possible to buy the tiny Brazilian lady fingers or sugar bananas. Red bananas, which come from Ecuador, have orange flesh and taste particularly good when cooked.

Buying and storing

Bananas are harvested when they are still green. By the time they reach stores in the northern hemisphere they have begun to ripen, and most are at their peak after being allowed to ripen in a warm room for a day or two. The skin of the fruit will become progressively darker, and will acquire brown speckles, but even at this stage, the flesh will probably be perfectly good to eat. Do not throw away very soft bananas; they can be used to make banana bread.

Preparing and serving

There's nothing tricky about preparing a banana – simply peel back the skin and eat. If you want to eat half a banana, fold the skin back across the uneaten piece, wrap the fruit well and it will still be edible the next day. Bananas are delicious fresh but can also be cooked. A popular way of preparing them in the Caribbean is to bake them, or cook them on the barbecue, with plenty of brown sugar and a dash of rum to caramelize.

Above: Bananas are an important crop in Latin America and the Caribbean; much of the world's supply comes from plantations in these areas.

OTHER FRUITS

Latin America and the Caribbean are also home to some more unusual fruits, including the following.

Ackees The only part of this bright red fruit that is edible is the creamy-coloured aril, which looks a bit like scrambled egg. Ackee has an interesting texture and a subtle flavour and is one of the key ingredients of the Jamaican dish salt fish and ackee. Canned ackees are available from Caribbean food stores.

Breadfruit This large green fruit has very starchy flesh. Although very ripe breadfruit can be eaten raw, they are more often roasted, as a Caribbean speciality, baked, boiled or fried. They are available fresh or canned.

Cherimoyas Indigenous to the region, cherimoyas have delicious creamy flesh that tastes like a cross between banana and pineapple, with a texture similar to papaya. The skin and seeds should not be eaten. Varieties include custard apples and soursops.

Prickly pears These are the fruit of a Central American cactus. Beneath the prickly skin, the flesh is sweet-scented, with a taste similar to melon. Prickly pear flesh can be eaten raw with a squeeze of lime juice and a sprinkling of chilli powder to bring out the flavour.

Right: Beneath the pink skin, the flesh of the prickly pear is vibrant red.

Above: Be sure to remove tamarillo skin before eating or cooking the tangy flesh.

Tamarillos Native to the west coast of South America, these shiny, bright red oval fruits are grown commercially in Argentina, Brazil, Colombia and Venezuela. The skin is very bitter and must be removed before the tangy flesh can be enjoyed. A tamarillo dip is the traditional accompaniment for *arepas*, the flat corn breads that are popular in Venezuela and Colombia.

Passion fruits These fragrant fruits come from Central and South America and the best-tasting variety is round and very dark-skinned. The greenish yellow pulp has an exquisite flavour and the seeds are edible, although some people prefer to remove them. Large yellow passion fruits that look rather like light bulbs are granadillas. These have greyish pulp and are neither as flavoursome nor as highly scented as passion fruits.

Above: Choose passion fruits with extra-dark skin as these are sweetest.

Plantains

These are a type of banana grown as a vegetable, but the name is also used for green sweet bananas. True plantains taste very bitter and must be cooked before being eaten. Treat them like potatoes – they are good when baked in their skins, or they can be boiled, mashed, baked or fried as chips. A popular snack on Spanish-speaking Caribbean islands is *tostones de plátano*, long slices of plantain that are partially fried, squashed flat and fried again until brown and crisp.

Below: Fresh plantains are prepared and cooked more like a vegetable than a fruit.

NUTS

Nutrient-rich nuts are a huge part of the Latin American diet, and they appear in various guises, most commonly as a thickening ingredient in both sweet and savoury sauces.

Coconuts The Latin American cuisine relies heavily on coconuts. The liquid they contain is used to flavour drinks and desserts, while the dense nutmeat is a valuable ingredient in almost everything, including soups, seafood and meat dishes and desserts. It is used fresh, dried or as coconut milk or cream, which can be bought canned.

Cashew nuts These are the fruit of an evergreen tree. Each nut grows out of the bottom of a fleshy bulge, which is called a cashew apple. Although not technically a fruit, it closely resembles one, rewarding the picker with crisp, juicy flesh. The nuts themselves are toxic and shelling is a tortuous business, but when released and detoxified, they make a tasty snack and are also used in drinks and sauces.

Pecan nuts These glossy red-skinned nuts are cultivated in northern Mexico, where they are often used in recipes, that hark back to the French occupation in the 19th century. Pecan nuts have a very high fat content so should be eaten sparingly.

Below: Many Latin American desserts are based on coconut or coconut milk.

Pine nuts The nuts of several native pine trees, including the Chilean araucaria and the Brazilian parana pine, are used in Latin American cooking. All are highly nutritious.

Almonds were introduced to Latin America by the Spanish, who cannily added the caveat that they could not be grown on a large scale, thus ensuring that the trade with their native country continued. They are still largely imported, so are fairly expensive and tend to be saved for more extravagant dishes or special occasions. Almonds are still used to make traditional Mexican chocolate, while almond paste is the basis of the luxurious sweetmeat, *turrón*.

Below: Cashew nuts are eaten as a snack with a cold beer or caipirinha.

Below: Almonds are mainly imported from Spain, while pecans and walnuts are native.

Below: Peanuts are a popular ingredient in savoury dishes, particularly with poultry.

Walnuts are grown in the highlands of central Mexico. Their bitter-sweet flavour makes them a popular ingredient in savoury dishes as well as desserts. They taste delicious when baked with potatoes and chillies.

Brazil nuts are the seeds of towering trees that grow wild in the Amazon rainforest. Inside the large husks are around 20 nuts, packed tightly together. Very high in oil, Brazil nuts go rancid quickly when shelled, so crack them at the last minute.

Peanuts These are actually pulses not nuts, and they grow just beneath the soil. They have been cultivated in Peru for centuries and are a valuable food crop, contributing protein and fat to the diet. Peanut brittle is a popular sweet treat, while savoury dishes include pork and potatoes in peanut sauce. Peanut oil and peanut butter are also used, the latter being the basis for a popular punch, which is often served in Trinidad with a shot of rum.

HERBS, SPICES AND FLAVOURINGS

Many of the herbs and spices used in Latin American cooking will be familiar to the foreign visitor. Bunches of thyme, basil, oregano, mint, parsley and coriander (cilantro) scent the air in city markets, and spices such as nutmeg, allspice and cinnamon add their warm aroma. Asian immigrants have introduced cumin, five-spice power and curry powder, but it is perhaps the local specialities that are of most interest to the food tourist: *epazote*, *palillo*, *guascas* and the fiery chilli sauces developed by Caribbean cooks.

THYME

Widely used, especially in Mexico, Colombia and the Caribbean, this robust herb lends its inimitable flavour to dishes such as rice and peas, okra fried rice, Colombian chicken hot-pot and thyme and lime chicken. The dried herb is included in the dry rub that is used to flavour *carnitas*.

Pebre

This hot coriander and chilli salsa from Chile is delicious with meats.

1 Whisk 15ml/1 tbsp red wine vinegar with 30ml/2 tbsp olive oil.

2 Add 2–3 aji mirasol chillies, seeded and very finely chopped, 1 finely chopped small onion, 2 crushed garlic cloves and 75ml/5 tbsp water.

3 Mix well, then stir in 90ml/6 tbsp chopped fresh coriander (cilantro). Cover and set aside for 2–3 hours at room temperature to allow the flavours to blend.

Below: Thyme is a popular flavouring in many Colombian dishes.

CORIANDER/CILANTRO

Native to Europe, coriander is grown in South America too, and is hugely popular, especially in Mexico and the Bahian cuisine of Brazil. Fresh coriander leaves go particularly well with fish. Chilli clam soup and Cuban seafood rice both owe their distinctive flavouring to this popular herb. It also goes well with avocado and is used in both guacamole and avocado soup. Mexican green tomato dishes inevitably include coriander.

Right: Use mint to make a refreshing mojito.

Below: Coriander is an essential ingredient in the Mexican salsa, guacamole.

MINT

South America cooks delight in using herbs in innovative ways. Mint and seafood is not an obvious combination, but their use of this familiar flavouring in chunky prawn chowder works extremely well. Mint is also used to flavour drinks and salads.

INDIGENOUS HERBS

Annatto/achiote The seeds of a tropical flowering tree, annatto has long been used as a flavouring and natural dye. The dried seeds have a mild flavour, with a hint of orange blossom. Annatto oil, pressed from the hard orange pulp that surrounds the seeds, is a popular flavouring and colouring for meat, fish and vegetable dishes. In the Yucatán peninsula and nearby Cuba, annatto seeds are often ground with cumin and oregano to make an aromatic rub for meats, such as spiced roast leg of lamb.

Epazote Also known as goose-foot, this herb is as commonplace in South America as oregano is on the islands of Greece. The dried leaves are crumbled and sold in jars. *Epazote* is widely used in central and southern Mexico, especially in bean dishes. The taste has been compared to anis.

Palillo This is an indigenous Peruvian herb. Dried and ground, it has little flavour and is mainly used to give food an attractive golden colour. Turmeric can be substituted, but use only half the amount suggested, as the flavour of turmeric can be overwhelming.

Guascas In Colombia, this herb is so common that it is sometimes viewed as a weed. The essential flavouring of the national dish, *ajiaco*, a delicious chicken soup, it is fairly difficult to obtain outside the country, except in dried and ground form. There is no real substitute as the flavour is unique, although it has been suggested that fennel comes close.

Huacatay comes from a plant that is closely related to the marigold. Pungent, with a rather unpleasant flavour, it is very much an acquired taste.

Caribbean spice mixes

These seasoning mixes are so frequently used in Caribbean recipes that it is perhaps worth making up a large amount and storing for future use.

Herb seasoning Chop 4 spring onions (scallions) and put them in a mortar. Add 1 chopped garlic clove and 15ml/1 tbsp each fresh coriander (cilantro), thyme and basil. Pound until smooth.

Spice seasoning Put 15ml/1 tbsp garlic granules in a bowl. Add 7.5ml/1½ tsp each of ground black pepper, paprika, celery salt and curry powder. Stir in 5ml/1 tsp caster (superfine) sugar. Mix well and store in a tightly sealed container in a dry, cool place.

Left: (Anticlockwise from top) Warm spices, such as allspice, cinnamon sticks, ground cinnamon and annatto (achiote) are popular throughout Latin America.

SPICES

The most popular spices in Caribbean and Latin American cooking are those with warm flavours, such as cinnamon, cloves, cumin, nutmeg and paprika. Several of these flavours are combined in the aptly named allspice, which comes from a type of tree related to the myrtle. Allspice berries are dark brown. When dried they resemble peppercorns. Both the whole berries and the ground spice are used in Latin American cooking. Ground allspice is one of the main flavourings in the traditional Caribbean speciality, salt fish and ackee, and also appears in the marinade for the popular jerk chicken.

Vanilla is another warm spice. The pods or beans come from a climbing tree orchid, which grows in parts of Central America. Added whole to warm milk or chocolate, they impart a wonderfully sweet and fragrant flavour. If just the seeds are required, slit the bean lengthways and carefully scrape them out with a sharp knife.

SWEET AND SOUR

Ever since sugar was introduced to Latin America in the 16th century, sweetmeats (*dulces*) have been enormously popular. Elaborately shaped and decorated, they are an everyday indulgence, as are caramel desserts, such as the flan, which resembles a caramel custard, but sometimes contains pineapple or coconut. Many cooks use unrefined sugar to make treats like these, selecting either *piloncillo*, the dark-brown Mexican sugar, or *panela*, the Colombian version.

As a contrast to all this sweetness, bitter flavours are also highly valued. Angostura bitters, an infusion of gentian root and herbs on a rum base, is often used to add a tart note to fish and meat dishes as well as drinks.

Below: On the island of Barbados, fresh grapefruit is often served with a dash of herb-flavoured Angostura bitters.

Dairy Products and Eggs

Dairy products came to Latin America relatively late, and although milk, cheese and eggs are important foodstuffs, they do not have as prominent a role as in Europe or North America.

CHEESE

Before the Spanish conquest in the 16th century, fresh milk was a rarity in Latin America. In Peru, indigenous llamas, vicuñas and alpacas that had been domesticated were occasionally milked, but cheesemaking was unknown until the arrival of Spanish missionaries. Nor did their presence spell instant conversion to cheesemaking since finding a ready supply of milk would remain problematic for some time. The native animals were deemed unsuitable and goats failed to thrive in the humid lowlands. It was only when dairy cattle were established in more temperature zones that cheesemaking was attempted on anything but a minor scale, and the monks who travelled with the conquerors taught local people.

Cow's milk was used to make *queso blanco* (white cheese) – the simple soft cheese that is now a familiar sight in most Latin American countries. In the upland areas where goats were farmed, some cheese was made, but sheep's milk was not used until fairly recently, when farmers in Chile began producing a sheep's milk cheese similar to that produced in the Pyrenées.

There are plenty of cattle in Argentina and Brazil, but they are mainly beef animals. Most of the cheese eaten in Brazil is imported, as the high humidity makes cheese production difficult. A fresh cheese – Minas Frescal – is made in the Minas Gerais region, north of Rio de Janeiro, together with a stretched curd cheese called Minas Prensado.

The influx of immigrants proved to be a trigger for cheese production in many parts of South America. In 19th century Argentina, homesick Italians developed a cheese that closely resembled Parmesan, Treboligiano, as well as a mozzarella-type cheese called Moliterno. Cheese similar to Edam and Gouda satisfied the longing of Dutch settlers on Aruba for familiar flavours.

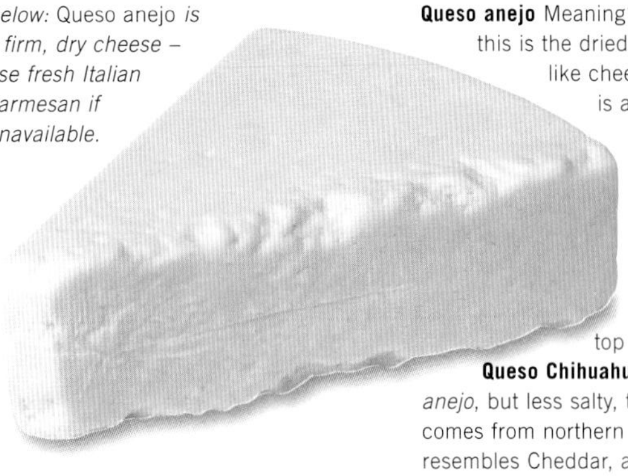

Below: Queso anejo *is a firm, dry cheese – use fresh Italian parmesan if unavailable.*

In Mexico, the demand for more European cheeses led to local production of cheeses such as Gruyère, Camembert and Port Salut, as well as a version of the Spanish cheese, Manchego. However, soft white cheeses remain the mainstay of the industry.

Queso blanco Made in most Latin American countries and eaten throughout the region, this white cow's milk cheese is traditionally produced from skimmed milk coagulated with lemon juice. Soft and crumbly, it is often used on enchiladas.

Queso fresco As the name, which means "fresh cheese" suggests, this is not a cheese for keeping. Young and unripened, it is usually eaten within a day or two of being made. It is mild and light, with a grainy, slightly crumbly texture. *Queso fresco* is actually the generic name for a number of cheeses, all of which share several common characteristics. It is often used for crumbling on top of finished dishes such as scrambled eggs, cooked *nopales* or other vegetables or bean dishes as a tasty garnish. *Queso fresco* has a fairly clean, sharp taste and is a good melting cheese so it is often used in tacos and on other tortilla-based snacks. If you can't find it in your local supermarket, substitute a good-quality mozzarella or ricotta.

Queso anejo Meaning"aged cheese", this is the dried version of a feta-like cheese. *Queso anejo* is a sharp, salty and fairly firm grating cheese similar to Parmesan, which makes a good substitute. It is often used for sprinkling on top of enchiladas

Queso Chihuahua Similar to *queso anejo*, but less salty, this originally comes from northern Mexico. It resembles Cheddar, and medium Cheddar can be used as a substitute. Alternatively, use the popular American cheese, Monterey Jack, which originated as *queso del pais* (country cheese) and was introduced to California by Spanish missionaries in the 18th century.

Asadero This slightly tart-tasting cheese is sometimes called *queso Oaxaca*, after the place in Mexico where it was originally made. The name *asadero* means "roasting cheese". It is a fairly stringy, supple cheese that is at its best when melted. It is ideal for stuffing fresh chillies, sweet (bell) peppers or other vegetables or meats, as it is unlikely to leak out during cooking. If *asadero* is unavailable, the closest equivalent is Italian mozzarella.

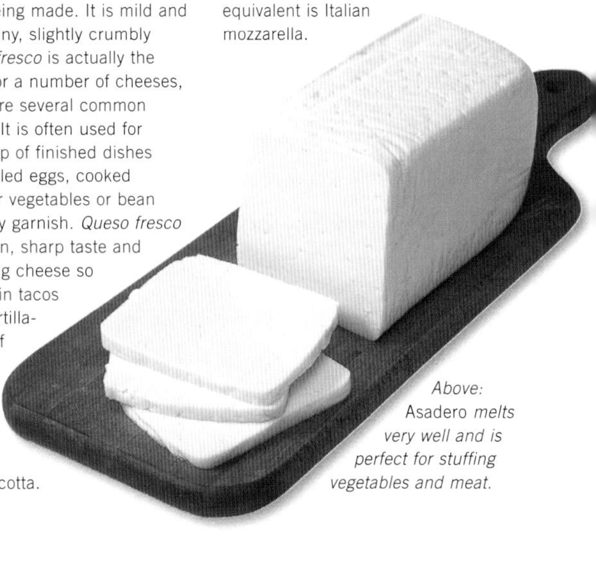

Above: Asadero *melts very well and is perfect for stuffing vegetables and meat.*

Above: When chickens were introduced to Latin America by the Spanish, hen's eggs quickly became popular and were added to many dishes.

EGGS

Until the Spanish arrived in Latin America, the only eggs eaten were those from game birds, ducks, wild geese, reptiles and insects. The Aztecs farmed wild turkeys, but although there is evidence of turkey eggs being used in religious festivals, the birds appeared to have been prized more for their plumage and meat. When chickens arrived on the scene, however, hen's eggs rapidly became a valued food, and today it would be hard to imagine Mexico without *huevos rancheros*, a complete egg-based breakfast, and *rompope*, a cinnamon eggnog; Brazil without *quindao*; or anywhere in Latin America without the traditional flan (caramel custard). Throughout the region, eggs are used in both sweet and savoury dishes. Hard-boiled eggs are often used as a garnish on top of stews or vegetable dishes.

MILK

As is the case in Spain, fresh milk is quite difficult to come by in this part of the world because of the heat and humidity. As a result, long-life, evaporated (unsweetened condensed) and condensed milks have become more popular. The use of these treated milks is simply a practical solution to the problem of keeping milk fresh in the heat, but several delicious dishes have evolved that make the most of these treated milks as ingredients. The most famous of these is *dulce de leche*, an incredibly sweet, caramel-flavoured concoction that is so thick and creamy it can be spread on bread like butter or jam. *Dulce de leche* is enomously popular among Latin American children. A rich bread and butter pudding from Barbados also makes the most of evaporated milk as one of its main ingredients.

Milk and cream are also used throughout the region in a similar way to in Europe – they are often combined with fruit to make refreshing drinks, added to rich desserts and used in many savoury sauces, stews and soups. Canned evaporated or condensed milk is nearly always used instead of fresh cream or milk in hot drinks, such as coffee and hot chocolate, adding a distinctive rich, thick sweetness.

Below: Milk and cream are often added to fresh fruit to make refreshing drinks.

Bajan bread and butter custard

This Caribbean variation of bread and butter pudding relies on evaporated milk for its rich flavour.

SERVES 4

3 thin slices buttered bread, crusts removed, plus extra butter
400g/14oz can evaporated milk
150ml/¼ pint/⅔ cup fresh milk
2.5ml/½ tsp mixed spice (pumpkin pie spice)
40g/1½oz/3 tbsp brown sugar
2 eggs
75g/3oz/½ cup sultanas (golden raisins)
30ml/2 tbsp rum
nutmeg

1 Lightly grease a baking dish with butter. Quarter each slice of bread and layer the pieces in the dish.

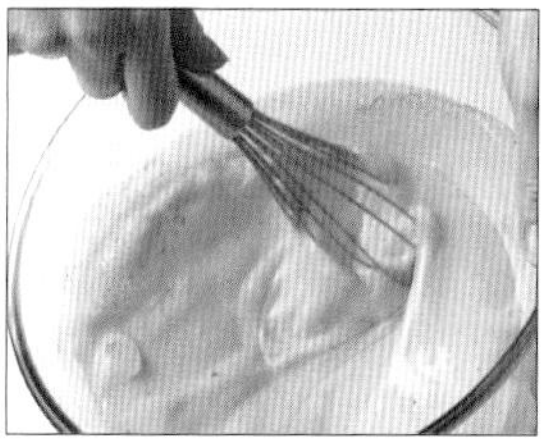

2 Whisk the milks, spice, sugar and eggs in a bowl. Pour over the bread and leave to stand for 30 minutes.

3 Meanwhile, soak the sultanas in the rum. Preheat the oven to 180°C/350°F/Gas 4.

4 Sprinkle the sultanas over the pudding, grate over a little nutmeg and bake for 30–45 minutes.

FISH AND SHELLFISH

When it comes to fish and shellfish, citizens of Latin America and the Caribbean are spoilt for choice. Every country except Bolivia and Paraguay has a coastline. You might expect the widest selection of fish to be available to the island dwellers of the Caribbean, but the finest seafood actually comes from the coastlines of Chile and Peru, where plankton brought up from the Antarctic by the icy Humboldt current provides a rich diet for the abundant sea life. The rivers and lakes teem with fresh fish, and both trout and salmon are farmed. The following list introduces just some of the fish available in Latin America, chosen either because they are particularly abundant or make a significant culinary contribution.

FRESH FISH

Snapper Two varieties of red snapper are to be found in the tropical waters of Central and South America. The American red snapper, which has lean white flesh with a very good flavour, is bright red all over, even including the eyes and fins. Its relative, the Caribbean red snapper, tends to be slightly smaller and is distinguished by its yellow eyes and paler belly. All snappers are very good to eat, whether baked, grilled (broiled), poached, steamed or pan-fried. The sweet, delicate flesh goes well with many types of fruit and fruit vegetables, such as mango or avocado. Caribbean snapper is often simply stuffed and baked, and sometimes wrapped in strips of bacon to keep the flesh juicy and tender.

Left: A large Caribbean red snapper can be stuffed and simply baked or grilled for a delicious meal.

Mahi mahi/dolphinfish/dorade Of all the many names for this flavoursome fish, dolphinfish is perhaps the most unfortunate, since it leads people to imagine, quite wrongly, that it is related to the dolphin. The mahi mahi looks like no other fish. It has an unusual square head and a long, tapering body, which makes it look somewhat like a baseball bat. The firm white flesh of mahi mahi has a delicious sweet flavour.

Mackerel Several varieties of king mackerel are fished off the coast of Latin America, including the *cero*, which is fairly abundant in the Gulf of Mexico, and the *sierra*, which frequents Pacific waters. Mackerel are at their most delicious when eaten extremely fresh, and are a popular choice to be "cooked" with lime juice and eaten as *escabeche*. When cooking mackerel, team it with robust or sharp flavours, to offset the richness.

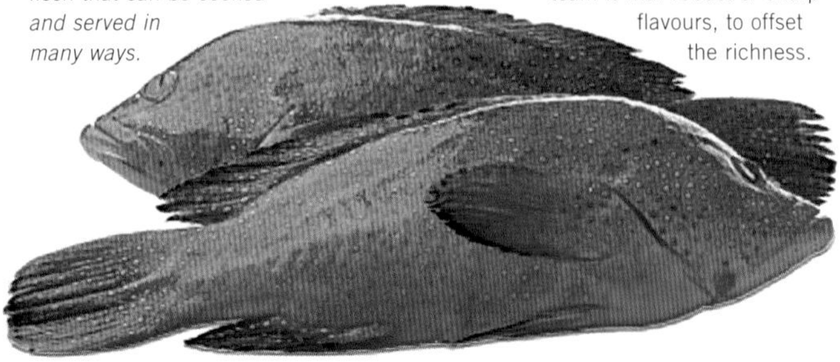

Below: Found in the Caribbean seas, warm-water groupers have fairly firm flesh that can be cooked and served in many ways.

Sea bass These look rather like salmon, with elegant, slim bodies and silvery scales. Various species are found in the Caribbean Sea and the Pacific Ocean. Sea bass can be grilled (broiled), baked, braised, poached, fried or steamed, and they taste particularly good when combined with spicy flavours. In Peru, where the striped bass or corvina is preferred, the fish is cooked with chillies, while in Argentina it is often stuffed and baked.

Grouper These rather glum-looking fish, with their characteristic pouty lips, are members of the sea bass family. The warm-water groupers, such as those that are found in the Caribbean Sea, tend to have firmer flesh than delicate sea bass, and are good for poaching as well as frying, baking or cooking on the barbecue.

Patagonian toothfish This large fish is commonly known as the Chilean sea bass. It does come from Chilean waters, but the sea bass label is not accurate because it belongs to a separate species. Famed for its fine flavour, the Patagonian toothfish is popular in the US and Asia. There have been concerns about overfishing in recent years.

Buying fish

When buying fish, make sure that it is as fresh as possible. This is particularly important if you are intending to serve it as ceviche. Here's what to look for:

- There should be no apparent odour, other than a pleasant, faint smell of the sea.
- The eyes should be clear, bright and slightly bulging.
- The flesh should be firm and elastic; if you press it lightly with your finger it should spring back.
- The gills should gape, revealing a red or rosy interior.
- The scales should be firmly attached, not flaking off.

Left: *Fresh trout are plentiful in Lake Titicaca, and are commonly eaten in the highlands of Peru and Bolivia.*

Swordfish are landed in the Gulf of Mexico and off the coast of Costa Rica from June to January and in Chile in late spring. The meaty flesh is low in fat and dries out quickly, so must be basted frequently if barbecued, or cooked in a sauce for the best results. Swordfish goes well with spicy flavours and Latin American cooks like to cook it with chillies and tomatoes. When buying swordfish, which is usually sold as steaks, check that the flesh is slightly translucent. It should be creamy white or pale pink, with the darker areas shading to a reddish-brown colour. Avoid steaks that look grey.

Pompano These are oily fish that taste similar to mackerel. They are available all year round, sometimes whole, but more often as fillets. There are several varieties in the warm seas off the coast of Central America, but the most common is the African pompano. This silvery, grey-finned fish has meaty flesh with a good, strong flavour. It is ideal for spicy dishes and goes well with chillies, coriander, red (bell) peppers and citrus fruit.

Congrio Found off the coasts of Chile and Peru, congrios resemble eels but are actually members of a distinctly separate species – *genypterus chilensis.* There are three types, all with firm, flavoursome flesh that flakes beautifully when cooked. This is one of the few fish to find its way into a poem. The Nobel prize-winning poet Pablo Neruda was so impressed with a bowl of congrio soup supped in his native Chile that he wrote an ode to the delicious fish.

Flying fish Also known as exocets, from which the name of the missile derives, these small fish really do look as if they are flying when you glimpse them leaping from the sea. Their propulsion comes from the tail and they stay in the air for several seconds, their large pectoral fins giving them lift. When freshly caught and pan-fried, flying fish taste delicious. Caribbean cooks like to rub them with a spicy mixture of garlic, herbs and hot pepper sauce before coating them in seasoned flour and frying them.

Above: Fresh swordfish steaks are delicious barbecued with a lime and chilli marinade.

Salt cod

Among the rations given to African slaves shipped over to work the sugar plantations was salt cod. They developed a taste for the rather unprepossessing looking food, and invented many recipes to make the most of its flavour. Some of these were based on those cooked by their Spanish or Portuguese masters, but they were often new. In Brazil, salt cod is served as a topping for baked eggs, while a Caribbean speciality is salt cod with scrambled eggs, spinach and bacon.

Below: Salt cod is used in many traditional Caribbean dishes.

Trout There are plenty of trout in the cooler regions of Latin America. Rainbow, brown and brook trout are found in the Patagonian lakes close to Bariloche, and the icy rivers that flow from the Andes to the sea in Peru are also a magnet for trout fishermen. Lake Titicaca, on the Andean highlands between Peru and Bolivia, also has a plentiful supply of trout. Trout has a fresh, clean flavour and, although it is often cooked very simply – either fried or grilled (broiled) – more inventive chefs delight in introducing unusual flavour combinations. One particularly tasty Caribbean dish combines spiced trout fillets with a rich wine and plantain sauce. The rosy flesh also looks lovely and tastes delicious when paired with fresh prawns (shrimp).

SHELLFISH

Latin America is a great place for shellfish. In the markets you'll not only come across familiar varieties, such as crabs and lobsters, but also rare and remarkable shellfish that look like algae-encrusted rocks, and sea urchins so large that their nickname – sea hedgehogs – seems entirely appropriate. In the Caribbean you can feast on conch, and in Brazil you can dine on some of the biggest prawns (shrimp) you are ever likely to encounter.

Crabs Both sea and land crabs are a delicacy in Latin America. There are many different varieties, from the soft-shelled blue crabs of the Atlantic and Gulf coasts to the mighty Patagonian king crabs. In Brazil, mangrove crabs are a great favourite, while Mexicans are partial to the California or Dungeness crab. Sweet and succulent, crab meat can be used in a wide variety of dishes. When carefully cooked, crab tastes good just as it is, but it also makes a great gumbo. Crab cakes are delicious. In Trinidad and Tobago, a favourite dish is a mixture of onion and crab meat in a rum sauce, served in crab shells.

Below: Crab meat is a Latin American delicacy, which can be added to soups or stews, alongside other seafood.

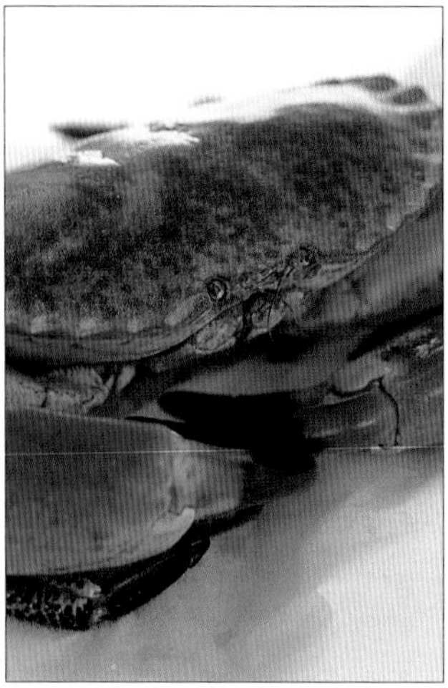

Above: Tender king prawns are often grilled with fresh coconut for a popular Brazilian street snack.

Prawns and shrimp Several different types of prawns and shrimp are found in the oceans surrounding the continent. The biggest and best are probably the Gulf shrimp, which are found in warm waters. Sometimes pinky grey in colour but more often brilliant scarlet, these are big and succulent. Prawns are always included on a cold mixed fish and shellfish platter but also feature in cooked dishes. They are often cooked with fresh coconut or coconut milk, an unusual combination but one that works extremely well.

Dried shrimp Tiny shrimp, tossed in dendê oil and dried in the sun until crunchy, are popular throughout Latin America, but particularly in Brazil's coastal Bahia region. They give flavour and texture to soups, stews and salads, and are an essential ingredient in the Brazilian dipping sauce, *vatapá*. To prepare dried shrimp, rinse them under cold running water, then soak in hot water for about 35 minutes. They are often ground before being used.

Mussels On the west coast of the continent, where the sea is often turbulent, mussels cling tenaciously to the rocks until prised off by chefs or diners. They inevitably form part of the pit-cooked seafood extravaganza, the Chilean *curanto*, and are also used in a variety of soups and stews. Their sweet, tender flesh is nutritious and they taste best when lightly steamed. Before cooking mussels, it is important to discard any that are not tightly closed, or which do not close when tapped. The opposite applies after cooking, when it is those mussels that have failed to open that must be discarded.

Clams Among the hundreds of different clams found in Latin America and the Caribbean, perhaps the most delicious are the *navajuelas* (razorshells) found off the coast of Chile and Peru. These clams have tubular brown shells. When packed in bundles, they look like bamboo sticks, with the soft creamy flesh of the animal protruding from one end. Razorshells are often served raw, but can be cooked. More familiar hard shell clams include quahogs and littlenecks, which are often used in *chupes* (chowders), and angelwing clams, which are harvested in Mexico, Cuba, Puerto Rico and Chile.

Below: Fresh mussels are abundant in Chile, where seafood is plentiful.

Above: Razorshell clams, also known as navajuelas, *can be cooked but are more often served raw.*

Scallops Easily identified by their fan-shaped shells, scallops are a source of two delectable treats: the sweet, tender white meat and the bright orange roe or "coral". In Latin America, scallops are widely enjoyed, especially on the western seaboard. Black scallops, which are found off the coast of Ecuador, are especially sought after. Scallops are often eaten raw, with just a squeeze of lime, but they can be cooked. Keep the cooking time short, however – a couple of minutes at most.

A Chilean extravaganza
The ultimate South American seafood experience has to be the Chilean *curanto*, a sort of clambake but with a much wider selection of fish and shellfish, including squid, mussels and scallops. A fire is made in a large stone-lined pit. When the stones are hot, the fish and shellfish are placed on top and covered with leaves. The pit is then sealed and only opened hours later when everything is cooked to perfection. One of the best places to sample a real *curanto* is on the island of Chiloe, otherwise, try the one-pot version called *curanto en olla*.

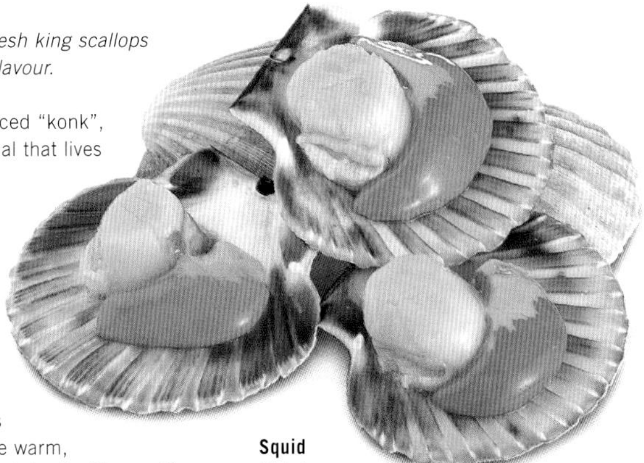

Right: Really fresh king scallops have the best flavour.

Conch Pronounced "konk", this is the animal that lives inside those big, beautiful pink-lined shells that many people display in their bathrooms. A large relative of the whelk, conches are found in the warm, shallow waters of the Caribbean. The pink flesh is tasty and chewy and good to eat, whether raw or cooked, but it must be beaten to tenderize it first. The meat is often used in chowders, but is also good delicately fried. In Barbados, fresh conch fritters are a great favourite, and are often served as a quick bar snack, alongside an ice-cold beer.
Abalone Like the conch, this is a gastropod, a sea creature with a single large foot for locomotion. Abalone feed exclusively on seaweed. They thrive in the cold waters off southern Chile, which are close to the world's largest kelp forests. Abalone are extremely difficult to prise from the rocks that they cling to, which helps to explain why they are fairly expensive. They are highly prized not only for their flesh, but also for their beautiful shells, which are lined with iridescent mother-of-pearl. Abalone has a delicious flavour but must be carefully prepared. Like conch, it needs to be tenderized carefully. Cynics sometimes suggest that the only way to do this successfully is to run it over with a truck, but beating with a wooden mallet usually does the trick.
Sea urchins There are over 800 species of sea urchin found all over the world, but only a few are edible. The ones found in Chile – called *erizos* – are unusually large, up to 10cm/4in across. Regarded as a gourmet delicacy, they are generally eaten raw. A tasty vinaigrette dressing may be offered, but lovers of sea urchins generally prefer them completely unadorned.

Squid
This is a very popular ingredient, especially in Mexico, Central America and the islands of the Caribbean. Squid has firm, lean, white flesh that can be tender and delicious when properly cooked. In Cuba, it forms part of a classic fish and shellfish rice dish, while in Chile it is combined with fresh chillies, potatoes and tomatoes to make a rich, warming stew. Small pan-fried squid can be found for sale along the coasts of South America as a delicious beach snack.

Below: Squid is a popular ingredient in Latin American cooking, with squid casserole a common dish in many areas.

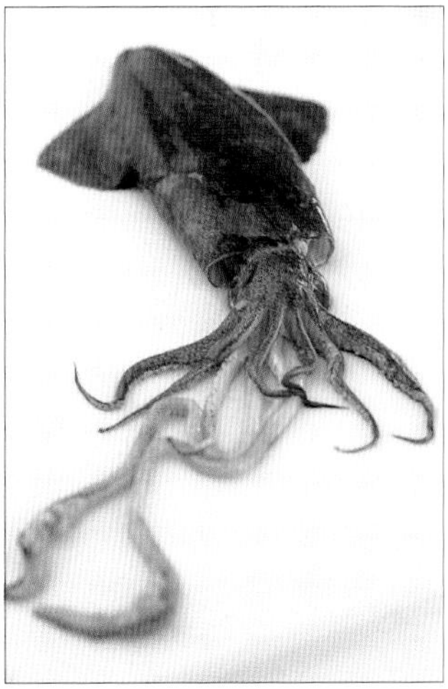

MEAT

Visit Argentina, and you could easily imagine that South America was some kind of monument to meat, yet it was not always so. Before the 16th century, cattle, sheep and pigs were unknown on the continent and the only meat that was consumed came from wild boar, game birds, including the wild turkey, cameloids, small mammals, iguanas, snakes and some other reptiles.

BEEF

Fanning out from either side of the Rio de la Plata are the pampas, large grassy plains that are home to some of the finest beef cattle in the world. Stretching for thousands of miles, the pampas cover the temperate zones of Argentina and Uruguay.

It was the early colonists who introduced beef cattle to the region, along with the European grasses that soon supplanted native varieties. Those first cattle, with horses and other farm animals, were kept in compounds, but inevitably many escaped and, finding the pampas very much to their liking, multiplied to form the nucleus of what would eventually become vast wild herds. With both wild horses and cattle at large, it was only a matter of time before gauchos, the South American cowboys, tamed the one and set about capturing the other. Such private enterprise could not continue indefinitely, however. By the end of the 19th century, much of this cattle country was in the hands of private ranchers, and the gauchos had to work for them if they wanted to maintain their chosen way of life. Cattle farming became big business and today much of the world's supply of beef comes not only from Argentina but also from Brazil, Peru and Colombia. Large tracts of rainforest have been cleared to make way for new cattle stations; something that is of considerable and rising concern to environmentalists.

In Latin America, and especially in Argentina and Brazil, beef consumption is high. Argentines eat around one and a half times as much beef as Americans, with much of it cooked over coals, whether in restaurants or at outdoor *asados*. That the meat should be cooked to perfection is a matter of pride. Whole rib sections or flanks of beef are cooked vertically, speared on iron rods that are set at an angle to prevent the juices from dripping on to the fire. Smaller portions are laid out on barbecue grills, some of which are as big as table tennis tables.

A Brazilian speciality is the *churrasco* or mixed grill, which includes excellent beef steaks. Variations on this traditional dish are a feature of special restaurants called *churrascarias* that also specialize in spit-roasts. Pot roasts are a popular choice too, and there are scores of different recipes for rich beef stews, often incorporating chillies, chorizo or other sausages, fresh or dried fruit or even fish and shellfish. Vegetables that cook down to a purée, like potatoes and pumpkin, are often used for thickening sauces, or the delicious juices are mopped up with farofa, a form of toasted cassava flour. Beef is also used to make meatballs or as a tasty and often spicy filling for empanadas, *humitas* or tamales.

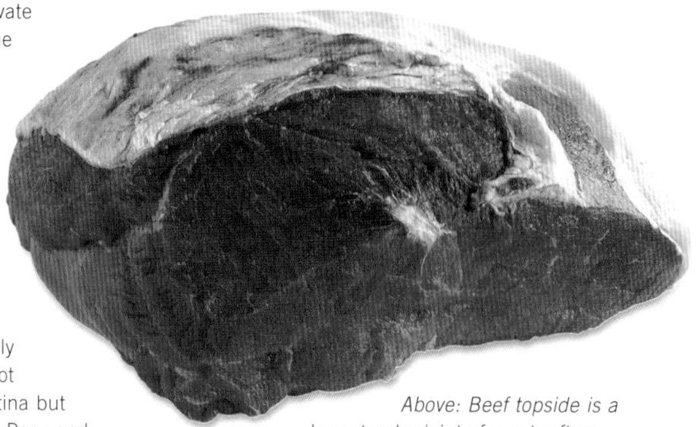

Above: Beef topside is a lean, tender joint of meat, often used for braising or pot-roasting.

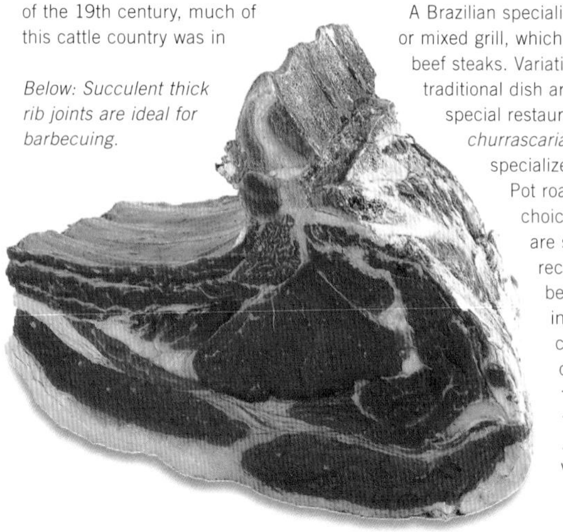

Below: Succulent thick rib joints are ideal for barbecuing.

Dried meat

In the heat of Latin America, meat tends to go off fairly quickly, so before refrigeration was an option it was necessary to find ways of preserving it. Chief among these was drying, a method that remains popular to this day. To make *cecina*, beef or pork is salted and partially dried, then treated with fresh lemon juice before being briefly air-dried again. During the process the meat acquires a robust flavour, and when it is tenderized it makes extremely good eating. *Cecina* is used to add a rich flavour to stews or as fillings for tortillas and tamales. More thoroughly dehydrated meat is *charqui* or *jerky*, which is produced by air-drying strips of meat in the icy Andean winds. Also available is *carne seca*, the traditional sun-dried salt beef of Brazil, a version of which is also produced in Colombia.

Carnitas
These crisp morsels of marinated meat, usually pork, are a popular Mexican snack, especially in Bajio, to the north of Mexico City.

The meat is cooked in lard, with garlic and oranges, and has a delicious flavour. *Carnitas* are served with salsa as an appetizer or used as a delicious filling for tacos or burritos.

LAMB

The main sheep-farming areas of Latin America are Patagonia, in the south of Argentina, and Uruguay. Sheep are also to be found on the Paramos, the high plateaux between the tree line and the snow line in Chile and Peru. Although lamb and mutton have historically been less popular than beef in Argentina, lamb is now gaining ground. Mutton and lamb are popular in Mexico and the islands of the Caribbean, featuring in dishes such as lamb pelau, lamb and lentil soup and "seasoned-up" lamb in spinach sauce. A favourite way of cooking lamb is to marinate it in a mixture of garlic and warm spices, including ground annatto (achiote) seeds, then roast it with sweet (bell) peppers and beans. The annatto gives the meat a rich red colour.

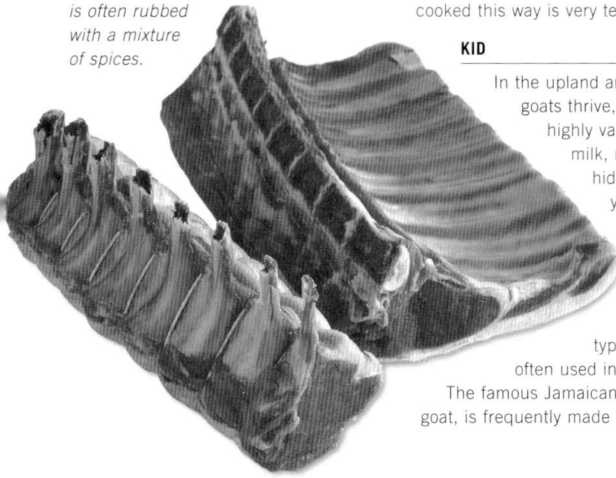

Below: Lamb is becoming more popular in South America and is often rubbed with a mixture of spices.

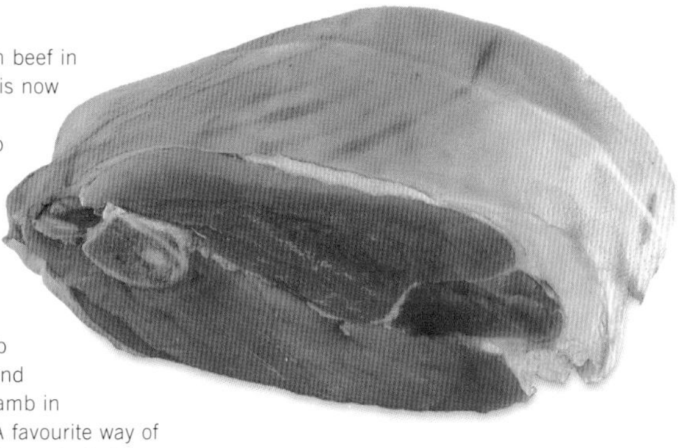

Above: The top end of a pork leg is excellent as a joint for roasting.

PORK

When Spanish and Portuguese colonists introduced pigs to Mexico and other parts of Latin America, there was jubilation, not just because the meat tasted so good, but also because the lard was such a valuable ingredient for frying and baking. Pork hasn't got the high profile that beef enjoys, but it is a popular meat, especially in Mexico, the Caribbean and Brazil, where pork ribs, smoked tongue and pork sausage feature in the national dish, *feijoada*. A favourite Caribbean treatment is to roast pork with rum, while in Argentina and Peru, meat is cooked in milk. Pork cooked this way is very tender.

KID

In the upland areas where goats thrive, they are highly valued for their milk, meat and hides. Kid – young goat – has a slighlty more gamey flavour than lamb, but the two types of meat are often used interchangeably. The famous Jamaican dish, curry goat, is frequently made using lamb instead, although the title makes it obvious that this wasn't always the case. As well as a slightly stronger flavour, kid is a little tougher than lamb, and therefore needs a longer cooking time for the best results.

Offal
Latin American cooks don't just eat offal, they celebrate it. Intestines, hearts, kidneys, tripe, pigs' feet – in fact all the animal parts eschewed in many other places around the world – are elevated to gourmet status by careful cooking with herbs, spices and sauces. Sausages of all types are also widely eaten, with chorizo being a particular favourite.

Below: Spanish-style chorizo and other dried sausages are often eaten in Latin America.

POULTRY

Although turkeys are native to Latin America and were first domesticated by the Aztecs, along with ducks, chickens were unknown until they were introduced by the Spanish and Portuguese colonists.

CHICKEN

As in many other places throughout the world, chickens can be found absolutely everywhere in Latin America: scratching in backyards, on sale at busy markets and on the menu at home and in restaurants. In the Caribbean, where there is seldom enough land to raise large food animals, chickens are a practical source of protein. Chicken is often grilled (broiled); cut into strips and simmered in soups; roasted for traditional Sunday lunch; rubbed with jerk seasoning and cooked over the coals; or stewed in delicious hot-pots thickened with okra, squash, cassava or peanut-based sauces. All over Latin America, and especially in Peru, you can find simple spit-roasted chickens – *pollos a la brasa* – on sale.

Jointing a duck

When preparing a duck, it is important to remember that there is not a great deal of meat on these birds. The simplest and fairest way of serving it is in four equal-sized portions, so the duck must be jointed before cooking.

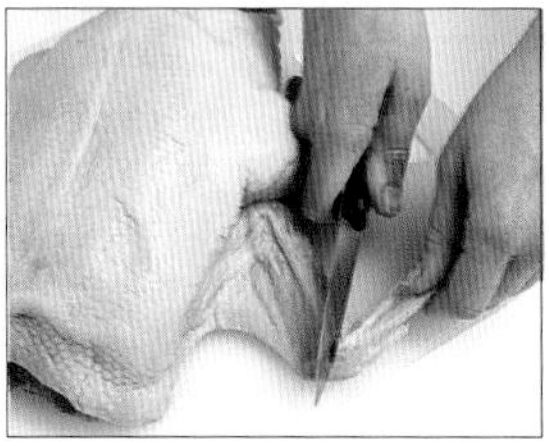

1 Place the whole bird, breast-up, on a chopping board. Remove the wing tips with poultry shears or a sharp knife and then cut the breast in half, working from the tail towards the neck.

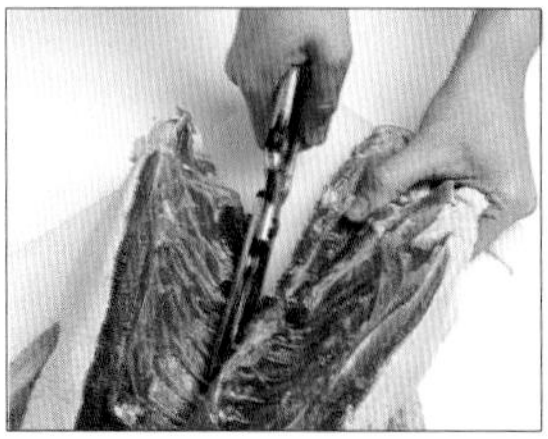

2 Continue cutting the bird in half, along either side of the backbone.

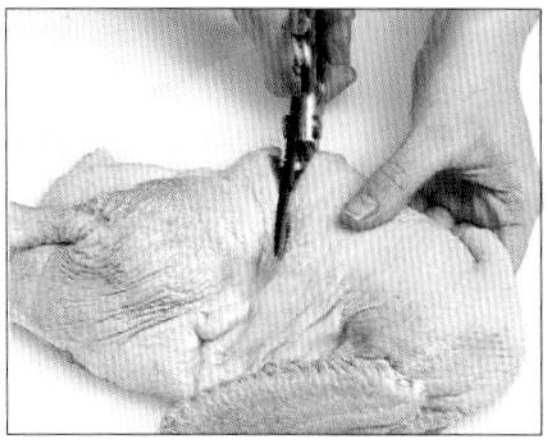

3 Cut each piece of duck roughly in half, cutting diagonally.

Below: Every part of Latin America and the Caribbean has its own favourite chicken recipe.

DUCK

The wild ducks that wintered in Mexico were hunted for food long before the arrival of the Spanish, and muscovy duck was just one of the more than 300 dishes on the menu when the renowned Aztec emperor, Montezuma, sat down to dine. Duck is also extremely popular in Peru, where it is often cooked with fresh coriander (cilantro) leaves. For lovers of duck, Latin America provides some delicious and unusual recipes, such as duck roasted with sweet potatoes and red wine, or cooked with rum.

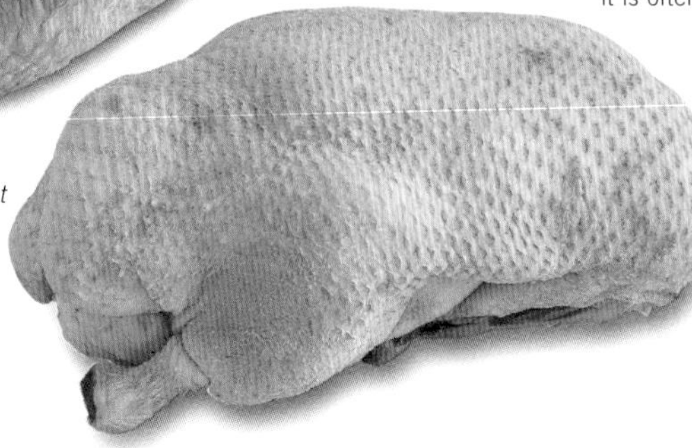

Right: Duck is eaten throughout the region – a tasty Caribbean speciality is duck in rum.

TURKEY

Two types of turkey are native to Latin America, one emerging in Yucatán and Guatemala and the other in Mexico. Turkeys were introduced to Europe by the Spanish and they soon became a popular choice in France, Italy and Britain. The wild birds were fast runners and strong fliers, and their bright feathers were highly prized for ceremonial head-dresses and jewellery, and to provide flights for arrows. The Aztecs were the first to domesticate wild turkeys, which they called *huexolotlin*. Aside from being a valuable food source, turkeys also had a strong religious significance, and two festivals were held every year in their honour. Probably the most famous Latin American dish involving turkey is the

Above: Quails are very small birds – for a main course, serve two per person.

Mexican *poblano mole*. There are many versions of this, all of which involve the bird being cooked in a thick, rich sauce, which contains numerous fresh or dried chillies and several pieces of rich, dark chocolate or cocoa powder. Turkey is often cooked with fresh fruit and tastes especially good with sweet, juicy mango in a traditional Caribbean dish.

GAME BIRDS

Wild birds were a vital part of the South American diet in the pre-Colombian era, and they are still hunted in many places today. Pheasant, partridge, quail and pigeon are all regularly eaten, along with several types of jungle bird, including some breeds of parrot. Pheasant is particularly good for roasting or stewing, young partridge is best simply roasted and served in their own cooking juices, while pigeon is delicious braised or cooked in a pigeon pie. The *curassow*, a large black bird with a distinctive crest of curved feathers, can be found from Mexico to Brazil. It is widely regarded as being the best game bird in Latin America, and is therefore in high demand, a fact that has led to over-hunting. Sadly, it has become an endangered species in some areas.

EXOTIC AND UNUSUAL MEATS

In Peru, guinea pigs (*cuyes*) have long been a favourite food. Domesticated in much the same way as chickens, roaming around backyards, they are cooked by similar methods. The vegetarian diet of *cuyes*, like rabbits, gives their meat a fairly light, delicate flavour. Roast *cuy* is sometimes on the menu at out-of-town restaurants and is readily available roasted at many Peruvian markets and on street stalls, but it is more often eaten at home.

Deer are hunted in forest regions, as are *moufflon*, a type of wild sheep, *peccaries*, which are similar to pigs, and wild goats. Llamas and other large cameloids were often cooked and eaten many centuries ago. In certain areas, they occasionally still are, but they tend to be more highly valued as pack animals. Subsistence hunters catch agoutis, tapirs, armadillos, capybara, monkeys, snakes, iguanas and even tortoises. Turtles are also considered a delicacy and are occasionally eaten, although some countries have made their capture and trade illegal.

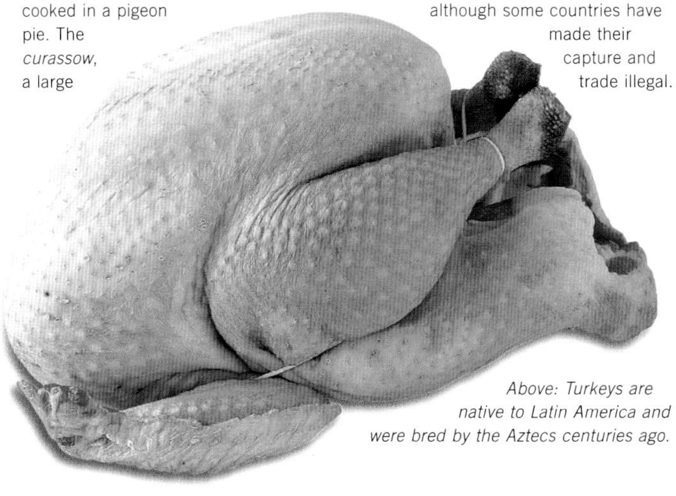

Above: Turkeys are native to Latin America and were bred by the Aztecs centuries ago.

Pheasant in green pipian sauce

This delicious recipe from the Yucatán peninsula can be used for almost any game bird.

SERVES 4

INGREDIENTS
30ml/2 tbsp oil
2 oven-ready pheasants, halved lengthways
1 onion, finely chopped
2 garlic cloves, crushed
275g/10oz can tomatillos
175g/6oz/generous 1 cup pepitas (pumpkin seeds), ground
15ml/1 tbsp annatto (achiote) seeds, ground
475ml/16fl oz/2 cups chicken stock
salt and ground black pepper
fresh coriander (cilantro), to garnish

1 Heat the oil in a frying pan and sauté the pheasant halves until lightly browned. Place them in a large roasting pan.

2 Purée the onion, garlic and tomatillos, with their juice, in a food processor or blender. Scrape the purée into a pan and add the pepitas and annatto seeds.

3 Stir in the stock and cook gently for 10 minutes, taking care not to burn. Leave to cool.

4 Preheat the oven to 180°C/350°F/Gas 4. Pour the sauce over the pheasant and bake for about 40 minutes, basting occasionally. Garnish with fresh coriander (cilantro) and serve immediately.

DRINKS

There are some delightful ways of slaking your thirst in Latin America, from sipping cool coconut juice or a refreshing fruit drink to sampling local wines and spirits. If the latter makes you sleepy, there is always strong coffee to wake you up, or a cup of chocolate to help you relax.

ALCOHOL-FREE DRINKS

Fruit drinks These are something of a speciality in many parts of Latin America and the Caribbean. *Sugos* and *refrescos* or *frescas* are always worth sampling and are particularly popular with children. Made while you wait, from whatever local fruit is available, these fruit drinks tend to be on the sweet side. Ice helps to take the edge off, but they can be served without sugar if preferred. One unusual drink, which is very popular in Brazil, is *guaraná*. Made from the berries of a tree sacred to Amazonian tribes, the drink is sold in both still and carbonated forms and is credited with a vast range of health-giving properties. In the English-speaking islands of the Caribbean, ginger beer is a popular drink, especially around Christmas time, as is *agua de Jamaica*, a refreshing drink made from the bright red sepals of a tropical plant.

Below: Ginger beer is a popular drink in some parts of the Caribbean.

The perfect cup

In Latin America, any time is the right time for full-bodied coffee, and visitors are often staggered by the strength of the brew and the amount consumed. To make a perfect cup, follow these directions:

- Use fresh, cold water that has not been chemically softened.
- Use 60–75ml/4–5 tbsp per 600ml/1 pint/2½ cups.
- Boil the water, then let it cool slightly before pouring it on to the ground coffee.
- If you are using a jug or cafetière (plunge pot) let the coffee stand for 3–4 minutes before pouring or plunging.
- Do not reheat coffee or keep it warm for long periods.

Coffee Two-thirds of the world's supply of coffee comes from Latin America and the Caribbean. Brazil is the leading grower and exporter, with Colombia second. Other important producers are Mexico, El Salvador, Guatemala, Costa Rica, Ecuador and Peru. Coffee is not native to Latin America, however. It was introduced, so the story goes, by a young naval officer called Gabriel de Clieu, who carried a small sapling with him when he sailed to the Caribbean from Europe in 1723. On the voyage, the ship was becalmed, but De Clieu used part of his own water ration to keep the sapling alive until he could plant it on his estate in Martinique. It was clearly a robust specimen, however, because in fewer than 60 years there

Below: Coffee beans must first be roasted before they can be ground.

were 18 million coffee trees on Martinique and production had spread to Central and South America.

There are about 50 species of coffee, but the only ones that are commercially significant are *Coffea arabica* and *Coffea canephora (robusta). Robusta* likes humid, tropical conditions and grows well below 600m/1,900ft, while *arabica* prefers the heights and is cultivated between 600 and 2,000m/1,900 and 6,500ft. The young trees do best in well-drained volcanic soil. They need plenty of sun, but cannot tolerate excessively high temperatures, so shade trees are planted between the rows.

Coffee trees are beautiful. They bear jasmine-scented white flowers up to three times a year, and these are followed by the berry-like fruit. These start off green, but gradually ripen to red, when the cherries, as they are called, are harvested. After picking, which must be done by hand for coffee of the highest quality, the cherries go through lengthy processing to release the pair of beans hidden inside each. Before the beans can be ground to make coffee, they must be roasted. Coffee connoisseurs in Latin America like to roast and grind their own beans at home every day, but most of us buy our beans ready-roasted. In some countries, a light roast is preferred, while in others a dark roast is favoured.

Discriminating drinkers demand specific types of coffee, such as Colombian Medellin, but most of what is exported has been blended, either to appeal to the majority or to persuade us to buy coffee tailored to a time of day: light for breakfast and full-bodied for after dinner, for instance.

Yerba maté

This herbal tea, made from the leaves of a plant that resembles holly, is popular in Argentina, Uruguay, Paraguay and southern Brazil. It is traditionally sipped through a silver straw from a hollow gourd, the *maté*, from which it takes its name.

Above: Good-quality chocolate is still produced in Bariloche, Patagonia.

Above: Hot chocolate is the perfect end to a meal, according to Montezuma.

Chocolate The cacao tree is indigenous to Latin America. One fifth of the world's production now comes from Brazil, with Ecuador only 2 per cent behind. The Olmecs, who inhabited Central America around 1200BC, are credited with discovering that the cacao bean could be transformed into a delicious drink, but it was the Maya and later the Aztecs who perfected the art. For the emperor Montezuma, the perfect end to one of his legendary feasts was a gold cup full of the frothy beverage.

The Aztecs credited cocoa with medicinal powers, and used the drink to treat all sorts of ailments. In this they were ahead of their time, for cocoa has been proven to be high in antioxidants, the natural compounds that are widely believed to reduce cholesterol levels, fight cancer and heart disease and delay signs of ageing. The drink the Aztecs enjoyed was not sweetened, but the natural bitterness of the chocolate was often offset by adding chillies and other warm spices, such as vanilla.

The Spanish first introduced chocolate to the rest of the world and the beverage was soon being drunk in sophisticated resorts and cities all over Europe. Although it is now as a form of confectionery that chocolate is best known and loved in Europe and the US, its main use in Latin America continues to be as a drink. Mexican chocolate is a delicate mixture of dark and bitter chocolate, sugar, ground almonds and cinnamon, and it tastes incredibly rich.

Swiss chocolate, Argentine-style

Although chocolate is more likely to be a drink than a sweet treat in Latin America, there is one place where bars of very good chocolate are regularly produced, and that is the beautiful Lake District of Patagonia. Descendants of Swiss, German and northern Italian immigrants have established a thriving chocolate industry in Bariloche, with many locals hand-making their own chocolates. This Andean village is a visual delight, known for its mountains, its lakes and the European look of its streets. The thriving chocolate industry helps to reinforce the town's decidedly Swiss character.

WINE

Much of South America is too hot for successful wine production. However, in Argentina and Chile, in the cool valleys on either side of the Andes, grapes flourish and wine is produced widely.

Argentina is the world's leading wine producer outside of Europe and the US, coming fifth in the global line-up. Until recently, Argentines drank most of the wine they produced themselves, but this is gradually changing. Despite producing less wine than Argentina, Chile has a bigger bite of the international market, and produces some highly regarded wines. Wine is also produced on a smaller scale in Uruguay, Brazil and Mexico.

Argentina

The first vines were planted in Argentina in the middle of the 16th century by Jesuit priests eager to ensure a steady supply of communion wine, Gradually the vineyards became established, and the industry gained a useful boost in the 18th and 19th centuries with the arrival of European viticulturists. They introduced many of the varieties that continue to dominate: Merlot, Cabernet Sauvignon, Chardonnay, Chenin and Pinot Noir.

Below: Parts of South America, particularly Chile and Argentina, are well known for both their red and white wines.

Most of Argentina's wine comes from the western part of the country, in an area stretching from Rio Negro in the south to La Rioja and Salta in the north. By far the most productive region is Mendoza, which has well over a thousand wineries, despite having very low rainfall. This is because the whole area lies in the rain shadow of the Andes. Paradoxically, however, it is thanks to the Andes that the grapes flourish, as the vines are fed by irrigation from snow and ice-melt.

It is for red wines that Argentina is best known. These include Cabernet Sauvignon, Syrah, Merlot, Malbec, Bonarda, Pinot Noir, Tempranillo and Sangiovese. Malbec is of particular interest. This black grape originated in France, but never fully realized its potential until it was introduced to South America. A wine with an intense, vibrant colour, Malbec has been described as having distinctive berry flavours, with hints of damson, liquorice and even chocolate.

Among the white wines produced are Chenin Blanc, Sauvignon Blanc, Chardonnay and Semillon. From the northern provinces of Salta and La Rioja comes Torrontés, a varietal that is believed to have Spanish antecedents, but which is now strongly established in its adoptive country. Fresh, fruity and deliciously dry, it is extremely popular.

Chile

Roughly one-third of the length of this slender ribbon of a country is given over to the growing of grapes. Although the northern part of the country is desert and the southern tip is too cold for wine production, the central temperate valleys have ideal conditions. The main wine-producing area stretches for just under 900km/550 miles from north of Santiago to Concepción. This part of the country has a Mediterranean climate similar to that enjoyed in South Africa's Western Cape, and because the moisture-laden clouds that roll in from the ocean drop their rain in winter on the Chilean side of the Andes, irrigation is not the problem it is on the other side of the mountains in Argentina.

Right: Red Stripe lager is one of Jamaica's most famous exports, and is popular throughout Europe and the USA.

Wine production began with the introduction of the rustic Pais grape to Chile in 1548, and owes its present character to the introduction of French vines in the middle of the 19th century. Established varieties like Cabernet Sauvignon, Cabernet Franc, Merlot, Malbec and Sauvignon Blanc soon flourished, and when European vineyards were devastated by a small insect – phylloxera – Chile was fortunately spared and made the most of this opportunity.

The Maipo Valley is the most famous wine-growing area of Chile and the site of some of the oldest established vineyards. It is well-known for producing excellent Cabernet Sauvignon. Also well known for reds are the Curicó and Colchagua Valleys, while some of the finest white wines come from the Aconcagua and Casablanca Valleys in the north. Mulchen, which is at the southern tip of the wine-producing region, is another white wine area, known especially for Sauvignon Blanc and Chardonnay wines.

Thanks to the huge north-south spread and a variety of microclimates, Chile has a wide range of both red and white wines, including several organic varieties. Aside from those varieties already mentioned, Merlot, Carmenère, Malbec, Syrah, Pinot Noir and Viognier are also successfully produced.

BEER

Best known for light, thin lager drunk straight from the bottle with a wedge of lime, Central and South American beer actually has a much richer tradition than is widely appreciated. The Mayans were brewing beer from fermented corn stalks long before Spanish conquistadors invaded, while, in northern Mexico, the Aztecs enjoyed a fermented drink made with sprouted maize. The Spanish settlers set up small breweries from the 16th century onwards, but beer came a poor second to distilled spirits, until German immigrants introduced lager to Mexico. Many of the brewing companies in existence today have German roots. Mexico remains the leading beer producer, followed by Brazil. Lager is the drink of choice and well-known brands include Corona Extra, Cuzco, Dos Equis, Sol and Tecate. These lagers go well with spicy Latin American food.
The Caribbean also has a strong beer culture and one of Jamaica's most famous exports is Red Stripe lager, now a familiar sight in the US and the UK.

SPIRITS

Latin America has given the world some fine spirits, including rum and tequila.
Rum Legend has it that rum was discovered after sugar-cane mash was left to ferment in the Caribbean sun

Above: The best rum in the world is still produced in the Caribbean.

soon after the first sugar plantations were established on the islands in the 16th century. In the early 18th century, it became standard practice for the British Navy to issue sailors with a daily ration of rum, largely because the spirit endured extremes of weather so much better than beer. At the same time, rum was becoming popular in Britain. Over the centuries, the spirit has been refined, and aged rums now have the same sort of prestige as that accorded to single malt whiskies. Rum is still largely produced in the Caribbean, and some of the world's finest rums come from Jamaica, Cuba, the Dominican Republic, Martinique, Barbados, Haiti and the British Virgin Islands. Rum is also produced in some parts of South America.
Cachaça Another cane spirit, *cachaça* is distilled from the first crush of the sugar cane. Also called *pinga* or *aguardente*, it is the national drink of Brazil and is often mixed with freshly squeezed lime juice and sugar to make the delicious and popular *caipirinha* cocktail, which is often enjoyed with meals.
Pisco A grape brandy, the birthplace of *pisco* is in some doubt. It originated either in Peru or Chile, depending on which of those countries your informant favours. Its one-time reputation for rough fieriness does not apply to the top grades of *pisco*, which have a delicate, fruity flavour.

TEQUILA

Tequila is, without doubt, the Mexican spirit which is best known outside the country. A specific type of *mescal*, it is becoming steadily more popular, especially among younger drinkers and those seeking the notorious cocktails based on the Margarita.

Below: Mexico's finest exports include mescal *(left) and* tequila blanco *(right).*

Liqueurs

Some of the world's most popular liqueurs originated in parts of Central America and the islands of the Caribbean. Curaçao, the bitter orange liqueur invented by Dutch settlers on the island of the same name, was the forerunner of Grand Marnier and Cointreau.
All are still made using Caribbean oranges. Tia Maria is a popular coffee liqueur from Jamaica. It is slightly sweeter than its Mexican rival, Kahlúa, while Toussaint, a coffee liqueur from Haiti, has a delectable strong espresso flavour that makes it extremely good for cooking as well as drinking.

The Spanish taught Mexicans the art of distilling, bringing about a new cultual era of alcohol and alcoholic spirit production. *Pulque*, the tasty national drink made from the cactus-type agave plant, was the perfect subject, and they began by distilling it to make *mescal*. This was then distilled a second time to produce tequila.

If *mescal* is brandy, then tequila is Cognac, and is subject to similar controls to those that are imposed by the French government on their famous spirit. There are also parallels with the production of Champagne, in that tequila production is tightly regulated and may only take place in specially designated areas. The producers have to be certified to use the name, and the certification process involves a large amount of checks, including the quality of the land on which the agave is grown, the blending of different types of the spirit, and the techniques used in preserving and aging.

It is thought that tequila takes its name from the plant from which it is sourced: *Agave tequilana*. However, it has also been suggested that the plant was named after the town in Jalisco where the drink was first made. The name means "volcano" in the local Indian dialect. Jalisco is also the home of *mariachi* music, which possibly explains how tequila gained its image.

Production

Tequila is made from the sap of the blue agave plant, which is not a cactus, as is commonly believed, but is related to the amaryllis. The leaves of each plant are cut away to leave the *piña*, which is then steam cooked. The juice is fermented, then distilled twice, the second time in a copper still, after which it is bottled or matured in casks. All aspects of the process are rigidly controlled and documented.

Flavour Variations

There are several different types of tequila, and innumerable brands of all of these. Each brand has a different flavour, determined by the soil and the climate where the agave was grown, the amount of sugar the agave contained and the finer details of the processing, including the cooking of the *piña* and the fermentation of the juice. Some tequilas are matured in casks, and the type of wood used, together with the duration of the aging process, will also influence the flavour of the finished product.

Not all tequilas are 100 per cent agave spirit; some are blended with cane spirit, but by law tequila must contain at least 51 per cent agave spirit. Blended tequilas are becoming less popular in foreign markets as consumers become more discriminating. At one time

Left: Mescal

Right: Tequila

Left: Tequila blanco

Below: Tequila and lime

Right: A bottle of Tequila anejo

you could walk into a bar in Britain or Europe and find only one type of tequila – and that was primarily used for making margaritas. However, the increasing popularity of Mexican food has led to a gradual rise in the popularity of tequila and a greater appreciation of the various types, and in some places today there are even specialist tequila bars, which stock a vast range of different types and brands of this exciting spirit.

Left: Margarita

Types of Tequila

Joven or blanco tequila has been bottled immediately after distillation. It is usually clear, but can sometimes be golden in colour. This classification also includes tequilas that have been aged for less than 60 days.

Reposada tequila is golden in colour and has been aged in oak for 2–6 months. It has a more rounded flavour than joven tequila.

Anejo tequila has been aged in oak for a year or more and has a rich golden colour.

Curados is the name given to blanco or joven tequila that has been naturally flavoured. Cinnamon sticks, chillies, almonds and vanilla pods are among the whole flavourings used, but essences and syrups can also be used.

Developing a Taste for Tequila

The best way to become a discriminating tequila drinker is to try as many different brands and types as possible. Compare and contrast them in terms of their appearance, bouquet, viscosity and flavour. Few tequilas taste of only one thing; most are a complex blend of flavours. They may taste sweet, earthy, woody, smooth or even smoky. It is a good idea to taste a new tequila against a familiar brand to give a standard for comparison.

Tequila Drinking

Drinking a shot of tequila in the classic manner, with a lick of salt beforehand and a wedge of lime after, is one of the best ways for Europeans to sample this drink. The method was originally adopted because the spirit was so crude that salt and lime were deemed necessary to make it palatable.

A natural progression from the tequila shot was the margarita. The rim of the glass is dipped in salt, the lime juice and tequila are combined and triple sec – orange liqueur – is added. A margarita may be served neat, as it comes out of the bottle, or over ice cubes, or "frozen" with crushed ice.

In Mexico, tequila is often sipped alternately with a glass of *sangrita*, a tomato juice flavoured with chillies and other seasonings. When the tequila and tomato juice are combined, the drink becomes a Bloody Maria. Tequila can also be enjoyed with orange juice and grenadine to make a Tequila Sunrise.

Below: Two types of Curados; bottles of blanco tequila that have had flavouring added. Here a few red chillies have been added to the bottle on the left, and three vanilla pods to the one on the right. The tequila will take on the flavour of the chilli or vanilla in just a few days.

Street Food and Snacks

Throughout the Caribbean and Latin America there is a tradition of street food. Market stalls, beach huts, bars and snack houses all offer sweet or savoury snacks, which make perfect accompaniments to fruit juice, cold beer or cocktails.

CASSAVA CHIPS

For a perfect sundowner, there's nothing quite like enjoying an ice-cold beer with some freshly cooked, golden cassava chips. Don't worry about cutting perfect-sized chips; they should be chunky and irregular, and extra crisp.

SERVES FOUR

INGREDIENTS
- 800g/1¾lb cassava
- vegetable oil, for frying
- salt

1 Peel the cassava and cut it lengthways into 5cm/2in-wide pieces. Then cut these pieces into slices, about 2cm/¾in thick.

2 Place the slices in a large pan of salted water and bring to the boil. Lower the heat until the water simmers and cover the pan.

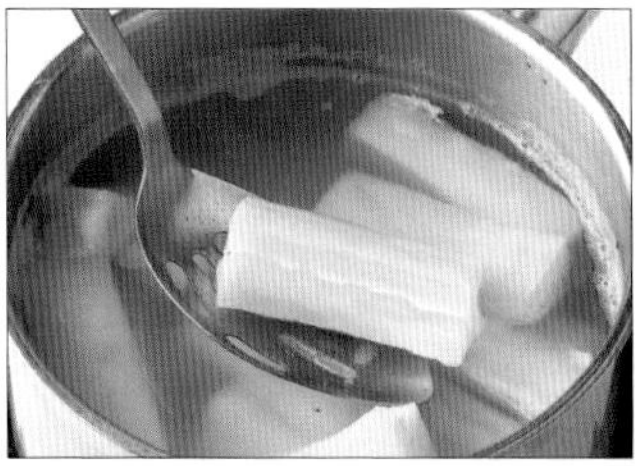

3 Cook the cassava for approximately 15 minutes, or until the slices are tender and just beginning to break up. Drain the cassava thoroughly and pat dry with kitchen paper.

4 Pour vegetable oil to a depth of 5cm/2in in a deep wide pan. Heat the oil, then add the cassava pieces. Fry for 3–4 minutes, turning occasionally, until the chips are golden and crisp all over. You may need to do this in batches.

5 Lift the chips from the pan with a slotted spoon and drain on kitchen paper. Season with salt and serve warm or at room temperature.

VARIATION

The chips are sometimes served with a sprinkling of grated Parmesan, in which case they will not need as much salt.

Cheese Tamales

Corn meal dumplings steamed in corn husks are to be found throughout South America. The recipe varies, with fresh corn kernels being used instead of corn meal on some occasions. There are many possible fillings; this recipe has one of the simplest.

MAKES TEN

INGREDIENTS

- 10 large dried corn husks or greaseproof (waxed) paper
- 75g/3oz/6 tbsp lard or white cooking fat, at room temperature
- 225g/8oz/2 cups *masa harina*
- 5ml/1 tsp salt
- 5ml/1 tsp baking powder
- 250–300ml/8–10fl oz/1–1¼ cups warm light vegetable stock
- 200g/7oz fresh white cheese, such as feta, roughly chopped

1 Place the corn husks in a bowl and pour over boiling water to cover. Soak for 30 minutes, until the husks become soft and pliable. Remove from the water and pat dry with a clean dishtowel.

2 Meanwhile put the lard or white cooking fat in a mixing bowl and beat with an electric whisk until light and fluffy. Test by dropping a small amount of the whipped lard into a cup of water. If it floats, it is ready to use.

3 Combine the *masa harina*, salt and baking powder in a separate bowl. Gradually add to the lard, beating in 45ml/3 tbsp at a time. As the mixture begins to thicken, start adding the stock, alternating the dry mixture and the stock until both have been used and the mixture is light and spreadable. If it feels tough, or dry to the touch, beat in a little more warm water, but don't add more stock, as the dough will already be flavoursome enough.

4 To assemble, lay the prepared corn husks on a board and spread about one-tenth of the *masa* mixture in the centre of each, leaving a small border at either side, with a larger border at the top and bottom.

5 Place a piece of cheese in the centre of the *masa* mixture. Fold one of the longer lengths of husk over, so that it covers the filling, then repeat with the opposite end. Close the package by folding over the two remaining sides, to make a neat parcel. Secure the tamales by tying each one with a piece of string or strip of corn husk.

6 Pile the tamales in a steamer basket placed over simmering water. Cover and steam for 1 hour. Check the level of the water occasionally, topping up if necessary. The tamales are ready when the dough comes away from the corn husk cleanly. Allow to stand for 10 minutes, then serve.

COOK'S TIP

Masa harina is a flour made with finely ground dried white corn kernels. It is most famously used to make corn tortillas, to which it imparts a nutty flavour. *Masa harina* can be found in Latin food stores and markets.

TORTILLA CHIPS

These are known as totopos in Mexico, and the term refers to both the fried tortilla strips used to garnish soups and the triangles of corn tortilla used for scooping salsa or dips. Use tortillas that are a few days old; fresh ones will not crisp up so well.

SERVES FOUR

INGREDIENTS
- 4–8 corn tortillas
- oil, for frying
- salt

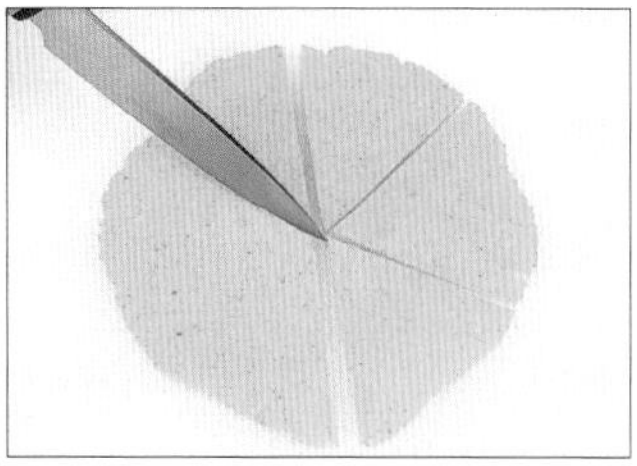

1 Cut each tortilla into six triangular wedges. Pour oil into a large frying pan to a depth of 1cm/½in, place the pan over a moderate heat and heat until very hot (see Cook's Tip).

2 Fry the tortilla wedges in the hot oil in small batches until they turn golden and are crisp. This will only take a few moments. Remove with a slotted spoon and drain on kitchen paper. Sprinkle with salt.

3 *Totopos* should be served warm. They can be cooled completely and stored in an airtight container for a few days, but will need to be reheated in a microwave or a warm oven before being served.

VARIATION
When fried, wheat flour tortillas do not crisp up as well as corn tortillas, but they make a delicious sweet treat when sprinkled with ground cinnamon and caster (superfine) sugar. Serve them hot with cream.

COOK'S TIP
The oil needs to be very hot for cooking the tortillas – test it by carefully adding one of the wedges. It should float and begin to bubble in the oil immediately.

PEPITAS

These little snacks are absolutely irresistible, especially if you include chipotle chillies. Their smoky flavour is the perfect foil for the nutty taste of the pumpkin seeds and the sweetness contributed by the sugar. Serve them with pre-dinner drinks.

SERVES FOUR

INGREDIENTS
- 130g/4½oz/1 cup pumpkin seeds
- 4 garlic cloves, crushed
- 1.5ml/¼ tsp salt
- 10ml/2 tsp crushed dried chillies
- 5ml/1 tsp caster (superfine) sugar
- a wedge of lime

COOK'S TIP
It is important to keep the pumpkin seeds moving as they cook. Watch them carefully and do not let them burn, or they will taste bitter.

1 Heat a small heavy-based frying pan, add the pumpkin seeds and dry fry for a few minutes, stirring constantly as they swell.

2 When all the seeds have swollen, add the garlic and cook for a few minutes more, stirring all the time. Add the salt and the crushed chillies and stir to mix. Turn off the heat, but keep the pan on the stove. Sprinkle sugar over the seeds and shake the pan to ensure that they are all coated.

3 Tip the *pepitas* into a bowl and serve with the wedge of lime for squeezing over the seeds. If the lime is omitted, the seeds can be cooled and stored in an airtight container for reheating later, but they are best served fresh.

TAMALES DE PICADILLO

In ancient times these little parcels made from corn husks, popular throughout the whole of Mexico, were cooked in the hot ashes of a camp fire.

MAKES TWELVE

INGREDIENTS

- 12 dried corn husks
- 50g/2oz/¼ cup lard or white cooking fat
- 150g/5oz/1 cup *masa harina*
- 2.5ml/½ tsp salt
- 5ml/1tsp baking powder
- 175ml/6fl oz/¾ cup chicken stock

For the picadillo

- 15ml/1 tbsp olive or corn oil
- 450g/1lb minced (ground) beef
- ½ onion, finely chopped
- 1 garlic clove, chopped
- 1 eating apple
- 225g/½lb tomatoes, peeled, seeded and chopped
- 1 or 2 drained pickled jalapeño chillies, seeded and chopped
- 25g/1oz raisins
- 1.5ml/¼ tsp ground cinnamon
- 1.5ml/¼ tsp ground cumin
- salt and ground black pepper

1 Soak the corn husks in warm water for about 30 minutes until pliable.

2 Meanwhile, make the picadillo. Heat the oil in a frying pan. Add the beef, chopped onion and garlic, and cook, stirring, until the beef is brown and the onion is tender.

3 Peel, core and chop the apple. Add the pieces to the pan with all of the remaining picadillo ingredients. Cook, uncovered, for about 20–25 minutes, stirring occasionally to prevent sticking.

4 In a bowl, cream the lard until it is light and fluffy. Mix the *masa harina* with the salt and baking powder, then gradually beat it into the lard, taking care not to add too much at once.

5 Warm the chicken stock slowly. It should not be hot or it will melt the lard.

6 Gradually beat enough of the chicken stock into the *masa* mixture to make a mushy dough. To see if the dough is ready, carefully place a small piece on top of a bowl of water. If it floats, the dough is ready; if it sinks, continue to beat the dough until the texture is light enough for it to float.

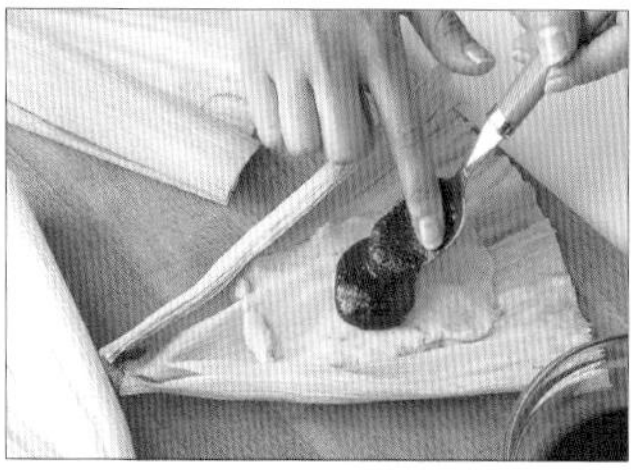

7 Drain a corn husk and lay it flat on a board. Spread about 30ml/2 tbsp of the dough down the centre part of the husk, leaving plenty of room all round for folding. Spoon 30ml/2 tbsp of the picadillo on to the centre of the dough.

8 Roll up the husk from one long side, so that the filling is completely enclosed, then fold the ends of the husks under. Make more tamales in the same way.

9 Prepare a steamer or use a metal colander and a deep pan into which the colander will fit with about 2.5cm/1in space all around.

10 Put the tamales in the steamer, folded ends under. Alternatively, place them in the colander and pour boiling water into the pan to within 2.5cm/1in of the bottom of the colander. Steam the tamales for about 1 hour, or until the dough comes away from the husk. Top up the water as required to prevent the tamales from drying.

11 Serve the tamales immediately, in the husk, leaving guests to open them at the table to reveal the delicious picadillo filling inside.

MIXED TOSTADAS

LIKE LITTLE EDIBLE PLATES, THESE TRADITIONAL MEXICAN FRIED TORTILLAS CAN SUPPORT ALMOST ANY INGREDIENTS YOU LIKE, SO LONG AS THEY ARE NOT TOO JUICY.

MAKES FOURTEEN

INGREDIENTS
- oil, for shallow frying
- 14 freshly prepared unbaked corn tortillas
- 225g/8oz/1 cup mashed red kidney or pinto beans
- 1 iceberg lettuce, shredded
- olive oil and vinegar dressing (optional)
- 2 cooked chicken breast portions, skinned and thinly sliced
- 225g/8oz guacamole
- 115g/4oz/1 cup coarsely grated mature (sharp) Cheddar cheese
- pickled jalapeño chillies, seeded and sliced, to taste

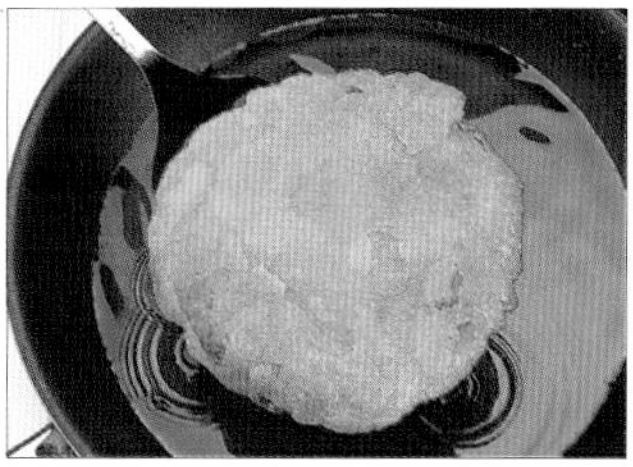

1 Heat the oil in a shallow frying pan and fry the corn tortillas one by one, until golden brown on both sides and crisp but not hard.

2 Spread each tortilla with a layer of mashed pinto or kidney beans. Put a layer of shredded lettuce (which can either be left plain or lightly tossed with a little dressing) over the beans.

3 Arrange chicken slices on top of the lettuce. Carefully spread over a layer of the guacamole and finally sprinkle over the grated cheese.

4 Arrange the mixed tostadas on a large platter and serve immediately, while still warm. Use your hands to eat tostadas as they are extremely messy.

VARIATIONS
- Instead of chicken, try using shredded pork, minced (ground) beef or turkey, or sliced chorizo.
- For a more authentic taste use *queso fresco* or feta cheese instead of Cheddar.

CHILLIES RELLENOS

STUFFED CHILLIES ARE POPULAR ALL OVER MEXICO. THE TYPE OF CHILLI USED DIFFERS FROM REGION TO REGION, BUT LARGER CHILLIES ARE OBVIOUSLY EASIER TO STUFF THAN SMALLER ONES. POBLANOS AND ANAHEIMS ARE QUITE MILD, BUT YOU CAN USE HOTTER CHILLIES IF YOU PREFER.

MAKES SIX

INGREDIENTS
- 6 fresh poblano or Anaheim chillies
- 2 potatoes (about 400g/14oz)
- 200g/7oz/scant 1 cup cream cheese
- 200g/7oz/1¾ cups grated mature (sharp) Cheddar cheese
- 5ml/1 tsp salt
- 2.5ml/½ tsp ground black pepper
- 2 eggs, separated
- 115g/4oz/1 cup plain (all-purpose) flour
- 2.5ml/½ tsp white pepper
- oil, for frying
- chilli flakes to garnish, optional

1 Make a neat slit down one side of each chilli. Place them in a dry frying pan over a moderate heat, turning them frequently until the skins blister.

2 Place the chillies in a strong plastic bag and tie the top to keep the steam in. Set aside for 20 minutes, then carefully peel off the skins and remove the seeds through the slits, keeping the chillies whole. Dry the chillies with kitchen paper and set them aside.

COOK'S TIP
Take care when making the filling; mix gently, trying not to break up the potato pieces.

VARIATION
Whole ancho (dried poblano) chillies can be used instead of fresh chillies, but will need to be reconstituted in water before they can be seeded and stuffed.

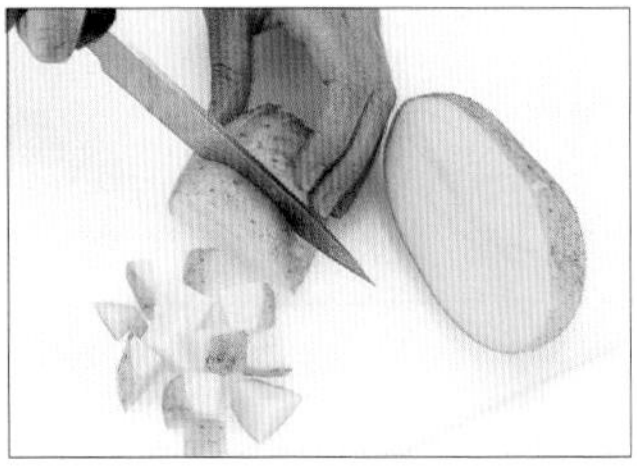

3 Scrub or peel the potatoes and cut them into 1cm/½in dice. Bring a large pan of water to the boil, add the potatoes and let the water return to boiling point. Lower the heat and simmer for 5 minutes or until the potatoes are just tender. Do not overcook. Drain them thoroughly.

4 Put the cream cheese in a bowl and stir in the grated cheese, with 2.5ml/½ tsp of the salt and the black pepper. Add the potato and mix gently.

5 Spoon some of the filling into each chilli. Put them on a plate, cover with clear film (plastic wrap) and chill for 1 hour so that the filling becomes firm.

6 Put the egg whites in a clean, grease-free bowl and whisk them to firm peaks. In a separate bowl, beat the yolks until pale, then fold in the whites. Scrape the mixture on to a large, shallow dish. Spread out the flour in another shallow dish and season it with the remaining salt and the white pepper.

7 Heat the oil for deep frying to 190°C/375°F. Coat a few chillies first in flour and then in egg before adding carefully to the hot oil.

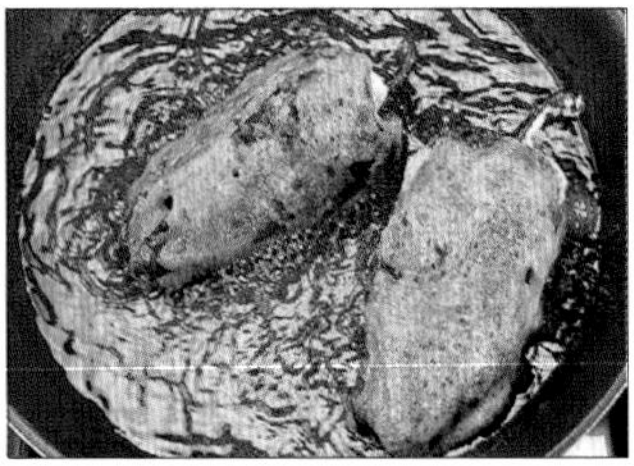

8 Fry the chillies in batches until golden and crisp. Drain on kitchen paper and serve hot, garnished with a sprinkle of chilli flakes for extra heat, if desired.

TORTAS

THE MULTI-LAYERED FILLING OF MEXICAN TORTAS OFFERS LOTS OF DIFFERENT TASTES AND TEXTURES. TRADITIONALLY THEY ARE MADE USING ROLLS CALLED TELERAS.

SERVES TWO

INGREDIENTS
- 2 fresh jalapeño chillies
- juice of ½ lime
- 2 French bread rolls or 2 pieces of French bread
- 115g/4oz/⅔ cup Refried Beans
- 150g/5oz roast pork
- 2 small tomatoes, sliced
- 115g/4oz Cheddar cheese, sliced
- small bunch of fresh coriander (cilantro)
- 30ml/2 tbsp crème fraîche

VARIATIONS
The essential ingredients of a *torta* are refried beans and chillies. Everything else is subject to change. Ham, chicken or turkey could all be used instead of pork, and lettuce is often added.

1 Cut the chillies in half, scrape out the seeds, then cut the flesh into thin strips. Put it in a bowl, pour over the lime juice and leave to stand.

2 If using rolls, slice them in half and remove some of the crumb so that they are slightly hollowed. If using French bread, slice each piece in half lengthways. Set the top of each piece of bread or roll aside and spread the bottom halves with the refried beans.

3 Cut the pork into thin shreds and put these on top of the refried beans. Top with the tomato slices. Drain the jalapeño strips and put them on top of the tomato slices. Add the cheese and sprinkle with coriander leaves.

4 Turn the top halves of the bread or rolls over, so that the cut sides are uppermost, and spread these with crème fraîche. Sandwich back together again and serve.

TAQUITOS WITH BEEF

MINIATURE SOFT CORN TORTILLAS MOULDED AROUND A TASTY FILLING AND SERVED WARM. UNLESS YOU HAVE ACCESS TO MINIATURE FRESH CORN TORTILLAS, YOU WILL NEED A TORTILLA PRESS.

SERVES TWELVE

INGREDIENTS

- 500g/1¼lb rump steak, diced into 1cm/½in pieces
- 2 garlic cloves, peeled and left whole
- 750ml/1¼ pints/3 cups beef stock
- 150g/5oz/1 cup *masa harina*
- pinch of salt
- 120ml/4fl oz/½ cup warm water
- 7.5ml/1½ tsp dried oregano
- 2.5ml/½ tsp ground cumin
- 30ml/2 tbsp tomato purée (paste)
- 2.5ml/½ tsp caster (superfine) sugar
- salt and ground black pepper
- shredded lettuce and Onion Relish, to serve

1 Put the beef and whole garlic cloves in a large pan and cover with the beef stock. Bring to the boil, lower the heat and simmer for 10–15 minutes, until the meat is tender. Using a slotted spoon, transfer the meat to a clean pan and set it aside. Reserve the stock.

2 Mix the *masa harina* and salt in a bowl. Add the warm water, a little at a time, to make a dough that can be worked into a ball. Knead on a lightly floured surface for 3–4 minutes until smooth, then wrap in clear film (plastic wrap) and leave to rest for 1 hour.

3 Divide the dough into 12 small balls. Open a tortilla press and line both sides with plastic (this can be cut from a new plastic sandwich bag).

4 Put a ball on the press and bring the top down to flatten it into a 5–6cm/2–2½in round. Flatten the remaining dough balls in the same way to make more tortillas. Carefully peel the plastic away from the tortilla and heat a griddle or frying pan until hot.

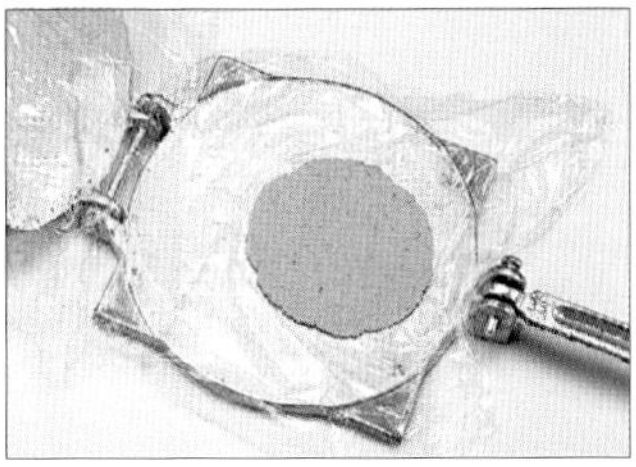

5 Cook each tortilla for 15–20 seconds on each side, and then for a further 15 minutes on the first side. Keep the tortillas warm and soft by folding them inside a slightly damp dishtowel.

6 Add the oregano, cumin, tomato purée and caster sugar to the pan containing the reserved beef cubes, with a couple of tablespoons of the reserved beef stock, or just enough to keep the mixture moist. Cook gently for a few minutes to combine the flavours.

7 Place a little of the lettuce on a warm tortilla. Top with a little of the filling and a little onion relish, fold in half and serve while still warm. Fill more tortillas in the same way.

PLANTAIN AND SWEET POTATO CHIPS

SALTY YET SWEET, THESE CRISP CHIPS ARE A CARIBBEAN SPECIALITY AND MAKE A DELICIOUS SNACK.

SERVES FOUR

INGREDIENTS
- 2 green plantains
- 1 small sweet potato
- oil, for deep-frying
- salt

VARIATIONS
For maximum crispness, it is important to use green plantains. If these are not available, substitute green bananas. Yam can be used instead of sweet potatoes. The vegetables must be soaked in cold salted water to prevent discoloration.

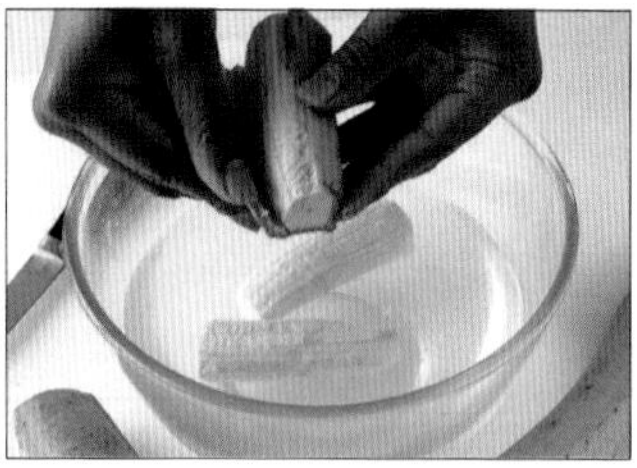

1 Using a small sharp knife, trim the plantains and cut them in half widthways. Peel by slitting the skin with a knife, following the natural ridges, then lifting it off. Place the peeled plantains in a bowl of cold, salted water.

2 Peel the sweet potato under cold running water, and add it to the plantains in the bowl.

3 Heat the oil in a large pan or deep-fryer. Remove the vegetables from the salted water, pat dry on kitchen paper and slice into thin rounds.

4 Fry the plantains and sweet potatoes in batches for about 2 minutes until crisp, then remove with a slotted spoon and drain on kitchen paper. Sprinkle with salt and serve when cool.

COCONUT KING PRAWNS

POPULAR THROUGHOUT THE CARIBBEAN ISLANDS, THESE BUTTERFLIED PRAWNS LOOK VERY PRETTY AND THEY TASTE WONDERFUL WHEN PARTNERED WITH A CRISP COCONUT AND CHIVE COATING.

SERVES FOUR

INGREDIENTS
- 12 raw king prawns (jumbo shrimp)
- 2 garlic cloves, crushed
- 15ml/1 tbsp lemon juice
- 50g/2oz/4 tbsp fine desiccated (dry unsweetened shredded) coconut
- 25g/1oz/⅔ cup chopped fresh chives
- 150ml/¼ pint/⅔ cup milk
- 2 eggs, beaten
- salt and ground black pepper
- oil, for deep-frying
- lime or lemon wedges and fresh flat leaf parsley, to garnish

COOK'S TIP
If raw king prawns (jumbo shrimp) are difficult to obtain, substitute cooked prawns. However, the raw prawns will absorb more flavour from the marinade, so they are the ideal choice.

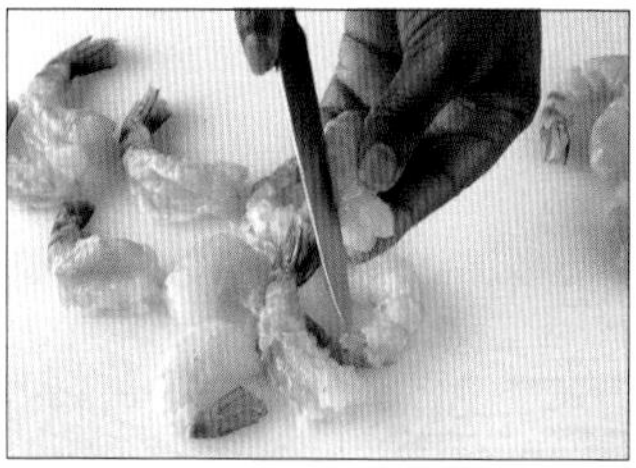

1 Peel and de-vein the prawns, leaving the tails intact, then deepen the incision made when de-veining the prawns, cutting from the back almost to the belly so that they can be opened out. Rinse the prawns under cold water and pat dry.

2 Mix the garlic and lemon juice with a little seasoning in a shallow dish, then add the prawns. Toss to coat, cover and marinate for about 1 hour.

3 Mix the coconut and chives in a separate shallow dish, and put the milk and eggs in two small bowls. Dip each prawn into the milk, then into the beaten egg and finally into the coconut and chive mixture.

4 Heat the oil in a large pan or deep-fryer and fry the prawns for about 1 minute, until golden. Lift out and drain on kitchen paper. Serve hot, garnished with lime or lemon wedges and parsley.

BUTTERFLIED PRAWNS IN CHILLI CHOCOLATE

ALTHOUGH THE COMBINATION OF HOT AND SWEET FLAVOURS MAY SEEM ODD, THIS IS A DELICIOUS SNACK. THE USE OF BITTER CHOCOLATE ADDS RICHNESS WITHOUT INCREASING THE SWEETNESS.

SERVES FOUR

INGREDIENTS
- 8 large raw prawns (shrimp), in the shell
- 15ml/1 tbsp seasoned flour
- 15ml/1 tbsp dry sherry
- juice of 4 clementines or 1 large orange
- 15g/½ oz unsweetened dark (bittersweet) chocolate, chopped
- 30ml/2 tbsp olive oil
- 2 garlic cloves, finely chopped
- 2.5cm/1in piece fresh root ginger, finely chopped
- 1 small red chilli, seeded and chopped
- salt and ground black pepper

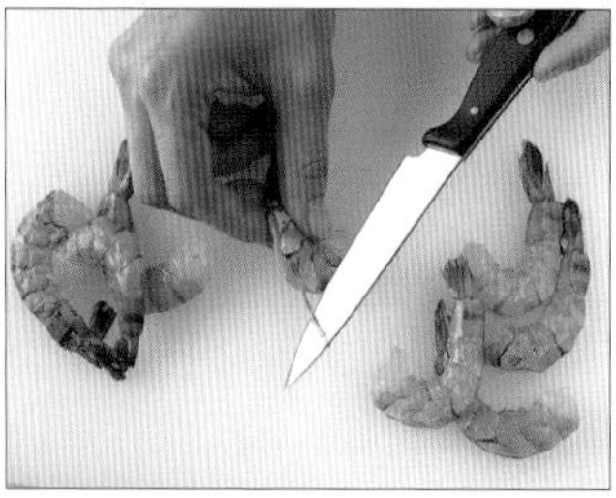

1 Peel the prawns, leaving just the tail sections intact. Make a shallow cut down the back of each prawn and carefully pull out and discard the dark intestinal tract. Turn over the prawns so that the undersides are uppermost, then carefully split them open from tail to top, using a small sharp knife, cutting almost, but not quite, through to the back.

2 Press the prawns down firmly to flatten them out. Coat with the seasoned flour and set aside.

3 Gently heat the sherry and clementine or orange juice in a small pan. When warm, remove from the heat and stir in the chopped chocolate until melted.

4 Heat the olive oil in a frying pan. Cook the garlic, ginger and chilli over a medium heat for 2 minutes, until golden. Remove with a slotted spoon and reserve. Add the prawns, cut side down, to the pan; cook for 2–3 minutes, until golden brown with pink edges. Turn and cook for a further 2 minutes. Be sure not to overcook the prawns, turning them only once to ensure that they are cooked through and yet retain succulence.

5 Return the garlic mixture to the pan and pour over the chocolate sauce. Cook for 1 minute, turning the prawns to coat them in the glossy sauce. Season to taste and serve hot.

DESERT NACHOS

TORTILLA CHIPS ARE LIVENED UP WITH JALAPEÑOS IN THIS QUICK-AND-EASY SNACK. SERVED WITH A VARIETY OF SPICY MEXICAN DIPS, THIS ALWAYS PROVES TO BE A POPULAR DISH.

SERVES TWO

INGREDIENTS
- 450g/1lb blue corn tortilla chips or ordinary tortilla chips, according to taste
- 45ml/3 tbsp chopped pickled jalapeño chillies, according to taste
- 12 black olives, sliced
- 225g/8oz/2 cups grated Cheddar cheese

To serve
- guacamole
- salsa
- sour cream
- a sprinkling of chopped coriander (cilantro) leaves
- lime wedges for squeezing

1 Preheat the oven to 180°C/350°F/ Gas 4. Put the tortilla chips in a 23 x 33cm/9 x 13in ovenproof dish and spread them out evenly. Sprinkle the jalapeños, olives and cheese evenly over the tortilla chips.

2 Place the prepared tortilla chips in the top of the oven and bake for 10–15 minutes, until the cheese melts. Serve the nachos immediately, with the guacamole, salsa, sour cream, coriander (cilantro) and lime.

EMPANADAS WITH ROPAS VIEJAS

The filling for these Mexican empanadas is traditionally made with meat that is cooked until it is so tender that it can be torn apart with forks. It resembles tattered cloth, which is how it came to be known as ROPA VIEJA, *which means "old clothes".*

SERVES SIX

INGREDIENTS
- 150g/5oz/1 cup *masa harina*
- 30ml/2 tbsp plain (all-pupose) flour
- 2.5ml/½ tsp salt
- 120–150ml/4–5fl oz/½–⅔ cup warm water
- 15ml/1 tbsp oil, plus extra, for frying
- 250g/9oz lean minced (ground) pork
- 1 garlic clove, crushed
- 3 tomatoes
- 2 ancho chillies
- ½ small onion
- 2.5ml/½ tsp ground cumin
- 2.5ml/½ tsp salt

1 Mix the *masa harina*, plain flour and salt in a bowl. Gradually add enough of the warm water to make a smooth, but not sticky, dough. Knead briefly, then shape into a ball, wrap in clear film (plastic wrap) and set aside.

2 Heat 15ml/1 tbsp oil in a pan. Add the minced pork and cook, stirring frequently, until it has browned evenly. Stir in the garlic and cook for 2 minutes more. Remove from the heat and set the pan aside.

3 Cut a cross in the base of each tomato, place them in a bowl and pour over boiling water. After 3 minutes plunge the tomatoes into a bowl of cold water. Drain. The skins will peel back easily from the crosses. Remove the skins completely. Chop the tomato flesh and put in a bowl.

4 Slit the ancho chillies and scrape out the seeds. Chop the chillies finely and add them to the tomatoes. Chop the onion finely and add it to the tomato mixture, with the ground cumin.

5 Stir the tomato mixture into the pan containing the pork and cook over a moderate heat for 10 minutes, stirring occasionally. Season with salt to taste.

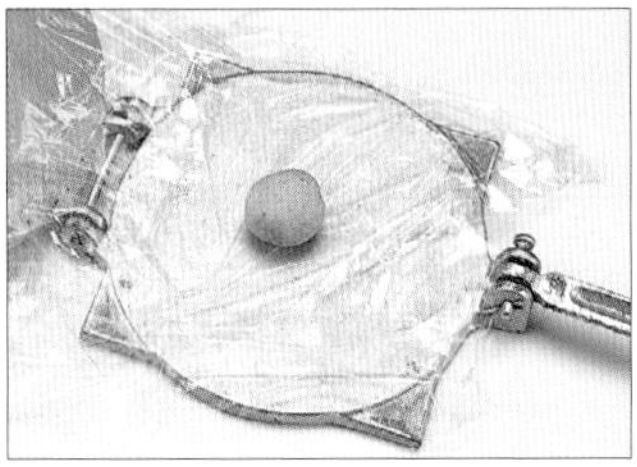

6 To make the tortillas, divide the empanada dough into 12 pieces and roll each piece into a ball. Open a tortilla press and line both sides with plastic (this can be cut from a new plastic sandwich bag). Put a ball of dough on the press and bring the top down to flatten it into a 7.5cm/3in round. Use the remaining dough balls to make more tortillas in the same way.

COOK'S TIP

If the empanada dough proves difficult to handle, a little oil or melted lard can be kneaded into the dough to help make it more pliable.

7 Spoon a little of the meat mixture on one half of each tortilla, working quickly to stop the dough from drying out. Dampen the edges of the dough with a little water and fold, turnover-style, to make the empanadas.

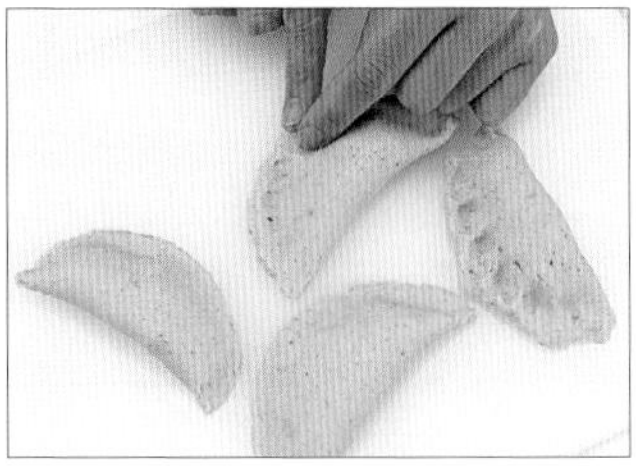

8 Seal the edges of the empanadas by pinching them between the index finger and thumb of the left hand and the index finger of the right hand.

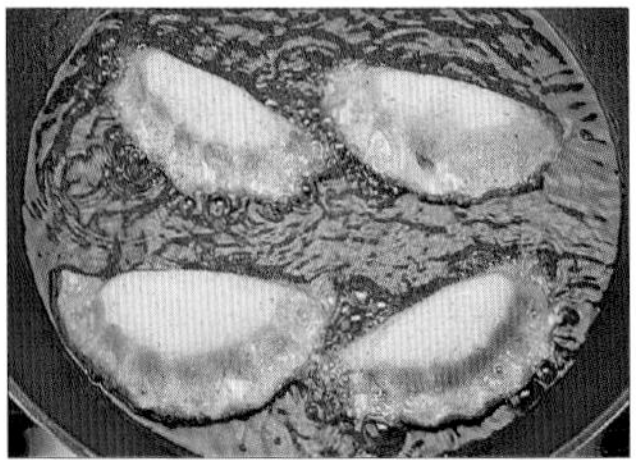

9 Heat a little oil in a large frying pan. When it is hot, fry the empanadas in batches until crisp and golden on both sides, turning at least once. Drain for a few minutes on kitchen paper, then serve hot or cold.

CHEESY EGGS

THESE DELICIOUS CARIBBEAN STUFFED EGGS ARE SIMPLE TO MAKE AND IDEAL FOR LAST-MINUTE PARTY SNACKS. SERVE THEM WITH A CRISP SALAD GARNISH AND DHAL PURI.

SERVES SIX

INGREDIENTS

- 6 eggs
- 15ml/1 tbsp mayonnaise
- 30ml/2 tbsp grated Cheddar cheese
- 2.5ml/½ tsp ground white pepper
- 10ml/2 tsp chopped fresh chives
- 2 radishes, thinly sliced, to garnish
- lettuce leaves, to serve

VARIATION

A variety of fillings can be used instead of Cheddar cheese. Canned sardines or tuna mayonnaise make a tasty alternative.

1 Cook the eggs in boiling water for about 10 minutes until hard-boiled. Lift out the eggs and place them in cold water. When cool, remove the shells.

2 Put the mayonnaise, Cheddar cheese, pepper and chives into a small bowl. Cut the hard-boiled eggs in half lengthways and carefully scoop out the yolks without breaking the whites, Add the yolks to the bowl.

3 Mash all the ingredients with a fork until well blended.

4 Fill each egg white with the egg yolk and cheese mixture, and arrange on a plate. Garnish with thinly sliced radishes and serve with crisp green lettuce leaves.

Red Enchiladas

THE METHOD OF FIRST DIPPING THE TORTILLAS IN SAUCE, THEN QUICKLY COOKING THEM IN OIL GIVES THE BEST FLAVOUR, ALTHOUGH THEY CAN BE DIPPED AFTER BEING QUICKLY FRIED.

SERVES SIX

INGREDIENTS
- 4 dried ancho chillies
- 450g/1lb tomatoes, peeled, seeded and chopped
- 1 onion, finely chopped
- 1 garlic clove, chopped
- 15ml/1 tbsp chopped fresh coriander (cilantro)
- lard or corn oil, for frying
- 250ml/8fl oz/1 cup sour cream
- 4 chorizo sausages, skinned and chopped
- 18 freshly prepared unbaked corn tortillas
- 50g/2oz/⅔ cup freshly grated Parmesan cheese
- salt and ground black pepper

1 Roast the ancho chillies in a dry frying pan over a medium heat for 1–2 minutes, shaking the pan frequently. When cool, carefully slit the chillies, remove and discard the stems and seeds, and tear the pods into pieces. Put the pieces into a bowl, add warm water to just cover, and soak for 20 minutes.

2 Tip the chillies, with a little of the soaking water, into a food processor. Add the tomatoes, onion, garlic and coriander and process. Stop the processor half way through blending, when the mixture is not yet smooth, to stir the ingredients and ensure that it becomes a smooth, unified purée.

3 Heat 15ml/1 tbsp lard or oil in a pan. Add the purée and cook gently over a medium heat, stirring, for 3–4 minutes. Season to taste with salt and pepper and then stir in the sour cream. Remove the pan from the heat and set it aside.

4 Heat a further 15ml/1 tbsp lard or oil in a small frying pan; sauté the chorizo for a few minutes until lightly browned. Moisten with a little of the sauce and set the pan aside.

5 Preheat the oven to 180°C/350°F/Gas 4. Heat 30ml/2 tbsp lard or oil in a frying pan. Dip a tortilla in the sauce and add to the pan. Cook for a few seconds, shaking the pan gently, turn over and briefly fry the other side.

6 Slide the tortilla on to a plate, top with some of the sausage mixture, and roll up. Pack the prepared tortillas in a single layer in an ovenproof dish. Pour the sauce over, sprinkle with Parmesan and bake for about 20 minutes.

TOSTADAS WITH TOMATO SALSA

A TOSTADA IS A CRISP, FRIED TORTILLA USED IN THIS RECIPE AS A BASE ON WHICH TO PILE THE TOPPING OF YOUR CHOICE. THIS VARIATION ON A SANDWICH MAKES A VERY TASTY SNACK.

SERVES SIX

INGREDIENTS

- 30ml/2 tbsp oil, plus extra for frying
- 1 onion, chopped
- 2 garlic cloves, chopped
- 2.5ml/½ tsp chilli powder
- 400g/14oz can pinto beans, drained
- 150ml/¼ pint/⅔ cup chicken stock
- 15ml/1 tbsp tomato purée (paste)
- 30ml/2 tbsp fresh coriander (cilantro)
- 6 wheat or corn tortillas
- 30ml/2 tbsp sour cream
- 50g/2oz/½ cup grated (shredded) Cheddar cheese

For the tomato salsa

- 1 small onion, chopped
- 1 garlic clove, crushed
- 2 fresh green chillies, seeded and finely chopped
- 450g/1lb tomatoes, chopped
- 30ml/2 tbsp fresh coriander (cilantro)

1 To make the salsa, put the onion and garlic in a serving bowl and stir in the chillies, tomatoes and fresh coriander. Season generously and mix well.

2 Heat 30ml/2 tbsp oil in a heavy-based frying pan and fry the chopped onion for 3–5 minutes until softened. Add the garlic and chilli powder, and fry for 1 minute, stirring constantly.

3 Add the beans. Pour in the stock and mix well. Mash the beans very roughly. Add the tomato purée, chopped coriander and seasoning to taste. Mix thoroughly and cook for a few minutes.

4 Fry 2 tortillas in hot oil for 1 minute, turning once, until crisp, then drain on kitchen paper. Fry the remaining tortillas in the same way.

5 Put a spoonful of the refried beans on each tostada, spoon over some tomato salsa, then some sour cream, sprinkle with grated Cheddar cheese and garnish with coriander.

COOK'S TIP

When you are in a hurry, you can use canned refried beans. Thin them with a little stock if necessary and cook them gently over a low heat for 5–10 minutes to ensure that they are properly heated through. Stir continuously to dissipate the heat and prevent burning.

ENCHILADAS WITH HOT TOMATO AND GREEN CHILLI SAUCE

In Mexico, chillies appear in almost every savoury dish, either as chilli powder or chopped, sliced or whole. By Mexican standards, this is a mild version of the popular chicken enchiladas. If you like your food hot, add extra chillies to the tomato sauce.

SERVES FOUR

INGREDIENTS
- 8 wheat tortillas
- 175g/6oz Cheddar cheese, grated
- 1 onion, finely chopped
- 350g/12oz cooked chicken, cut into small chunks
- 300ml/½ pint/1¼ cups sour cream
- 1 avocado, sliced and tossed in lemon juice, to garnish

For the sauce
- 1–2 fresh green chillies
- 15ml/1 tbsp vegetable oil
- 1 onion, chopped
- 1 garlic clove, crushed
- 400g/14oz can chopped tomatoes
- 30ml/2 tbsp tomato purée (paste)
- salt and ground black pepper

1 To make the sauce, cut the chillies in half lengthways and carefully remove the cores and seeds. Slice the chillies very finely.

2 Heat the oil in a frying pan and fry the onion and garlic for about 3–4 minutes until softened. Stir in the tomatoes, tomato purée and chillies. Simmer gently, uncovered, for 12–15 minutes, stirring frequently.

3 Pour the sauce into a food processor or blender, and process until smooth. Return to the heat and cook very gently, uncovered, for a further 15 minutes. Season to taste, then set aside.

4 Preheat the oven to 180°C/350°F/Gas 4. Butter a shallow ovenproof dish. Take one tortilla and sprinkle with some cheese and chopped onion, about 40g/1½oz of chicken and 15ml/1 tbsp of sauce. Pour over 15ml/1 tbsp of sour cream, roll up and place seam- side down in the dish.

5 Make 7 more enchiladas to fill the dish. Pour the remaining sauce over and sprinkle with the remaining cheese and onion. Bake for 25–30 minutes until the top is golden. Serve with the remaining sour cream, either poured over or in a separate container, and garnish with the sliced avocado.

Chicken Flautas

Crisp-fried Mexcian tortillas with a chicken and cheese filling make a delicious light meal, especially when served with a spicy tomato salsa. The secret is to make sure that the oil is sufficiently hot to prevent the flutes from absorbing too much of it.

MAKES TWELVE

INGREDIENTS
- 2 skinless, boneless chicken breasts
- 1 onion
- 2 garlic cloves
- 15ml/1 tbsp vegetable oil
- 90g/3½oz feta cheese, crumbled
- 12 corn tortillas, freshly made or a few days old
- oil, for frying
- salt and ground black pepper

For the salsa
- 3 tomatoes, peeled, seeded and chopped
- juice of ½ lime
- small bunch of fresh coriander (cilantro), chopped
- ½ small onion, finely chopped
- 3 fresh fresno chillies or similar fresh green chillies, seeded and chopped

1 Start by making the salsa. Mix the tomatoes, lime juice, coriander, onion and chillies in a bowl. Season with salt to taste and set aside.

2 Put the chicken breasts in a large pan, add water to cover and bring to the boil. Lower the heat and simmer for 15–20 minutes or until the chicken is cooked. Remove the chicken from the pan and let it cool a little. Using two forks, shred the chicken into small pieces. Set it aside.

3 Chop the onion finely and crush the garlic. Heat the oil in a frying pan, add the onion and garlic and fry over a low heat for about 5 minutes, or until the onion has softened but not coloured. Add the shredded chicken, with salt and pepper to taste. Mix well, remove from the heat and stir in the feta.

4 Before they can be rolled, soften the tortillas by steaming three or four at a time on a plate over boiling water for a few moments until they are pliable. Alternatively, wrap them in microwave-safe film and then heat them in a microwave oven on full power for about 30 seconds.

5 Place a spoonful of the chicken filling on one of the tortillas and roll tightly to make a neat cylinder. Secure with a cocktail stick (toothpick). Immediately cover the roll with clear film (plastic wrap) to prevent the tortilla from drying out and splitting. Fill and roll the remaining tortillas in the same way.

6 Pour oil into a frying pan to a depth of 2.5cm/1in. Heat it until a small cube of bread, added to the oil, rises to the surface and bubbles at the edges before turning golden. Remove the cocktail sticks, then add the flutes to the pan, a few at a time.

7 Fry the flutes for 2–3 minutes until golden, turning frequently. Drain on kitchen paper and serve at once, with the salsa.

COOK'S TIP

You might find it easier to keep the cocktail sticks (toothpicks) in place until after the flutes have been fried, but do remove them before serving.

BLACK-EYED BEAN AND SHRIMP FRITTERS

THIS BRAZILIAN SNACK, LOCALLY KNOWN AS ACARAJÉ, *IS FROM BAHIA, A REGION HIGHLY INFLUENCED BY ITS AFRICAN SLAVE HERITAGE. WOMEN FRY THESE PATTIES TO ORDER. THEY ARE THEN CUT OPEN AND FILLED WITH VARIOUS SAUCES, ALL DELECTABLE BUT VERY MESSY TO EAT.*

MAKES TEN

INGREDIENTS

- 250g/9oz/1¼ cups black-eyed beans (peas)
- 40g/1½oz/¼ cup dried shrimp
- 1 onion, roughly chopped
- palm oil and vegetable oil, for frying
- salt
- chilli oil, to serve

For the filling

- 30ml/2 tbsp palm oil
- 115g/4oz/⅔ cup dried shrimp
- 1 large onion, thinly sliced
- 2 fresh hot red chillies, seeded and finely chopped

1 Put the black-eyed beans in a large bowl and cover with plenty of water. Soak overnight to loosen the skins. Drain, then soak for a further 30 minutes in hot (but not boiling) water.

2 Drain the beans and tip them on to a board. Rub them between your hands to separate them from their skins. The patties will be very dry if the skins are not removed.

3 Transfer the beans to a bowl and pour over cold water to cover. The loose skins will begin to rise to the surface. Remove them with a slotted spoon and throw them away. Stir the beans to encourage more skins to float to the surface, continuing until all the skins have been removed. You'll be able to chart your progress easily, as the beans lose their distinctive "eye" when peeled. Drain.

4 Blend the dried shrimp and onion in a food processor until smooth. Add the beans and blend to a thick purée. Season with salt.

5 Mix equal quantities of palm oil and vegetable oil to a depth of about 5cm/2in in a deep pan. Form the *acarajé* mixture into 10 oval shapes. Heat the oil and fry half of the fritters for 5 minutes or until golden. Lift out with a slotted spoon and drain on kitchen paper. Between batches, skim the oil to remove any burnt bits.

6 Make the filling. Heat the oil in a frying pan. When hot, add the dried shrimp and sauté for 2–3 minutes until golden. Lift out with a slotted spoon and drain on kitchen paper. Lower the heat and stir in the onion slices. Cook for 5 minutes until soft, then add the chilli. Sauté for 1 minute and set aside.

7 Cut each fritter open lengthways and fill with the onion mixture. Add a couple of dried shrimp and drizzle with chilli oil.

Beef Empanadas

You'll find these pastry turnovers throughout Latin America, with Colombia's being perhaps the most famous. They come with a variety of fillings, including beef, pork, vegetables and cheese. What better way for using up leftovers?

MAKES TWENTY

INGREDIENTS

- 225g/8oz/2 cups plain (all-purpose) flour
- 2.5ml/½ tsp salt
- 90g/3½oz/scant ½ cup cold butter, cut into small chunks
- juice of ½ lime
- 50ml/2fl oz/¼ cup lukewarm water
- vegetable oil, for deep-frying
- chilli salsa, to serve (optional)

For the filling

- 450g/1lb beef shin or leg (shank)
- 60ml/4 tbsp olive oil
- 1.5ml/¼ tsp ground cumin
- 1 garlic clove, crushed
- 10ml/2 tsp paprika
- 250ml/8fl oz/1 cup light beef stock
- 450g/1lb potatoes, peeled and cubed
- 2 tomatoes, finely chopped
- 3 spring onions (scallions), finely chopped
- salt and ground black pepper

1 Make the filling. Cut the beef into large chunks and chop in a food processor until finely diced, but not minced (ground). This will tenderize the meat, cutting the cooking time.

2 Heat 30ml/2 tbsp of the olive oil in a wide, heavy pan over a high heat. Add the beef chunks and sauté until golden brown. Push the beef to the side and add the cumin, crushed garlic and paprika to the pan. Reduce the heat and cook, stirring gently, for around 2 minutes, until the spices begin to release their delicious aroma.

3 Stir in the stock and bring to the boil. Cover and cook over a low heat for 30 minutes. Stir in the potatoes, tomatoes and spring onions. Cook for 15 minutes more, or until the beef and potatoes are tender. Season with salt and pepper to taste, then leave to cool.

4 Meanwhile, place the flour and salt in a food processor. Add the small chunks of butter and pulse until the mixture resembles fine breadcrumbs. Combine the lime juice and water and slowly pour into the food processor, with the motor still running. As soon as the pastry comes together, tip it on to a floured surface and gently knead to a soft dough. Shape into a ball, wrap in clear film (plastic wrap) and chill for at least 20 minutes.

5 On a floured surface roll out the pastry until it is very thin. Cut out 6cm/2½in circles, using a pastry (cookie) cutter.

6 Spoon about 7.5ml/1½ tsp of the filling into the centre of a pastry circle, then brush the edges with water. Fold the pastry over to form a half-moon, then press around the edges to seal. Repeat with the rest of the pastry.

7 Pour vegetable oil to a depth of 5cm/2in into a deep frying pan. Heat the oil, then add five or six empanadas. Fry for 5 minutes until golden brown, turning halfway through cooking. Remove from the pan with a slotted spoon and drain. Repeat with the remaining empanadas. Serve with a little chilli salsa, if using.

SOPES WITH PICADILLO

These are small, thick tortillas with crimped edges, made with masa harina, and are filled like tarts. They are an acquired taste as they remain "doughy" when cooked, but they can become quite addictive. The filling – picadillo – is very popular in Mexico and is used in many different recipes.

SERVES SIX

INGREDIENTS

250g/9oz/scant 2 cups *masa harina*
2.5ml/½ tsp salt
50g/2oz/¼ cup chilled lard
300ml/½ pint/1¼ cups warm water
15ml/1 tbsp vegetable oil
250g/9oz lean minced (ground) beef
2 garlic cloves, crushed
1 red pepper, seeded and chopped
60ml/4 tbsp dry sherry
15ml/1 tbsp tomato purée (paste)
2.5ml/½ tsp ground cumin
5ml/1 tsp ground cinnamon
1.5ml/¼ tsp ground cloves
2.5ml/½ tsp ground black pepper
25g/1oz/3 tbsp raisins
25g/1oz/¼ cup slivered almonds
fresh parsley sprigs, to garnish

1 Put the *masa harina* and salt in a large bowl. Grate the chilled lard into the bowl and rub it into the dry ingredients until no visible pieces remain. Add the warm water, a little at a time, to make a dough that can be worked into a ball. Knead the dough on a lightly floured surface for 3–4 minutes until smooth. Set aside.

2 Heat the oil in a large pan. Add the minced beef and cook over a high heat, stirring until it has browned. Stir in the garlic and continue cooking for 2–3 minutes, stirring occasionally.

3 Stir in the red pepper, sherry, tomato purée and spices. Cook for 5 minutes more, then add the raisins and the slivered almonds. Lower the heat and simmer for 10 minutes. The meat should be cooked through and the mixture moist, but not wet. Keep hot.

4 Divide the dough into six balls. Open a tortilla press and line both sides with plastic (this can be cut from a new plastic sandwich bag). Put a ball of dough on the press and bring the top down to flatten it into a 10cm/4in round, thicker than the conventional tortilla. Use the remaining dough balls to make five more rounds.

5 Heat a griddle or frying pan until hot. Add one of the rounds and fry until the underside is beginning to brown and blister. Turn the round over and cook the other side briefly, until the colour is just beginning to change. Slide on to a plate and crimp the rim to form a raised edge. Fill with the spicy beef and keep hot while cooking and filling the remaining tartlets. Garnish with parsley.

COOK'S TIP

Take care that the dough for the *sopes* does not become dry. Wrap it in clear film (plastic wrap) while it is set aside.

PANUCHOS

THESE STUFFED TORTILLAS ARE A BIT FIDDLY TO MAKE, BUT WELL WORTH THE EFFORT. THIS DISH IS PARTICULARLY POPULAR IN THE YUCATÁN REGION OF MEXICO.

SERVES SIX

INGREDIENTS
- 150g/5oz/1 cup *masa harina*
- pinch of salt
- 120ml/4fl oz/½ cup warm water
- 2 skinless, boneless chicken breasts
- 5ml/1 tsp dried oregano
- 150g/5oz/about 1 cup *Frijoles de Olla* (bean paste)
- 2 hard-boiled eggs, sliced
- oil, for shallow frying
- salt and ground black pepper
- sliced onions, to serve

1 Mix the *masa harina* and salt in a large bowl. Add the warm water, a little at a time, to make a dough that can be worked into a ball. Knead on a lightly floured surface for 3–4 minutes until smooth, then wrap in clear film (plastic wrap) and leave to rest for 1 hour.

2 Put the chicken in a pan, add the dried oregano and pour in water to cover. Bring to the boil, then lower the heat and simmer for 10 minutes or until the chicken is cooked. Remove the chicken from the pan, discard the water and let the chicken cool a little. Using two forks, shred the chicken into small pieces. Set it aside.

3 Divide the dough into 12 small pieces and roll into balls. Open a tortilla press and line both sides with plastic (this can be cut from a new plastic sandwich bag). Put a dough ball on the press and flatten it into a 6cm/2½in round. Use the remaining dough balls to make more tortillas in the same way.

4 Cook each tortilla in a hot frying pan for 15–20 seconds on each side. After a further 15 seconds on one side remove and wrap in a clean dishtowel.

5 Cut a slit in each tortilla, about 1cm/½in deep around the rim. Put a spoonful of the bean paste and a slice of hard-boiled egg in each slit.

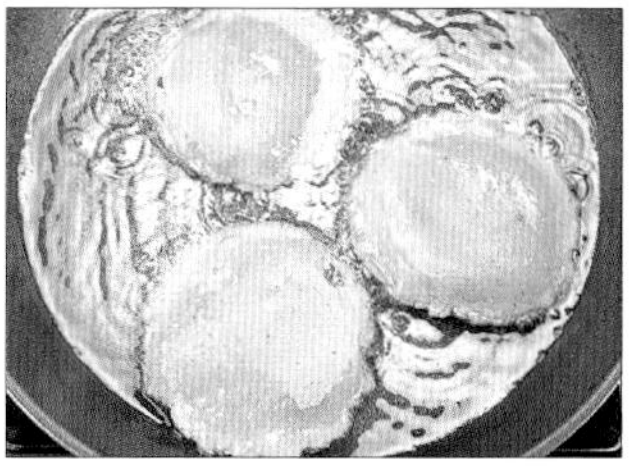

6 Heat the oil for shallow frying in a large frying pan. Fry the tortilla pockets until they are crisp and golden brown on all sides, turning at least once during cooking. Drain them on kitchen paper and place on six individual serving plates. Top with a little of the shredded chicken and some onion relish. Season to taste and serve immediately.

QUESADILLAS

THESE CHEESE-FILLED TORTILLAS ARE THE MEXICAN EQUIVALENT OF TOASTED SANDWICHES. SERVE THEM AS SOON AS THEY ARE COOKED, OR THEY WILL BECOME CHEWY. IF YOU ARE MAKING THEM FOR A CROWD, FILL AND FOLD THE TORTILLAS AHEAD OF TIME, BUT ONLY COOK THEM TO ORDER.

SERVES FOUR

INGREDIENTS

- 200g/7oz mozzarella, Monterey Jack or mild Cheddar cheese
- 1 fresh fresno chilli (optional)
- 8 wheat flour tortillas, about 15cm/6in across
- onion relish or salsa, to serve

VARIATIONS

Spread a thin layer of your favourite Mexican salsa on the tortilla before adding the cheese, or add a few pieces of cooked chicken or prawns (shrimp) before folding the tortilla in half.

1 If using mozzarella cheese, it must be drained thoroughly and then patted dry and sliced into thin strips. Monterey Jack and Cheddar cheese should both be coarsely grated, as finely grated cheese will melt and ooze away when cooking. Set the cheese aside in a bowl.

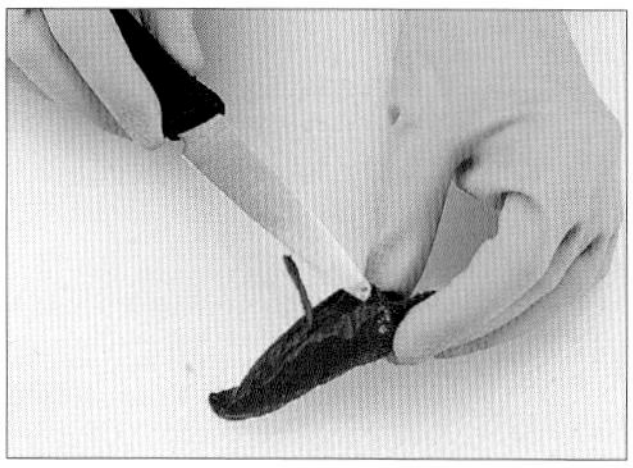

2 If using the chilli, spear it on a long-handled metal skewer and roast it over the flame of a gas burner until the skin blisters and darkens. Do not let the flesh burn. Alternatively, dry fry it in a griddle pan until the skin is scorched. Place the roasted chilli in a strong plastic bag and tie the top to keep the steam in. Set aside for 20 minutes.

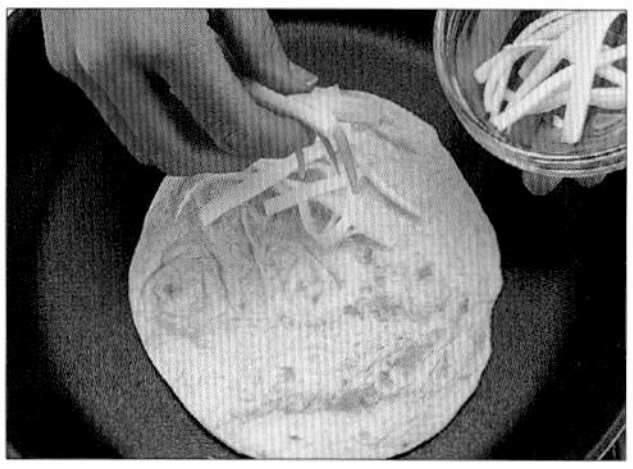

3 Remove the chilli from the bag and peel off the skin. Cut off the stalk, then slit the chilli and scrape out the seeds. Cut the flesh into eight thin strips.

4 Warm a large frying pan or griddle. Place one tortilla on the pan or griddle at a time, sprinkle about an eighth of the cheese on to one half and add a strip of chilli, if using. Fold the tortilla over the cheese and press the edges together gently to seal. Cook the filled tortilla for 1 minute, then turn over and cook the other side for 1 minute.

5 Remove the filled tortilla from the pan or griddle, cut it into three triangles or four strips and serve at once, with the onion relish or tomato salsa.

MEXICAN RICE

VERSIONS OF THIS DISH – A RELATIVE OF SPANISH RICE – ARE POPULAR ALL OVER CENTRAL AND SOUTH AMERICA, AND CAN ALSO BE FOUND IN THE CARIBBEAN TOO. CLASSIFIED AS A SOPA SECA OR DRY SOUP, IT IS A DELICIOUS MEDLEY OF RICE, TOMATOES AND AROMATIC FLAVOURINGS. THE STOCK IS LARGELY ABSORBED BY THE TIME THE DISH IS READY.

SERVES SIX

INGREDIENTS

- 200g/7oz/1 cup long grain rice
- 200g/7oz can chopped tomatoes in tomato juice
- ½ onion, roughly chopped
- 2 garlic cloves, roughly chopped
- 30ml/2 tbsp vegetable oil
- 450ml/¾ pint/scant 2 cups chicken stock
- 2.5ml/½ tsp salt
- 3 fresh fresno chillies or other fresh green chillies, trimmed
- 150g/5oz/1 cup frozen peas (optional)
- ground black pepper

1 Put the rice in a large bowl and pour over boiling water to cover. Stir once, then leave to stand for 10 minutes. Tip into a strainer, rinse under cold water, drain again and set aside to dry slightly.

2 Meanwhile, pour the tomatoes and juice into a food processor or blender, add the onion and garlic and process until smooth.

3 Heat the oil in a large, heavy-based pan, add the rice and cook over a moderate heat until it becomes a delicate golden brown. Stir occasionally to ensure that the rice does not stick to the bottom of the pan.

4 Add the tomato mixture and stir over a moderate heat until all the liquid has been absorbed. Stir in the stock, salt, whole chillies and peas, if using. Continue to cook the mixture, stirring occasionally, until all the liquid has been absorbed and the rice is just tender.

5 Remove the pan from the heat, cover it with a tight-fitting lid and leave it to stand in a warm place for 5–10 minutes. Remove the chillies, fluff up the rice lightly and serve, sprinkled with black pepper. The chillies may be used as a garnish, if you like.

COOK'S TIP

Do not stir the rice too often after adding the stock or the grains will break down and the mixture will become starchy.

PAN-FRIED SQUID

VISIT A BEACH BAR ANYWHERE ALONG THE COAST OF SOUTH AMERICA AND THIS IS PRECISELY THE TYPE OF SNACK YOU ARE LIKELY TO FIND ON SALE.

SERVES FOUR

INGREDIENTS
- 1kg/2¼lb fresh small squid
- 30ml/2 tbsp olive oil
- 2 garlic cloves, crushed
- 1 fresh red chilli, seeded and finely chopped
- 45ml/3 tbsp *cachaça*
- juice of 1 lime
- salt
- chunks of bread, to serve

1 Clean the squid under cold water. Pull the tentacles away from the body. The squid's entrails will come out easily. Remove the piece of cartilage from inside the body cavity and discard it.

VARIATION
If you cannot find *cachaça*, replace it with white rum or vodka.

2 Wash the body and peel away the membrane that covers it. Cut between the tentacles and head, discarding the head and entrails. Leave the tentacles whole, but discard the hard beak in the middle. Cut the body into small pieces.

3 Heat the oil over a high heat. Add the garlic, chilli and squid. Season with salt and cook for 2–3 minutes, until the squid is opaque and lightly charred.

4 Pour in the *cachaça* and continue cooking the squid until most of the liquid has evaporated. Remove the pan from the heat and then stir in the lime juice.

5 Tip the squid on to a plate and serve with chunks of bread to soak up the delicious cooking juices. Offer cocktail sticks (toothpicks) for picking up the pieces of squid.

FRIED WHITEBAIT WITH CAYENNE PEPPER

FOR THE PERFECT BEACH SNACK, TRY THESE CRISP, SPICY, BITESIZE FISH WITH A SQUEEZE OF LIME.

SERVES FOUR

INGREDIENTS
- 50g/2oz/½ cup plain (all-purpose) flour
- 1.5ml/¼ tsp cayenne pepper
- 250g/9oz whitebait
- vegetable oil, for deep-frying
- salt and ground black pepper
- lime wedges, to serve

VARIATIONS
Small fresh anchovies are also delicious cooked whole in this way. Alternatively, make up a mixed platter using whitebait, squid and prawns (shrimp).

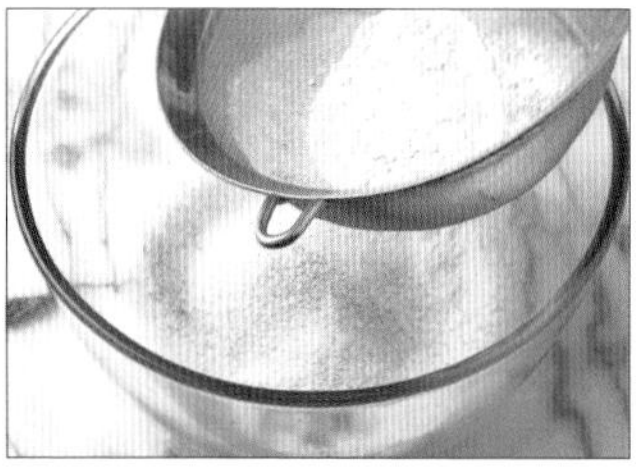

1 Sift the flour and cayenne pepper into a deep bowl or large shallow dish. Season with plenty of salt and ground black pepper.

2 Thoroughly coat the whitebait in the seasoned flour, then shake off any excess flour and make sure the whitebait are separate. Do this in batches, placing the coated fish on a plate ready for frying.

3 Pour oil to a depth of 5cm/2in into a deep wide pan. Heat the oil until very hot, then add a batch of whitebait and fry for 2–3 minutes until golden. Remove from the pan with a slotted spoon and drain on kitchen paper. Repeat with the remaining whitebait.

4 Pile the fried whitebait on a plate, season with salt and serve immediately with the lime wedges.

EGGS WITH CHORIZO

In Mexico, there are two types of chorizo sausage. The first is freshly made and sold loose; the second is packed in sausage skins and air-dried, like Spanish chorizo. This is a recipe for the former. Freshly made chorizo can be used in a number of savoury dishes, but is particularly good with scrambled egg, as here.

SERVES FOUR

INGREDIENTS

- 25g/1oz/2 tbsp lard
- 500g/1¼lb minced (ground) pork
- 3 garlic cloves, crushed
- 10ml/2 tsp dried oregano
- 5ml/1 tsp ground cinnamon
- 2.5ml/½ tsp ground cloves
- 2.5ml/½ tsp ground black pepper
- 30ml/2 tbsp dry sherry
- 5ml/1 tsp caster (superfine) sugar
- 5ml/1 tsp salt
- 6 eggs
- 2 tomatoes, peeled, seeded and finely diced
- ½ small onion, finely chopped
- 60ml/4 tbsp milk or single (light) cream
- fresh oregano sprigs, to garnish
- warm corn or wheat-flour tortillas, to serve

1 Melt the lard in a large frying pan over a moderate heat. Add the pork mince and cook until browned, stirring frequently. Stir in the garlic, dried oregano, cinnamon, cloves and black pepper. Cook for 3–4 minutes more.

2 Add the sherry, caster sugar and salt to the mince, stir well and cook for 3–4 minutes until the flavours are blended. Remove from the heat.

3 Put the eggs in a bowl. Beat lightly to mix, then stir in the finely diced tomatoes and chopped onion.

4 Return the chorizo mixture to the heat. Heat it through and pour in the egg mixture. Cook, stirring constantly, until the egg is almost firm.

5 Stir in the milk or cream and check the seasoning. Garnish with fresh oregano and serve with warm corn or wheat-flour tortillas.

CHILLIES IN CHEESE SAUCE

This makes an excellent starter, light lunch or dip to serve with drinks. The chillies and tequila give it quite a kick.

SERVES FOUR TO SIX

INGREDIENTS

- 4 fresh green fresno chillies
- 15ml/1 tbsp vegetable oil
- ½ red onion, finely chopped
- 500g/1¼lb/5 cups grated Monterey Jack cheese
- 30ml/2 tbsp crème fraîche
- 150ml/¼ pint/⅔ cup double (heavy) cream
- 2 firm tomatoes, peeled
- 15ml/1 tbsp reposada tequila
- Tortilla Chips, to serve

COOK'S TIP

Cross-cut the base of a tomato and cover with boiling water. Plunge into cold water and the skin will peel easily.

1 Place the chillies in a dry frying pan over a moderate heat, turning them frequently until the skin blisters and darkens. Place the chillies in a strong plastic bag and tie the top to keep the steam in. Set aside for 20 minutes, then carefully peel off the skins. Slit the chillies and scrape out the seeds, then cut the flesh into thin strips. Cut these in half lengthways.

2 Heat the oil in a frying pan and fry the onion over a moderate heat for 5 minutes, until it is beginning to soften. Add the cheese, crème fraîche and cream. Stir over a low heat until the cheese melts and the mixture becomes a rich, creamy sauce. Stir in the thick chilli strips.

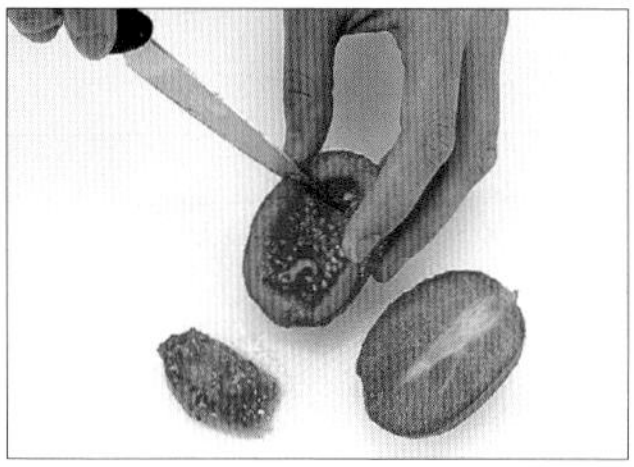

3 Cut the tomatoes in half and scrape out the seeds. Cut the flesh into 1cm/½in pieces and stir these into the sauce.

4 Just before serving, stir in the tequila. Pour the sauce into a serving dish and serve warm, with the tortilla chips.

MOLETTES

THIS IS THE MEXICAN VERSION OF BEANS ON TOAST. SOLD BY STREET TRADERS AROUND MID-MORNING, THEY MAKE THE PERFECT SNACK FOR THOSE WHO HAVE MISSED BREAKFAST.

SERVES FOUR

INGREDIENTS
- 4 crusty finger rolls
- 50g/2oz/¼ cup butter, softened
- 225g/8oz/1⅓ cups Refried Beans
- 150g/5oz/1¼ cups grated medium Cheddar cheese
- green salad leaves, to garnish
- 120ml/4fl oz/½ cup salsa, to serve

1 Cut the rolls in half, then take a sliver off the base so that they lie flat. Remove a little of the crumb. Spread them lightly with enough butter to crisp.

2 Arrange the rolls on a baking sheet and grill for about 5 minutes, or until they are crisp and golden. Meanwhile, heat the refried beans over a low heat in a small pan.

3 Scoop the beans into the rolls, then sprinkle the grated cheese on top. Put back under the grill until the cheese melts. Serve with the tomato salsa and garnish with salad leaves.

EGGS MOTULENOS

IN A TASTY AND FILLING BREAKFAST OR MIDDAY SNACK, BLACK BEANS, WHICH ARE ALSO KNOWN AS TURTLE BEANS, ARE TOPPED WITH EGGS AND CHILLI SAUCE AND SURROUNDED BY PEAS AND HAM.

SERVES FOUR

INGREDIENTS
- 225g/8oz/generous 1 cup black beans, soaked overnight in water
- 1 small onion, finely chopped
- 2 garlic cloves
- small bunch of fresh coriander (cilantro), chopped
- 150g/5oz/1 cup frozen peas
- 4 corn tortillas
- 30ml/2 tbsp oil
- 4 eggs
- 150g/5oz cooked ham, diced
- 60ml/4 tbsp hot chilli sauce
- 75g/3oz feta cheese, crumbled
- salt and ground black pepper
- salsa, to serve

1 Drain the beans, rinse them under cold water and drain again. Put them in a pan, add the onion and garlic and water to cover. Bring to the boil, then simmer for 40 minutes. Stir in the coriander, with salt and pepper to taste, and keep the beans hot.

2 Cook the peas in a small pan of boiling water until they are just tender. Drain and set aside. Wrap the tortillas in foil and place them on a plate. Stand the plate over a pan of boiling water and steam them for about 5 minutes. Alternatively, wrap them in microwave-safe film and heat them in a microwave on full power for about 30 seconds.

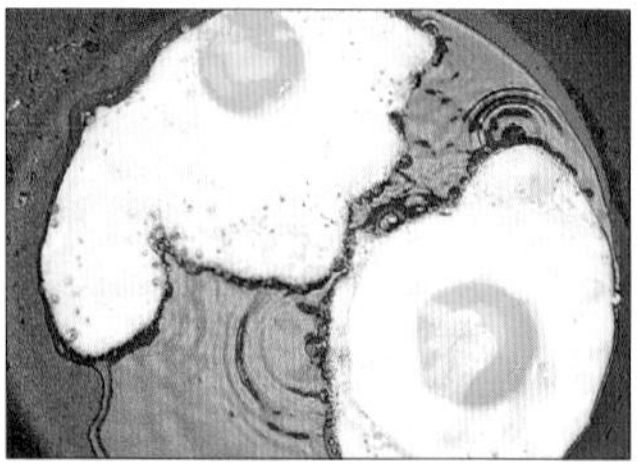

3 Heat the oil in a frying pan and fry the eggs until the whites are set. Lift them on to a plate and keep them warm while you quickly heat the ham and peas in the oil remaining in the pan.

4 Place the tortillas on warmed plates and top each one with some beans. Place an egg on each tortilla, spoon over 15ml/1 tbsp hot chilli sauce, then surround each egg with some peas and ham. Sprinkle feta over the peas and serve at once, with salsa on the side.

EGGS RANCHEROS

THERE ARE MANY VARIATIONS ON THIS POPULAR MEXICAN DISH, WHICH IS GREAT FOR BREAKFAST OR BRUNCH. THE COMBINATION OF CREAMY EGGS WITH ONION, CHILLI AND TOMATOES WORKS VERY WELL.

SERVES FOUR FOR BREAKFAST

INGREDIENTS

- 2 corn tortillas, several days old
- oil, for frying
- 2 fresh green jalapeño chillies
- 1 garlic clove
- 4 spring onions (scallions)
- 1 large tomato
- 8 eggs, beaten
- 150ml/¼ pint/⅔ cup single (light) cream
- small bunch of fresh coriander (cilantro), finely chopped
- salt and ground black pepper

1 Cut the tortillas into long strips. Pour oil into a frying pan to a depth of 1cm/½in. Heat the oil until it is very hot.

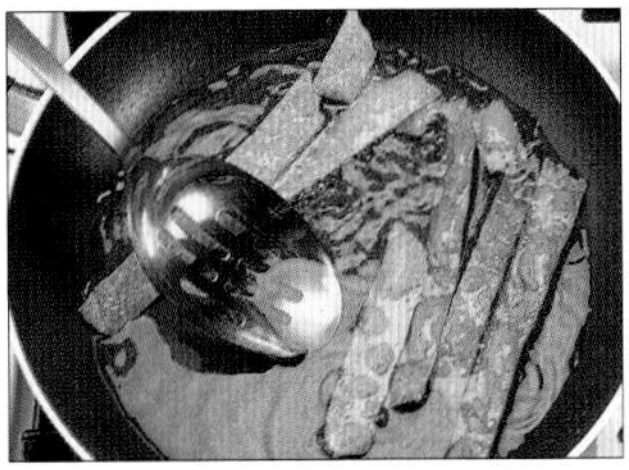

2 Fry the tortilla strips in batches for a minute or two until they are crisp and golden, turning them occasionally, then drain on kitchen paper.

COOK'S TIP
When cooking the tortilla strips it is important that the oil is the correct temperature. To test if the oil is ready to use, carefully add a strip of tortilla. If the strip floats and the oil immediately bubbles around its edges, the oil is ready.

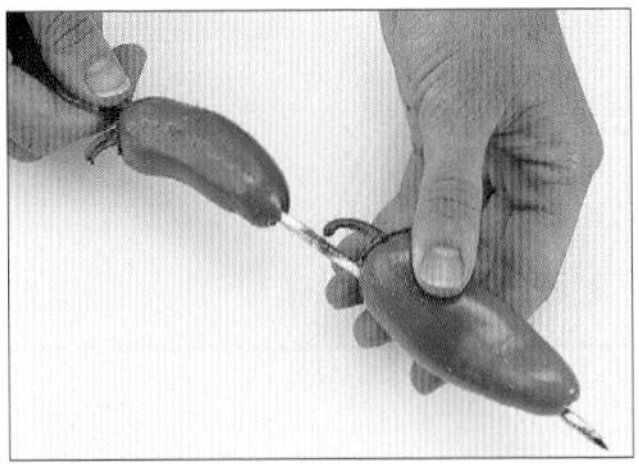

3 Spear the chillies on a long-handled metal skewer and roast them over the flame of a gas burner until the skins blister and darken. Do not let the flesh burn. Alternatively, dry fry them in a griddle pan until the skins are scorched. Place them in a strong plastic bag and tie the top to keep the steam in. Set aside for 20 minutes.

4 Meanwhile, crush the garlic and chop the spring onions finely. Cut a cross in the base of the tomato. Place it in a heatproof bowl and pour over boiling water to cover. After 3 minutes lift the tomato out using a slotted spoon and plunge it into a bowl of cold water. Leave for a few minutes to cool.

5 Drain the tomato, remove the skin and cut it into four pieces. Using a teaspoon scoop out the seeds and the core, then dice the flesh finely.

6 Remove the chillies from the bag and peel off the skins. Cut off the stalks, then slit the chillies and scrape out the seeds. Chop the flesh finely. Put the eggs in a bowl, season with salt and pepper and beat lightly.

7 Heat 15ml/1 tbsp oil in a large frying pan. Add the garlic and spring onions and fry gently for 2–3 minutes until soft. Stir in the diced tomato and cook for 3–4 minutes more, then stir in the chillies and cook for 1 minute.

8 Pour the eggs into the pan and stir until they start to set. When only a small amount of uncooked egg remains visible, stir in the cream so that the cooking process is slowed down and the mixture cooks to a creamy mixture rather than a solid mass.

9 Stir the chopped coriander into the scrambled egg. Arrange the tortilla strips on four serving plates and spoon the eggs over. Serve at once.

MEXICAN TORTILLA PARCELS

SEEDED GREEN CHILLIES ADD JUST A FLICKER OF FIRE TO THE SPICY TOMATO FILLING IN THESE PARCELS, WHICH ARE PERFECT AS A MAIN COURSE, APPETIZER OR SNACK.

SERVES FOUR

INGREDIENTS
- 675g/1½lb tomatoes
- 60ml/4 tbsp sunflower oil
- 1 large onion, finely sliced
- 1 garlic clove, crushed
- 10ml/2 tsp cumin seeds
- 2 fresh green chillies, seeded and chopped
- 30ml/2 tbsp tomato purée (paste)
- 1 vegetable stock (bouillon) cube
- 200g/7oz can corn, drained
- 15ml/1 tbsp chopped fresh coriander (cilantro)
- 115g/4oz/1 cup grated Cheddar cheese
- 8 wheat tortillas
- fresh coriander (cilantro), shredded lettuce and sour cream, to serve

1 Peel the tomatoes: place them in a heatproof bowl, add boiling water to cover and leave for 30 seconds. Lift out with a slotted spoon and plunge into a bowl of cold water. Leave for 1 minute, then drain. Slip the skins off the tomatoes and chop the flesh.

2 Heat half the oil in a frying pan and fry the onion with the garlic and cumin seeds for 5 minutes, until the onion softens. Add the chillies and tomatoes, then stir in the tomato purée. Crumble the stock cube over, stir well and cook gently for 5 minutes, until the chilli is soft but the tomato has not completely broken down. Stir in the sweetcorn and fresh coriander and heat gently to warm through. Keep warm.

3 Sprinkle grated cheese in the middle of each tortilla. Spoon some tomato mixture over the cheese. Fold over one edge of the tortilla, then the sides and finally the remaining edge, to enclose the filling completely.

4 Heat the remaining oil in a frying pan and fry the filled tortillas for 1–2 minutes on each side until golden and crisp. Lift them out carefully with tongs and drain on kitchen paper. Serve immediately, with coriander, shredded lettuce and sour cream.

COOK'S TIP

Mexican wheat tortillas (sometimes described as wheatflour tortillas) are available in most supermarkets. They are handy to keep in the pantry as a wrapping for a variety of vegetable mixtures.

CARIBBEAN CRAB CAKES

CRAB MEAT MAKES WONDERFUL FISH CAKES, AS EVIDENCED WITH THESE GUTSY MORSELS. SERVED WITH A RICH TOMATO DIP, THEY BECOME GREAT PARTY FOOD TOO, ON "STICKS".

MAKES ABOUT FIFTEEN

INGREDIENTS
- 225g/8oz white crab meat (fresh, frozen or canned)
- 115g/4oz cooked potatoes, mashed
- 30ml/2 tbsp fresh herb seasoning
- 2.5ml/½ tsp mild mustard
- 2.5ml/½ tsp ground black pepper
- ½ fresh hot chilli pepper, finely chopped
- 5ml/1 tsp fresh oregano
- 1 egg, beaten
- plain (all-purpose) flour, for dredging
- vegetable oil, for frying
- lime wedges and coriander (cilantro) sprigs, to garnish
- fresh whole chilli peppers, to garnish

For the tomato dip
- 15g/½oz/1 tbsp butter or margarine
- ½ onion, finely chopped
- 2 canned plum tomatoes, chopped
- 1 garlic clove, crushed
- 150ml/¼ pint/⅔ cup water
- 5–10ml/1–2 tsp malt vinegar
- 15ml/1 tbsp chopped coriander (cilantro)
- ½ hot fresh chilli pepper, chopped

1 To make the crab cakes, mix together the crab meat, potatoes, herb seasoning, mustard, peppers, oregano and egg in a large bowl. Chill the mixture in the bowl for at least 30 minutes.

2 Meanwhile, make the tomato dip to accompany the crab cakes. Melt the butter or margarine in a small pan over a medium heat.

3 Add the onion, tomatoes and garlic and sauté for about 5 minutes until the onion is tender. Add the water, vinegar, coriander and hot chilli pepper. Bring to the boil then reduce the heat and simmer for 10 minutes.

4 Transfer the mixture to a food processor or blender and blend to a smooth paste. Pour into a bowl. Keep warm or chill as wished.

5 Using a spoon, shape the crab into rounds and dredge with flour, shaking off the excess. Heat a little oil in a frying pan and fry, a few at a time, for 2–3 minutes on each side. Drain on kitchen paper and keep warm in a low oven while cooking the remainder.

6 Serve with the tomato dip and garnish with lime wedges, coriander sprigs and whole chillies.

Spiced Plantain Chips

Plantains are more starchy than the bananas to which they are related, and must be cooked before being eaten. In Latin America the fruit is used much as a potato would be. This snack has a lovely sweet taste, which is balanced by the heat from the chilli powder and sauce. Cook the chips just before you plan to serve them.

SERVES FOUR AS AN APPETIZER OR SNACK

INGREDIENTS

- 2 large plantains
- oil, for shallow frying
- 2.5ml/½ tsp chilli powder
- 5ml/1 tsp ground cinnamon
- hot chilli sauce, to serve

COOK'S TIP

Plantain skins are very dark, almost black, when the fruit is ready to eat. If they are green when you buy them, allow them to ripen at room temperature for a few days before use.

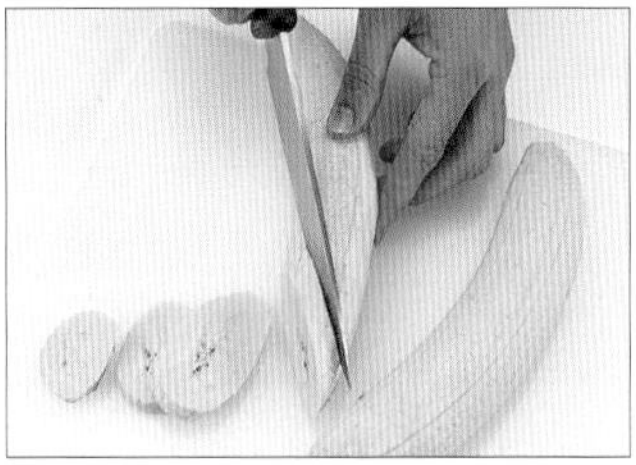

1 Peel the plaintains. Cut off and throw away the ends, then slice the fruit into rounds, cutting slightly on the diagonal to give larger, flatter slices.

2 Pour the oil for frying into a small frying pan, to a depth of about 1cm/½in. Heat the oil until it is very hot, watching it closely all the time. Test by carefully adding a slice of plantain; it should float and the oil should immediately bubble up around it.

3 Fry the plantain slices in small batches or the temperature of the oil will drop. When they are golden brown remove from the oil with a slotted spoon and drain on kitchen paper.

4 Mix the chilli powder with the cinnamon. Put the plantain chips on a serving plate, sprinkle them with the chilli and cinnamon mixture and serve immediately, with a small bowl of hot chilli sauce for dipping.

POPCORN WITH LIME AND CHILLI

IF THE ONLY POPCORN YOU'VE HAD CAME OUT OF A CARTON AT THE CINEMA, TRY THIS MEXICAN SPECIALITY. THE LIME JUICE AND CHILLI POWDER ARE INSPIRED ADDITIONS, AND THE SNACK IS QUITE A HEALTHY CHOICE TO SERVE WITH DRINKS.

MAKES ONE LARGE BOWL

INGREDIENTS
- 30ml/2 tbsp vegetable oil
- 225g/8oz/1¼ cups corn kernels for popcorn
- 10ml/2 tsp chilli powder
- juice of 2 limes

1 Heat the oil in a large, heavy-based frying pan until it is very hot. Add the popcorn and immediately cover the pan with a lid and reduce the heat.

2 After a few minutes the corn should start to pop. Resist the temptation to lift the lid to check. Shake the pan occasionally so that all corn will be cooked and browned.

3 When the sound of popping corn has stopped, quickly remove the pan from the heat and allow to cool slightly. Take off the lid and with a spoon lift out and discard any corn kernels that have not popped. The uncooked corn will have fallen to the bottom of the pan and is completely inedible.

4 Add the chilli powder. Shake the pan again and again to make sure that all of the corn is covered with a colourful dusting of chilli.

5 Tip the popcorn into a large bowl and keep warm. Add a squeeze of lime juice immediately before serving.

SOUPS

The colonizers of Latin America and the Caribbean introduced soup to the region, transforming their original recipes by using local ingredients. Light soups, such as heart of palm soup, are ideal as an appetizer, while heartier soups, such as chilli clam broth, make excellent light meals.

VERMICELLI SOUP

THIS POPULAR MEXICAN SOUP, DELICIOUS AS AN APPETIZER, DRAWS INSPIRATION FROM TRADITIONAL ITALIAN CUISINE, USING INGREDIENTS SUCH AS VERMICELLI, GARLIC AND PARMESAN CHEESE.

SERVES FOUR

INGREDIENTS
- 30ml/2 tbsp olive or corn oil
- 50g/2oz/⅓ cup vermicelli
- 1 onion, roughly chopped
- 1 garlic clove, chopped
- 450g/1lb tomatoes, peeled, seeded and roughly chopped
- 1 litre/1¾ pints/4 cups chicken stock
- 1.5ml/¼ tsp sugar
- 15ml/1 tbsp finely chopped fresh coriander (cilantro)
- salt and ground black pepper
- chopped fresh coriander, to garnish
- 25g/1oz/¼ cup freshly grated Parmesan cheese, to serve

COOK'S TIP
Vermicelli burns easily, so move it about in the frying pan and remove from the heat as soon as it is brown.

1 Heat the olive or corn oil in a shallow frying pan and gently sauté the vermicelli over a moderate heat until golden brown. Take care not to let the strands burn. Remove the vermicelli with a slotted spoon and drain thoroughly on kitchen paper.

2 Purée the chopped onion, garlic and tomatoes in a food processor until smooth. Return the frying pan to the heat. When the oil is hot, add the purée.

3 Cook the tomato purée, stirring constantly, for about 5 minutes.

4 Transfer the purée to a pan. Add the vermicelli and pour in the stock. Season to taste. Stir in the coriander, bring to the boil, then lower the heat, cover the pan and simmer until the vermicelli is tender.

5 Serve sprinkled with chopped coriander, with the Parmesan on the side.

TOMATO SOUP

THE TASTE OF FRESH CORIANDER ADDS A MEXICAN FLAVOUR TO THIS CLASSIC TOMATO SOUP RECIPE. SPRINKLE GENEROUSLY WITH BLACK PEPPER AND SERVE WITH CRUSTY BREAD FOR A SATISFYING LUNCH.

SERVES FOUR

INGREDIENTS
- 15ml/1 tbsp corn or peanut oil
- 1 onion, finely chopped
- 900g/2lb tomatoes, peeled, seeded and chopped
- 475ml/16fl oz/2 cups chicken stock
- 2 large fresh coriander (cilantro) sprigs
- salt and ground black pepper

1 Heat the oil in a pan and gently fry the finely chopped onion, stirring frequently, for about 5 minutes, or until it is soft and translucent but not brown.

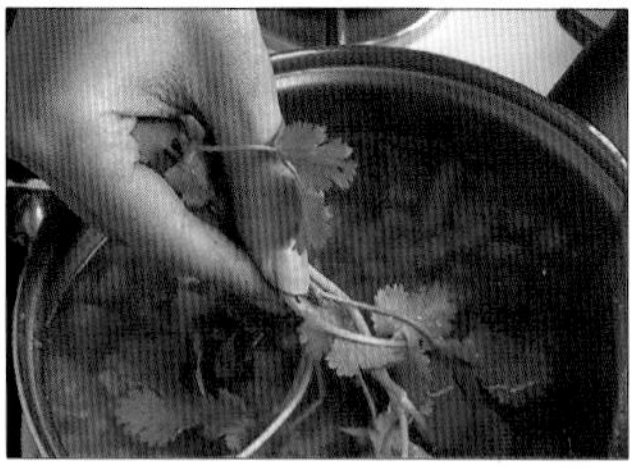

2 Add the chopped tomatoes, chicken stock and coriander sprigs to the pan. Bring to the boil, then lower the heat, cover the pan and simmer gently for about 15 minutes.

3 Remove and discard the coriander. Press the soup through a sieve and return it to the clean pan. Season and heat through. Serve sprinkled with ground black pepper.

Creamy Heart of Palm Soup

This delicate soup has a luxurious, creamy, almost velvety texture. The subtle yet distinctive flavour of the palm hearts is like no other, although it is mildly reminiscent of artichokes and asparagus. Serve with fresh bread for a satisfying lunch.

SERVES FOUR

INGREDIENTS
- 25g/1oz/2 tbsp butter
- 10ml/2 tsp olive oil
- 1 onion, finely chopped
- 1 large leek, finely sliced
- 15ml/1 tbsp plain (all-purpose) flour
- 1 litre/1¾ pints/4 cups well-flavoured chicken stock
- 350g/12oz potatoes, peeled and cubed
- 2 x 400g/14oz cans hearts of palm, drained and sliced
- 250ml/8fl oz/1 cup double (heavy) cream
- salt and ground black pepper
- cayenne pepper and chopped fresh chives, to garnish

1 Heat the butter and oil in a large pan over a low heat. Add the onion and leek and stir well until coated in butter. Cover and cook for 5 minutes until softened and translucent.

2 Sprinkle over the flour. Cook, stirring, for 1 minute.

3 Pour in the stock and add the potatoes. Bring to the boil, then lower the heat and simmer for 10 minutes. Stir in the hearts of palm and the cream, and simmer gently for 10 minutes.

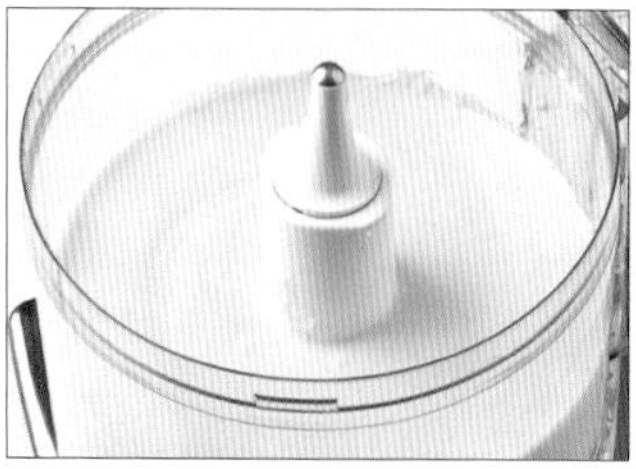

4 Process in a blender or food processor until smooth. Return the soup to the pan and heat gently, adding a little water if necessary. The consistency should be thick but not too heavy. Season with salt and ground black pepper.

5 Ladle the soup into heated bowls and garnish each with a pinch of cayenne pepper and a scattering of fresh chives. Serve immediately.

VARIATION

For a richer, buttery flavour, add the flesh of a ripe avocado when blending.

PEANUT AND POTATO SOUP WITH CORIANDER

Peanut soup is a firm favourite throughout Central and South America, and is particularly popular in Bolivia and Ecuador. As in many Latin American recipes, the ground nuts are used as a thickening agent, with unexpectedly delicious results.

SERVES SIX

INGREDIENTS
- 60ml/4 tbsp peanut oil
- 1 onion, finely chopped
- 2 garlic cloves, crushed
- 1 red (bell) pepper, seeded and chopped
- 250g/9oz potatoes, peeled and diced
- 2 fresh red chillies, seeded and chopped
- 200g/7oz canned chopped tomatoes
- 150g/5oz/1¼ cups unsalted peanuts
- 1.5 litres/2½ pints/6¼ cups beef stock
- salt and ground black pepper
- 30ml/2 tbsp chopped fresh coriander (cilantro), to garnish

1 Heat the oil in a large heavy pan over a low heat. Stir in the onion and cook for 5 minutes, until beginning to soften. Add the garlic, pepper, potatoes, chillies and tomatoes. Stir well to coat the vegetables evenly in the oil, cover and cook for 5 minutes, until softened.

2 Meanwhile, toast the peanuts by gently cooking them in a large dry frying pan over a medium heat. Keep a close eye on them, moving the peanuts around the pan until they are evenly golden. Take care not to burn them.

3 Set 30ml/2 tbsp of the peanuts aside, to use as garnish. Transfer the remaining peanuts to a food processor and process until finely ground. Add the vegetables and process again until smooth.

4 Return the mixture to the pan and stir in the beef stock. Bring to the boil, then lower the heat and simmer for 10 minutes.

5 Pour the soup into heated bowls. Garnish with a generous scattering of coriander and the remaining peanuts.

COOK'S TIP
Replace the unsalted peanuts with peanut butter if you like. Use equal quantities of chunky and smooth peanut butter for the ideal texture.

TLALPEÑO-STYLE SOUP

This simple chicken soup originates from Tlalpan, a suburb of Mexico City. The soup is made more substantial by the addition of cheese and chickpeas.

SERVES SIX

INGREDIENTS
- 1.5 litres/2½ pints/6¼ cups chicken stock
- ½ chipotle chilli, seeded
- 2 skinless, boneless chicken breasts
- 1 medium avocado
- 4 spring onions (scallions), finely sliced
- 400g/14oz can chickpeas, drained
- salt and ground black pepper
- 75g/3oz/¾ cup grated Cheddar cheese, to serve

1 Pour the stock into a large pan and add the dried chilli. Bring to the boil, add the whole chicken breasts, then lower the heat and simmer for about 10 minutes or until the chicken is cooked. Remove the chicken from the pan and let it cool a little.

2 Using two forks, shred the chicken into small pieces. Set it aside. Pour the stock and chilli into a blender or food processor and process until smooth. Return the stock to the pan.

COOK'S TIP
When buying the avocado for this soup choose one that is slightly under-ripe, which makes it easier to handle when peeling and slicing.

3 Cut the avocado in half, remove the skin and seed, then slice the flesh into 2cm/¾in pieces. Add it to the stock, with the spring onions and chickpeas. Return the shredded chicken to the pan, with salt and pepper to taste, and heat gently.

4 Spoon the soup into heated bowls. Sprinkle grated cheese on top of each portion and serve immediately.

CORN SOUP

Quick and easy to prepare, this colourful soup has a sweet and creamy flavour. It is a favourite all over Mexico, especially for children.

SERVES SIX

INGREDIENTS
- 2 red (bell) peppers
- 30ml/2 tbsp vegetable oil
- 1 medium onion, finely chopped
- 500g/1¼lb/3–4 cups corn niblets, thawed if frozen
- 750ml/1¼ pints/3 cups chicken stock
- 150ml/¼ pint/⅔ cup single (light) cream
- salt and ground black pepper

1 Dry fry the peppers in a griddle pan over a moderate heat, turning them frequently until the skins are blistered all over. Place them in a strong plastic bag and tie the top to keep the steam in. Set aside for 20 minutes, then remove the peppers from the bag and peel off the skin.

2 Cut the peppers in half and scoop out the seeds and cores. Set one aside. Cut the other into 1cm/½in dice.

3 Heat the oil in a large pan. Add the onion and fry over a low heat for about 10 minutes, until it is translucent and soft. Stir in the diced pepper and corn and fry for 5 minutes over a moderate heat.

4 Spoon the contents of the pan into a food processor, pour in the chicken stock and process until almost smooth. This processing can be done in batches if necessary.

5 Return the soup to the pan and reheat it. Stir in the cream, with salt and pepper to taste. Core, seed and cut the reserved pepper into thin strips and add half of these to the pan. Serve the soup in heated bowls, garnished with the remaining pepper strips.

COOK'S TIP
Look out for roasted red peppers in jars. These come ready-skinned and are useful in all sorts of recipes. Used here, they make a quick soup even speedier.

Chilled Coconut Soup

Refreshing, cooling and not too filling, this soup is the perfect antidote to hot weather. At a formal meal in Mexico it would be served after a starter, to refresh the palate before the main course.

SERVES SIX

INGREDIENTS

- 1.2 litres/2 pints/5 cups milk
- 225g/8oz/2⅔ cups desiccated (dry, unsweetened shredded) coconut
- 400ml/14fl oz/1⅔ cups coconut milk
- 400ml/14fl oz/1⅔ cups chicken stock
- 200ml/7fl oz/scant 1 cup double (heavy) cream
- 2.5ml/½ tsp salt
- 2.5ml/½ tsp ground white pepper
- 5ml/1 tsp caster (superfine) sugar
- small bunch of fresh coriander (cilantro)

1 Pour the milk into a large pan. Bring it to the boil, stir in the coconut, lower the heat and allow to simmer for 30 minutes. Spoon the mixture into a food processor and process until smooth. This may take a while – up to 5 minutes – so pause frequently and scrape down the sides of the bowl.

2 Rinse the pan to remove any coconut, pour in the processed mixture and add the coconut milk. Stir in the chicken stock (home-made, if possible, which gives a better flavour than a stock or bouillon cube), cream, salt, pepper and sugar. Bring the mixture to the boil, stirring occasionally, then lower the heat and cook for 10 minutes.

3 Reserve a few coriander leaves to garnish, then chop the rest finely and stir into the soup. Pour the soup into a large bowl, let it cool, then cover and put in the refrigerator until chilled. Just before serving, taste the soup and adjust the seasoning, as chilling will alter the taste. Serve in chilled bowls, garnished with the coriander leaves.

AVOCADO SOUP

THIS DELICIOUS AND VERY PRETTY SOUP IS PERFECT FOR DINNER PARTIES AND HAS A FRESH, DELICATE FLAVOUR. YOU MIGHT WANT TO ADD A DASH MORE LIME JUICE JUST BEFORE SERVING FOR ADDED ZEST.

SERVES FOUR

INGREDIENTS
- 2 large ripe avocados
- 300ml/½ pint/1¼ cups crème fraîche
- 1 litre/1¾ pints/4 cups well-flavoured chicken stock
- 5ml/1 tsp salt
- juice of ½ lime
- small bunch of fresh coriander (cilantro)
- 2.5ml/½ tsp freshly ground black pepper

COOK'S TIP
Because this soup contains avocados, it may discolour if left to stand, so make it just before serving.

1 Cut the avocados in half, remove the peel and lift out the stones. Mash the flesh coarsely and place it in a food processor with 45–60ml/3–4 tbsp of the crème fraîche. Process until smooth.

2 Heat the chicken stock in a pan. When it is hot, but still below simmering point, stir in the rest of the crème fraîche, with the salt.

3 Add the lime juice to the avocado mixture, process briefly to mix, then gradually stir the mixture into the hot stock. Heat gently but do not let the mixture approach boiling point.

4 Chop the coriander. Pour the soup into individual heated bowls and sprinkle each portion with coriander and black pepper. Serve immediately.

Fish and Sweet Potato Soup

The subtle sweetness of the potato combines with the stronger flavours of fish and oregano to make this an appetizing soup, popular throughout the Caribbean.

SERVES FOUR

INGREDIENTS
- 175g/6oz white fish fillet, skinned
- ½ onion, chopped
- 1 sweet potato, about 175g/6oz, peeled and diced
- 1 small carrot, about 50g/2oz, chopped
- 5ml/1 tsp chopped fresh oregano or 2.5ml/½ tsp dried oregano
- 2.5ml/½ tsp ground cinnamon
- 1.35 litres/2¼ pints/5½ cups fish stock
- 75ml/5 tbsp single (light) cream
- chopped fresh parsley, to garnish

1 Remove any bones from the fish and put it in a pan. Add the onion, sweet potato, carrot, oregano, cinnamon and half of the stock. Bring to the boil, then simmer for 20 minutes or until the potatoes are cooked.

2 Leave to cool, then pour into a food processor and blend until smooth.

3 Return the soup to the pan, stir in the remaining fish stock and gently bring to the boil. Reduce the heat.

4 Stir the cream into the soup, then gently heat it through without boiling. If the soup boils the cream will curdle. Serve hot, garnished with the chopped parsley.

Caribbean Vegetable Soup

This hearty vegetable soup is filling enough to be served on its own for lunch, but strips of cooked meat, poultry or fish can also be added.

SERVES FOUR

INGREDIENTS
- 25g/1oz/2 tbsp butter or margarine
- 1 onion, chopped
- 1 garlic clove, crushed
- 2 carrots, sliced
- 1.5 litres/2½ pints/6¼ cups vegetable stock
- 2 bay leaves
- 2 fresh thyme sprigs
- 1 celery stick, finely chopped
- 2 green bananas, peeled and quartered
- 175g/6oz white yam or eddoe, peeled and cubed
- 25g/1oz/2 tbsp red lentils
- 1 chayote (christophene), peeled and chopped
- 25g/1oz/2 tbsp macaroni (optional)
- salt and ground black pepper
- chopped spring onion (scallion), to garnish

1 Melt the butter or margarine in a pan and fry the onion, garlic and carrots for a few minutes, stirring occasionally. Add the stock, bay leaves and thyme, and bring to the boil.

2 Add the celery, green bananas, white yam or eddoe, lentils, chayote and macaroni, if using. Season with salt and ground black pepper and simmer for 25 minutes or until the vegetables are cooked through. Serve garnished with chopped spring onion.

VARIATION

Use other root vegetables, such as potatoes or sweet potatoes, if yam or eddoes are not available.

MEXICAN BEAN CHILLI WITH NACHOS

STEAMING BOWLS OF BEEF CHILLI SOUP, PACKED WITH BEANS, ARE DELICIOUS TOPPED WITH CRUSHED TORTILLAS AND CHEESE. POP THE BOWLS UNDER THE GRILL TO MELT THE CHEESE, IF YOU LIKE.

SERVES FOUR

INGREDIENTS

- 45ml/3 tbsp olive oil
- 350g/12oz rump (round) steak, cut into small cubes
- 2 onions, chopped
- 2 garlic cloves, crushed
- 2 green chillies, seeded and chopped
- 30ml/2 tbsp mild chilli powder
- 5ml/1 tsp ground cumin
- 2 bay leaves
- 30ml/2 tbsp tomato purée (paste)
- 900ml/1½ pints/3¾ cups beef stock
- 2 x 400g/14oz cans mixed beans, drained and rinsed
- 45ml/3 tbsp chopped fresh coriander (cilantro)
- salt and ground black pepper

For the topping

- bag of plain tortilla chips, lightly crushed
- 225g/8oz/2 cups Monterey Jack cheese, grated

1 Heat the oil in a large pan over a high heat and brown the meat all over. Use a draining spoon to remove it from the pan. Reduce the heat and add the onions, garlic and chillies, then cook for 4–5 minutes, until softened.

2 Add the chilli powder and ground cumin, and cook for a further 2 minutes. Return the meat to the pan, then stir in the bay leaves, tomato purée and beef stock. Bring to the boil.

3 Reduce the heat, cover and simmer for about 45 minutes or until the meat is tender.

4 Put a quarter of the beans into a bowl, mash with a potato masher and stir into the soup to thicken it. Add the remaining beans and simmer for 5 minutes. Season and stir in the coriander. Ladle into bowls and spoon tortilla chips on top. Pile grated cheese over the tortilla chips and serve.

VARIATION

Use Cheddar cheese instead of Monterey Jack if you prefer.

ROASTED PUMPKIN SOUP WITH PUMPKIN CRISPS

THE PUMPKIN IS ROASTED WHOLE, THEN SPLIT OPEN AND SCOOPED OUT TO MAKE THIS DELICIOUS SOUP; TOPPED WITH CRISP STRIPS OF FRIED PUMPKIN, IT IS A REAL TREAT.

SERVES SIX TO EIGHT

INGREDIENTS

- 1.5kg/3–3½lb pumpkin
- 90ml/6 tbsp olive oil
- 2 onions, chopped
- 3 garlic cloves, chopped
- 7.5cm/3in piece of fresh root ginger, grated
- 5ml/1 tsp ground coriander
- 2.5ml/½ tsp ground turmeric
- pinch of cayenne pepper
- 1 litre/1¾ pints/4 cups vegetable stock
- salt and ground black pepper
- 15ml/1 tbsp sesame seeds and fresh coriander (cilantro) leaves, to garnish

For the pumpkin crisps

- wedge of fresh pumpkin, seeded
- 120ml/4fl oz/½ cup olive oil

1 Preheat the oven to 200°C/400°F/Gas 6. Prick the pumpkin around the top several times with a fork. Brush the pumpkin with plenty of the oil and bake for 45 minutes or until tender. Leave until cool enough to handle.

2 Take care when cutting the pumpkin as there may still be a lot of hot steam inside. When cool enough to handle, scoop out and discard the seeds. Scoop out and chop the flesh.

3 Heat about 60ml/4 tbsp of the remaining oil (you may not have to use all of it) in a large pan and add the onions, garlic and ginger, then cook gently for 4–5 minutes. Add the coriander, turmeric and cayenne, and cook for 2 minutes. Stir in the pumpkin flesh and stock. Bring to the boil, reduce the heat and simmer for about 20 minutes, until tender.

4 Cool the soup slightly, then purée it in a food processor or blender until smooth. Return the soup to the rinsed-out pan and season well.

COOK'S TIP

If only very large pumpkins are available, simply cut off two or three large wedges weighing 1.5kg/3–3½lb in total. Brush them with oil and roast as above for 20–30 minutes or until tender.

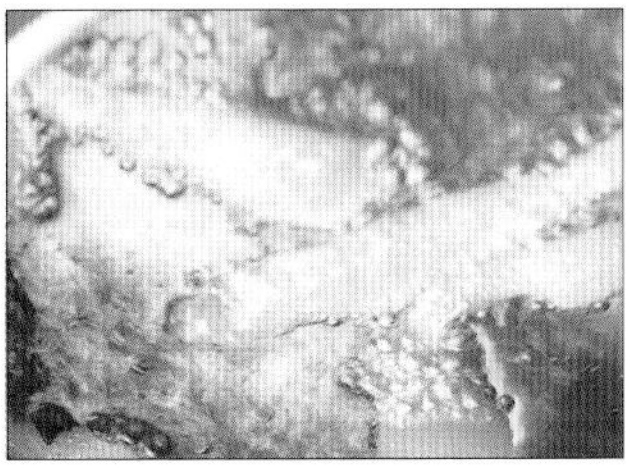

5 Meanwhile, prepare the pumpkin crisps. Using a swivel-blade potato peeler, pare long thin strips off the wedge of pumpkin. Heat the oil in a small pan and fry the strips in batches for 2–3 minutes, until crisp. Drain on kitchen paper.

6 Reheat the soup and ladle it into bowls. Top with the pumpkin crisps and garnish each portion with sesame seeds and coriander leaves.

South American Red Bean Soup

This soup is in Tex-Mex style, and it is served with a cooling avocado and lime salsa. If you relish chillies, add a little more cayenne for a truly fiery experience.

SERVES SIX

INGREDIENTS
- 30ml/2 tbsp olive oil
- 2 onions, chopped
- 2 garlic cloves, chopped
- 10ml/2 tsp ground cumin
- 1.5ml/¼ tsp cayenne pepper
- 15ml/1 tbsp paprika
- 15ml/1 tbsp tomato purée (paste)
- 2.5ml/½ tsp dried oregano
- 400g/14oz can chopped tomatoes
- 2 x 400g/14oz cans red kidney beans, drained and rinsed
- 900ml/1½ pints/3¾ cups water
- salt and ground black pepper
- Tabasco sauce, to serve

For the guacamole salsa
- 2 avocados
- 1 small red onion, finely chopped
- 1 green chilli, seeded and finely chopped
- 15ml/1 tbsp chopped fresh coriander (cilantro)
- juice of 1 lime

1 Heat the oil in a large, heavy-based pan and add the onions and garlic. Cook for about 4–5 minutes, until softened. Add the cumin, cayenne and paprika, and cook for 1 minute, stirring continuously.

2 Stir in the tomato purée and cook for a few seconds, then stir in the oregano. Add the chopped tomatoes, kidney beans and water.

3 Bring the tomato and bean mixture to the boil and simmer for 15–20 minutes. Cool the soup slightly, then purée it in a food processor or blender until smooth. Return to the rinsed-out pan and add seasoning to taste.

4 To make the guacamole salsa, halve, stone and peel the avocados, then dice them finely. Place in a small bowl and gently, but thoroughly, mix with the finely chopped red onion and chilli, and the coriander and lime juice.

5 Reheat the soup and ladle into bowls. Spoon a little guacamole salsa into the middle of each bowl and serve, offering Tabasco sauce for those who want to spice up their soup.

CORN AND RED CHILLI CHOWDER

SWEETCORN AND CHILLIES MAKE GOOD BEDFELLOWS, AND HERE THE COOL COMBINATION OF CREAMED CORN AND MILK IS THE PERFECT FOIL FOR THE RAGING HEAT OF THE CHILLIES.

SERVES SIX

INGREDIENTS

- 2 tomatoes, skinned
- 1 onion, roughly chopped
- 375g/13oz can creamed corn
- 2 red peppers, halved and seeded
- 15ml/1 tbsp olive oil, plus extra for brushing
- 3 red chillies, seeded and chopped
- 2 garlic cloves, chopped
- 5ml/1 tsp ground cumin
- 5ml/1 tsp ground coriander
- 600ml/1 pint/2½ cups milk
- 350ml/12fl oz/1½ cups chicken stock
- 3 corn cobs, kernels removed
- 450g/1lb potatoes, finely diced
- 60ml/4 tbsp double (heavy) cream
- 60ml/4 tbsp chopped fresh parsley
- salt and ground black pepper

1 Process the tomatoes and onion in a blender until smooth. Add the corn and process again, then set aside. Preheat the grill (broiler) to high.

2 Put the peppers and chillies, skin sides up, on a grill rack and brush with oil. Grill (broil) for 8–10 minutes, until the skins blister. Transfer to a bowl and cover with clear film (plastic wrap), then leave to cool. Peel and dice.

3 Heat the oil in a large saucepan and add the chopped chillies and garlic. Cook, stirring, for 2–3 minutes, until softened.

4 Add the ground cumin and coriander, and cook for a further 1 minute. Stir in the corn purée and cook for about 8 minutes, stirring occasionally.

5 Pour in the milk and stock, then stir in the corn kernels, potatoes, red pepper and seasoning to taste. Cook for 15–20 minutes, until the corn and potatoes are tender.

6 Pour into deep bowls and add the cream, then scatter over the chopped parsley and serve at once.

TORTILLA SOUP

THERE ARE SEVERAL MEXICAN TORTILLA SOUPS. THIS ONE IS AN AGUADA *– OR LIQUID – VERSION, AND IS INTENDED FOR SERVING AS A STARTER OR LIGHT MEAL. IT IS VERY EASY AND QUICK TO PREPARE, OR MAKE IT IN ADVANCE AND FRY THE TORTILLA MEZES AS IT REHEATS. THE CRISP TORTILLA PIECES ADD AN UNUSUAL TEXTURE.*

SERVES FOUR

INGREDIENTS
- 4 corn tortillas
- 15ml/1 tbsp vegetable oil, plus extra, for frying
- 1 small onion, finely chopped
- 2 garlic cloves, crushed
- 400g/14oz can plum tomatoes, drained
- 1 litre/1¾ pints/4 cups chicken stock
- small bunch of fresh coriander (cilantro)
- salt and ground black pepper

1 Using a sharp knife, cut each tortilla into four or five strips, each measuring about 2cm/¾in wide.

2 Pour vegetable oil to a depth of 2cm/¾in into a heavy-based frying pan. Heat until a small piece of tortilla, added to the oil, floats on the top and bubbles at the edges.

3 Add a few tortilla strips to the hot oil and fry for a few minutes until crisp and golden brown all over, turning them occasionally. Remove with a slotted spoon and drain on a double layer of kitchen paper. Cook the remaining tortilla strips in the same way.

4 Heat the 15ml/1 tbsp vegetable oil i n a large heavy-based pan. Add the chopped onion and garlic and cook over a moderate heat for 2–3 minutes, stirring constantly with a wooden spatula, until the onion is soft and translucent. Do not let the garlic turn brown or it will give the soup a bitter taste.

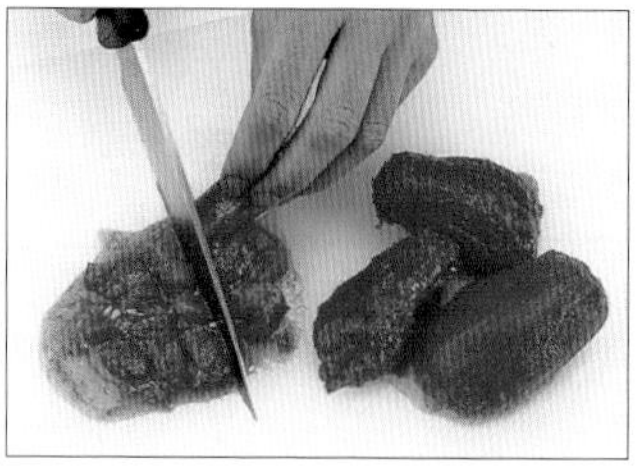

5 Chop the tomatoes using a large sharp knife and add them to the onion mixture in the pan. Pour in the chicken stock and stir well. Bring to the boil, then lower the heat and allow to simmer for about 10 minutes, until the liquid has reduced slightly.

6 Chop the coriander. Add to the soup, reserving a little to use as a garnish. Season to taste.

7 Place a few of the crisp tortilla pieces in the bottom of four warmed soup bowls. Ladle the soup on top. Sprinkle each portion with the reserved chopped coriander and serve.

COOK'S TIP

An easy way to chop the coriander (cilantro) is to put the leaves in a mug and snip with a pair of scissors. Hold the scissors vertically in both hands and work the blades back and forth until the coriander is finely chopped.

Jamaican Rice and Bean Soup with Salt Cod

Based on the classic Caribbean dish of rice and peas, this recipe is made with black-eyed beans, but kidney beans or, more traditionally, pigeon peas can be used instead.

SERVES SIX

INGREDIENTS
- 15ml/1 tbsp sunflower oil
- 75g/3oz/6 tbsp butter
- 115g/4oz thick rindless bacon rashers (strips), cut into lardons
- 1 onion, chopped
- 2 garlic cloves, chopped
- 1 red chilli, seeded and chopped
- 225g/8oz/generous 1 cup long grain rice
- 2 fresh thyme sprigs
- 1 cinnamon stick
- 400g/14oz can black-eyed beans, drained and rinsed
- 900ml/1½ pints/3¾ cups water
- 350g/12oz salt cod, soaked for 24 hours, changing the water several times
- plain (all-purpose) flour, for dusting
- 400g/14oz can coconut milk
- 175g/6oz baby spinach leaves
- 30ml/2 tbsp chopped fresh parsley
- salt and ground black pepper

1 Heat the oil and 25g/1oz/2 tbsp of the butter in a large, heavy-based pan. Add the bacon lardons and cook for 3–4 minutes, until golden. Stir in the onion, garlic and chilli and cook for a further 4–5 minutes.

2 Add the rice, stir well and cook for 1–2 minutes, until the grains are translucent. Stir in the thyme, cinnamon stick and black-eyed beans and cook for 1–2 minutes. Pour in the water and bring to the boil. Reduce the heat to low and cook for 25–30 minutes.

3 Meanwhile, wash the soaked salt cod under cold running water. Pat dry with kitchen paper and remove the skin. Cut into generous bite-size pieces and toss in the flour until evenly coated. Shake off the excess flour.

4 Melt the remaining butter in a large, heavy-based frying pan. Add the cod, in batches if necessary, and cook for 4–5 minutes until tender and golden. Remove the cod and set aside.

5 Stir the coconut milk into the cooked rice and beans. Remove the cinnamon stick and cook the soup for 2–3 minutes. Stir in the spinach and cook for a further 2–3 minutes.

6 Add the cod and chopped parsley, season to taste with salt and pepper, and heat through. Ladle the soup into bowls and serve.

COOK'S TIP
Lardons are neat strips of fatty meat, such as belly of pork or streaky (fatty) bacon. They are thicker and slightly longer than matchsticks. Cut them from very thick bacon rashers (strips) or from a joint of bacon or gammon.

AVOCADO AND LIME SOUP

INSPIRED BY GUACAMOLE, THE POPULAR AVOCADO DIP, THIS CREAMY SOUP RELIES ON GOOD-QUALITY RIPE AVOCADOS FOR ITS FLAVOUR AND COLOUR.

SERVES FOUR

INGREDIENTS

- 3 ripe avocados
- juice of 1½ limes
- 1 garlic clove, crushed
- handful of ice cubes
- 400ml/14fl oz/1⅔ cups vegetable stock, chilled
- 400ml/14fl oz/1⅔ cups milk, chilled
- 150ml/¼ pint/⅔ cup soured cream, chilled
- few drops of Tabasco sauce
- salt and ground black pepper
- fresh coriander (cilantro) leaves, to garnish
- extra virgin olive oil, to serve

For the salsa

- 4 tomatoes, peeled, seeded and finely diced
- 2 spring onions (scallions), trimmed and chopped
- 1 fresh green chilli, seeded and chopped
- 15ml/1 tbsp chopped fresh coriander (cilantro)
- juice of ½ lime

1 Prepare the salsa first. Mix all the ingredients and season well. Chill in the refrigerator until required.

2 Halve and stone the avocados. Scoop the flesh out of the avocado skins and place in a food processor or blender. Add the lime juice, garlic, ice cubes and 150ml/¼ pint/⅔ cup of the vegetable stock.

3 Process the soup until smooth. Pour into a large bowl and stir in the remaining stock, the milk, soured cream, Tabasco sauce and seasoning.

4 Ladle the soup into bowls or glasses and spoon a little salsa on top. Add a splash of olive oil to each portion and garnish with fresh coriander leaves. Serve at once.

COOK'S TIPS

- It is easy to remove the stone from an avocado. Halve the avocado and simply tap the stone firmly with the blade of a large knife. Twist the knife gently and the stone will pop out.
- This soup may discolour if it is left standing for too long, but the flavour will not be spoilt. Give it a quick whisk just before serving.

CRAB, COCONUT AND CORIANDER SOUP

QUICK AND EASY TO PREPARE, THIS SOUP HAS ALL THE FLAVOURS ASSOCIATED WITH THE BAHIA REGION OF BRAZIL: CREAMY COCONUT, PALM OIL, FRAGRANT CORIANDER AND, OF COURSE, CHILLI.

SERVES FOUR

INGREDIENTS

- 30ml/2 tbsp olive oil
- 1 onion, finely chopped
- 1 celery stick, finely chopped
- 2 garlic cloves, crushed
- 1 fresh red chilli, seeded and chopped
- 1 large tomato, peeled and chopped
- 45ml/3 tbsp chopped fresh coriander (cilantro)
- 1 litre/1¾ pints/4 cups fresh crab or fish stock
- 500g/1¼ lb crab meat
- 250ml/8fl oz/1 cup coconut milk
- 30ml/2 tbsp palm oil
- juice of 1 lime
- salt
- hot chilli oil and lime wedges, to serve

1 Heat the olive oil in a pan over a low heat. Stir in the onion and celery, and sauté gently for 5 minutes, until softened and translucent. Stir in the garlic and chilli and cook for a further 2 minutes.

2 Add the tomato and half the coriander and increase the heat. Cook, stirring, for 3 minutes, then add the stock. Bring to the boil, then simmer for 5 minutes.

3 Stir the crab, coconut milk and palm oil into the pan and simmer over a very low heat for a further 5 minutes. The consistency should be thick, but not stew-like, so add some water if needed.

4 Stir in the lime juice and remaining coriander, then season with salt to taste. Serve in heated bowls with the chilli oil and lime wedges on the side.

CHILLI CLAM BROTH

THIS SOUP OF SUCCULENT CLAMS IN A TASTY STOCK COULD NOT BE EASIER TO PREPARE. POPULAR IN COASTAL AREAS OF COLOMBIA, IT MAKES THE PERFECT LUNCH ON A HOT SUMMER'S DAY.

SERVES SIX

INGREDIENTS

- 30ml/2 tbsp olive oil
- 1 onion, finely chopped
- 3 garlic cloves, crushed
- 2 fresh red chillies, seeded and finely chopped
- 250ml/8fl oz/1 cup dry white wine
- 400ml/14fl oz can plum tomatoes, drained
- 1 large potato, about 250g/9oz, peeled and diced
- 400ml/14fl oz/1⅔ cups fish stock
- 1.3kg/3lb fresh clams
- 15ml/1 tbsp chopped fresh coriander (cilantro)
- 15ml/1 tbsp chopped fresh flat leaf parsley
- salt
- lime wedges, to garnish

1 Heat the oil in a pan. Add the onion and sauté for 5 minutes over a low heat. Stir in the garlic and chillies and cook for a further 2 minutes. Pour in the wine and bring to the boil, then simmer for 2 minutes.

2 Add the tomatoes, diced potato and stock. Bring to the boil, cover and lower the heat so that the soup simmers.

3 Season with salt and cook for 15 minutes, until the potatoes are beginning to break up and the tomatoes have made a rich sauce.

4 Meanwhile, wash the clams thoroughly under cold running water. Gently tap any that are open, and discard them if they do not close.

5 Add the clams to the soup, cover the pan and cook for about 3–4 minutes, or until the clams have opened, then stir in the chopped herbs. Season with salt to taste.

6 Check over the clams and throw away any that have failed to open. Ladle the soup into warmed bowls. Offer the lime wedges separately, to be squeezed over the soup just before eating.

Chunky Prawn Chupe

Chowders, known as chupes in South America, are a meal in themselves. Potatoes are always included, but the other ingredients vary. This is a seafood version.

SERVES SIX

INGREDIENTS
- 500g/1¼lb raw king prawns (jumbo shrimp)
- 750ml/1¼ pints/3 cups fish stock
- 1 carrot, finely chopped
- 2 celery sticks, thinly sliced
- 45ml/3 tbsp annatto (achiote) oil
- 1 large onion, finely chopped
- 1 red (bell) pepper, seeded and diced
- 2 garlic cloves, crushed
- 2 fresh red chillies, seeded and chopped
- 5ml/1 tsp turmeric
- 1 large tomato, peeled and chopped
- 675g/1½lb potatoes, peeled and cut into 2.5cm/1in cubes
- 115g/4oz/1 cup fresh or frozen peas
- 15ml/1 tbsp chopped fresh mint
- 15ml/1 tbsp chopped fresh coriander (cilantro)
- salt

1 Peel the prawns and set them aside. Place the shells in a large pan with the fish stock, carrot and celery. Bring to the boil, then simmer over a low heat for 20 minutes. Strain into a bowl or jug (pitcher) and set the stock aside.

VARIATION
Traditionally this soup would be made using *huacatay*, a pungent Peruvian herb that tastes like a cross between mint and coriander (cilantro).

2 Heat the oil in a large pan over a low heat. Stir in the onion and red pepper and sauté for 5 minutes. Stir in the garlic, chillies and turmeric and cook for a further 2 minutes.

3 Add the chopped tomato and potatoes to the pan, season to taste with salt and cook for about 10 minutes, allowing the tomato to break down slightly and the potatoes to absorb the flavours of the other ingredients.

4 Pour in the strained stock and bring to the boil. Lower the heat and simmer for 15 minutes, or until the potatoes are cooked through.

5 Stir the prawns and peas into the soup and simmer for 4–5 minutes, or until the prawns become opaque. Finally, stir in the mint and coriander, and serve in warmed bowls.

CARIBBEAN SALT COD WITH CREAMED YAM

INSPIRED BY THE INGREDIENTS OF THE CARIBBEAN, THIS COLOURFUL CHUNKY SOUP IS SERVED IN DEEP BOWLS AROUND A CHIVE-FLAVOURED SWEET YAM MASH.

SERVES SIX

INGREDIENTS
- 200g/7oz salt cod, soaked for 24 hours, changing the water several times
- 15ml/1 tbsp olive oil
- 1 garlic clove, chopped
- 1 onion, chopped
- 1 green chilli, seeded and chopped
- 6 plum tomatoes, peeled and chopped
- 250ml/8fl oz/1 cup white wine
- 2 bay leaves
- 900ml/1½ pints/3¾ cups water
- 225g/8oz okra
- 225g/8oz callaloo or spinach
- 30ml/2 tbsp chopped fresh parsley
- salt and ground black pepper

For the creamed yam
- 675g/1½lb yam
- juice of 1 lemon
- 50g/2oz/¼ cup butter
- 30ml/2 tbsp double (heavy) cream
- 15ml/1 tbsp chopped fresh chives

1 Drain and skin the salt cod, then rinse it under cold running water. Cut the flesh into bite-size pieces, removing any bones, and set aside.

2 Heat the oil in a heavy pan. Add the garlic, onion and chilli, and cook for 4–5 minutes until softened and the onions are transparent.

3 Add the salt cod and cook for 3–4 minutes. Stir in the tomatoes, wine and bay leaves and bring to the boil. Pour in the water, bring to the boil, then simmer for 10 minutes.

4 Meanwhile, trim the stalk ends off the okra and cut the pods into chunks. Add to the soup and cook for 10 minutes. Stir in the callaloo or spinach and cook for 5 minutes, until the okra is tender.

5 Meanwhile, prepare the creamed yam. Peel the yam and cut it into large dice, then place in a pan with the lemon juice and add cold water to cover. Bring to the boil and cook for 15–20 minutes, until tender. Drain well, then return the yam to the pan and dry it out over the heat for a few seconds. Mash with the butter and cream, and season well. Stir in the chives.

6 Season the soup and stir in the chopped parsley. Spoon portions of creamed yam into the centres of six soup bowls and ladle over the soup.

SPICED LAMB SOUP

THE COMBINATION OF LAMB WITH PUMPKIN AND GREEN BANANAS, AND PLENTY OF SPICES, MAKES THIS UNUSUAL SOUP FULL OF FLAVOUR. IT IS SUBSTANTIAL ENOUGH TO MAKE A COMPLETE MEAL.

SERVES FOUR

INGREDIENTS

- 115g/4oz/1 cup split black-eyed beans (peas), soaked overnight
- 675g/1½lb neck (US shoulder) of lamb, cut into medium chunks
- 5ml/1 tsp chopped fresh thyme
- 2 bay leaves
- 1.2 litres/2 pints/5 cups water
- 1 onion, sliced
- 225g/8oz pumpkin, diced
- 2 black cardamom pods
- 7.5ml/1½ tsp ground turmeric
- 15ml/1 tbsp chopped coriander (cilantro)
- 2.5ml/½ tsp caraway seeds
- 1 green chilli, seeded and chopped
- 2 green bananas
- 1 carrot
- salt and ground black pepper

1 Drain the black-eyed beans, place them in a large pan and cover with fresh cold water.

2 Bring the beans to the boil, boil rapidly for 10 minutes and then reduce the heat and simmer, covered for 40–50 minutes, until tender, adding more water if necessary. Remove from the heat and set aside to cool.

3 Meanwhile, put the lamb in a large pan, add the thyme, bay leaves and water and bring to the boil. Cover and simmer for 1 hour, until tender.

4 Add the onion, pumpkin, cardamoms, turmeric, coriander, caraway, chilli and seasoning and stir. Bring back to a simmer and then cook, uncovered, for 15 minutes, until the pumpkin is tender.

5 When the beans are cool, spoon into a blender or food processor with their liquid and blend to a smooth purée.

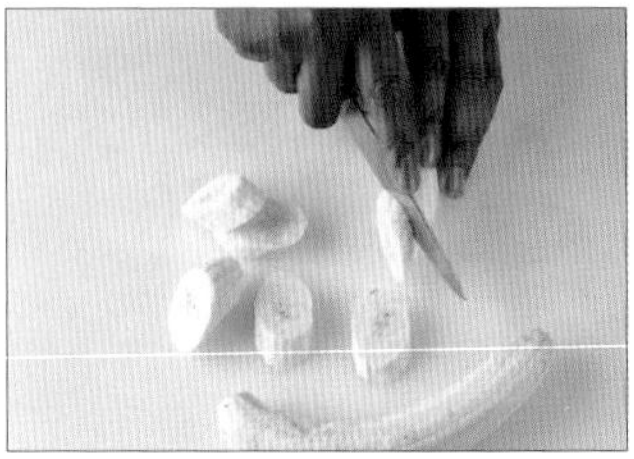

6 Cut the bananas into medium slices and the carrot into thin slices. Stir into the soup with the beans and cook for 10–12 minutes. Season and serve.

Plantain Soup with Corn and Chilli

This colourful soup is ideal for vegetarians if made with vegetable rather than chicken stock. The pinch of nutmeg adds a unique flavour.

SERVES FOUR

INGREDIENTS

25g/1oz/2 tbsp butter or margarine
1 onion, finely chopped
1 garlic clove, crushed
275g/10oz yellow plantains, peeled and sliced
1 large tomato, peeled and chopped
175g/6oz/1 cup corn kernels
5ml/1 tsp dried tarragon, crushed
900ml/1½pints/3¾ cups vegetable or chicken stock
1 green chilli, seeded and chopped
pinch of grated nutmeg
salt and ground black pepper

1 Melt the butter or margarine in a pan over a medium heat, add the onion and garlic and cook for a few minutes until soft. Add the plantain, tomato and corn and cook for 5 minutes.

2 Add the tarragon, vegetable stock, chilli and salt and pepper and simmer for about 10 minutes, or until the plantain is tender. Stir in the nutmeg and serve immediately.

KALE, CHORIZO AND POTATO SOUP

THIS HEARTY WINTER SOUP HAS A SPICY KICK TO IT, WHICH COMES FROM THE CHORIZO SAUSAGE. THE SOUP BECOMES MORE POTENT IF CHILLED OVERNIGHT AND IT IS WORTH BUYING THE BEST POSSIBLE CHORIZO SAUSAGE TO IMPROVE THE FLAVOUR.

SERVES SIX TO EIGHT

INGREDIENTS

- 225g/8oz kale, stems removed
- 225g/8oz chorizo sausage
- 675g/1½lb red potatoes
- 1.75 litres/3 pints/7½ cups vegetable stock
- 5ml/1 tsp ground black pepper
- pinch cayenne pepper (optional)
- 12 slices French bread, grilled
- salt and ground black pepper

1 Place the kale in a food processor and process for a few seconds to chop it finely.

2 Prick the sausages and place in a pan with enough water to cover. Simmer for 15 minutes. Drain and cut into thin slices.

3 Boil the potatoes for about 15 minutes or until tender. Drain, and place in a bowl, then mash adding a little of the cooking liquid to form a thick paste.

4 Bring the stock to the boil and add the kale. Add the chorizo and simmer for 5 minutes. Add the potato paste gradually, and simmer for 20 minutes. Season with black pepper and cayenne.

5 Place bread slices in each bowl, and pour the soup over. Serve sprinkled with pepper.

CORN AND SWEET POTATO SOUP

THE COMBINATION OF CORN AND SWEET POTATO GIVES THIS SOUP A REAL DEPTH OF FLAVOUR AS WELL AS MAKING IT LOOK VERY COLOURFUL. IT MAKES A HEARTY APPETIZER OR CAN BE A MEAL IN ITSELF WITH A CHUNK OF BREAD OR SOME TORTILLA CHIPS AND SALSA ON THE SIDE.

SERVES SIX

INGREDIENTS

- 15ml/1 tbsp olive oil
- 1 onion, finely chopped
- 2 garlic cloves, crushed
- 1 small red chilli, seeded and finely chopped
- 1.75 litres/3 pints/7½ cups vegetable stock
- 10ml/2 tsp ground cumin
- 1 medium sweet potato, diced
- ½ red (bell) pepper, finely chopped
- 450g/1lb corn kernels
- salt and ground black pepper
- lime wedges, to serve

1 Heat the oil in a heavy pan and fry the onion for 5 minutes until softened. Add the garlic and chilli and fry for a further 2 minutes.

2 Add 300ml/½ pint/1¼ cups of the vegetable stock, and simmer for about 10 minutes.

3 Mix the cumin with a little stock to form a paste and then stir into the soup. Add the diced sweet potato, stir and simmer for 10 minutes. Season and stir again.

4 Add the pepper, corn and remaining stock and simmer for 10 minutes. Process half of the soup until smooth and then stir into the chunky soup. Season and serve with lime wedges for squeezing over.

Beef and Cassava Soup

This simple, tasty soup is almost a stew. Such soups, made in one pot, are everyday fare in Latin America. The addition of wine is not traditional, but it enhances the flavour.

SERVES FOUR

INGREDIENTS

- 450g/1lb stewing beef, cubed
- 1.2 litres/2 pints/5 cups beef stock
- 300ml/½ pint/1¼ cups white wine
- 15ml/1 tbsp soft brown sugar
- 1 onion, finely chopped
- 1 bay leaf
- 1 bouquet garni
- 1 fresh thyme sprig
- 15ml/1 tbsp tomato purée (paste)
- 1 large carrot, sliced
- 275g/10oz cassava or yam, peeled and cubed
- 50g/2oz fresh spinach, chopped
- a little hot pepper sauce, to taste
- salt and ground black pepper

1 Mix the cubed beef, stock, white wine, sugar, chopped onion, bay leaf, bouquet garni, thyme and tomato purée in a large pan. Bring to the boil, then cover and simmer very gently for about 1¼ hours. If you want very tender meat, allow about 2–2¼ hours.

2 Add the sliced carrot, cubed cassava or yam, spinach and a few drops of hot pepper sauce. Season with salt and ground black pepper to taste and simmer for a further 15 minutes until the meat and vegetables are both tender. Serve in heated bowls.

LAMB AND LENTIL SOUP

Lentils are popular on Caribbean islands, such as Trinidad and Tobago, where they were introduced by South-East Asian labourers recruited to work the sugar cane plantations.

SERVES FOUR

INGREDIENTS
- 1.5–1.75 litres/2½–3 pints/6¼–7½ cups water or stock
- 900g/2lb neck of lamb, cut into pieces
- ½ onion, chopped
- 1 garlic clove, crushed
- 1 bay leaf
- 1 clove
- 2 fresh thyme sprigs
- 225g/8oz potatoes
- 175g/6oz/¾ cup red lentils
- 600ml/1 pint/2½ cups water
- salt and ground black pepper
- chopped fresh parsley

1 Pour 1.5 litres/2½ pints/6¼ cups of the water or stock into a large pan and add the lamb, chopped onion, crushed garlic, bay leaf, clove and thyme sprigs. Bring to the boil, then lower the heat and simmer gently for about 1 hour, until the lamb is tender.

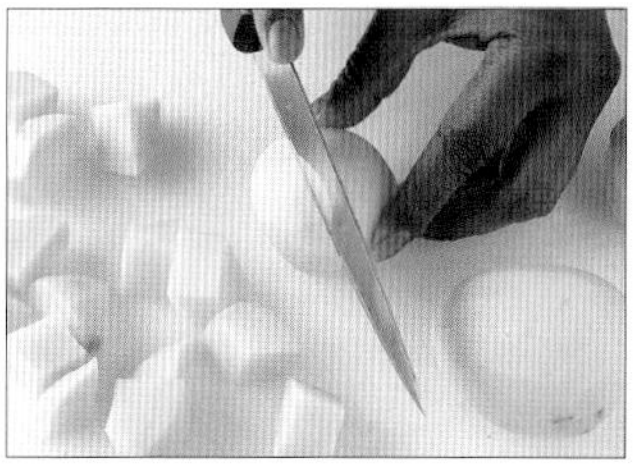

2 Peel the potatoes and cut them into rough 2.5cm/1in cubes. Add them to the soup in the pan and cook for a further 5 minutes.

3 Add the red lentils to the pan, stirring them gently into the stock, then season the soup to taste with a little salt and plenty of ground black pepper. Add approximately 300ml/½ pint/1¼ cups of warm water to completely cover the meat and vegetables.

4 Bring the soup back to the boil, then lower the heat, cover and simmer for 25 minutes or until the lentils are cooked, stirring occasionally. Add a little more water during cooking if the soup becomes too thick. Just before serving, stir in the chopped parsley.

Fish

Fish plays an important part in Latin-American cuisine and the most popular recipes rely on the freshest fish cooked simply. In parts of Brazil and the Caribbean, where the local cuisine has been shaped by African slave influences, richly flavoured fish stews are more popular.

BAKED SEA BASS WITH COCONUT

This elegant Colombian dish is ideal for a dinner party. The bay leaves give a depth of flavour to the chilli and coconut sauce.

SERVES FOUR

INGREDIENTS
- 1 whole large sea bass, about 900g/2lb, cleaned
- 2 fresh red chillies, seeded and finely chopped
- 1 onion, finely sliced
- 2 garlic cloves, crushed
- juice of 1 lime
- 15ml/1 tbsp olive oil
- 2 bay leaves
- 200ml/7fl oz/scant 1 cup coconut milk
- salt

VARIATION
For a complete meal, cook some vegetables in the roasting pan with the sea bass. Sliced carrots, fennel or/and courgettes (zucchini) would all go well with the coconut sauce.

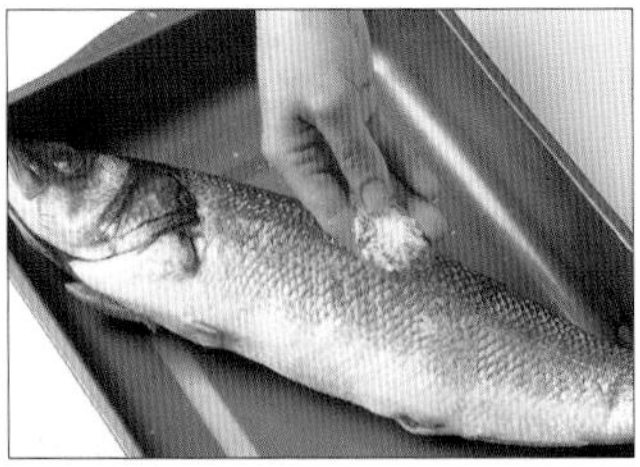

1 Preheat the oven to 180°C/350°F/Gas 4. Thoroughly rinse the fish inside and out, then pat dry with kitchen paper. Place in a large roasting pan and season all over with salt.

2 Generously sprinkle the chopped chillies, onion, garlic, lime juice and olive oil over the fish. Add the bay leaves to the pan and bake the fish in the oven for about 15 minutes.

3 Pour the coconut milk over the fish and return it to the oven for a further 10 minutes, or until the flesh flakes easily when tested with the tip of a sharp knife.

4 Cut along the back of the fish. This will release the flesh from the bones, making it easy to divide into portions. Serve with the sauce. A rice dish would make a good accompaniment.

PAN-FRIED SEA BREAM WITH LIME AND TOMATO SALSA

The most popular way of cooking a fresh piece of fish is to pan fry it or grill it. In this recipe a simple salsa is flashed in the pan at the end of cooking, to make a light sauce.

SERVES FOUR

INGREDIENTS
- 4 sea bream fillets
- juice of 2 limes
- 30ml/2 tbsp chopped coriander (cilantro)
- 1 fresh red chilli, seeded and finely chopped
- 2 spring onions (scallions), sliced
- 45ml/3 tbsp olive oil, plus extra to serve
- 2 large tomatoes, diced
- salt
- cooked white rice, to serve

1 Place the fish fillets in a shallow china or glass dish large enough to hold them all in a single layer.

2 Mix the lime juice, coriander, chilli and spring onions in a jug (pitcher). Stir in half the oil, then pour this marinade over the fish. Cover and marinate for around 15–20 minutes. Do not be tempted to marinate the fish for longer than this or the acid in the marinade will start to "cook" it.

3 Heat the remaining oil in a large heavy frying pan over a high heat. Lift each piece of fish from the marinade and pat dry with kitchen paper.

4 Season the fish with salt and place in the hot pan, skin side down. Cook for 2 minutes, then turn and cook for a further 2 minutes, until the flesh is opaque all the way through.

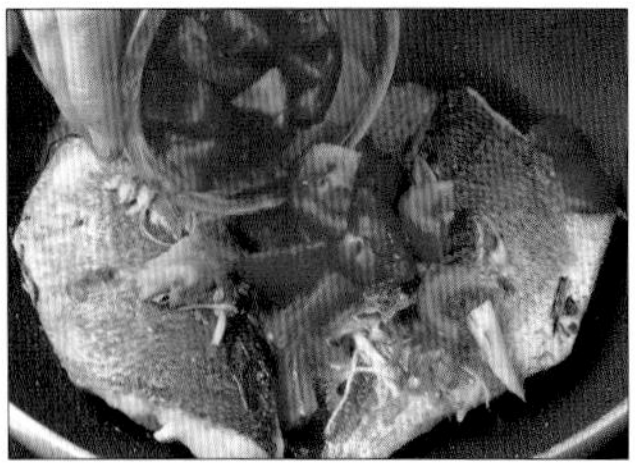

5 Add the marinade and the chopped tomatoes to the pan. Bring the sauce to the boil and cook for about 1 minute, until the tomatoes are lightly cooked but still retain their shape. Drizzle a little olive oil over the fish and serve on individual warm plates, with white rice and the tomato salsa.

HALIBUT WITH PEPPERS AND COCONUT MILK

THIS AROMATIC DISH, KNOWN LOCALLY AS MOQUECA *COMES FROM THE STATE OF BAHIA, ON THE EAST COAST OF BRAZIL. COOKED AND SERVED IN AN EARTHENWARE DISH, IT IS USUALLY ACCOMPANIED BY WHITE RICE AND FLAVOURED CASSAVA FLOUR TO SOAK UP THE DELICIOUS SAUCE.*

SERVES SIX

INGREDIENTS
- 6 halibut, cod, haddock or monkfish fillets, each about 115g/4oz
- juice of 2 limes
- 8 fresh coriander (cilantro) sprigs
- 2 fresh red chillies, seeded and chopped
- 3 tomatoes, sliced into thin rounds
- 1 red (bell) pepper, seeded and sliced into thin rounds
- 1 green (bell) pepper, seeded and sliced into thin rounds
- 1 small onion, sliced into thin rounds
- 200ml/7fl oz/scant 1 cup coconut milk
- 60ml/4 tbsp palm oil
- salt
- cooked white rice, to serve

For the flavoured cassava flour
- 30ml/2 tbsp palm oil
- 1 medium onion, thinly sliced
- 250g/9oz/2¼ cups cassava flour

1 Place the fish fillets in a large, shallow dish and pour over water to cover. Pour in the lime juice and set aside for 30 minutes. Drain the fish thoroughly and pat dry with kitchen paper. Arrange the fish in a single layer in a heavy pan which has a tight-fitting lid.

2 Sprinkle the coriander and chillies over the fish, then top with a layer each of tomatoes, peppers and onion. Pour the coconut milk over, cover and leave to stand for 15 minutes before cooking.

3 Season with salt, then place the pan over a high heat and cook until the coconut milk comes to the boil. Lower the heat and simmer for 5 minutes. Remove the lid, pour in the palm oil, cover again and simmer for 10 minutes.

4 Meanwhile make the flavoured cassava flour. Heat the oil in a large frying pan over a very low heat. Stir in the onion slices and cook for 8–10 minutes until soft and golden. Stir in the cassava flour and cook, stirring constantly, for 1–2 minutes until lightly toasted and evenly coloured by the oil. Season with salt.

5 Serve the *moqueca* with the rice and flavoured cassava flour.

CARIBBEAN FISH STEAKS

West Indian cooks love spices, and use them to good effect. This quick and easy recipe is a typical example of how chillies, cayenne and allspice can be used with lime to add an exotic accent to a tomato sauce for fish.

SERVES FOUR

INGREDIENTS

- 45ml/3 tbsp sunflower oil
- 6 shallots
- 1 garlic clove
- 1 fresh green chilli, seeded and finely chopped
- 400g/14oz can chopped tomatoes
- 2 bay leaves
- 1.5ml/¼ tsp cayenne pepper
- 5ml/1 tsp ground allspice
- juice of 2 limes
- 4 cod steaks
- 5ml/1 tsp muscovado (molasses) sugar
- 10ml/2 tsp angostura bitters
- salt

VARIATION

This unusual and exotic sauce is also good over grilled (broiled) pork chops.

1 Slowly heat the oil in a frying pan. Finely chop the shallots and add them to the frying pan. Cook for 5 minutes until soft. Crush a peeled garlic clove into the frying pan and add the chilli. Cook for a further 2 minutes, then stir in the tomatoes, bay leaves, cayenne pepper, allspice and lime juice, with a little salt to taste.

2 Cook gently for 15 minutes, then add the cod steaks and baste with the tomato sauce. Cover and cook for 10 minutes. Transfer the steaks to a warmed dish and keep hot while you prepare the sauce. Stir the sugar and angostura bitters into the sauce, simmer for 2 minutes, then pour over the fish.

SALMON IN MANGO AND GINGER SAUCE

MANGO AND SALMON MAY SEEM UNLIKELY PARTNERS, BUT THE FLAVOURS COMPLEMENT EACH OTHER VERY WELL, ESPECIALLY WHEN THE DISTINCT FLAVOUR OF TARRAGON IS ADDED TO THE EQUATION.

SERVES TWO

INGREDIENTS

- 2 salmon steaks, each about 275g/10oz
- a little lemon juice
- 1–2 garlic cloves, crushed
- 5ml/1 tsp dried tarragon, crushed
- 2 shallots, roughly chopped
- 1 tomato, roughly chopped
- 1 large ripe mango, peeled, stoned (pitted) and chopped
- 150ml/¼ pint/⅔ cup fish stock or water
- 15ml/1 tbsp syrup from a jar of preserved ginger
- 25g/1oz/2 tbsp butter
- salt and ground black pepper

1 Place the salmon steaks in a single layer in a shallow dish and sprinkle with the lemon juice, garlic, tarragon and salt and pepper. Cover and set aside in the refrigerator for at least 1 hour.

2 Meanwhile, place the shallots, tomato and mango in a blender or food processor and blend until smooth. Add the fish stock or water and the ginger syrup, blend again and set aside.

3 Melt the butter in a frying pan and cook the salmon steaks for about 3 minutes on each side.

4 Add the mango purée, cover and simmer for a further 5 minutes, until the salmon is cooked and flakes easily.

5 Transfer the salmon to plates. Heat the sauce, adjust the seasoning and pour over the salmon. Serve hot.

FRIED SNAPPER WITH AVOCADO

THE COMBINATION OF CRISP FRIED FISH AND SILKY SMOOTH AVOCADO WORKS EXTREMELY WELL IN THIS RECIPE. IN THE ISLANDS OF THE CARIBBEAN, WHERE THIS RECIPE ORIGINATED, THE FISH IS OFTEN SERVED WITH FRIED DUMPLINGS OR HARD-DOUGH BREAD.

SERVES FOUR

INGREDIENTS

- 1 lemon
- 4 red snappers, each about 225g/8oz, prepared
- 10ml/2 tsp spice seasoning
- flour, for dusting
- oil, for frying
- 2 avocados and cooked corn, sliced widthways, to serve
- chopped fresh parsley and lime slices, to garnish

1 Squeeze the lemon juice both inside and outside the fish, and sprinkle with the spice seasoning. Place the fish in a shallow dish, cover and set aside in a cool place to marinate for a few hours.

2 Lift the marinated fish out of the dish and dust thoroughly with the flour, shaking off any excess.

3 Heat the oil in a large non-stick frying pan over a medium heat. Add the fish and fry gently for about 10 minutes on each side.

4 Meanwhile, cut the avocados in half, remove the stones (pits) and cut in half again. Peel away the skin and cut the flesh into thin strips.

5 When the fish are cooked through and the skin is crisp and brown, transfer them to warmed serving plates. Add the avocado and corn slices. Garnish with the chopped parsley and lime slices and serve immediately.

COOK'S TIP

Using two frying pans will allow you to cook all four fish simultaneously. Alternatively, cook two and keep them hot in a covered dish in a warm oven while cooking the remaining pair.

Salt Cod for Christmas Eve

This Mexican dish is milder than the similar Spanish dish, Bacaldo a la Vizcaina. It is eaten on Christmas Eve throughout Mexico.

SERVES SIX

INGREDIENTS

- 450g/1lb dried salt cod
- 105ml/7 tbsp extra virgin olive oil
- 1 onion, halved and thinly sliced
- 4 garlic cloves, crushed
- 2 x 400g/14oz cans chopped tomatoes in tomato juice
- 75g/3oz/¾ cup slivered almonds
- 75g/3oz/½ cup pickled jalapeño chilli slices
- 115g/4oz/1 cup green olives stuffed with pimiento
- small bunch of fresh parsley, finely chopped
- salt and ground black pepper
- fresh flat-leaved parsley, to garnish
- crusty bread, to serve

1 Put the cod in a large bowl and pour over enough cold water to cover. Soak for 24 hours, changing the water at least five times during this period.

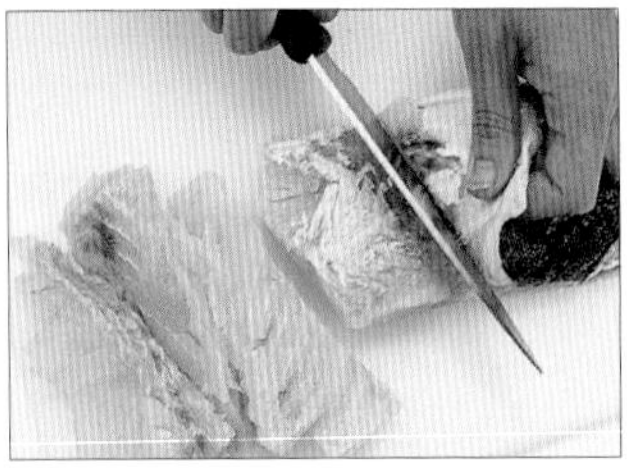

2 Drain the cod and remove the skin using a large sharp knife. Shred the flesh finely using two forks, and put it into a bowl. Set it aside.

3 Heat half the oil in a large frying pan. Add the onion slices and fry over a moderate heat until the onion has softened and is translucent.

4 Remove the onion from the pan and set aside. Make sure you transfer the oil with the onion as it is an important flavouring in this dish and mustn't be discarded. Add the remaining olive oil to the pan. When the oil is hot but not smoking, add the crushed garlic and fry gently for 2 minutes.

5 Add the canned tomatoes and their juice to the pan with the garlic. Cook over a medium-high heat for about 20 minutes, stirring occasionally, until the mixture has reduced and thickened.

COOK'S TIPS

- Salt cod is available in specialist fishmongers, Spanish delicatessens and West Indian stores.
- Any leftovers can be used to fill burritos or empanadas.

6 Meanwhile, spread out the slivered almonds in a single layer in a large heavy-based frying pan. Toast them over a moderate heat for a few minutes, shaking the pan lightly throughout the process so that they turn golden brown all over. Do not let them burn.

7 Add the jalapeño chilli slices and stuffed olives to the toasted almonds.

8 Stir in the shredded fish, mixing it in thoroughly, and cook for 20 minutes more, stirring occasionally, until the mixture is almost dry.

9 Season to taste, add the parsley and cook for a further 2–3 minutes. Garnish with parsley leaves and serve in heated bowls, with crusty bread.

Ceviche with Red Onion, Avocado and Sweet Potato

Ceviche is a South American dish of fish marinated in citrus juice and onion, which has a similar effect to cooking, making the fish opaque and firm in texture.

SERVES SIX AS A STARTER

INGREDIENTS
- 500–675g/1¼–1½lb white fish fillets, skinned
- 1 red onion, thinly sliced
- pinch of dried red chilli flakes
- grated rind of 1 small lime and juice of 5 limes
- 450–500g/1–1¼lb sweet potatoes
- 75ml/5 tbsp mild olive oil
- 15–25ml/3–5 tsp rice vinegar
- 2.5–5ml/½–1 tsp caster (superfine) sugar
- 2.5 ml/½ tsp ground toasted cumin seeds
- ½–1 fresh red or green chilli, seeded and finely chopped
- 1 large or 2 small avocados, peeled, stoned and sliced
- 225g/8oz peeled cooked prawns (shrimp)
- 45ml/3 tbsp chopped fresh coriander (cilantro)
- 30ml/2 tbsp roasted peanuts, chopped
- salt and ground black pepper

1 Cut the fish into strips or chunks. Sprinkle half the onion in a glass dish and lay the fish on top. Add the chilli flakes and pour in the lime juice. Cover and chill for 2–3 hours, spooning the lime juice over the fish once or twice. Drain, and discard the onion.

2 Steam or boil the sweet potatoes for 20–25 minutes, or until just tender. Peel and slice, or cut into wedges.

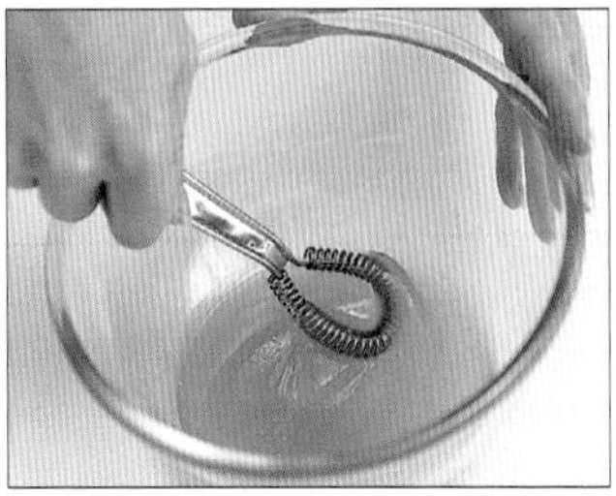

3 Place the oil in a bowl and whisk in the rice vinegar and sugar to taste, then add the cumin, season, and whisk in the fresh chilli and grated lime rind.

4 In a glass bowl, toss together the fish, sweet potatoes, avocado slices, prawns and most of the coriander, and the dressing.

5 Toss in the remaining half of the sliced red onion. Sprinkle with the remaining coriander and the peanuts and serve at once.

COOK'S TIP
Choose orange-fleshed sweet potatoes if you can for this dish.

SEARED TUNA STEAKS WITH RED ONION SALSA

RED ONIONS ARE IDEAL FOR THIS SALSA, NOT ONLY FOR THEIR MILD AND SWEET FLAVOUR, BUT ALSO BECAUSE THEY LOOK SO APPETIZING. SALAD, RICE OR BREAD ARE GOOD ACCOMPANIMENTS.

SERVES FOUR

INGREDIENTS

- 4 tuna loin steaks, each weighing about 175–200g/6–7oz
- 5ml/1 tsp cumin seeds, toasted and crushed
- pinch of dried red chilli flakes
- grated rind and juice of 1 lime
- 30–60ml/2–4 tbsp extra virgin olive oil
- salt and ground black pepper
- lime wedges and fresh coriander (cilantro) sprigs, to garnish

For the salsa

- 1 small red onion, finely chopped
- 200g/7oz red or yellow cherry tomatoes, roughly chopped
- 1 avocado, peeled, stoned and chopped
- 2 kiwi fruit, peeled and chopped
- 1 fresh red chilli, seeded and finely chopped
- 15g/½oz fresh coriander (cilantro), chopped
- 6 fresh mint sprigs, leaves only, chopped
- 5–10ml/1–2 tsp Thai fish sauce (*nam pla*)
- 5ml/1 tsp muscovado (molasses) sugar

1 Wash the tuna steaks and pat dry. Sprinkle with half the cumin, the dried chilli, salt, pepper and half the lime rind. Rub in 30ml/2 tbsp of the oil and set aside in a glass or china dish for about 30 minutes.

2 Meanwhile, make the salsa. Mix the onion, tomatoes, avocado, kiwi fruit, fresh chilli, chopped coriander and mint. Add the remaining cumin, the rest of the lime rind and half the lime juice. Add Thai fish sauce and sugar to taste. Set aside for 15–20 minutes, then add more Thai fish sauce, lime juice and olive oil if required.

3 Heat a ridged cast-iron grill pan. Cook the tuna, allowing about 2 minutes on each side for rare tuna or a little longer for a medium result.

4 Serve the tuna steaks garnished with lime wedges and coriander sprigs. Serve the salsa separately or spoon on to the plates with the tuna.

RED SNAPPER WITH CORIANDER AND ALMONDS

THIS SIMPLE TREATMENT IS PERFECT FOR RED SNAPPER, A FISH THAT IS VERY POPULAR IN MEXICO WHERE FRESH RED SNAPPER CAN BE PICKED UP FROM MARKET STALLS ON THE COAST.

SERVES FOUR

INGREDIENTS

- 75g/3oz/¾ cup plain (all purpose) flour
- 4 red snapper fillets
- salt and ground black pepper
- 75g/3oz/6 tbsp butter
- 15ml/1 tbsp vegetable oil
- 75g/3oz/¾ cup flaked almonds
- grated rind and juice of 1 lime
- small bunch of fresh coriander (cilantro), finely chopped
- warm wheat-flour tortillas, to serve

COOK'S TIP

Warm the tortillas by wrapping them in foil and steaming them on a plate over boiling water for a few minutes. Alternatively, wrap them in microwave-safe film and heat them in a microwave on full power for about 30 seconds.

1 Preheat the oven to 140°C/275°F/ Gas 1. Spread out the flour in a shallow dish and add seasoning. Dry the fish fillets with kitchen paper, then coat each fillet in the seasoned flour.

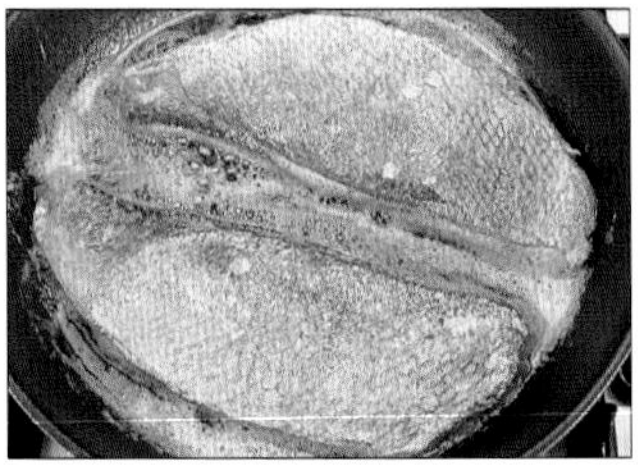

2 Heat the butter and oil in a frying pan. Add the snapper fillets, in batches if necessary, and cook for 2 minutes. Turn the fillets over carefully and cook the other side until golden.

3 Using a fish slice, carefully transfer the fillets to a shallow dish and keep them warm in the oven. Add the almonds to the fat remaining and fry them for 3–4 minutes, until golden.

4 Add the lime rind, juice and coriander to the almonds in the frying pan and stir well. Heat through for 1–2 minutes, then pour the mixture over the fish. Serve with warm wheat-flour tortillas.

VERACRUZ-STYLE RED SNAPPER

THIS IS A CLASSIC MEXICAN DISH, WHICH BORROWS BAY LEAVES AND OLIVES FROM SPAIN TO GO WITH THE NATIVE CHILLIES TO CREATE AN EASY-TO-MAKE, TASTY MEAL.

SERVES FOUR

INGREDIENTS

- 4 whole red snapper, cleaned
- juice of 2 limes
- 4 garlic cloves, crushed
- 5ml/1 tsp dried oregano
- 2.5ml/½ tsp salt
- drained bottled capers, to garnish
- lime wedges, to serve (optional)

For the sauce

- 120ml/4fl oz/½ cup olive oil
- 2 bay leaves
- 2 garlic cloves, sliced
- 4 fresh jalapeño chillies, seeded and cut in strips
- 1 onion, thinly sliced
- 8 fresh tomatoes
- 75g/3oz/½ cup pickled jalapeño chilli slices
- 15ml/1 tbsp soft dark brown sugar
- 2.5ml/½ tsp ground cloves
- 2.5ml/½ tsp ground cinnamon
- 150g/5oz/1¼ cups green olives stuffed with pimiento

1 Preheat the oven to 180°C/350°F/Gas 4. Rinse the fish inside and out, then pat dry with kitchen paper. Place in a single layer in a large roasting tin .

2 Mix the lime juice, garlic, oregano and salt in a small bowl. Pour the mixture over the fish. Bake for about 30 minutes, or until the flesh flakes easily when tested with the tip of a sharp knife.

3 Meanwhile, make the sauce. Heat the olive oil in a pan, add the bay leaves, garlic and chilli strips; fry over a low heat for 3–4 minutes.

4 Add the onion slices to the oil in the pan and cook for 3–4 minutes more, until all the onion is softened and translucent.

5 Cut a cross in the base of each tomato. Place them in a heatproof bowl and pour over boiling water to cover. After 3 minutes, lift the tomatoes out on a slotted spoon and plunge them into a bowl of cold water. Drain. The skins will have begun to peel back from the crosses.

6 Skin the tomatoes completely, then cut them in half and squeeze out the seeds. Chop the flesh finely and add it to the onion mixture. Cook for 3–4 minutes, until the tomato is starting to soften.

7 Add the pickled jalapeños, brown sugar, ground cloves and cinnamon to the sauce. Cook for 10 minutes, stirring frequently, then stir the olives into the sauce and pour a little over each fish. Garnish with the capers and serve with lime wedges, if you like. A rice dish would make a good accompaniment.

PICKLED FISH

This delicious dish has a lovely rounded flavour as the sweetness of the vegetables balances out the sharpness of the pickled fish. Add a garnish of capers and chilli strips.

SERVES FOUR

INGREDIENTS

- 900g/2lb white fish fillets
- 60ml/4 tbsp freshly squeezed lime or lemon juice
- 300ml/½ pint/1¼ cups olive or corn oil
- 2 whole cloves
- 6 peppercorns
- 2 garlic cloves
- 2.5ml/½ tsp ground cumin
- 2.5ml/½ tsp dried oregano
- 2 bay leaves
- 1 drained canned jalapeño chilli, seeded, and cut into strips
- 1 onion, thinly sliced
- 250ml/8fl oz/1 cup white wine vinegar
- 250ml/8fl oz/1 cup olive or corn oil
- salt

For the garnish

- sprigs of fresh herbs such as oregano, coriander (cilantro) or parsley

1 Cut the fish fillets into eight equal size pieces and arrange them in a single layer in a shallow dish. Drizzle with the lime or lemon juice. Cover and leave to marinate for 15 minutes, turning the fillets once.

2 Lift out the fillets with a spatula, pat them dry with kitchen paper and season with salt. Heat 60ml/4 tbsp of the oil in a frying pan and sauté the fish until lightly golden brown. Transfer to a platter and set aside.

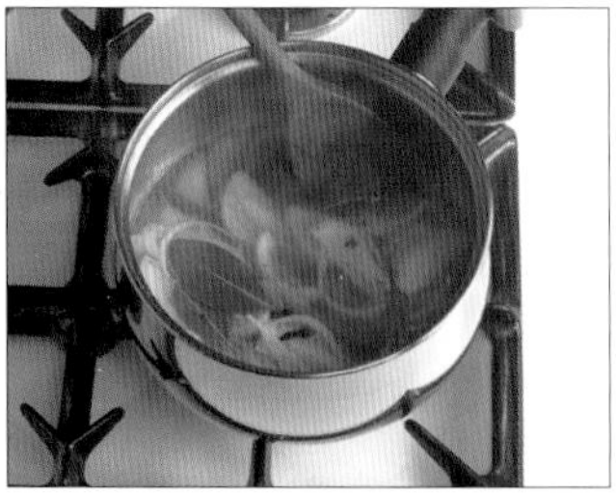

3 Combine the cloves, peppercorns, garlic, cumin, oregano, bay leaves, chilli and vinegar in a pan. Bring to the boil, add the jalapeño chilli and onion, then simmer for 3–4 minutes.

4 Add the remaining oil, and bring to a simmer. Pour over the fish. Cool, cover and chill for 24 hours. To serve, lift out the fillets with a spatula and arrange on a serving dish. Garnish with fresh herbs.

CITRUS FISH WITH CHILLIES

LEMON IS THE NATURAL FLAVOURING FOR WHITE FISH, AND IN THIS DISH THE BAKED LEMONY FLAVOURS INFUSE THE FISH WITH A WONDERFUL TANGY RICHNESS.

SERVES FOUR

INGREDIENTS

4 halibut or cod steaks
juice of 1 lemon
5ml/1 tsp garlic granules
5ml/1 tsp paprika
5ml/1 tsp ground cumin
4ml/3/4 tsp dried tarragon
about 60ml/4 tbsp olive oil
flour, for dusting
300ml/½ pint/1¼ cups fish stock
2 red chillies, seeded and finely chopped
30ml/2 tbsp chopped fresh coriander (cilantro)
1 red onion, cut into rings
salt and ground black pepper

1 Place the fish in a shallow bowl and mix together the lemon juice, garlic, paprika, cumin, tarragon and a little salt and pepper. Spoon over the lemon mixture, cover loosely with clear film (plastic wrap) and marinate for a few hours or overnight in the refrigerator.

2 Heat the oil in a frying pan, dust the fish with flour and fry for a few minutes each side, until golden brown all over.

3 Pour the fish stock around the fish and simmer, covered, for about 5 minutes, until the fish is thoroughly cooked through.

4 Add the chopped red chillies and 15ml/1 tbsp of the coriander to the pan. Simmer for 5 minutes.

5 Transfer the fish and sauce to a serving plate and keep warm.

6 Wipe the pan with kitchen paper, heat some olive oil and stir-fry the onion rings until speckled brown. Sprinkle over the fish with the remaining chopped coriander and serve.

Mexican Spicy Fish

In Mexico fish is often marinated in a spicy mixture before cooking. Here the fish is flavoured with cumin, cinnamon and annato, a traditional Mexican spice.

SERVES SIX

INGREDIENTS

- 1.5kg/3–3½lb striped bass or any non-oily white fish, cut into 6 steaks
- 120ml/4fl oz/½ cup corn oil
- 1 large onion, thinly sliced
- 2 garlic cloves, chopped
- 350g/12oz tomatoes, sliced
- 2 drained canned jalapeño chillies, rinsed and sliced

For the marinade

- 4 garlic cloves, crushed
- 5ml/1 tsp black peppercorns
- 5ml/1 tsp dried oregano
- 2.5ml/½ tsp ground cumin
- 5ml/1 tsp ground annatto
- 2.5ml/½ tsp ground cinnamon
- 120ml/4fl oz/½ cup mild white vinegar
- salt

1 Arrange the fish steaks in a single layer in a shallow dish. Make the marinade. Using a pestle, grind the garlic and black peppercorns in a mortar. Add the dried oregano, cumin, annatto and cinnamon and mix to a paste with the vinegar. Add salt to taste and spread the marinade on both sides of each of the fish steaks. Cover and leave in a cool place for 1 hour.

2 Select a flameproof dish large enough to hold the fish in a single layer and pour in enough of the oil to coat the base. Arrange the fish in the dish with any remaining marinade.

3 Top the fish with the onion, garlic, tomatoes and chillies and pour the rest of the oil over the top.

4 Cover the dish and cook over a low heat on top of the stove for 15–20 minutes, or until the fish is no longer translucent. Serve immediately, garnished with flat leaf parsley.

SALT COD IN MILD CHILLI SAUCE

DRIED SALT COD IN A GREAT FAVOURITE THROUGHOUT LATIN AMERICA. THIS PREPARATION ORIGINATED FROM SPAIN AND PORTUGAL, WHERE IT REMAINS POPULAR TODAY.

SERVES SIX

INGREDIENTS
- 900g/2lb dried salt cod
- 1 onion, chopped
- 2 garlic cloves, chopped

For the sauce
- 6 dried ancho chillies
- 1 onion, chopped
- 2.5ml/½ tsp dried oregano
- 2.5ml/½ tsp ground coriander
- 1 serrano chilli, seeded and chopped
- 45ml/3 tbsp corn oil
- 750ml/1¼ pints/3 cups fish or chicken stock
- salt

For the garnish
- 1 fresh green chilli, sliced

1 Soak the cod in cold water for several hours, depending on how hard and salty it is. Change the water once or twice during soaking.

2 Drain the fish and transfer it to a pan. Pour in enough water to cover. Bring to a gentle simmer and cook for about 15 minutes, until the fish is tender. Drain, reserving the stock. Remove any skin or bones from the fish and cut it into 4cm/1½in pieces.

3 Make the sauce. Remove the stems and shake out the seeds from the ancho chillies. Tear the pods into pieces, put in a bowl of warm water and soak until they are soft. Drain and put into a food processor with the onion, oregano, coriander and serrano chilli. Process to a purée.

4 Heat the oil in a frying pan and cook the purée, stirring, for about 5 minutes. Stir in the fish or chicken stock and simmer for 3–4 minutes. Add the prepared cod and simmer for a few minutes longer to heat the fish through and blend the flavours. Serve garnished with the sliced chilli.

Red Snapper Burritos

Fish makes a great filling for a tortilla, especially when it is succulent red snapper mixed with rice, chilli and tomatoes.

SERVES SIX

INGREDIENTS
- 3 red snapper fillets
- 90g/3½ oz/½ cup long grain white rice
- 30ml/2 tbsp vegetable oil
- 1 small onion, finely chopped
- 5ml/1 tsp ground achiote seed (annatto powder)
- 1 pasilla or similar dried chilli, seeded and ground
- 75g/3oz/¾ cup slivered almonds
- 200g/7oz can chopped tomatoes in tomato juice
- 150g/5oz/1¼ cups grated Monterey Jack or mild Cheddar cheese
- 8 x 20cm/8in wheat-flour tortillas
- fresh flat leaf parsley to garnish
- lime wedges (optional)

1 Preheat the grill (broiler). Cook the fish on an oiled rack for 5 minutes, turning once. When cool, remove the skin and flake the fish. Set it aside.

2 Meanwhile, put the rice in a pan, cover with cold water, cover and bring to the boil. Drain, rinse and drain again.

3 Heat the oil in a pan and fry the onion until soft and translucent. Stir in the ground achiote (annatto powder) and the chilli and cook for 5 minutes.

4 Add the rice, stir well, then stir in the fish and almonds. Add the tomatoes, with their juice. Cook over a moderate heat until the juice is absorbed and the rice is tender. Stir in the cheese and remove from the heat. Warm the tortillas.

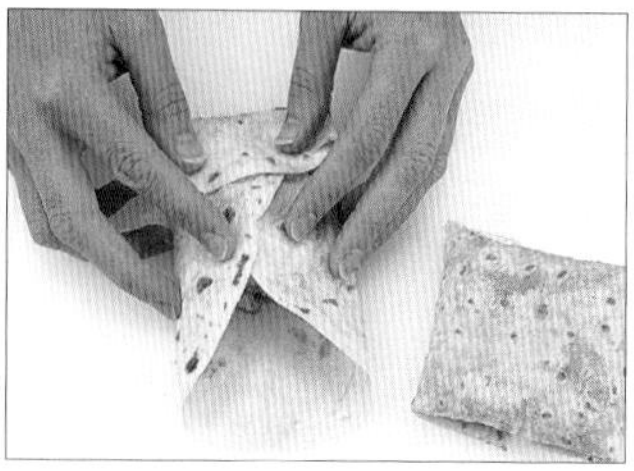

5 Divide the filling among the tortillas and fold them as shown, to make neat parcels. Garnish with fresh parsley and serve with lime wedges, if liked. A green salad makes a good accompaniment.

SEA BASS WITH ORANGE CHILLI SALSA

THE CITRUS SALSA HAS A FRESHNESS WHICH PROVIDES THE PERFECT CONTRAST TO THE WONDERFUL FLAVOUR OF FRESH SEA BASS.

SERVES FOUR

INGREDIENTS
- 4 sea bass fillets
- salt and ground black pepper
- fresh coriander (cilantro), to garnish

For the salsa
- 2 fresh green chillies
- 2 oranges or pink grapefruit
- 1 small onion

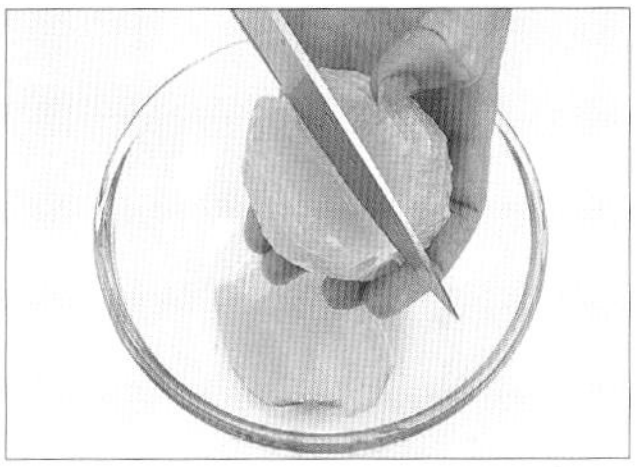

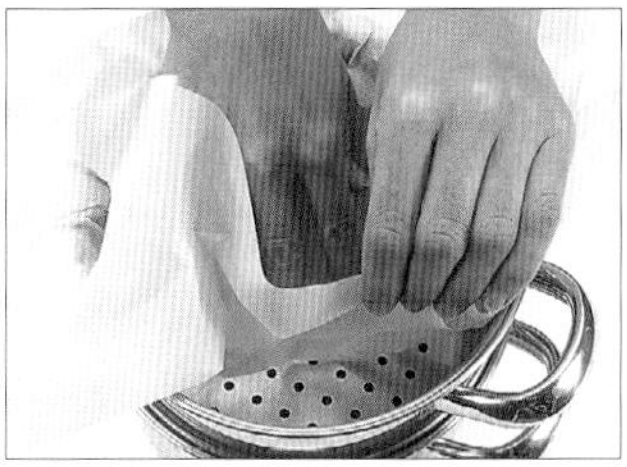

1 Make the salsa. Roast the chillies in a dry griddle pan until the skins are blistered, being careful not to let the flesh burn. Put them in a strong plastic bag and tie the top to keep the steam in. Set aside for 20 minutes.

COOK'S TIP

If the fish has not been scaled, do this by running the back of a small filleting knife against the grain of the scales. They should come away cleanly. Rinse and pat dry with kitchen paper.

2 Slice the top and bottom off each orange or grapefruit and cut off all the peel and pith. Cut between the membranes and put each segment in a bowl.

3 Remove the chillies from the bag and peel off the skins. Cut off the stalks, then slit the chillies and scrape out the seeds. Chop the flesh finely. Cut the onion in half and slice it thinly. Add the onion and chillies to the orange pieces and mix lightly. Season and chill.

4 Season the sea bass fillets. Line a steamer with baking parchment, allowing extra to hang over the sides to enable the fish to be lifted out after cooking. Place the empty steamer over a pan of water and bring to the boil.

5 Place the fish in a single layer in the steamer. Cover with a lid and steam for about 8 minutes or until just cooked. Garnish with fresh coriander and serve with the salsa and a vegetable side dish of your choice.

Fried Sole with Lime

Simple fish dishes like this one capitalize on the delicious flavour of good fresh fish.

SERVES FOUR

INGREDIENTS
- 75g/3oz/¾ cup plain (all-purpose) flour
- 10ml/2 tsp garlic salt
- 5ml/1 tsp ground black pepper
- 4 sole fillets
- oil, for frying
- juice of 2 limes
- small bunch of fresh parsley, chopped, plus extra sprigs, to garnish
- fresh salsa, to serve

COOK'S TIP
Make sure the oil is hot enough when you add the fish, or it will be absorbed by the fish and the dish will be too greasy.

1 Mix the flour, garlic salt and pepper together. Spread out the seasoned flour mixture in a shallow dish. Pat the sole fillets dry with kitchen paper, then turn them in the seasoned flour until they are evenly coated.

2 Pour oil into a wide frying pan to a depth of 2.5cm/½in. Heat it until a cube of bread added to the oil rises to the surface and browns in 45–60 seconds.

3 Add the fish, in batches if necessary, and fry for 3–4 minutes. Lift each fillet out and drain it on kitchen paper. Transfer to a heated serving dish.

4 Squeeze the juice of half a lime over each piece of fish and sprinkle with the chopped parsley. Serve immediately, with a fresh salsa to complement the fish. Garnish with parsley sprigs. New potatoes would also go well.

Baked Salmon with a Guava Sauce

Guavas have a creamy flesh with a slight citrus tang, which makes them the perfect fruit for a sauce to serve with salmon. The sauce works well with other grilled fish and is also good with chicken or turkey.

SERVES FOUR

INGREDIENTS
- 6 ripe guavas
- 45ml/3 tbsp vegetable oil
- 1 small onion, finely chopped
- 120ml/4fl oz/½ cup well-flavoured chicken stock
- 10ml/2 tsp hot pepper sauce
- 4 salmon steaks
- salt and ground black pepper
- strips of red (bell) pepper to garnish

COOK'S TIP
Ripe guavas have yellow skin and succulent flesh that ranges in colour from white to deep pink or salmon red. They are exceptionally rich in vitamin C. Ripe fruit will keep in the refrigerator for a few days; green guavas will need to be placed in a warm spot until they ripen.

1 Cut each guava in half. Scoop the seeded soft flesh into a sieve placed over a bowl. Press it through the sieve, discard the seeds and skin and set the pulp aside.

2 Heat 30ml/2 tbsp of the oil in a frying pan. Fry the chopped onion for about 4 minutes over a moderate heat until softened and translucent.

3 Stir in the guava pulp, with the chicken stock and hot pepper sauce. Cook, stirring constantly, until the sauce thickens. Keep it warm until needed.

4 Brush the salmon steaks on one side with a little of the remaining oil. Season with salt and pepper. Heat a griddle or ridged grill (broiler) pan until very hot and add the salmon steaks, oiled side down. Cook for 2–3 minutes, until the underside is golden, then brush the surface with oil, turn each salmon steak over and cook the other side until the fish is cooked and flakes easily when tested with the tip of a sharp knife.

5 Transfer each steak to a warmed plate. Serve, garnished with strips of red pepper on a pool of sauce. A fresh green salad is a good accompaniment.

Trout in Wine Sauce with Plantain

Exotic fish from the warm Caribbean waters, such as mahi mahi or grouper, would add a distinctive flavour to this tasty dish, which is eaten throughout the region. If you cannot find exotic fish, however, trout is ideal, or you can use any filleted white fish.

SERVES FOUR

INGREDIENTS
- 4 trout fillets
- spice seasoning, for dusting
- 25g/1oz/2 tbsp butter or margarine
- 1–2 garlic cloves
- 150ml/¼ pint/⅔ cup white wine
- 150ml/¼ pint/⅔ cup fish stock
- 10ml/2 tsp clear honey
- 15–30ml/1–2 tbsp chopped fresh parsley
- 1 yellow plantain
- salt and ground black pepper
- oil, for frying
- green salad, to serve

1 Season the trout fillets by coating them in the spice seasoning. Place in a shallow dish, cover with cling film (plastic wrap) and marinate in a cool place for at least 1 hour.

2 Melt the butter or margarine in a large frying pan and heat gently for 1 minute. Add the fish fillets. Sauté for about 5 minutes, until cooked through, turning carefully once. Transfer to a plate and keep hot.

3 Add the garlic, white wine, fish stock and honey to the pan and bring to the boil, stirring. Lower the heat and simmer to reduce slightly. Return the fish to the pan and spoon over the sauce. Sprinkle with the parsley and simmer gently for 2–3 minutes.

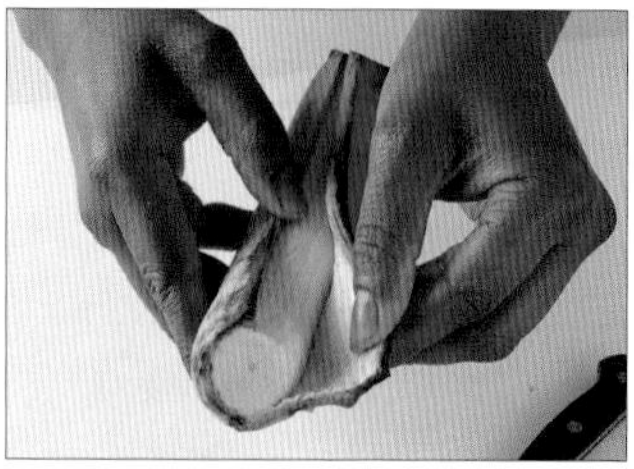

4 Meanwhile, peel the plantain, and cut it into rounds. Heat a little oil in a small frying pan and fry the plantain slices for 2–3 minutes, until golden, turning once. Transfer the fish to warmed serving plates. Stir the sauce, season and pour over the fish. Serve with the fried plantain and a green salad.

COOK'S TIP

Plantains belong to the banana family and can be green, yellow or brown, depending on how ripe they are. Unlike bananas, they must be cooked.

ESCHOVISHED FISH

THIS PICKLED FISH DISH IS OF SPANISH ORIGIN AND IS VERY POPULAR THROUGHOUT THE CARIBBEAN ISLANDS. IT GOES BY VARIOUS NAMES, INCLUDING ESCOVITCH AND CAVEACHED FISH, BUT NO MATTER WHAT THE NAME, IT INEVITABLY TASTES DELICIOUS.

SERVES SIX

INGREDIENTS
- 900g/2lb cod fillet
- ½ lemon
- 15ml/1 tbsp spice seasoning
- flour, for dusting
- oil, for frying
- lemon wedges, to garnish

For the sauce
- 30ml/2 tbsp vegetable oil
- 1 onion, sliced
- ½ red (bell) pepper, sliced
- ½ chayote (christophene), peeled, seeded and cut into small pieces
- 2 garlic cloves, crushed
- 120ml/4fl oz/½ cup malt vinegar
- 75ml/5 tbsp water
- 2.5ml/½ tsp ground allspice
- 1 bay leaf
- 1 small fresh Scotch bonnet or Habañero chilli, chopped
- 15ml/1 tbsp soft brown sugar
- salt and ground black pepper

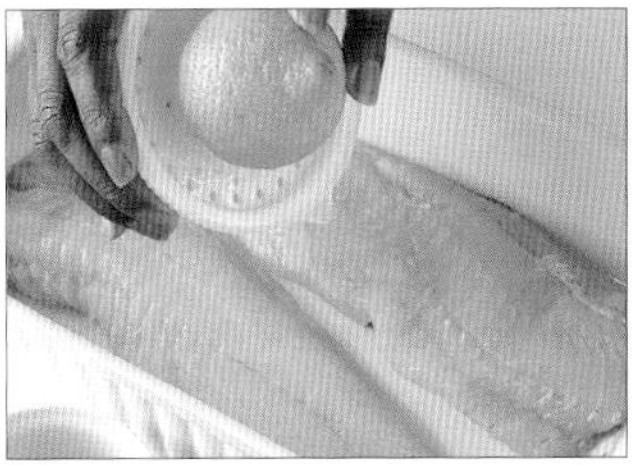

1 Place the fish in a shallow dish, squeeze over the lemon juice, then sprinkle with the spice seasoning. Pat the seasoning into the fish using your hands, then cover and leave to marinate in a cool place for at least 1 hour.

2 Cut the cod fillet across into 7.5cm/3in pieces. Dust the pieces of fish with a little flour, shaking off any excess.

3 Heat the oil in a heavy frying pan and fry the fish pieces for 2–3 minutes, turning occasionally, until they are golden brown and crisp. Using a fish slice or slotted spoon, lift the cooked fish pieces out of the pan and place in a serving dish. Keep hot.

4 Make the sauce. Heat the oil in a frying pan and fry the onion for 4–5 minutes. Add the pepper, chayote and garlic and stir-fry for 2 minutes.

5 Pour in the vinegar, then add the water, allspice, bay leaf, chilli and sugar. Simmer for 5 minutes, then season. Leave to stand for 10 minutes, then pour the sauce over the fish. Serve hot, garnished with the lemon wedges.

VARIATION

Cod fillets are very expensive so, if they are available, try using whole red snapper or red mullet, which are often used for this dish in the Caribbean.

CHARGRILLED TUNA WITH FIERY PEPPER PURÉE

TUNA IS AN OILY FISH THAT BARBECUES WELL AND IS MEATY ENOUGH TO COMBINE SUCCESSFULLY WITH STRONG FLAVOURS – EVEN HOT CHILLI, AS IN THIS RED PEPPER PURÉE, WHICH IS EXCELLENT SERVED WITH CRUSTY BREAD OR TORTILLAS.

SERVES FOUR

INGREDIENTS
- 4 tuna steaks, about 175g/6oz each
- finely grated rind and juice of 1 lime
- 30ml/2 tbsp olive oil
- salt and freshly ground black pepper
- lime wedges, to serve

For the pepper purée
- 2 red (bell) peppers, halved
- 45ml/3 tbsp olive oil, plus extra for brushing
- 1 small onion
- 2 garlic cloves, crushed
- 2 red chillies
- 1 slice white bread, crusts removed, diced
- salt

1 Trim any skin from the tuna and place the steaks in a single layer in a wide dish. Sprinkle over the lime rind and juice, olive oil, salt and black pepper. Cover with clear film (plastic wrap) and chill in the refrigerator until required.

2 To make the pepper purée, brush the pepper halves with a little olive oil and cook them, skin-side down, on a hot barbecue, until the skin is charred and blackened. Place the onion in its skin on the barbecue and cook until browned, turning it occasionally.

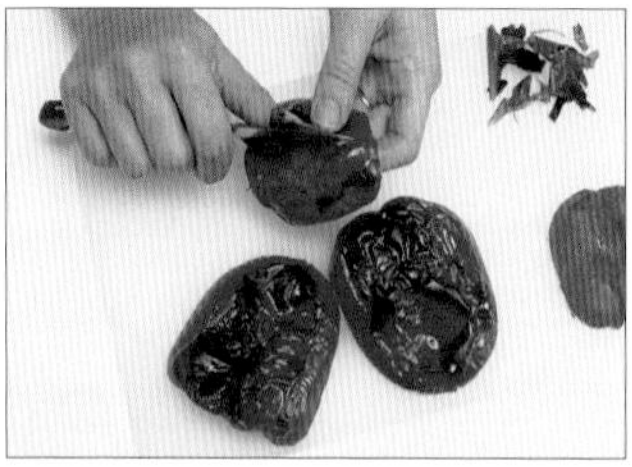

3 Leave the peppers and onion until cool enough to handle, then remove the skins, using a sharp kitchen knife.

4 Place the cooked peppers and onion with the garlic, chillies, bread and olive oil in a food processor. Process until smooth. Add salt to taste.

5 Drain the tuna steaks from the marinade and cook them on a hot barbecue for 8–10 minutes, turning once, until golden brown. Serve the steaks with the pepper purée and lime wedges, with crusty bread if you like.

COOK'S TIP

The pepper purée can be made in advance, cooking the peppers and onion under a hot grill (broiler); keep it in the refrigerator until you cook the fish.

MACKEREL ESCABECHE

THIS TRADITIONAL WAY OF PRESERVING FISH IN VINEGAR, WAS BROUGHT TO LATIN AMERICA BY THE SPANISH AND PORTUGUESE. OILY FISH, SUCH AS MACKEREL AND SARDINES, LEND THEMSELVES PARTICULARLY WELL TO THIS TREATMENT. IT TAKES AT LEAST A DAY, SO ALLOW PLENTY OF TIME.

SERVES SIX

INGREDIENTS
- 12 small mackerel fillets
- juice of 2 limes
- 90ml/6 tbsp olive oil
- 2 red onions, thinly sliced
- 2 garlic cloves, thinly sliced
- 2 bay leaves
- 6 black peppercorns
- 120ml/4fl oz/½ cup red wine vinegar
- 50g/2oz/½ cup plain (all-purpose) flour
- salt and ground black pepper

1 Place the mackerel fillets side by side in a large, shallow glass or china dish. Pour over the lime juice. Season with salt and pepper and cover. Marinate in the refrigerator for 20–30 minutes, but no longer.

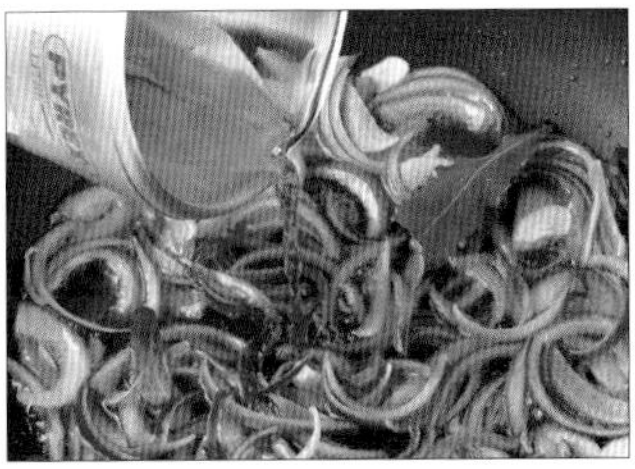

2 Meanwhile, heat half the oil in a frying pan. Add the onions and cook over a low heat for 10 minutes, until softened but not coloured. Stir in the garlic and cook for 2 minutes.

3 Add the bay leaves, peppercorns and vinegar to the pan and simmer over a very low heat for 5 minutes.

COOK'S TIP
If you are planning to keep the fish for more than one day, make sure it is completely immersed in the vinegar, then top with a thin layer of olive oil. Cover tightly. It will keep in the refrigerator for up to 1 month.

4 Pat the mackerel fillets dry and coat them in the flour. Heat the remaining oil in a large frying pan and fry the fish, in batches, for 2 minutes on each side.

5 Return the fish to the dish in which they were originally marinated. Pour the vinegar marinade over the fish. Leave to marinate for 24 hours before serving.

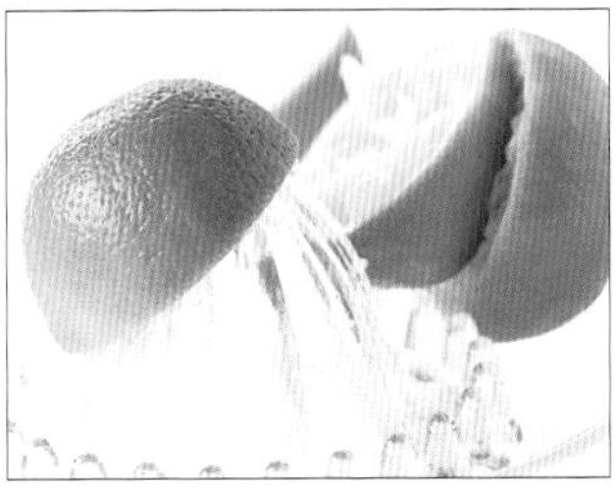

SALMON WITH TEQUILA CREAM SAUCE

USE REPOSADA TEQUILA, WHICH IS LIGHTLY AGED, FOR THE SAUCE IN THIS MEXICAN DISH. IT HAS A SMOOTHER, MORE ROUNDED FLAVOUR, WHICH GOES WELL WITH THE CREAM.

SERVES FOUR

INGREDIENTS

3 fresh jalapeño chillies
45ml/3 tbsp olive oil
1 small onion, finely chopped
150ml/¼ pint/⅔ cup fish stock
grated rind and juice of 1 lime
120ml/4fl oz/½ cup single (light) cream
30ml/2 tbsp reposada tequila
1 firm avocado
4 salmon fillets
salt and ground white pepper
strips of green (bell) pepper and fresh flat leaf parsley, to garnish

1 Roast the chillies in a frying pan until the skins are blistered, being careful not to let the flesh burn. Put them in a strong plastic bag and tie the top to keep the steam in. Set aside for 20 minutes.

2 Heat 15ml/1 tbsp of the oil in a pan. Add the onion and fry for 3–4 minutes, then add the stock, lime rind and juice. Cook for 10 minutes, until the stock starts to reduce. Remove the chillies from the bag and peel off the skins, slit and scrape out the seeds.

3 Stir the cream into the onion and stock mixture. Slice the chilli flesh into strips and add to the pan. Cook over a gentle heat, stirring constantly, for 2–3 minutes. Season to taste with salt and white pepper.

4 Stir the tequila into the onion and chilli mixture. Leave the pan over a very low heat. Peel the avocado, remove the stone and slice the flesh. Brush the salmon fillets on one side with a little of the remaining oil.

5 Heat a frying pan or ridged grill (broiler) pan until very hot and add the salmon, oiled side down. Cook for 2–3 minutes, until the underside is golden, then brush the top with oil. Turn over and cook the other side until the fish is cooked and flakes easily when tested with the tip of a sharp knife.

6 Serve on a pool of sauce, with the avocado slices. Garnish with strips of green pepper and fresh parsley. This dish is good with fried potatoes.

YUCATÁN-STYLE SHARK STEAK

A FIRM-FLESHED FISH, SHARK IS WIDELY AVAILABLE, EITHER FRESH OR FROZEN. IT NEEDS CAREFUL WATCHING, AS OVERCOOKING WILL MAKE IT DRY AND TOUGH, BUT THE FLAVOUR IS EXCELLENT.

SERVES FOUR

INGREDIENTS

- grated rind and juice of 1 orange
- juice of 1 small lime
- 45ml/3 tbsp white wine
- 30ml/2 tbsp olive oil
- 2 garlic cloves, crushed
- 10ml/2 tsp ground achiote seed (annatto powder)
- 2.5ml/½ tsp cayenne pepper
- 2.5ml/½ tsp dried marjoram
- 5ml/1 tsp salt
- 4 shark steaks
- fresh oregano leaves, to garnish
- 4 wheat-flour tortillas and any suitable salsa, to serve

COOK'S TIP

Shark freezes successfully, with little or no loss of flavour on thawing, so use frozen steaks if you can't find fresh.

1 Put the orange rind and juice in a shallow non-metallic dish which is large enough to hold all the shark steaks in a single layer. Add the lime juice, white wine, olive oil, garlic, ground achiote seed (annatto powder), cayenne, marjoram and salt. Mix well.

2 Add the shark steaks to the dish and spoon the marinade over them. Cover and set aside for 1 hour, turning once.

3 Heat a griddle pan until very hot and cook the marinated shark steaks for 2–3 minutes on each side. Alternatively, they are very good cooked on the barbecue, so long as they are cooked after the coals have lost their fierce initial heat. Do not overcook.

4 Garnish the shark steaks with oregano and serve with the tortillas and salsa. A green vegetable would also go well.

Swordfish Tacos

It is important not to overcook swordfish, or it can be tough and dry. Cooked correctly, however, it is absolutely delicious and makes a great change from beef or chicken as a taco filling.

SERVES SIX

INGREDIENTS
- 3 swordfish steaks
- 30ml/2 tbsp vegetable oil
- 2 garlic cloves, crushed
- 1 small onion, chopped
- 3 fresh green chillies, seeded and chopped
- 3 tomatoes
- small bunch of fresh coriander (cilantro), chopped
- 6 fresh corn tortillas
- ½ iceberg lettuce, shredded
- salt and ground black pepper
- lemon wedges, to serve (optional)

1 Preheat the grill (broiler). Put the swordfish on an oiled rack over a grill pan and cook for 2–3 minutes on each side. When cool, remove the skin and flake the fish into a bowl.

2 Heat the oil in a pan. Add the garlic, onion and chillies and fry for 5 minutes or until the onion is soft and translucent.

3 Cut a cross in the base of each tomato and pour over boiling water. After 3 minutes plunge into cold water. Remove the skins and seeds and chop the flesh into 1cm/½in dice.

4 Add the tomatoes and swordfish to the onion mixture. Cook for 5 minutes over a low heat. Add the coriander and cook for 1–2 minutes. Season to taste.

5 Wrap the tortillas in foil and steam on a plate over boiling water until pliable. Place some shredded lettuce and fish mixture on each tortilla. Fold in half and serve with lemon wedges, if you like.

Chargrilled Swordfish with Chilli and Lime Sauce

Swordfish is a prime candidate for the barbecue, as long as it is not overcooked. It tastes wonderful with a spicy sauce whose fire is tempered with crème fraîche.

SERVES FOUR

INGREDIENTS
- 2 fresh serrano chillies
- 4 tomatoes
- 45ml/3 tbsp olive oil
- grated rind and juice of 1 lime
- 4 swordfish steaks
- 2.5ml/½ tsp salt
- 2.5ml/½ tsp ground black pepper
- 175ml/6fl oz/¾ cup crème fraîche
- fresh flat leaf parsley, to garnish

1 Roast the chillies in a dry griddle pan, put in a plastic bag and tie the top. Set aside for 20 minutes, then peel off the skins. Cut off the stalks, scrape out the seeds and slice the flesh.

2 Cut a cross in the base of each tomato. Place them in a heatproof bowl and pour over boiling water to cover. After 3 minutes, lift the tomatoes out on a slotted spoon and plunge them into a bowl of cold water. Drain. The skins will have begun to peel back from the crosses. Remove all the skin from the tomatoes, then cut them in half and squeeze out the seeds. Chop the flesh into 1cm/½in pieces.

3 Heat 15ml/1 tbsp of the oil in a small pan and add the strips of chilli, with the lime rind and juice. Cook for 2–3 minutes, then stir in the tomatoes. Cook for 10 minutes, stirring the mixture occasionally, until the tomato is pulpy.

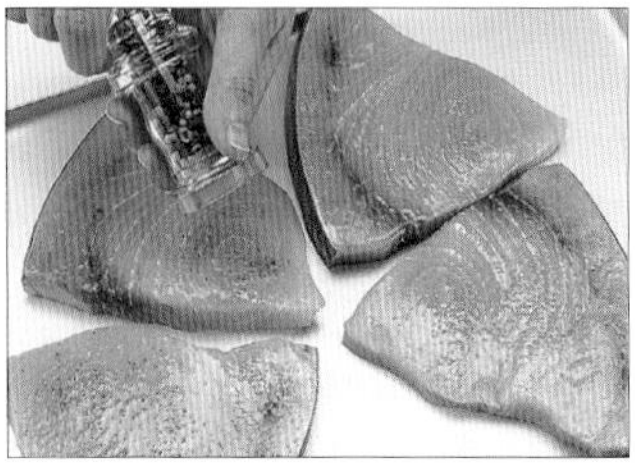

4 Brush the fish with olive oil and season. Barbecue or grill (broil) for 3–4 minutes, turning once. Meanwhile, stir the crème fraîche into the sauce, heat it gently and pour over the fish. Serve garnished with fresh parsley. Chargrill some vegetables as well.

MARINATED RED MULLET

This popular Latin American recipe is based on a Spanish way of cooking fish en escabeche by first frying it, then marinating it. If you are unable to find fresh mullet, snapper, sea bream or tilapia are all good alternatives.

SERVES SIX

INGREDIENTS
- 7.5ml/1½ tsp mild Spanish paprika, preferably Spanish smoked pimentón
- 45ml/3 tbsp plain (all-purpose) flour
- 120ml/4fl oz/½ cup olive oil
- 6 red mullet, each weighing about 300g/11oz, filleted
- 2 aubergines (eggplants), sliced or cut into long wedges
- 2 red or yellow (bell) peppers, seeded and thickly sliced
- 1 large red onion, thinly sliced
- 2 garlic cloves, sliced
- 15ml/1 tbsp sherry vinegar
- juice of 1 lemon
- brown sugar, to taste
- 15ml/1 tbsp chopped fresh oregano
- 18–24 black olives
- 45ml/3 tbsp chopped fresh flat leaf parsley
- salt and ground black pepper

1 Mix 5ml/1 tsp of the paprika with the flour and season well with salt and black pepper. Heat half the oil in a large frying pan. Dip the fish into the flour, turning to coat both sides, and fry for 4–5 minutes, until browned on each side. Place the fish in a glass or china dish suitable for marinating it.

2 Add 30ml/2 tbsp of the remaining oil to the pan and fry the aubergine wedges until softened and browned. Drain thoroughly on a piece of kitchen paper to remove excess oil, then add the aubergine to the fish.

3 Add another 30ml/2 tbsp oil to the pan and cook the peppers and onion gently for 6–8 minutes, until softened but not browned. Add the garlic and remaining paprika, then cook for a further 2 minutes. Stir in the sherry vinegar and lemon juice with 30ml/2 tbsp water and heat until simmering. Season to taste with a pinch of sugar.

4 Stir in the oregano and olives, then spoon over the fish. Set aside to cool, then cover and marinate in the fridge for several hours or overnight.

5 About 30 minutes before serving, bring the fish and vegetables back to room temperature. Stir in the parsley just before serving.

Cod Caramba

This colourful Mexican dish, with its contrasting crunchy topping and tender fish filling, can be made with any economical white fish such as coley or haddock. Serve with a tasty green salad for a hearty midweek supper.

SERVES SIX

INGREDIENTS
- 450g/1lb cod fillets
- 225g/8oz smoked cod fillets
- 300ml/½ pint/1¼ cups fish stock
- 50g/2oz/¼ cup butter
- 1 onion, sliced
- 2 garlic cloves, crushed
- 1 green and 1 red (bell) pepper, seeded and diced
- 2 courgettes (zucchini), diced
- 115g/4oz/⅔ cup drained canned or thawed frozen corn kernels
- 2 tomatoes, peeled and chopped
- juice of 1 lime
- Tabasco sauce
- salt, ground black pepper and cayenne pepper

For the topping
- 75g/3oz tortilla chips
- 50g/2oz/½ cup grated Cheddar cheese
- coriander (cilantro) sprigs, to garnish
- lime wedges, to serve

1 Lay the fish in a shallow pan and pour over the fish stock. Bring to the boil, lower the heat, cover and poach for about 8 minutes, until the flesh flakes easily. Leave to cool slightly, then remove the skin and separate the flesh into large flakes. Keep hot.

2 Melt the butter in a pan, add the onion and garlic and cook gently over a low heat until soft and translucent. Add the peppers, stir and cook for about 2 minutes. Stir in the courgettes and cook for 3 minutes more, until all the vegetables are tender.

3 Stir in the corn and tomatoes, then add lime juice and Tabasco to taste. Season with salt, black pepper and cayenne. Cook for 2 minutes to heat the corn and tomatoes, then stir in the fish and transfer to a dish that can safely be used under the grill (broiler).

4 Preheat the grill. Make the topping by crushing the tortilla chips, then mixing in the grated cheese. Add cayenne pepper to taste and sprinkle over the fish. Place the dish under the grill until the topping is crisp and brown. Garnish with coriander sprigs and lime wedges.

Creole Fish Stew

This is a simple dish that looks as good as it tastes. It is a good choice for a dinner party, but remember to allow time for marinating the fish.

SERVES SIX

INGREDIENTS
- 2 whole red bream, porgy or large snapper, prepared and cut into 2.5cm/1in pieces
- 30ml/2 tbsp spice seasoning
- 30ml/2 tbsp malt vinegar
- flour, for dusting
- oil, for frying

For the sauce
- 30ml/2 tbsp vegetable oil
- 15ml/1 tbsp butter or margarine
- 1 onion, finely chopped
- 275g/10oz fresh tomatoes, peeled and finely chopped
- 2 garlic cloves, crushed
- 2 fresh thyme sprigs
- 600ml/1 pint/2½ cups fish stock or water
- 2.5ml/½ tsp ground cinnamon
- 1 fresh hot chilli, chopped
- 1 red and 1 green (bell) pepper, seeded and finely chopped
- salt
- fresh oregano sprigs, to garnish

1 Toss the pieces of fish with the spice seasoning and vinegar in a bowl. Cover and set aside to marinate for at least 2 hours at cool room temperature or overnight in the refrigerator.

COOK'S TIP
Take care when preparing the chilli as the capsaicin it contains is a powerful irritant and will burn the skin. Wear gloves if possible and avoid touching your face until you have removed them. Leave the chilli seeds in, or remove them for a slightly milder result.

2 When ready to cook, place a little flour in a large shallow bowl and use to coat the fish pieces, shaking off any excess flour.

3 Heat a little oil in a large frying pan. Add the fish pieces and fry for about 5 minutes, turning the pieces carefully, until golden brown, then set aside. Do not worry if the fish is not quite cooked through; it will finish cooking in the sauce.

4 To make the sauce, heat the oil and butter or margarine in a frying pan and stir-fry the onion for 5 minutes. Add the tomatoes, garlic and thyme and simmer for a further 5 minutes. Stir in the stock or water, cinnamon and chilli.

5 Add the fish pieces and the chopped peppers. Simmer until the fish is cooked and the stock has reduced to a thick sauce. Season with salt. Serve hot, garnished with the oregano.

SALT FISH AND ACKEE

This is a classic Jamaican dish, that is also popular throughout the Caribbean. It is often served with boiled green bananas as well as fried dumplings.

SERVES FOUR

INGREDIENTS

- 450g/1lb salt cod
- 25g/1oz/2 tbsp butter or margarine
- 30ml/2 tbsp vegetable oil
- 1 onion, chopped
- 2 garlic cloves, crushed
- 225g/8oz tomatoes, chopped
- ½ hot chilli, chopped (optional)
- 2.5ml/½ tsp ground black pepper
- 2.5ml/½ tsp dried thyme
- 2.5ml/½ tsp ground allspice
- 30ml/2 tbsp chopped spring onion (scallion)
- 540g/1lb 6oz can ackees, drained
- fried dumplings, to serve

1 Place the salt cod in a bowl and pour in enough cold water to cover. Leave to soak for at least 24 hours, changing the water about five times. Drain and rinse in fresh cold water.

2 Put the salt cod in a large pan of cold water. Bring the water to the boil, then remove the fish and leave it to cool on a plate. Carefully remove and discard the skin and bones, then flake the fish and set it aside.

3 Heat the butter or margarine and oil in a large heavy frying pan over a medium heat. Add the onion and garlic and sauté for 5 minutes. Stir in the tomatoes, with the chilli, if using, and cook gently for a further 5 minutes.

4 Add the salt cod, black pepper, thyme, allspice and spring onion, stir to mix, then stir in the ackees, taking care not to crush them. If you prefer a more moist dish, add a little water or stock. Serve hot with fried dumplings.

ESCABECHE

A classic dish that the Mexicans inherited from the Spanish, Escabeche is often confused with Ceviche, which consists of marinated raw fish. In Escabeche, the raw fish is initially marinated in lime juice, but is then cooked before being pickled.

SERVES FOUR

INGREDIENTS
- 900g/2lb whole fish fillets
- juice of 2 limes
- 300ml/½ pint/1¼ cups olive oil
- 6 black peppercorns
- 3 garlic cloves, sliced
- 2.5ml/½ tsp ground cumin
- 2.5ml/½ tsp dried oregano
- 2 bay leaves
- 50g/2oz/⅓ cup pickled jalapeño chilli slices, chopped
- 1 onion, thinly sliced
- 250ml/8fl oz/1 cup white wine vinegar
- 150g/5oz/1¼ cups green olives stuffed with pimiento, to garnish

1 Place the fish fillets in a single layer in a shallow non-metallic dish. Pour the lime juice over, turn the fillets over once to ensure that they are completely coated, then cover the dish and leave to marinate for 15 minutes.

2 Drain the fish in a colander, then pat the fillets dry with kitchen paper. Heat 60ml/4 tbsp of the oil in a frying pan, add the fish fillets and sauté for 5–6 minutes, turning once, until they are golden brown. Use a fish slice (metal spatula) to transfer them to a shallow dish that will hold them in a single layer.

3 Heat 30ml/2 tbsp of the remaining oil in a frying pan. Add the peppercorns, garlic, ground cumin, oregano, bay leaves and jalapeños, and cook over a low heat for 2 minutes, then increase the heat, add the onion slices and vinegar and bring to the boil. Lower the heat and simmer for 4 minutes.

4 Remove the pan from the heat and carefully add the remaining oil. Stir well, then pour the mixture over the fish. Leave to cool, then cover the dish and marinate for 24 hours in the refrigerator.

5 When you are ready to serve, drain off the liquid and garnish the pickled fish with the stuffed olives. Salad leaves would make a good accompaniment.

COOK'S TIP

Use the largest frying pan you have when cooking the fish. If your pan is too small, it may be necessary to cook them in batches. Do not overcrowd the pan as they will cook unevenly.

CHILEAN SQUID CASSEROLE

THIS HEARTY STEW IS IDEAL ON A COLD EVENING. THE POTATOES DISINTEGRATE TO THICKEN AND ENRICH THE SAUCE, MAKING A WARMING, COMFORTING MAIN COURSE.

SERVES SIX

INGREDIENTS
- 800g/1¾lb squid
- 45ml/3 tbsp olive oil
- 5 garlic cloves, crushed
- 4 fresh jalapeño chillies, seeded and finely chopped
- 2 celery sticks, diced
- 500g/1¼lb small new potatoes or baby salad potatoes, scrubbed, scraped or peeled and quartered
- 400ml/14fl oz/1⅔ cups dry white wine
- 400ml/14fl oz/1⅔ cups fish stock
- 4 tomatoes, diced
- 30ml/2 tbsp chopped fresh flat leaf parsley
- salt
- white rice or *arepas* (corn breads), to serve

1 Clean the squid under cold water. Pull the tentacles away from the body. The squid's entrails will come out easily. Remove the cartilage from inside the body cavity and discard it. Wash the body thoroughly.

2 Pull away the membrane that covers the body. Cut between the tentacles and head, discarding the head and entrails. Leave the tentacles whole but discard the hard beak in the middle. Cut the body into thin rounds.

COOK'S TIP

Adding the tomatoes and parsley at the end gives a real freshness to the sauce. If you'd prefer an even heartier dish, add these ingredients to the pan with the potatoes. Replace the white wine with a Chilean cabernet sauvignon.

3 Heat the oil, add the garlic, chillies and celery and cook for 5 minutes. Stir in the potatoes, then add the wine and stock. Bring to the boil, then simmer, covered, for 25 minutes.

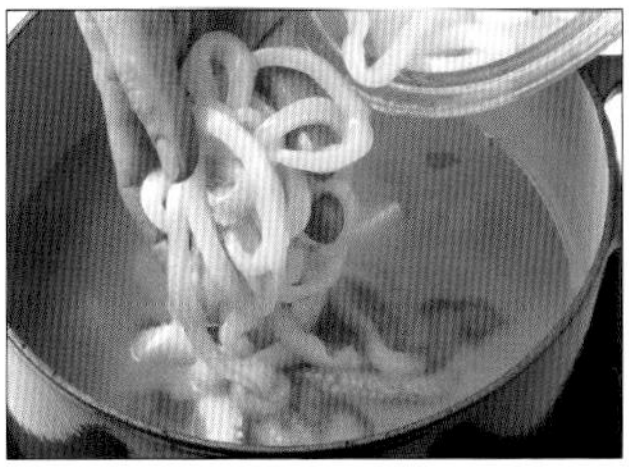

4 Remove from the heat and stir in the squid, tomatoes and parsley. Cover the pan and leave to stand until the squid is cooked. Serve immediately.

Jamaican Fish Curry

This recipe uses some of the most common spices in Caribbean cuisine, where the influence of India is clearly visible. The taste is for strong, pungent flavours rather than fiery heat, and the rice is an integral part of the dish.

SERVES FOUR

INGREDIENTS
- 2 halibut steaks, total weight about 500–675g/1¼–1½lb
- 30ml/2 tbsp groundnut oil
- 2 cardamom pods
- 1 cinnamon stick
- 6 allspice berries
- 4 cloves
- 1 large onion, chopped
- 3 garlic cloves, crushed
- 10–15ml/2–3 tsp grated fresh root ginger
- 10ml/2 tsp ground cumin
- 5ml/1 tsp ground coriander
- 2.5ml/½ tsp cayenne pepper, or to taste
- 4 tomatoes, peeled, seeded and chopped
- 1 sweet potato, about 225g/8oz, cut into 2cm/¾in cubes
- 475ml/16fl oz/2 cups fish stock or water
- 115g/4oz piece of creamed coconut
- 1 bay leaf
- 225g/8oz/generous 1 cup white long grain rice
- salt

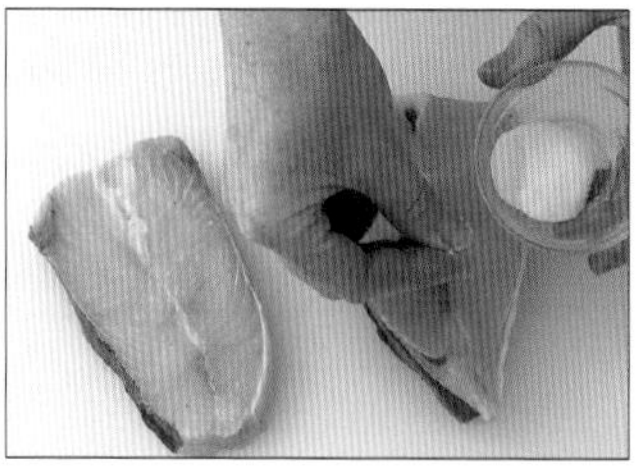

1 Rub the halibut steaks well with salt and set aside.

2 Heat the oil in a flameproof casserole dish and stir-fry the cardamom pods, cinnamon stick, allspice berries and cloves for about 3 minutes to release the delicate aromas.

3 Add the chopped onion, crushed garlic and grated ginger. Continue cooking for about 4–5 minutes over a gentle heat, stirring frequently, until the onion is soft.

4 Add the ground cumin, coriander and cayenne pepper and cook briefly, stirring all the time.

5 Stir in the tomatoes, sweet potato, fish stock or water, creamed coconut and bay leaf. Season well with salt. Bring to the boil, then lower the heat, cover and simmer for about 15–18 minutes, until the sweet potato is tender.

6 Cook the rice according to your preferred method. Meanwhile, add the halibut steaks to the pan of curry sauce and spoon the sauce over to cover them completely. Cover the pan with a tight-fitting lid and simmer gently for about 10 minutes until the fish is just tender and flakes easily.

7 Spoon the rice into a warmed serving dish, spoon over the curry sauce and arrange the halibut steaks on top. Garnish with chopped coriander (cilantro), if you like, and serve immediately.

VARIATION

Other types of fish can be used, although the strong taste of the sauce makes it a good recipe for white fish with hearty flavours. Try cod and haddock, or more meaty fish and shellfish such as swordfish, monkfish or prawns (shrimp).

COOK'S TIP

Sweet potato discolours very quickly when cut. If preparing ingredients in advance, put the cubes of potato into a bowl of cold water with 30–45ml/2–3 tbsp lemon juice until ready to use.

Pueblo Fish Bake

The lime juice is a perfect partner for the trout, which is an oily fish. Marinating means that the fish is beautifully tender when cooked.

SERVES FOUR

INGREDIENTS
- 2 fresh pasilla chillies
- 4 rainbow trout, cleaned
- 4 garlic cloves
- 10ml/2 tsp dried oregano
- juice of 2 limes
- 50g/2oz/½ cup slivered almonds
- salt and ground black pepper

1 Roast the chillies in a dry frying pan or griddle pan until the skins are blistered, being careful not to let the flesh burn. Put them in a strong plastic bag and tie the top to keep the steam in. Set aside for 20 minutes.

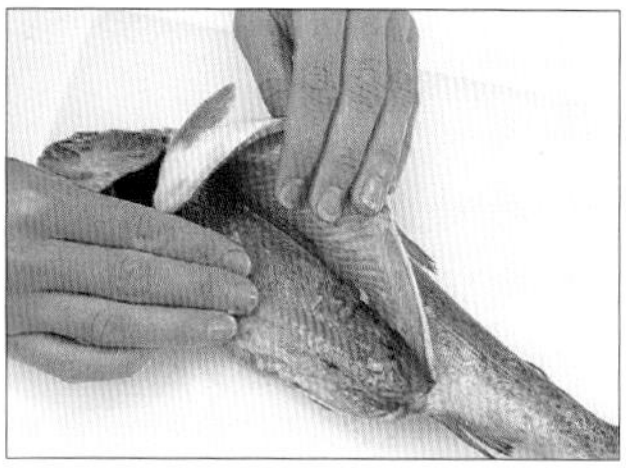

2 Meanwhile, rub a little salt into the cavities in the trout, to ensure they are completely clean, then rinse them under cold running water. Drain and pat dry with kitchen paper.

COOK'S TIP
Cooking fish in a paper parcel means that it stays very moist. Trout cooks perfectly by this method, but you could use other fish – try tuna steaks, small mackerel or salmon fillets.

3 Remove the chillies from the bag and peel off the skins. Cut off the stalks, then slit the chillies and scrape out the seeds. Chop the flesh roughly and put it in a mortar. Crush with a pestle until the mixture forms a paste.

4 Place the chilli paste in a shallow dish that will hold all the trout in a single layer. Slice the garlic lengthways and add to the dish.

5 Add the oregano and 10ml/2 tsp salt, then stir in the lime juice and pepper to taste. Add the trout, turning to coat them in the mixture. Cover the dish and set aside for at least 30 minutes, turning the trout again halfway through.

6 Preheat the oven to 200°C/400°F/Gas 6. Have ready four pieces of kitchen foil, each large enough to wrap a trout. Top each sheet with a piece of baking parchment of the same size.

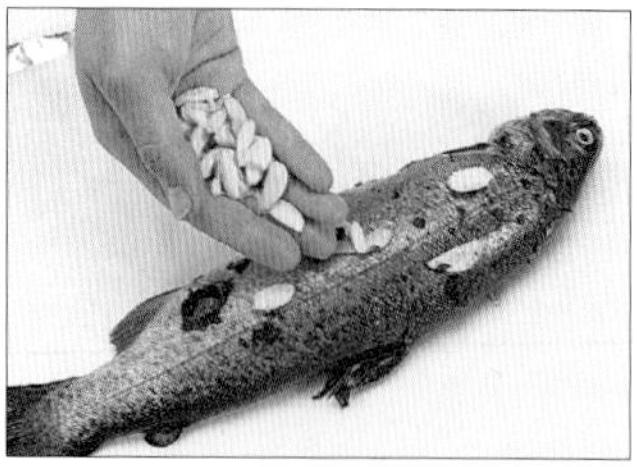

7 Place one of the trout on one of the pieces of paper, moisten with the marinade, then sprinkle about a quarter of the almonds over the top.

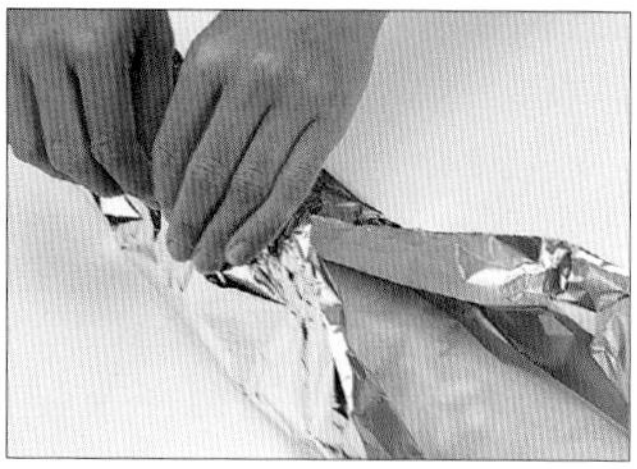

8 Bring up the sides of the paper and fold over to seal in the fish, then fold the foil over to make a neat parcel. Make three more parcels in the same way, then place them side by side in a large roasting tin.

9 Transfer the parcels to the oven and bake for 25 minutes. Put each parcel on an individual plate, or open them in the kitchen and serve unwrapped if you prefer. This dish goes well with new potatoes and cooked fresh vegetables.

Shellfish

Surrounded on all sides by the sea, it is not surprising that Mexico and the Caribbean produce so many wonderful dishes based on shellfish, many barbecued or grilled with light flavouring and spices. Whether served as a snack, main meal or in a salad, freshness is the vital attribute.

CHILEAN SEAFOOD PLATTER

FRESHNESS IS IMPORTANT FOR THIS RAW SEAFOOD APPETIZER, SO CHILEAN COOKS USE THE PRIME CATCH OF THE DAY, INCLUDING EXOTIC SHELLFISH. YOU CAN USE WHATEVER IS AVAILABLE LOCALLY.

SERVES SIX

INGREDIENTS
- 450g/1lb raw king prawns (jumbo shrimp)
- 12 clams
- 12 mussels
- 6 scallops
- 6 oysters
- 12 razor clams
- lime wedges, to serve

For the salsa
- 60ml/4 tbsp chopped fresh coriander (cilantro)
- 15ml/1 tbsp chopped fresh flat leaf parsley
- 2 shallots, finely chopped
- 1 fresh green chilli, seeded and finely chopped
- juice of 2 limes
- 30ml/2 tbsp olive oil
- salt

1 Combine the salsa ingredients in a bowl and season to taste. Make the salsa a few hours in advance, if possible, so that the delicate flavours have time to develop.

2 Bring a pan of salted water to the boil. Plunge the prawns into the water and remove from the pan as soon as they turn pink. Refresh the prawns in a bowl of cold water, drain and set aside.

COOK'S TIP
If you prefer to cook the shellfish, it could be steamed quickly and then refreshed in cold water before being served. Do not overcook the shellfish, or it will become tough.

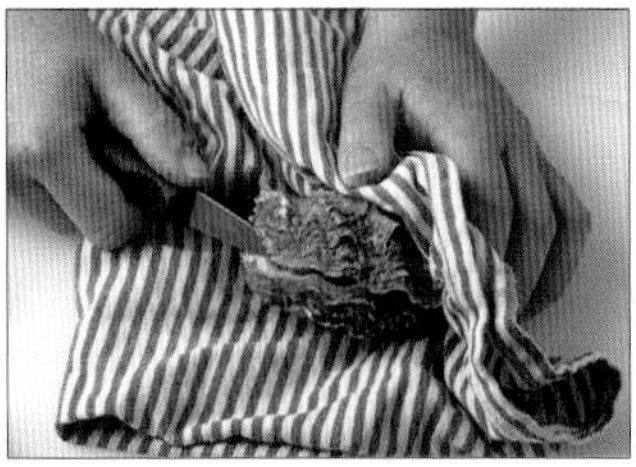

3 Use an oyster knife to open the raw shellfish. Push the point of the knife into the hinge, then twist to loosen. Push the knife along the edge of the whole shell so it can be opened.

4 Use the knife to loosen the fish from their shells and carefully remove the black "string" that runs along the edge of the scallop.

5 Arrange the seafood, in the shells, on a platter and serve with the fresh coriander and chilli salsa, and lime wedges, if you like. Eat immediately.

PRAWN AND SCALLOP CEVICHE

THIS FAMOUS DISH IS PARTICULARLY POPULAR ALONG MEXICO'S WESTERN SEABOARD, IN PLACES SUCH AS ACAPULCO. IT CONSISTS OF VERY FRESH RAW FISH, "COOKED" BY THE ACTION OF LIME JUICE.

SERVES SIX

INGREDIENTS

200g/7oz raw peeled prawns (shrimp)
200g/7oz shelled scallops
200g/7oz squid, cleaned and cut into serving pieces
7 limes
3 tomatoes
1 small onion
1 ripe avocado
20ml/4 tbsp chopped fresh oregano, or 10ml/2 tsp dried
5ml/1 tsp salt
ground black pepper
fresh oregano sprigs, to garnish
crusty bread and lime wedges, to serve (optional)

1 Spread out the prawns, scallops and squid in a non-metallic bowl. Squeeze six of the limes and pour the juice over the mixed seafood to cover it. Cover the dish with clear film (plastic wrap) and set aside for 8 hours or overnight.

2 Drain the seafood in a colander to remove the excess lime juice, then pat it dry with kitchen paper. Place the prawns, scallops and squid in a bowl.

3 Cut the tomatoes in half, squeeze out the seeds, then dice the flesh. Cut the onion in half, then slice it thinly. Cut the avocado in half lengthways, remove the stone and peel, then cut the flesh into 1cm/½in dice.

4 Add the tomatoes, onion and avocado to the seafood with the oregano and seasoning. Squeeze the remaining lime and pour over the juice. Garnish with oregano and serve, with crusty bread and lime wedges, if you like.

PRAWNS WITH ALMOND SAUCE

GROUND ALMONDS ADD AN INTERESTING TEXTURE TO THE CREAMY, PIQUANT SAUCE THAT ACCOMPANIES THIS MEXICAN DISH.

SERVES SIX

INGREDIENTS
- 1 ancho or similar dried chilli
- 30ml/2 tbsp vegetable oil
- 1 onion, chopped
- 3 garlic cloves, roughly chopped
- 8 tomatoes
- 5ml/1 tsp ground cumin
- 120ml/4fl oz/½ cup chicken stock
- 130g/4½ oz/generous 1 cup ground almonds
- 175ml/6fl oz/¾ cup crème fraîche
- ½ lime
- 900g/2lb cooked peeled prawns (shrimp)
- salt
- fresh coriander (cilantro) and spring onion (scallion) strips, to garnish
- cooked rice and tortillas, to serve

1 Place the dried chilli in a heatproof bowl and pour over boiling water to cover. Leave to soak for 30 minutes until softened. Drain, remove the stalk, then slit the chilli and scrape out the seeds with a small sharp knife. Chop the flesh roughly and set it aside.

2 Heat the oil in a frying pan and fry the onion and garlic until soft.

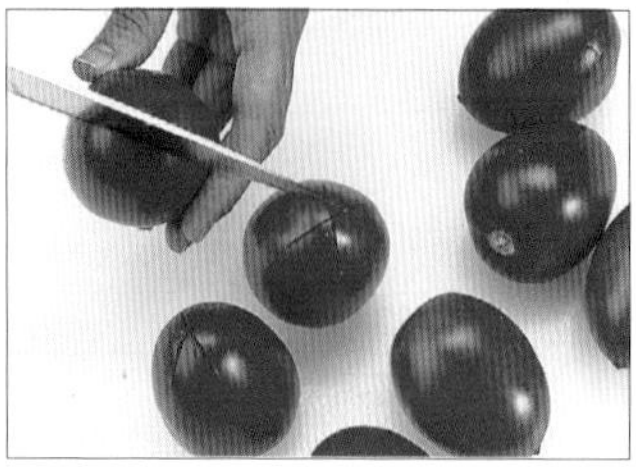

3 Cut a cross in the base of each tomato. Place them in a heatproof bowl and pour over boiling water to cover. After 3 minutes, lift the tomatoes out on a slotted spoon and plunge them into a bowl of cold water. Drain. The skins will have begun to peel back.

4 Skin the tomatoes completely, then cut them in half and scoop out the seeds. Chop the flesh into 1cm/½in cubes and add it to the onion mixture, with the chopped chilli. Stir in the ground cumin and cook for 10 minutes, stirring occasionally.

5 Tip the mixture into a food processor or blender. Add the stock and process on high speed until smooth.

6 Pour the mixture into a large pan, add the ground almonds and stir over a low heat for 2–3 minutes. Stir in the crème fraîche until is has been incorporated completely.

7 Squeeze the juice from the lime and stir it into the sauce. Season with salt to taste, then increase the heat and bring the sauce to simmering point.

8 Add the prawns and heat for 2–3 minutes, depending on size, until warmed through. Serve on a bed of rice and offer warm tortillas separately.

VARIATIONS

Try this sauce with other types of fish, too. Adding just a few prawns (shrimp) and serving it over steamed sole would make a very luxurious dish. The sauce is also very good with chicken.

PRAWNS IN GARLIC BUTTER

THIS QUICK AND EASY MEXICAN DISH IS PERFECT FOR SERVING TO FRIENDS WHO DON'T MIND GETTING THEIR HANDS STICKY. PROVIDE A PLATE FOR THE SHELLS AND OFFER WARM TORTILLAS FOR MOPPING UP THE DELECTABLE JUICES.

SERVES SIX

INGREDIENTS

- 900g/2lb raw tiger prawns (shrimp), in their shells, thawed if frozen
- 115g/4oz/½ cup butter
- 15ml/1 tbsp vegetable oil
- 6 garlic cloves, crushed
- grated rind and juice of 2 limes
- small bunch of fresh coriander (cilantro), chopped
- warm tortillas, to serve
- lemon slices, for the finger bowls

1 Rinse the prawns in a colander, remove their heads and leave them to drain. Heat the butter and oil in a large frying pan, add the garlic and fry over a low heat for 2–3 minutes.

2 Add the lime rind and juice. Cook, stirring constantly, for 1 minute more.

COOK'S TIP

Cook the prawns in a large frying pan or cast-iron flameproof dish that can be taken directly to the table, so that they retain their heat until they are served.

3 Add the prawns and cook them for 2–3 minutes until they turn pink. Remove from the heat, sprinkle with coriander and serve with the warm tortillas. Give each guest a finger bowl filled with water and a slice of lemon, for cleaning their fingers after shelling the prawns, and provide paper napkins.

PRAWN SALAD

IN MEXICO, THIS SALAD WOULD FORM THE FISH COURSE IN A FORMAL MEAL, BUT IT IS SO GOOD THAT YOU'LL WANT TO SERVE IT ON ALL SORTS OF OCCASIONS. IT IS PERFECT FOR A BUFFET LUNCH.

SERVES FOUR

INGREDIENTS

- 450g/1lb cooked peeled prawns (shrimp)
- juice of 1 lime
- 3 tomatoes
- 1 ripe but firm avocado
- 30ml/2 tbsp hot chilli sauce
- 5ml/1 tsp sugar
- 150ml/¼ pint/⅔ cup soured cream
- 2 Little Gem (Bibb) lettuces
- salt and ground black pepper
- fresh basil leaves and strips of green (bell) pepper to garnish

1 Put the prawns in a large bowl, add the lime juice and salt and pepper. Toss lightly, then leave to marinate.

2 Cut a cross in the base of each tomato. Place them in a heatproof bowl and pour over boiling water to cover.

3 After 3 minutes, lift the tomatoes out on a slotted spoon and plunge them into a bowl of cold water. Drain. The skins will have begun to peel back easily from the crosses.

4 Skin the tomatoes completely, then cut them in half and squeeze out the seeds. Chop the flesh into 1cm/½in cubes and add it to the prawns.

5 Cut the avocado in half, remove the skin and seed, then slice the flesh into 1cm/½in chunks. Add it to the prawn and tomato mixture.

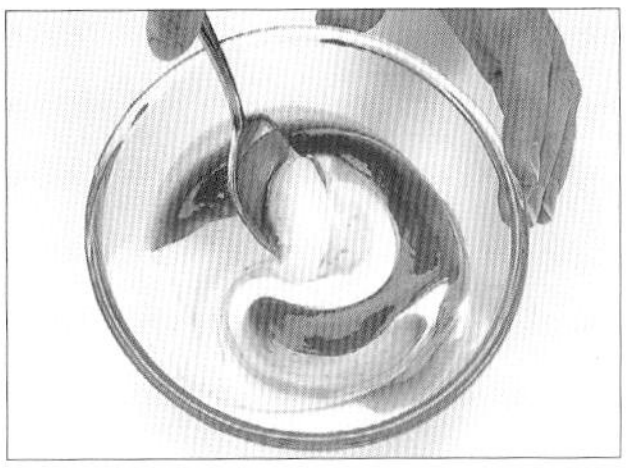

6 Mix the hot chilli sauce, sugar and soured cream in a bowl. Fold into the prawn mixture. Line a bowl with lettuce leaves, then top with the prawn mixture. Cover and chill for at least 1 hour, then garnish with fresh basil and strips of green pepper. Crusty bread makes a perfect accompaniment.

Crab with Green Rice

This is a popular dish in the western coastal areas of Mexico. Prawns (shrimp) can be used instead of crab meat and the dish also works well with warm corn tortillas.

SERVES FOUR

INGREDIENTS
- 225g/8oz/generous 1 cup long grain white rice
- 500g/1¼lb/3⅓ cups drained canned tomatillos
- bunch of fresh coriander (cilantro)
- 1 onion, roughly chopped
- 3 poblano or other fresh green chillies, seeded and chopped
- 3 garlic cloves
- 45ml/3 tbsp olive oil
- 500g/1¼lb crab meat
- 300ml/½ pint/1¼ cups fish stock
- 60ml/4 tbsp dry white wine
- salt
- spring onions (scallions), to garnish

1 Put the rice in a heatproof bowl, pour over boiling water to cover and leave to stand for 20 minutes. Drain thoroughly.

2 Put the tomatillos in a food processor or blender and process until smooth. Chop half the coriander and add to the tomatillo purée, with the onion, chillies and garlic. Process again until smooth.

3 Heat the oil in a large pan. Add the rice and fry over a moderate heat for 5 minutes, until all the oil has been absorbed. Stir occasionally to prevent the rice from sticking.

4 Stir in the tomatillo mixture, with the crab meat, stock and wine. Cover and cook over a low heat for about 20 minutes or until all the liquid has been absorbed. Stir occasionally and add a little more liquid if the rice starts to stick to the pan. Add salt as required, then spoon into a dish and garnish with the remaining coriander and sliced spring onions. Green salad and lime wedges make good accompaniments.

SCALLOPS WITH GARLIC AND CORIANDER

SHELLFISH IS OFTEN COOKED VERY SIMPLY IN MEXICO, HOT CHILLI SAUCE AND LIME BEING POPULAR INGREDIENTS IN MANY FISH RECIPES.

SERVES FOUR

INGREDIENTS

- 20 scallops
- 2 courgettes (zucchini)
- 75g/3oz/6 tbsp butter
- 15ml/1 tbsp vegetable oil
- 4 garlic cloves, chopped
- 30ml/2 tbsp hot chilli sauce
- juice of 1 lime
- small bunch of fresh coriander (cilantro), finely chopped

COOK'S TIP

Oil can withstand higher temperatures than butter, but butter gives fried food added flavour. Using a mixture, as here, provides the perfect compromise.

1 If you have bought scallops in their shells, open them. Hold a scallop shell in the palm of your hand, with the flat side uppermost. Insert the blade of a knife close to the hinge that joins the shells and prise them apart. Run the blade of the knife across the inside of the flat shell to cut away the scallop. Only the white adductor muscle and the orange coral are eaten, so pull away and discard all other parts. Rinse the scallops under cold running water.

2 Cut the courgettes in half, then into four pieces. Melt the butter in the oil in a large frying pan. Add the courgettes and fry until soft. Remove from the pan. Add the garlic and fry until golden. Stir in the hot chilli sauce.

3 Add the scallops to the sauce. Cook, stirring constantly, for 1–2 minutes only. Stir in the lime juice, chopped coriander and courgette pieces. Serve immediately on warmed plates.

King Prawns in a Coconut and Nut Cream

For this Brazilian recipe, coconut milk is used to make VATAPÁ, *a luxurious sauce thickened with cashews, peanuts and breadcrumbs, then used to cook prawns.*

4 Grind the peanuts and cashew nuts in a food processor until they become a fine powder. Stir into the pan and cook for about 1 minute more.

SERVES SIX

INGREDIENTS

- 130g/4½oz/2¼ cups fresh white breadcrumbs
- 105ml/7 tbsp coconut milk
- 30 raw king prawns (jumbo shrimp), about 900g/2lb
- 400ml/14fl oz/1⅔ cups fish stock
- 2 large tomatoes, roughly chopped
- 1 onion, quartered
- 2 fresh red chillies, seeded and roughly chopped
- 130g/4½oz dried shrimps
- 45ml/3 tbsp palm oil
- 2 garlic cloves, crushed
- 25g/1oz fresh root ginger, grated
- 75g/3oz/¾ cup roasted peanuts
- 50g/2oz/½ cup cashew nuts
- 60ml/4 tbsp coconut cream
- juice of 1 lime
- salt and ground black pepper
- chopped fresh coriander (cilantro) and hot chilli oil, to serve

1 Place the breadcrumbs in a bowl and stir in the coconut milk. Leave to soak for at least 30 minutes. Purée, in a blender or food processor, then scrape into a bowl and set aside.

2 Meanwhile, peel the fresh prawns and set them aside in a cool place. Place the shells in a pan and add the fish stock and tomatoes. Bring to the boil, then simmer over a low heat for 30 minutes. Strain into a bowl, pressing the prawn shells against the sides of the sieve with a wooden spoon to extract as much flavour as possible. Reserve the prawn stock but discard the shells.

3 Put the onion, chillies and dried shrimps in a blender or food processor and blend to a purée. Scrape into a large pan and stir in the palm oil. Cook over a very low heat for 5 minutes. Add the garlic and ginger and cook for a further 2 minutes.

5 Stir in the breadcrumb purée and prawn stock and bring to the boil. Reduce the heat and continue to cook, stirring constantly, for 6–8 minutes, until thick and smooth.

6 Add the coconut cream, lime juice and prawns. Stir over the heat for 3 minutes until the prawns are cooked through and the *vatapá* resembles a thin porridge. If necessary, stir in a little water. Season with salt and black pepper.

7 Serve immediately, adding a scattering of chopped coriander and a couple of drops of chilli oil to each portion. Cooked white rice makes a good accompaniment.

VARIATIONS

- Instead of prawns, try using white fish.
- For chicken *vatapá*, replace the prawns with chicken pieces, seasoned and pan-fried in a little olive oil until tender. Use chicken stock rather than fish stock.

STUFFED CRAB

SERVE THIS SIMPLE DISH AS AN APPETIZER FOR A DINNER PARTY. A TRADITIONAL BRAZILIAN RECIPE, IT IS USUALLY SERVED EITHER IN CRAB SHELLS OR SMALL EARTHENWARE DISHES.

SERVES SIX

INGREDIENTS

- 400g/14oz crab meat
- juice of 1 lime
- 50g/2oz/1 cup fresh breadcrumbs
- 105ml/7 tbsp full-fat (whole) milk
- 25g/1oz/2 tbsp butter
- 1 onion, finely chopped
- 2 garlic cloves, crushed
- 2 tomatoes, finely chopped
- 15ml/1 tbsp chopped fresh flat leaf parsley
- 2 egg yolks, plus extra for glazing
- 15ml/1 tbsp dried breadcrumbs
- 15ml/1 tbsp grated Parmesan cheese
- salt
- lemon wedges, to serve

1 Place the crab meat in a large glass bowl and squeeze over the lime juice. Marinate for about 20 minutes. Meanwhile, put the breadcrumbs in a separate bowl with the milk and leave to soak for 10 minutes.

2 Melt the butter in a pan over a low heat. Add the chopped onion and cook gently for 10 minutes until softened. Stir in the crushed garlic and cook for 1 minute more. Drain the crab meat and squeeze out all of the excess liquid from the breadcrumbs.

COOK'S TIP

The crab mixture can be prepared in advance. Spoon it into the individual crab shells or bowls and cover. Keep refrigerated until needed, then add the topping and bake in a preheated oven at 200°C/400°F/Gas 6 for 10–15 minutes.

3 Add the crab meat, tomatoes and breadcrumbs to the pan and stir well to combine. Return to a medium heat and cook, stirring, for 4–5 minutes. Stir in the chopped parsley and season to taste with salt and ground pepper – the mixture should actually taste over-seasoned at this stage.

4 Lower the heat and add the egg yolks, stirring vigorously for 1 minute. Do not allow the mixture to boil.

5 Preheat the grill (broiler). Transfer the mixture to six empty crab shells, or small ovenproof dishes and brush with beaten egg yolk. Combine the dried breadcrumbs and Parmesan and sprinkle a thin coating over the crab meat. Grill (broil) for 3–4 minutes, until golden. Serve with the lemon wedges.

CRAB AND CORN GUMBO

A typically Creole dish, this is thickened with a classic nut-brown roux. It is popular on the Caribbean islands of Martinique and St Barts.

SERVES FOUR

INGREDIENTS
- 25g/1oz/2 tbsp butter or margarine
- 25g/1oz/¼ cup plain (all-purpose) flour
- 15ml/1 tbsp vegetable oil
- 1 onion, finely chopped
- 115g/4oz okra, trimmed and chopped
- 2 garlic cloves, crushed
- 15ml/1 tbsp finely chopped celery
- 600ml/1 pint/2½ cups fish stock
- 150ml/¼ pint/⅔ cup sherry
- 15ml/1 tbsp tomato ketchup
- 2.5ml/½ tsp dried oregano
- 1.5ml/¼ tsp ground mixed spice (pumpkin pie spice)
- 10ml/2 tsp Worcestershire sauce
- dash of hot pepper sauce
- 2 fresh corn cobs, sliced
- 450g/1lb crab claws
- fresh coriander (cilantro), to garnish

1 Melt the butter or margarine in a large heavy pan over a low heat. Add the flour and stir together to make a roux.

2 Cook for about 10 minutes, stirring constantly to prevent the mixture from burning. The roux will turn golden brown and then darken. As soon as it becomes a rich nut brown, turn the roux on to a plate, scraping it all out of the pan, and set aside.

3 Heat the oil in the same pan over a medium heat, add the chopped onion, the okra, garlic and celery and stir well. Cook for about 2–3 minutes, then add the fish stock, sherry, tomato ketchup, dried oregano, mixed spice, Worcestershire sauce and a dash of hot pepper sauce.

4 Bring to the boil, then lower the heat and simmer gently for about 10 minutes or until all the vegetables are tender. Add the roux, stirring it thoroughly into the sauce, and cook for about 3–4 minutes, until thickened.

5 Add the corn cobs and crab claws and continue to simmer gently over a low heat for about 10 minutes, until both are cooked through.

6 Spoon on to warmed serving plates and garnish with a few sprigs of fresh coriander. Serve immediately.

COOK'S TIP

The roux must not be allowed to burn. Stir it constantly over a low heat. If dark specks appear in the roux, it must be discarded and a fresh roux made.

PRAWN AND POTATO OMELETTE

MORE LIKE A SPANISH TORTILLA THAN A FRENCH OMELETTE, THIS DISH MAKES A DELICIOUS LUNCH WHEN SERVED WITH A FRESH LEAFY GREEN SALAD. THE SWEET PRAWNS ARE COOKED GENTLY INSIDE THE OMELETTE, STAYING TENDER AND SUCCULENT.

SERVES SIX

INGREDIENTS

- 200g/7oz potatoes, peeled and diced
- 30ml/2 tbsp olive oil
- 1 onion, finely sliced
- 2.5ml/½ tsp paprika
- 2 large tomatoes, peeled, seeded and chopped
- 200g/7oz peeled raw prawns (shrimp)
- 6 eggs
- 2.5ml/½ tsp baking powder
- salt

1 Cook the potatoes in a pan of salted boiling water for about 10 minutes or until tender.

2 Meanwhile, pour the oil into a 23cm/9in frying pan which can safely be used under the grill (broiler). Place over a medium heat. Add the onion slices and stir well to coat evenly in the oil. Cook for 5 minutes until the onions begin to soften. Sprinkle over the paprika and cook for 1 minute more.

3 Stir in the tomatoes. Drain the cooked potatoes thoroughly and add them to the pan. Stir gently to mix. Increase the heat and cook for 10 minutes, or until the mixture has thickened and the potatoes have absorbed the flavour of the tomatoes. Remove from the heat and stir in the prawns.

4 Preheat the grill. Beat the eggs, stir in the baking powder and salt. Pour into the pan and mix thoroughly. Cover and cook for 8–10 minutes until the omelette has almost set, then finish under the grill.

Cuban Seafood Rice

This is the perfect dish for a large gathering. The more people you make it for, the more types of seafood you can add, and the tastier it will become.

SERVES EIGHT

INGREDIENTS

- 450g/1lb raw tiger prawns (shrimp)
- 1 litre/1¾ pints/4 cups fish stock
- 450g/1lb squid
- 16 clams
- 16 mussels
- 60ml/4 tbsp olive oil
- 1 onion, finely chopped
- 1 fresh red chilli, seeded and finely chopped
- 2 garlic cloves, crushed
- 350g/12oz/1⅔ cups long grain rice
- 45ml/3 tbsp chopped fresh coriander (cilantro)
- juice of 2 limes
- salt and ground black pepper

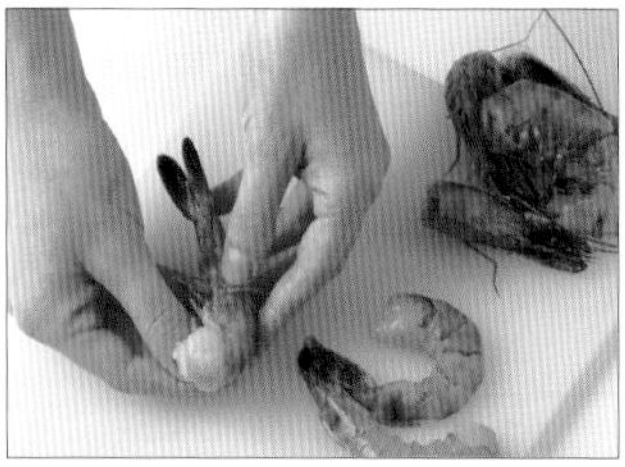

1 Peel the prawns and set them aside. Place the shells in a pan and add the fish stock. Bring to the boil, then simmer for 15 minutes. Strain into a bowl, discarding the shells.

2 Clean the squid under cold running water. Pull the tentacles away from the body. The squid's entrails will come out easily. Remove the clear piece of cartilage from inside the body cavity and discard it. Wash the body thoroughly.

3 Pull away the purplish-grey membrane that covers the body. Now cut between the tentacles and head, discarding the head and entrails. Leave the tentacles whole but discard the hard beak in the middle. Cut the body into thin rounds.

4 Scrub the clams and mussels under cold running water. Pull away the "beard" from the mussels and discard any open shells that fail to close when tapped. Place the shellfish in a bowl, cover with a wet piece of kitchen paper and put in the refrigerator until needed.

COOK'S TIP

Live shellfish are best kept in a cool moist environment. Place them in a bowl covered with wet kitchen paper and store them in the refrigerator.

5 Pour half the olive oil into a pan with a tight fitting lid. Place over a high heat. When the oil is very hot, add the squid and season well. Stir-fry for 2–3 minutes, until the squid curls and begins to brown. Remove the pieces from the pan with a slotted spoon and set aside.

6 Add the prawns to the pan and cook for 2 minutes. The moment they turn pink, remove them from the heat.

7 Pour the remaining oil into the pan. Stir in the onion and sauté over a low heat for 5 minutes. Add the chilli and garlic and cook for 2 minutes. Tip in the rice, and cook, stirring, for 1 minute, until lightly toasted but not coloured.

8 Add the prawn stock and bring to the boil. Cover, lower the heat and simmer, for 15–18 minutes.

9 Add the clams and mussels and cover the pan. Cook for 3–4 minutes, until their shells open. Remove from the heat and discard any that have remained closed. Stir the cooked squid, prawns, coriander and lime juice into the rice. Season and serve immediately.

Pumpkin and Prawns with Dried Shrimp

This Caribbean recipe is an excellent way of making a small amount of seafood go a long way. The dried shrimps and cooked prawns are delicious with the spiced pumpkin.

SERVES FOUR

INGREDIENTS

- 50g/2oz/⅓ cup dried shrimps
- 30ml/2 tbsp vegetable oil
- 25g/1oz/2 tbsp butter or margarine
- 1 red onion, chopped
- 800g/1¾lb pumpkin, peeled and chopped
- 225g/8oz peeled cooked prawns (shrimp)
- 2.5ml/½ tsp ground cinnamon
- 2.5ml/½ tsp five-spice powder
- 2 garlic cloves, chopped
- 2 tomatoes, chopped
- chopped fresh parsley and lime wedges, to garnish

1 Rinse the dried shrimps under cold water and put them in a bowl. Pour in enough hot water to cover, then leave them to soak for about 35 minutes.

2 Meanwhile, heat the oil and butter or margarine in a large frying pan. Add the onion and sauté over a medium heat for 5 minutes, until soft.

3 Add the pumpkin and cook for about 5–6 minutes, until it starts to soften. Tip in the peeled prawns and the dried shrimps with their soaking water. Stir in the cinnamon, five-spice powder and chopped garlic.

4 Add the tomatoes and cook over a gentle heat, stirring occasionally, until the pumpkin is soft.

5 Spoon on to a warmed serving plate and serve hot, garnished with the chopped parsley and lime wedges.

SPICY PRAWNS WITH CORNMEAL

THESE CRISPY FRIED PRAWNS WITH A CORNMEAL COATING AND A CHEESE TOPPING ARE TRULY DELICIOUS WHEN SERVED WITH A SPICY TOMATO SALSA AND LIME WEDGES TO EASE THE HEAT.

SERVES FOUR

INGREDIENTS
- 115g/4oz/¾ cup cornmeal
- 5–10ml/1–2 tsp cayenne pepper
- 2.5ml/½ tsp ground cumin
- 5ml/1 tsp salt
- 30ml/2 tbsp chopped fresh coriander (cilantro)
- 900g/2lb large raw prawns (shrimp), peeled and deveined
- flour, for dredging
- ¼ cup vegetable oil
- 115g/4oz/1 cup grated Cheddar cheese

To serve
- lime wedges
- salsa

1 Preheat the grill (broiler) to hot. In a large mixing bowl, combine the cornmeal, cayenne, cumin, salt and chopped coriander.

2 Coat the prawns lightly in flour, then dip them in water and roll them in the cornmeal mixture to coat.

3 Heat the oil in a non-stick frying pan. When hot, add the prawns, in several batches if necessary. Cook them until they are opaque throughout, for about 2–3 minutes on each side. Drain on kitchen paper.

4 Place the prawns in a large ovenproof dish, or in individual dishes. Sprinkle the cheese evenly over the top. Grill (broil) about 8cm/3in from the heat until the cheese melts and is lightly browned, for about 2–3 minutes.

5 Serve immediately, with lime wedges and tomato salsa.

VARIATIONS

Chopped fresh flat leaf parsley may be substituted for coriander (cilantro). Grated Monterey Jack cheese may be used in place of Cheddar.

Fisherman's Stew

This is just the sort of one-pot meal you can imagine Mexican fishermen cooking for themselves, using freshly caught shellfish and a few vegetables.

SERVES SIX

INGREDIENTS

- 500g/1¼lb mussels
- 3 onions
- 2 garlic cloves, sliced
- 300ml/½ pint/1¼ cups fish stock
- 12 scallops
- 450g/1lb cod fillet
- 30ml/2 tbsp olive oil
- 1 large potato, about 200g/7oz
- few sprigs of fresh thyme, chopped
- 1 red and 1 green (bell) pepper
- 120ml/4fl oz/½ cup dry white wine
- 250ml/8fl oz/1 cup crème fraîche
- 275g/10oz raw peeled prawns (shrimp)
- 75g/3oz/¾ cup grated mature Cheddar cheese
- salt and ground black pepper
- fresh thyme sprigs, to garnish

1 Clean the mussel shells, removing any beards. Discard any that stay open when tapped. Rinse in cold water.

2 Pour water to a depth of 2.5cm/1in into a large, deep frying pan. Chop one onion and add it to the pan, with the sliced garlic. Bring to the boil, then add the mussels and cover the pan tightly.

3 Cook the mussels for 5–6 minutes, shaking the pan occasionally. Remove them as they open, discarding any that remain shut. Remove the mussels from their shells and set them aside.

4 Strain the cooking liquid through a sieve lined with muslin (cheesecloth) to remove any remaining sand. Make up the liquid with fish stock to 300ml/½ pint/1¼ cups.

5 If you have bought scallops in their shells, open them: hold a scallop shell in the palm of your hand, with the flat side uppermost. Insert the blade of a knife close to the hinge that joins the shells and prise apart. Run the blade of the knife across the inside of the flat shell to cut away the scallop. Only the white adductor muscle and the orange coral are eaten, so pull away and discard all other parts. Rinse the scallops under cold running water to remove any grit or sand, then put them in a bowl and set them aside.

6 Cut the cod into large cubes and put it in a bowl. Season with salt and pepper and set aside.

7 Cut the remaining onions into small wedges. Heat the olive oil in a large pan and fry the onion wedges for 2–3 minutes. Slice the potato about 1cm/½in thick and add to the pan, with the fresh chopped thyme. Cover and cook for about 15 minutes, until the potato has softened.

8 Core the peppers, remove the cores and seeds, then dice the flesh. Add to the onion and potato mixture and cook for a few minutes. Stir in the mixed mussel and fish stock, with the wine and crème fraîche.

9 Bring to just below boiling point, then add the cod and scallops. Lower the heat and simmer for 5 minutes, then add the prawns. Simmer for a further 3–4 minutes more, until all the seafood is cooked. Stir in the mussels and warm through for 1–2 minutes. Season the sauce if necessary. Spoon into bowls, garnish with the thyme sprigs and sprinkle with the cheese. Crusty bread would be an ideal accompaniment.

MEAT

The gaucho nations of Argentina, Paraguay and Uruguay are real meat-eaters, and large cuts of beef, lamb and pork are cooked whole at their famous barbecues. Richly flavoured stews and pot roasts are also popular, made with herbs, spices and fruits, or as a combination of mixed meats, as in the Brazilian national dish Feijoada.

THE GAUCHO BARBECUE

THERE IS NO BETTER WAY OF ENJOYING THE PRESTIGIOUS PAMPAS BEEF THAN WITH A TRADITIONAL BARBECUE. THE MEAT IS COOKED SIMPLY, WITH NO NEED FOR RUBS OR MARINADES, THEN ENJOYED WITH A DELICIOUS SELECTION OF SALADS AND SALSAS.

SERVES SIX

INGREDIENTS

- 50g/2oz/¼ cup coarse sea salt
- 200ml/7fl oz/ scant 1 cup warm water
- 6 pork sausages
- 1kg/2¼lb beef short ribs
- 1kg/2¼lb rump (round) steak, in one piece
- salads, salsas and breads, to serve

COOK'S TIP

Regularly basting the meat in salted water keeps it moist and succulent.

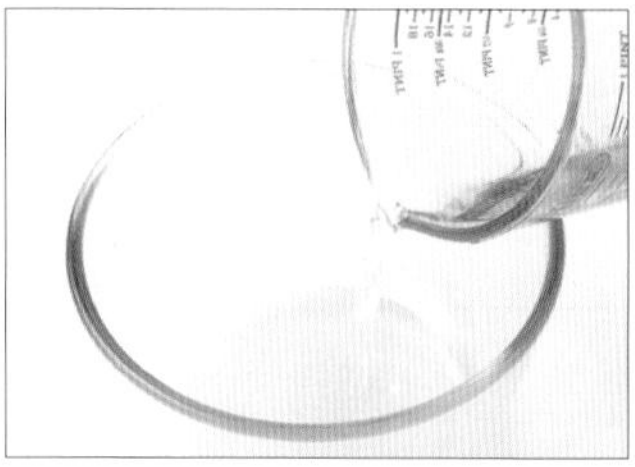

1 Dissolve the sea salt in the warm water in a bowl. Leave to cool.

2 Prepare the barbecue. If you are using a charcoal grill, light the coals about 40 minutes before you want to start cooking. Wait until the coals are no longer red but are covered in white ash. Occasionally add coals to the barbecue to maintain this temperature.

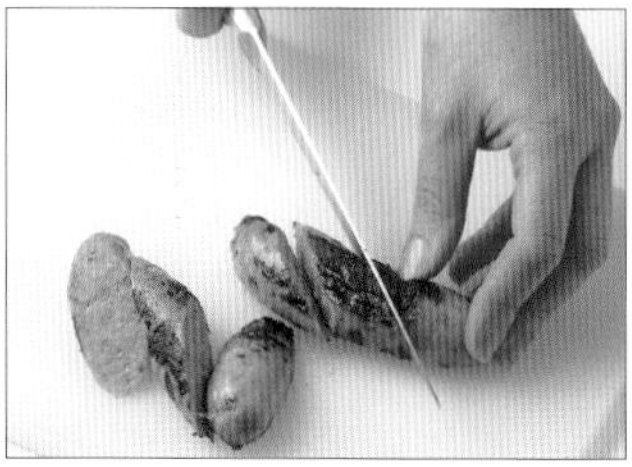

3 Start by cooking the sausages, which should take 15–20 minutes depending on the size. Once cooked on all sides, slice the sausages thickly and arrange on a plate. Let guests help themselves while you cook the remaining meats.

4 The short ribs should be placed bony side down on the grill. Cook for 15 minutes, turn, brush the cooked side of each rib with brine and grill for a further 25–30 minutes. Slice and transfer to a plate for guests to help themselves.

5 Place the whole rump steak on the grill and cook for 5 minutes, then turn over and baste the browned side with brine. Continue turning and basting in this way for 20–25 minutes in total, until the meat is cooked to your liking. Allow the meat to rest for 5 minutes, then slice thinly and serve with salads, salsa and bread.

VARIATION

A selection of meat cuts can be used, from sirloin to flank steak or chuck steak. Sweetbreads, skewered chicken hearts and kidneys are popular additions to the Gaucho barbecue, as well as chicken, lamb and pork. The star of the show, however, will always be the beef.

BEEF STUFFED WITH EGGS AND SPINACH

THIS TRADITIONAL ARGENTINIAN DISH MAKES A GREAT LUNCH WHEN SERVED COLD WITH A SALAD, BUT CAN ALSO BE SERVED HOT FOR DINNER WITH SOME BOILED POTATOES. ITS NAME, MATAMBRE *("KILL HUNGER") IS SOMEWHAT UNFAIR; FOR ALTHOUGH FILLING, IT IS NOT A HEAVY DISH.*

SERVES SIX

INGREDIENTS

- 60ml/4 tbsp olive oil
- 1 small carrot, finely chopped
- 1 celery stick, finely chopped
- 1 onion, finely chopped
- 2 eggs
- 675g/1½ lb flank steak
- 250g/9oz spinach, trimmed
- 2.5ml/½ tsp cayenne pepper
- 1.5 litres/2½ pints/6¼ cups beef stock
- salt and ground black pepper
- boiled potatoes or salad, to serve

1 Heat half the olive oil in a frying pan over a medium heat. Add the carrot, celery and onion and sauté for 5 minutes, until soft and beginning to colour.

2 Meanwhile, hard-boil the eggs. Place them in a pan with cold water to cover. Bring to the boil, then lower the heat to a simmer. Cook for 10 minutes then lift out and cool in a bowl of cold water. Shell the eggs, then slice them thinly.

3 Season the steak generously with salt and ground black pepper. Spread the cooked onion mixture over the beef, leaving a 1cm/½in border round the edge. Arrange the spinach over the onion, then top with the egg. Season with extra salt and cayenne pepper.

COOK'S TIP

Flank steak is ideal for slow cooking, becoming so tender you can almost cut it with a fork. If you cannot get flank, skirt steak is very similar.

4 Roll the meat up tightly, being careful not to lose any of the stuffing. Tie with string four or five times along the length of the roll.

5 Heat the remaining oil in a pan. Add the beef roll to the pan and cook on all sides until golden brown. Pour in the stock, then bring to the boil. Lower the heat, cover and simmer gently for 1½–2 hours, until very tender.

6 Remove the beef from the stock and slice it as thinly as possible. Serve hot with boiled potatoes or as part of a buffet or picnic.

CARBONADA CRIOLLA

MEAT AND FRUIT ARE OFTEN COMBINED IN ARGENTINIAN COOKING, AND THIS COLOURFUL STEW IS A PRIME EXAMPLE. THE TENDER BEEF COOKED IN RED WINE BALANCES THE SWEETNESS OF THE PEACHES, POTATOES AND PUMPKIN. MAKE SURE THE PUMPKIN FITS IN YOUR OVEN.

SERVES EIGHT

INGREDIENTS

- 1 large pumpkin, about 5kg/11lb
- 60ml/4 tbsp olive oil
- 1kg/2¼lb braising steak, cut into 2.5cm/1in cubes
- 1 large onion, finely chopped
- 3 fresh red chillies, seeded and chopped
- 2 garlic cloves, crushed
- 1 large tomato, roughly chopped
- 2 fresh bay leaves
- 600ml/1 pint/2½ cups beef stock
- 350ml/12fl oz/1½ cups red wine
- 500g/1¼lb potatoes, peeled and cut into 2cm/¾in cubes
- 500g/1¼lb sweet potatoes, peeled and cut into 2cm/¾in cubes
- 1 corn cob, cut widthways into 6 slices
- 3 peaches, peeled, stoned (pitted) and cut into thick wedges
- salt and ground black pepper

1 Wash the outside of the pumpkin. Using a sharp knife, carefully cut a slice off the top 6cm/2½in from the stem, to make a lid. Using a spoon, scoop out the seeds and stringy fibres and discard. Scoop out some of the flesh, leaving a shell about 2cm/¾in thick inside of the pumpkin. Cut the flesh you have removed into 1cm/½in pieces.

COOK'S TIP

Calabaza is a large West Indian pumpkin with a greenish orange skin that is often used for *carbonada criolla*. Look for it in Caribbean markets.

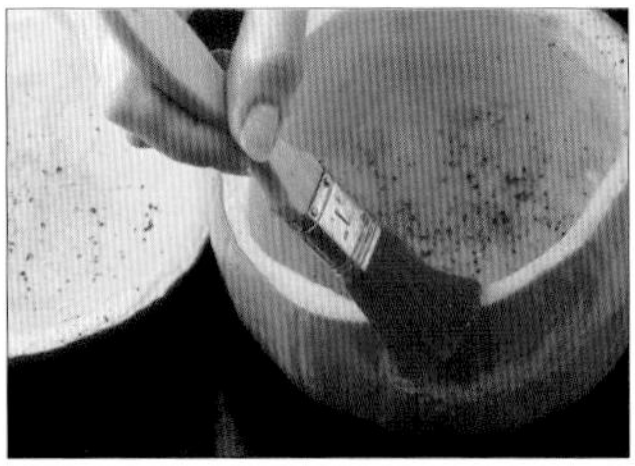

2 Brush the inside of the pumpkin and the flesh side of the lid with a little olive oil. Season with salt and ground black pepper. Place both pumpkin and lid on a baking sheet, flesh-side up. Set aside.

3 Preheat the oven to 200°C/400°F/Gas 6. Heat half the remaining oil in a large heavy pan over a high heat. Add the beef, season and sauté for 8–10 minutes, until golden brown, then remove with a slotted spoon – you may need to do this in batches. Avoid adding too much beef to the pan or it will steam rather than brown.

4 Lower the heat and add the remaining oil to the pan. Stir in the onion and chillies, and sauté for 5 minutes. Scrape the base of the pan with a wooden spoon, to loosen any sediment. Add the garlic and tomato and cook for 2 minutes more.

5 Return the meat to the pan and add the bay leaves, stock and red wine. Bring to the boil, then lower the heat to a gentle simmer. Cook for 1 hour or until the meat is tender.

6 Place the baking sheet containing the pumpkin and its lid in the oven and bake for 30 minutes.

7 Add the potatoes, sweet potatoes, pieces of pumpkin and corn to the stew. Pour in more liquid if needed and bring to the boil. Reduce the heat to a simmer, cover and cook for 15 minutes.

8 Finally add the peach wedges and season with salt and black pepper to taste. Spoon the stew into the partially cooked pumpkin, cover with the pumpkin lid and bake for 15 minutes or until the pumpkin is tender.

9 Carefully lift the filled pumpkin on to a large, strong platter and take it to the table. Ladle the stew on to plates, then cut the empty pumpkin into six to eight wedges, depending on the number of people to be served.

GARLIC AND CHILLI MARINATED BEEF WITH CORN-CRUSTED ONION RINGS

FRUITY, SMOKY AND MILD MEXICAN CHILLIES COMBINE WELL WITH GARLIC IN THIS MARINADE FOR GRILLED STEAK. POLENTA MAKES A CRISP COATING FOR THE ACCOMPANYING FRIED ONION RINGS.

SERVES FOUR

INGREDIENTS

- 20g/¾oz large mild dried red chillies (such as *mulato* or *pasilla*)
- 2 garlic cloves, plain or smoked, finely chopped
- 5ml/1 tsp ground toasted cumin seeds
- 5ml/1 tsp dried oregano
- 60ml/4 tbsp olive oil
- 4 × 175–225g/6–8oz beef steaks (rump, round or rib-eye)
- salt and ground black pepper

For the onion rings

- 2 onions, sliced into rings
- 250ml/8fl oz/1 cup milk
- 75g/3oz/¾ cup coarse cornmeal or polenta
- 2.5ml/½ tsp dried red chilli flakes
- 5ml/1 tsp ground toasted cumin seeds
- 5ml/1 tsp dried oregano
- vegetable oil, for deep-frying

1 Cut the stalks from the chillies and discard the seeds. Toast the chillies in a dry frying pan for 2–4 minutes, until they give off their aroma. Place the chillies in a bowl, cover with warm water and leave to soak for 20–30 minutes. Drain and reserve the water.

2 Process the chillies to a paste with the garlic, cumin, oregano and oil in a food processor. Add a little soaking water, if needed. Season with pepper.

3 Wash and dry the steaks, rub the chilli paste all over them and leave to marinate for up to 12 hours.

4 For the onion rings, soak the onions in the milk for 30 minutes. Mix the cornmeal, chilli, cumin and oregano, and season with salt and pepper.

5 Heat the oil for deep-frying to 160–180°C/325–350°F, or until a cube of day-old bread turns brown in about a minute.

6 Drain the onion rings and dip each one into the cornmeal mixture, coating it thoroughly. Fry for 2–4 minutes, until browned and crisp. Do not overcrowd the pan, but cook in batches. Lift the onion rings out of the pan with a slotted spoon and drain on kitchen paper.

7 Heat a barbecue or cast-iron grill (broiler) pan. Season the steaks with salt and grill (broil) for about 4 minutes on each side for a medium result; reduce or increase this time according to how rare or well done you like steak. Serve the steaks with the onion rings.

MEXICAN SPICY BEEF TORTILLA

THIS DISH IS NOT UNLIKE A LASAGNE, EXCEPT THAT THE SPICY MEAT IS MIXED WITH RICE AND IS LAYERED BETWEEN MEXICAN TORTILLAS, WITH A HOT SALSA SAUCE FOR AN EXTRA KICK.

SERVES FOUR

INGREDIENTS

- 1 onion, chopped
- 2 garlic cloves, crushed
- 1 fresh red chilli, seeded and thinly sliced
- 350g/12oz rump (round) steak, cut into small cubes
- 15ml/1 tbsp oil
- 225g/8oz/2 cups cooked long grain rice
- beef stock, to moisten
- 3 large wheat tortillas

For the salsa picante

- 2 x 400g/14oz cans chopped tomatoes
- 2 garlic cloves, halved
- 1 onion, quartered
- 1–2 fresh red chillies, seeded and roughly chopped
- 5ml/1 tsp ground cumin
- 2.5–5ml/½–1 tsp cayenne pepper
- 5ml/1 tsp fresh oregano or 2.5ml/½ tsp dried oregano
- tomato juice or water, if required

For the cheese sauce

- 50g/2oz/4 tbsp butter
- 50g/2oz/½ cup plain (all-purpose) flour
- 600ml/1 pint/2½ cups milk
- 115g/4oz/1 cup grated Cheddar cheese
- salt and ground black pepper

1 Preheat the oven to 180°C/350°F/Gas 4. Make the salsa picante. Place the tomatoes, garlic, onion and chillies in a blender or food processor and process until smooth. Pour into a small pan, add the spices and oregano and season with salt.

2 Gradually bring the mixture to the boil, stirring occasionally. Boil for 1–2 minutes, then lower the heat, cover with a lid and simmer gently for about 15 minutes. The sauce should be thick, but of a pouring consistency. If it is too thick, dilute it with a little fresh tomato juice or water.

3 Make the cheese sauce. Melt the butter in a pan and stir in the flour. Cook for 1 minute. Add the milk, stirring all the time until the sauce boils and thickens. Stir in all but 30ml/2 tbsp of cheese and season to taste. Cover the pan with a lid and set aside.

4 Mix the onion, garlic and chilli in a bowl. Add the steak cubes and mix well.

5 Heat the oil in a frying pan and stir-fry the meat mixture for about 10 minutes, until the meat cubes have browned and the onion is soft. Stir in the rice and enough beef stock to moisten. Season to taste with salt and freshly ground black pepper.

6 Pour about a quarter of the cheese sauce into the bottom of a round ovenproof dish. Add a tortilla and then spread over half the salsa followed by half the meat mixture.

7 Repeat these layers, then add half the remaining cheese sauce and the final tortilla. Pour over the remaining cheese sauce and sprinkle the reserved grated cheese on top. Bake in the preheated oven for about 15–20 minutes, or until golden on top.

TACOS WITH SHREDDED BEEF

In Mexico tacos are most often made with soft corn tortillas, which are filled and folded in half. It is unusual to see the crisp shells of corn which are so widely used in Tex-Mex cooking. Tacos are always eaten in the hand.

SERVES SIX

INGREDIENTS
- 450g/1lb rump steak, diced
- 150g/5oz/1 cup *masa harina*
- 2.5ml/½ tsp salt
- 120ml/4fl oz/½ cup warm water
- 10ml/2 tsp dried oregano
- 5ml/1 tsp ground cumin
- 30ml/2 tbsp oil
- 1 onion, thinly sliced
- 2 garlic cloves, crushed
- fresh coriander (cilantro), to garnish
- shredded lettuce, lime wedges and salsa, to serve

1 Put the steak in a deep frying pan and pour over water to cover. Bring to the boil, then lower the heat and simmer for 1–1½ hours.

2 Meanwhile, make the tortilla dough. Mix the *masa harina* and salt in a large mixing bowl. Add the warm water, a little at a time, to make a dough that can be worked into a ball. Knead the dough on a lightly floured surface for 3–4 minutes until smooth, then wrap the dough in clear film (plastic wrap) and leave to rest for 1 hour.

3 Put the meat on a board, let it cool slightly, then shred it, using two forks. Put the meat in a bowl. Divide the tortilla dough into six equal balls.

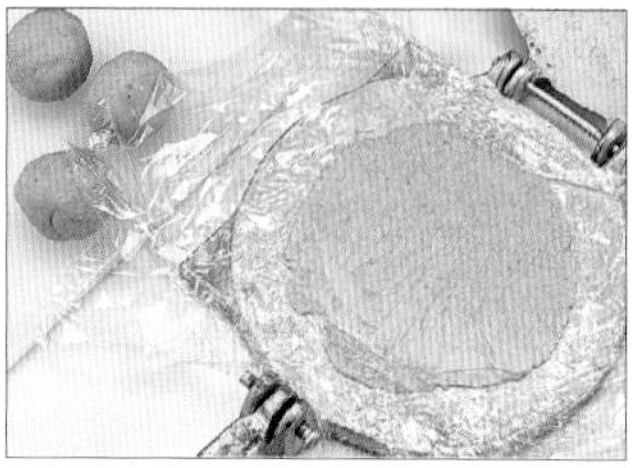

4 Open a tortilla press and line both sides with plastic (this can be cut from a new plastic sandwich bag). Put each ball on the press and flatten it into a 15–20cm/6–8in round.

5 Heat a griddle or frying pan until hot. Cook each tortilla for 15–20 seconds on each side, and then for a further 15 seconds on the first side. Keep the tortillas warm and soft by folding them inside a slightly damp dishtowel.

6 Add the oregano and cumin to the shredded meat and mix well. Heat the oil in a frying pan and fry the onion and garlic for 3–4 minutes until softened. Add the spiced meat mixture and toss over the heat until heated through.

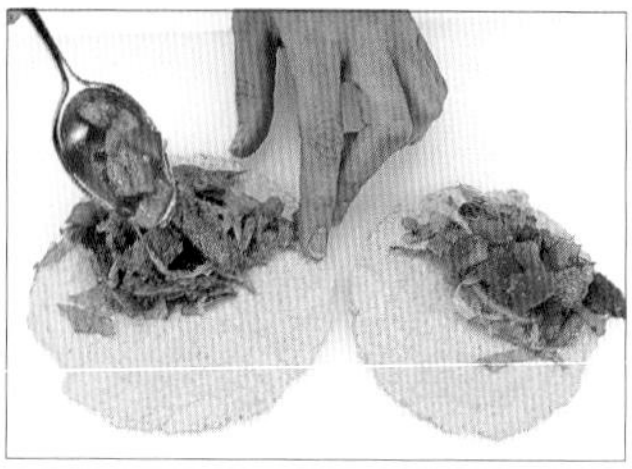

7 Place some shredded lettuce on a tortilla, top with shredded beef and salsa, fold in half and serve with lime wedges. Garnish with fresh coriander.

BEEF ENCHILADAS WITH RED SAUCE

ENCHILADAS ARE USUALLY MADE WITH CORN TORTILLAS, ALTHOUGH IN PARTS OF NORTHERN MEXICO FLOUR TORTILLAS ARE SOMETIMES USED.

SERVES THREE TO FOUR

INGREDIENTS

- 500g/1¼lb rump steak, cut into 5cm/2in cubes
- 2 ancho chillies, seeded
- 2 pasilla chillies, seeded
- 2 garlic cloves, crushed
- 10ml/2 tsp dried oregano
- 2.5ml/½ tsp ground cumin
- 30ml/2 tbsp vegetable oil
- 7 fresh corn tortillas
- shredded onion and flat leaf parsley, to garnish
- mango salsa, to serve

1 Put the steak in a deep frying pan and cover with water. Bring to the boil, then lower the heat and simmer for 1–1½ hours, or until very tender.

2 Meanwhile, put the dried chillies in a bowl and pour over the hot water. Leave to soak for 30 minutes, then tip the contents of the bowl into a blender and whizz to a smooth paste.

3 Drain the steak and let it cool, reserving 250ml/8fl oz/1 cup of the cooking liquid. Meanwhile, fry the garlic, oregano and cumin in the oil for 2 minutes.

4 Stir in the chilli paste and the reserved cooking liquid from the beef. Tear one of the tortillas into small pieces and add it to the mixture. Bring to the boil, then lower the heat. Simmer for 10 minutes, stirring occasionally, until the sauce has thickened. Shred the steak, using two forks, and stir into the sauce, heat through for a few minutes..

5 Spoon some of the meat mixture on to each tortilla and roll it up to make an enchilada. Keep the enchiladas in a warmed dish until you have rolled them all. Garnish with shreds of onion and fresh flat leaf parsley and then serve immediately with the mango salsa.

VARIATION

For a richer version place the rolled enchiladas side by side in a gratin dish. Pour over 300ml/½ pint/1¼ cups soured cream and 75g/3oz/¾ cup grated Cheddar cheese. Place under a preheated grill (broiler) for 5 minutes or until the cheese melts and the sauce bubbles. Serve at once, with the salsa.

BLACK BEAN CHILLI CON CARNE

FRESH GREEN AND DRIED RED CHILLIES ADD PLENTY OF FIRE TO THIS CLASSIC TEX-MEX DISH OF TENDER BEEF COOKED IN A RICH AND SPICY TOMATO SAUCE.

SERVES SIX

INGREDIENTS
- 225g/8oz/1¼ cups dried black beans
- 500g/1¼lb braising steak
- 30ml/2 tbsp vegetable oil
- 2 onions, chopped
- 1 garlic clove, crushed
- 1 fresh green chilli, seeded and finely chopped
- 15ml/1 tbsp paprika
- 10ml/2 tsp ground cumin
- 10ml/2 tsp ground coriander
- 400g/14oz can chopped tomatoes
- 300ml/½ pint/1¼ cups beef stock
- 1 dried red chilli, crumbled
- 5ml/1 tsp hot pepper sauce
- 1 fresh red (bell) pepper, seeded and chopped
- salt
- fresh coriander (cilantro), to garnish
- boiled rice, to serve

1 Put the beans in a large pan. Cover with cold water, bring to the boil and boil vigorously for about 10 minutes. Drain, tip into a bowl, cover with cold water and leave to soak overnight.

2 Preheat the oven to 150°C/300°F/Gas 2. Cut the steak into small dice. Heat the oil in a large, flameproof casserole. Add the onion, garlic and green chilli and cook gently for 5 minutes until soft. Transfer the mixture to a plate.

3 Increase the heat to high, add the meat to the casserole and brown on all sides, then stir in the paprika, ground cumin and ground coriander.

4 Add the tomatoes, beef stock, dried chilli and hot pepper sauce. Drain the beans and add them to the casserole, with enough water to cover. Bring to simmering point, cover and cook in the oven for about 2 hours. Stir occasionally and add extra water, if necessary, to prevent the casserole from drying.

5 Season the casserole with salt and add the chopped red pepper. Replace the lid, return the casserole to the oven and cook for about 30 minutes more, or until the meat and beans are tender. Sprinkle over the fresh coriander and serve with boiled rice.

VARIATION

Use minced (ground) beef in place of the braising steak.

COOK'S TIP

Red kidney beans are traditionally used in chilli con carne, but in this recipe black beans are used instead. They are the same shape and size as red kidney beans but have a shiny black skin.

SPICY MEATBALLS WITH TOMATO SAUCE

Wherever you go in Latin America, you'll find a different interpretation of this hearty family dish. Spanish in origin, the meatballs are often made with pork or veal, or a mixture of meats, and known as albondigas.

SERVES FOUR

INGREDIENTS
- 500g/1¼lb minced (ground) beef
- 3 garlic cloves, crushed
- 1 small onion, finely chopped
- 50g/2oz/1 cup fresh breadcrumbs
- 2.5ml/½ tsp ground cumin
- 1 egg, beaten
- 50g/2oz/½ cup plain (all-purpose) flour
- 60ml/4 tbsp olive oil
- salt
- cooked white rice, to serve

For the sauce
- 30ml/2 tbsp olive oil
- 1 small onion, thinly sliced
- 2 red (bell) peppers, seeded and diced
- 2 fresh red chillies, seeded and chopped
- 2 garlic cloves, crushed
- 150ml/¼ pint/⅔ cup canned chopped tomatoes
- 400ml/14fl oz/1⅔ cups light beef stock
- ground black pepper

COOK'S TIP

An electric frying pan is ideal for cooking the meatballs, as its large surface area will allow you to fry them in one or two batches, and there is plenty of room for reheating them in the sauce.

1 Place all the meatball ingredients, except the flour and oil, in a large bowl. Using your hands, mix until thoroughly combined. Season with salt and shape the mixture into even-size balls. Wet your hands to prevent the mixture from sticking. Dust lightly with flour.

2 Heat the oil in a large frying pan and cook the meatballs, in batches, for 6–8 minutes or until golden. When all the meatballs have been browned, wipe the pan clean with kitchen paper.

3 Pour the olive oil into the pan and cook the onion and peppers over a low heat for 10 minutes, until soft. Add the chillies and garlic, and cook for a further 2 minutes. Pour in the tomatoes and stock, and bring to the boil. Lower the heat, cover the pan and simmer for 15 minutes. Season to taste.

4 Add the meatballs to the pan and spoon the sauce over them. Bring back to the boil, then cover and simmer for 10 minutes. Serve with rice.

FEIJOADA

This mixed meat and black bean stew is indisputably the national dish of Brazil and is traditionally served for Saturday lunch. It's impossible to make a good feijoada for fewer than ten people, since there are so many different types of meat involved. The meats can vary, but the beans have to be very small and black.

SERVES 12

INGREDIENTS

- 1kg/2¼lb/5½ cups black turtle beans
- 1 smoked pig's tongue, optional
- 500g/1¼lb *carne seca* or beef jerky
- 250g/9oz salted pork ribs
- 350g/12oz smoked streaky (fatty) bacon, in one piece
- 500g/1¼lb smoked pork ribs
- 300g/11oz pork sausages
- 300g/11oz smoked chorizo
- 2 fresh bay leaves
- 60ml/4 tbsp vegetable oil
- 5 garlic cloves, crushed
- salt
- fresh orange slices, peeled, to serve
- cooked white rice
- toasted cassava flour
- stir-fried kale
- chilli oil

1 Wash the beans in running water, then place in a bowl with cold water to cover. Soak overnight. Rinse the tongue, *carne seca* or beef jerky, and salted pork ribs in cold running water and place in a separate bowl. Pour over water to cover and soak for 8 hours, or overnight, changing the soaking water three or four times.

2 Drain the beans and place them in a very large heavy pan. Pour in enough water to cover, and bring to the boil over a high heat. Skim the surface, then lower the heat. Cover the pan and simmer for 1 hour.

3 Meanwhile, drain the soaked meats, rinse them again under cold running water and transfer to a second large heavy pan. Add the streaky bacon and smoked pork ribs, then cover with water. Bring to the boil over a high heat, skim the surface, then cover the pan. Lower the heat and simmer for 1 hour.

4 Transfer the cooked meats, with their cooking liquid, to the pan with the beans. Add the pork sausages, chorizo and bay leaves. If necessary, add more water to cover. Bring to the boil, skim the surface, cover, and continue simmering for about 30 minutes.

5 Heat the oil in a large frying pan over a low heat. Add the crushed garlic cloves and cook, stirring, for about 2 minutes, being careful not to let it burn.

6 Ladle some beans from the large pan into the frying pan and fry, mashing the beans with a wooden spoon. Return the mashed beans to the meat mixture and lower the heat for 5 minutes. Taste the stew and add some salt if needed.

7 Lift the meats from the pan and cut them into even-size pieces. Arrange on a platter, keeping each type of meat separate. Spoon a ladleful of beans over the meats. Pour the remaining beans into a large serving bowl.

8 Take the beans and meats to the table with a platter of peeled, sliced oranges, cooked white rice, toasted cassava flour, stir-fried kale and chilli oil.

COOK'S TIPS

- *Carne seca*, a Brazilian beef jerky, can be bought in Brazilian or Portuguese food stores. You can make a *feijoada* without it, but it won't be as rich.
- Toasted cassava flour is sold in Latin American or Portuguese food stores. Here it is served from the packet, but it can be flavoured with palm oil or eggs.

Stuffed Butterfly of Beef with Cheese and Chilli Sauce

This recipe had its origins in northern Mexico or in New Mexico, which is beef country. It is a good way to cook steaks, either under the grill or on the barbecue.

SERVES FOUR

INGREDIENTS

- 4 fresh serrano chillies
- 115g/4oz/½ cup full-fat soft cheese
- 30ml/2 tbsp reposada tequila
- 30ml/2 tbsp oil
- 1 onion
- 2 garlic cloves
- 5ml/1 tsp dried oregano
- 2.5ml/½ tsp salt
- 2.5ml/½ tsp ground black pepper
- 175g/6oz/1½ cups grated medium Cheddar cheese
- 4 fillet steaks, at least 2.5cm/1in thick

1 Dry roast the chillies in a griddle pan over a moderate heat, turning them frequently until the skins are blistered but not burnt. Put them in a strong plastic bag and tie the top to keep the steam in. Set aside for 20 minutes.

2 Remove the chillies from the bag, slit them and scrape out the seeds with a sharp knife. Cut the flesh into long narrow strips, then cut each strip into several shorter strips.

3 Put the full-fat soft cheese in a small heavy-based pan and stir over a low heat until it has melted. Add the chilli strips and the tequila and stir to make a smooth sauce. Keep warm over a very low heat.

4 Heat the oil in a frying pan and fry the onion, garlic and oregano for about 5 minutes over a moderate heat, stirring frequently until the onion has browned. Season with the salt and pepper.

5 Remove the pan from the heat and stir in the grated cheese so that it melts into the onion mixture.

6 Cut each steak almost but not quite in half across its width, so that it can be opened out, butterfly-fashion. Preheat the grill (broiler) to its highest setting.

7 Spoon a quarter of the cheese and onion filling on to one side of each steak and close the other side over it. Place the steaks in a grill pan and grill (broil) for 3–5 minutes on each side, depending on how you like your steak. Serve on heated plates with the vegetables of your choice, and with the cheese and chilli sauce poured over.

COOK'S TIP

One of the easiest ways of testing whether a steak is cooked is by touch. A steak that is very rare or "blue" will feel soft to the touch; the meat will be relaxed. A rare steak will feel like a sponge, and will spring back when lightly pressed. A medium-rare steak offers more resistance, while a well-cooked steak will feel very firm.

Hearty Beef Stew

Brown ale enriches this Caribbean beef stew and gives it a real kick. Vary the amount to suit your taste, but don't overdo it or you will overwhelm the taste of the paprika.

SERVES FOUR

INGREDIENTS

- 50g/2oz/⅓ cup black-eyed beans (peas)
- 25g/1oz/2 tbsp butter or margarine
- 1 onion, chopped
- 675g/1½ lb stewing beef, cubed
- 5ml/1 tsp paprika
- 2 garlic cloves, crushed
- 10ml/2 tsp ground cinnamon
- 10ml/2 tsp sugar
- 600ml/1 pint/2½ cups beef stock
- 150ml/¼ pint/⅔ cup brown ale
- 45ml/3 tbsp evaporated (unsweetened condensed) milk
- salt and ground black pepper
- steamed baby patty-pan squash

1 Put the black-eyed beans in a bowl and pour over water to cover. Leave to soak overnight, then drain, tip into a large pan, cover with water and bring to the boil. Boil rapidly for 3–4 minutes, then reduce the heat.

2 Simmer the beans for 30 minutes or until tender, but still quite firm. Drain the beans, reserving the cooking liquid.

3 Melt the butter or margarine in a large pan and sauté the onion for a few minutes. Add the beef, paprika, garlic, cinnamon and sugar and fry for about 5 minutes, stirring frequently.

4 Pour in the beef stock and brown ale, cover and cook gently for 1½ hours, until the beef is almost cooked.

5 Add the evaporated milk and beans. Season with salt and pepper and continue cooking until the beans and beef are tender. Serve with steamed baby patty-pan squash.

OXTAIL AND BUTTER BEANS

This is a traditional Caribbean stew – old-fashioned, economical and full of goodness. It requires patience because of the long cooking time. There is not much meat on the oxtail, so it is necessary to buy a large amount.

SERVES FOUR

INGREDIENTS

- 1.6kg/3½lb oxtail, chopped into pieces
- 1 onion, finely chopped
- 3 bay leaves
- 4 fresh thyme sprigs
- 3 whole cloves
- 1.75 litres/3 pints/7½ cups water
- 175g/6oz/scant 1 cup dried butter (lima) beans, soaked overnight
- 2 garlic cloves, crushed
- 15ml/1 tbsp tomato purée (paste)
- 400g/14oz can chopped tomatoes
- 5ml/1 tsp ground allspice
- 1 fresh hot chilli
- salt and ground black pepper

1 Put the pieces of oxtail in a large heavy pan, add the chopped onion, bay leaves, thyme and cloves and cover with water. Bring to the boil.

2 Reduce the heat, cover the pan and simmer gently for at least 2½ hours or until the meat is very tender. If the meat looks like it might dry out, add a little extra water, being careful not to add too much at one time.

3 Meanwhile, drain the butter beans and tip them into a large pan. Pour in water to cover. Bring to the boil, lower the heat and simmer for about 1–1¼ hours or until just tender. Drain and set aside until ready to use.

COOK'S TIP

Unless you are confident using a meat cleaver to chop the oxtail into short lengths, ask your butcher to do it for you.

VARIATION

Haricot (navy) beans can be used in the same way as butter beans in the recipe.

4 When the oxtail is cooked, add the garlic, tomato purée, tomatoes, allspice, and chilli, and season. Add the beans, simmer for 20 minutes, then serve.

"Seasoned-Up" Lamb in Spinach Sauce

In the Caribbean, especially on the English-speaking islands, you will often hear dishes described as "seasoned up". This refers to the use of a spicy rub or marinade, a technique that works well with cheaper cuts of meat.

SERVES FOUR

INGREDIENTS
- 675g/1½lb boneless lamb, cubed
- 2.5ml/½ tsp ground ginger
- 2.5ml/½ tsp dried thyme
- 30ml/2 tbsp olive oil
- 1 onion, chopped
- 2 garlic cloves, crushed
- 15ml/1 tbsp tomato purée (paste)
- ½ fresh hot chilli, chopped (optional)
- 600ml/1 pint/2½ cups lamb stock or water
- 115g/4oz fresh spinach, finely chopped
- salt and ground black pepper

1 Put the lamb cubes in a dish. Sprinkle over the ginger and thyme, season and mix well to coat. Cover and marinate for at least 2 hours or overnight in the refrigerator.

2 Heat the olive oil in a heavy pan, add the onion and garlic and fry gently for 5 minutes or until the onion is soft.

3 Add the lamb with the tomato purée and chilli, if using. Fry over a medium heat for about 5 minutes, stirring frequently, then add the lamb stock or water. Cover and simmer for about 30 minutes, until the lamb is tender.

4 Stir in the spinach and simmer for around 8 minutes. Serve hot.

Lamb Pelau

Indian immigrants introduced the pilau to the Caribbean. The name has changed slightly, but rice dishes like this one remain true to their origins.

SERVES FOUR

INGREDIENTS
- 450g/1lb stewing lamb
- 15ml/1 tbsp curry powder
- 1 onion, finely chopped
- 2 garlic cloves, crushed
- 2.5ml/½ tsp dried thyme
- 2.5ml/½ tsp dried oregano
- 1 fresh or dried chilli
- 25g/1oz/2 tbsp butter or margarine, plus extra for serving
- 600ml/1 pint/2½ cups beef stock, chicken stock or coconut milk
- 5ml/1 tsp ground black pepper
- 2 tomatoes, chopped
- 10ml/2 tsp sugar
- 30ml/2 tbsp chopped spring onion (scallion)
- 450g/1lb/2½ cups basmati rice
- spring onion strips, to garnish

1 Cut the lamb into cubes and place in a dish. Add the curry powder, onion, garlic, herbs and chilli and stir well. Cover with clear film (plastic wrap) and leave to marinate for 1 hour.

2 Melt the butter or margarine in a pan and fry the lamb for 5–10 minutes. Pour in the stock or coconut milk, bring to the boil, then lower the heat and simmer for 35 minutes or until tender.

3 Add the black pepper, tomatoes, sugar, chopped spring onion and rice. Stir well and reduce the heat. Make sure that the rice is covered by 2.5cm/1in of liquid; add a little water if necessary. Cover the pan; simmer the pelau for 25 minutes or until the rice has absorbed the liquid and is cooked. Spoon into a serving bowl and stir in a little extra butter or margarine. Garnish with spring onion strips and serve.

LAMB STEW WITH CHILLI SAUCE

THE CHILLIES IN THIS MEXICAN STEW ADD DEPTH AND RICHNESS TO THE SAUCE, WHILE THE POTATO SLICES ENSURE THAT IT IS SUBSTANTIAL ENOUGH TO SERVE ON ITS OWN.

SERVES SIX

INGREDIENTS

- 6 guajillo chillies, seeded
- 2 pasilla chillies, seeded
- 250ml/8fl oz/1 cup hot water
- 3 garlic cloves, peeled
- 5ml/1 tsp ground cinnamon
- 2.5ml/½ tsp ground cloves
- 2.5ml/½ tsp ground black pepper
- 15ml/1 tbsp vegetable oil
- 1kg/2¼lb lean boneless lamb shoulder, cut into 2cm/¾in cubes
- 400g/14oz potatoes, scrubbed and cut into 1cm/½in thick slices
- salt
- strips of red (bell) pepper and fresh oregano to garnish

COOK'S TIP

When frying the lamb, don't be tempted to cook too many cubes at one time, as the meat will steam rather than fry.

1 Snap or tear the dried chillies into large pieces, put them in a bowl and pour over the hot water. Leave to soak for 30 minutes, then tip the contents of the bowl into a food processor or blender. Add the garlic and spices. Process until smooth.

2 Heat the oil in a large pan. Add the lamb cubes, in batches, and stir-fry over a high heat until the cubes are browned on all sides.

3 Return all the lamb cubes to the pan, spread them out, then cover them with a layer of potato slices. Add salt to taste. Put a lid on the pan and cook over a medium heat for 10 minutes.

4 Pour over the chilli mixture and mix well. Replace the lid and simmer over a low heat for about 1 hour or until the meat and the potato are tender. Serve with a rice dish if you like, and garnish with red pepper and fresh oregano.

ALBONDIGAS

These family-favourite Mexican meatballs are delicious, and the chipotle chilli gives the sauce a distinctive, slightly smoky flavour.

SERVES FOUR

INGREDIENTS
- 225g/8oz minced (ground) pork
- 225g/8oz lean minced (ground) beef
- 1 onion, finely chopped
- 50g/2oz/1 cup fresh white breadcrumbs
- 5ml/1 tsp dried oregano
- 2.5ml/½ tsp ground cumin
- 2.5ml/½ tsp salt
- 2.5ml/½ tsp ground black pepper
- 1 egg, beaten
- oil, for frying
- fresh oregano sprigs, to garnish

For the sauce
- 1 chipotle chilli, seeded
- 15ml/1 tbsp vegetable oil
- 1 onion, finely chopped
- 2 garlic cloves, crushed
- 175ml/6fl oz/¾ cup beef stock
- 400g/14oz can chopped tomatoes
- 105ml/7 tbsp passata (bottled strained tomatoes)

1 Mix the minced pork and beef in a bowl. Add the onion, breadcrumbs, oregano, cumin, salt and pepper. Mix with clean hands until all the ingredients are well combined.

2 Stir in the egg, mix well, then roll into 4cm/1½in balls. Put these on a baking sheet and chill while you prepare the sauce.

3 Soak the dried chilli in hot water to cover for 15 minutes. Heat the oil in a pan and fry the onion and garlic for 3–4 minutes until softened.

4 Drain the chilli, reserving the soaking water, then chop it and add it to the onion mixture. Fry for 1 minute, then stir in the beef stock, tomatoes, passata and soaking water, with salt and pepper to taste. Bring to the boil, lower the heat and simmer, stirring occasionally, while you cook the meatballs.

5 Heat the oil for frying in a frying pan and fry the meatballs in batches for about 5 minutes, turning them occasionally, until browned.

6 Drain off the oil and transfer all the meatballs to a shallow casserole. Pour over the sauce and simmer for 10 minutes, stirring gently from time to time so that the meatballs are coated but do not disintegrate. Garnish with the oregano and serve. Plain white rice makes a good accompaniment.

COOK'S TIP

Dampen your hands before shaping the meatballs and the mixture will be less likely to stick.

Spiced Roast Leg of Lamb

Peppers and beans are delicious cooked with this spiced lamb – the beans soak up the meat juices and combine with sweet red peppers to make a succulent one-pot meal.

SERVES SIX

INGREDIENTS

- 1 leg of lamb, about 1.8kg/4lb
- 4 garlic cloves, crushed
- 5ml/1 tsp ground cumin
- 10ml/2 tsp ground annatto (achiote) seeds
- 10ml/2 tbsp sweet paprika
- 5ml/1 tsp dried oregano
- 45ml/3 tbsp olive oil
- 3 red (bell) peppers, cored, seeded and thickly sliced
- 2 x 400g/14oz can black-eyed beans (peas), drained
- 105ml/7 tbsp dry white wine
- salt and ground black pepper
- cooked white rice or polenta, to serve

COOK'S TIP

Look for ground annatto in South American or Caribbean markets, or replace with saffron or turmeric.

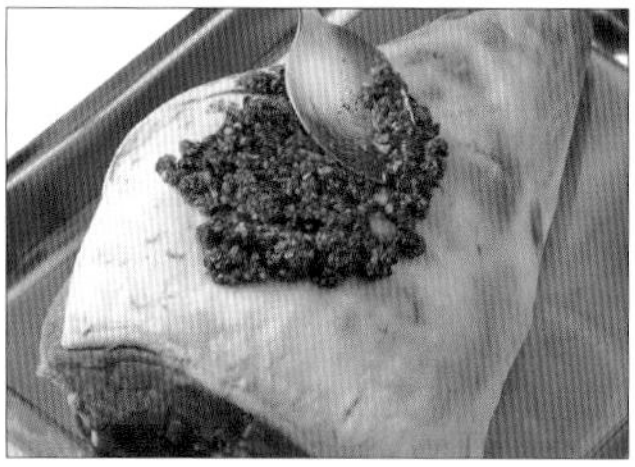

1 Weigh the lamb and calculate the cooking time. For medium-cooked lamb, allow 20 minutes per 450g/1lb, plus 20 minutes. Allow either 5 minutes more or less per 450/1lb for rare and well-done meat.

2 Mix the garlic, cumin, annatto, paprika and oregano in a bowl. Stir in half the olive oil. Using a spoon, rub the paste all over the lamb. Cover and marinate in a cool place for 2–3 hours.

3 Preheat the oven to 180°C/350°F/Gas 4. Place the lamb in a roasting pan with the peppers and beans. Pour in the wine and drizzle with the remaining oil. Season, then roast for the calculated time. Check occasionally, adding water if the vegetables begin to dry out.

4 When the lamb is cooked, remove from the oven and cover the meat loosely with foil. Leave to rest for 15 minutes, then serve with rice or polenta.

Rabbit in Coconut Milk

This unusual dish comes from Colombia. The rabbit is stewed in a lightly spiced tomato sauce, and when it is almost ready, coconut milk is stirred in to enrich the sauce.

SERVES FOUR

INGREDIENTS

- 1 rabbit, cut into 8 pieces (ask your butcher to do this for you)
- 3 garlic cloves, crushed
- 1.5ml/¼ tsp paprika
- 1.5ml/¼ tsp ground cumin
- 45ml/3 tbsp olive oil
- 1 large onion, thinly sliced
- 1 bay leaf
- 400g/14oz can plum tomatoes, drained and roughly chopped
- 150ml/¼ pint/⅔ cup chicken stock
- 250ml/8fl oz/1 cup coconut milk
- salt and ground black pepper
- white rice or boiled potatoes, to serve

1 Wash the rabbit under cold water, then pat the pieces dry with kitchen paper. Combine the garlic, paprika and cumin in a bowl and rub the mixture all over the rabbit. Cover with clear film (plastic wrap) and leave to marinate for 1 hour, or overnight in the refrigerator.

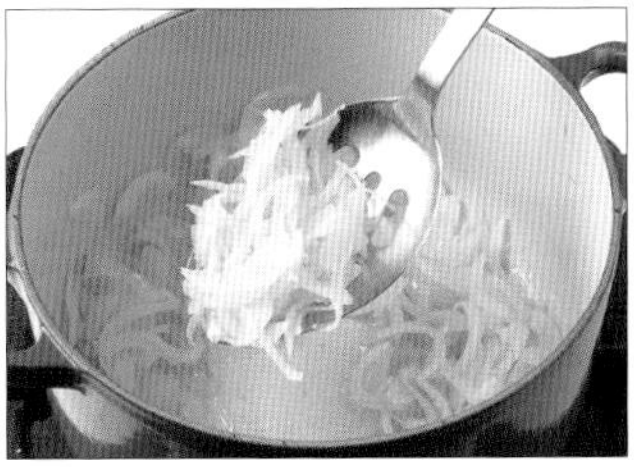

2 Heat the oil in a pan, add the onion slices and cook for 5 minutes, until tender. Remove the onion with a slotted spoon and set aside.

3 Add the rabbit to the oil remaining in the pan, season and cook until golden. Do this over a very low heat to avoid burning the spices.

4 Return the onion slices to the pan and add the bay leaf. Stir in the tomatoes and stock and bring to the boil. Lower the heat, cover and simmer for 45 minutes.

VARIATION

This dish is often made with chicken rather than rabbit. The ingredients remain the same, but the cooking time should be reduced by 15 minutes.

5 Stir in the coconut milk. Continue to simmer, uncovered, for a further 15 minutes, until the rabbit is tender and the sauce has thickened. Serve immediately with white rice or boiled potatoes.

CARIBBEAN LAMB CURRY

THIS JAMAICAN DISH IS POPULARLY KNOWN AS CURRIED GOAT OR CURRY GOAT, ALTHOUGH KID, LAMB OR MUTTON ARE EQUALLY LIKELY TO BE USED TO MAKE IT.

SERVES SIX

INGREDIENTS

- 900g/2lb boned leg of mutton or lamb
- 50g/2oz/4 tbsp curry powder
- 3 garlic cloves, crushed
- 1 large onion, chopped
- leaves from 4 fresh thyme sprigs, or 5ml/1 tsp dried thyme
- 3 bay leaves
- 5ml/1 tsp ground allspice
- 30ml/2 tbsp vegetable oil
- 50g/2oz/¼ cup butter or margarine
- 900ml/1½ pints/3¾ cups lamb stock or water
- 1 fresh hot chilli, chopped
- fresh coriander (cilantro) sprigs, to garnish
- cooked rice, to serve

1 Cut the meat into 5cm/2in cubes, discarding excess fat and any gristle. Place it in a large bowl.

2 Add the curry powder, garlic, onion, thyme, bay leaves, allspice and oil. Mix well, then cover the bowl and place in the refrigerator. Marinate for at least 3 hours or overnight.

3 Melt the butter or margarine in a large heavy pan. Add the seasoned mutton or lamb and fry over a medium heat for about 10 minutes, turning the meat frequently.

4 Stir in the stock or water and chilli, and bring to the boil. Lower the heat, cover and simmer for 1½ hours or until the meat is tender. Garnish with coriander and serve with rice.

PORK WITH PINEAPPLE

THIS UNUSUAL DISH FROM MEXICO COMBINES THE SWEET, JUICY TASTE OF FRESH PINEAPPLE WITH FIERY HOT CHILLIES, AND THE REFRESHING TANG OF COOL MINT.

SERVES SIX

INGREDIENTS

- 30ml/2 tbsp corn oil
- 900g/2lb boneless pork shoulder or loin, cut into 5cm/2in cubes
- 1 onion, finely chopped
- 1 large red (bell) pepper, seeded and finely chopped
- 1 or more jalapeño chillies, seeded and finely chopped
- 450g/1lb fresh pineapple chunks
- 8 fresh mint leaves, chopped
- 250ml/8fl oz/1 cup chicken stock
- salt and ground black pepper
- fresh mint sprigs, to garnish
- boiled rice, to serve

1 Heat the oil in a large frying pan and sauté the pork in batches until the cubes are lightly coloured. Transfer the pork to a flameproof casserole, leaving the oil behind in the pan.

2 Add the chopped onion, red pepper and the chillies to the oil remaining in the pan. Sauté until the onion is tender, then add to the casserole with the pineapple. Stir to mix.

3 Add the mint leaves, then cover the casserole with a tight-fitting lid.

4 Simmer gently for about 2 hours, or until the pork is tender.

5 Season to taste, garnish the casserole with fresh sprigs of mint and serve with plain boiled rice. Serve immediately, while still hot.

COOK'S TIP

If fresh pineapple is not available, use pineapple chunks from a can. Make sure it is canned in its own juice, however, and not in syrup or other fruit juice.

STUFFED LOIN OF PORK

PORK FEATURES TWICE IN THIS DELICIOUS AND LUXURIOUS DISH, WHICH CONSISTS OF A ROAST LOIN STUFFED WITH A RICH MINCED (GROUND) PORK MIXTURE. THE PERFECT CENTREPIECE FOR A SPECIAL OCCASION DINNER, IT IS SERVED IN MEXICO AT WEDDINGS AND SIMILAR CELEBRATIONS.

SERVES SIX

INGREDIENTS

- 1.5kg/3–3½lb boneless pork loin, butterflied ready for stuffing

For the stuffing

- 50g/2oz/⅓ cup raisins
- 120ml/4fl oz/½ cup dry white wine
- 15ml/1 tbsp vegetable oil
- 1 onion, diced
- 2 garlic cloves, crushed
- 2.5ml/½ tsp ground cloves
- 5ml/1 tsp ground cinnamon
- 500g/1¼lb minced (ground) pork
- 150ml/¼ pint/⅔ cup vegetable stock
- 2 tomatoes
- 50g/2oz/½ cup chopped almonds
- 2.5ml/½ tsp each salt and ground black pepper

1 Make the stuffing. Put the raisins and wine in a bowl. Set aside. Heat the oil in a large pan, add the onion and garlic and cook for 5 minutes over a low heat.

2 Add the cloves and cinnamon, then the pork. Cook, stirring, until the pork has browned. Add the stock. Simmer, stirring frequently, for 20 minutes.

3 While the pork is simmering, peel the tomatoes. Cut a cross in the base of each tomato, then put them both in a heatproof bowl. Pour over boiling water to cover. Leave the tomatoes in the water for 3 minutes, then lift them out on a slotted spoon and plunge them into a bowl of cold water. Drain. The skins will have begun to peel back from the crosses.

4 Remove the skins completely, then chop the flesh.

5 Stir the tomatoes and almonds into the mince mixture, add the raisins and wine. Cook until the mixture has reduced to a thick sauce. Leave to cool.

6 Preheat the oven to 180°C/350°F/ Gas 4. Open out the pork loin and trim it neatly. Season the minced pork stuffing with salt and pepper to taste. Spread over the surface of the meat in a neat layer, taking it right to the edges and keeping it as even as possible.

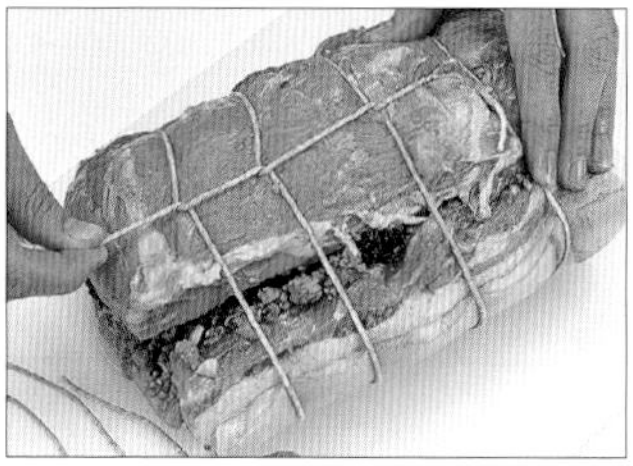

7 Roll up the pork loin carefully and tie it at intervals with kitchen string. Weigh the pork and calculate the cooking time at 30 minutes per 450g/1lb, plus another 30 minutes.

8 Put the stuffed pork joint in a roasting tin, season with salt and pepper and roast for the calculated time. When the joint is cooked, transfer it to a meat platter, place a tent of foil over it, and let it stand for 10 minutes before carving and serving with the roast vegetables of your choice.

COOK'S TIP

Your butcher will prepare the pork loin for you, if you give him or her plenty of notice.

ENCHILADAS WITH PORK AND GREEN SAUCE

THE GREEN TOMATILLO SAUCE PROVIDES A TART CONTRAST TO THE PORK FILLING IN THIS POPULAR MEXICAN DISH. CASCABELS ARE DRIED CHILLIES WHICH RATTLE WHEN SHAKEN.

SERVES THREE TO FOUR

INGREDIENTS

- 500g/1¼lb pork shoulder, diced
- 1 cascabel chilli
- 30ml/2 tbsp oil
- 2 garlic cloves, crushed
- 1 onion, finely chopped
- 300g/11oz/scant 2 cups drained canned tomatillos
- 6 fresh corn tortillas
- 75g/3oz/¾ cup grated Monterey Jack or mild Cheddar cheese

1 Put the diced pork in a pan and pour over water to cover completely. Bring to the boil, lower the heat and simmer for 40 minutes.

2 Meanwhile, soak the dried chilli in hot water for 30 minutes until softened. Drain, remove the stalk, then slit the chilli and scrape out the seeds.

3 Drain the pork and let it cool slightly, then shred it, using two forks. Put the pork in a bowl and set it aside.

4 Heat the oil in a frying pan and fry the garlic and onion for 3–4 minutes until translucent. Chop and add the chilli with the tomatillos. Cook, stirring constantly, until the tomatillos start to break up. Lower the heat and simmer the sauce for 10 minutes more. Cool slightly, then purée in a blender.

5 Preheat the oven to 180°C/350°F/Gas 4. Soften the tortillas by wrapping them in foil and steaming on a plate over boiling water for a few minutes until they are pliable. Alternatively, wrap them in microwave-safe film and heat in a microwave on full power for about 30 seconds.

6 Spoon one-sixth of the shredded pork on to the centre of a tortilla and roll it up to make an enchilada. Place it in a shallow baking dish which is large enough to hold all the enchiladas in a single layer. Fill and roll the remaining tortillas and add them to the dish.

7 Pour the sauce over the enchiladas to cover completely. Sprinkle evenly with cheese. Bake for 25–30 minutes or until the cheese bubbles. Serve immediately. Tomato salad makes a good accompaniment for this dish.

PORK IN GREEN SAUCE WITH CACTUS

CHILE VERDE IS A CLASSIC SAUCE. THE INCLUSION OF CACTUS PIECES – A POPULAR INGREDIENT IN MEXICAN COOKING – GIVES THIS DISH AN INTRIGUING FLAVOUR WHICH WILL DOUBTLESS PROVE A GOOD TALKING POINT AT THE DINNER TABLE.

SERVES FOUR

INGREDIENTS
- 30ml/2 tbsp vegetable oil
- 500g/1¼lb pork shoulder, cut into 2.5cm/1in cubes
- 1 onion, finely chopped
- 2 garlic cloves, crushed
- 5ml/1 tsp dried oregano
- 3 fresh jalapeño chillies, seeded and chopped
- 300g/11oz/scant 2 cups drained canned tomatillos
- 150ml/¼ pint/⅔ cup vegetable stock
- 300g/11oz jar *nopalitos*, drained
- salt and ground black pepper
- warm fresh corn tortillas, to serve

COOK'S TIP

Nopalitos are cactus paddles which have been cut into strips and pickled in vinegar or packed in brine. Look for them in speciality food shops.

1 Heat the oil in a large pan. Add the pork cubes and cook over a high heat, turning several times until browned all over. Add the onion and garlic and fry gently until soft, then stir in the oregano and chopped jalapeños. Cook for 2 minutes more.

2 Tip the canned tomatillos into a blender, add the stock and process until smooth. Add to the pork mixture, cover and cook for 30 minutes.

3 Meanwhile, soak the *nopalitos* in cold water for 10 minutes. Drain, then add to the pork and continue cooking for about 10 minutes or until the pork is cooked through and tender.

4 Season the mixture with salt and plenty of ground black pepper. Serve with warm corn tortillas.

TAMALES FILLED WITH SPICED PORK

THESE TAMALES ARE AMONG THE MOST ANCIENT OF MEXICAN FOODS. AT ONE TIME THE NEAT LITTLE CORN HUSK PARCELS FILLED WITH PLAIN, SAVOURY OR SWEET MASA DOUGH WERE COOKED IN THE ASHES OF A WOOD FIRE. TODAY THEY ARE MORE LIKELY TO BE STEAMED, BUT THE THRILL OF UNWRAPPING THEM REMAINS THE SAME.

SERVES SIX

INGREDIENTS

- 500g/1¼lb lean pork, cut into 5cm/2in cubes
- 750ml/1¼ pints/3 cups chicken stock
- 600g/1lb 6oz/4½ cups *masa harina*
- 450g/1lb/2 cups lard, softened
- 30ml/2 tbsp salt
- 12 large or 24 small dried corn husks
- 2 ancho chillies, seeded
- 15ml/1 tbsp vegetable oil
- ½ onion, finely chopped
- 2 or 3 garlic cloves, crushed
- 2.5ml/½ tsp allspice berries
- 2 dried bay leaves
- 2.5ml/½ tsp ground cumin
- lime wedges, to serve (optional)

1 Put the pork cubes in a large pan. Pour over water to cover. Bring to the boil, lower the heat and simmer for about 40 minutes.

2 Meanwhile, heat the chicken stock in a separate pan. Put the *masa harina* in a large bowl and add the hot stock, a little at a time, to make a stiff dough.

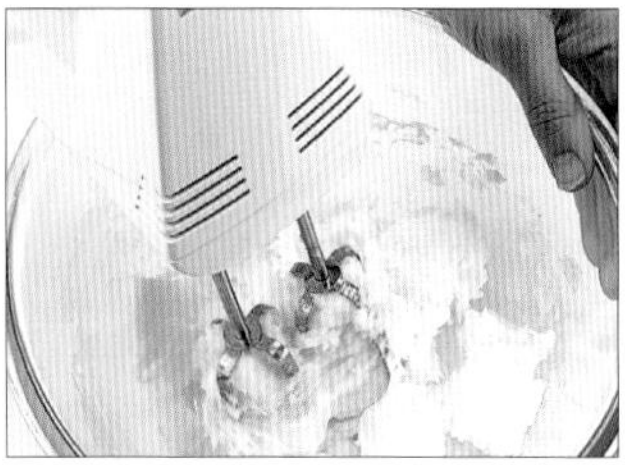

3 Put the lard in another bowl and beat with an electric whisk until light and fluffy, as when beating butter for a cake. Test by dropping a small amount of the whipped lard into a cup of water. If it floats, it is ready for use.

4 Continue to beat the lard, gradually adding the *masa* dough. When all of it has been added and the mixture is light and spreadable, beat in the salt. Cover closely with clear film (plastic wrap) to prevent the mixture from drying out.

5 Put the corn husks in a bowl and pour over boiling water to cover. Leave to soak for 30 minutes. Soak the seeded chillies in a separate bowl of hot water for the same time. Drain the pork, reserving 105ml/7 tbsp of the cooking liquid, and chop the meat finely.

6 Heat the oil in a large pan and fry the onion and garlic over a moderate heat for 2–3 minutes. Drain the chillies, chop them finely and add them to the pan. Put the allspice berries and bay leaves in a mortar, grind them with a pestle, then work in the ground cumin. Add to the onion mixture and stir well. Cook for 2–3 minutes more. Add the chopped pork and reserved cooking liquid and continue cooking over a moderate heat until all the liquid is absorbed. Leave to cool slightly.

7 Drain the corn husks and pat them dry in a clean dishtowel. Place one large corn husk (or overlap two smaller ones) on a board. Spoon about one-twelfth of the *masa* mixture on to the centre of the husk wrapping and spread it almost to the sides.

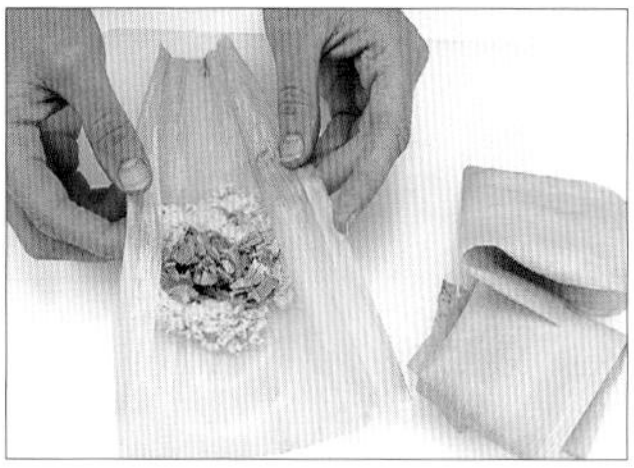

8 Place a spoonful of the meat mixture on top of the *masa*. Fold the two long sides of the corn husk over the filling, then bring up each of the two shorter sides in turn, to make a neat parcel. Slide one of the two short sides inside the other, if possible, to prevent the parcel from unravelling, or tie with string or strips of the corn husk.

9 Place the *tamales* in a steamer basket over a pan of steadily simmering water and steam for 1 hour, topping up the water as needed. To test if the *tamales* are ready, unwrap one. The filling should peel away from the husk cleanly. Pile the *tamales* on a plate, leave to stand for 10 minutes, then serve with lime wedges, if liked. Guests unwrap their own *tamales* at the table.

Pork Roasted with Herbs, Spices and Rum

In the Caribbean, this spicy roast pork is a favourite dish that is usually cooked on a barbecue and served on special occasions as part of a buffet.

SERVES EIGHT

INGREDIENTS

- 2 garlic cloves, crushed
- 45ml/3 tbsp soy sauce
- 15ml/1 tbsp malt vinegar
- 15ml/1 tbsp finely chopped celery
- 30ml/2 tbsp chopped spring onion (scallion)
- 7.5ml/1½ tsp dried thyme
- 5ml/1 tsp dried sage
- 2.5ml/½ tsp ground mixed spice (pumpkin pie spice)
- 10ml/2 tsp curry powder
- 120ml/4fl oz/½ cup rum
- 15ml/1 tbsp demerara (raw) sugar
- 1.6kg/3½lb boned loin of pork
- salt and ground black pepper
- spring onion (scallion) curls, to garnish
- creamed sweet potato, to serve

For the sauce

- 25g/1oz/2 tbsp butter or margarine, diced
- 15ml/1 tbsp tomato purée (paste)
- 300ml/½ pint/1¼ cups chicken or pork stock
- 15ml/1 tbsp chopped fresh parsley
- 15ml/1 tbsp demerara (raw) sugar
- hot pepper sauce, to taste

1 In a bowl, mix the garlic, soy sauce, vinegar, celery, spring onion, thyme, sage, spice, curry powder, rum, and sugar. Add a little salt and pepper.

2 Open out the pork and slash the meat, without cutting through it completely. Place it in a shallow dish. Spread most of the spice mixture all over the pork, pressing it well into the slashes. Rub the outside of the joint with the remaining mixture, cover the dish with clear film (plastic wrap) and chill in the refrigerator overnight.

COOK'S TIP

In the Caribbean, pork is baked until it is very well done, so reduce the cooking time if you prefer meat slightly more moist. To get the full flavour from the marinade, start preparation the day before.

3 Preheat the oven to 190°C/375°F/Gas 5. Roll the meat up, then tie it tightly in several places with strong cotton string to hold the meat together.

4 Spread a large piece of foil across a roasting pan and place the marinated pork loin in the centre. Baste the pork with a few spoonfuls of the marinade and wrap the foil around the meat.

5 Roast the pork in the oven for 1¾ hours, then slide the foil out from under the meat and discard it. Baste the pork with any remaining marinade and cook for a further 1 hour. Check occasionally that the meat is not drying out and baste with the pan juices.

6 Meanwhile, make the sauce. Transfer the pork to a warmed serving dish, cover with foil and leave to stand in a warm place for 15 minutes. Pour the pan juices into a pan. Add the butter or margarine, tomato purée, stock, parsley and sugar, with hot pepper sauce and salt to taste. Simmer until reduced.

7 Serve the pork sliced, with the creamed sweet potato. Garnish with the spring onion curls and serve the sauce separately.

TOSTADAS WITH SHREDDED PORK AND SPICES

CRISP FRIED TORTILLAS TOPPED WITH REFRIED BEANS AND SPICED SHREDDED PORK MAKE A LIGHT MEAL OR LUNCH AND ARE POPULAR FOR PARTIES AND FESTIVALS.

SERVES SIX

INGREDIENTS
- 6 corn tortillas, freshly made or a few days old
- oil, for frying

For the topping
- 500g/1¼lb pork shoulder, cut into 2.5cm/1in cubes
- 2.5ml/½ tsp salt
- 15ml/1 tbsp oil
- 1 small onion, halved and sliced
- 1 garlic clove, crushed
- 1 pasilla chilli, seeded and ground
- 5ml/1 tsp ground cinnamon
- 2.5ml/½ tsp ground cloves
- 175g/6oz/1 cup Refried Beans
- 90ml/6 tbsp soured cream
- 2 tomatoes, seeded and diced
- 115g/4oz feta cheese, crumbled
- fresh oregano sprigs, to garnish

COOK'S TIP

In Mexico, the local fresh goat's or cow's cheese – *queso fresco* – would be used; feta is the nearest equivalent.

1 Make the topping. Place the pork cubes in a pan, pour over water to cover and bring to the boil. Lower the heat, cover and simmer for 40 minutes. Drain, discarding the cooking liquid. Shred the pork, using two forks. Put it in a bowl and season with the salt.

2 Heat the oil in a large frying pan. Add the onion, garlic, chilli and spices. Stir over the heat for 2–3 minutes, then add the shredded meat and cook until the meat is thoroughly heated and has absorbed the flavourings. Heat the refried beans in a small pan.

3 Meanwhile, cook the tortillas. Pour oil into a frying pan to a depth of 2cm/¾in. Heat the oil and fry one tortilla at a time, pressing down with a fish slice (metal spatula) or pair of tongs to keep it flat. As soon as a tortilla is crisp, lift it out and drain it on kitchen paper.

4 Place each tortilla on a plate. Top with refried beans. Add a little of the meat mixture, then spoon 15ml/1 tbsp of the soured cream over each. Divide the chopped tomato among the tostadas and top with the crumbled feta. Serve at once, garnished with fresh oregano.

Pork in Milk

Italian immigrants first took this Tuscan recipe to Argentina. In Peru, raisins and several sweet spices are added, but for this version only cloves are used, giving a subtle flavour.

SERVES SIX

INGREDIENTS
- 1kg/2¼lb pork loin, on the bone
- 25g/1oz/2 tbsp butter
- 15ml/1 tbsp olive oil
- 1 litre/1¾ pints/4 cups full-fat (whole) milk
- 3 whole cloves
- 4 garlic cloves, peeled but left whole
- 1 bay leaf
- juice of 2 lemons
- salt and ground black pepper
- boiled potatoes, to serve

COOK'S TIP
The milk will curdle because of the addition of lemon juice. Don't be tempted to strain it, or you'll lose half the flavour. When you blend it, it will become perfectly smooth again.

1 Preheat the oven to 180°C/350°F/ Gas 4. Season the pork and select a roasting pan that will hold it snugly. Heat the butter and oil in the roasting pan over a medium heat. When the butter has melted, add the pork and baste it all over. Cook for 10–15 minutes, turning, until golden brown all over.

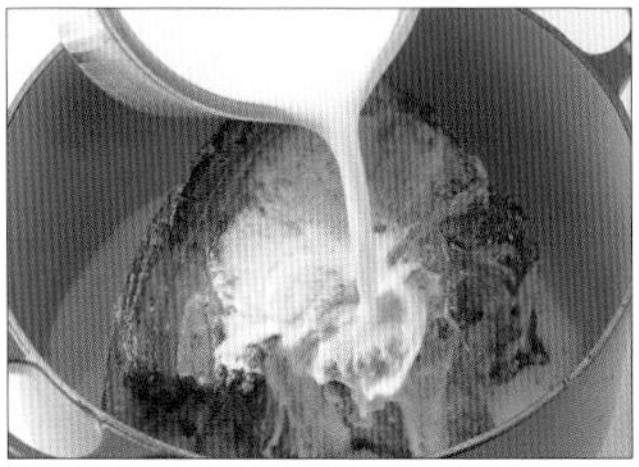

2 Pour in the milk and add the cloves, garlic, bay leaf and lemon juice. Cook in the oven for 1¾–2 hours.

3 Remove the roasting pan from the oven and transfer the pork loin to a serving platter to rest for 5 minutes. Skim the fat from the cooking liquid and, using a teaspoon, remove the cloves and bay leaf. Place the pan on the hob (stovetop) and boil over a high heat until the sauce is reduced by half.

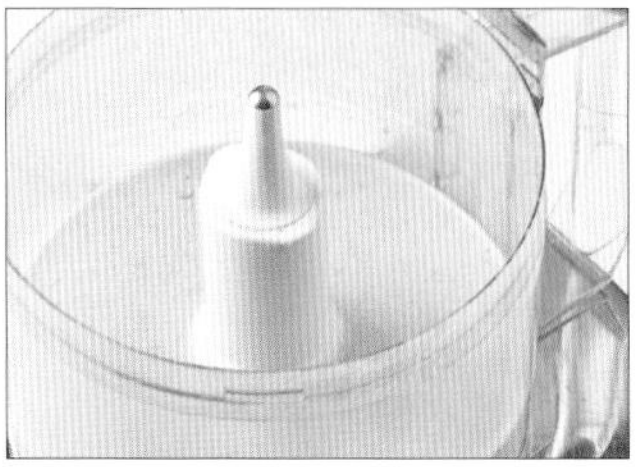

4 Process the sauce in a food processor until smooth. Carve the pork and serve it with the sauce and boiled potatoes.

Baked Ham with Orange and Lime

The delicious citrus glaze on this ham contrasts beautifully with the sweetness of the meat for this perfect Sunday lunch dish. Plain rice and black beans, those favourite Latin American side dishes, are the obvious accompaniment.

SERVES EIGHT

INGREDIENTS
- 1 green gammon (unsmoked cured ham), about 2kg/4½lb
- grated rind of 1 orange
- grated rind of 1 lime
- 1 bay leaf
- 3 fresh parsley stalks
- 6 black peppercorns
- 5 garlic cloves, crushed
- 15ml/1 tbsp dried oregano
- 2 fresh red chillies, seeded and finely chopped
- juice of 1 orange
- juice of 2 limes
- 30ml/2 tbsp soft brown sugar
- ground black pepper

1 Put the gammon in a large pan and pour in cold water to cover. Add the orange and lime rind, the bay leaf, parsley and peppercorns. Bring to the boil over a high heat, cover and lower the heat so that the water is bubbling at a gentle simmer. Cook the gammon for about 2 hours.

2 Preheat the oven to 220°C/425°F/ Gas 7. When the gammon is cooked, remove the pan from the heat. Leave until the gammon is cool enough to handle, then transfer it to a chopping board. Carefully pull away the skin, leaving the fat on the meat.

3 Mix the crushed garlic, oregano, chopped chillies, orange and lime juice and sugar in a bowl and stir well to combine. Add a generous amount of ground black pepper. Rub the mixture all over the gammon, coating it evenly. Transfer to a roasting pan and bake for 20–25 minutes or until golden.

4 Slice the ham and serve. Alternatively, enjoy as part of a buffet or picnic.

CARNITAS

In Mexico these succulent little pieces of meat, literally translated as "little meats", can be eaten as part of a main dish or used to fill tacos or burritos. They are also served with salsa as snacks or ANTOJITOS *(nibbles).*

SERVES EIGHT AS AN APPETIZER, SIX AS A MAIN COURSE

INGREDIENTS
- 2 dried bay leaves
- 10ml/2 tsp dried thyme
- 5ml/1 tsp dried marjoram
- 1.5kg/3–3½lb mixed boneless pork (loin and leg)
- 3 garlic cloves
- 2.5ml/½ tsp salt
- 200g/7oz/scant 1 cup lard
- 1 orange, cut into 8 wedges
- 1 small onion, thickly sliced
- warm wheat-flour tortillas, to serve

For the salsa
- bunch of fresh coriander (cilantro)
- 1 white onion
- 8–10 pickled jalapeño chilli slices
- 45ml/3 tbsp freshly squeezed orange juice

1 Crumble the bay leaves into a mortar. Add the dried thyme and dried marjoram and grind the mixture with a pestle to a fine powder.

COOK'S TIP

If the *carnitas* are to be served in tacos or burritos, shred or chop them. Make the chunks about half the given size if serving them as *antojitos*. Reduce the cooking time accordingly.

2 Cut the pork into 5cm/2in cubes and place it in a non-metallic bowl. Add the herbs and salt. Using your fingers, rub the spice mixture into the meat. Cover and marinate for at least 2 hours, preferably overnight.

3 To make the salsa, remove the stems from the coriander and chop the leaves roughly. Cut the onion in half, then slice each half thinly. Finely chop the jalapeño chilli slices.

4 Mix all the salsa ingredients in a bowl, pour over the freshly squeezed orange juice and toss gently to mix. Cover and chill until required.

5 Heat the lard in a flame-proof casserole. Add the pork mixture, with the oranges, garlic cloves and onion. Brown the pork cubes on all sides.

6 Using a slotted spoon, lift out the onion and garlic and discard. Cover the casserole and continue to cook over a low heat for about 1½ hours.

7 Remove the lid and lift out and discard the orange wedges. Continue to cook the mixture, uncovered, until all the meat juices have been absorbed and the pork cubes are crisp on the outside and tender and moist inside. Serve with warm tortillas and the salsa.

Pork Casserole with Onions, Chilli and Dried Fruit

Inspired by South American cooking, a mole – paste – of chilli, shallots and nuts is added to this casserole of pork and onions. Part of the mole is added at the end of cooking to retain its fresh flavour. Serve with rice and a green salad.

SERVES SIX

INGREDIENTS

- 25ml/1½ tbsp plain (all-purpose) flour
- 1kg/2¼lb shoulder or leg of pork, cut into 5cm/2in cubes
- 45–60ml/3–4 tbsp olive oil
- 2 large onions, chopped
- 2 garlic cloves, finely chopped
- 600ml/1 pint/2½ cups fruity white wine
- 105ml/7 tbsp water
- 115g/4oz ready-to-eat prunes
- 115g/4oz ready-to-eat dried apricots
- grated rind and juice of 1 small orange
- pinch of muscovado (molasses) sugar (optional)
- 30ml/2 tbsp chopped fresh parsley
- ½–1 fresh green chilli, seeded and finely chopped (optional)
- salt and ground black pepper

For the mole

- 3 *ancho* chillies and 2 *pasilla* chillies (or other varieties of large, medium-hot dried red chillies)
- 30ml/2 tbsp olive oil
- 2 shallots, chopped
- 2 garlic cloves, chopped
- 1 fresh green chilli, seeded and chopped
- 10ml/2 tsp ground coriander
- 5ml/1 tsp mild Spanish paprika or *pimentón*
- 50g/2oz/½ cup blanched almonds, toasted
- 15ml/1 tbsp chopped fresh oregano or 2.5ml/½ tsp dried oregano

1 Make the mole paste first. Toast the dried chillies in a dry frying pan over a low heat for 1–2 minutes, until they are aromatic, then soak them in warm water for 30 minutes.

2 Drain the chillies, reserving the soaking water, and discard their stalks and seeds. Preheat the oven to 160°C/325°F/Gas 3.

3 Heat the oil in a small frying pan and fry the shallots, garlic, fresh green chilli and ground coriander over a very low heat for 5 minutes.

4 Transfer the shallot mixture to a food processor or blender and add the drained chillies, paprika or *pimentón*, almonds and oregano. Process the mixture, adding 45–60ml/3–4 tbsp of the chilli soaking liquid to make a workable paste.

5 Season the flour with salt and black pepper, then use to coat the pork. Heat 45ml/3 tbsp of the olive oil in a large, heavy-based frying pan and fry the pork, stirring frequently, until sealed on all sides. Transfer the pork cubes to a flameproof casserole.

6 If necessary, add the remaining oil to the frying pan and cook the onions and garlic gently for 8–10 minutes, stirring occasionally.

7 Add the wine and water to the frying pan. Cook for 2 minutes. Stir in half the mole paste, bring back to the boil and bubble for a few seconds before pouring over the pork.

8 Season lightly with salt and pepper and stir to mix, then cover and cook in the oven for 1½ hours.

9 Increase the oven temperature to 180°C/350°F/Gas 4. Stir in the prunes, apricots and orange juice. Test the seasoning, adding the muscovado sugar if necessary, cover and cook for another 30–45 minutes.

10 Place the casserole over a direct heat and stir in the remaining mole paste. Simmer, stirring once or twice, for 5 minutes. Serve sprinkled with the orange rind, chopped parsley and fresh chilli, if using.

TORTILLA PIE WITH CHORIZO

THIS IS A POPULAR MEXICAN BREAKFAST DISH, KNOWN AS CHILAQUILES. *THE FRIED TORTILLA STRIPS STAY CRISP IN THE TOMATILLO, CREAM AND CHEESE SAUCE.*

SERVES SIX

INGREDIENTS

- 25g/1oz/2 tbsp lard or 30ml/2 tbsp vegetable oil
- 500g/1¼lb minced (ground) pork
- 3 garlic cloves, crushed
- 10ml/2 tsp dried oregano
- 5ml/1 tsp ground cinnamon
- 2.5ml/½ tsp ground cloves
- 2.5ml/½ tsp ground black pepper
- 30ml/2 tbsp dry sherry
- 5ml/1 tsp caster (superfine) sugar
- 5ml/1 tsp salt
- 12 corn tortillas, freshly made or a few days old
- oil, for frying
- 350g/12oz/3 cups grated Monterey Jack or mild Cheddar cheese
- 300ml/½ pint/1¼ cups crème fraîche

For the tomatillo sauce

- 300g/11oz/scant 2 cups drained canned tomatillos
- 60ml/4 tbsp stock or water
- 2 fresh serrano chillies, seeded and roughly chopped
- 2 garlic cloves
- bunch of fresh coriander (cilantro)
- 120ml/4fl oz/½ cup soured cream

1 Preheat the oven to 180°C/350°F/Gas 4. Heat the lard or oil in a large pan. Add the minced pork and crushed garlic. Stir over a moderate heat until the meat has browned, then stir in the oregano, cinnamon, cloves and pepper. Cook for 3–4 minutes more, stirring all the time, then add the sherry, sugar and salt. Stir for 3–4 minutes until all the flavours are blended, then remove the pan from the heat.

2 Cut the tortillas into 2cm/¾in strips. Pour oil into a frying pan to a depth of 2cm/¾in and heat to 190°C/375°F. Fry the tortilla strips in batches until crisp and golden brown all over.

3 Spread half the minced pork mixture in a baking dish. Top with half the tortilla strips and grated cheese, then add dollops of crème fraîche. Repeat the layers. Bake for 20–25 minutes, or until bubbling.

4 To make the sauce, put all the ingredients except the soured cream in a food processor or blender. Reserve a little coriander for sprinkling. Process until smooth. Scrape into a pan, bring to the boil, then lower the heat and simmer for 5 minutes.

5 Stir the soured cream into the sauce, with salt and pepper to taste. Pour the mixture over the layer bake and serve immediately, sprinkled with coriander.

SCRAMBLED EGGS WITH CHORIZO

This popular Mexican dish is often eaten for breakfast. Dried, Spanish-style chorizo gives the eggs a rich golden colour and delicious smoky flavour. Buy the sausage in one piece and slice it just before cooking.

SERVES FOUR

INGREDIENTS
- 15ml/1 tbsp olive oil
- 150g/5oz dried chorizo, cut into 1cm/½in slices
- 2.5ml/½ tsp paprika
- 8 eggs, lightly beaten
- salt
- country bread and green salad, to serve

VARIATION
For extra fire and spice, add a dash of a hot pepper sauce, such as Tabasco, to the beaten egg mixture.

1 Heat the oil in a large frying pan over a medium heat and pan-fry the chorizo slices for 1–2 minutes, until browned and crisp.

COOK'S TIP
The chorizo will brown very quickly, so do not leave it to cook unattended, or it may burn.

2 Add the paprika, stir for 30 seconds, then pour in the beaten eggs. Season lightly with salt. As the eggs start to set, break them up with a fork.

3 Remove the pan from the heat when the mixture is still quite moist; it will continue cooking off the heat. Serve with the bread and a green salad.

POULTRY

Chicken is the meat most frequently eaten in the Caribbean and Latin America. The Caribbean Sunday roast is extremely popular, but for delicious weekday meals try thyme and lime chicken, or chicken with okra. Colombian chicken hot-pot and carapulcra*, a chicken and pork dish from Peru, are both national dishes. Turkey and duck are also popular throughout the region.*

CUBAN CHICKEN PIE

THIS IS A GREAT FAMILY MEAL, PERFECT FOR A SUNDAY LUNCH. THE FILLING, WHICH INCLUDES CAPERS, OLIVES AND RAISINS, PROVIDES A FLAVOURSOME CONTRAST TO THE CRISP CORN TOPPING.

SERVES SIX

INGREDIENTS
- 1 chicken, about 1.6kg/3½lb
- 6 peppercorns
- 1 bay leaf
- 3 fresh parsley sprigs
- 30ml/2 tbsp olive oil
- 1 large onion, finely chopped
- 2 hard-boiled eggs, chopped
- 2 tomatoes, roughly chopped
- 50g/2oz/½ cup pitted green olives, roughly chopped
- 15ml/1 tbsp drained bottled capers
- 65g/2½oz/scant ½ cup raisins
- salt and ground black pepper

For the topping
- 500g/1¼lb/3⅓ cups drained canned or thawed frozen corn kernels
- 90g/3½oz butter
- 10ml/2 tsp caster (superfine) sugar
- 3 eggs, lightly beaten
- salt

1 Put the chicken in a large, heavy pan and add enough water to cover. Add the peppercorns, bay leaf and parsley and bring to the boil over a high heat. Lower the heat, cover and simmer gently for 1 hour or until cooked through.

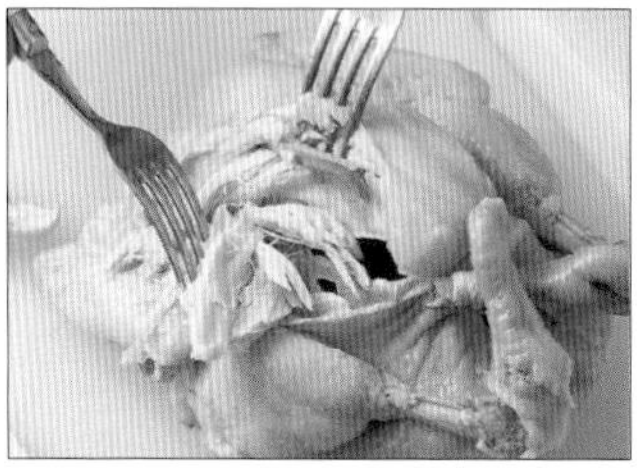

2 Allow the chicken to cool in the cooking liquid. When cold enough to handle, lift the chicken out of the pan and, using two forks, shred the flesh roughly. Discard the skin and bones.

3 Make the topping. Tip the corn kernels into a blender or food processor and purée until smooth. Melt the butter in a pan over a low heat. Stir in the puréed corn and sugar. Season generously with salt and cook, stirring, for 10 minutes, until the mixture thickens and comes away from the sides of the pan.

4 Remove from the heat and leave to cool for 10 minutes, then slowly stir in the beaten eggs, a little at a time. Set the topping mixture aside.

5 Preheat the oven to 180°C/350°F/Gas 4. Heat the oil in a large frying pan and stir in the chopped onion. Cook gently for 5 minutes, until soft and translucent, and season with salt and black pepper to taste.

6 Stir in the chopped hard-boiled eggs, chopped tomatoes, olives, capers and raisins. Fold in the shredded chicken, making sure that it is well distributed throughout the mixture.

7 Spoon the pie filling into a 25 x 20cm/10 x 8in baking dish. Using a spoon, spread the corn topping evenly over the top of the chicken filling and bake for 45 minutes, until golden brown. Leave to stand for about 10 minutes before serving on warm plates.

VARIATION
Shortcrust pastry can be used instead of the corn topping.

CHICKEN WITH OKRA

SERVE THIS CLASSIC BRAZILIAN DISH FOR A FAMILY SUPPER. IT IS TOTALLY FUSS-FREE, TAKING VERY LITTLE TIME AND EFFORT TO PREPARE.

SERVES FOUR

INGREDIENTS
- 15ml/1 tbsp olive oil
- 4 chicken thighs
- 1 large onion, finely chopped
- 2 garlic cloves, finely crushed
- 2 fresh red chillies, seeded and finely chopped
- 120ml/4fl oz/½ cup water
- 350g/12oz okra
- 2 large tomatoes, finely chopped
- salt
- boiled white rice or polenta, to serve
- hot chilli oil (optional)

COOK'S TIP

As okra cooks, the pods release a sticky juice, which coats and flavours the chicken. If you don't like this sticky texture, however, cook the pods whole, simply trimming off the tops but not cutting into the pods themselves.

1 Heat the oil in a wide pan over a low heat. Season the chicken thighs with salt and add them to the pan, skin side down. Cook until golden brown, turn them over and add the chopped onion.

2 Sauté for 5 minutes, until the onion has softened; then add the garlic and chopped chillies. Cook for a further 2 minutes. Add half the water to the pan and bring to the boil. Lower the heat, cover and cook for 30 minutes.

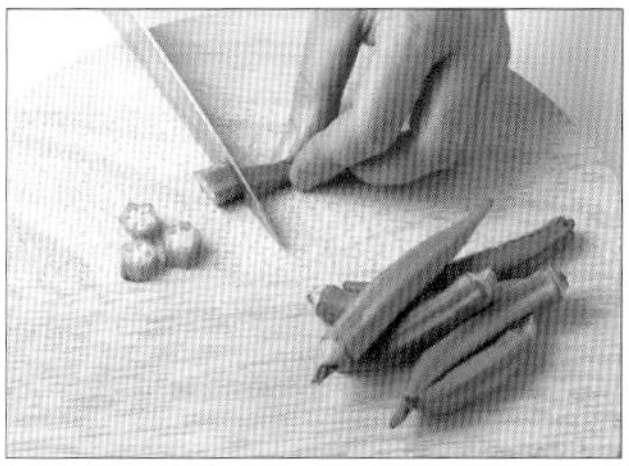

3 Trim the okra and slice into thin rounds. Add to the pan with the tomatoes. Season with salt and pour in the remaining water. Cover and simmer gently for about 10–15 minutes, or until the chicken pieces are tender and fully cooked. The chicken is ready when the flesh can be pulled off the bone easily.

4 Serve immediately with boiled white rice or polenta, and offer some hot chilli oil on the side.

BURRITOS WITH CHICKEN AND RICE

In Mexico, burritos are a very popular light meal or lunch. The secret of a successful burrito is to have all the filling neatly packaged inside the tortilla for easy eating, so these meals are seldom served with a pour-over sauce or a knife and fork.

SERVES FOUR

INGREDIENTS
- 90g/3½oz/½ cup long grain rice
- 15ml/1 tbsp vegetable oil
- 1 onion, chopped
- 2.5ml/½ tsp ground cloves
- 5ml/1 tsp dried, or fresh oregano
- 200g/7oz can chopped tomatoes in tomato juice
- 2 skinless, boneless chicken breasts
- 150g/5oz/1¼ cups grated Monterey Jack or mild Cheddar cheese
- 60ml/4 tbsp soured cream (optional)
- 8 x 20–25cm/8–10in fresh wheat-flour tortillas
- salt
- fresh oregano, to garnish (optional)

1 Bring a pan of lightly salted water to the boil. Add the rice and cook for 8 minutes. Drain, rinse thoroughly and then drain again.

2 Heat the oil in a large pan. Add the onion, with the ground cloves and oregano, and fry for 2–3 minutes. Stir in the rice and tomatoes and cook over a low heat until all the tomato juice has been absorbed. Set the pan aside.

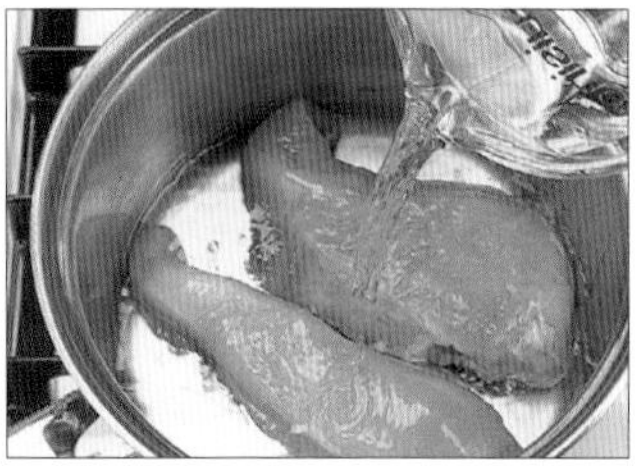

3 Put the chicken breasts in a large pan, pour in enough water to cover and bring to the boil. Lower the heat and simmer for about 10 minutes or until the chicken is cooked through. Lift the chicken out of the pan, put on a plate and cool slightly.

4 Preheat the oven to 160°C/325°F/ Gas 3. Shred the chicken by pulling the flesh apart with two forks, then add the chicken to the rice mixture, with the grated cheese. Stir in the soured cream, if using.

COOK'S TIP

If you use very fresh tortillas, you may be able to dispense with the cocktail sticks (toothpicks). Secure the tortilla parcels by damping the final fold with water. When you lay the burritos in the dish, place the folded surfaces down.

5 Wrap the tortillas in foil and place them on a plate. Stand the plate over boiling water for about 5 minutes. Alternatively, wrap in microwave-safe film and heat in a microwave on full power for 1 minute.

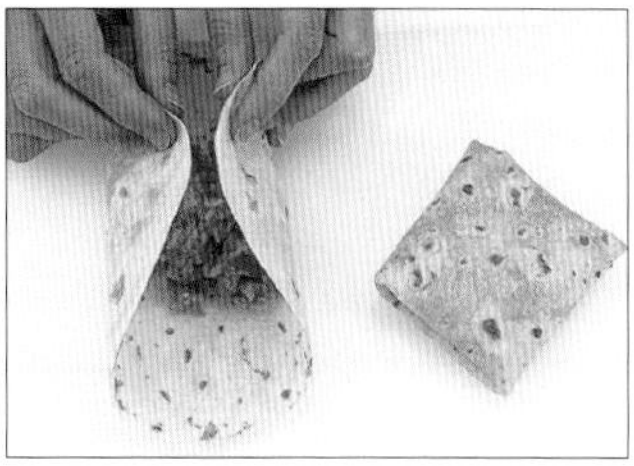

6 Spoon one-eighth of the filling into the centre of a tortilla and fold in both sides. Fold the bottom up and the top down to form a parcel. Secure with a cocktail stick (toothpick).

7 Put the filled burrito in a shallow dish or casserole, cover with foil and keep warm in the oven while you make seven more. Remove the cocktail sticks before serving, sprinkled with fresh oregano.

Chicken and Tomatillo Chimichangas

These fried burritos are a common sight in the restaurants and cafés that line the Mexican border with Texas, although they are not so well known further south.

SERVES FOUR

INGREDIENTS

- 2 skinless, boneless chicken breasts
- 1 chipotle chilli, seeded
- 15ml/1 tbsp vegetable oil
- 2 onions, finely chopped
- 4 garlic cloves, crushed
- 2.5ml/½ tsp ground cumin
- 2.5ml/½ tsp ground coriander
- 2.5ml/½ tsp ground cinnamon
- 2.5ml/½ tsp ground cloves
- 300g/11oz/scant 2 cups drained canned tomatillos
- 400g/14oz/2⅓ cups cooked pinto beans
- 8 x 20–25cm/8–10in fresh wheat-flour tortillas
- oil, for frying
- salt and ground black pepper

1 Put the chicken breasts in a large pan, pour over water to cover and add the chilli. Bring to the boil, lower the heat and simmer for 10 minutes or until the chicken is cooked through and the chilli has softened. Remove the chilli and chop it finely. Lift the chicken breasts out of the pan and put them on a plate. Leave to cool slightly, then shred with two forks.

2 Heat the oil in a frying pan. Fry the onions until translucent, then add the garlic and ground spices and cook for 3 minutes more. Add the tomatillos and pinto beans. Cook over a moderate heat for 5 minutes, stirring constantly to break up the tomatillos and some of the beans. Simmer gently for 5 minutes more. Add the chicken and seasoning.

3 Wrap the tortillas in foil and place them on a plate. Stand the plate over boiling water for about 5 minutes until they become pliable. Alternatively, wrap them in microwave-safe film and heat them in a microwave on full power for 1 minute.

4 Spoon one-eighth of the bean filling into the centre of a tortilla, fold in both sides, then fold the bottom up and the top down to form a neat parcel. Secure with a cocktail stick (toothpick).

5 Heat the oil in a large frying pan. Remove the sticks and fry the chimichangas in batches, turning once. Remove them from the oil with a slotted spoon and drain on kitchen paper.

COOK'S TIP

The word "pinto" means speckled, which aptly describes these attractive dried beans. If you prepare them yourself, they will need to be soaked overnight in water, then cooked in unsalted boiling water for 1–1¼ hours until tender.

DRUNKEN CHICKEN

TEQUILA IS THIS CHICKEN'S TIPPLE, AND THE DISH HAS A DELICIOUS SWEET-AND-SOUR FLAVOUR. SERVE IT WITH GREEN OR YELLOW RICE AND FLOUR TORTILLAS TO MOP UP THE SAUCE.

SERVES FOUR

INGREDIENTS

- 150g/5oz/scant 1 cup raisins
- 120ml/4fl oz/½ cup sherry
- 115g/4oz/1 cup plain (all-purpose) flour
- 2.5ml/½ tsp salt
- 2.5ml/½ tsp ground black pepper
- 45ml/3 tbsp vegetable oil
- 8 skinless chicken thighs, bone-in
- 1 onion, halved and thinly sliced
- 3 garlic cloves, crushed
- 2 tart eating apples, such as Granny Smith
- 115g/4oz/1 cup slivered almonds
- 1 ripe plantain, peeled and sliced
- 350ml/12fl oz/1½ cups well-flavoured chicken stock
- 250ml/8fl oz/1 cup tequila
- fresh herbs, chopped, to garnish

1 Put the raisins in a bowl and pour the sherry over. Set aside to plump up. Season the flour with the salt and pepper and spread it out on a large, flat dish or soup plate. Heat 30ml/2 tbsp of the oil in a large frying pan. Dip each chicken thigh in turn in the seasoned flour, then fry in the hot oil until browned, turning occasionally. Drain on kitchen paper.

2 Heat the remaining vegetable oil in a large, deep frying pan. Add the onion slices and crushed garlic and cook for 2–3 minutes. Meanwhile, peel, core and dice the apples.

3 Add the diced apple to the onion mixture with the almonds and plantain slices. Cook, stirring occasionally, for 3–4 minutes, then add the soaked raisins, with any free sherry. Add the chicken pieces to the pan.

4 Pour the stock and tequila over the chicken mixture. Cover the pan with a lid and cook for 15 minutes, then take off the lid and cook for 10 minutes more or until the sauce has reduced by about half.

5 Check that the chicken thighs are cooked by lifting one out of the pan and piercing it in the thickest part with a sharp knife or skewer. Any juices that come out should be clear. If necessary, cook the chicken for a little longer before serving, sprinkled with chopped fresh herbs.

Colombian Chicken Hot-Pot

Colombians are justifiably proud of this national dish. Traditionally, three native varieties of potatoes are used, each with a different texture, to create a tasty thick broth. The addition of coriander and corn provides a complementary sweetness.

SERVES EIGHT

INGREDIENTS

- 1.6kg/3½lb chicken
- 3 spring onions (scallions)
- 2 bay leaves
- 6 fresh coriander (cilantro) sprigs
- 6 whole black peppercorns
- 675g/1½lb floury potatoes, peeled and cut into 1cm/½in chunks
- 675g/1½lb waxy potatoes, peeled and cut into 1cm/½in chunks
- 675g/1½lb baby new potatoes or salad potatoes
- 2 corn cobs, each cut into 4 pieces
- salt
- capers and sour cream, to serve

For the avocado salsa

- 1 hard-boiled egg
- 1 large ripe avocado
- 1 spring onion (scallion), finely chopped
- 15ml/1 tbsp chopped fresh coriander (cilantro)
- 1 fresh green chilli, seeded and finely chopped
- salt

1 Put the chicken in a large pan or flameproof casserole and cover with water. Add the spring onions (scallions), bay leaves, coriander sprigs and peppercorns. Season, bring to the boil and skim the surface of the liquid.

2 Reduce the heat to a gentle simmer, cover and cook for 1 hour or until the chicken is tender and fully cooked. Remove from the heat and allow the chicken to cool in the cooking liquid.

3 Drain the chicken, reserving the cooking liquid to use as stock. Place the chicken on a board and cut it into 8 pieces. It should be so tender that the legs are easy to pull off.

4 Separate the thighs from the drumsticks. Use a knife to cut between the two breasts, then gently ease the meat off the bone. Cut the breasts in half, set the chicken pieces aside on a plate and discard the rest of the carcass.

5 Skim the fat from the top of the cooking liquid, then strain it into a clean pan. Bring to the boil. Add the floury and waxy potatoes and simmer for 15 minutes. Stir in the new potatoes or salad potatoes and corn and simmer for a further 20 minutes.

6 By this time, the floury potatoes will have broken up and they will have helped to thicken the liquid. The waxy potatoes should be soft and partly broken. The new or salad potatoes should be tender but still whole. Return the chicken pieces to the pan and reheat gently but thoroughly.

7 Meanwhile, make the fresh avocado salsa. Peel and roughly chop the hard-boiled egg. Using a fork, mash it in a small bowl.

8 Just before serving, cut the avocado in half lengthways and, using a teaspoon, scoop the flesh into a separate bowl. Mash well with a fork, then stir in the chopped hard-boiled egg until thoroughly combined. Add the spring onion, fresh coriander and chilli, mix well, then season to taste with salt.

9 Serve the chicken mixture in a heated casserole or earthenware dish, with bowls of hot tomato salsa, capers and sour cream on the side, if you like.

COOK'S TIP

The quality and flavour of the chicken stock in this dish will depend entirely on what kind of chicken you use. It is worth spending a bit more and buying the best bird you can find, preferably free range, corn-fed or organic. You will really taste the difference.

CHICKEN WITH CHIPOTLE SAUCE

IT IS IMPORTANT TO SEEK OUT CHIPOTLE CHILLIES FOR THIS MEXICAN RECIPE, AS THEY IMPART A WONDERFULLY RICH AND SMOKY FLAVOUR TO THE CHICKEN BREASTS. THE PURÉE CAN BE MADE AHEAD OF TIME, MAKING THIS A VERY EASY RECIPE FOR ENTERTAINING.

SERVES SIX

INGREDIENTS

6 chipotle chillies
200ml/7fl oz/scant 1 cup water
chicken stock
3 onions
6 boneless chicken breasts
45ml/3 tbsp vegetable oil
salt and ground black pepper
fresh oregano to garnish

1 Put the dried chillies in a bowl and pour over hot water to cover. Leave to stand for about 30 minutes until very soft. Drain, reserving the soaking water in a measuring jug. Cut off the stalk from each chilli, then slit them lengthways and scrape out the seeds with a small sharp knife.

2 Preheat the oven to 180°C/350°F/Gas 4. Chop the flesh of the chillies roughly and put it in a food processor or blender. Add enough chicken stock to the soaking water to make it up to 400ml/14fl oz/1⅔ cups. Pour it into the processor or blender and process at maximum power until smooth.

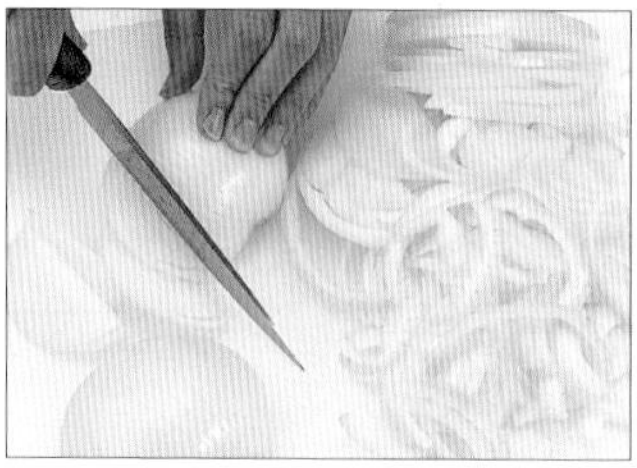

3 Peel the onions. Using a sharp knife, cut them in half, then slice them thinly. Separate the slices.

4 Remove the skin from the chicken breasts and trim off any stray pieces of fat or membrane.

5 Heat the oil in a large frying pan, add the onions and cook over a low to moderate heat for about 5 minutes, or until they have softened but not coloured, stirring occasionally.

6 Using a slotted spoon, transfer the onion slices to a casserole that is large enough to hold all the chicken breasts in a single layer. Sprinkle the onion slices with a little salt and ground black pepper.

COOK'S TIP

If you are particularly fond of chipotle chillies and like a spicy, hot sauce, you may wish to use more than six.

7 Arrange the chicken breasts on top of the onion slices. Sprinkle with a little salt and several grindings of black pepper.

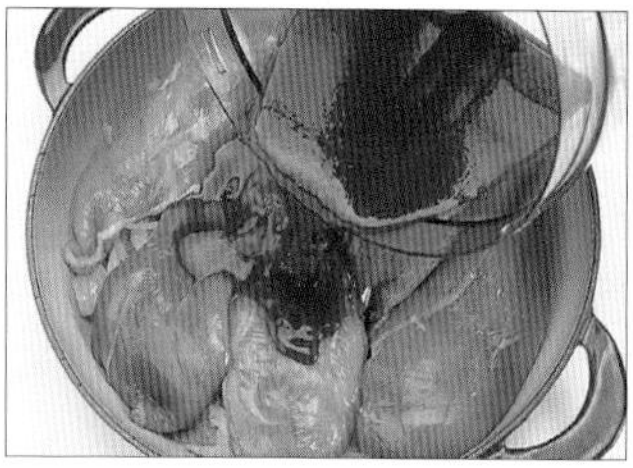

8 Pour the chipotle purée over the chicken breasts, making sure that each piece is evenly coated.

9 Place the casserole in the preheated oven and bake for 45 minutes–1 hour or until the chicken is cooked through, but still moist and tender. Garnish with fresh oregano, and serve with boiled white rice.

Spinach and Potato Stuffed Chicken Breasts

This dish consists of large chicken breasts filled with a herby spinach mixture, topped with butter and baked until mouth-wateringly tender.

SERVES SIX

INGREDIENTS

- 115g/4oz floury potatoes, diced
- 115g/4oz spinach leaves, finely chopped
- 1 egg, beaten
- 30ml/2 tbsp chopped fresh coriander (cilantro)
- 4 large chicken breasts
- 50g/2oz/4 tbsp butter

For the sauce

- 400g/14oz can chopped tomatoes
- 1 garlic clove, crushed
- 150ml/¼ pint/⅔ cup hot chicken stock
- 30ml/2 tbsp chopped fresh coriander
- salt and ground black pepper
- fried mushrooms, to serve

1 Preheat the oven to 180°C/350°F/Gas 4. Boil the potatoes in a large pan of lightly salted boiling water for 15 minutes or until tender. Drain the potatoes, place them in a large bowl and roughly mash with a fork.

2 Stir the spinach into the potato with the egg and coriander. Season with salt and pepper to taste.

3 Cut almost all the way through the chicken breasts and open out to form a pocket in each. Spoon the filling into the centre and fold the chicken back over again. Secure with cocktail sticks (toothpicks) and place in a roasting tin.

4 Dot with butter and cover with foil. Bake for 25 minutes. Remove the foil and cook for a further 10 minutes until the chicken is golden.

5 Meanwhile, to make the sauce heat the tomatoes, garlic and stock in a pan. Boil rapidly for 10 minutes. Season and stir in the coriander. Remove the chicken from the oven and serve with the sauce and fried mushrooms.

COOK'S TIP

Young spinach leaves have a sweeter flavour and are ideal for this dish.

MOLE POBLANO DE GUAJOLOTE

Mole Poblano de Guajolote is the great festive dish of Mexico. It is served at any special occasion, be it a birthday, wedding or family get-together. Rice, beans, tortillas and Guacamole are the traditional accompaniments.

SERVES SIX–EIGHT

INGREDIENTS

- 2.75–3.6kg/6–8lb turkey, cut into serving pieces
- 1 onion, chopped
- 1 garlic clove, chopped
- 90ml/6 tbsp lard or corn oil
- salt
- fresh coriander (cilantro) and 30ml/2 tbsp toasted sesame seeds, to garnish

For the sauce

- 6 dried ancho chillies
- 4 dried pasilla chillies
- 4 dried mulato chillies
- 1 drained canned chipotle chilli, seeded and chopped (optional)
- 2 onions, chopped
- 2 garlic cloves, chopped
- 450g/1lb tomatoes, peeled and chopped
- 1 stale tortilla, torn into pieces
- 50g/2oz/⅓ cup seedless raisins
- 115g/4oz/1 cup ground almonds
- 45ml/3 tbsp sesame seeds, ground
- 2.5ml/½ tsp coriander seeds, ground
- 5ml/1 tsp ground cinnamon
- 2.5ml/½ tsp ground anise
- 1.5ml/¼ tsp ground black peppercorns
- 60ml/4 tbsp lard or corn oil
- 40g/1½oz unsweetened (bitter) chocolate, broken into squares
- 15ml/1 tbsp sugar
- salt and ground pepper

1 Put the turkey pieces in a pan or flameproof casserole large enough to hold them in one layer. Add the onion and garlic, and enough cold water to cover. Season with salt, bring to a simmer, cover and cook for about 1 hour, or until the turkey pieces are thooughly cooked.

2 Meanwhile, put the ancho, pasilla and mulato chillies in a dry frying pan over a low heat and roast them for a few minutes, shaking the pan frequently.

3 Remove the stems and shake out the seeds. Tear the pods into pieces and put these into a small bowl. Add sufficient warm water to just cover and soak, turning occasionally, for 30 minutes, until soft.

4 Lift out the turkey pieces and pat them dry with kitchen paper. Reserve the stock in a measuring jug (pitcher). Heat the lard or oil in a large frying pan and sauté the turkey pieces until lightly browned all over. Transfer to a plate and set aside. Reserve the oil that is left in the frying pan.

5 Tip the chillies, with the water in which they have been soaked, into a food processor. Add the chipotle chilli, if using, with the onions, garlic, tomatoes, tortilla, raisins, ground almonds and spices. Process to a purée. Do this in batches if necessary.

6 Add the oil to the frying pan used for sautéing the turkey. Heat the mixture, then add the chilli and spice paste. Cook, stirring, for 5 minutes.Transfer the mixture to the pan or casserole in which the turkey was originally cooked. Stir in 475ml/16fl oz/2 cups of the turkey stock.

7 Add the chocolate and season with salt and pepper. Cook over a low heat until the chocolate has melted. Stir in the sugar. Add the turkey, cover and simmer gently for 30 minutes.

Peanut Chicken

The rich sauce for this popular Caribbean dish is best made with smooth peanut butter, although it can also be made with ground peanuts.

SERVES FOUR

INGREDIENTS
- 900g/2lb boneless chicken breast portions, skinned and cut into cubes
- 2 garlic cloves, crushed
- 2.5ml/½ tsp dried thyme
- 2.5ml/½ tsp ground black pepper
- 15ml/1 tbsp curry powder
- 15ml/1 tbsp lemon juice
- 25g/1oz/2 tbsp butter or margarine
- 1 onion, chopped
- 45ml/3 tbsp chopped tomatoes
- 1 fresh hot chilli, seeded and chopped
- 30ml/2 tbsp smooth peanut butter
- 450ml/¾ pint/scant 2 cups warm water
- salt
- fresh coriander (cilantro) sprigs, to garnish
- fried plantain, to serve
- okra, to serve

1 Put the chicken in a large bowl and stir in the garlic, thyme, black pepper, curry powder, lemon juice and a little salt. Cover and marinate in a cool place for 3–4 hours.

2 Melt the butter or margarine in a large pan. Add the onion, sauté gently for 5 minutes, then add the seasoned chicken. Fry over a medium heat for 10 minutes, turning frequently, and then stir in the tomatoes and chilli.

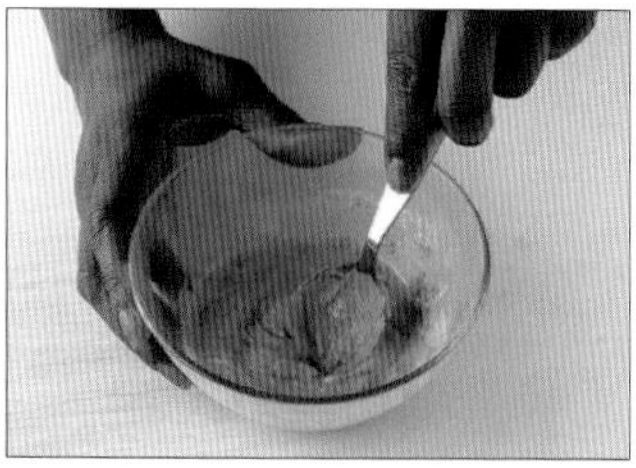

3 In a small bowl, blend the peanut butter to a smooth paste with a little of the warm water and stir this paste into the chicken mixture.

4 Gradually stir in the remaining water, then simmer gently for about 30 minutes or until the chicken is fully cooked. Add a little more water if the sauce begins to dry out. Garnish with sprigs of fresh coriander and serve hot with slices of fried plantain and okra.

Breast of Turkey with Mango and Wine

Fresh tropical mango and warm cinnamon combine to give a real taste of the Caribbean.

SERVES FOUR

INGREDIENTS
- 4 turkey breast fillets
- 1 small ripe mango
- 1 garlic clove, crushed
- 1.5ml/¼ tsp ground cinnamon
- 15ml/1 tbsp finely chopped fresh parsley
- 15ml/1 tbsp crushed cream crackers (oyster crackers)
- 40g/1½oz/3 tbsp butter or margarine
- 1 garlic clove, crushed
- 6 shallots, sliced
- 150ml/¼ pint/⅔ cup white wine
- salt and ground black pepper
- diced fresh mango and chopped fresh parsley, to garnish

1 Cut a slit horizontally into each turkey fillet to make a pocket. Using a sharp knife, peel the mango and cut the flesh off the stone (pit). Finely chop enough of the flesh to make 30ml/2 tbsp and roughly dice the remainder.

2 Mix the garlic, cinnamon, parsley, cracker crumbs and finely chopped mango in a bowl. Add 15ml/1 tbsp of the butter or margarine with salt and pepper to taste and mash together.

3 Spoon a little of the mango mixture into each of the pockets in the turkey breast fillets and close, securing with a wooden cocktail stick (toothpick) if necessary. Season with a little extra ground black pepper.

4 Melt the remaining butter in a frying pan and sauté the crushed garlic and sliced shallots for about 5 minutes. Add the turkey fillets and cook for 15 minutes, turning once. Add the wine, cover and simmer for 5–10 minutes, until the turkey is cooked. Add the mango, heat, and serve garnished with parsley.

CHICKEN FAJITAS

IN MEXICO THIS DISH IS POPULAR FOR CASUAL ENTERTAINING. FAJITAS ARE FLOUR TORTILLAS THAT ARE BROUGHT TO THE TABLE FRESHLY COOKED, STILL WARM. GUESTS SELECT AND ADD THEIR OWN FILLINGS BEFORE FOLDING THE TORTILLAS AND TUCKING IN.

SERVES SIX

INGREDIENTS
- 3 skinless, boneless chicken breasts
- grated rind and juice of 2 limes
- 30ml/2 tbsp caster (superfine) sugar
- 10ml/2 tsp dried oregano
- 2.5ml/½ tsp cayenne pepper
- 5ml/1 tsp ground cinnamon
- 2 onions
- 3 (bell) peppers (1 red, 1 yellow or orange, and 1 green)
- 45ml/3 tbsp vegetable oil
- guacamole, salsa and soured cream, to serve

For the tortillas
- 250g/9oz/2¼ cups plain (all-purpose) flour, sifted
- 1.5ml/¼ tsp baking powder
- pinch of salt
- 50g/2oz/¼ cup lard
- 60ml/4 tbsp warm water

1 Slice the chicken breasts into 2cm/¾in wide strips and place these in a large bowl. Add the lime rind and juice, caster sugar, oregano, cayenne and cinnamon. Mix thoroughly. Set aside to marinate for at least 30 minutes.

COOK'S TIP
Tortilla dough can be very difficult to roll out thinly. If the dough is breaking up try placing each ball between two sheets of clean plastic (this can be cut from a new sandwich bag). Roll out, turning over, still inside the plastic, until the tortilla is the right size.

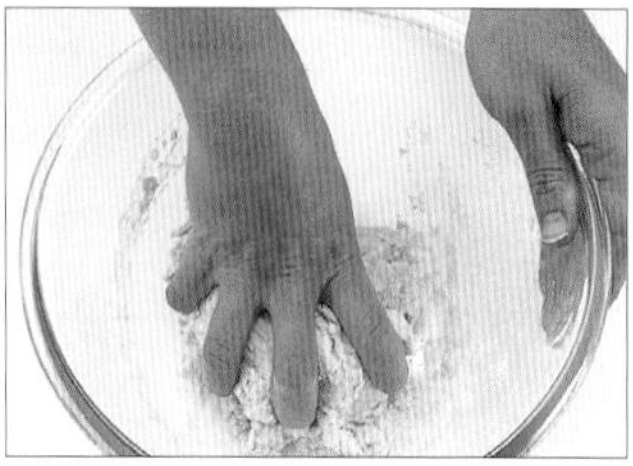

2 Meanwhile, make the tortillas. Mix the flour, baking powder and salt in a large bowl. Rub in the lard, then add the warm water, a little at a time, to make a stiff dough. Knead this on a lightly floured surface for 10–15 minutes until it is smooth and elastic.

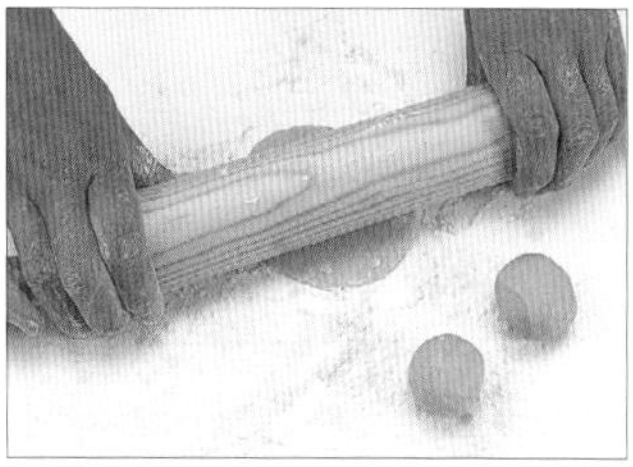

3 Divide the dough into 12 small balls, then roll each ball to a 15cm/6in round. Cover the rounds with clear film (plastic wrap) to keep them from drying out while you prepare the vegetables.

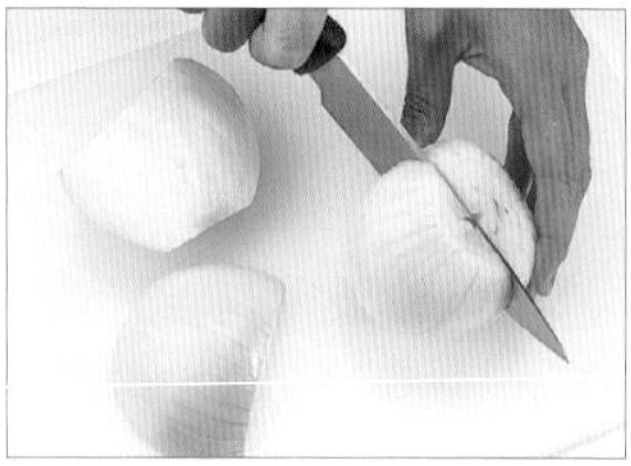

4 Cut the onions in half and slice them thinly. Cut the peppers in half, remove the cores and seeds, then slice the flesh into 1cm/½in wide strips.

5 Heat a large frying pan or griddle and cook each tortilla in turn for about 1 minute on each side, or until the surface colours and begins to blister. Keep the cooked tortillas warm and pliable by wrapping them in a clean, dry dishtowel.

6 Heat the oil in a large frying pan. Stir-fry the marinated chicken for 5–6 minutes, then add the peppers and onions and cook for 3–4 minutes more, until the chicken strips are cooked through and the vegetables are soft and tender, but still juicy.

7 Spoon the chicken mixture into a serving bowl and take it to the table with the cooked tortillas, guacamole, salsa and soured cream. Keep the tortillas wrapped and warm.

8 To serve, each guest takes a warm tortilla, spreads it with a little salsa, adds a spoonful of guacamole and piles some of the chicken mixture in the centre. The final touch is to add a small dollop of soured cream. The tortilla is then folded over the filling and eaten in the hand.

Barbecued Jerk Chicken

Jerk seasoning is a blend of herbs and spices that is rubbed into meat before it is cooked over charcoal sprinkled with pimiento berries. In Jamaica, jerk seasoning was originally used only for pork, but jerked chicken tastes just as good.

SERVES FOUR

INGREDIENTS
- 8 chicken pieces
- oil, for brushing
- salad leaves, to serve

For the jerk seasoning
- 5ml/1 tsp ground allspice
- 5ml/1 tsp ground cinnamon
- 5ml/1 tsp dried thyme
- 1.5ml/¼ tsp freshly grated nutmeg
- 10ml/2 tsp demerara (raw) sugar
- 2 garlic cloves, crushed
- 15ml/1 tbsp finely chopped onion
- 15ml/1 tbsp chopped spring onion (scallion)
- 15ml/1 tbsp vinegar
- 30ml/2 tbsp oil
- 15ml/1 tbsp lime juice
- 1 fresh hot chilli pepper, chopped
- salt and ground black pepper

1 Make the jerk seasoning. Combine the ground allspice, cinnamon, thyme, grated nutmeg, sugar, garlic, both types of onion, vinegar, oil, lime juice and chilli pepper in a small bowl. Use a fork to mash them together until a thick paste is formed. Season to taste with a little salt and plenty of ground black pepper.

2 Make several lengthways slits in the flesh on the chicken pieces. Place the chicken pieces in a dish and spoon the jerk seasoning over them. Use your hands to rub the seasoning into the chicken, especially into the slits.

3 Cover with clear film (plastic wrap) and marinate for at least 4–6 hours or overnight in the refrigerator.

4 Preheat the grill (broiler) or prepare the barbecue. Shake off any excess seasoning from the chicken and brush the pieces with oil. Either place on a baking sheet and grill (broil) for 45 minutes, or cook on the barbecue for about 30 minutes. Whichever method you choose, it is important to turn the chicken pieces frequently. Serve hot with salad leaves.

COOK'S TIP

The flavour is best if you marinate the chicken overnight. If cooking on the barbecue, sprinkle the charcoal with aromatic herbs, such as rosemary or bay leaves, for even more flavour.

THYME AND LIME CHICKEN

LIMES GROWN IN LATIN AMERICA TEND TO BE PALER THAN THE ONES IN OUR SUPERMARKETS, BUT THEY ARE JUICY AND FULL OF FLAVOUR. THIS CARIBBEAN RECIPE, WHICH COMBINES THEM WITH FRAGRANT THYME, IS A GREAT VEHICLE FOR THEM.

SERVES FOUR

INGREDIENTS
- 8 chicken thighs
- 30ml/2 tbsp chopped spring onion (scallion)
- 10ml/2 tsp chopped fresh thyme or 5ml/1 tsp dried thyme
- 2 garlic cloves, crushed
- juice of 2 limes or 1 lemon
- 75g/3oz/6 tbsp butter, melted
- salt and ground black pepper
- cooked rice, to serve

To garnish
- lime slices
- fresh coriander (cilantro) sprigs

1 Put the chicken thighs skin side down in a baking dish or roasting pan. Using a sharp knife, make a lengthways slit along the thigh bone of each. Mix the spring onion with a little salt and pepper and press the mixture into the slits.

2 Mix the thyme, garlic and lime or lemon juice in a small bowl. Add 50g/2oz/4 tbsp of the butter and mix well, then spoon a little of the mixture over each chicken thigh, spreading evenly.

3 Spoon the remaining butter evenly over the top of the chicken pieces. Cover the dish tightly with clear film (plastic wrap) and leave to marinate for at least 3–4 hours in the refrigerator. For the best flavour, prepare the chicken the day before and leave to marinate overnight.

4 Preheat the oven to 190°C/375°F/Gas 5. Remove the film and cover the chicken with foil. Bake for about 1 hour, then remove the foil and cook for a further 5–10 minutes, until the chicken turns golden brown. Garnish with lime slices and fresh coriander and serve with rice.

Chicken, Pork and Potatoes in Peanut Sauce

This traditional Peruvian dish, known as CARAPULCRA, *is made with* PAPASECA *(dried potatoes), which break up when cooked to thicken the sauce. The same effect is achieved here by using floury potatoes, the kind that disintegrate when cooked for a long time.*

SERVES SIX

INGREDIENTS

- 75g/3oz/¾ cup unsalted peanuts
- 60ml/4 tbsp olive oil
- 3 chicken breast portions, halved
- 500g/1¼ lb boneless pork loin, cut into 2cm/¾ in pieces
- 1 large onion, chopped
- 30–45ml/2–3 tbsp water
- 3 garlic cloves, crushed
- 5ml/1 tsp paprika
- 5ml/1 tsp ground cumin
- 500g/1¼ lb floury potatoes, peeled and thickly sliced
- 550ml/18fl oz/scant 2½ cups vegetable stock
- salt and ground black pepper
- cooked rice, to serve

To garnish

- 2 hard-boiled eggs, sliced
- 50g/2oz/½ cup pitted black olives
- chopped fresh flat leaf parsley

1 Place the peanuts in a large dry frying pan over a low heat. Toast for about 2–3 minutes, until golden all over. Watch them closely, shaking the pan frequently, as they have a tendency to burn. Leave to cool, then process in a food processor until finely ground.

2 Heat half the olive oil in a heavy pan. Add the chicken pieces, season with salt and ground black pepper and cook for 10 minutes, until golden brown all over. Transfer the pieces of chicken to a plate, using a slotted spoon.

3 Heat the remaining oil in the pan. When it is very hot, add the pork. Season and sauté for 3–4 minutes, until golden brown. Transfer to the plate containing the chicken pieces.

4 Lower the heat and stir the onion into the oil in the pan. Cook for 5 minutes, adding the water if it begins to stick. Stir in the garlic, paprika and cumin and cook for 1 minute more.

5 Add the potatoes, stir and cover the pan. Cook for 3 minutes. Add the peanuts and stock. Bring to the boil, and simmer gently for 20–30 minutes.

6 Return the chicken and pork to the pan and bring to the boil. Lower the heat, replace the lid and simmer for 6–8 minutes, until the meat is fully cooked. Avoid overcooking the meat or it will become tough and stringy.

7 Garnish the stew with the egg slices, black olives and chopped parsley. Serve with the rice.

COOK'S TIP

If you cannot locate unsalted peanuts, buy a pack of salted ready-roasted peanuts, wash them under cold running water, then pat dry and grind.

SPICY FRIED CHICKEN

THIS TRADITIONAL CARIBBEAN CRISPY CHICKEN DISH IS SUPERB EATEN HOT OR COLD. SERVED WITH A SALAD OR VEGETABLES, IT MAKES A DELICIOUS LUNCH AND IS ALSO IDEAL FOR PICNICS OR SNACKS.

SERVES FOUR

INGREDIENTS

- 4 chicken drumsticks
- 4 chicken thighs
- 10ml/2 tsp curry powder
- 2.5ml/½ tsp garlic granules or 1 garlic clove, crushed
- 2.5ml/½ tsp ground black pepper
- 2.5ml/½ tsp paprika
- about 300ml/½ pint/1¼ cups milk
- oil, for deep frying
- 50g/2oz/½ cup plain (all-purpose) flour
- salt
- dressed salad leaves, to serve

1 Sprinkle the chicken pieces with curry powder, garlic, pepper, paprika and a little salt. Rub into the chicken, then cover and marinate for at least 2 hours, or overnight in the refrigerator.

2 Preheat the oven to 180°C/350°F/Gas 4. Cover the chicken with milk and leave to stand for a further 15 minutes.

3 Heat the oil in a large pan or deep-fryer and tip the flour on to a plate. Dip the chicken pieces in flour and add to the oil, taking care not to overcrowd the pan. Fry until golden, but not fully cooked.

4 Remove the chicken pieces with a slotted spoon and place on a baking sheet. Continue until all the chicken pieces have been fried.

5 Place the baking sheet in the oven and bake the chicken for around 30 minutes. Serve hot or cold with dressed salad leaves.

SUNDAY ROAST CHICKEN

MUCH OF THE PREPARATION FOR THIS DISH IS DONE THE NIGHT BEFORE, MAKING IT IDEAL FOR A FAMILY LUNCH. THE CHICKEN IS SUCCULENT AND FULL OF FLAVOUR, WITH A RICH GRAVY.

SERVES SIX

INGREDIENTS
- 1.6kg/3½lb chicken
- 5ml/1 tsp paprika
- 5ml/1 tsp dried thyme
- 2.5ml/½ tsp dried tarragon
- 5ml/1 tsp garlic granules or 1 garlic clove, crushed
- 15ml/1 tbsp lemon juice
- 30ml/2 tbsp clear honey
- 45ml/3 tbsp dark rum
- melted butter, for basting
- 300ml/½ pint/1¼ cups chicken stock
- lime quarters, to garnish

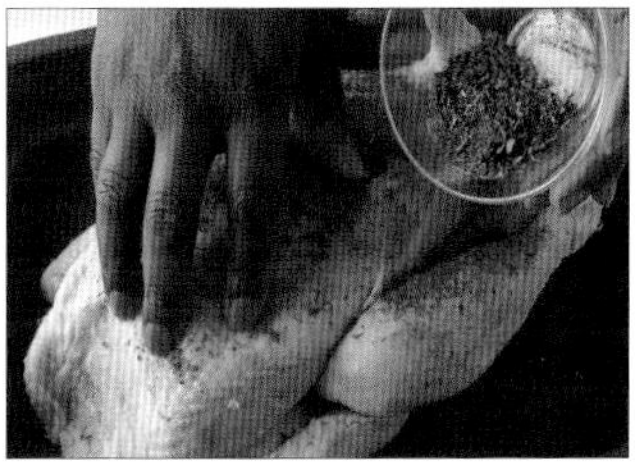

1 Place the chicken in a roasting pan and sprinkle with paprika, thyme, tarragon, garlic and salt and pepper. Rub the mixture all over the chicken, including underneath the skin. Cover with clear film (plastic wrap) and leave to marinate for at least 2 hours or overnight in the refrigerator.

2 Preheat the oven to 190°C/375°F/Gas 5. Mix the lemon, honey and rum in a bowl. Stir well, then pour over and under the chicken skin, rubbing it in well to ensure the flavours are absorbed.

3 Spoon melted butter all over the chicken, then transfer to the oven and roast for 1½–2 hours, until fully cooked.

VARIATION
Extra herbs and rum can be used to make a richer, tastier gravy, if you like.

4 Transfer the chicken to a serving dish while you make the gravy. Pour the pan juices into a small pan. Add the chicken stock. Simmer for 10 minutes or until the gravy has reduced and thickened slightly. Adjust the seasoning and pour into a serving jug (pitcher). Garnish the chicken with the lime and serve.

TURKEY MOLE

A MOLE IS A RICH STEW, TRADITIONALLY SERVED ON A FESTIVE OCCASION IN MEXICO. THE WORD COMES FROM THE AZTEC "MOLLI", MEANING A CHILLI-FLAVOURED SAUCE. THERE ARE MANY DIFFERENT TYPES, INCLUDING THE FAMOUS MOLE POBLANO DE GUAJALOTE. *TOASTED NUTS, FRUIT AND CHOCOLATE ARE AMONG THE CLASSIC INGREDIENTS; THIS VERSION INCLUDES COCOA POWDER.*

SERVES FOUR

INGREDIENTS

- 1 ancho chilli, seeded
- 1 guajillo chilli, seeded
- 115g/4oz/¾ cup sesame seeds
- 50g/2oz/½ cup whole blanched almonds
- 50g/2oz/½ cup shelled unsalted peanuts, skinned
- 1 small onion
- 2 garlic cloves
- 50g/2oz/¼ cup lard or 60ml/4 tbsp vegetable oil
- 50g/2oz/⅓ cup canned tomatoes
- 1 ripe plantain
- 50g/2oz/⅓ cup raisins
- 75g/3oz/½ cup ready-to-eat prunes, stoned
- 5ml/1 tsp dried oregano
- 2.5ml/½ tsp ground cloves
- 2.5ml/½ tsp crushed allspice berries
- 5ml/1 tsp ground cinnamon
- 25g/1oz/¼ cup cocoa powder (unsweetened)
- 4 turkey breast steaks
- fresh oregano, to garnish (optional)

1 Soak both types of dried chilli in a bowl of hot water for 30 minutes, then lift them out and chop them roughly. Reserve 250ml/8fl oz/1 cup of the soaking liquid.

COOK'S TIP

It is important to use good quality cocoa powder, which is unsweetened.

2 Spread out the sesame seeds in a heavy-based frying pan. Toast them over a moderate heat, shaking the pan lightly so that they turn golden all over. Do not let them burn, or the sauce will taste bitter. Set aside 45ml/3 tbsp of the toasted seeds for the garnish and tip the rest into a bowl. Toast the almonds and peanuts in the same way and add them to the bowl.

3 Chop the onion and garlic finely. Heat half the lard or oil in a frying pan, cook the chopped onion and garlic for 2–3 minutes, then add the chillies and tomatoes. Cook gently for 10 minutes.

4 Peel the plantain and slice it into short diagonal slices. Add it to the onion mixture with the raisins, prunes, dried oregano, spices and cocoa. Stir in the 250ml/8fl oz/1 cup of the reserved water in which the chillies were soaked. Bring to the boil, stirring, then add the toasted sesame seeds, almonds and peanuts. Cook for 10 minutes, stirring frequently, then remove from the heat and allow to cool slightly.

5 Blend the sauce in batches in a food processor or blender until smooth. The sauce should be fairly thick, but a little water may be added if necessary.

6 Heat the remaining lard or oil in a flameproof casserole. Add the turkey and brown over a moderate heat.

7 Pour the sauce over the steaks and cover the casserole with foil and a tight-fitting lid. Cook over a gentle heat for 20–25 minutes or until the turkey is cooked, and the sauce has thickened. Sprinkle with sesame seeds and chopped oregano, and serve with a rice dish and warm tortillas.

Peruvian Duck with Rice

Duck is very popular in Peru. In this recipe, the rice is cooked in the same liquid as the duck, so it absorbs the aromatic flavours of the herbs and spices.

SERVES SIX

INGREDIENTS
- 2 fresh red chillies, seeded
- 4 garlic cloves, roughly chopped
- 5 fresh coriander (cilantro) stalks
- 5ml/1 tsp ground cumin
- 3 duck legs
- salt and ground black pepper
- 1 large onion, finely chopped
- 650ml/1 pint/2½ cups chicken stock
- 250ml/8fl oz/1 cup red wine
- 350g/12oz/1¾ cups long grain rice
- 115g/4oz/1 cup frozen peas, thawed
- 15ml/1 tbsp chopped fresh coriander, to garnish

VARIATION
If you find duck too fatty for your tastes, try making this dish with chicken legs or rabbit. It will be just as delicious.

1 Put the fresh chillies, garlic cloves, coriander stalks and ground cumin in a blender or food processor and process to a thick paste.

2 Cut the duck legs in half to separate the thigh from the drumstick. Place in a large heavy pan with a tight-fitting lid. Place over a low heat. Season the duck with salt and ground black pepper. Cook until golden brown on all sides, set the duck aside and pour away most of the fat, leaving about 30ml/2 tbsp.

3 Add the onion to the pan and cook gently for 5 minutes. Stir in the chilli and coriander paste and cook for a further 2 minutes. Return the duck to the pan, pour in the stock and wine and bring to the boil. Cover, reduce the heat and simmer for 45 minutes.

4 Stir the rice into the pan, replace the lid and cook for 18–20 minutes. Stir in the peas and remove from the heat. Leave to stand for 5 minutes and serve with a sprinkling of chopped coriander.

Drunken Duck

This is a lovely dish for a dinner party. The duck and sweet potatoes cook in the red wine and warm spices, creating a rich, almost chocolate-like sauce.

SERVES FOUR

INGREDIENTS
- 1 duck, about 2.25kg/5lb
- 1 large onion, thinly sliced
- 2.5ml/½ tsp crushed dried chillies
- 2 garlic cloves, crushed
- 1.5ml/¼ tsp ground cloves
- 1.5ml/¼ tsp ground allspice
- 2.5ml/½ tsp ground cinnamon
- 800g/1¾ lb sweet potatoes, peeled and cut into thick wedges
- 250ml/8fl oz/1 cup red wine
- 250ml/8fl oz/1 cup chicken stock
- salt and ground black pepper
- polenta or cooked rice, to serve

1 Preheat the oven to 200°C/400°F/Gas 6. Season the inside and outside of the duck. Place the duck in a large flameproof casserole over a low heat and cook, turning occasionally, until the skin has released some of its fat and turned a rich golden brown. Transfer the duck to a plate.

2 Pour away most of the duck fat from the pan, leaving about 30ml/2 tbsp. Return the casserole to the heat, add the onion and crushed chillies and stir well to coat in the fat, incorporating any sediment on the bottom of the pan.

3 Cook for 5 minutes until the onion is soft and translucent. Stir in the garlic and spices and cook for 1 minute more.

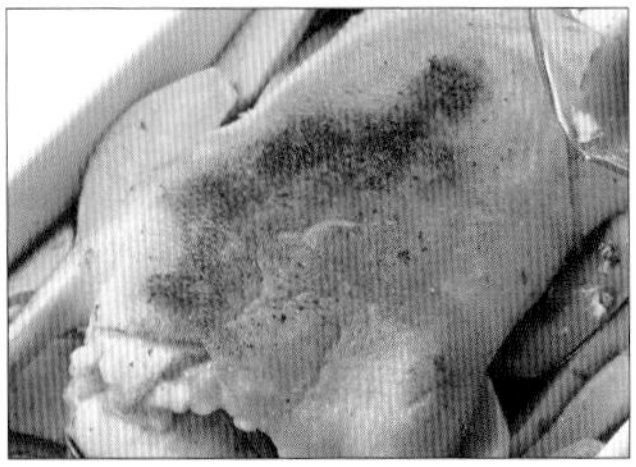

4 Return the duck to the casserole, arrange the sweet potatoes around it and pour in the wine and stock. Bring to the boil and cover. Move the dish to the oven and cook for 1¼–1½ hours.

5 Skim the fat from the top of the sauce and serve with soft polenta or plain rice.

Vegetarian Dishes and Salads

Although vegetarianism is not widespread in the Caribbean and Latin America, root vegetables, corn and what might be considered exotic fruit and vegetables, such as heart of palm and okra, are used extensively. The salads in this chapter can either be enjoyed as a light lunch, as an appetizer or as side dishes.

Corn Soufflé

Latin American soufflés are quite different from their French counterparts. For example, this one will rise only slightly, yet the texture will still be light and airy.

SERVES SIX

INGREDIENTS
- 75g/3oz/6 tbsp butter
- 300g/11oz sweet potato, peeled and cubed
- 300g/11oz pumpkin, peeled and cubed
- 300g/11oz/scant 2 cups frozen corn kernels, thawed
- 3 spring onions (scallions), roughly chopped
- 150g/5oz Cheddar cheese, grated
- 5 eggs
- salt and ground black pepper

1 Preheat the oven to 180°C/350°F/Gas 4. Using 15g/½oz/1 tbsp of the butter, grease a 28 x 18cm/11 x 7in baking dish. Cook the sweet potato and pumpkin in a pan of lightly salted boiling water for 10 minutes, until tender. Drain and set aside.

2 Put 250g/9oz/1½ cups of corn kernals into a food processor. Add the chopped spring onions and process until smooth. Melt the remaining butter in a pan and stir in the corn and onion mixture. Cook, stirring, over a low heat, for about 1–2 minutes.

3 Add the cheese, stirring until it has melted. Season generously with salt and pepper. Remove from the heat.

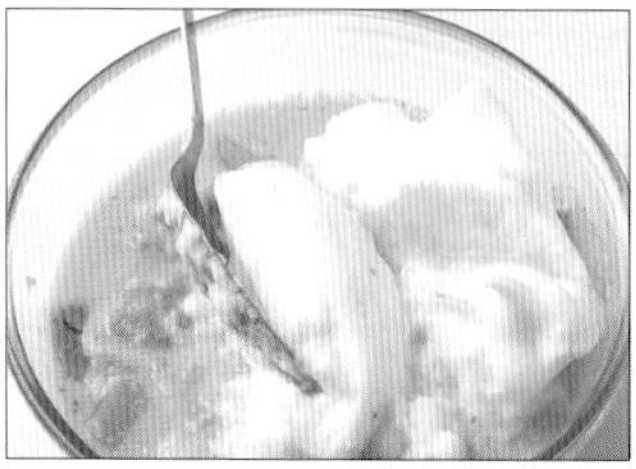

4 Separate three of the eggs and add the remaining whole eggs to the bowl containing the yolks. Mix lightly, then stir the yolk mixture into the pan. Add the sweet potato, pumpkin and remaining corn. Whisk the egg whites until stiff, then fold them into the soufflé mixture.

5 Transfer the mixture to the prepared dish and place the dish in a roasting pan. Pour in hot water to come halfway up the side of the dish and bake for 35–40 minutes, until golden. If the soufflé still wobbles when shaken gently, cook for a further 5–10 minutes. Leave to cool, then serve.

COOK'S TIP

For the best results, whisk the egg whites with a pinch of salt in a clean glass or metal bowl. When they are very stiff and no longer slide around the bowl when it is moved, they are ready for use.

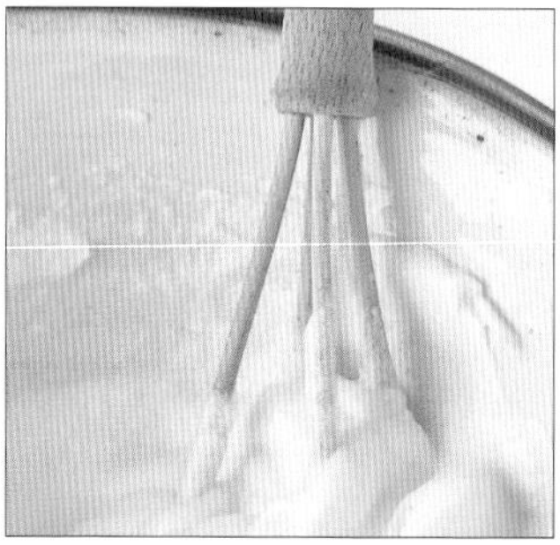

Layered Potato Bake with Cheese

Inspired by the Peruvian side dish, Ocopa Arequipena, this family-sized potato cake in a spicy cheese and walnut sauce is substantial enough for a main course.

SERVES SIX

INGREDIENTS
- 105ml/7 tbsp olive oil
- 1 large onion, chopped
- 2 garlic cloves, crushed
- 5ml/1 tsp crushed dried chillies
- 130g/4½ oz/generous 1 cup walnut halves
- 130g/4½ oz/generous ½ cup fresh cheese, such as ricotta
- 105ml/7 tbsp warm water
- 3 eggs
- 450g/1lb large potatoes, peeled
- butter, for greasing
- 65g/2½ oz/scant ¾ cup pitted black olives
- 4 pimientos, cut into strips
- salt

1 Heat 30ml/2 tbsp of the oil in a small pan over a low heat. Add the chopped onion and sauté gently for 5 minutes, until softened. Stir in the garlic and crushed dried chillies and cook for a further 2 minutes.

2 Put the walnuts in a blender or food processor. Blend until smooth, then add the cooked onion mixture, with the cheese and remaining olive oil. Season generously with salt and pour in the warm water. Blend to make a smooth paste. Set aside.

3 Put the eggs in a small pan of cold water. Bring to the boil, then lower the heat to a simmer. Cook for 10 minutes then cool in a bowl of cold water.

4 Add the potatoes to a pan of salted water and cover. Bring to the boil, then simmer for 10 minutes. Drain and refresh under cold water. Drain again and cut into 1cm/½in slices. Shell the eggs and cut them into slices.

5 Preheat the oven to 180°C/350°F/Gas 4. Grease a 28 x 18cm/11 x 7in baking dish with butter. Arrange a layer of potatoes in the dish and generously spread with the prepared paste. Top with egg slices and a sprinkling of olives and pimiento strips. Continue layering until all the ingredients have been used, finishing with olives and pimientos.

6 Bake for 30 minutes, until the potatoes are very tender. Leave to cool for 5 minutes before serving.

FRIJOLES

IN THE YUCATÁN PENINSULA, WHERE THESE SPICY BEANS ARE VERY POPULAR, BLACK HARICOT BEANS ARE COOKED WITH THE MEXICAN HERB EPAZOTE.

SERVES SIX TO EIGHT

INGREDIENTS
- 350g/12oz/1¾ cups dried red kidney, pinto or black haricot beans, picked over and rinsed
- 2 onions, finely chopped
- 2 garlic cloves, chopped
- 1 bay leaf
- 1 or more serrano chillies (small fresh green chillies)
- 30ml/2 tbsp corn oil
- 2 tomatoes, peeled, seeded and chopped
- salt
- sprigs of fresh bay leaves, to garnish

1 Put the beans into a pan and add cold water to cover by 2.5cm/1in.Add half the onion, half the garlic, the bay leaf and chilli(es). Bring to the boil and boil vigorously for 10 minutes. Put the beans and liquid into an earthenware pot or large pan, cover and cook over a low heat for 30 minutes. Add boiling water if the mixture becomes dry.

2 When the beans begin to wrinkle, add 15ml/1 tbsp of the corn oil and cook for a further 30 minutes, or until the beans are tender. Add salt to taste and cook for 30 minutes more.

3 Remove the beans from the heat. Heat the remaining oil in a small frying pan and sauté the remaining onion and garlic until the onion is soft. Add the tomatoes and cook for 2–3 minutes.

5 Spoon 45ml/3 tbsp of the beans into the tomato mixture. Mash to a paste. Stir this into the beans to thicken the liquid. Cook for just long enough to heat through, if necessary. Serve the beans in small bowls and garnish with sprigs of fresh bay leaves.

BLACK BEAN BURRITOS

BURRITOS – STUFFED TORTILLAS – ARE ONE OF THE MOST POPULAR SNACK FOODS IN MEXICO. IN THIS RECIPE THEY ARE STUFFED WITH SPICY BEANS AND TOPPED WITH A CHEESE SAUCE.

SERVES FOUR

INGREDIENTS
- 175g/6oz/1 cup dried black beans, soaked overnight and drained
- 1 bay leaf
- 45ml/3 tbsp sea salt
- 1 small red onion, chopped
- 225g/8oz/2 cups grated cheese
- 45ml/3 tbsp chopped pickled jalapeños
- 15ml/1 tbsp chopped coriander (cilantro)
- 750ml/1¼ pints/3 cups tomato salsa
- 8 flour tortillas
- diced avocado, to serve

1 Place the beans in a pan. Add water to cover and the bay leaf. Bring to the boil, cover and simmer for 30 minutes. Add the salt and continue simmering for about 30 minutes, until tender. Drain and cool slightly. Discard the bay leaf.

2 Preheat the oven to 180°C/350°F/Gas 4. Grease an ovenproof dish.

3 Combine the beans, onion, half the cheese, the jalapeños, coriander and one-third of the salsa. Stir and season.

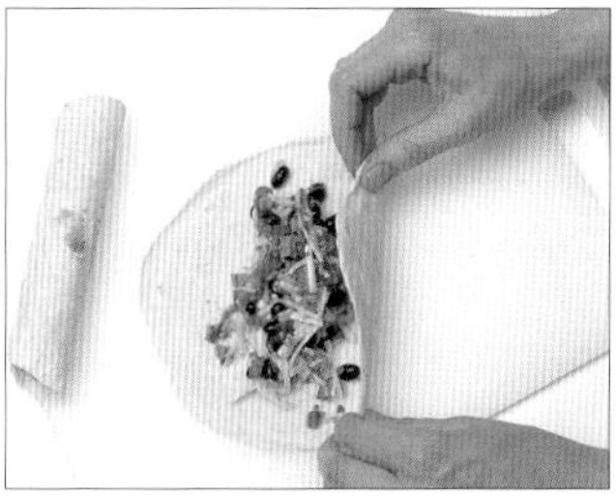

4 Place one tortilla on a clean work surface. Spread a large spoonful of the filling down the middle, then roll it up to enclose the filling completely. Place the burrito in the prepared dish, seam side down. Repeat this process with the remaining tortillas until the dish is full.

5 Sprinkle the remaining cheese over the burritos, in an even line right down the middle. Bake in the oven for about 15 minutes, or until the cheese melts completely and starts to bubble and brown. Do not overheat as the edges of the tortilla will become dry and crisp.

6 Serve the bean burritos immediately, garnished with diced avocado and the remaining salsa. To make a more hearty meal, serve with a side salad, a potato salad or a mixed bean salad.

Chilli Cheese Tortilla with Fresh Tomato Salsa

Good warm or cold, this is like a sliced potato quiche without the pastry base, well spiked with chilli. The salsa can be made without the chilli if you prefer.

SERVES FOUR

INGREDIENTS

- 45ml/3 tbsp sunflower or olive oil
- 1 small onion, thinly sliced
- 2–3 fresh green jalapeño chillies, seeded and sliced
- 200g/7oz cold cooked potato, thinly sliced
- 120g/4¼oz/generous 1 cup cheese, grated (use a firm but not hard cheese, such as Double Gloucester, Monterey Jack or Manchego)
- 6 eggs, beaten
- salt and ground black pepper
- fresh herbs, to garnish

For the salsa

- 500g/1¼lb tomatoes, peeled, seeded and finely chopped
- 1 fresh mild green chilli, seeded and finely chopped
- 2 garlic cloves, crushed
- 45ml/3 tbsp chopped fresh coriander (cilantro)
- juice of 1 lime
- 2.5ml/½ tsp salt

1 To make the salsa, put the tomatoes in a bowl and add the chopped chilli, garlic, coriander, lime juice and salt. Mix well and set aside.

2 Heat 15ml/1 tbsp of the oil in a large omelette pan and gently fry the onion and jalapeños for 5 minutes, stirring until softened. Add the potato and cook for 5 minutes until lightly browned, keeping the slices whole.

3 Using a slotted spoon, transfer the vegetables to a warm plate. Wipe the pan with kitchen paper, then add the remaining oil and heat until really hot. Return the vegetables to the pan. Scatter the cheese over the top. Season.

4 Pour in the beaten eggs, making sure that they seep under the vegetables. Cook the tortilla over a low heat, without stirring, until set. Serve hot or cold, cut into wedges, garnished with fresh herbs and with the salsa on the side.

POTATO AND ONION TORTILLA

THIS DEEP-SET TORTILLA WITH SLICED POTATOES AND ONIONS IS A STAPLE SNACK OR DISH ORIGINATING FROM SPAIN AND POPULAR THROUGHOUT LATIN AMERICA. ADD CHEESE, HERBS AND OTHER VEGETABLES TO MAKE THIS INTO A MORE HEARTY MEAL.

SERVES THREE TO FOUR

INGREDIENTS

- 2,800g/1¾ lb medium potatoes
- 100ml/3½ fl oz/scant ½ cup extra virgin olive oil
- 2 onions, thinly sliced
- 6 eggs
- sprigs of coriander (cilantro) or parsley, to garnish

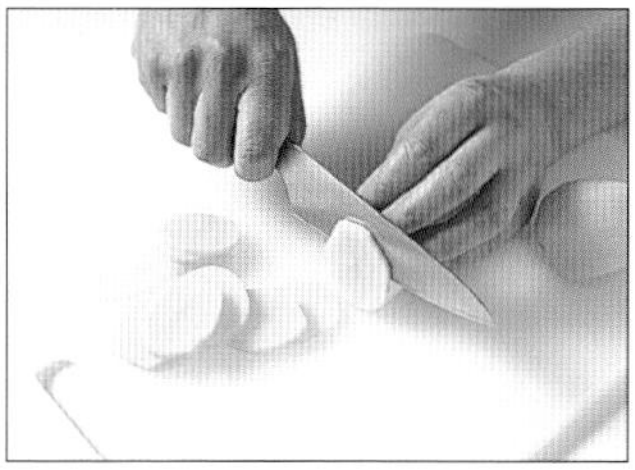

1 Peel and thinly slice the potatoes and onions. Set the onions to one side.

2 Heat 75ml/5 tbsp of the oil in a frying pan and cook the potatoes, turning frequently, for 10 minutes.

3 Add the onions and seasoning, turning occasionally. Continue to cook gently for a further 10 minutes, until the onions are transparent and golden and the potaotes are tender.

4 Meanwhile, break the eggs into a bowl and beat them. Add a little seasoning. Add the potatoes and onions and mix gently. Leave to stand for 10 minutes.

5 Wipe out the pan with kitchen paper and heat the remaining oil in it. Pour the egg, potato and onion mixture into the pan and spread it out in an even layer. Cover and cook over a very gentle heat for 20 minutes, until the eggs are just set. Serve cut into wedges.

HEART OF PALM PIE

The delicate creamy filling in this pie contrasts beautifully with the crumbly pastry. This recipe can also be used to make small Brazilian EMPADINHAS *– baby savoury pies – not to be confused with* EMPANADAS*, the little turnovers.*

SERVES EIGHT

INGREDIENTS
- 500g/1¼lb/5 cups plain (all-purpose) flour
- 5ml/1 tsp salt
- 175g/6oz/¾ cup butter
- 75g/3oz/6 tbsp lard or white cooking fat
- 1 egg yolk
- 45ml/3 tbsp cold water

For the filling
- 25g/1oz/2 tbsp butter
- 1 large onion, finely chopped
- 4 garlic cloves, crushed
- 15ml/1 tbsp plain (all-purpose) flour
- 200ml/7fl oz/scant 1 cup full-fat (whole) milk
- 2 hard-boiled eggs, roughly chopped
- 1 large tomato, peeled, seeded and cubed
- 1 fresh red chilli, seeded and finely chopped
- 2 x 400g/14oz cans heart of palm, drained and cut into 2cm/¾in slices
- 15ml/1 tbsp chopped fresh flat leaf parsley
- salt and ground black pepper

To glaze
- 1 egg yolk
- 15ml/1 tbsp water

1 Place the flour, salt, butter and lard or cooking fat in a food processor and process until the mixture resembles fine breadcrumbs. With the motor still running, add the egg yolk and the cold water. As soon as the mixture comes together, transfer to a floured surface. Knead it lightly until smooth. Divide the pastry into two rounds, one slightly larger than the other, wrap both in cling film (plastic wrap) and place in the refrigerator while you make the filling.

2 Melt the butter in a frying pan over a low heat. Stir in the chopped onion and cook for 5 minutes until soft. Add the garlic and cook for a further 2 minutes.

3 Stir the flour into the pan and cook, stirring, for 1 minute. Remove from the heat and slowly pour in the milk, a little at a time, stirring to prevent any lumps from forming.

4 Return to the heat and cook, stirring constantly, for 2 minutes to make a thin white sauce. Remove from the heat and stir in the chopped hard-boiled eggs, cubed tomato, chilli, palm hearts and parsley. Season with salt and pepper.

5 Preheat the oven to 190°C/375°F/Gas 5. Place a large baking sheet on the central shelf so that it heats up.

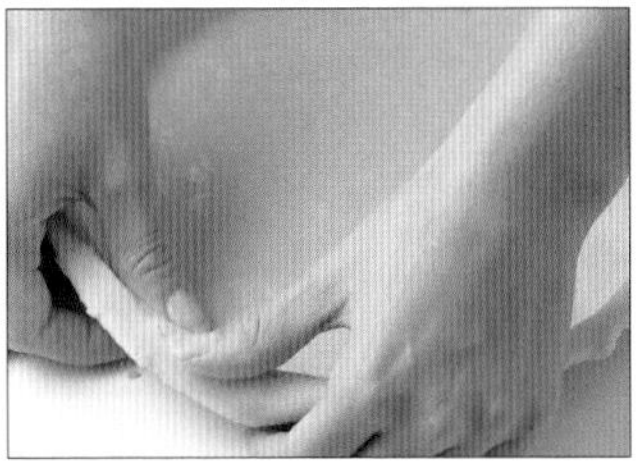

6 On a floured surface, roll out the larger piece of pastry and line the base and sides of a 23cm/9in round loose-based quiche pan. The pastry will be very crumbly, so it may tear in a few places. Should this happen, use your fingers to push the pastry together again. There should be no gaps.

7 Add the filling, then roll out the remaining pastry and use to top the pie. Do not worry about any small gaps in the pastry, as they add to the rustic character of the dish.

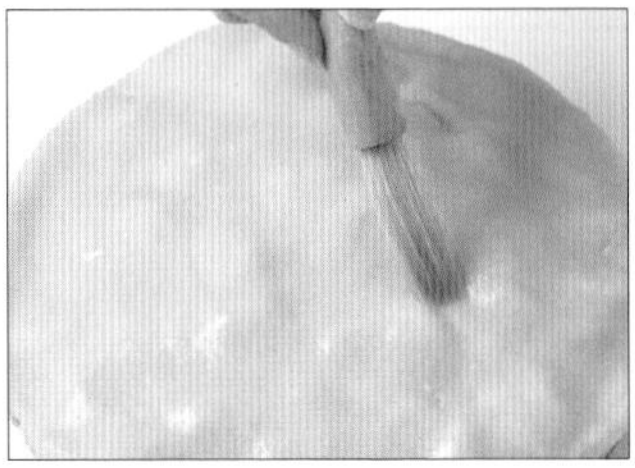

8 Make the glaze by mixing the egg yolk with the water. Using a pastry brush glaze the pastry, then place the quiche pan on the heated baking sheet and bake the pie for 45 minutes, until the pastry is golden.

9 Leave the pie to cool for 5 minutes on a wire rack before removing it from the pan and putting it on to a large plate. Serve warm or at room temperature.

COOK'S TIP

Cooking the pie on a heated baking sheet ensures that the pastry cooks thoroughly, avoiding a soggy base.

MACARONI CHEESE PIE

MACARONI CHEESE IS A FAVOURITE DISH ON THE ISLAND OF BARBADOS, WHERE IT IS OFTEN SERVED AS AN ACCOMPANIMENT, INSTEAD OF A STARCHY VEGETABLE SUCH AS POTATO. THIS TREATMENT MAKES AN EXCELLENT VEGETARIAN MAIN COURSE.

SERVES FOUR

INGREDIENTS
- 225g/8oz/2 cups macaroni
- 40g/1½oz/3 tbsp butter or margarine
- 20g/¾oz/3 tbsp plain (all-purpose) flour
- 450ml/¾ pint/scant 2 cups milk
- 5ml/1 tsp mild mustard
- 2.5ml/½ tsp ground cinnamon
- 175g/6oz mature (sharp) Cheddar cheese, grated
- 1 egg, beaten
- 15ml/1 tbsp butter or margarine
- 25g/1oz/2 tbsp chopped spring onion (scallion)
- 40g/1½oz/3 tbsp canned chopped tomatoes
- 115g/4oz/⅔ cup corn kernels
- salt and ground black pepper
- chopped fresh parsley, to garnish

1 Heat the oven to 180°C/350°F/Gas 4. Cook the macaroni in a pan of salted boiling water for 10 minutes. Drain, rinse under cold water and drain again.

2 Melt 25g/1oz/2 tbsp of the butter in a pan and add the flour. Cook for 1 minute, then add the milk, whisking constantly. Heat until the mixture boils, then simmer gently for 5–10 minutes.

3 Stir in the mustard and cinnamon, with two-thirds of the cheese. Season to taste. Cook gently, stirring frequently, until the cheese has melted, then remove from the heat and whisk in the egg. Cover closely and set aside.

4 Heat the remaining butter or margarine in a small frying pan and cook the spring onion, chopped tomatoes and corn over a gentle heat for 5–10 minutes.

5 Tip half the cooked macaroni into a greased ovenproof dish. Pour over half the cheese sauce and mix well, then spoon the tomato and corn mixture evenly over the mixture.

6 Tip the remaining macaroni into the pan containing the cheese sauce, stir well and then spread carefully over the tomato and corn mixture.

7 Top with the remaining grated cheese. Bake for about 45 minutes, or until the top is golden and bubbly. If possible, leave to stand for 30 minutes before serving, garnished with parsley.

RED BEAN CHILLI

SATISFYING, SPICY AND SIMPLE TO PREPARE, THIS VEGETARIAN CARIBBEAN VERSION OF THE CLASSIC MEXICAN CHILLI IS COMFORT FOOD AT ITS BEST. EXPERIMENT WITH DIFFERENT TYPES OF CHILLI PEPPERS, INCLUDING DRIED VARIETIES LIKE THE MEXICAN CHIPOTLES.

SERVES FOUR

INGREDIENTS

- 30ml/2 tbsp vegetable oil
- 1 onion, chopped
- 400g/14oz can chopped tomatoes
- 2 garlic cloves, crushed
- 300ml/½ pint/1¼ cups white wine
- about 300ml/½ pint/1¼ cups vegetable stock
- 115g/4oz/1 cup red lentils
- 2 fresh thyme sprigs or 5ml/1 tsp dried thyme
- 10ml/2 tsp ground cumin
- 45ml/3 tbsp dark soy sauce
- ½ fresh hot chilli, seeded and finely chopped
- 5ml/1 tsp ground mixed spice (pumpkin pie spice)
- 15ml/1 tbsp oyster sauce (optional)
- 225g/8oz can red kidney beans, drained
- 10ml/2 tsp sugar
- salt
- boiled white rice with corn, to serve

1 Heat the oil in a pan and fry the onion for 2–3 minutes, until slightly softened.

2 Add the tomatoes and garlic, cook for about 10 minutes, then stir in the white wine and vegetable stock.

VARIATION
This vegetarian chilli can be adapted to accommodate meat-eaters by substituting either minced (ground) beef or lamb for the lentils.

3 Stir in the lentils, thyme, cumin, soy sauce, chilli, spice and oyster sauce, if using.

COOK'S TIP
Fiery chillies can irritate the skin, so always wash your hands thoroughly after handling them and avoid touching your eyes.

4 Cover and simmer for 40 minutes or until the lentils are cooked, stirring occasionally and adding more water if the lentils begin to dry out.

5 Stir in the kidney beans and sugar and cook for 10 minutes more. Season to taste and serve with boiled white rice and corn.

Peppers Stuffed with Beans

Stuffed peppers are a popular Mexican dish. A special version – Chiles en Nogada – is served on 28 August to mark Independence Day. The green peppers are served with a fresh walnut sauce and pomegranate seeds to represent the colours of the Mexican flag.

SERVES SIX

INGREDIENTS

- 6 large green (bell) peppers
- 2 eggs, separated
- 2.5ml/½ tsp salt
- corn oil, for frying
- plain (all-purpose) flour, for dusting
- 120ml/4fl oz/½ cup whipping cream
- 115g/4oz/1 cup grated Cheddar cheese
- fresh coriander (cilantro) sprigs, to garnish

For the beans

- 350g/12oz/1¼ cups dried red kidney, pinto or black haricot (navy) beans
- 2 onions, finely chopped
- 2 garlic cloves, finely chopped
- 1 bay leaf
- 1 or more serrano chillies
- 120–150ml/8–10 tbsp corn oil
- 2 tomatoes, peeled and chopped

1 Put the beans into a pan and add cold water to cover. Add half the chopped onion, half the garlic, the bay leaf and the chillies. Boil vigorously for about 10 minutes. Transfer the beans and liquid into a large flameproof casserole or pan, then cover and cook over a low heat for 30 minutes.

2 Add 15ml/1 tbsp of the corn oil to the beans and cook for a further 30 minutes or until the beans are tender. Add salt to taste and cook for 30 minutes more.

3 Remove the beans from the heat. Heat the remaining oil in a small frying pan and sauté the remaining onion and garlic until soft. Add the tomatoes and cook for a few minutes more. Add the tomato and onion mixture to the beans.

4 Roast the peppers over a gas flame or under a medium grill (broiler), turning occasionally, until the skins have blackened and blistered. Transfer the peppers to a plastic bag, secure the top and leave for 15 minutes.

5 Meanwhile, heat 30ml/2 tbsp of the oil in a large frying pan. Add about 45ml/3 tbsp of the beans. Mash them with a wooden spoon or potato masher, gradually adding more beans and oil until they have formed a heavy paste.

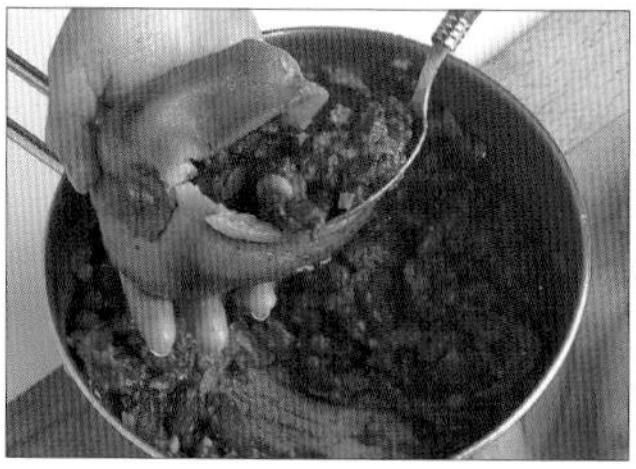

6 Preheat the oven to 180°C/350°F/Gas 4. Remove the peppers from the bag. Hold each pepper in turn under cold running water and rub off the skins. Slit the peppers down one side and remove the seeds and ribs. Stuff with the beans.

7 Beat the egg whites in a bowl until they stand in firm peaks. In another bowl, beat the yolks together with the salt. Fold gently into the whites.

8 Pour the corn oil into a large frying pan to a depth of about 2.5cm/1in and heat. Spread out the flour in a shallow bowl or dish.

9 Dip the filled peppers in the flour and then in the egg mix. Fry in batches until golden brown all over. Arrange the peppers in an ovenproof dish. Pour over the cream and sprinkle with the cheese. Bake for 30 minutes or until the topping is golden brown and the peppers are hot. Serve garnished with fresh coriander.

BLACK-EYED BEAN STEW WITH SPICY PUMPKIN

THIS WONDERFULLY WARM AND TASTY DISH IS A HEARTY WINTER FAVOURITE IN CENTRAL AMERICA AND THE CARIBBEAN, ALTHOUGH IT CAN ALSO BE FOUND THROUGHOUT MEXICO. THE PUMPKIN ADDS A SWEETNESS, MAKING THIS DELICIOUS COMFORT DISH.

SERVES THREE TO FOUR

INGREDIENTS

- 225g/8oz/1¼ cups black-eyed beans (peas), soaked overnight
- 1 onion, chopped
- 1 green or red (bell) pepper, seeded and chopped
- 2 garlic cloves, chopped
- 1 vegetable stock (bouillon) cube
- 1 thyme sprig or 5ml/1 tsp dried thyme
- 5ml/1 tsp paprika
- 2.5ml/½ tsp mixed (apple pie) spice
- 2 carrots, sliced
- 15–30ml/1–2 tbsp palm oil
- salt and hot pepper sauce

For the spicy pumpkin

- 675g/1½lb pumpkin
- 1 onion
- 25g/1oz/2 tbsp butter or margarine
- 2 garlic cloves, crushed
- 3 tomatoes, peeled and chopped
- 2.5ml/½ tsp ground cinnamon
- 10ml/2 tsp curry powder
- pinch of grated nutmeg
- 300ml/½ pint/⅔ cup water
- salt, hot pepper sauce and ground black pepper

1 Drain the beans, place in a pan and cover with water. Bring to the boil.

2 Add the onion, green or red pepper, garlic, stock cube, herbs and spices. Simmer for 45 minutes, or until the beans are just tender. Season to taste with salt and a little hot pepper sauce.

3 Add the carrots and palm oil and continue cooking for 10–12 minutes, until the carrots are cooked, adding a little more water if necessary. Remove from the heat and set aside.

4 To make the spicy pumpkin, cut the pumpkin into cubes and finely chop the onion.

5 Melt the butter or margarine in a large pan and add the pumpkin, onion garlic, tomatoes, spices and water. Stir well to combine and simmer until the pumpkin is soft.

6 Season to taste with salt, hot pepper sauce and black pepper. Serve with the black-eyed beans.

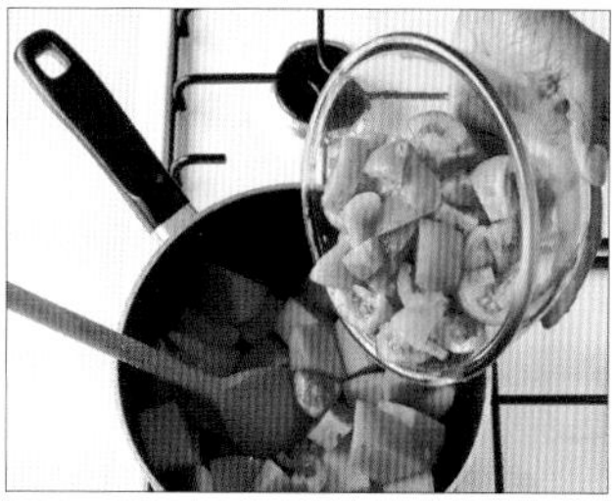

SPICY VEGETABLE CHOW MEIN

Chow mein is popular in Guyana, where it is usually made with shredded chicken or prawns. This vegetarian version can be adapted to suit all tastes.

SERVES THREE

INGREDIENTS

- 225g/8oz egg noodles
- 115g/4oz/¾ cup fine green beans
- 30–45ml/2–3 tbsp vegetable oil
- 2 garlic cloves, crushed
- 1 onion, chopped
- 1 small red (bell) pepper, chopped
- 1 small green (bell) pepper, chopped
- 2 celery sticks, finely chopped
- 2.5ml/½ tsp five-spice powder
- 1 vegetable stock (bouillon) cube
- 2.5ml/½ tsp ground black pepper
- 15ml/1 tbsp soy sauce (optional)
- salt

COOK'S TIP
Shredded omelette or sliced hard-boiled eggs are popular garnishes for chow mein.

1 Cook the noodles in a large pan of salted boiling water for 10 minutes or according to the instructions on the packet. Drain and cool. Blanch the beans.

2 Heat the oil in a wok or large frying pan and stir-fry the garlic, onion, red and green pepper, beans and celery, tossing them together to mix.

3 Add the five-spice powder, vegetable stock cube and ground black pepper, stir well and cook for 5 minutes until the vegetables are just tender but still slightly crunchy.

4 Stir in the noodles and soy sauce, if using. Taste the chow mein and season with salt if required. Serve immediately.

AUBERGINES STUFFED WITH SWEET POTATO

Slices of aubergine rolled around a sweet potato and cheese filling make an unusual Caribbean supper dish, or try them as an appetizer for a vegetarian meal.

SERVES FOUR

INGREDIENTS

- 225g/8oz/l cup sweet potatoes, peeled and quartered
- 2.5ml/½ tsp chopped fresh thyme
- 75g/3oz/¾ cup Cheddar cheese, diced
- 25g/1oz/2 tbsp chopped spring onion (scallion)
- 15ml/1 tbsp each chopped red and green (bell) pepper
- 1 garlic clove, crushed
- 2 large aubergines (eggplants)
- 30ml/2 tbsp plain (all-purpose) flour
- 15ml/1 tbsp spice seasoning
- olive oil, for frying
- butter, for greasing
- 2 tomatoes, sliced
- salt and ground black pepper
- chopped fresh parsley, to garnish

1 Preheat the oven to 180°C/350°F/Gas 4. Cook the sweet potatoes in a pan of boiling water for 15–20 minutes, until tender, then drain and mash.

2 Add the thyme, cheese, spring onion, peppers and garlic. Mix well and season.

3 Cut each aubergine lengthways into four slices. Mix the flour and spice seasoning on a plate and dust over each aubergine slice.

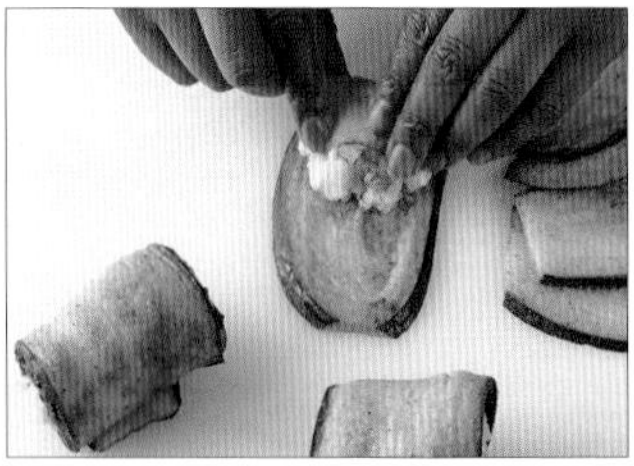

4 Heat a little oil in a large frying pan and fry each aubergine slice until browned, but not fully cooked. Drain and cool. Spoon a little of the potato mixture into the middle of each aubergine slice and roll up.

5 Butter two large pieces of foil and cover with the slices of tomato. Place four rolls on each piece of foil. Wrap up the parcels and bake for 20 minutes. Serve hot, garnished with the parsley.

Tomato Rice and Beans with Avocado Salsa

Mexican-style rice and beans make a delicious supper dish. Spoon on to tortillas and serve with a tangy salsa. Alternatively, serve as an accompaniment to a spicy stew.

SERVES FOUR

INGREDIENTS

- 40g/1½oz/¼ cup dried or 75g/3oz/½ cup canned kidney beans, rinsed and drained
- 8 tomatoes, halved and seeded
- 2 garlic cloves, chopped
- 1 onion, sliced
- 45ml/3 tbsp olive oil
- 225g/8oz/generous 1 cup long grain brown rice, rinsed
- 600ml/1 pint/2½ cups vegetable stock
- 2 carrots, diced
- 75g/3oz/¾ cup green beans
- salt and ground black pepper
- 4 wheat-flour tortillas and sour cream, to serve

For the avocado salsa

- 1 avocado
- juice of 1 lime
- 1 small red onion, diced
- 1 small fresh red chilli, seeded and chopped
- 15ml/1 tbsp chopped fresh coriander (cilantro)

1 If using dried kidney beans, place in a bowl, cover with cold water and leave to soak overnight, then drain and rinse well. Place in a pan with enough water to cover and bring to the boil. Boil rapidly for 10 minutes, then reduce the heat. Simmer for 40–50 minutes until tender; drain and set aside.

2 Make the avocado salsa. Halve and stone (pit) the avocado. Peel and dice the flesh, then toss it in the lime juice. Add the onion, chilli and coriander. Mix well.

3 Preheat the grill (broiler) to high. Place the tomatoes, garlic and onion on a baking tray. Pour over 15ml/1 tbsp of the oil and toss to coat. Grill (broil) for 10 minutes or until the tomatoes and onions are softened, turning once. Set aside to cool. Heat the remaining oil in a pan, add the rice and cook for 2 minutes, stirring, until light golden.

4 Purée the cooled tomatoes and onion in a food processor or blender, then add the mixture to the rice and cook for a further 2 minutes, stirring frequently. Pour in the vegetable stock, then cover and cook gently for 20 minutes, stirring occasionally.

5 Stir 30ml/2 tbsp of the kidney beans into the salsa. Add the rest to the rice mixture with the carrots and green beans, and cook for 10 minutes until the vegetables are tender. Season well. Remove the pan from the heat and leave to stand, covered, for 15 minutes.

6 Warm the tortillas and place one on each serving plate. Spoon the hot rice and bean mixture on top. Serve immediately, with the avocado salsa and a bowl of sour cream.

LEEK, SQUASH AND TOMATO GRATIN

COLOURFUL AND SUCCULENT, YOU CAN USE VIRTUALLY ANY KIND OF SQUASH FOR THIS AUTUMN GRATIN, FROM PATTY PANS AND ACORN SQUASH TO PUMPKINS.

SERVES FOUR TO SIX

INGREDIENTS

- 450g/1lb peeled and seeded squash, cut into 1cm/½in slices
- 60ml/4 tbsp olive oil
- 450g/1lb leeks, cut into thick, diagonal slices
- 675g/1½lb tomatoes, peeled and thickly sliced
- 2.5ml/½ tsp ground toasted cumin seeds
- 300ml/½ pint/1¼ cups single (light) cream
- 1 fresh red chilli, seeded and sliced
- 1 garlic clove, finely chopped
- 15ml/1 tbsp chopped fresh mint
- 30ml/2 tbsp chopped fresh parsley
- 60ml/4 tbsp fine white breadcrumbs
- salt and ground black pepper

VARIATION

For a curried version of this dish, use ground coriander as well as cumin, and coconut milk instead of cream. Use fresh coriander (cilantro) instead of the mint and parsley.

1 Steam the squash over boiling salted water for 10 minutes.

2 Heat half the oil in a frying pan and cook the leeks gently for 5–6 minutes until lightly coloured. Try to keep the slices intact. Preheat the oven to 190°C/375°F/Gas 5.

3 Layer all the squash, leeks and tomatoes in a 2 litre/3½ pint/8 cup gratin dish, arranging them in rows. Season with salt, pepper and cumin.

4 Pour the cream into a small pan and add the sliced chilli and chopped garlic. Bring to the boil over a low heat then stir in the mint. Pour the mixture evenly over the layered vegetables, using a rubber spatula to scrape all the sauce out of the pan.

5 Cook for 50–55 minutes, or until the gratin is bubbling and tinged brown. Sprinkle the parsley and breadcrumbs on top and drizzle over the remaining oil. Bake for another 15–20 minutes until the breadcrumbs are browned and crisp. Serve immediately.

Bean and Tomato Casserole

Juicy tomatoes and filling cannellini beans baked – a great dish for a cold day.

SERVES FOUR

INGREDIENTS
- 45ml/3 tbsp extra virgin olive oil or sunflower oil
- 45ml/3 tbsp chopped fresh flat leaf parsley
- 400g/14oz can cannellini beans, rinsed and drained
- 1kg/2¼lb firm ripe tomatoes
- 5ml/1 tsp caster (superfine) sugar
- 40g/1½oz/scant 1 cup day-old breadcrumbs
- 2.5ml/½ tsp chilli powder or paprika
- salt
- chopped fresh parsley, to garnish
- rye bread, to serve

1 Preheat the oven to 200°C/400°F/Gas 6. Brush a large ovenproof dish with 15ml/1 tbsp of the oil.

2 Sprinkle the chopped flat leaf parsley over the base of the dish and cover with the beans. Cut the tomatoes into even slices, discarding the two end slices of each. Arrange the slices of tomato in the dish over the beans so that they overlap slightly. Sprinkle them with a little salt and the sugar.

3 In a mixing bowl, stir together the breadcrumbs, the remaining olive or sunflower oil and chilli powder or paprika, whichever you are using.

4 Sprinkle the crumb mixture over the tomatoes, and bake in the oven for 50 minutes. Serve hot or cold, garnished with chopped parsley and accompanied by rye bread.

Mixed Vegetable Casserole

The vegetables in this rich tomato sauce can be varied according to season.

SERVES FOUR

INGREDIENTS
- 1 aubergine (eggplant), diced into 2.5cm/1in pieces
- 115g/4oz/½ cup okra, halved lengthways
- 115g/4oz/1 cup frozen or fresh peas or petits pois (baby peas)
- 115g/4oz/¾ cup green beans, cut into 2.5cm/1in pieces
- 400g/14oz can flageolet (small cannellini) beans, rinsed and drained
- 4 courgettes (zucchini), cut into 1cm/½in pieces
- 2 onions, finely chopped
- 450g/1lb maincrop potatoes, diced into 2.5cm/1in pieces
- 1 red (bell) pepper, seeded and sliced
- 400g/14oz can chopped tomatoes
- 150ml/¼ pint/⅔ cup vegetable stock
- 60ml/4 tbsp olive oil
- 75ml/5 tbsp chopped fresh parsley
- 5ml/1 tsp paprika
- salt
- crusty bread, to serve

For the topping
- 6 tomatoes, sliced
- 1 courgette (zucchini), sliced

1 Slice the tomatoes and courgettes for the topping.

2 Put all the other ingredients in an ovenproof dish, combine them well.

3 Preheat the oven to 190°C/375°F/Gas 5. Arrange alternate slices of tomato and courgette attractively on the top of the other vegetables.

4 Put the lid on or cover the casserole tightly with foil. Bake in the oven for 60–70 minutes until all the vegetables are tender. Remove the lid or foil for the last 15 minutes to brown the topping slightly, if you like. Serve either hot or cold with wedges of crusty bread.

COOK'S TIP
For the finest flavour, use extra virgin olive oil in the bake and vine-ripened or home-grown tomatoes for the topping.

Spinach Plantain Rounds

This delectable way of serving plantains is popular throughout the Caribbean islands. The plantains must be fairly ripe, but still firm. The rounds can be served either hot or cold, with a salad, or as a vegetable accompaniment.

SERVES FOUR

INGREDIENTS
- 2 large ripe plantains
- oil, for frying
- 15g/½oz/2 tbsp butter or margarine
- 25g/1oz/2 tbsp finely chopped onion
- 2 garlic cloves, crushed
- 450g/1lb fresh spinach, chopped
- pinch of freshly grated nutmeg
- 1 egg, beaten
- wholemeal (whole-wheat) flour, for dusting
- salt and ground black pepper

1 Using a small sharp knife, carefully cut each plantain lengthways into four pieces.

2 Heat a little oil in a large frying pan and fry the pieces of plantain on both sides until golden brown but not fully cooked. Lift out and drain on kitchen paper. Reserve the oil in the pan.

3 Melt the butter or margarine in a separate pan and sauté the onion and garlic for 2–3 minutes, until the onion is soft. Add the spinach and nutmeg, with salt and pepper to taste. Cover and cook for about 5 minutes, until the spinach has wilted. Cool, then tip into a sieve (strainer) and press out any excess moisture.

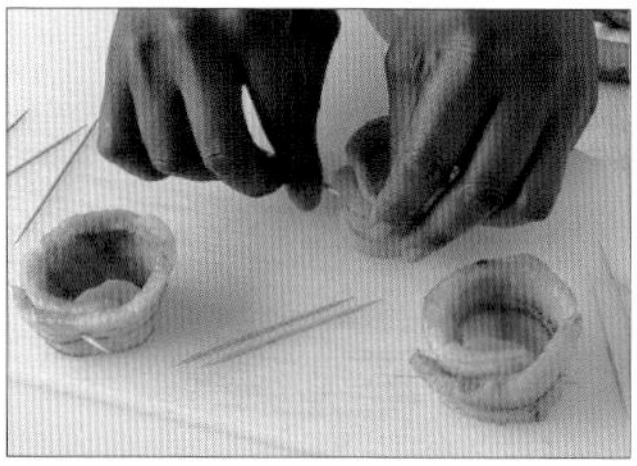

4 Curl the plantain pieces into rings and secure each ring with half a wooden cocktail stick (toothpick). Pack each ring with a little of the spinach mixture.

5 Place the egg and flour in two separate shallow dishes. Add a little more oil to the frying pan, if necessary, and heat until medium hot. Dip the plantain rings in the egg and then in the flour and fry on both sides for 1–2 minutes until golden brown. Drain on kitchen paper and serve.

PEPPERY BEAN SALAD

THIS PRETTY CARIBBEAN SALAD USES CANNED BEANS FOR SPEED AND CONVENIENCE. THE CONTRAST BETWEEN THE CRISP RADISHES AND PEPPERS AND THE SOFTER TEXTURE OF THE BEANS IS ONE REASON WHY IT WORKS SO WELL. THE TASTY DRESSING PLAYS A PART, TOO.

SERVES SIX

INGREDIENTS
- 425g/15oz can kidney beans, drained
- 425g/15oz can black-eyed beans (peas), drained
- 425g/15oz can chickpeas, drained
- ¼ red (bell) pepper
- ¼ green (bell) pepper
- 6 radishes
- 15ml/1 tbsp chopped spring onion (scallion)
- sliced spring onion, to garnish

For the dressing
- 5ml/1 tsp ground cumin
- 15ml/1 tbsp tomato ketchup
- 30ml/2 tbsp olive oil
- 15ml/1 tbsp white wine vinegar
- 1 garlic clove, crushed
- 2.5ml/½ tsp hot pepper sauce
- salt

1 Drain the canned beans and chickpeas into a colander and rinse them thoroughly under cold running water. Shake off the excess water and tip them into a large salad bowl.

2 Core, seed and roughly chop the peppers. Trim the radishes and slice them thinly. Add to the beans with the chopped pepper and spring onion.

3 In a small bowl, mix the ground cumin, ketchup, olive oil, white wine vinegar and garlic. Add the hot pepper sauce and a little salt to taste and stir again until thoroughly mixed.

4 Pour the dressing over the salad and mix thoroughly with a fork. Cover with clear film (plastic wrap) and chill for at least 1 hour before serving, garnished with sliced spring onion.

COOK'S TIP

For maximum flavour, it is best to allow the ingredients to marinate for at least 3–4 hours.

Avocado and Grapefruit Salad

This is a light, refreshing lunch-time salad. The buttery texture of the avocados, combines with the tanginess of the grapefruit to make the perfect summer dish. Serve it as a light main course or as an accompaniment to barbecued meats.

SERVES FOUR

INGREDIENTS
- 90ml/6 tbsp olive oil
- 30ml/2 tbsp white wine vinegar
- 1 pink grapefruit
- 2 large ripe avocados
- 1 cos or romaine lettuce, separated into leaves
- salt and ground black pepper

1 Using a balloon whisk or a fork, whisk the olive oil and white wine vinegar together in a large bowl, season to taste with salt and ground black pepper and vigorously whisk again.

VARIATIONS

Try other fruit combinations. Mango and strawberries go well together, as do papaya and limes.

2 Slice the top and bottom off the grapefruit. Peel the fruit by running a small knife all around it, between the peel and flesh. Make sure all the bitter pith is removed. Hold the grapefruit over the bowl containing the dressing and cut carefully between the membranes, so that all the segments fall into the bowl. Squeeze the remaining pulp over the bowl to extract all the juice.

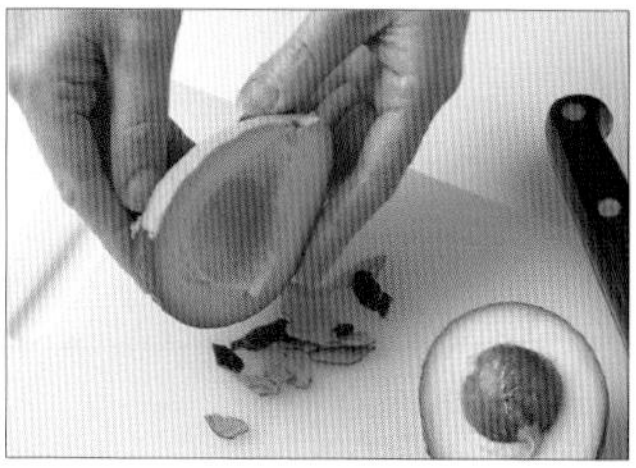

3 Run a knife around the length of the avocados. Twist the sides in opposite directions to separate the halves. Use a large spoon to remove the stone (pit), then peel the halves. Slice the flesh and cover these with the dressing, to stop them from discolouring.

4 Tear the lettuce into pieces and add to the bowl. Toss to coat. Adjust the seasoning to taste and serve.

QUINOA SALAD WITH CITRUS DRESSING

QUINOA IS A TYPE OF GRAIN GROWN IN THE ANDES. A STAPLE FOOD OF THE REGION, IT HAS BEEN CULTIVATED SINCE THE TIME OF THE INCAS AND AZTECS. QUINOA IS PACKED WITH PROTEIN AND IS ALSO GLUTEN FREE, SO IT IS IDEAL FOR VEGETARIANS AND THOSE WHO ARE GLUTEN INTOLERANT.

SERVES SIX

INGREDIENTS

- 175g/6oz/1 cup quinoa
- 90ml/6 tbsp olive oil
- juice of 2 limes
- juice of 1 large orange
- 2 fresh green chillies, seeded and finely chopped
- 2 garlic cloves, crushed
- ½ cucumber, peeled
- 1 large tomato, seeded and cubed
- 4 spring onions (scallions), sliced
- 30ml/2 tbsp chopped fresh mint
- 15ml/1 tbsp chopped fresh flat leaf parsley
- salt

COOK'S TIP

Quinoa can also be eaten plain as an accompaniment to meat or fish dishes.

1 Put the quinoa in a sieve (strainer), rinse thoroughly under cold water, then tip into a large pan. Pour in cold water to cover and bring to the boil. Lower the heat and simmer for 10–12 minutes, until tender. Drain and leave to cool.

2 Make a dressing by whisking the oil with the citrus juices. Stir in the chillies and garlic and season with salt.

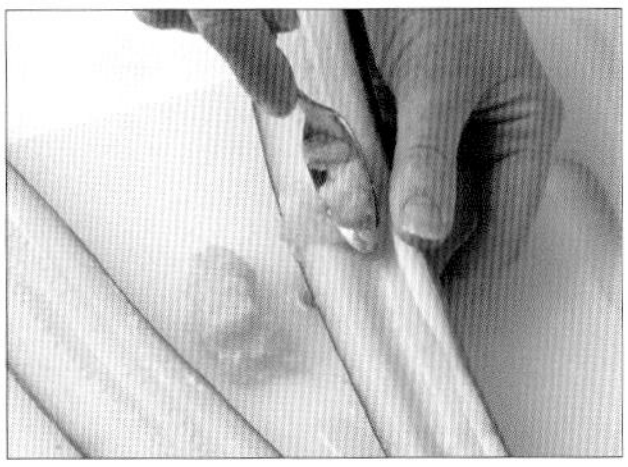

3 Cut the cucumber in half lengthways and, using a teaspoon, scoop out and discard the seeds. Cut into 5mm/¼in slices and add to the cooled quinoa with the tomato, spring onions and herbs. Toss well to combine.

4 Pour the dressing over the salad and toss again until well mixed. Check the seasoning and serve.

OKRA AND TOMATO SALAD

For this salad the okra is cooked as little as possible, keeping it crunchy. Serve as a side salad, or stir in some baby spinach for a memorable main course.

SERVES FOUR

INGREDIENTS
- 60ml/4 tbsp olive oil
- 15ml/1 tbsp red wine vinegar
- 1 red onion, very thinly sliced
- 3 tomatoes, peeled and seeded
- 400g/14oz okra
- salt and ground black pepper

1 In a large bowl, whisk together the olive oil and red wine vinegar. Season with salt and ground black pepper. Toss the slices of red onion into the dressing and leave to marinate while you prepare and cook the okra.

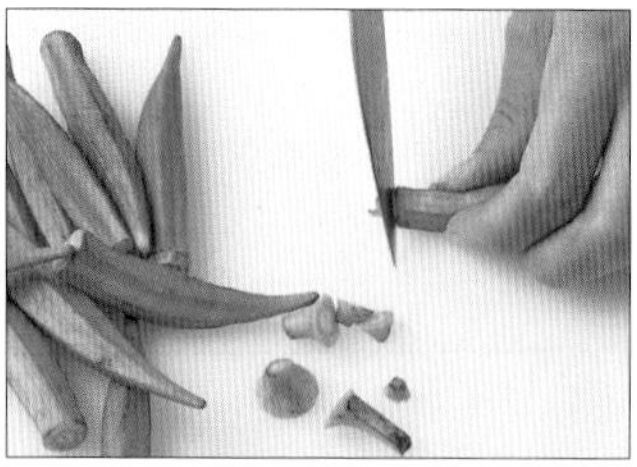

2 Trim the tough stalks from the okra, but avoid cutting into the pods, otherwise you will release a sticky liquid. Cook the okra in a pan of lightly salted boiling water for 4–5 minutes, until just tender. Drain and dry on kitchen paper. Leave the small okra whole, but cut any larger ones diagonally in half.

3 Stir the cooked okra into the dressing, mix thoroughly and leave to marinate for about 20–25 minutes.

4 Cut the tomatoes into thin wedges and add them to the bowl. Gently toss them together with the okra. Season to taste with salt and ground black pepper and serve immediately.

TOMATO, HEART OF PALM AND ONION SALAD

This simple salad can be assembled in minutes. It is an excellent dish for introducing anyone to the delicate flavour of palm hearts.

SERVES FOUR

INGREDIENTS
- 4 beefsteak tomatoes
- 1 small onion, thinly sliced
- 400g/14oz can hearts of palm

For the dressing
- juice of 1 lime
- 10ml/2 tsp Dijon mustard
- 60ml/4 tbsp olive oil
- salt and ground black pepper

COOK'S TIP
If the tomatoes are not perfectly ripe, sprinkle the slices with a large pinch of caster (superfine) sugar, to help bring out their sweetness.

1 Cut the tomatoes into 1cm/½in slices and arrange on a large serving platter. Sprinkle the thin onion slices over the tomatoes and season to taste with salt and ground black pepper.

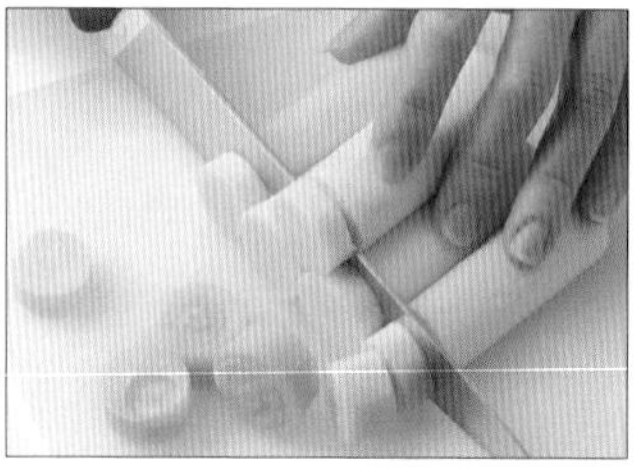

2 Drain the canned hearts of palm thoroughly, cut them into 1cm/½in slices and sprinkle the slices over the tomatoes and onions.

3 Make the dressing by whisking the lime juice, mustard and oil in a bowl. Season with salt and ground pepper. Drizzle over the salad and serve.

VARIATION
If you cannot get hearts of palm, this salad will be just as delicious using artichoke hearts instead.

CHAYOTES WITH CORN AND CHILLIES

Shaped like pears or avocados, chayotes are members of the squash family and have rather a bland taste. However, they marry extremely well with other ingredients, such as the corn and roasted jalapenos in this Mexican medley.

SERVES SIX

INGREDIENTS
- 4 fresh jalapeño chillies
- 3 chayotes
- oil, for frying
- 1 red onion, finely chopped
- 3 garlic cloves, crushed
- 225g/8oz/1⅓ cups corn kernels, thawed if frozen
- 150g/5oz/⅔ cup cream cheese
- 5ml/1 tsp salt (optional)
- 25g/1oz/⅓ cup freshly grated Parmesan cheese

1 Dry roast the fresh jalapeño chillies in a griddle pan, turning them frequently so that the skins blacken but do not burn. Place them in a plastic bag, tie the top securely, and set them aside for 20 minutes.

2 Meanwhile, peel the chayotes, cut them in half and remove the seed from each of them. Cut the flesh into 1cm/½in cubes.

COOK'S TIP
Chayotes go by several names, including christophene and choko. Store them in a plastic bag in the refrigerator and they will keep for up to 1 month.

3 Heat the oil in a frying pan. Add the onion, garlic,chayote cubes and corn. Fry over a moderate heat for 10 minutes, stirring occasionally.

4 Remove the jalapeños from the bag, peel off the skins and remove any stems. Cut them in half, scrape out the seeds, then cut the flesh into strips.

5 Add the chillies and cream cheese to the pan, stirring gently, until the cheese melts. Place in a serving dish.

6 Stir in salt, if needed, then spoon into a warmed dish. Sprinkle with Parmesan cheese and serve. This makes a good accompaniment for cold roast meats.

SPINACH SALAD

YOUNG SPINACH LEAVES MAKE A WELCOME CHANGE FROM LETTUCE AND ARE EXCELLENT IN THIS MEXICAN SALAD. THE ROASTED GARLIC IS AN INSPIRED ADDITION TO THE DRESSING.

SERVES SIX

INGREDIENTS
- 500g/1¼lb baby spinach leaves
- 50g/2oz/⅓ cup sesame seeds
- 50g/2oz/¼ cup butter
- 30ml/2 tbsp olive oil
- 6 shallots, sliced
- 8 fresh serrano chillies, seeded and cut into strips
- 4 tomatoes, sliced

For the dressing
- 6 roasted garlic cloves
- 120ml/4fl oz/½ cup white wine vinegar
- 2.5ml/½ tsp ground white pepper
- 1 bay leaf
- 2.5ml/½ tsp ground allspice
- 30ml/2 tbsp chopped fresh thyme, plus extra sprigs, to garnish

COOK'S TIP
To roast individual garlic cloves simply place in a roasting tray in a moderate oven for about 15 minutes until soft.

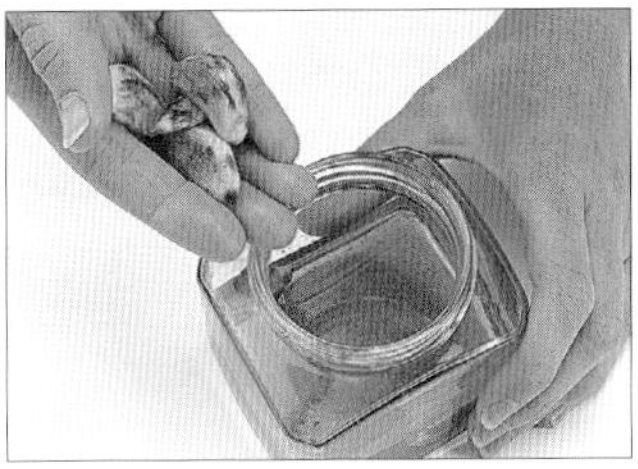

1 Make the dressing. Remove the skins from the garlic when cool, then chop and combine with the vinegar, pepper, bay leaf, allspice and chopped thyme in a jar with a screw-top lid. Close the lid tightly, shake well, then put the dressing in the refrigerator until needed.

2 Wash the spinach leaves and dry them in a salad spinner or clean dishtowel. Put them in a plastic bag in the refrigerator.

3 Toast the sesame seeds in a dry frying pan, shaking frequently over a moderate heat until golden. Set aside.

4 Heat the butter and oil in a frying pan. Fry the shallots for 4–5 minutes, until softened, then stir in the chilli strips and fry for 2–3 minutes more.

5 In a large bowl, layer the spinach with the shallot and chilli mixture, and the tomato slices. Pour over the dressing. Sprinkle with sesame seeds and serve, garnished with thyme sprigs.

BAKED SWEET POTATO SALAD

THIS SALAD HAS A TRULY TROPICAL TASTE, BLENDING THE CREAMINESS OF THE NATURAL YOGURT WITH THE HEARTINESS OF THE SWEET POTATO. IT IS IDEAL SERVED WITH CARIBBEAN DISHES.

SERVES FOUR TO SIX

INGREDIENTS

1kg/2¼lb sweet potatoes

For the dressing

45ml/3 tbsp chopped fresh coriander (cilantro)
juice of 1 lime
150ml/¼ pint/⅔ cup natural (plain) yogurt

For the salad

1 red (bell) pepper, seeded and finely diced
3 celery sticks, finely diced
¼ red skinned onion, finely chopped
1 red chilli, finely chopped
salt and ground black pepper
coriander (cilantro) leaves, to garnish

1 Preheat the oven to 200°C/400°F/Gas 6. Wash the potatoes, pierce them all over, and bake in the oven for 40 minutes or until tender.

2 Meanwhile, mix the dressing ingredients together in a bowl and season to taste. Chill while you prepare the remaining ingredients.

3 In a large bowl mix the red pepper, celery, onion and chilli together.

4 Remove the potatoes from the oven and when cool enough to handle, peel them. Cut the potatoes into cubes and add them to the bowl. Drizzle the dressing over and toss carefully. Season again to taste and serve, garnished with fresh coriander.

WARM HAZELNUT AND PISTACHIO SALAD

TWO KINDS OF CRUNCHY NUTS TURN ORDINARY POTATO SALAD INTO A REALLY SPECIAL ACCOMPANIMENT. SERVE WITH COLD SLICED MEAT OR ON ITS OWN AS A VEGETARIAN MEAL.

SERVES FOUR

INGREDIENTS
- 900g/2lb small new or salad potatoes
- 30ml/2 tbsp hazelnut or walnut oil
- 60ml/4 tbsp sunflower oil
- juice of 1 lemon
- 25g/1oz/¼ cup hazelnuts
- 15 pistachio nuts
- salt and ground black pepper
- sprigs of flat leaf parsley, to garnish

VARIATION

Use chopped walnuts in place of the hazelnuts. Buy the broken pieces of nut, which are less expensive than walnut halves, but chop them smaller before adding to the salad.

1 Cook the potatoes in their skins in boiling salted water for about 10–15 minutes, until tender.

2 Drain the potatoes well and leave to cool slightly.

3 Meanwhile mix the hazelnut or walnut oil with the sunflower oil and lemon juice. Season well.

4 Using a sharp knife, roughly chop the nuts.

5 Put the cooled potatoes into a large bowl and pour the dressing over. Toss to combine.

6 Sprinkle the salad with the chopped nuts. Serve immediately, garnished with flat leaf parsley.

JALAPEÑO AND PRAWN SALAD

PICKLED JALAPEÑO CHILLI GIVES A DISTINCTIVE SPICY FLAVOUR TO THIS DELICIOUS SALAD. IN MEXICO, IT IS QUITE USUAL TO SERVE SUCH A HEARTY SALAD AS A SEPARATE COURSE.

SERVES FOUR

INGREDIENTS
- 1 iceberg lettuce or 2 Little Gem (Bibb) lettuces
- 60ml/4 tbsp mayonnaise
- 60ml/4 tbsp sour cream
- 350g/12oz/3 cups cooked peeled prawns (shrimp), thawed if frozen
- 75g/3oz/½ cup cooked green beans, chopped
- 75g/3oz/½ cup cooked carrots, chopped
- ½ cucumber, chopped
- 2 hard-boiled eggs, coarsely chopped
- 1 drained pickled jalapeño chilli, seeded and chopped
- salt

1 Line a large salad bowl or platter with the lettuce leaves. You can also chop the middle part of the lettuce up and combine it with the other ingredients.

2 Mix the mayonnaise and sour cream together in a small bowl and set aside.

3 Combine the prawns, beans, carrot, cucumber, eggs and chilli in a separate bowl. Season with salt.

4 Fold the mayonnaise and sour cream mixture into the prawns and pile into the lined salad bowl to serve.

BROAD BEAN, MUSHROOM AND CHORIZO SALAD

THIS SALAD CAN BE SERVED AS A FIRST COURSE OR AS PART OF A BUFFET MENU. FRESH BROAD BEANS ARE PREFERABLE FOR THEIR TASTE, BUT FROZEN ONES COULD BE SUBSTITUTED.

SERVES FOUR

INGREDIENTS
- 225g/8oz shelled broad beans
- 175g/6oz chorizo sausage
- 60ml/4 tbsp extra virgin olive oil
- 225g/8oz brown cap mushrooms, sliced
- handful of fresh chives
- salt and freshly ground black pepper

COOK'S TIP
This salad can be prepared a day in advance and stored in the refrigerator until needed, although it may not remain fresh and crisp for longer than a day, and the quality of the food will reduce if you keep it for longer periods. Remove from the refrigerator a few hours beforehand in order to allow the salad to reach room temperature before serving.

1 Cook the broad beans in a large pan of boiling, salted water until just tender. You can test them by breaking them in half and watching to see if they snap easily. If they begin to give between your fingers they will be cooked sufficiently. Drain and refresh under cold running water.

2 If the beans are large, peel away the tough outer skins and discard them, setting aside the paler core.

3 Remove the skin from the chorizo sausage and cut it into small chunks. Heat the oil in a frying pan, add the chorizo and cook for 2 minutes. Empty into a bowl with the mushrooms, mix well and leave aside to cool.

4 Chop half the chives and stir the beans and chopped chives into the mushroom mixture. Season to taste. Serve the salad at room temperature, garnished with the remaining chives.

Nopalitos Salad

Nopalitos – strips of pickled cactus paddles – are sold in cans or jars, and are very useful for making quick and easy salads like this one from Mexico.

SERVES FOUR

INGREDIENTS

- 300g/11oz/scant 2 cups drained canned *nopalitos*
- 1 red (bell) pepper
- 30ml/2 tbsp olive oil
- 2 garlic cloves, sliced
- ½ red onion, thinly sliced
- 120ml/4fl oz/½ cup cider vinegar
- small bunch of fresh coriander (cilantro), chopped
- salt

1 Preheat the grill (broiler). Put the *nopalitos* in a bowl. Pour over water to cover and set aside for 30 minutes. Drain, replace with fresh water and leave to soak for a further 30 minutes.

2 Place the halves of the red pepper cut side down in a grill pan. Grill (broil) until the skins blister and char, then put the pepper halves in a strong plastic bag, tie the top securely to keep the steam in, and set aside for 20 minutes.

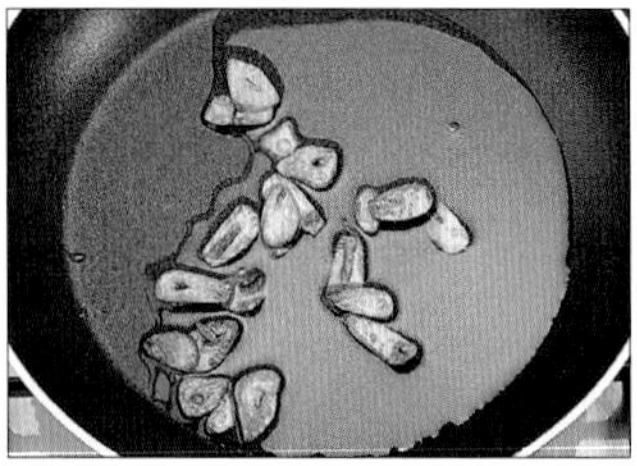

3 Heat the oil in a small frying pan and fry the garlic over a low heat until the slices start to turn golden. Using a slotted spoon, transfer them to a salad bowl. Pour the garlic-flavoured oil into a jug and set it aside to cool.

4 Add the red onion slices to the salad bowl, then pour over the vinegar. Remove the red pepper from the bag, peel off the skins, then cut the flesh into thin strips. Add to the salad bowl.

5 Drain the *nopalitos* thoroughly and add them to the salad, with the cool garlic-flavoured oil and a little salt, to taste. Toss lightly, then chill until needed. Sprinkle the chopped coriander over just before serving. This is delicious served with crusty bread.

JICAMA, CHILLI AND LIME SALAD

A VERY TASTY, CRISP VEGETABLE, THE JICAMA *IS SOMETIMES CALLED THE MEXICAN POTATO. UNLIKE POTATO, HOWEVER, IT CAN BE EATEN RAW AS WELL AS COOKED. THIS MAKES A GOOD SALAD OR A REFRESHING APPETIZER TO SERVE WITH DRINKS AND COCKTAILS.*

SERVES FOUR

INGREDIENTS

- 1 *jicama*
- 2.5ml/½ tsp salt
- 2 fresh serrano chillies
- 2 limes

COOK'S TIP

Look for *jicama* in Oriental supermarkets, as it is widely used in Chinese cooking. It goes by several names and you may find it labelled as either yam bean or Chinese turnip.

Residents of Mexico recognize *jicama* as one of the four elements used for "The Festival of the Dead", celebrated on November 1. It is prepared in the same way as described here and enjoyed as a snack or nibble with drinks.

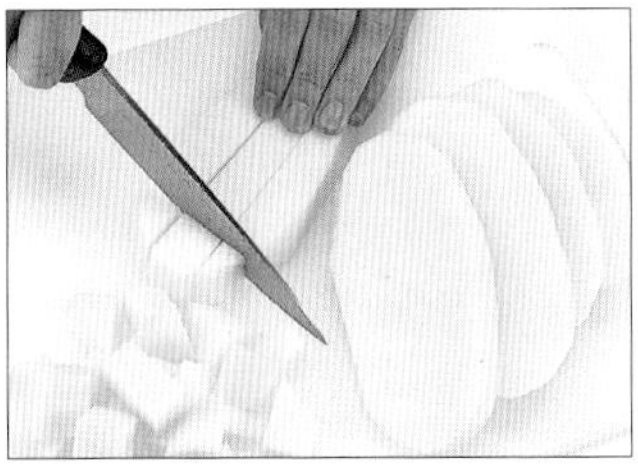

1 Peel the *jicama* with a potato peeler or knife, then cut it into 2cm/¾in cubes. Put these in a large bowl, add the salt and toss well.

2 Cut the chillies in half, scrape out the seeds with a sharp knife, then cut the flesh into fine strips. Grate one of the limes thinly, removing only the coloured part of the skin, then cut the lime in half and squeeze the juice.

3 Add the chillies, lime rind and juice to the *jicama* and mix thoroughly to ensure that all the *jicama* cubes are coated. Cut the other lime into wedges.

4 Cover and chill for at least 1 hour before serving with lime wedges. If the salad is to be served as an appetizer with drinks, transfer the *jicama* cubes to little bowls and offer them with cocktail sticks (toothpicks) for spearing.

CHAYOTE SALAD

COOL AND REFRESHING, THIS MEXICAN SALAD IS IDEAL ON ITS OWN OR WITH FISH OR CHICKEN DISHES. THE SOFT FLESH OF THE CHAYOTES ABSORBS THE FLAVOUR OF THE DRESSING BEAUTIFULLY.

SERVES FOUR

INGREDIENTS
- 2 *chayotes*
- 2 firm tomatoes
- 1 small onion, finely chopped
- finely sliced strips of fresh red and green chilli, to garnish

For the dressing
- 2.5ml/½ tsp Dijon mustard
- 2.5ml/½ tsp ground anise
- 90ml/6 tbsp white wine vinegar
- 60ml/4 tbsp olive oil
- salt and ground black pepper

1 Bring a pan of water to the boil. Peel the *chayotes*, cut them in half and remove the seeds. Add them to the boiling water. Lower the heat and simmer for 20 minutes or until the *chayotes* are tender. Drain and set them aside to cool.

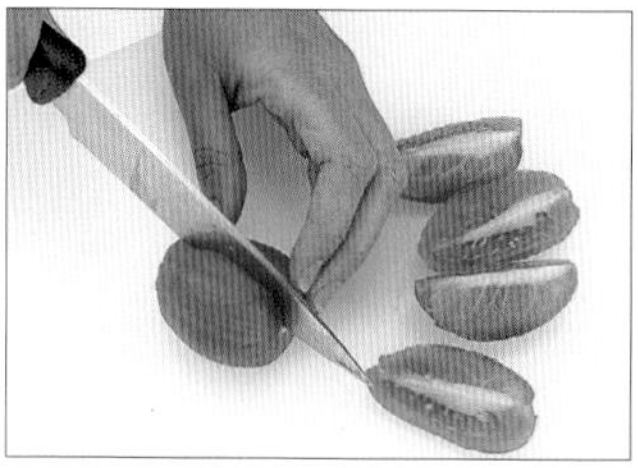

2 Meanwhile, peel the tomatoes. Cut a cross in the base of each tomato. Place them in a heatproof bowl and pour over boiling water to cover. After 3 minutes, lift the tomatoes out on a slotted spoon and plunge them into a bowl of cold water. Drain. The skins will have begun to peel back from the crosses. Remove the skins completely and cut the tomatoes into wedges.

3 Make the dressing by combining all the ingredients in a screw top jar. Close the lid tightly and shake the jar vigorously.

4 Cut the *chayotes* into wedges and place in a bowl with the tomato and onion. Pour over the dressing and serve garnished with strips of fresh red and green chilli.

Caesar Salad

Caesar Salad actually originated in Mexico, and takes its name from the chef, Caesar Cardini, who invented it in his restaurant in Tijuana in 1924.

SERVES FOUR

INGREDIENTS
- 2 large garlic cloves, peeled and left whole
- 60ml/4 tbsp extra virgin olive oil
- 4 slices of bread, crusts removed, cubed
- 1 cos or Romaine lettuce, separated into leaves
- 6 drained canned anchovy fillets
- shavings of Parmesan cheese, to garnish

For the dressing
- 1 egg
- 10ml/2 tsp Dijon mustard
- generous dash of Worcestershire sauce
- 30ml/2 tbsp lemon juice
- 30ml/2 tbsp extra virgin olive oil
- salt and freshly ground black pepper

1 Cut one garlic clove in half and rub it around the inside of a salad bowl. Put the remaining garlic in a large frying pan. Add the oil and heat gently for 5 minutes, then discard the garlic. Add the bread cubes to the hot oil, in batches if necessary, and fry them until they are crisp on all sides. Drain on kitchen paper.

2 Line the salad bowl with the cos or Romaine leaves. Carefully cut the anchovy fillets in half lengthways and distribute them among the lettuce leaves. Toss the leaves to spread the flavour of the anchovies.

3 Crack the egg into a food processor or blender, with the Dijon mustard, Worcestershire sauce and lemon juice. Season and process to blend briefly, then add the oil with the motor running.

4 Pour the dressing thickly over the salad in the bowl and toss lightly. Add the garlic croûtons. Transfer to a serving bowl, sprinkle with Parmesan shavings and serve.

Green Bean and Chilli Pepper Salad

This colourful red and green salad, garnished with beans and green and black olives, is just the thing for a light summer lunch dish or as part of a cold buffet.

SERVES FOUR

INGREDIENTS
- 350g/12oz/2¼ cups cooked green beans, quartered
- 2 red (bell) peppers, seeded and chopped
- 2 spring onions (scallions), chopped
- 1 or more pickled serrano chillies, rinsed, seeded and chopped
- 1 iceberg lettuce, coarsely shredded, or mixed salad leaves
- olives, to garnish

For the dressing
- 45ml/3 tbsp red wine vinegar
- 135ml/9 tbsp olive oil
- salt and ground black pepper

1 Combine the cooked green beans, chopped peppers, chopped spring onions and chillies in a salad bowl.

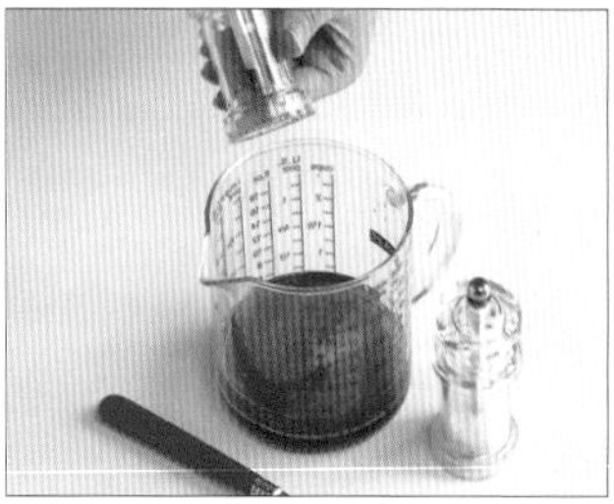

2 Make the salad dressing. Pour the red wine vinegar into a bowl or jug (pitcher). Add salt and ground black pepper to taste, then gradually whisk in the olive oil until well combined.

3 Pour the salad dressing over the prepared vegetables and toss lightly together to mix and coat thoroughly.

4 Line a large platter with the shredded lettuce leaves and arrange the salad attractively on top. Garnish with the olives and serve.

MANGO, TOMATO AND RED ONION SALAD

This salad makes a delicious appetizer and is often eaten on the islands of the Caribbean. Under-ripe mango contributes a subtle sweetness that goes well with the tomato.

SERVES FOUR

INGREDIENTS

- 1 firm under-ripe mango
- 2 large tomatoes or 1 beefsteak tomato, sliced
- ½ cucumber, peeled and thinly sliced
- ½ red onion, sliced into rings
- 1 garlic clove, crushed
- 30ml/2 tbsp sunflower or vegetable oil
- 15ml/1 tbsp lemon juice
- 2.5ml/½ tsp hot pepper sauce
- salt and ground black pepper
- sugar, to taste
- chopped chives, to garnish

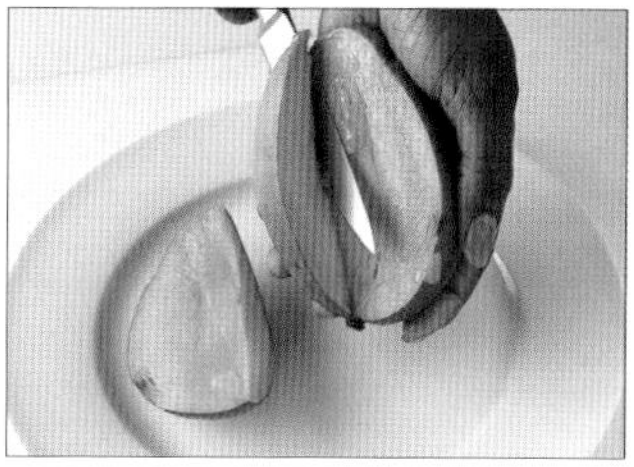

1 Using a sharp knife, cut a thick slice or "cheek" from either side of the mango stone. Peel away the skin and slice the flesh into thin strips. Peel the remaining mango, remove the rest of the flesh and slice it thinly.

2 Arrange a layer of tomato slices on a large serving plate or platter. Top with the cucumber slices, followed by the mango, and finish off with the thin slices of red onion.

3 Make the salad dressing. Crush the garlic clove into a small glass bowl. Add the oil, lemon juice, hot pepper sauce, salt, ground black pepper and sugar, if you like. Using a balloon whisk or a fork, whisk these ingredients together until thoroughly mixed.

4 Drizzle the dressing evenly over the salad and garnish with chopped chives. Serve immediately.

COOK'S TIP

Choose the freshest, ripest tomatoes available for the best flavour.

Peruvian Salad

This is a spectacular-looking salad that could be served as a side dish or a light lunch. In Peru, white rice would be used, but brown rice adds an interesting texture and flavour.

SERVES FOUR

INGREDIENTS
- 225g/8oz/2 cups cooked long grain brown or white rice
- 15ml/1 tbsp chopped fresh parsley
- 1 red (bell) pepper
- 1 small onion, sliced into rings
- olive oil, for sprinkling
- 115g/4oz green beans, halved
- 50g/2oz/½ cup baby corn
- 4 quail's eggs, hard-boiled and halved
- 25–50g/1–2oz Spanish ham, cut into thin slices (optional)
- 1 small avocado
- lemon juice, for sprinkling
- 75g/3oz mixed salad leaves
- 15ml/1 tbsp capers
- about 10 stuffed olives, halved

For the dressing
- 1 garlic clove, crushed
- 60ml/4 tbsp olive oil
- 45ml/3 tbsp sunflower oil
- 30ml/2 tbsp lemon juice
- 45ml/3 tbsp natural (plain) yogurt
- 2.5ml/½ tsp mustard
- 2.5ml/½ tsp granulated sugar
- salt and ground black pepper

1 Make the dressing by placing all the ingredients in a bowl and whisking with a fork or whisk until smooth. Alternatively, place the ingredients in an empty jam jar, screw the lid on tightly and shake well.

2 Put the cooked rice into a large, glass salad bowl and spoon in half the dressing. Add the chopped parsley, stir well and set aside.

3 Cut the pepper in half, remove the seeds and pith, then place the halves cut side down in a small roasting pan. Add the onion rings. Sprinkle the onion with a little olive oil, place the pan under a hot grill (broiler) and cook for 5–6 minutes until the pepper blackens and blisters and the onion turns golden. You may need to stir the onion once or twice so that it cooks evenly.

4 Stir the onion in with the rice. Put the pepper in a plastic bag and knot the top. When the steam has loosened the skin on the pepper halves and they are cool enough to handle, peel them and cut the flesh into thin strips.

5 Cook the green beans in boiling water for 2 minutes, then add the corn and cook for 1–2 minutes more. Place in a large mixing bowl and add the red pepper strips, quail's eggs and ham.

6 Peel and dice the avocado. Put the salad leaves in a separate mixing bowl, add the avocado and mix lightly. Arrange the salad leaves and avocado on top of the rice. In a separate bowl, stir about 45ml/3 tbsp of the dressing into the green bean and pepper mixture. Pile this on top of the salad. Sprinkle the capers and stuffed olives on top and serve the salad with the remaining dressing.

PUMPKIN SALAD

RED WINE VINEGAR BRINGS OUT THE SWEETNESS OF THE PUMPKIN. NO SALAD LEAVES ARE USED, JUST PLENTY OF FRESH PARSLEY. EATEN THROUGHOUT LATIN AMERICA, IT IS GREAT FOR A COLD BUFFET.

SERVES FOUR

INGREDIENTS

- 1 large red onion, peeled and very thinly sliced
- 200ml/7fl oz/scant 1 cup olive oil
- 60ml/4 tbsp red wine vinegar
- 675g/1½ lb pumpkin, peeled and cut into 4cm/1½ in pieces
- 40g/1½ oz/¾ cup fresh flat leaf parsley leaves, chopped
- salt and ground black pepper

VARIATIONS

Try replacing the pumpkin with sweet potatoes. Wild rocket (arugula) or fresh coriander (cilantro) can be used instead of the parsley, if you prefer.

1 Mix the onion, olive oil and vinegar in a large bowl. Stir well to combine.

2 Put the pumpkin in a large pan of cold salted water. Bring to the boil, then lower the heat and simmer gently for 15–20 minutes. Drain.

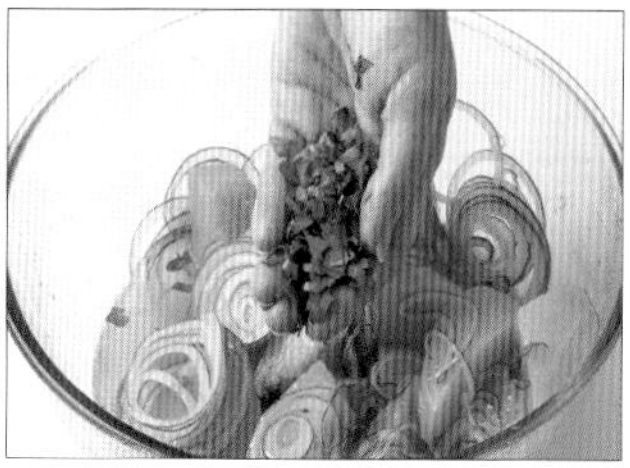

3 Immediately add the drained pumpkin to the bowl containing the dressing and toss lightly with your hands. Leave to cool. Stir in the chopped parsley, cover with clear film (plastic wrap) and chill. Allow the salad to come back to room temperature before serving.

Side Dishes

Traditionally, Mexican, Caribbean and Latin American meals consist of a meat, fish or poultry dish accompanied by rice, beans or potatoes and a combination of side dishes, such as rice and peas, or stir-fried kale. Each contributes its own unique flavour and character to a meal.

Plain Rice

Rice is a staple food in many parts of Latin America – it is eaten at most meals with anything and everything, and is often accompanied by black beans.

SERVES FOUR

INGREDIENTS
- 200g/7oz/1 cup long grain rice
- 30ml/2 tbsp vegetable oil
- 2 garlic cloves, crushed
- 450ml/¾ pint/scant 2 cups water
- salt

COOK'S TIP
If the rice is still tough after steaming, add a little water, cover and return to the heat for a few minutes. If, instead, the rice is still sticky, return to the heat and cook over a very low heat with the lid off, until the excess moisture has evaporated.

1 Rinse the rice in a large bowl of cold water, then drain thoroughly in a fine sieve (strainer). Pour the oil into a heavy pan that has a tight-fitting lid. Heat gently, then add the garlic and cook, stirring, for 1 minute. Add the rice and stir for 2 minutes, until the grains are lightly toasted.

2 Pour in the water and season with salt. Bring to the boil, cover and lower the heat again to a very gentle simmer. Cook for 18 minutes, without lifting the lid. Remove from the heat and leave the rice to rest, covered, for 5 minutes. Transfer to a serving bowl and fluff up with a fork before taking to the table.

Black Beans

You'll find beans on most Latin tables, whatever the day of the week or occasion. The recipe will vary slightly, depending on the country, the availability of additional ingredients and personal choice. Chillies and other spices are often included.

SERVES SIX

INGREDIENTS
- 450g/1lb/2½ cups black turtle beans, soaked overnight in water to cover
- 115g/4oz smoked streaky (fatty) bacon, in one piece
- 1 bay leaf
- 30ml/2 tbsp vegetable oil
- 2 garlic cloves, crushed
- salt

COOK'S TIP
Do not season the beans until they are cooked, or they will become tough. As the sauce thickens, the beans have a tendency to stick, so stir frequently after returning the refried beans to the pan.

1 Drain the beans and put them in a large heavy pan. Cover generously with cold water. Add the bacon and bay leaf and bring to the boil. Skim the surface of the liquid, then lower the heat to a simmer. Cook for at least 1 hour or until the beans are tender, topping up the water if necessary.

2 Heat the oil in a pan over a medium heat. Cook the garlic for 2 minutes. Add two ladles of cooked beans and fry for 2–3 minutes, breaking up the beans.

3 Tip the refried beans back into the pan and season. Simmer over a very low heat for 10 minutes, then serve.

Coconut Rice

Deliciously moist and full of flavour, coconut rice is an excellent accompaniment for all sorts of main dishes – this Colombian version is particularly good with fish.

SERVES FOUR

INGREDIENTS
- 3 x 400ml/14fl oz cans coconut milk
- 5ml/1 tsp light brown sugar
- 200g/7oz/1 cup long grain rice
- salt
- 15g/½oz/1 tbsp butter

COOK'S TIP
Canned coconut milk is available sweetened as well as plain – be sure to buy the unsweetened, plain type for savoury cooking.

To make your own coconut milk, heat a coconut in the oven for 20 minutes, then crack it open and remove the flesh. Blend it in a food processor and then press it through a muslin or cloth.

1 Pour the coconut milk into a large pan that has a tight-fitting lid. Stir in the sugar. Bring to the boil and simmer until the liquid is reduced by half.

VARIATION
This tasty side dish is equally good when made with other varieties of rice. Depending on preference, try using short-grain, medium-grain or basmati.

2 Add the rice to the pan, season with salt and bring to the boil. Lower the heat to a simmer and cook, stirring often, for 5 minutes.

3 Stir the butter into the rice and cover the pan tightly. Simmer gently for a further 15 minutes, then remove from the heat. Leave covered for 5 minutes before transferring to a serving bowl.

TOASTED CASSAVA FLOUR WITH EGG AND BACON

Brazilian cooks make great use of FAROFA, *flavoured toasted cassava flour, sprinkling it over meat or fish dishes to mop up the juices. Try this version with rice and beans.*

SERVES SIX

INGREDIENTS
- 15g/½oz/1 tbsp butter
- 90g/3½oz streaky (fatty) bacon, in one piece
- 2 eggs, lightly beaten
- 15ml/1 tbsp water
- 225g/8oz/2 cups toasted cassava flour
- 15ml/1 tbsp chopped fresh parsley
- salt

COOK'S TIP

Cassava flour resembles dried breadcrumbs. Look for it in Latin American or Portuguese stores, where it will be labelled *farinha de mandioca.* It is sometimes called cassava meal.

1 Melt the butter in a pan over a low heat. Dice the bacon and add to the pan. Sauté for 5 minutes, until golden.

2 Mix the eggs with the water in a cup or small bowl. Tip the mixture into the pan and stir until it starts to set. The eggs should have the consistency of soft scrambled eggs – do not overcook them.

3 Add the cassava flour and stir vigorously over the heat for 1 minute, until thoroughly combined. Remove from the heat and stir in the chopped parsley. Season to taste with salt and transfer to a bowl to serve.

Green Rice

This rice seldom features on menus in Mexican restaurants, but it is often made in the home. Extra chillies and green pepper can be diced and added at the end, if you like.

SERVES FOUR

INGREDIENTS
- 2 fresh green chillies, preferably poblanos
- 1 small green (bell) pepper
- 200g/7oz/1 cup long grain white rice
- 1 garlic clove, roughly chopped
- bunch of fresh coriander (cilantro)
- small bunch of fresh flat leaf parsley
- 475ml/16fl oz/2 cups chicken stock
- 30ml/2 tbsp vegetable oil
- 1 small onion, finely chopped
- salt

1 Dry roast the chillies and green pepper in a griddle pan, turning them frequently so that the skins blacken but the flesh does not burn. Place them in a strong plastic bag, tie the top securely and set aside for 20 minutes.

2 Put the rice in a heatproof bowl, pour over boiling water to cover and leave to stand for 20 minutes.

3 Drain the rice, rinse well under cold water and drain again. Remove the chillies and peppers from the bag and peel off the skins. Remove any stalks, then slit the vegetables and scrape out the seeds with a sharp knife.

4 Put the roasted vegetables in a food processor, with the garlic. Strip off the leaves from the coriander and parsley stalks, reserve some for the garnish and add the rest to the processor. Pour in half the chicken stock and process until smooth. Add the rest of the stock and process the purée again.

5 Heat the oil in a pan, add the onion and rice and fry for 5 minutes over a moderate heat until the rice is golden and the onion translucent. Stir in the purée. Lower the heat, cover and cook for 25–30 minutes or until all the liquid is absorbed and the rice is just tender. Add salt and garnish with the reserved herbs. Served with lime wedges, this rice goes extremely well with fish.

Yellow Rice

This rice dish owes its striking colour and distinctive flavour to ground achiote seed, which is derived from annatto.

SERVES SIX

INGREDIENTS
- 200g/7oz/1 cup long grain white rice
- 30ml/2 tbsp vegetable oil
- 5ml/1 tsp ground achiote seed (annatto powder)
- 1 small onion, finely chopped
- 2 garlic cloves, crushed
- 475ml/16fl oz/2 cups chicken stock
- 50g/2oz/⅓ cup drained pickled jalapeño chilli slices, chopped
- salt
- fresh coriander (cilantro), to garnish

COOK'S TIP
Achiote, the seed of the annatto tree, is used as a food colouring and flavouring throughout Latin America. You can buy it in specialist spice shops and ethnic food stores.

1 Put the rice in a heatproof bowl, pour over boiling water to cover and leave to stand for 20 minutes. Drain, rinse under cold water and drain again.

2 Heat the oil in a pan, add the ground achiote seed (annatto powder) and cook for 2–3 minutes. Add the onion and garlic and cook for 3–4 minutes or until the onion is translucent. Stir in the rice and cook for 5 minutes.

3 Pour in the stock, mix well and bring to the boil. Lower the heat, cover the pan with a tight-fitting lid and simmer for 25–30 minutes, until all the liquid has been absorbed.

4 Add the chopped jalapeños to the pan and stir to distribute them evenly. Add salt to taste, then spoon into a heated serving dish and garnish with the fresh coriander (cilantro). Serve immediately.

Rice and Peas

It may seem odd that a dish with kidney beans as a primary ingredient is called rice and peas, but in Jamaica, where it originated, fresh pigeon peas were originally used. Since the peas are seasonal, the dish is more often made with dried kidney beans.

SERVES SIX

INGREDIENTS
- 200g/7oz/1 cup red kidney beans
- 2 fresh thyme sprigs
- 50g/2oz piece of creamed coconut or 120ml/4fl oz/½ cup coconut cream
- 2 bay leaves
- 1 onion, finely chopped
- 2 garlic cloves, crushed
- 2.5ml/½ tsp ground allspice
- 1 red or green (bell) pepper, seeded and chopped
- 600ml/1 pint/2½ cups water
- 450g/1lb/2½ cups long grain rice
- salt and ground black pepper

1 Put the red kidney beans in a large bowl. Pour in enough cold water to cover the beans generously. Cover the bowl and leave the beans to soak overnight.

2 Drain the beans and tip them into a large pan with a tight-fitting lid. Pour in enough water to cover the beans. Bring to the boil and boil for 10 minutes, then lower the heat and simmer for 1½ hours or until the beans are tender.

3 Add the thyme, creamed coconut or coconut cream, bay leaves, onion, garlic, allspice and pepper. Season and stir in the measured water.

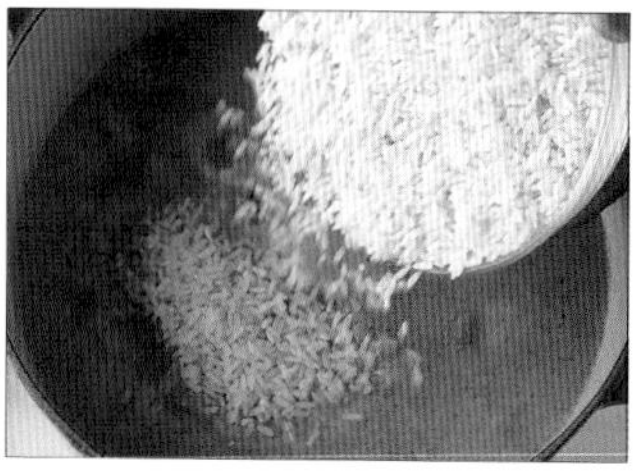

4 Bring to the boil and add the rice. Stir well, reduce the heat and cover the pan. Simmer for 25–30 minutes, until all the liquid has been absorbed. Serve as an accompaniment to fish, meat or vegetarian dishes.

Cou-Cou

This tasty okra and mashed cornmeal pudding is a Bajan national dish. Traditionally, it is served with fresh flying fish cooked in a Caribbean gravy, but it can also be served with any other fish, meat or vegetable stew.

SERVES FOUR

INGREDIENTS
- 115g/4oz okra, trimmed and roughly chopped
- 225g/8oz/1½ cups coarse cornmeal
- 600ml/1 pint/2½ cups water or coconut milk
- 25g/1oz/2 tbsp butter
- salt and ground black pepper

COOK'S TIP
Adding unsweetened coconut milk instead of water will give your cou-cou a special, rich flavour.

1 Bring a pan of water seasoned with a little salt and pepper to the boil. Add the chopped okra and cook for about 10 minutes. Remove the okra with a slotted spoon and set it aside.

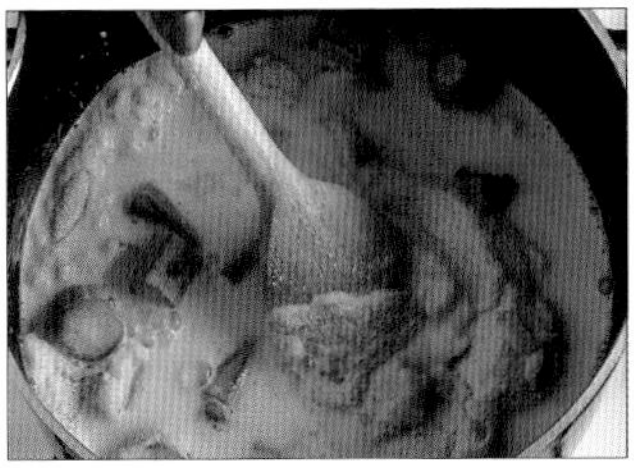

2 Pour away half the liquid from the pan, then return the pan to the heat. Return the okra to the pan, then gradually beat in the cornmeal.

3 Cook on a very low heat, beating the mixture vigorously. Gradually add the measured water or coconut milk, beating after each addition to prevent the mixture from sticking to the pan and burning.

4 Cover and cook for about 20 minutes, beating occasionally. The cou-cou is cooked when the cornmeal granules are soft. Cover with foil and then a lid to keep the mixture moist and hot until required. Spread with butter before serving.

Buttered Spinach and Rice

The layer of fresh cooked spinach in this popular Caribbean dish is said to have been the result of a happy accident. It was intended for a separate dish, but the cook forgot to add it so simply used it to top the rice instead.

SERVES FOUR

INGREDIENTS
- 40g/1½oz/3 tbsp butter or margarine
- 1 onion, finely chopped
- 2 fresh tomatoes, chopped
- 450g/1lb/2½ cups basmati rice, rinsed
- 2 garlic cloves, crushed
- 600ml/1 pint/2½ cups stock or water
- 350g/12oz fresh spinach, shredded
- salt and ground black pepper
- 2 tomatoes, sliced, to garnish

COOK'S TIP
If you are unable to get fresh spinach, use frozen leaf spinach instead. Thaw and drain approximately 225g/8oz frozen spinach and cook on top of the rice for about 5 minutes. If you prefer, finely shredded spring greens (collards) make a delicious alternative to spinach.

1 Melt 25g/1oz/2 tbsp of butter or margarine in a large pan with a tight-fitting lid. Gently fry the onion for 3–4 minutes, until soft and translucent. Stir in the fresh chopped tomatoes.

2 Add the basmati rice and crushed garlic, gently cook for 5 minutes, then gradually add the stock or water, stirring constantly. Season to taste with plenty of salt and ground black pepper.

3 Cover and simmer gently for 10–15 minutes, until the rice is almost cooked, then reduce the heat to low.

4 Spread the spinach in a thick layer over the rice. Cover the pan and cook over a low heat for 5–8 minutes, until the spinach has wilted. Spoon into a serving dish, dot the remaining butter over the top and garnish with the sliced tomatoes. Serve immediately.

Creamed Sweet Potatoes

Similar to traditional mashed potatoes, this Caribbean speciality uses white sweet potatoes instead of the orange variety. The grated nutmeg adds an extra, irresistible sweetness.

SERVES FOUR

INGREDIENTS
- 900g/2lb sweet potatoes
- 50g/2oz/¼ cup butter
- 45ml/3 tbsp single (light) cream
- freshly grated nutmeg
- 15ml/1 tbsp chopped fresh chives
- salt and ground black pepper

COOK'S TIP
If you cannot get white sweet potatoes, white yams make a good substitute, especially poona (Ghanaian) yam.

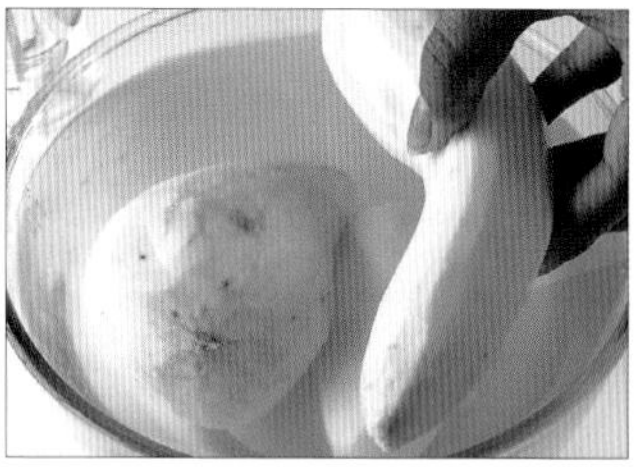

1 Peel the sweet potatoes under cold running water and place in a bowl of salted water to prevent them from discolouring. Cut them into large chunks and place in a pan of cold water. Cook, covered, for 20–30 minutes until tender.

2 Drain the potatoes and return them to the dry pan. Add the butter, cream, nutmeg, chives and seasoning. Mash with a potato masher and then fluff up with a fork. Serve warm as an accompaniment to a curry or stew.

Colombian Cheesy Potatoes

Tender new potatoes topped with a creamy cheese and tomato sauce make a delicious side dish, which is great served with meat, poultry or fish dishes.

SERVES SIX

INGREDIENTS

- 1kg/2¼lb new or salad potatoes
- 25g/1oz/2 tbsp butter
- 4 spring onions (scallions), thinly sliced
- 2 large tomatoes, peeled, seeded and chopped
- 200ml/7fl oz/scant 1 cup double (heavy) cream
- 90g/3½oz/1 cup grated mozzarella
- salt and ground black pepper

1 Place the potatoes in a large pan of salted cold water. Cover and bring to the boil. Lower the heat and simmer for 18–20 minutes, until tender.

2 Meanwhile, melt the butter in a frying pan over a low heat, add the spring onions and cook gently, stirring occasionally, for 5 minutes, until softened. Stir in the tomatoes and cook for a further 2–3 minutes, stirring occasionally, until the tomatoes break up.

3 Drain the potatoes and put them in a warmed serving bowl. Add the cream to the onion and tomato mixture, bring to the boil, then add the cheese, stirring until it melts. Season with salt and pepper to taste. Pour the hot sauce over the potatoes and serve immediately.

CARIBBEAN POTATO SALAD

Colourful vegetables in a creamy smooth dressing make this piquant Caribbean salad ideal to serve on its own or with grilled or cold meats.

SERVES SIX

INGREDIENTS
- 900g/2lb small waxy or salad potatoes, with the skins rubbed off
- 2 red (bell) peppers, seeded and diced
- 2 celery sticks, finely chopped
- 1 shallot, finely chopped
- 2 or 3 spring onions (scallions), finely chopped
- 1 mild fresh green chilli, seeded and finely chopped
- 1 garlic clove, crushed
- 10ml/2 tsp finely chopped chives
- 10ml/2 tsp finely chopped basil
- 15ml/1 tbsp finely chopped parsley
- 15ml/1 tbsp single (light) cream
- 30ml/2 tbsp salad cream
- 15ml/1 tbsp mayonnaise
- 5ml/1 tsp Dijon mustard
- 7.5ml/1½ tsp sugar
- chopped chives, to garnish
- chopped red chilli, to garnish

1 Cook the potatoes in a large pan of boiling water until tender but still firm. Drain and leave to one side. When cool enough to handle, cut the cooked potatoes into 2.5cm/1in cubes and place in a large salad bowl.

2 Add all the vegetables to the potatoes in the salad bowl, together with the chopped chilli, crushed garlic and all the chopped herbs.

3 Mix together the cream, salad cream, mayonnaise, mustard and sugar in a small bowl. Stir well until the mixture is thoroughly combined and forms a smooth dressing.

4 Pour the dressing over the potato mixture and stir gently to coat evenly. Serve immediately, garnished with the chopped chives and chopped red chilli.

VARIATIONS

Try adding other vegetables to this potato salad, such as tomatoes for flavour or lightly cooked green beans for a tasty crunch. Many traditional potato salads also include a coarsely chopped hard-boiled egg. This would work just as well in this Caribbean version, if you like.

POTATOES WITH CHORIZO AND GREEN CHILLIES

MEXICANS MAKE THEIR OWN CHORIZO SAUSAGE, SOMETIMES USING IT FRESH, BUT ALSO PUTTING IT INTO CASINGS TO DRY, WHEN IT RESEMBLES THE SPANISH VERSION WHICH IS NOW POPULAR THE WORLD OVER. TYPICAL OF PEASANT FOOD, IT IS BASED ON THE COMBINATION OF STRONGLY FLAVOURED MEAT MIXED WITH PLENTY OF POTATO TO HELP IT GO FURTHER.

SERVES FOUR TO SIX

INGREDIENTS

- 900g/2lb potatoes, peeled and diced
- 30ml/2 tbsp vegetable oil
- 2 garlic cloves, crushed
- 4 spring onions (scallions), trimmed and chopped
- 2 fresh jalapeño chillies, seeded and diced
- 300g/11oz chorizo sausage, skinned
- 150g/5oz/1¼ cups grated Monterey Jack or Cheddar cheese
- salt (optional)

1 Bring a large pan of water to the boil and add the potatoes. When the water returns to the boil, lower the heat and simmer the potatoes for 5 minutes. Tip the potatoes into a colander and drain thoroughly. Without breaking the potatoes, dice them into cubes.

COOK'S TIP

Use firm-textured potatoes such as Desiree, Pentland Dell and Estima for this dish. If you can't find Monterey Jack, look for a mature (sharp) Gouda, or use a medium mature Cheddar.

2 Heat the oil in a large frying pan, add the crushed cloves of garlic, chopped spring onions and diced chillies and cook for 3–4 minutes. Add the diced potato and cook until the cubes begin to brown a little.

3 Cut the chorizo into small cubes and add these to the pan. Cook the mixture for 5 minutes more, until the sausage has heated through.

4 Season with salt if necessary, then add the cheese. Mix quickly but carefully, trying not to break up the cubes of potato. Serve immediately, while the cheese is still melting.

Red Cauliflower

Vegetables are seldom served plain in Mexico. The cauliflower here is flavoured with a simple tomato salsa and fresh cheese. The salsa could be any table salsa; tomatillo is particularly good. The contrast with the texture and mild flavour of the cauliflower makes for a tasty dish.

SERVES SIX

INGREDIENTS

- 1 small onion
- 1 lime
- 1 medium cauliflower
- 400g/14oz can chopped tomatoes
- 4 fresh serrano chillies, seeded and finely chopped
- 1.5ml/¼ tsp caster (superfine) sugar
- 75g/3oz feta cheese, crumbled
- salt
- chopped fresh flat leaf parsley, to garnish

COOK'S TIP

Use a zester for the lime, if have you have one. This handy little tool enables you to pare off tiny strips of the rind, leaving the pith behind.

1 Chop the onion very finely and place in a bowl. With a zester peel away the zest of the lime in thin strips. Add to the chopped onion.

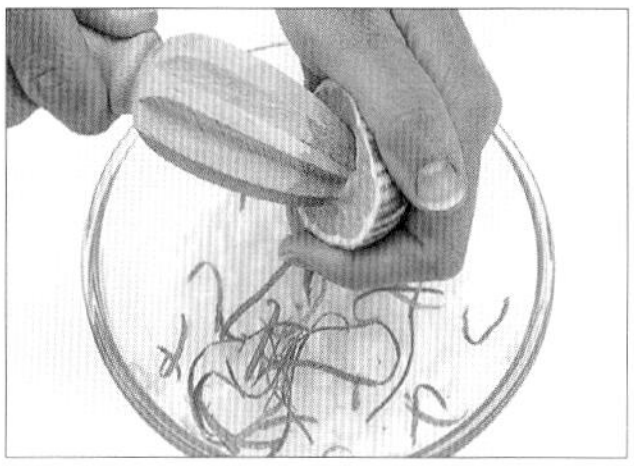

2 Cut the lime in half and add the juice from both halves to the onions and lime zest mixture. Set aside so that the lime juice can soften the onion. Cut the cauliflower into florets.

3 Tip the tomatoes into a pan and add the chillies and sugar. Heat gently. Meanwhile, place the cauliflower in a pan of boiling water and cook gently for 5–8 minutes until tender.

4 Add the onions to the tomato salsa, with salt to taste, stir in and heat through, then spoon about a third of the salsa into a serving dish.

5 Arrange the drained cauliflower florets on top of the salsa and spoon the remaining salsa on top.

6 Sprinkle with the feta, which should soften a little on contact. Serve immediately, sprinkled with chopped fresh flat leaf parsley.

Green Lima Beans in Tomato Sauce

Make the most of fresh lima beans or broad beans by teaming them with tomatoes and fresh chillies in this simple accompaniment.

SERVES FOUR

INGREDIENTS

- 450g/1lb fresh lima beans or broad (fava) beans
- 30ml/2 tbsp olive oil
- 1 onion, finely chopped
- 2 garlic cloves, crushed
- 400g/14oz can plum tomatoes, drained and chopped
- 25g/1oz/about 3 tbsp drained pickled jalapeño chilli slices, chopped
- salt
- fresh coriander (cilantro) and lemon slices, to garnish

COOK'S TIP

Pickled chillies are often hotter than roasted chillies – taste one before adding to the recipe and adjust the quantity to suit your taste.

1 Bring a pan of lightly salted water to the boil. Add the lima beans or broad beans and cook for 15 minutes, or until just tender.

2 Meanwhile, heat the olive oil in a frying pan, add the onion and garlic and sauté until the onion is translucent. Add the tomatoes and continue to cook, stirring, until the mixture thickens.

3 Add the chilli slices and cook for 1–2 minutes. Season with salt to taste.

4 Drain the beans and return them to the pan. Pour over the tomato mixture and stir over the heat for a few minutes. If the sauce thickens too quickly add a little water. Spoon into a serving dish, garnish with the coriander and lemon slices and serve.

Green Beans with Eggs

This is an unusual way of cooking green beans, but it tastes delicious. Try this dish for a light supper or as an accompaniment to a simple roast.

SERVES SIX

INGREDIENTS

- 300g/11oz string beans, topped, tailed and halved
- 30ml/2 tbsp vegetable oil
- 1 onion, halved and thinly sliced
- 3 eggs
- salt and ground black pepper
- 50g/2oz/½ cup grated Monterey Jack or mild Cheddar cheese
- strips of lemon rind, to garnish

VARIATION

Freshly grated Parmesan can be used instead of the Monterey Jack or Cheddar cheese for a sharper flavour.

1 Bring a pan of water to the boil, add the beans and cook for 5–6 minutes or until tender. Drain the beans in a colander, rinse under cold water to preserve the bright colour, then drain the beans once more.

2 Heat the oil in a frying pan and fry the onion slices for 3–4 minutes until soft and translucent. Break the eggs into a bowl and beat them with seasoning.

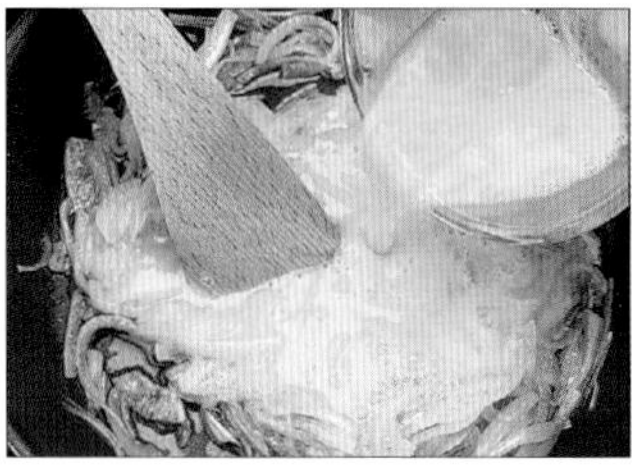

3 Add the egg mixture to the onion. Cook slowly over a moderate heat, stirring constantly so that the egg is lightly scrambled. The egg should be moist throughout. Do not overcook.

4 Add the beans to the pan and cook for a few minutes until warmed through. Tip the mixture into a heated serving dish, sprinkle with the grated cheese and lemon rind and serve.

COURGETTES WITH CHEESE AND GREEN CHILLIES

This is a very tasty way to serve courgettes, often a rather bland vegetable, and the dish looks good too. Serve it as a vegetarian main dish or an unusual side dish.

SERVES SIX AS AN ACCOMPANIMENT

INGREDIENTS

- 30ml/2 tbsp vegetable oil
- ½ onion, thinly sliced
- 2 garlic cloves, crushed
- 5ml/1 tsp dried oregano
- 2 tomatoes
- 50g/2oz/⅓ cup drained pickled jalapeño chilli slices, chopped
- 500g/1¼lb courgettes (zucchini)
- 115g/4oz/½ cup cream cheese, cubed
- salt and ground black pepper
- fresh oregano sprigs, to garnish

1 Heat the oil in a frying pan. Add the onion, garlic and dried oregano. Fry for 3–4 minutes, until the onion is soft and translucent.

2 Cut a cross in the base of each tomato. Place in a heatproof bowl and cover with boiling water. Leave in the water for 3 minutes, then lift out on a slotted spoon and plunge into a bowl of cold water. Drain. The skins will have begun to peel back from the crosses. Remove the skins, cut the tomatoes in half and squeeze out the seeds. Chop the flesh into strips.

3 Top and tail the courgettes, then cut them lengthways into 1cm/½in wide strips. Slice the strips into matchsticks.

4 Stir the courgettes into the onion mixture and fry for 10 minutes, stirring occasionally, until just tender. Add the tomatoes and chopped jalapeños and cook for 2–3 minutes more.

5 Add the cream cheese. Reduce the heat to the lowest setting. As the cheese melts, stir gently to coat the courgettes. Season with salt, pile into a heated dish and serve, garnished with fresh oregano. If serving as a main dish, rustic bread makes a good accompaniment.

COURGETTE TORTE

THIS DISH LOOKS RATHER LIKE A SPANISH OMELETTE, WHICH IS TRADITIONALLY SERVED AT ROOM TEMPERATURE. SERVE WARM OR PREPARE IT IN ADVANCE AND LEAVE TO COOL, BUT DO NOT REFRIGERATE.

SERVES FOUR TO SIX

INGREDIENTS
- 500g/1¼lb courgettes (zucchini)
- 60ml/4 tbsp vegetable oil
- 1 small onion
- 3 fresh jalapeño chillies, seeded and cut in strips
- 3 large eggs
- 50g/2oz/½ cup self-raising (self-rising) flour
- 115g/4oz/1 cup grated Monterey Jack or mild Cheddar cheese
- 2.5ml/½ tsp cayenne pepper
- 15g/½oz/1 tbsp butter
- salt

1 Preheat the oven to 180°C/350°F/ Gas 4. Top and tail the courgettes, then slice them thinly.

2 Heat the oil in a large frying pan. Add the courgettes and cook for a few minutes, turning them over at least once, until they are soft and beginning to brown. Using a slotted spoon, transfer them to a bowl. Slice the onion and add it to the oil remaining in the pan, with most of the jalapeño strips, reserving some for the garnish.

3 Fry until the onions have softened and are golden. Using a slotted spoon, add the onions and jalapeños to the courgettes. Place them to one side and cover.

4 Beat the eggs in a large bowl under blended and slightly frothy. Add the self-raising flour, cheese and cayenne. Mix well with a fork, then gently pour in the courgette mixture and stir, adding salt to taste.

5 Grease a 23cm/9in round shallow ovenproof dish with the butter. Pour in the courgette mixture and bake for 30 minutes until risen, firm to the touch and golden. Allow to cool.

PUMPKIN WITH SPICES

ROASTED PUMPKIN HAS A WONDERFUL, RICH FLAVOUR. EAT IT STRAIGHT FROM THE SKIN, EAT THE SKIN TOO, OR SCOOP OUT THE COOKED FLESH, ADD A SPOONFUL OF SALSA AND WRAP IT IN A WARM TORTILLA. IT ALSO MAKES FLAVOURSOME SOUPS AND SAUCES.

SERVES SIX

INGREDIENTS
- 1kg/2¼lb pumpkin
- 50g/2oz/¼ cup butter, melted
- 10ml/2 tsp hot chilli sauce
- 2.5ml/½ tsp salt
- 2.5ml/½ tsp ground allspice
- 5ml/1 tsp ground cinnamon
- chopped fresh herbs, to garnish
- salsa and crème fraîche, to serve

COOK'S TIP
Green, grey or orange-skinned pumpkins all roast well. The orange-fleshed varieties are the most colourful when it comes to cooking.

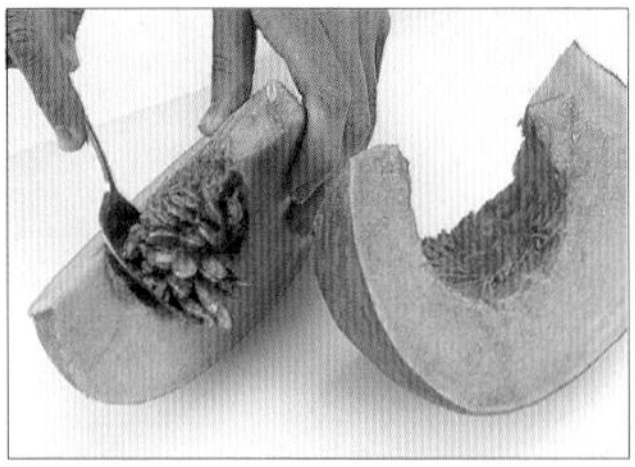

1 Preheat the oven to 220°C/425°F/ Gas 7. Cut the pumpkin into large pieces. Scoop out and discard the fibre and seeds, then put the pumpkin pieces in a roasting tin.

2 Mix the melted butter and chilli sauce and drizzle the mixture evenly over the pumpkin pieces.

3 Put the salt in a small bowl and add the ground allspice and cinnamon. Sprinkle the mixture over the pumpkin.

4 Roast for 25 minutes or until the pumpkin flesh yields when pressed gently. Serve on a heated platter and offer the tomato salsa and crème fraîche separately.

POTATO CAKES

QUICK AND EASY TO MAKE, THESE MEXICAN POTATO CAKES ARE VERY MOREISH. SERVE THEM WITH SALSA AS A LIGHT MEAL, OR AS AN ACCOMPANIMENT TO ROAST OR PAN-FRIED MEATS. IF YOU WANT TO SPICE THEM UP A LITTLE, ADD A FEW EXTRA CHILLI PEPPERS.

MAKES TEN

INGREDIENTS

- 600g/1lb 6oz potatoes
- 115g/4oz/1 cup grated Cheddar cheese
- 2.5ml/½ tsp salt
- 50g/2oz/⅓ cup drained pickled jalapeño chilli slices, finely chopped (optional)
- 1 egg, beaten
- small bunch of fresh coriander (cilantro), finely chopped
- plain (all-purpose) flour, for shaping
- oil, for shallow frying
- salsa, to serve

1 Peel the potatoes and halve them if large. Add them to a large pan of cold water. Bring to the boil and cook for about 30 minutes, until tender. Drain, return to the pan and mash. The mash should not be smooth.

2 Scrape the potato into a bowl and stir in the grated cheese, with the salt and the chopped jalapeños, if using. Stir in the beaten egg and most of the chopped coriander and mix to a dough.

3 When the dough is cool enough to handle, put it on a board. With floured hands, divide it into ten pieces of equal size. Shape each piece into a ball, then flatten to a cake.

4 Heat the oil in a large frying pan. Fry the potato cakes for 2–3 minutes over a moderate heat. Turn them over and cook until both sides are golden. Pile on a platter and sprinkle with salt.

FRIED PLANTAINS

THESE ARE THE PERFECT ACCOMPANIMENT TO HIGHLY SPICED AND SEASONED FOODS. THEIR SWEET FLAVOUR PROVIDES AN INTERESTING CONTRAST.

SERVES FOUR

INGREDIENTS
- 4 ripe plantains
- 75g/3oz/6 tbsp butter
- 10ml/2 tsp vegetable oil
- strips of spring onion (scallion) and red (bell) pepper, to garnish

COOK'S TIP
Ripe plantains have dark, almost black skins. Do not use under-ripe plantains, which are very hard and do not soften on cooking.

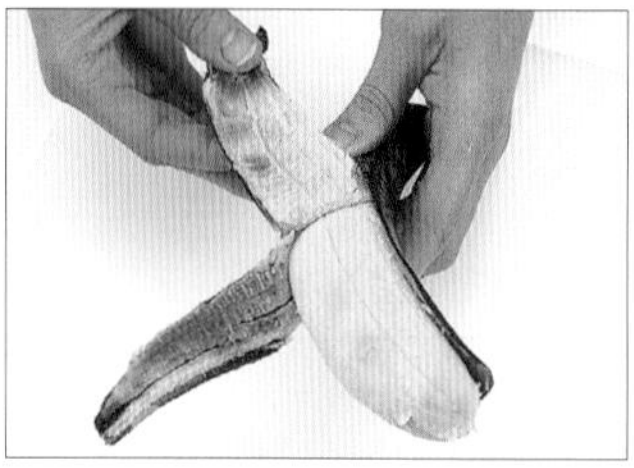

1 Peel the plantains, cut them in half lengthways, then cut them in half again. Melt the butter with the oil in a large frying pan.

2 Add the plantains to the pan in a single layer and fry for 8–10 minutes, turning halfway through. Spoon into a heated dish and serve, garnished with strips of spring onion and red pepper.

FRIED POTATOES

THESE MAKE THE PERFECT ACCOMPANIMENT FOR CHORIZO, BEANS AND MEATY DISHES SUCH AS CARNITAS AND ROAST PORK. THEY ALSO MAKE EXCELLENT BREAKFAST OR BRUNCH SIDE DISHES, AND GO VERY WELL WITH EGGS AND BACON, ESPECIALLY THOSE DONE THE MEXICAN WAY.

SERVES FOUR

INGREDIENTS
- 6 fresh jalapeño chillies
- 60ml/4 tbsp vegetable oil
- 1 onion, finely chopped
- 450g/1lb waxy potatoes, scrubbed and cut in 1cm/½in cubes
- few sprigs of fresh oregano, chopped plus extra sprigs, to garnish
- 75g/3oz/1 cup freshly grated Parmesan cheese (optional)

1 Dry roast the jalapeños in a griddle pan, turning them frequently so that the skins blacken but do not burn. Place them in a strong plastic bag and tie the top to keep the steam in. Set aside for 20 minutes.

2 Remove the jalapeños from the bag, peel off the skins and remove any stems. Cut them in half, scrape out the seeds, then chop the flesh finely.

3 Meanwhile, heat half the oil in a large heavy-based frying pan which has a lid. Add the onion and fry, stirring occasionally, for 3–4 minutes, until translucent, then add the potato cubes.

4 Stir to coat the potato cubes in oil, then cover the pan and cook over a moderate heat for 20–25 minutes, until the potatoes are tender. Shake the pan occasionally to prevent sticking.

5 When the potatoes are tender, push them to the side of the frying pan, then add the remaining oil.

6 When the oil is hot, spread out the potatoes again and add the chopped jalapeños. Cook over a high heat for 5–10 minutes, stirring carefully so that the potatoes turn golden brown all over but do not break up.

7 Add the chopped oregano, with the grated Parmesan, if using. Mix gently, spoon on to a heated serving dish and garnish with extra oregano sprigs. Serve as part of a cooked breakfast or brunch.

Potato and Onion Tortilla with Broad Beans

The classic tortilla or Spanish omelette includes nothing more than onions, potato, eggs and olive oil. Adding chopped herbs and a few skinned broad beans makes this a very summery dish to enjoy at lunch, or cut it into small pieces and serve as a Spanish tapas.

SERVES TWO

INGREDIENTS

- 45ml/3 tbsp olive oil
- 2 Spanish onions, thinly sliced
- 300g/11oz waxy potatoes, cut into 1cm/½in dice
- 250g/9oz/1¾ cups shelled broad (fava) beans
- 5ml/1 tsp chopped fresh thyme or summer savory
- 6 large eggs
- 45ml/3 tbsp mixed chopped chives and chopped flat leaf parsley
- salt and ground black pepper

1 Heat 30ml/2 tbsp of the oil in a 23cm/9in deep non-stick frying pan. Add the onions and potatoes and stir to coat. Cover and cook gently, stirring frequently, for 20–25 minutes until the potatoes are cooked and the onions collapsed. Do not let the mixture brown.

2 Meanwhile, cook the beans in boiling salted water for 5 minutes. Drain well and set aside to cool.

3 When the beans are cool enough to handle, peel off the grey outer skins. Add the beans to the frying pan, together with the thyme or summer savory, and season with salt and pepper to taste. Stir well to mix and cook for a further 2–3 minutes.

4 Beat the eggs with salt and pepper to taste and the mixed herbs, then pour over the potatoes and onions and increase the heat slightly. Cook gently until the egg on the bottom sets and browns, gently pulling the omelette away from the sides of the pan and tilting it to allow the uncooked egg to run underneath.

5 Invert the tortilla on to a plate. Add the remaining oil to the pan and heat until hot. Slip the tortilla back into the pan, uncooked side down, and cook for another 3–5 minutes to allow the underneath to brown. Slide the tortilla out on to a plate. Divide as wished, and serve warm rather than piping hot.

Bean Feast with Tomato and Avocado Salsa

This is a very quick and easy recipe using canned beans, although it could be made with dried beans. They would need to be soaked overnight, boiled hard for 10 minutes, then simmered for 1–1½ hours until tender.

SERVES FOUR

INGREDIENTS

- 15ml/1 tbsp olive oil
- 1 small onion, finely chopped
- 3 garlic cloves, finely chopped
- 1 fresh red Ancho chilli, seeded and finely chopped
- 1 red (bell) pepper, seeded and coarsely chopped
- 2 plum tomatoes, chopped
- 2 bay leaves
- 10ml/2 tsp chopped fresh oregano
- 10ml/2 tsp ground cumin
- 5ml/1 tsp ground coriander
- 2.5ml/½ tsp ground cloves
- 15ml/1 tbsp soft dark brown sugar
- 400g/14oz can red kidney beans, rinsed and drained
- 400g/14oz can flageolet (small cannellini) beans, rinsed and drained
- 400g/14oz can borlotti beans, rinsed and drained
- 300ml/½ pint/1¼ cups vegetable stock
- salt and ground black pepper
- fresh coriander (cilantro), to garnish

For the salsa

- 1 ripe, but firm, avocado
- 45ml/3 tbsp fresh lime juice
- 1 small red onion
- 1 small fresh hot green chilli
- 5 ripe plum tomatoes
- 45ml/3 tbsp chopped fresh coriander (cilantro)

1 Heat the oil and fry the onion for 3 minutes, until transparent. Add the garlic, chilli, pepper, herbs and spices.

2 Stir well and cook for a further 3 minutes, then add the sugar, beans and stock, and cook for 8 minutes. Season with salt and plenty of ground black pepper.

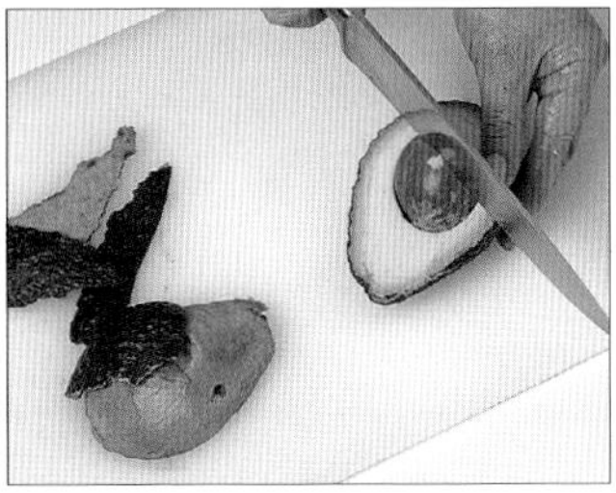

3 To make the salsa, peel the avocado, cut it in half around the stone (pit), then remove the stone by striking it with the blade of a large, sharp knife and lifting it out cleanly. Cut the flesh into 1cm/½in dice. Place in a mixing bowl with the lime juice and stir to mix.

4 Chop the red onion and slice the chilli, discarding the seeds. Plunge the tomatoes into boiling water, leave for 30 seconds and then peel away the skin. Chop the tomatoes.

5 Add the onion, chilli, tomatoes and coriander to the avocado. Season with black pepper and stir to mix. Spoon the beans into a warmed serving dish or into 4 serving bowls. Serve with the tomato and avocado salsa and garnish with sprigs of fresh coriander.

CORN WITH CREAM

IN MEXICO, THIS WOULD BE MADE WITH "HEAVY CREAM", THE AMERICAN EQUIVALENT OF DOUBLE CREAM, BUT THE SAUCE HAS A BETTER CONSISTENCY WHEN MADE WITH FULL-FAT SOFT CHEESE, ADDING A LOVELY, HEARTY FLAVOUR TO THE DISH.

SERVES SIX

INGREDIENTS

- 4 corn cobs
- 50g/2oz/¼ cup butter
- 1 small onion, finely chopped
- 115g/4oz/⅔ cup drained pickled jalapeño chilli slices
- 130g/4½oz/⅔ cup full-fat soft cheese
- 25g/1oz/⅓ cup freshly grated Parmesan cheese, plus shavings, to garnish
- salt and ground black pepper

1 Strip off the husks from the corn and pull off the silks. Place the cobs in a bowl of water and use a vegetable brush to remove any remaining silks. Stand each cob in turn on a board and slice off the kernels, cutting as close to the cob as possible.

2 Melt the butter in a pan, add the chopped onion and fry for 4–5 minutes, stirring occasionally, until the onion has softened and is translucent.

3 Add the corn kernels and cook for 4–5 minutes, until they are just tender. Chop the jalapeños finely and stir them into the corn mixture.

4 Stir in the soft cheese and the grated Parmesan. Cook over a low heat until both cheeses have melted and the corn kernels are coated in the mixture. Season to taste, tip into a heated dish and serve, topped with shredded Parmesan.

VARIATION

A simplified version of this dish is sold on street stalls in Mexico. Whole cooked corn cobs are dipped in cream, then sprinkled with crumbled fresh cheese. Next time you barbecue, try this as an appetizer. Alternatively, put whole corn cobs in a shallow baking dish and bake them in an oven preheated to 200°C/400°F/Gas 6 for 30 minutes, until tender and golden. Pour over 120ml/4fl oz/½ cup soured cream or crème fraîche, then sprinkle with 30ml/2 tbsp freshly grated Parmesan cheese. The corn can also be brushed with butter and grilled (broiled), but it must not be too close to the heat, or it will burn.

FRIJOLES DE OLLA

TRAVELLERS OFTEN SAY THAT "BEANS IN A POT", AS IT IS TRANSLATED, TASTE DIFFERENT IN MEXICO FROM THOSE COOKED ANYWHERE ELSE. THE SECRET IS, QUITE LITERALLY, IN THE POT. TRADITIONALLY, CLAY POTS ARE USED, WHICH GIVE THE BEANS A WONDERFUL, SLIGHTLY EARTHY FLAVOUR.

SERVES FOUR

INGREDIENTS
- 250g/9oz/1¼ cups dried pinto beans, soaked overnight in water to cover
- 1.75 litres/3 pints/7½ cups water
- 2 onions
- 10 garlic cloves, peeled and left whole
- bunch of fresh coriander (cilantro)
- salt

For the toppings
- 2 fresh red fresno chillies
- 1 tomato, peeled and chopped
- 2 spring onions (scallions), finely chopped
- 60ml/4 tbsp soured cream
- 50g/2oz feta cheese

1 Drain the beans, rinse them under cold water and drain again. Put the water in a large pan, bring to the boil and add the beans.

2 Cut the onions in half and add them to the pan, with the whole garlic cloves. Bring to the boil again, then lower the heat and simmer for 1½ hours, until the beans are tender and there is only a little liquid remaining.

3 While the beans are cooking, prepare the toppings. Spear the chillies on a long-handled metal skewer and roast them over the flame of a gas burner until the skins blister and darken. Do not let the flesh burn.

4 Put the roasted chillies in a strong plastic bag and tie the top immediately to keep the steam in. Set aside for 20 minutes.

5 Remove the chillies from the bag and peel off the skins. If they do not easily come loose, they may not have been cooked enough and you should roast them further. Cut off the stalks, then slit the chillies and scrape out the seeds. Cut the flesh into thin strips and put it in a bowl. Spoon all the other toppings into separate bowls.

6 Ladle about 250ml/8fl oz/1 cup of the beans and liquid into a food processor or blender. Process to a smooth purée. If you prefer, simply mash the beans with a potato masher; try to achieve a smooth paste.

7 Return the purée to the pan, and stir in. Chop and add the coriander, reserving some leaves to garnish, season with salt and mix well. Ladle into warmed individual bowls and take them to the table with the toppings.

8 Serve the beans with the toppings and add coriander to garnish. Crumble a little feta cheese over each portion.

POTATOES WITH RED CHILLIES

IF YOU LIKE CHILLIES, YOU'LL LOVE THESE POTATOES! IF YOU'RE NOT A FAN OF FIERY FLAVOURS, THEN SIMPLY LEAVE OUT ALL THE CHILLI SEEDS AND USE THE FLESH BY ITSELF.

SERVES FOUR

INGREDIENTS

- 12–14 small new or salad potatoes, halved
- 30ml/2 tbsp vegetable oil
- 2.5ml/½ tsp crushed dried red chillies
- 2.5ml/½ tsp white cumin seeds
- 2.5ml/½ tsp fennel seeds
- 2.5ml/½ tsp crushed coriander seeds
- 5ml/1 tsp salt
- 1 onion, sliced
- 1–4 fresh red chillies, chopped
- 15ml/1 tbsp chopped fresh coriander (cilantro), plus extra, to garnish

COOK'S TIP

To prepare fresh chillies, slit down one side and scrape out the seeds. Finely slice or chop the flesh. Wear rubber gloves if you have very sensitive skin.

1 Cook the potatoes in boiling salted water until tender but still firm. Remove from the heat and drain off the water. Set aside until needed.

2 In a deep frying pan, heat the oil over a medium-high heat, then reduce the heat to medium. Add the crushed chillies, cumin, fennel and coriander seeds and salt and fry, stirring, for 30–40 seconds.

3 Add the sliced onion and fry until golden brown. Then add the potatoes, red chillies and coriander and stir well.

4 Reduce the heat to very low, then cover and cook for 5–7 minutes. Serve the potatoes hot, garnished with more fresh coriander.

CORN WITH A GARLIC BUTTER CRUST

WHETHER YOU ARE CATERING FOR VEGETARIANS OR SERVING THIS WITH MEAT DISHES, IT WILL DISAPPEAR IN A FLASH. THE CHARRED GARLIC BUTTER CRUST ADDS A NEW DIMENSION TO THE COBS.

SERVES SIX

INGREDIENTS

- 6 ripe corn cobs
- 225g/8oz/1 cup butter
- 30ml/2 tbsp olive oil
- 2 garlic cloves, crushed
- 115g/4oz/1 cup wholemeal (whole-wheat) breadcrumbs
- 15ml/1 tbsp chopped fresh parsley
- salt and freshly ground black pepper

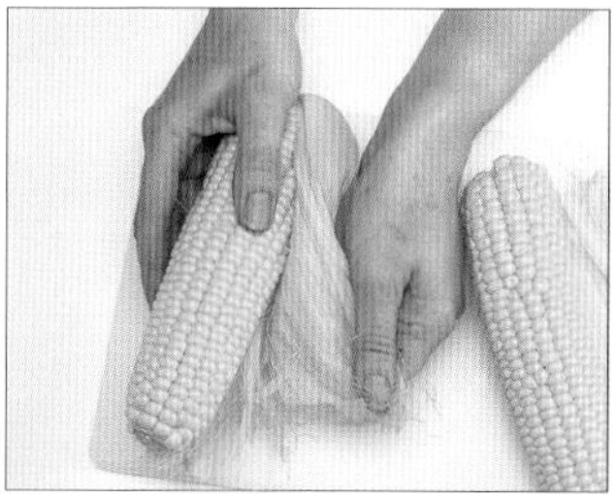

1 Pull off the husks and silks and boil the corn cobs in a large pan of salted water until tender. Drain the corn cobs and leave to cool.

2 Melt the butter in a pan and add the olive oil, crushed garlic, salt and freshly ground black pepper, and stir to blend. Pour the mixture into a shallow dish.

3 In another shallow dish, blend the breadcrumbs and chopped fresh parsley. Roll the corn cobs in the melted butter mixture and then in the breadcrumbs until they are well coated.

4 Cook the corn cobs on a hot barbecue for about 10 minutes, turning them frequently, until the breadcrumbs are golden brown. Serve hot with skewers or forks to hold the cobs.

Vegetables in Peanut and Chilli Sauce

This dish makes a wonderful slash of colour and taste to a meal. Make it as an accompaniment for hearty pork, lamb and poultry dishes.

SERVES FOUR

INGREDIENTS

- 15ml/1 tbsp palm or vegetable oil
- 1 onion, chopped
- 2 garlic cloves, crushed
- 400g/14oz can tomatoes, puréed
- 45ml/3 tbsp smooth peanut butter
- 750ml/1¼ pint/3⅔ cups water
- 5ml/1 tsp dried thyme
- 1 green chilli, seeded and chopped
- 1 vegetable stock (bouillon) cube
- 2.5ml/½ tsp ground allspice
- 2 carrots
- 115g/4oz white cabbage
- 175g/6oz okra
- 1/2 red (bell) pepper
- 150ml/¼ pint/⅔ cup vegetable stock

1 Heat the oil in a large pan and cook the onion and garlic over a medium heat for 5 minutes, stirring frequently. When the onions are soft and transparent, add the tomatoes and peanut butter and stir well.

2 Stir in the water, thyme, chilli, stock cube, allspice and a little salt. Bring to the boil, lower the heat and simmer gently, uncovered, for about 35 minutes.

3 Cut the carrots into sticks, slice the cabbage, trim the okra and seed and slice the red pepper.

4 Place the vegetables in a pan with the stock, bring to the boil and cook until tender but still with a little "bite".

5 Drain the vegetables and place in a warmed serving dish. Pour the sauce over the top and serve.

Chilli Courgettes

Calabacitas is an extremely easy recipe to make, and it is also delicious chilled. Use young tender courgettes that remain sweet and crisp after cooking.

SERVES FOUR

INGREDIENTS

- 30ml/2 tbsp corn oil
- 450g/1lb young courgettes (zucchini), sliced
- 1 onion, finely chopped
- 2 garlic cloves, chopped
- 450g/1lb tomatoes, peeled, seeded and chopped
- 2 drained canned jalapeño chillies, rinsed, seeded and chopped
- 15ml/1 tbsp chopped fresh coriander (cilantro)
- salt
- fresh coriander, to garnish

1 Heat the oil in a flameproof casserole and fry the onions and garlic until soft. Add all the remaining ingredients, except the salt.

2 Cover with water and bring to simmering point. Cover and cook over a low heat for about 30 minutes, until the courgettes are tender, checking from time to time that the dish is not drying out. If it is, add a little tomato juice, stock or water.

3 Season with salt to taste, and serve the Mexican way as a separate course in a bowl for each of your guests. Alternatively, serve as an accompaniment to any plainly cooked meat or poultry. Place it in a colourful serving dish and garnish with fresh coriander (cilantro).

Refried Beans

These are not actually fried twice, but they are cooked twice, first as Frijoles de Olla and then by frying in lard. If the only refried beans you've tried have been the canned ones, you may have found them rather bland. These, however, are superb.

SERVES FOUR

INGREDIENTS
- 25g/1oz/2 tbsp lard
- 2 onions, finely chopped
- 5ml/1 tsp ground cumin
- 5ml/1 tsp ground coriander
- 1 quantity Frijoles de Olla, without the toppings
- 3 garlic cloves, crushed
- small bunch of fresh coriander (cilantro) or 4–5 dried avocado leaves
- 50g/2oz feta cheese
- salt

1 Melt the lard in a large frying pan. Add the onions, cumin and ground coriander. Cook gently over a low heat for about 30 minutes or until the onions caramelize and become soft.

2 Add a ladleful of the soft, cooked beans. Fry them for only a few minutes, simply to heat. Mash the beans into the onions as they cook, using a fork or a potato masher. Continue until all the beans have been added, a little at a time, then stir in the crushed garlic.

3 Lower the heat and cook the beans to form a thick paste. Season with salt and spoon into a warmed serving dish. Chop the coriander or crumble the avocado leaves, and sprinkle most of them over the beans. Crumble the feta cheese over the top, then garnish with the reserved sprigs or leaves.

FRIJOLES CHARROS

THESE "COWBOY BEANS" TASTE RATHER LIKE BOSTON BAKED BEANS, BUT WITH RATHER MORE PUNCH. THE FLAVOUR IMPROVES ON KEEPING, SO MAKE IT THE DAY BEFORE YOU INTEND TO SERVE IT.

SERVES SIX

INGREDIENTS
- 2 x 400g/14oz cans pinto beans
- 120ml/4fl oz/½ cup Mexican beer
- 115g/4oz/⅔ cups drained pickled jalapeño chilli slices
- 2 tomatoes, peeled and chopped
- 5ml/1 tsp ground cinnamon
- 175g/6oz bacon fat
- 1 onion, chopped
- 2 garlic cloves, crushed
- 175g/6oz rindless smoked lean bacon, diced
- 45ml/3 tbsp soft dark brown sugar
- wheat-flour tortillas, to serve

1 Put the drained pinto beans in a pan. Stir in the beer and cook over a high heat for 5 minutes, until some of the beer has been absorbed.

2 Lower the heat slightly and stir in the chopped jalapeños chilli, then add the tomatoes and cinnamon. Continue to cook, stirring occasionally, for about 10 minutes.

3 Meanwhile, heat the bacon fat in a frying pan until the fat runs. The quantity suggested should yield about 45ml/3 tbsp bacon fat.

4 Discard the bacon, then add the onion and garlic to the pan and fry for about 5 minutes, until browned. Using a slotted spoon, lift out the garlic and onions and stir them into the beans.

5 Add the diced smoked bacon to the fat remaining in the frying pan and fry until crisp. Add the bacon and any remaining fat to the beans and mix well.

6 Stir in the sugar. Cook the bean and bacon mixture over a low heat, stirring constantly, until the sugar is dissolved. Serve immediately or spoon into a bowl, leave to cool, cover, then chill for reheating next day. Serve with warmed wheat-flour tortillas.

Okra Fried Rice

Okra was introduced to mainland South America and the islands of the Caribbean by the African slaves who were brought over to work the sugar plantations. It became an important and much-valued ingredient.

SERVES FOUR

INGREDIENTS

- 15ml/1 tbsp butter or margarine
- 30ml/2 tbsp vegetable oil
- 1 garlic clove, crushed
- ½ red onion, finely chopped
- 115g/4oz okra, trimmed
- 30ml/2 tbsp diced green and red (bell) peppers
- 2.5ml/½ tsp dried thyme
- 2 fresh green chillies, finely chopped
- 2.5ml/½ tsp five-spice powder
- 1 vegetable stock (bouillon) cube
- 30ml/2 tbsp soy sauce
- 15ml/1 tbsp chopped fresh coriander (cilantro)
- 225g/8oz/2 cups cooked long grain white rice
- salt and ground black pepper
- fresh coriander, to garnish

1 Melt the butter or margarine in the oil in a frying pan or wok. Add the garlic and onion, and cook over a medium heat for 5 minutes, until the onion is soft but not browned.

2 Trim the okra, cutting off the stalks and points, then thinly slice the pods. Add to the pan or wok and cook gently for 6–7 minutes.

3 Add the green and red peppers, thyme, chillies and five-spice powder. Cook for 3 minutes, then crumble in the stock cube.

4 Add the soy sauce, chopped coriander and rice, and heat through, stirring well. Season with salt and pepper. Spoon into a dish and serve hot, garnished with the coriander sprigs.

Aubergines with Garlic and Spring Onions

This is a superb way of serving aubergines. It can be made even more delicious by adding little strips of smoked salmon at the last minute and letting them just warm through.

SERVES FOUR

INGREDIENTS

- 45ml/3 tbsp vegetable oil
- 2 garlic cloves, crushed
- 3 tomatoes, peeled and chopped
- 900g/2lb aubergines (eggplants), cut into chunks
- 150ml/¼ pint/⅔ cup vegetable stock or water
- 30ml/2 tbsp soy sauce
- 60ml/4 tbsp chopped spring onion (scallion)
- ½ red (bell) pepper, seeded and chopped
- 1 fresh hot chilli, seeded and chopped
- 30ml/2 tbsp chopped fresh coriander (cilantro)
- salt and ground black pepper

1 Heat the oil in a wok or frying pan and fry the garlic and tomatoes for 3–4 minutes. Add the aubergines and toss with the garlic and tomatoes.

2 Pour in the stock or water and cover the pan. Simmer gently until the aubergines are very soft. Stir in the soy sauce and half of the spring onion.

3 Add the red pepper and chilli to the aubergine. Season with salt and pepper to taste. Mix well.

4 Stir in the coriander and sprinkle with the remaining spring onion. Spoon the aubergine mixture into a dish and serve at once. Alternatively, allow to cool until warm before serving.

CASSAVA WITH A CITRUS SALSA

This dish consists of diced cassava in a classic Cuban sauce called mojo. *When the cooked cassava is coated in the sharp dressing, it becomes imbued with the delicious flavours of fresh orange, lime and garlic.*

SERVES FOUR

INGREDIENTS
- 800g/1¾ lb cassava, peeled and cut into chunks
- 2 garlic cloves, crushed
- juice of 1 small orange
- juice of 1 lime
- 45ml/3 tbsp olive oil
- 15ml/1 tbsp chopped fresh flat leaf parsley
- salt

VARIATION
Mojo is also delicious with cooked pumpkin and sweet potatoes.

1 Cook the cassava in a large pan of salted boiling water for 20–25 minutes, until beginning to break up. Drain in a colander and then transfer to a large serving plate.

2 Mix the garlic, orange juice and lime juice in a bowl. Whisk in the oil, season with salt and stir in the parsley. Drizzle the dressing over the cooked cassava and serve.

STIR-FRIED SPRING GREENS

Spring greens are very popular in Brazil. They are eaten with meat and are the traditional accompaniment to feijoada. Garlic enhances their slightly bitter flavour, and they taste even better when cooked with bacon and chillies.

SERVES SIX

INGREDIENTS
- 450g/1lb spring greens (collards)
- 15ml/1 tbsp vegetable oil
- 150g/5oz smoked streaky (fatty) bacon, in one piece
- 2 garlic cloves, crushed
- 1.5ml/¼ tsp crushed dried chillies
- salt

VARIATIONS
- If you cannot find spring greens, use curly kale or Savoy cabbage instead. These may not be as vibrant in colour, but the taste will be very similar.
- Cubed pancetta can be used instead of the bacon.

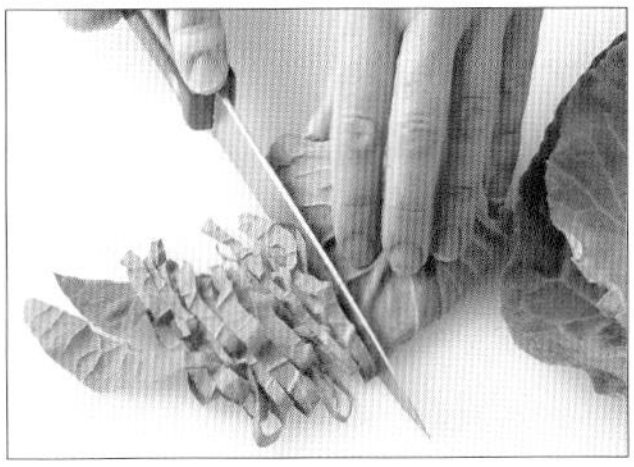

1 Cut off the hard stalks from the spring greens. Lay the leaves flat on top of each other and roll into a tight cigar-shape. Slice very thinly, using a sharp knife.

2 Heat the oil in a large frying pan over a low heat. Cut the bacon into small cubes and sauté in the oil for 5 minutes, or until golden brown. Lift the cubes out of the pan with a slotted spoon and drain on kitchen paper.

3 Increase the heat, add the crushed garlic and dried chillies to the oil remaining in the pan, and stir-fry for about 30 seconds.

4 Add the shredded spring greens and toss over the heat until just tender. Season to taste with salt, stir in the cooked bacon cubes and serve immediately.

Corn Sticks

This traditional Caribbean recipe produces perfect corn bread in a loaf tin. Alternatively, if you can find the moulds, it can be used to make attractive corn sticks.

MAKES FORTY

INGREDIENTS
- 225g/8oz/2 cups plain (all-purpose) flour
- 225g/8oz/2 cups fine corn meal
- 50ml/10 tsp bicarbonate of soda (baking soda)
- 2.5ml/½ tsp salt
- 60ml/4 tbsp demerara (raw) sugar
- 450ml/¾ pint/scant 2 cups milk
- 2 eggs
- 50g/2oz/4 tbsp butter or margarine

COOK'S TIP
Because there is such a lot of bicarbonate of soda used in this recipe, the corn meal mixture begins to rise as soon as the liquid is added, so make sure you bake straight away.

1 Preheat the oven to 190°C/375°F/Gas 5 and grease either corn bread moulds, if you can find them, or a 900g/2lb loaf tin (pan).

2 Sift together the flour, corn meal, bicarbonate of soda, salt and sugar into a large bowl. In a separate bowl, whisk the milk and eggs, then stir into the flour mixture.

3 Melt the butter or margarine in a small pan and stir gradually into the corn meal mixture.

4 Carefully spoon the thick mixture into the moulds or tin. Bake the corn sticks for about 15 minutes. If using a loaf tin, you will need to bake for around 30–35 minutes, until the corn bread is golden and hollow sounding when tapped.

MUSHROOMS WITH CHIPOTLE CHILLIES

THESE SPICY MUSHROOMS COULDN'T BE EASIER TO PREPARE. SERVE THEM AS AN APPETIZER, OR AS AN ACCOMPANIMENT TO MEAT AND POULTRY DISHES WITH SOME BREAD TO SOAK UP THE JUICES.

SERVES SIX

INGREDIENTS
- 450g/1lb/4 cups button (white) mushrooms
- 60ml/4 tbsp olive oil
- 1 onion, finely chopped
- 2 garlic cloves, chopped
- 2 drained canned chipotle chillies, rinsed and sliced
- salt
- chopped fresh coriander (cilantro), to garnish

COOK'S TIP
Never wash mushrooms as they quickly absorb water and lose their flavour. Wipe them with kitchen paper or a clean, damp cloth.

1 Wipe the mushrooms gently and carefully with kitchen paper. Heat the olive oil in a large frying pan and add the mushrooms, finely chopped onion, chopped garlic and sliced chillies. Stir to coat in oil.

2 Cook the mixture over a medium heat for 6–8 minutes, stirring occasionally, until the onions and mushrooms are tender. Season to taste with salt and serve on small plates, sprinkled with a little chopped fresh coriander.

SALSAS

Mexican and Latin American cuisine is known for its salsas. Whether hot and spicy or cool and refreshing, these are served as a relish or stirred into dishes. There are delicious salsas to complement all kinds of foods, from shellfish or barbecued meat to tortillas and enchiladas.

ARGENTINIAN BARBECUE SALSA

THIS COMBINATION OF FINELY CHOPPED VEGETABLES AND TART DRESSING IS THE PERFECT PARTNER FOR ALL TYPES OF GRILLED MEATS, SO IT IS NOT SURPRISING TO FIND BOWLS OF FRESH SALSA CREOLLA ON THE TABLE WHENEVER A BARBECUE OR ASADO IS BEING PEPARED. SIMILAR BARBECUE SALSAS CAN ALSO BE FOUND IN BRAZIL, URUGUAY AND PARAGUAY.

SERVES SIX AS AN ACCOMPANIMENT

INGREDIENTS

- 2 fresh green chillies, seeded and very finely chopped
- 1 garlic clove, crushed
- 1 onion, very finely chopped
- 1 large tomato, peeled, seeded and very finely chopped
- 15ml/1 tbsp finely chopped fresh flat leaf parsley
- salt
- 105ml/7 tbsp olive oil
- 30ml/2 tbsp red wine vinegar

1 Combine the chopped chillies, crushed garlic, onion and tomato in a bowl. Stir in the chopped parsley and season to taste with salt.

2 Pour in the oil and vinegar and stir well. Allow the flavours to mingle for at least 1 hour before serving with grilled (broiled) or barbecued meats.

HOT CHILLI SALSA

CONTRARY TO POPULAR BELIEF, LATIN FOOD IS NOT INTRINSICALLY SPICY. IT IS THE HOT CHILLI OILS AND SALSAS, ADDED TO DISHES AT THE TABLE, THAT FAN THE FLAMES.

MAKES ONE SMALL JAR

INGREDIENTS

- 10 fresh red chillies, roughly chopped
- 1 large tomato, peeled and quartered
- 2 garlic cloves
- juice of 1 lime
- 60ml/4 tbsp olive oil
- salt

COOK'S TIP

Treat this salsa with extreme caution. Just the oil is enough to add serious heat to a dish, especially if the salsa has had a chance to age. A couple of drops of the oil are enough for most people!

1 Place the chillies, tomato and garlic in a food processor, then process the mixture until smooth.

2 Scrape the mixture into a small frying pan and place over a medium heat. Season with salt and cook, stirring, for 10 minutes, until the sauce is thick.

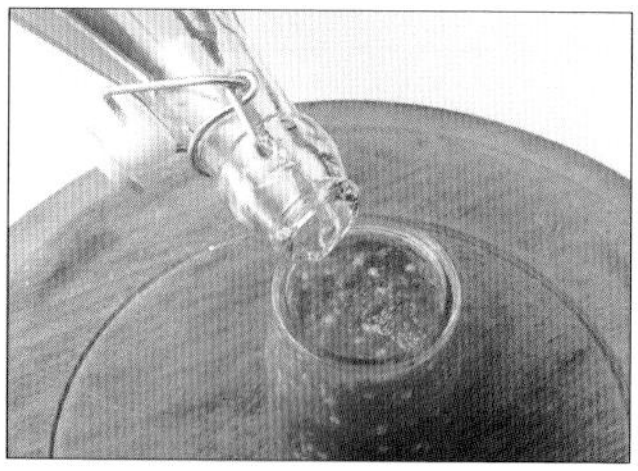

3 Remove from the heat and stir in the freshly squeezed lime juice. Transfer to a sterilized airtight jar and top with a thin film of olive oil before tightly screwing on the lid. As long as the sauce always has a film of oil on top, it will keep for ages at room temperature or in the refrigerator.

Green Tomatillo Sauce

This sauce, with its distinctive green colour and sharp taste, is a popular choice for pouring over enchiladas. When the cream is added, it is perfect for poached fish or with chicken breasts. Fresh tomatillos are difficult to obtain outside Mexico, but the sauce can be made with canned tomatillos. Instructions for both versions are given here.

SERVES FOUR AS A SAUCE FOR A MAIN COURSE

INGREDIENTS

- 300g/11oz fresh tomatillos, plus 120ml/4fl oz/½ cup stock or water **or** 300g/11oz drained canned tomatillos, plus 60ml/4 tbsp/¼ cup stock or water
- 2 fresh serrano chillies
- 4 garlic cloves, crushed
- 15ml/1 tbsp vegetable oil
- bunch of fresh coriander (cilantro)
- 120ml/4fl oz/½ cup double (heavy) cream (optional)
- salt

1 If using fresh tomatillos, remove the husks and cut the tomatillos into quarters. Place them in a pan and add the stock or water. Cook over a moderate heat for 8–10 minutes until the flesh is soft and transparent.

2 Remove the stalks from the chillies, slit them and scrape out the seeds with a small knife. Chop the flesh roughly and place it in a food processor or blender with the garlic.

3 Add the tomatillos to the processor or blender with their cooking liquid and process for a few minutes until almost smooth. If using drained canned tomatillos, simply quarter and put in the blender or food processor with the smaller amount of stock or water and the chopped chillies and garlic. Process until almost smooth.

4 Heat the oil in a heavy-based frying pan and add the processed tomatillo purée. Reduce the heat and cook gently, stirring, for about 5 minutes until the sauce thickens. Be sure to keep stirring the sauce all the time, since it can easily catch and burn.

5 Chop the coriander and add it to the sauce, with salt to taste. Cook for a few minutes, stirring occasionally.

6 Stir in the cream, if using, and warm the sauce through. Do not let it boil after adding the cream. Serve at once.

GUACAMOLE

ONE OF THE BEST LOVED MEXICAN SALSAS, THIS BLEND OF CREAMY AVOCADO, TOMATOES, CHILLIES, CORIANDER AND LIME NOW APPEARS ON TABLES THE WORLD OVER. BOUGHT GUACAMOLE USUALLY CONTAINS MAYONNAISE, WHICH HELPS TO PRESERVE THE AVOCADO, BUT THIS IS NOT AN INGREDIENT IN TRADITIONAL RECIPES.

SERVES EIGHT AS AN ACCOMPANIMENT

INGREDIENTS

- 4 medium tomatoes
- 4 ripe avocados, preferably fuerte
- juice of 1 lime
- ½ small onion
- 2 garlic cloves
- small bunch of fresh coriander (cilantro), chopped
- 3 fresh red fresno chillies
- salt
- tortilla chips, to serve

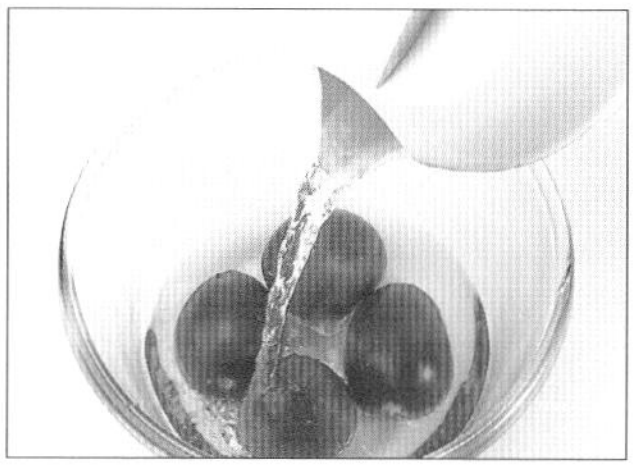

1 Cut a cross in the base of each tomato. Place the tomatoes in a heatproof bowl and pour over boiling water to cover.

2 Leave the tomatoes in the water for 3 minutes, then lift them out using a slotted spoon and plunge them into a bowl of cold water. Drain. The skins will have begun to peel back from the crosses. Remove the skins completely. Cut the tomatoes in half, remove the seeds with a teaspoon, then chop the flesh roughly and set it aside.

COOK'S TIP

Smooth-skinned fuerte avocados are native to Mexico, so would be ideal for this dip. If they are not available, use any avocados, but make sure they are ripe. To test, gently press the top of the avocado; it should give a little.

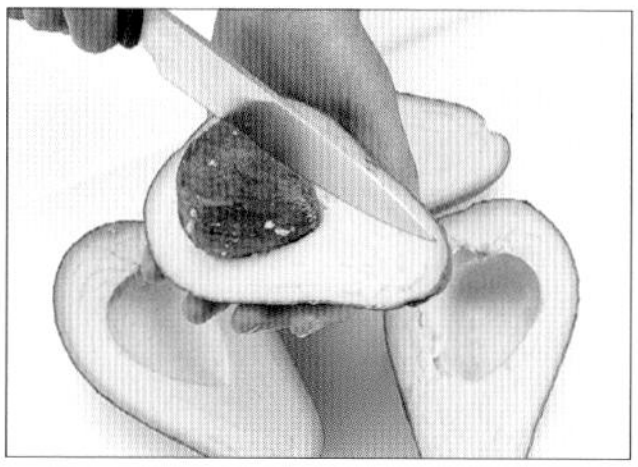

3 Cut the avocados in half then remove the stones (pits). Scoop the flesh out of the shells and place it in a food processor or blender. Process until almost smooth, then scrape into a bowl and stir in the lime juice.

4 Chop the onion finely, then crush the garlic. Add both to the avocado and mix well. Stir in the coriander.

5 Remove the stalks from the chillies, slit them and scrape out the seeds with a small sharp knife. Chop the chillies finely and add them to the avocado mixture, with the chopped tomatoes. Mix well.

6 Check the seasoning and add salt to taste. Cover with clear film (plastic wrap) and chill for 1 hour before serving as a dip with tortilla chips. If it is well covered, guacamole will keep in the refrigerator for 2–3 days.

Pinto Bean Salsa

These beans have a pretty, speckled appearance. The smoky flavour of the chipotle chillies and the herby taste of the pasilla chilli contrast well with the tart tomatillos. Unusually, these are not cooked.

SERVES FOUR AS AN ACCOMPANIMENT

INGREDIENTS

- 130g/4½oz/generous ½ cup pinto beans, soaked overnight in water to cover
- 2 chipotle chillies
- 1 pasilla chilli
- 2 garlic cloves, peeled
- ½ onion
- 200g/7oz fresh tomatillos
- salt

1 Drain the beans and put them in a large pan. Pour in water to cover and place the lid on the pan. Bring to the boil, lower the heat slightly and simmer the beans for 45–50 minutes or until tender. They should still have a little bite and should not have begun to disintegrate. Drain, rinse under cold water, then drain again and tip into a bowl. Leave the beans until cold.

COOK'S TIP

Canned tomatillos can be substituted, but to keep a clean, fresh flavour add a little lime juice.

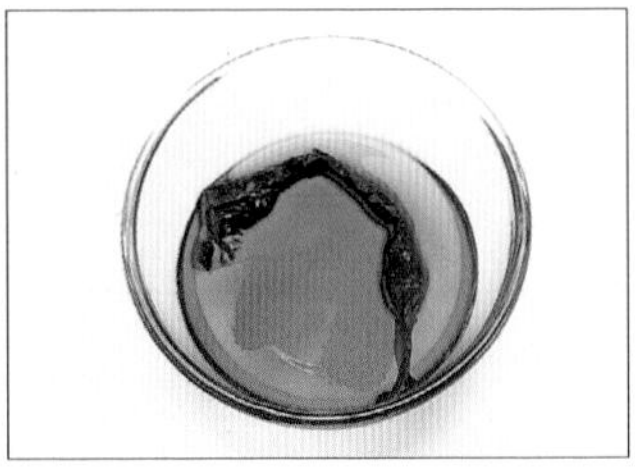

2 Soak the chipotle and pasilla chillies in hot water for about 10 minutes until softened. Drain, reserving the soaking water. Remove the stalks, then slit each chilli and scrape out the seeds with a small sharp knife. Chop the flesh finely and mix it to a smooth paste with a little of the soaking water.

3 Roast the garlic in a dry frying pan over a moderate heat for a few minutes until the cloves start to turn golden. Crush them and add them to the beans.

4 Chop the onion and tomatillos and stir them into the beans. Add the chilli paste and mix well. Add salt to taste, cover and chill before serving.

Black Bean Salsa

This salsa has a very striking appearance. It is rare to find a black sauce and it provides a wonderful contrast to the more common reds and greens on the plate. The pasado chillies add a subtle citrus flavour.

SERVES FOUR AS AN ACCOMPANIMENT

INGREDIENTS

- 130g/4½oz/generous ½ cup black beans, soaked overnight in water to cover
- 1 pasado chilli
- 2 fresh red fresno chillies
- 1 red onion
- grated rind and juice of 1 lime
- 30ml/2 tbsp Mexican beer (optional)
- 15ml/1 tbsp olive oil
- small bunch of fresh coriander (cilantro), chopped
- salt

1 Drain the beans and put them in a large pan. Pour in water to cover and place the lid on the pan. Bring to the boil, lower the heat slightly and simmer the beans for about 40 minutes or until tender. They should still have a little bite and should not have begun to disintegrate. Drain, rinse under cold water, then drain again and leave the beans until cold.

2 Soak the pasado chilli in hot water for about 10 minutes until softened. Drain, remove the stalk, then slit the chilli and scrape out the seeds with a small sharp knife. Chop the flesh finely.

COOK'S TIP

Mexican beer is a lager-type beer. Few brands are to be found in this country, but the most popular, *Dos Equis* (Double X), is readily available.

3 Spear the fresno chillies on a long-handled metal skewer and roast them over the flame of a gas burner until the skins blister and darken. Do not let the flesh burn. Alternatively, dry fry them in a griddle pan until the skins are scorched. Then place the roasted chillies in a strong plastic bag and tie the top to keep the steam in. Set aside for 20 minutes.

4 Meanwhile, chop the red onion finely. Remove the chillies from the bag and peel off the skins. Slit them, remove the seeds and chop them finely.

5 Tip the beans into a bowl and add the onion and both types of chilli. Stir in the lime rind and juice, beer, oil and coriander. Season with salt and mix well. Chill before serving.

Chipotle Sauce

The smoky flavour of this sauce makes it ideal for barbecued food, either as a marinade or as an accompaniment. It is also wonderful stirred into cream cheese as a sandwich filling with chicken. Chipotle chillies are smoked dried jalapeño chillies.

SERVES SIX AS AN ACCOMPANIMENT

INGREDIENTS
- 500g/1¼lb tomatoes
- 5 chipotle chillies
- 3 garlic cloves, roughly chopped
- 150ml/¼ pint/⅔ cup red wine
- 5ml/1 tsp dried oregano
- 60ml/4 tbsp clear honey
- 5ml/1 tsp American mustard
- 2.5ml/½ tsp ground black pepper
- salt

1 Preheat the oven to 200°C/400°F/ Gas 6. Cut the tomatoes into quarters and place them in a roasting tin. Roast for 45 minutes–1 hour, until they are charred and softened.

2 Meanwhile, soak the chillies in a bowl of cold water to cover for about 20 minutes or until soft. Remove the stalks, slit the chillies and scrape out the seeds with a small sharp knife. Chop the flesh roughly.

3 Remove the tomatoes from the oven, let them cool slightly, then remove the skins. If you prefer a smooth sauce, remove the seeds. Chop the tomatoes and put them in a blender or food processor. Add the chopped chillies and garlic with the red wine. Process until smooth, then add the oregano, honey, mustard and black pepper. Process briefly to mix, then taste and season with salt.

4 Scrape the mixture into a small pan. Place over a moderate heat and stir until the mixture boils. Lower the heat and simmer the sauce for about 10 minutes, stirring occasionally, until it has reduced and thickened. Spoon into a bowl and serve hot or cold.

Guajillo Chilli Sauce

This sauce can be served over enchiladas or steamed vegetables. It is also good with meats such as pork, and a little makes a fine seasoning for soups or stews. Made from dried chillies, it has a well rounded, fruity flavour and is not too hot.

SERVES FOUR AS AN ACCOMPANIMENT

INGREDIENTS
- 2 tomatoes, total weight about 200g/7oz
- 2 red (bell) peppers, cored, seeded and quartered
- 3 garlic cloves, in their skins
- 2 ancho chillies
- 2 guajillo chillies
- 30ml/2 tbsp tomato purée (paste)
- 5ml/1 tsp dried oregano
- 5ml/1 tsp soft dark brown sugar
- 300ml/½ pint/1¼ cups chicken stock

1 Preheat the oven to 200°C/400°F/ Gas 6. Cut the tomatoes into quarters and place them in a roasting tin with the peppers and whole garlic cloves. Roast for 45 minutes–1 hour, until the tomatoes and peppers are slightly charred and the garlic has softened.

2 Put the peppers in a strong plastic bag and tie the top to keep the steam in. Set aside for 20 minutes. Remove the skin from the tomatoes. Meanwhile, soak the chillies in boiling water for 15 minutes until soft.

3 Remove the peppers from the bag and rub off the skins. Cut them in half, remove the cores and seeds, then chop the flesh roughly and put it in a food processor or blender. Drain the chillies, remove the stalks, then slit them and scrape out the seeds with a sharp knife. Chop the chillies roughly and add them to the peppers.

4 Add the roasted tomatoes to the food processor or blender. Squeeze the roasted garlic out of the skins and add to the tomato mixture, with the tomato purée, oregano, brown sugar and stock. Process until smooth.

5 Pour the mixture into a pan, place over a moderate heat and bring to the boil. Lower the heat and simmer for 10–15 minutes until the sauce has reduced to about half. Transfer to a bowl and serve immediately or, if serving cold, cover, leave to cool, then chill until required. The sauce will keep in the refrigerator for up to a week.

ROASTED TOMATO SALSA

SLOW ROASTING THESE TOMATOES TO A SEMI-DRIED STATE RESULTS IN A VERY RICH, FULL-FLAVOURED SWEET SAUCE. THE COSTENO AMARILLO CHILLI IS MILD AND HAS A FRESH LIGHT FLAVOUR, MAKING IT THE PERFECT PARTNER FOR THE RICH TOMATO TASTE. THIS SALSA IS GREAT WITH TUNA OR SEA BASS AND MAKES A MARVELLOUS SANDWICH FILLING WHEN TEAMED WITH CREAMY CHEESE.

SERVES SIX AS AN ACCOMPANIMENT

INGREDIENTS
- 500g/1¼lb tomatoes
- 8 small shallots
- 5 garlic cloves
- sea salt
- 1 fresh rosemary sprig
- 2 costeno amarillo chillies
- grated rind and juice of ½ small lemon
- 30ml/2 tbsp extra virgin olive oil
- 1.5ml/¼ tsp soft dark brown sugar

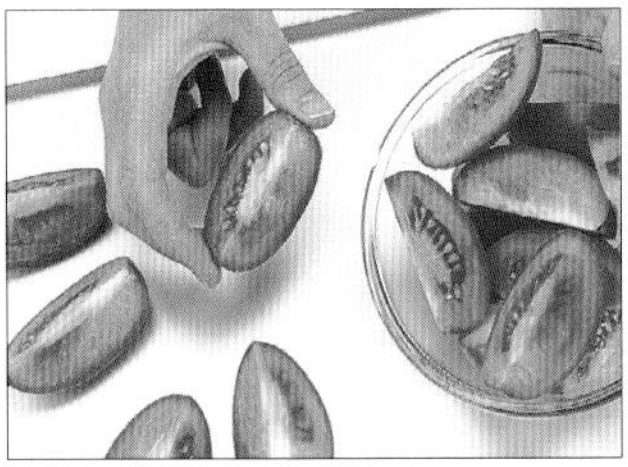

1 Preheat the oven to 160°C/325°F/ Gas 3. Cut the tomatoes into quarters and place them on a baking tray.

2 Peel the shallots and garlic and add them to the roasting tin. Sprinkle with sea salt. Roast in the oven for 1¼ hours or until the tomatoes are beginning to dry. Do not let them burn or blacken or they will have a bitter taste.

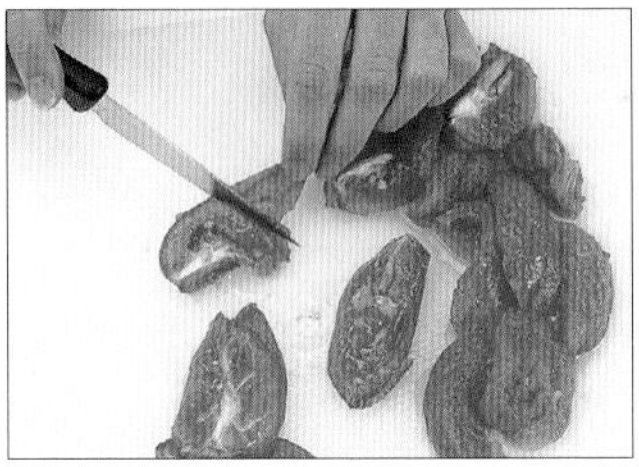

3 Leave the tomatoes to cool, then peel off the skins and chop the flesh finely. Place in a bowl. Remove the outer layer of skin from any shallots that have toughened.

4 Using a large, sharp knife, chop the shallots and garlic roughly, place them with the tomatoes in a bowl and mix.

5 Strip the rosemary leaves from the woody stem and chop them finely. Add half to the tomato and shallot mixture and mix lightly.

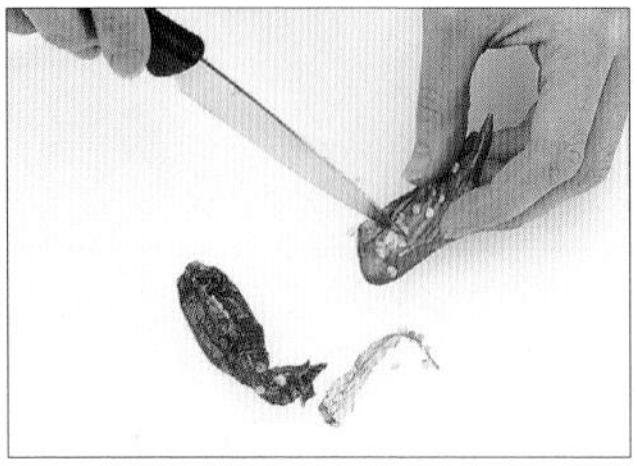

6 Soak the chillies in hot water for about 10 minutes until soft. Drain, remove the stalks, slit them and scrape out the seeds with a sharp knife. Chop the flesh finely and add it to the tomato mixture.

7 Stir in the lemon rind and juice, the olive oil and the sugar. Mix well, taste and add more salt if needed. Cover and chill for at least an hour before serving, sprinkled with the remaining rosemary. It will keep for up to a week in the refrigerator.

COOK'S TIP

Use plum tomatoes or vine tomatoes, which have more flavour than tomatoes that have been grown for their keeping properties rather than their flavour. Cherry tomatoes make delicious roast tomato salsa and there is no need to peel them after roasting.

TAMARILLO SAUCE

THIS UNUSUAL PERUVIAN SAUCE MAKES A DELICIOUS DIP FOR SERVING WITH AREPAS *– THOSE IRRESISTIBLE CORN MEAL GRIDDLE CAKES THAT ARE FREQUENTLY FILLED WITH SOFT WHITE CHEESE. ALTERNATIVELY, ITS DELICIOUS, HOT AND SPICY FLAVOUR CONTRASTS BEAUTIFULLY WITH THE NATURAL SWEETNESS OF FRESH GRILLED SEAFOOD.*

SERVES FOUR AS AN ACCOMPANIMENT

INGREDIENTS
- 450g/1lb fresh tamarillos
- 2.5ml/½ tsp ground ginger
- 1.5ml/¼ tsp ground cinnamon
- 1 fresh red chilli, seeded and chopped
- 1 small onion, finely chopped
- 5ml/1 tsp light brown sugar
- 105ml/7 tbsp water
- 30ml/2 tbsp olive oil
- salt

COOK'S TIP
If tamarillos are heavier than they look, they will be ripe and juicy.

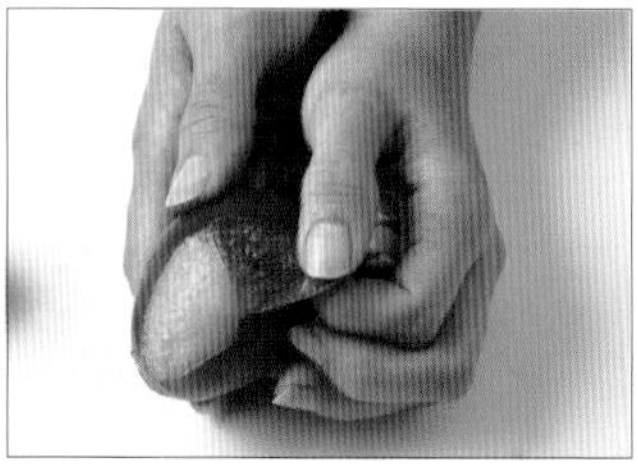

1 Place the whole fresh tamarillos in a large pan of boiling water for about 30 seconds. Drain, refresh in cold water, then carefully remove the peel with a sharp knife and discard it. Roughly chop the tamarillos.

2 Place the ginger and cinnamon in a small heavy pan over a low heat. Stir the mixture for 30 seconds, until the spices release their aroma. Add the chopped tamarillos, chilli, onion, sugar and water.

3 Bring to the boil, lower the heat, cover and simmer for 20 minutes. Remove the lid and continue cooking until the sauce thickens. Stir in the oil and season with salt. Serve with grilled (broiled) seafood.

AVOCADO SALSA

There are many versions of avocado salsa, including the classic Mexican guacamole. Here the ingredients are chopped and diced, rather than mashed, which adds texture and allows all the delicious flavours to remain distinct. Prepare this salsa at the last minute to avoid the avocados discolouring.

SERVES FOUR AS AN ACCOMPANIMENT

INGREDIENTS

- 1 large ripe avocado
- juice of 1 lime
- 15ml/1 tbsp red wine vinegar
- 1 tomato, peeled, seeded and chopped
- 1 green (bell) pepper, seeded and diced
- 1 red onion, finely chopped
- 1 fresh red chilli, seeded and finely chopped
- 45ml/3 tbsp olive oil
- salt

1 Prepare the avocado. Run a sharp knife around the whole length of the avocado, cutting right in until you touch the stone (pit). Twist the two sides of the split avocado in opposite directions to separate the two halves.

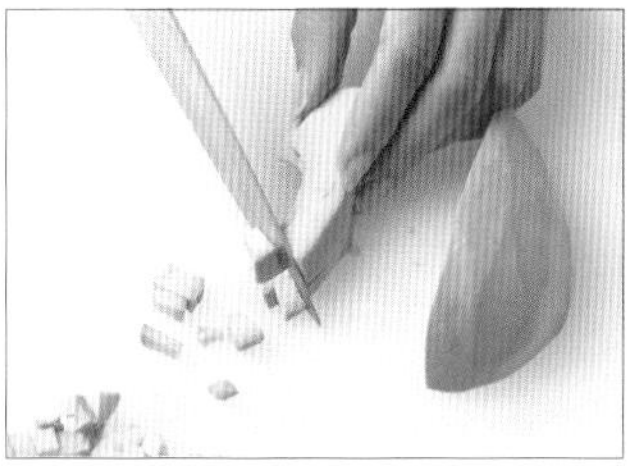

2 Use a large spoon to remove the large stone, then peel both halves of the avocado. Dice the flesh and put it in a bowl with the lime juice.

3 Stir the vinegar, tomato, pepper, onion and chilli into the avocado and lime juice mixture. Gradually add the olive oil, mixing well.

COOK'S TIP

If there is any delay before serving this salsa, add the avocado stone to the mixture. This will prevent any discoloration. Remember to remove the stone before serving though.

4 Season to taste with salt and serve with tortilla chips, or as an accompaniment to meat, fish or poultry.

Jicama Salsa

The jicama is a round, brown root vegetable with a texture somewhere between that of water chestnut and crisp apple. It can be eaten raw or cooked, and is always peeled. Look for jicamas in ethnic food stores.

SERVES FOUR AS AN ACCOMPANIMENT

INGREDIENTS
- 1 small red onion
- juice of 2 limes
- 3 small oranges
- 1 *jicama*, about 450g/1lb
- ½ cucumber
- 1 fresh red fresno chilli

1 Cut the onion in half, then slice each half finely. Place in a bowl, add the lime juice and leave to soak while you prepare the remaining ingredients.

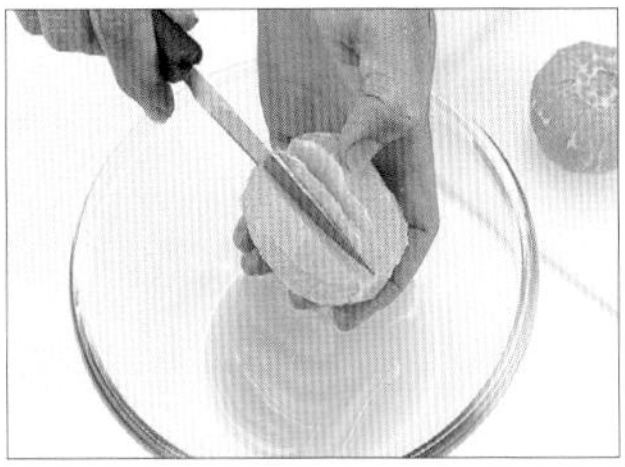

2 Slice the top and bottom off each orange. Stand an orange on a board, then carefully slice off all the peel and pith. Hold the orange over a bowl and cut carefully between the membranes so that the segments fall into the bowl. Having cut out all the segments, squeeze the pulp over the bowl to extract the remaining juice.

3 Peel the *jicama* and rinse it in cold water. Cut it into quarters, then slice finely. Add to the bowl of orange juice.

COOK'S TIP
The juices of citrus fruits are very useful in preserving colour and freshness, and add more than flavouring to a recipe. For instance, lemon juice added to sliced apples keeps them white. Guacamole retains its colour for two to three days if lime juice is added. In this recipe the lime juice will slightly soften the finely sliced onion.

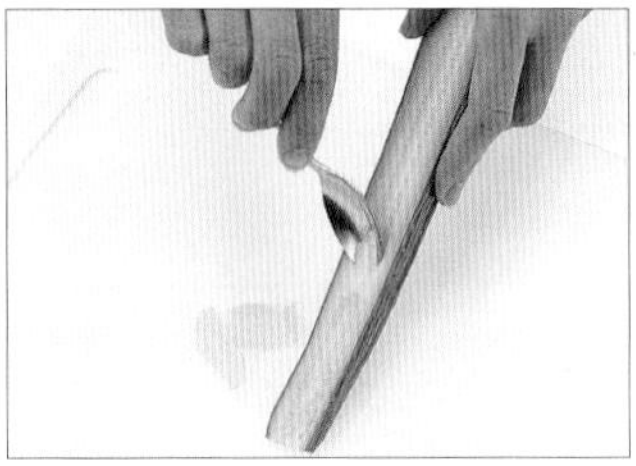

4 Cut the cucumber in half lengthways, then use a teaspoon to scoop out the seeds. Slice the cucumber and add to the bowl. Remove the stalk from the chilli, slit it and scrape out the seeds with a small sharp knife. Chop the flesh finely and add to the bowl.

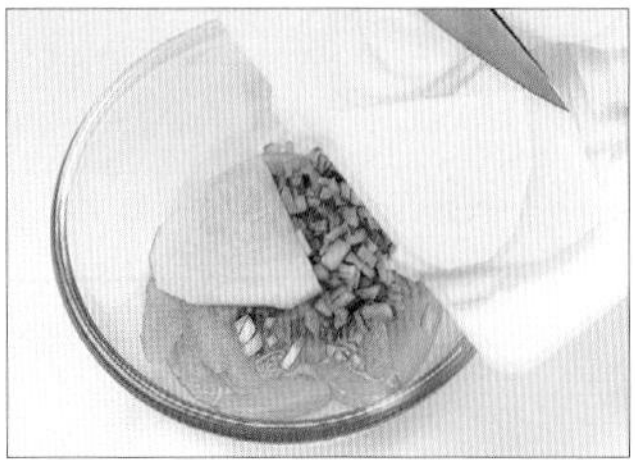

5 Add the sliced onion to the bowl, with any remaining lime juice, and mix well. Cover and leave to stand at room temperature for at least 1 hour before serving. If not serving immediately, put the salsa in the refrigerator; it will keep for 2–3 days.

SWEET POTATO SALSA

VERY COLOURFUL AND DELIGHTFULLY SWEET, THIS SALSA MAKES THE PERFECT ACCOMPANIMENT TO HOT, SPICY MEXICAN DISHES.

SERVES FOUR AS AN ACCOMPANIMENT

INGREDIENTS

- 675g/1½lb sweet potatoes
- juice of 1 small orangc
- 5ml/1 tsp crushed dried jalapeño chillies
- 4 small spring onions (scallions)
- juice of 1 small lime (optional)
- salt

COOK'S TIP

This fresh and tasty salsa is also very good served with a simple grilled salmon fillet or other fish dishes, and makes a delicious accompaniment to veal escalopes or grilled chicken breasts.

1 Peel the sweet potatoes and dice the flesh finely. Bring a pan of water to the boil. Add the sweet potato and cook for 8–10 minutes, until just soft. Drain off the water, cover the pan and put it back on the hob, having first turned off the heat. Leave the sweet potato for about 5 minutes to dry out, then tip into a bowl and set aside.

2 Mix the orange juice and crushed dried chillies in a bowl. Chop the spring onions finely and add them to the juice and chillies.

3 When the sweet potatoes are cool, add the orange juice mixture and toss carefully until all the pieces are well coated. Cover the bowl and chill for at least 1 hour, then taste and season with salt. Stir in the lime juice if you prefer a fresher taste. The salsa will keep for 2–3 days in a covered bowl in the refrigerator.

Nopales Salsa

Nopales are the tender, fleshy leaves or "paddles" of an edible cactus known variously as the cactus pear and the prickly pear cactus. This grows wild in Mexico, but is also cultivated. The most familiar type sold in Mexican markets has dark green ovals with tiny thorns. Fresh nopales are difficult to track down outside Mexico, but if you do locate a supply, look for paddles that are firm and smooth skinned.

SERVES FOUR AS AN ACCOMPANIMENT

INGREDIENTS

- 2 fresh red fresno chillies
- 250g/9oz *nopales* (cactus paddles)
- 3 spring onions (scallions)
- 3 garlic cloves, peeled
- ½ red onion
- 100g/3½oz fresh tomatillos
- 2.5ml/½ tsp salt
- 150ml/¼ pint/⅔ cup cider vinegar

1 Spear the chillies on a long-handled metal skewer and roast them over the flame of a gas burner until the skins blister and darken. Do not let the flesh burn. Alternatively, dry fry them in a griddle pan until the skins are scorched. Place the roasted chillies in a strong plastic bag and tie the top to keep the steam in. Set aside for 20 minutes.

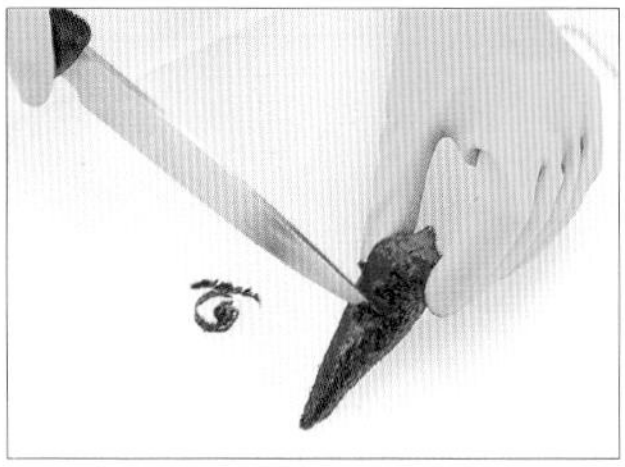

2 Remove the chillies from the bag and peel off the skins. Cut off the stalks, then slit the chillies and scrape out the seeds. Chop the chillies roughly and set them aside.

COOK'S TIP

Fresh *nopales* are sometimes available from specialist fruit and vegetable stores. Like okra, they yield a sticky gum, and are best boiled before being used. Fresh cactus will lose about half its weight during cooking. Look out for canned *nopales* (sometimes sold as *nopalitos*) packed in water or vinegar.

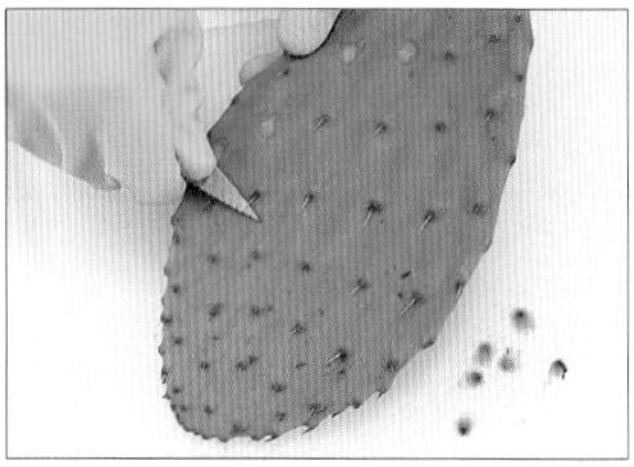

3 Carefully remove the thorns from the nopales. Wearing gloves or holding each cactus paddle in turn with kitchen tongs, cut off the bumps that contain the thorns with a sharp knife.

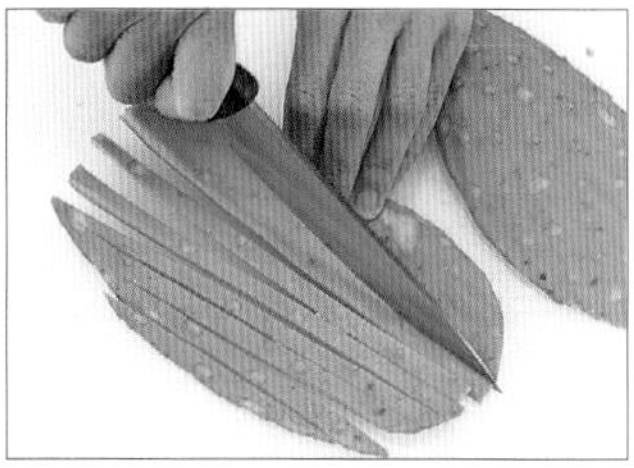

4 Cut off and discard the thick base from each cactus paddle. Rinse the paddles well and cut them into strips then cut the strips into small pieces.

5 Bring a large pan of lightly salted water to the boil. Add the cactus paddle strips, spring onions and garlic. Boil for 10–15 minutes, until the paddle strips are just tender.

6 Drain the mixture in a colander, rinse under cold running water to remove any remaining stickiness, then drain again. Discard the spring onions and garlic.

7 Chop the red onion and the tomatillos finely. Place in a bowl and add the cactus and chillies.

8 Spoon the mixture into a large preserving jar, add the salt, pour in the vinegar and seal. Put the jar in the refrigerator for at least 1 day, turning the jar occasionally to ensure that the *nopales* are marinated. The salsa will keep in the refrigerator for up to 10 days.

Chilli Bean Dip

This creamy and spicy dip made from kidney beans is best served warm with triangles of golden brown toasted pitta bread or a generous helping of crunchy tortilla chips.

SERVES FOUR TO SIX AS AN ACCOMPANIMENT

INGREDIENTS

- 2 garlic cloves
- 1 onion
- 2 fresh green chillies
- 30ml/2 tbsp vegetable oil
- 5–10ml/1–2 tsp hot chilli powder
- 400g/14oz can kidney beans
- 75g/3oz/¾ cup grated mature (sharp) Cheddar cheese
- 1 red chilli, seeded
- salt and freshly ground black pepper
- freshly shaved strips of chilli, to garnish

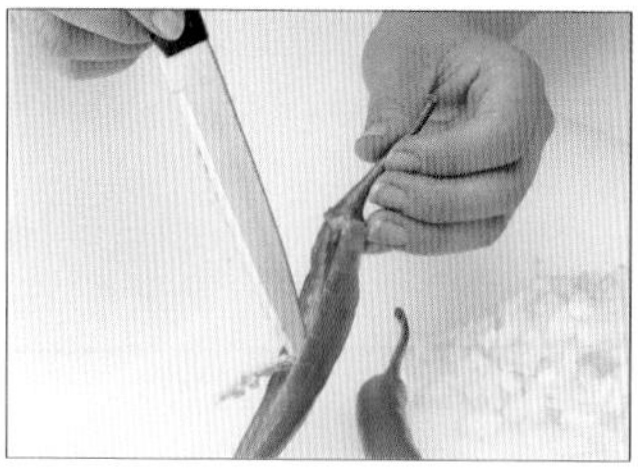

1 Finely chop the garlic and onion. Seed and finely chop the fresh green chillies.

2 Heat the oil in a frying pan and add the garlic, onion, green chillies and chilli powder. Cook gently for about 5 minutes, stirring frequently, until the onions are softened.

3 Drain the can of kidney beans, reserving the can juice. Blend all but 30ml/2 tbsp of the beans to a purée in a food processor or blender.

4 Add the puréed beans to the pan with 30–45ml/2–3 tbsp of the reserved can juice. Heat gently, stirring to mix well.

5 Stir in the whole kidney beans and the grated Cheddar cheese. Cook gently for about 2–3 minutes, stirring until all the cheese melts. Add salt and plenty of freshly ground black pepper to taste.

6 Cut the fresh red chilli into tiny strips. Spoon the dip into four individual serving bowls and sprinkle the chilli strips over the top of each one. Serve warm.

Cook's Tip

For a dip with a coarser texture, do not purée the kidney beans in a food processor or blender; instead, mash them with a potato masher.

Piquant Pineapple Relish

This fruity sweet and sour relish is really excellent when it is served with grilled chicken or bacon slices.

SERVES FOUR TO SIX AS AN ACCOMPANIMENT

INGREDIENTS

- 400g/14oz can crushed pineapple in natural juice
- 30ml/2 tbsp light muscovado (brown) sugar
- 30ml/2 tbsp wine vinegar
- 1 garlic clove
- 4 spring onions (scallions)
- 2 red chillies
- 10 fresh basil leaves
- salt and ground black pepper

1 Drain the crushed pineapple pieces thoroughly and reserve about 60ml/4 tbsp of the juice.

2 Place the juice in a small pan with the muscovado sugar and wine vinegar, then heat gently, stirring, until the sugar dissolves. Remove the pan from the heat and add salt and pepper to taste.

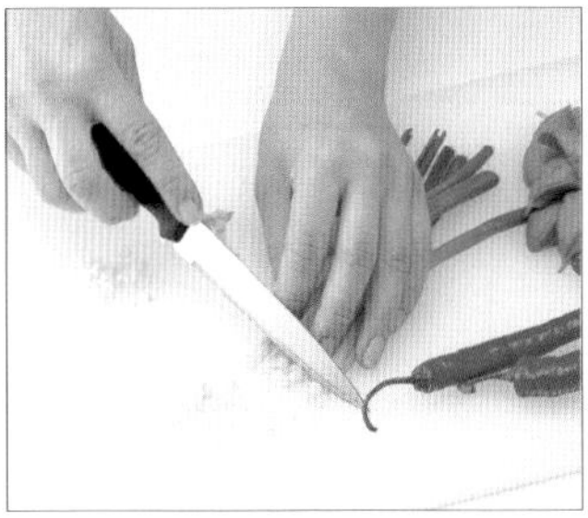

3 Finely chop the garlic and spring onions. Halve the chillies, remove the seeds and finely chop the flesh. Finely shred the basil.

4 Place the pineapple, garlic, spring onions and chillies in a bowl. Mix well and pour in the sauce. Leave to cool for 5 minutes, then stir in the basil.

MANGO SALSA

THIS HAS A FRESH, FRUITY TASTE AND IS PERFECT WITH FISH OR AS A CONTRAST TO RICH, CREAMY DISHES. THE BRIGHT COLOURS MAKE IT AN ATTRACTIVE ADDITION TO ANY TABLE.

SERVES FOUR AS AN ACCOMPANIMENT

INGREDIENTS
- 2 fresh red fresno chillies
- 2 ripe mangoes
- ½ white onion
- bunch of fresh coriander (cilantro)
- grated rind and juice of 1 lime

1 To peel the chillies spear them on a long-handled metal skewer and roast them over the flame of a gas burner until the skins blister and darken. Do not let the flesh burn. Alternatively, dry fry them in a griddle pan until the skins are scorched.

2 Place the roasted chillies in a strong plastic bag and tie the top to keep the steam in. Set aside for 20 minutes.

COOK'S TIP
Mangoes, in season, are readily available nowadays, but are usually sold unripe. Keep in a warm room for 24 hours or until they are just soft to the touch. Do not allow to ripen beyond this point.

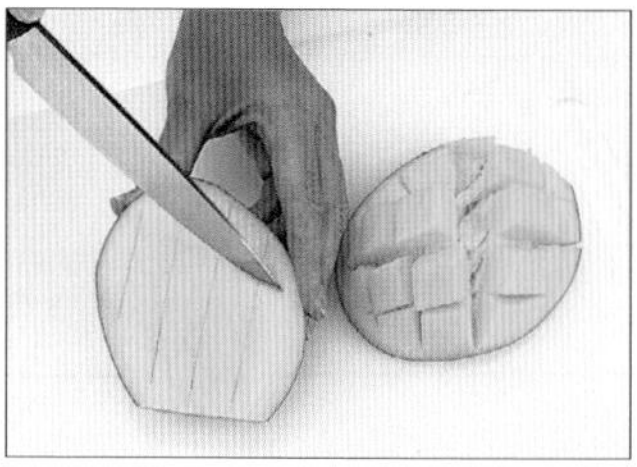

3 Meanwhile, put one of the mangoes on a board and cut off a thick slice close to the flat side of the stone. Turn the mango round and repeat on the other side. Score the flesh on each thick slice with criss-cross lines at 1cm/½in intervals, taking care not to cut through the skin. Repeat with the second mango.

4 Fold the mango halves inside out so that the mango flesh stands proud of the skin, in neat dice. Carefully slice these off the skin and into a bowl. Cut off the flesh adhering to each stone, dice it and add it to the bowl.

5 Remove the roasted chillies from the bag and carefully peel off the skins. Cut off the stalks, then slit the chillies and scrape out the seeds.

6 Chop the white onion and the coriander finely and add them to the diced mango. Chop the chilli flesh finely and add it to the mixture in the bowl, together with the lime rind and juice. Stir well to mix, cover and chill for at least 1 hour before serving. The salsa will keep for 2–3 days in the refrigerator.

ROASTED TOMATO AND CORIANDER SALSA

ROASTING THE TOMATOES GIVES A GREATER DEPTH TO THE FLAVOUR OF THIS SALSA, WHICH ALSO BENEFITS FROM THE WARM, ROUNDED FLAVOUR OF ROASTED CHILLIES.

SERVES SIX AS AN ACCOMPANIMENT

INGREDIENTS
- 500g/1¼lb tomatoes
- 2 fresh serrano chillies
- 1 onion
- juice of 1 lime
- bunch of fresh coriander (cilantro)
- salt

1 Preheat the oven to 200°C/400°F/ Gas 6. Cut the tomatoes into quarters and place them in a roasting tin. Add the chillies. Roast for 45 minutes–1 hour, until the tomatoes and chillies are charred and softened.

2 Place the roasted chillies in a strong plastic bag. Tie the top to keep the steam in and set aside for 20 minutes. Leave the tomatoes to cool slightly, then remove the skins and dice the flesh.

3 Chop the onion finely, then place in a bowl and add the lime juice and the chopped tomatoes.

4 Remove the chillies from the bag and peel off the skins. Cut off the stalks, then slit the chillies and scrape out the seeds with a sharp knife. Chop the chillies roughly and add them to the onion mixture. Mix well.

5 Chop the coriander and add most to the salsa. Add salt, cover and chill for at least 1 hour before serving, sprinkled with the remaining coriander. This salsa will keep in the refrigerator for 1 week.

Chayote Salsa

Chayote – or vegetable pear, as it is sometimes called – is a gourd-like fruit, shaped like a large pear. Several varieties grow in Mexico, the most common being white-fleshed and smooth-skinned, with a taste reminiscent of cucumber. Chayotes should be peeled before being eaten raw or cooked. The seed, which looks rather like a large, flat almond, is edible. The contrast between the crisp chayote, *cool melon and hot habañero sauce makes this a spectacular salsa.*

SERVES SIX AS AN ACCOMPANIMENT

INGREDIENTS

- 1 chayote, about 200g/7oz
- ½ small Galia melon
- 10ml/2 tsp habañero sauce or similar hot chilli sauce
- juice of 1 lime
- 2.5ml/½ tsp salt
- 2.5ml/½ tsp sugar

COOK'S TIP

In some countries, chayotes are called christophenes or choko. They are also used in Chinese cooking, so will be found in Oriental stores.

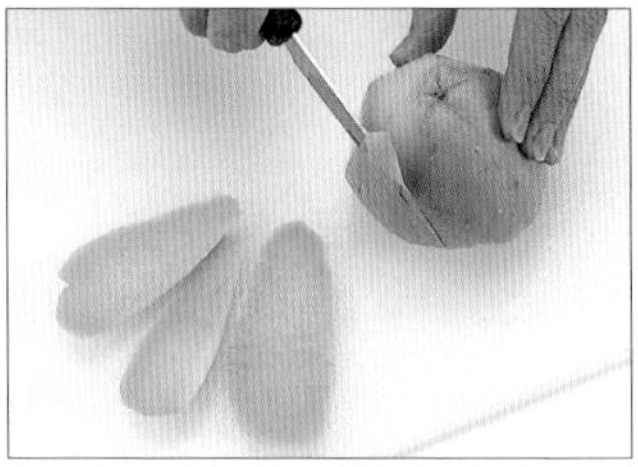

1 Peel the *chayote*, then cut slices of flesh away from the stone. Cut the slices into thin strips. Cut the melon in half, scoop the seeds out, and cut each half into two pieces. Remove the skin and cut the flesh into small cubes. Place in a bowl with the *chayote* strips.

2 Mix the chilli sauce, lime juice, salt and sugar in a bowl or jug. Stir until all the sugar has dissolved. Pour over the melon and *chayote* mixture and mix thoroughly. Chill for at least 1 hour before serving. The salsa will keep for up to 3 days in the refrigerator.

PUMPKIN SEED SAUCE

The ancestors of modern-day Mexicans didn't believe in wasting food, as this traditional recipe proves. It is based upon pumpkin seeds, the flesh having been used for another dish, and has a delicious nutty flavour. It is great served over steamed or boiled nopales (cactus paddles) and is also delicious with cooked chicken or rack of lamb.

SERVES FOUR AS AN ACCOMPANIMENT

INGREDIENTS

- 130g/4½oz raw pumpkin seeds
- 500g/1¼lb tomatoes
- 2 garlic cloves, crushed
- 300ml/½ pint/1¼ cups chicken stock, preferably freshly made
- 15ml/1 tbsp vegetable oil
- 45ml/3 tbsp red chilli sauce
- salt (optional)

1 Preheat the oven to 200°C/400°F/ Gas 6. Heat a heavy-based frying pan until very hot. Add the pumpkin seeds and dry fry them, stirring constantly over the heat. The seeds will start to swell and pop, but they must not be allowed to scorch (see Cook's Tip). When all the seeds have popped remove the pan from the heat.

2 Cut the tomatoes into quarters and place them on a baking tray. Roast in the hot oven for 45 minutes–1 hour, until charred and softened. Allow to cool slightly, then remove the skins using a small sharp knife.

3 Put the pumpkin seeds in a food processor and process until smooth. Add the tomatoes and process for a few minutes, then add the garlic and stock and process for 1 minute more.

COOK'S TIP

When dry frying the pumpkin seeds, don't stop stirring for a moment or they may scorch, which would make the sauce bitter. It is a good idea to stand back a little as some of the hot seeds may fly out of the pan.

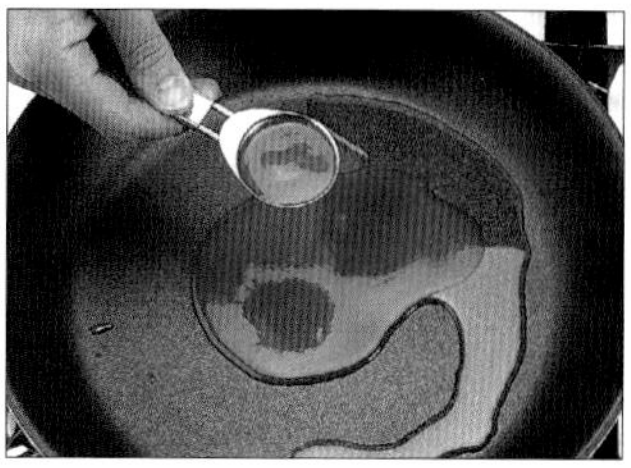

4 Heat the oil in a large frying pan. Add the red chilli sauce and cook, stirring constantly, for 2–3 minutes. Add the pumpkin seed mixture and bring to the boil, stirring all the time.

5 Simmer the sauce for 20 minutes, stirring frequently until the sauce has thickened and reduced by about half. Taste and add salt, if needed. Serve over meat or vegetables or cool and chill. The sauce will keep for up to a week in the refrigerator.

Fiery Citrus Salsa

This unusual salsa makes a fantastic marinade for shellfish, such as grilled or barbecued prawns or shrimp. It is also delicious drizzled over barbecued meat.

SERVES 4

INGREDIENTS
- 1 orange
- 1 green apple
- 2 fresh red chillies
- 1 garlic clove
- 8 fresh mint leaves
- juice of 1 lemon
- salt and freshly ground black pepper

1 Using a sharp knife, remove the peel and pith from the orange and, working over a bowl to catch the juices, cut out the segments. Squeeze any remaining juice into the bowl.

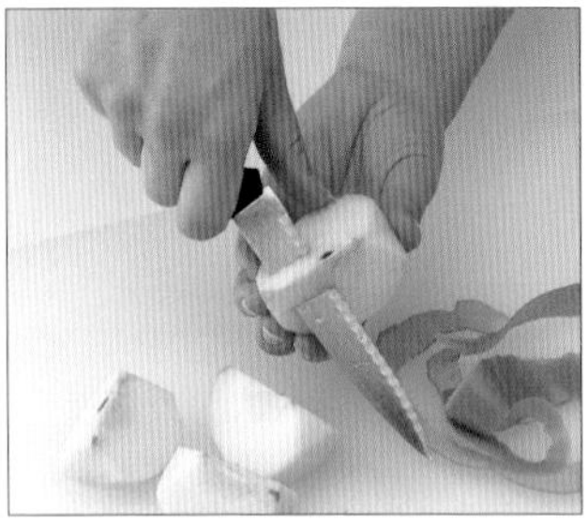

2 Use a sharp kitchen knife to peel the apple and slice it into thin wedges. Make sure that you remove and discard the whole apple core and any tough parts of the apple that may affect the crisp texture of the salsa.

3 Halve the chillies and remove the seeds, then place them in a blender or food processor with the orange segments and juice, apple wedges, garlic and mint.

4 Process until smooth. With the motor running, slowly pour in the lemon juice. Season to taste with salt and freshly ground black pepper and serve immediately.

GRILLED CORN-ON-THE-COB SALSA

THIS IS AN UNUSUAL SALSA AND CONTAINS DELICIOUSLY SWEET VEGETABLES. USE CHERRY TOMATOES FOR AN EXTRA SPECIAL FLAVOUR, AND COMBINE WITH THE RIPEST AND FRESHEST CORN ON THE COB.

SERVES FOUR

INGREDIENTS
- 2 corn on the cob
- 30ml/2 tbsp melted butter
- 4 tomatoes
- 8 spring onions (scallions)
- 1 garlic clove
- 30ml/2 tbsp fresh lemon juice
- 30ml/2 tbsp olive oil
- Tabasco sauce, to taste

1 Remove the husks and silky threads covering the corn on the cob. Brush the cobs with the melted butter and gently cook on the barbecue or grill (broil) for 20–30 minutes, turning occasionally, until tender and tinged brown.

2 To remove the kernels, stand each cob upright on a chopping board and use a large, heavy knife to slice down the length of the cob.

3 Plunge the tomatoes into boiling water for 30 seconds. Remove with a slotted spoon; cool in cold water. Slip off the skins and dice the tomato flesh.

4 Place 6 spring onions on a chopping board and chop finely. Crush and chop the garlic and then mix together with the corn and tomato in a small bowl.

5 Stir the lemon juice and olive oil together, adding Tabasco sauce, salt and pepper to taste.

6 Pour this mixture over the salsa and stir well. Cover the salsa and leave to steep at room temperature for 1–2 hours before serving. Garnish with the remaining spring onions.

COOK'S TIP

Make this salsa in summer when fresh cobs of corn are readily available.

Orange, Tomato and Chive Salsa

Fresh chives and sweet oranges provide a very cheerful combination of flavours. This is an unusual salsa that is a very good accompaniment to salads.

SERVES FOUR AS AN ACCOMPANIMENT

INGREDIENTS
- 2 large, sweet oranges
- 1 beefsteak tomato, or 2 plum tomatoes if not available
- bunch of fresh chives
- 1 garlic clove
- 30ml/2 tbsp extra virgin olive oil or grapeseed oil
- sea salt

1 Slice the base off 1 orange so that it will stand firmly on a chopping board. Using a large sharp knife, remove the peel by slicing from the top to the bottom of the orange. Repeat with the second orange.

2 Working over a bowl, segment each orange in turn. Slice towards the middle of the fruit, and slightly to one side of a segment, and then gently twist the knife to release the orange segment. Repeat. Squeeze any juice from the remaining membrane.

3 Roughly chop the orange segments and add them to the bowl with the collected orange juice. Halve the tomato and use a teaspoon to scoop the seeds into the bowl. With a sharp knife, finely dice the flesh and add to the oranges and juice in the bowl.

4 Hold the bunch of chives neatly together and use a pair of kitchen scissors to snip them into the bowl.

5 Thinly slice the garlic and stir it into the orange mixture. Pour over the olive oil, season with sea salt and stir well to mix. Serve the salsa within 2 hours.

SOUR CREAM DIP

THIS COOLING TOMATO AND PEPPER DIP IS A PERFECT ACCOMPANIMENT TO HOT AND SPICY DISHES. ALTERNATIVELY, SERVE IT AS A SNACK WITH THE FIERIEST TORTILLA CHIPS YOU CAN FIND.

SERVES TWO AS AN ACCOMPANIMENT

INGREDIENTS
- 1 small yellow (bell) pepper
- 2 tomatoes
- 30ml/2 tbsp chopped fresh parsley
- 150ml/¼ pint/⅔ cup sour cream
- grated (shredded) lemon rind, to garnish

VARIATIONS
- Vary the colour combinations by using yellow, orange or red peppers with red or yellow tomatoes. Green pepper with yellow tomatoes looks good with the chopped parsley.
- Use Greek (US strained plain) yogurt or crème fraîche instead of sour cream.
- Use finely diced avocado or cucumber in place of the pepper.

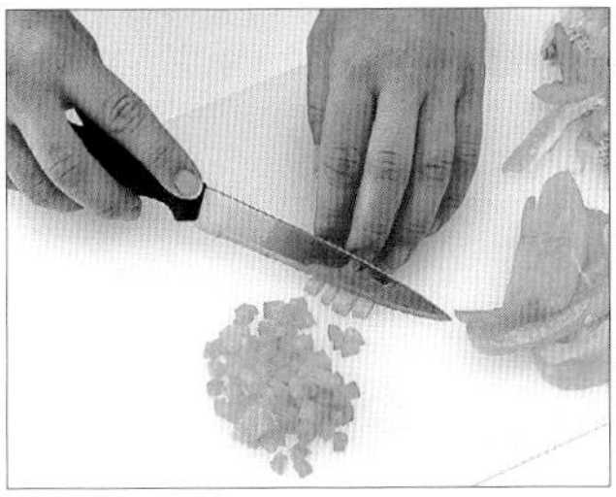

1 Halve the pepper lengthways. Remove the core and seeds, then cut the flesh into tiny dice.

2 Halve the tomatoes, then scoop out and discard the seeds and cut the flesh into tiny dice.

3 Stir the pepper and tomato dice and the chopped parsley into the sour cream and mix well.

4 Spoon the dip into a small bowl and chill. Garnish by sprinkling with grated lemon rind before serving.

CHILLI STRIPS WITH LIME

THIS FRESH RELISH IS IDEAL FOR SERVING WITH STEWS, RICE DISHES OR BEAN DISHES. THE OREGANO ADDS A SWEET NOTE AND THE ABSENCE OF SUGAR OR OIL MAKES THIS A VERY HEALTHY CHOICE.

MAKES ABOUT 60ML/4 TBSP

INGREDIENTS
- 10 fresh green chillies
- ½ white onion
- 4 limes
- 2.5ml/½ tsp dried oregano
- salt

COOK'S TIP
This method of roasting chillies is ideal if you need more than one or two, or if you do not have a gas burner. To roast over a burner, spear the chillies, four or five at a time, on a long-handled metal skewer and hold them over the flame until the skins blister.

1 Roast the chillies in a griddle pan over a moderate heat until the skins are charred and blistered. The flesh should not be allowed to blacken as this might make the salsa bitter. Place the roasted chillies in a strong plastic bag and tie the top to keep the steam in. Set aside for 20 minutes.

2 Meanwhile, slice the onion very thinly and put it in a large bowl. Squeeze the limes and add the juice to the bowl, with any pulp that gathers in the strainer. The lime juice will soften the onion. Stir in the oregano.

3 Remove the chillies from the bag and peel off the skins. If the skins do not come off easily, you may need to griddle them for longer, placing them once again in a the bag to cool. Slit them, scrape out the seeds with a small sharp knife, then cut the chillies into long strips, which are called "rajas".

4 Add the chilli strips to the onion mixture, blend well and season with salt to taste.

5 Cover the bowl and chill for at least 1 day before serving, to allow the flavours to blend. The salsa will keep for up to 2 weeks in a covered bowl in the refrigerator.

Onion Relish

This popular relish, known as Cebollas en Escabeche, *is typical of the Yucatán region of Mexico and is often served with chicken, fish or turkey.*

MAKES ONE SMALL JAR

INGREDIENTS
- 2 fresh red fresno chillies
- 5ml/1 tsp allspice berries
- 2.5ml/½ tsp black peppercorns
- 5ml/1 tsp dried oregano
- 2 white onions
- 2 garlic cloves, peeled
- 100ml/3½fl oz/⅓ cup white wine vinegar
- 200ml/7fl oz/scant cup cider vinegar
- salt

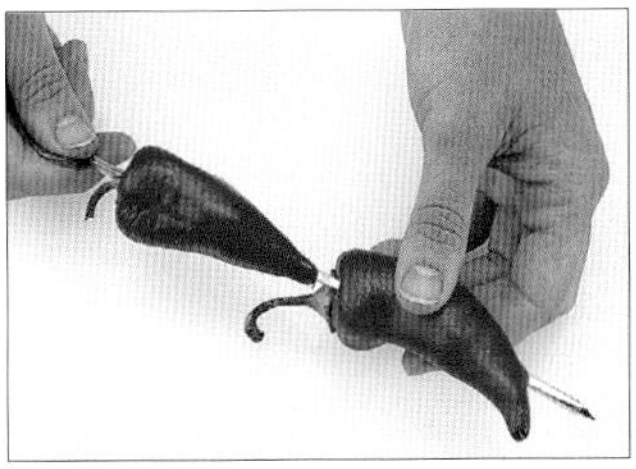

1 Spear the fresno chillies on a long-handled metal skewer and roast them over the flame of a gas burner until the skins blister. Do not let the flesh burn. Alternatively, dry fry them in a griddle pan until the skins are scorched. Place the roasted chillies in a strong plastic bag and tie the top to keep the steam in. Set aside for 20 minutes.

2 Meanwhile, place the allspice, black peppercorns and oregano in a mortar or food processor. Grind slowly by hand with a pestle or process until coarsely ground.

3 Cut the onions in half and slice them thinly. Put them in a bowl. Dry roast the garlic in a heavy-based frying pan until golden, then crush and add to the onions in the bowl.

4 Remove the chillies from the bag and peel off the skins. Slit the chillies, scrape out the seeds with a small sharp knife, then chop them.

COOK'S TIP
White onions have a pungent flavour and are good in this salsa; Spanish onions can also be used. Shallots also make an exellent pickle.

5 Add the ground spices to the onion mixture, followed by the chillies. Stir in both vinegars. Add salt to taste and mix thoroughly. Cover the bowl and chill for at least 1 day before use.

Habañero Salsa

This is a very fiery salsa with an intense heat level. A dab on the plate alongside a meat or fish dish adds a fresh, clean taste, but this is not for the faint-hearted. Habañero chillies, also called Scotch bonnets, are very hot. Lantern-shaped, they range in colour from yellow to a deep orange red. Costeno amarillo chillies are yellow when fresh and have a sharp citrus flavour.

SERVE SPARINGLY

INGREDIENTS
- 5 dried roasted habañero chillies
- 4 dried costeno amarillo chillies
- 3 spring onions, finely chopped
- juice of ½ large grapefruit or 1 Seville orange
- grated rind and juice of 1 lime
- bunch of fresh coriander (cilantro)
- salt

1 Soak the habañero and costeno amarillo chillies in hot water for about 10 minutes until softened. Drain, reserving the soaking water.

2 Wear rubber gloves to handle the habañeros. Remove the stalks from all chillies, then slit them and scrape out the seeds with a small sharp knife. Chop the chillies roughly.

3 Put the chillies in a food processor and add a little of the soaking liquid. Purée to a fine paste. Do not lean over the processor – the fumes may burn your face. Remove the lid and scrape the mixture into a bowl.

4 Put the chopped spring onions in another bowl and add the fruit juice, with the lime rind and juice. Roughly chop the coriander.

5 Carefully add the coriander to the chilli mixture and mix very thoroughly. Add salt to taste. Cover and chill for at least 1 day before use. Serve the salsa very sparingly.

Adobo Seasoning

Adobo means vinegar sauce, and this adobo is a chilli vinegar paste used for marinating pork chops or steaks. Adobos are widely used in the cooking of the Yucatán in Mexico.

MAKES ENOUGH TO MARINATE SIX CHOPS OR STEAKS

INGREDIENTS
- 1 small head of garlic
- 5 ancho chillies
- 2 pasilla chillies
- 15ml/1 tbsp dried oregano
- 5ml/1 tsp cumin seeds
- 6 cloves
- 5ml/1 tsp coriander seeds
- 10cm/4in piece of cinnamon stick
- 10ml/2 tsp salt
- 120ml/4fl oz/½ cup white wine vinegar

1 Preheat the oven to 180°C/350°F/ Gas 4. Cut a thin slice off the top of the head of garlic, so that the inside of each clove is exposed. Wrap the head of garlic in foil. Roast for 45–60 minutes or until the garlic is soft.

2 Meanwhile, slit the chillies and scrape out the seeds. Put the chillies in a blender or a mortar. Add the oregano, cumin seeds, cloves, coriander seeds, cinnamon stick and salt. Process or grind with a pestle to a fine powder.

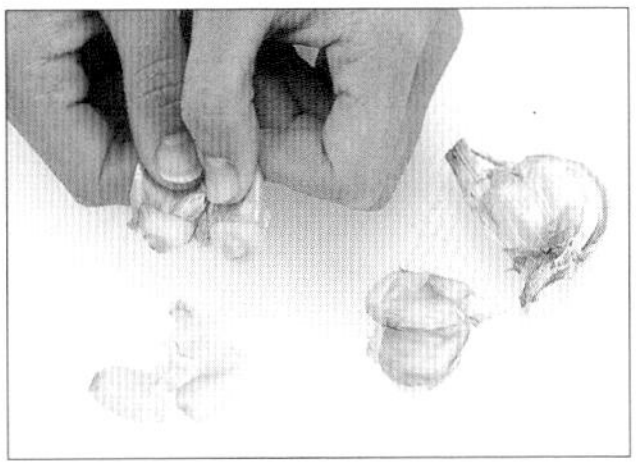

3 Remove the garlic from the oven. When it is cool enough to handle, squeeze the garlic pulp out of each clove and grind into the spice mix.

4 Add the wine vinegar to the spice and garlic mixture and process or grind until a smooth paste forms. Spoon into a bowl and leave to stand for 1 hour, to allow the flavours to blend. Spread over pork chops or steaks as a marinade, before grilling (broiling) or barbecuing.

Red Rub

This "rub" or dry paste is frequently used in the Yucatán region of Mexico for seasoning meat. The mixture is rubbed on to the surface of the meat, which is then wrapped in banana leaves and cooked slowly in a pib, a heated stone-lined hole in the ground. Meat cooked this way is referred to as pibil-style. Try using the rub on pork chops or chicken pieces before oven baking or barbecuing.

MAKES ENOUGH FOR ONE JOINT OF MEAT OR FOUR CHICKEN BREASTS

INGREDIENTS
- 10ml/2 tsp achiote (annatto) seeds
- 5ml/1 tsp black peppercorns
- 5ml/1 tsp allspice berries
- 5ml/1 tsp dried oregano
- 2.5ml/½ tsp ground cumin
- 5ml/1 tsp freshly squeezed lime juice
- 1 small Seville orange or ½ grapefruit

1 Put the achiote (annatto) seeds in a mortar and grind them with a pestle to a fine powder. Alternatively, use a food processor. Add the peppercorns, grind again, then repeat the process with the allspice berries. Mix in the oregano and ground cumin.

2 Add the lime juice to the spice mixture. Squeeze the orange or grapefruit and add the juice to the spice mixture a teaspoonful at a time until a thick paste is produced. Don't be tempted to substitute a sweet orange if Seville oranges are out of season; the spice mixture must be tart.

3 Allow the paste to stand for at least 30 minutes so the spices absorb the juice. The correct consistency for the paste is slightly dry and crumbly. When ready to use, rub the paste on to the surface of the meat, then leave to marinate for at least 1 hour before cooking, preferably overnight. The rub will keep for up to 1 week in a covered bowl in the refrigerator, after which time some of the flavour will be lost.

COOK'S TIP

Achiote is the rusty red seed of the annatto, a tropical American tree. It is used in Mexico for flavouring and colouring cheeses, butter and smoked fish. It is also used in Indian cooking and can be purchased from ethnic food stores.

Red Salsa

Use this as a condiment with fish or meat dishes, or as a dipping sauce for baked potato wedges. It is often added to rice dishes.

MAKES ABOUT 250ML/8FL OZ/1 CUP

INGREDIENTS
- 3 large tomatoes
- 15ml/1 tbsp olive oil
- 3 ancho chillies
- 2 pasilla chillies
- 2 garlic cloves, peeled and left whole
- 2 spring onions (scallions)
- 10ml/2 tsp soft dark brown sugar
- 2.5ml/½ tsp paprika
- juice of 1 lime
- 2.5ml/½ tsp dried oregano
- salt

1 Preheat the oven to 200°C/400°F/ Gas 6. Quarter the tomatoes and place in a roasting tin. Drizzle over the oil. Roast for about 40 minutes until slightly charred, then remove the skin.

2 Soak the chillies in hot water for about 10 minutes. Drain, remove the stalks, slit and then scrape out the seeds. Chop finely. Dry roast the garlic in a heavy-based pan until golden.

3 Finely chop most of the spring onions, retaining the top part of one for garnishing. Place the chopped onion in a bowl with the sugar, paprika, lime juice and oregano. Slice the remaining spring onion diagonally and set aside for the garnish.

4 Put the skinned tomatoes and chopped chillies in a food processor or blender and add the garlic cloves. Process until smooth.

5 Add the sugar, paprika, lime juice, spring onions and oregano to the blender. Process for a few seconds, then taste and add salt as required. Spoon into a saucepan and warm through before serving, or place in a bowl, cover and chill until required. Garnish with the sliced spring onion. The salsa will keep, covered, for up to 1 week in the refrigerator.

Breads and Cakes

European-style breads and cakes are available in most parts of the Caribbean and Latin America, but the recipes have evolved to reflect regional traditions, with corn meal often being used instead of wheat flour. The breads make good accompaniments while the cakes are often eaten for breakfast or as snacks.

Corn Tortillas

To prepare these delicious Mexican specialities, make sure you have ready a tortilla press and a small plastic bag, cut open and halved crossways.

MAKES ABOUT 14

INGREDIENTS
275g/10oz/2½ cups *masa harina*
250–350ml/8–12fl oz/
1–1½ cups water

COOK'S TIP
Tortillas are very easy to make but it is important to get the dough texture right. If it is too dry and crumbly, add a little water; if it is too wet, add more *masa harina*. If you misjudge the pressure needed for flattening the ball of dough to a neat circle on the tortilla press, just scrap it off, re-roll it and try again.

1 Put the *masa harina* into a bowl and stir in 250ml/8fl oz/1 cup of the water, mixing it to a soft dough that just holds together. If it is too dry, add a little more water. Cover the bowl with a cloth and set aside for 15 minutes.

2 Preheat the oven to 150°C/300°F/Gas 2. Open the tortilla press and line both sides with the prepared plastic sheets. Preheat a griddle until hot.

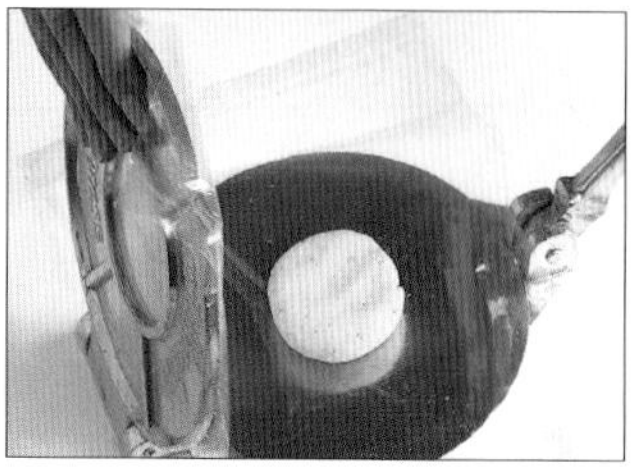

3 Knead the dough lightly and shape into 14 balls. Put a ball on the press and bring the top down firmly to flatten the dough out into a round.

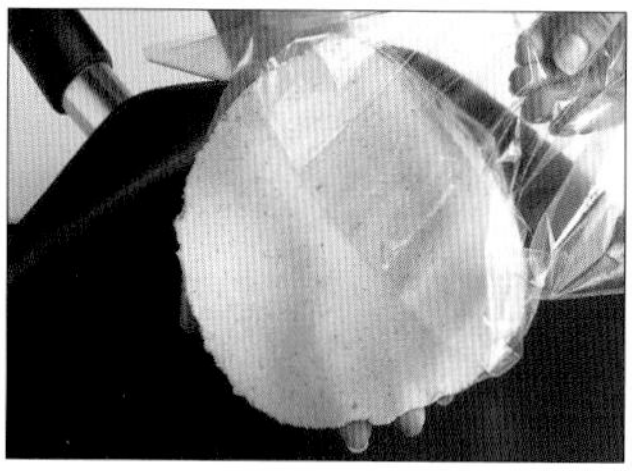

4 Open the press. Peel off the top layer of plastic and, using the bottom layer, lift the tortilla out of the press. Peel off the bottom plastic and flip the tortilla on to the hot griddle.

5 Cook for 1 minute and turn over and cook for a minute more. Wrap in foil and keep warm. Repeat for the other tortillas.

FLOUR TORTILLAS

THESE ARE MORE COMMON THAN CORN TORTILLAS IN THE NORTH OF MEXICO, FROM SONORA TO CHIHUAHUA, WHERE WHEAT IS GROWN. FOR THE BEST RESULTS, USE A GOOD QUALITY PLAIN FLOUR.

MAKES ABOUT 14

INGREDIENTS
- 225g/8oz/2 cups plain (all-purpose) flour
- 5ml/1 tsp salt
- 15ml/1 tbsp lard or vegetable fat
- 120ml/4fl oz/½ cup water

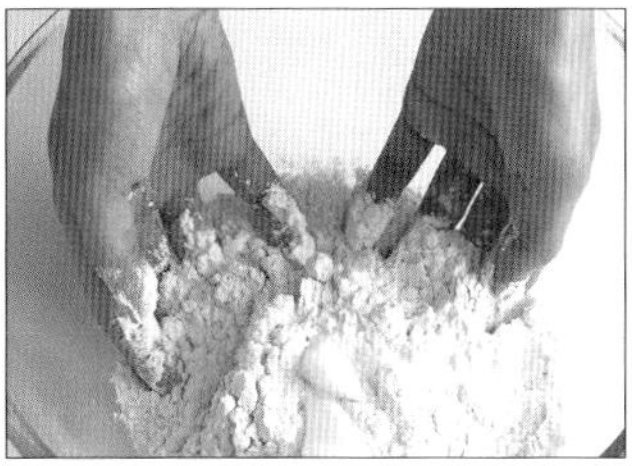

1 Sift the flour and salt into a large mixing bowl. Gradually rub in the lard or vegetable fat using your fingertips until the mixture resembles coarse breadcrumbs.

2 Gradually add the water and mix to a soft dough. Knead lightly, form into a ball, cover with a cloth and leave to rest for 15 minutes.

3 Carefully divide the dough into about 14 portions and form these portions into small balls. One by one, roll out each ball of dough on a lightly floured wooden board to a round measuring about 15cm/6in. Trim the rounds if necessary.

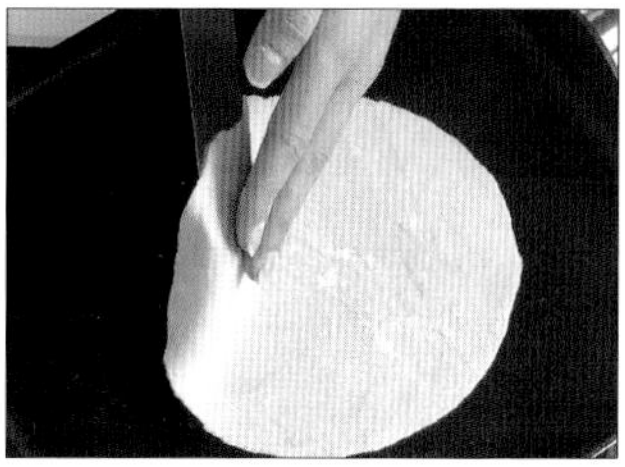

4 Heat an ungreased griddle or frying pan over a moderate heat. Cook the tortillas for about 1½–2 minutes on each side. Turn over with a palette knife or metal spatula when the bottom begins to brown. Wrap in foil and keep warm in the oven until ready to serve.

COOK'S TIP

Make flour tortillas whenever *masa harina* is difficult to find. To keep them soft and pliable, make sure they are kept warm until ready to serve, and eat as soon as possible.

Dhal Puri

Known as rotis *in their native India, these tasty flat breads can also be made with white flour. A traditional Caribbean favourite,* dhal puri *are delicious with meat, fish or vegetable dishes and are ideal for mopping up leftover sauces.*

MAKES ABOUT 15

INGREDIENTS
- 450g/1lb/4 cups self-raising (self-rising) flour
- 115g/4oz/1 cup wholemeal (whole-wheat) flour
- 350ml/12fl oz/1½ cups cold water
- 30ml/2 tbsp oil, plus extra for frying
- salt, to taste

For the filling
- 350g/12oz/1½ cups yellow split peas
- 15ml/1 tbsp ground cumin
- 2 garlic cloves, crushed

1 Sift the dry ingredients into a bowl, then tip in the grain remaining in the sieve. Add the water a little at a time, and knead gently until a soft dough forms. Continue kneading until supple, but do not over-work the dough.

2 Add the oil to the dough and continue to knead it until it is completely smooth. Put the dough in a plastic bag or wrap in clear film (plastic wrap). Place in a cool room or in the refrigerator and leave to rest for at least 30 minutes, or overnight if possible.

3 To make the filling, put the split peas in a large pan, pour over water to cover and cook for about 10–15 minutes, until half cooked – they should be tender on the outside, but still firm in the middle. Allow the water to evaporate during cooking, until the pan is almost dry, but add a little extra water to prevent burning, if necessary.

4 Spread out the peas on a tray. When cool, grind to a paste, using a mortar and pestle or food processor. Mix with the cumin and garlic.

5 Divide the dough into about 15 balls, Slightly flatten each ball, put about 15ml/1 tbsp of the split pea mixture into the centre and fold over the edges.

6 Dust a rolling pin and a board with flour and roll out the dhal puri, taking care not to overstretch the dough, until they are about 18cm/7in in diameter.

7 Heat a little oil in a frying pan. Cook the dhal puris for about 3 minutes on each side until light brown. Serve as soon as the last one is cooked.

FRIED DUMPLINS

IN THE CARIBBEAN AND GUYANA THESE FRIED DUMPLINS ARE SIMPLY CALLED "BAKES". THEY ARE USUALLY SERVED WITH SALT FISH OR FRIED FISH, BUT CAN BE EATEN QUITE SIMPLY WITH BUTTER AND JAM OR CHEESE, WHICH CHILDREN ESPECIALLY LOVE.

MAKES ABOUT TEN

INGREDIENTS
- 450g/1lb/4 cups self-raising (self-rising) flour
- 10ml/2 tsp sugar
- 2.5ml/½ tsp salt
- 300ml/½ pint/1¼ cups milk
- oil, for frying

COOK'S TIP
Mix and knead the dough gently to avoid overworking it and making it tough. A quite light touch is all that is needed to make the dough smooth.

1 Sift the flour, sugar and salt into a large bowl, add the milk and mix and knead until a smooth dough forms.

2 Divide the dough into ten balls, kneading each ball with floured hands. Press the balls gently to flatten them into 7.5cm/3in rounds.

3 Heat a little oil in a non-stick frying pan over medium heat. Place half the dumplins in the pan, reduce the heat to low and fry for about 15 minutes, until they are golden brown, turning once.

4 Stand the dumplins on their sides for a few minutes to brown the edges, before removing them from the pan and draining thoroughly on kitchen paper. Serve immediately, while still warm.

CORN GRIDDLE CAKES

KNOWN AS AREPAS, THESE ARE A STAPLE BREAD IN SEVERAL LATIN AMERICAN COUNTRIES, PARTICULARLY COLOMBIA AND VENEZUELA. EAT THEM FILLED WITH SOFT WHITE CHEESE, AS HERE, OR PLAIN AS AN ACCOMPANIMENT. WITH THEIR CRISP CRUST AND CHEWY INTERIOR, AREPAS CAN BECOME STALE VERY QUICKLY, SO ARE BEST EATEN PIPING HOT.

MAKES 15

INGREDIENTS
- 200g/7oz/1¾ cups *masarepa* (or *masa harina*)
- 2.5ml/½ tsp salt
- 300ml/½ pint/1¼ cups water
- 15ml/1 tbsp oil
- 200g/7oz fresh white cheese, such as queso fresco or mozzarella, roughly chopped

1 Combine the *masarepa* or *masa harina* and salt in a bowl. Gradually stir in the water to make a soft dough, then set aside for about 20 minutes.

2 Divide the dough into 15 equal-sized balls, then, using your fingers, flatten each ball into a circle, approximately 1cm/½in thick.

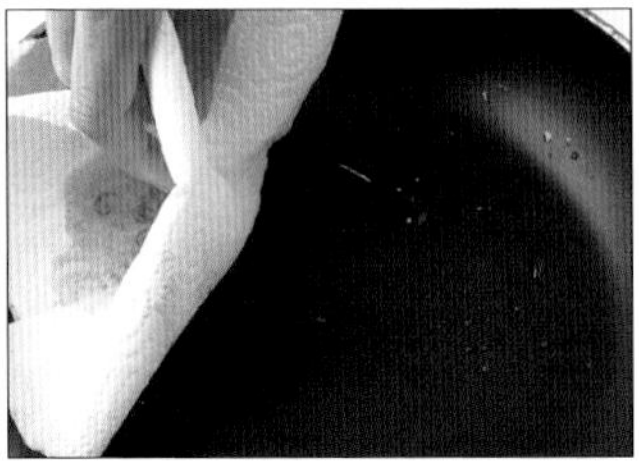

3 Heat 5ml/1 tsp of the oil in a large, heavy frying pan over a medium heat. Using a piece of kitchen paper, gently wipe the surface of the frying pan, leaving it just lightly greased.

4 Place five of the *arepas* in the frying pan. Cook for about 4 minutes, then flip over and cook for a further 4 minutes. The *arepas* should be lightly blistered on both sides.

5 Open the *arepas* and fill each with a few small pieces of fresh white cheese. Return to the pan to cook until the cheese begins to melt. Remove from the heat and keep warm.

6 Cook the remaining ten *arepas* in the same way, oiling the pan and wiping with kitchen paper between batches, to ensure it is always lightly greased. Serve the *arepas* while still warm so that the melted cheese is soft and runny.

COOK'S TIP

Masarepa is a flour made with the white corn grown in the Andes. Look for it in Latin American food stores. If not available, replace it with *masa harina*, the flour used to make tamales. The result will not be quite as delicate, but the *arepas* will be equally delicious.

VARIATION

Instead of cheese, try a delicious beef filling. Simply fry some minced (ground) beef in oil with ½ chopped onion, 1 small red chilli, finely chopped, 1 crushed garlic clove, ground black pepper and fresh thyme. When thoroughly cooked, stuff the mixture inside the *arepas*.

Paraguayan Corn Bread

This moist corn meal bread is so rich and flavoursome that it can easily be eaten on its own. It tastes best when eaten warm, especially when covered with melting butter.

MAKES ONE LOAF

INGREDIENTS
- 75g/3oz/6 tbsp butter
- 1 large onion, finely chopped
- 400ml/14fl oz/1⅔ cups full-fat (whole) milk
- 225g/8oz/2 cups corn meal
- 175g/6oz mozzarella cheese, roughly grated
- 2 large eggs, separated
- salt and ground black pepper

1 Preheat the oven to 200°C/400°F/Gas 6. Using 15g/½oz/1 tbsp of the butter, grease a loaf tin (pan). Melt a further 25g/1oz/2 tbsp of the butter in a large pan over a low heat and fry the onions for 5 minutes until softened.

COOK'S TIP
If you can't get hold of corn meal, use instant polenta instead.

2 Pour in the milk and stir until heated, without allowing it to boil. Still stirring, add the corn meal in a steady stream. Continue to stir until the mixture is smooth.

3 Remove from the heat and stir in the cheese and remaining butter. When both have melted, season with salt and ground pepper.

4 Whisk the egg whites in a bowl until they hold their shape. Stir the egg yolks into the corn meal mixture, then gently fold in the egg whites.

5 Tip the mixture into the prepared loaf tin. Bake for 35–40 minutes, or until a skewer comes out clean when inserted in the bread. Turn out onto a wire rack to cool a little. Cut into slices and serve.

MEXICAN "BREAD OF THE DEAD"

A CELEBRATORY LOAF MADE FOR ALL SOULS' DAY, WHEN MEXICANS PAY THEIR RESPECTS TO THE SOULS OF THE DEAD, IT IS TRADITIONALLY DECORATED WITH A DOUGH SKULL, BONES AND TEARS.

MAKES ONE LARGE LOAF

INGREDIENTS

- 3 star anise
- 90ml/6 tbsp cold water
- 675g/1½ lb/6 cups unbleached white bread flour, plus extra for sprinkling
- 5ml/1 tsp salt
- 115g/4oz/½ cup caster (superfine) sugar
- 25g/1oz fresh yeast
- 175ml/6fl oz/¾ cup lukewarm water
- 3 eggs
- 60ml/4 tbsp orange-flavoured liqueur
- 115g/4oz/½ cup butter, melted
- grated rind of 1 orange
- icing (confectioners') sugar, for dusting

1 Grease a 26cm/10½ in fluted round cake tin (pan). Place the star anise in a small pan and add the cold water. Bring to the boil and boil for 3–4 minutes, or until the liquid has reduced to 45ml/3 tbsp. Discard the star anise and leave the liquid to cool.

2 Sift the flour and salt together into a large bowl. Stir in the sugar and make a well in the centre.

3 In a jug (pitcher), dissolve the yeast in the lukewarm water. Pour into the centre of the flour and mix in, using your fingers, until a smooth, thick batter forms. Sprinkle over a little more flour, cover with clear film (plastic wrap) and leave the batter in a warm place for 30 minutes, or until the mixture starts to bubble.

4 Beat the eggs, the reserved liquid flavoured with star anise, orange liqueur and melted butter together. Gradually incorporate into the flour mixture to form a smooth dough.

5 Turn out the dough on to a lightly floured surface and gently knead in the orange rind. Knead for 5–6 minutes until smooth and elastic.

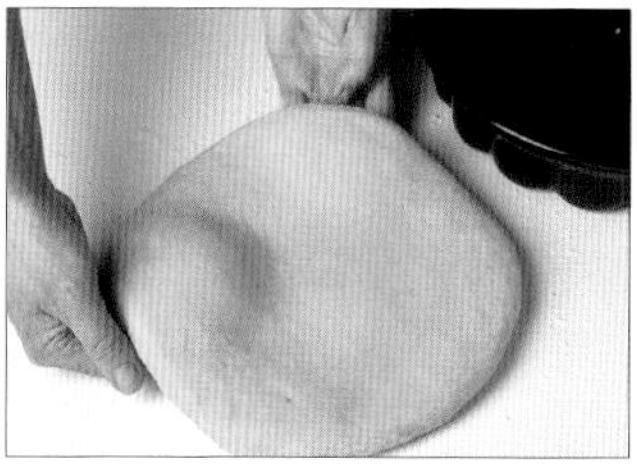

6 Shape the dough into a 26cm/10½ in round and place in the prepared tin. Cover with lightly oiled clear film and leave to rise, in a warm place, for 2–3 hours, or until doubled in bulk.

7 Meanwhile, preheat the oven to 190°C/375°F/Gas 5. Bake the loaf for 45–50 minutes, or until golden. Turn out on to a wire rack to cool. Dust with icing sugar to serve.

VARIATION

Top the baked bread with orange-flavoured icing. Blend 60g/2oz/½ cup icing sugar and 15–30ml/1–2 tbsp orange liqueur. Pour the icing over the bread and let it dribble down the sides.

MANGO TEA BREAD

THIS FRUITY TEA BREAD WITH A COCONUT TOPPING MAKES A DELICIOUS TEATIME TREAT.

MAKES TWO LOAVES

INGREDIENTS

- 285g/10oz/2½ cups plain (all-purpose) flour
- 10ml/2 tsp bicarbonate of soda (baking soda)
- 10ml/2 tsp ground cinnamon
- 2.5ml/½ tsp salt
- 115g/4oz/½ cup margarine, at room temperature
- 3 eggs, at room temperature
- 300g/10½oz/1½ cups sugar
- 125ml/4fl oz vegetable oil
- 1 large ripe mango, peeled and chopped
- 90g/3¼oz desiccated (dry unsweetened shredded) coconut
- 70g/2½oz raisins

1 Preheat the oven to 350°F/180°C/Gas 4. Line the bottom and sides of two 9 x 5in (23 x 13cm) loaf tins (pans) with baking parchment and grease.

2 Sift together the flour, bicarbonate of soda, cinnamon and salt. Set aside.

3 With an electric mixer, cream the margarine until soft. Beat in the eggs and sugar until light and fluffy. Beat in the oil. Fold the dry ingredients into the creamed ingredients in three batches.

4 Fold in the mangoes, two-thirds of the coconut and the raisins.

5 Spoon the batter into the tins.

6 Sprinkle over the remaining coconut. Bake until a skewer inserted in the centre comes out clean, about 50–60 minutes. Let stand for 10 minutes before turning out on to a rack to cool completely.

COURGETTE TEA BREAD

SERVE THIS UNUSUAL SAVOURY TEABREAD SLICED, WITH PATS OF BUTTER FOR SPREADING.

MAKES ONE LOAF

INGREDIENTS

- 50g/2oz/1¼ cups butter
- 3 eggs
- 250ml/8fl oz vegetable oil
- 300g/10½oz/1½ cups sugar
- 2 medium unpeeled courgettes (zucchini), grated
- 285g/10oz/2½ cups plain (all-purpose) flour
- 10ml/2 tsp bicarbonate of soda (baking soda)
- 5ml/1tsp baking powder
- 5ml/1tsp salt
- 5ml/1tsp ground cinnamon
- 5ml/1tsp grated nutmeg
- 1.25ml/¼ tsp ground cloves
- 115g/4oz/1 cup walnuts, chopped

1 Preheat the oven to 350°F/180°C/Gas 4. Line the bottom and sides of a 9 x 5in (23 x 13cm) loaf tin (pan) with baking parchment and grease.

2 In a small pan, melt the butter over low heat. Set aside.

3 With an electric mixer, beat the eggs and oil together until thick. Beat in the sugar. Stir in the melted butter and courgettes. Set aside.

4 Sift the dry ingredients and fold in the courgettes and walnuts. Pour into the tin and bake for 60–70 minutes. Let stand 10 minutes before turning out.

Buñuelos

These lovely little puffs look like miniature doughnuts and taste so good it is hard not to over-indulge. Make them for brunch, or simply serve them with a cup of Cafe con Leche or Cafe de Olla.

MAKES 12

INGREDIENTS

- 225g/8oz/2 cups plain (all-purpose) flour
- pinch of salt
- 5ml/1 tsp baking powder
- 2.5ml/½ tsp ground anise
- 115g/4oz/½ cup caster (superfine) sugar
- 1 large (US extra large) egg
- 120ml/4fl oz/½ cup milk
- 50g/2oz/¼ cup butter
- oil, for deep frying
- 10ml/2 tsp ground cinnamon
- cinnamon sticks, to decorate

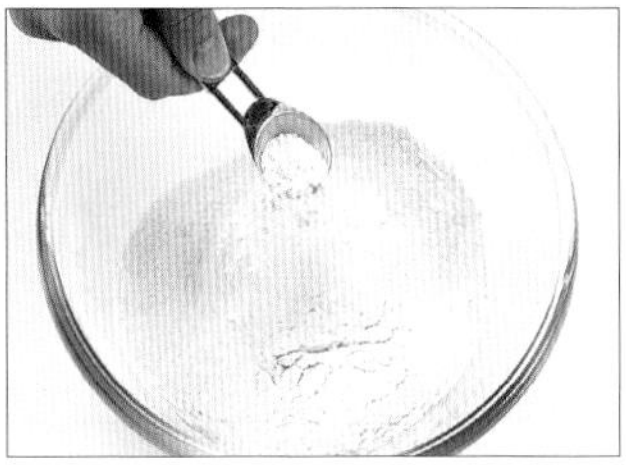

1 Sift the flour, salt, baking powder and ground anise into a mixing bowl. Add 30ml/2 tbsp of the caster sugar.

2 Place the egg and milk in a small jug and whisk well with a fork. Melt the butter in a small pan.

3 Pour the egg mixture and milk gradually into the flour, stirring all the time, until well blended, then add the melted butter. Mix first with a wooden spoon and then with your hands to make a soft dough.

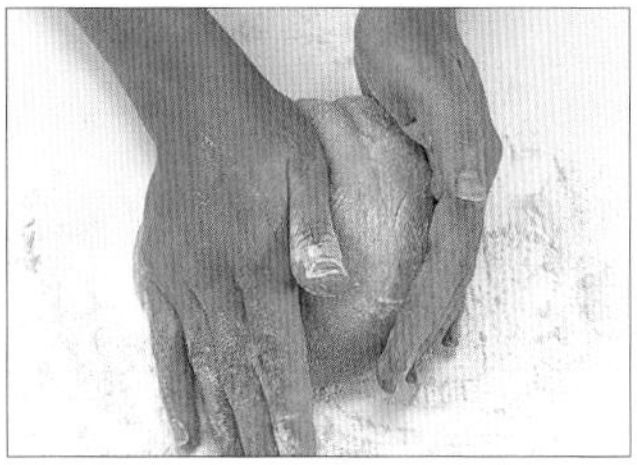

4 Lightly flour a work surface, tip the dough on to it and knead for about 10 minutes, until smooth.

5 Divide the dough into 12 pieces and roll into balls. Slightly flatten each ball with your hand and then make a hole in the centre with the floured handle of a wooden spoon.

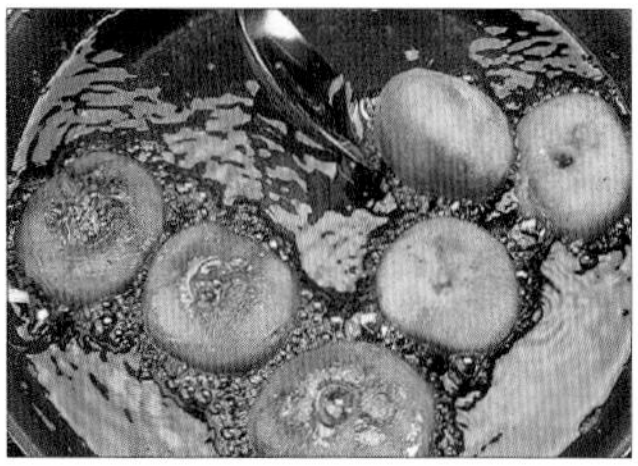

6 Heat the oil for deep frying to a temperature of 190°C/375°F, or until a cube of dried bread, added to the oil, floats and then turns a golden colour in 30–60 seconds. Fry the *buñuelos* in small batches until they are puffy and golden brown, turning them once or twice during cooking. As soon as they are golden, lift them out of the oil using a slotted spoon and lie them on a double layer of kitchen paper to drain.

7 Mix the remaining caster sugar with the ground cinnamon in a small bowl. Add the *buñuelos*, one at a time, while they are still warm, toss them in the mixture until they are lightly coated and either serve at once or leave to cool. Decorate with cinnamon sticks.

COOK'S TIP

Buñuelos are sometimes served with syrup for dunking, although they are perfectly delicious without. To make the syrup, mix 175g/6oz/¾ cup soft dark brown sugar and 450ml/¾ pint/ scant 2 cups water in a small pan. Add a cinnamon stick and heat, stirring until the sugar has dissolved. Bring to the boil, then lower the heat and simmer for 15 minutes without stirring. Cool slightly before serving with the *buñuelos*.

GARBANZO CAKE

THIS IS A MOIST CAKE, WITH A TEXTURE LIKE THAT OF CHRISTMAS PUDDING. IT IS FLAVOURED WITH ORANGE AND CINNAMON AND TASTES WONDERFUL IN THIN SLICES, WITH FRESH MANGO OR PINEAPPLE AND A SPOONFUL OF NATURAL YOGURT.

SERVES SIX

INGREDIENTS

- 2 x 275g/10oz cans chickpeas, drained
- 4 eggs, beaten
- 225g/8oz/1 cup caster (superfine) sugar
- 5ml/1 tsp baking powder
- 10ml/2 tsp ground cinnamon
- grated rind and juice of 1 orange
- cinnamon sugar (see Cook's Tip), for sprinkling

COOK'S TIP

To make cinnamon sugar, mix 50g/2oz/¼ cup caster sugar with 5ml/1 tsp ground cinnamon.

1 Preheat the oven to 180°C/350°F/Gas 4. Tip the chickpeas into a colander, drain them thoroughly, then rub them between the palms of your hands to loosen and remove the skins. Rinse any bits of skin away and put the chickpeas in a food processor and process until smooth.

2 Spoon the purée into a bowl and gently stir in the eggs, sugar, baking powder, cinnamon, orange rind and orange juice. Grease and line a 450g/1lb loaf tin (pan).

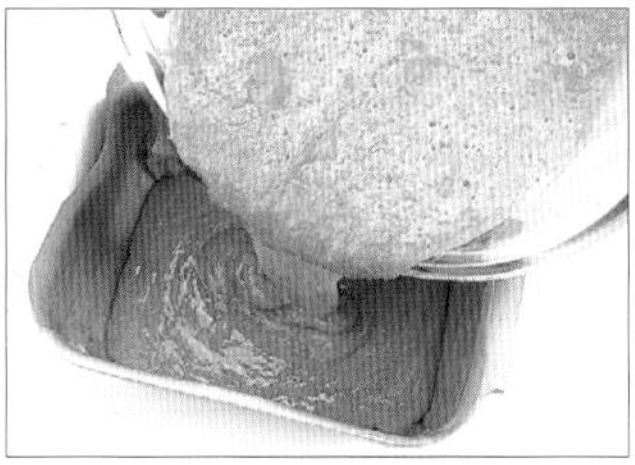

3 Pour the cake mixture into the loaf tin, level the surface and bake for about 1½ hours or until a skewer inserted into the centre comes out clean.

4 Remove the cake from the oven and leave to stand, in the tin, for about 10 minutes. Remove from the tin, place on a wire rack and sprinkle with the cinnamon sugar. Leave to cool completely before serving. Try serving this with sliced fresh pineapple.

Pecan Cake

This cake is an example of the French influence on Mexican cooking. It is traditionally served with cajeta *– sweetened boiled milk – but whipped cream or crème fraîche can be used instead. Try serving the cake with a few redcurrants for a splash of colour.*

SERVES EIGHT TO TEN

INGREDIENTS

- 115g/4oz/1 cup pecan nuts
- 115g/4oz/½ cup butter, softened
- 115g/4oz/½ cup soft light brown sugar
- 5ml/1 tsp vanilla essence (extract)
- 4 large eggs, separated
- 75g/3oz/¾ cup plain (all-purpose) flour
- pinch of salt
- 12 whole pecan nuts, to decorate
- *cajeta*, whipped cream or crème fraîche, to serve

For drizzling

- 50g/2oz/¼ cup butter
- 120ml/4fl oz/scant ½ cup clear honey

1 Preheat the oven to 180°C/350°F/Gas 4. Grease a 20cm/8in round springform cake tin (pan). Toast the pecan nuts in a dry frying pan for 5 minutes, shaking frequently. Grind in a blender or food processor. Place in a bowl.

2 Cream the butter with the sugar in a mixing bowl, then beat in the vanilla essence and egg yolks.

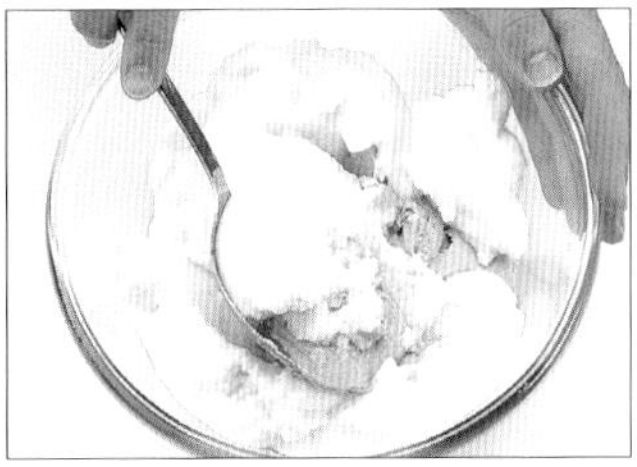

3 Add the flour to the ground nuts and mix well. Whisk the egg whites with the salt in a grease-free bowl until soft peaks form. Fold the whites into the butter mixture, then gently fold in the flour and nut mixture. Spoon the mixture into the prepared cake tin and bake for 30 minutes or until a skewer inserted in the centre comes out clean.

4 Cool the cake in the tin for 5 minutes, then remove the sides of the tin. Stand the cake on a wire rack until cold.

5 Remove the cake from the base of the tin if necessary, then return it to the rack and arrange the pecans on top. Transfer to a plate. Melt the butter in a small pan, add the honey and bring to the boil, stirring. Lower the heat and simmer for 3 minutes. Pour over the cake. Serve with *cajeta*, whipped cream or crème fraîche.

Caribbean Fruit and Rum Cake

This popular cake is eaten at Christmas, weddings and other special occasions. It is known as black cake, because the traditional recipe uses burnt sugar.

MAKES ONE CAKE

INGREDIENTS
- 450g/1lb/2 cups currants
- 450g/1lb/3 cups raisins
- 225g/8oz/1 cup pitted prunes
- 115g/4oz/⅔ cup mixed (candied) peel
- 5ml/1 tsp ground mixed spice (pumpkin pie spice)
- 90ml/6 tbsp rum, plus more if needed
- 300ml/½ pint/1¼ cups sherry, plus more if needed
- 400g/14oz/1¾ cups soft dark brown sugar
- 450g/1lb/4 cups self-raising (self-rising) flour
- 450g/1lb/2 cups butter, softened
- 10 eggs, beaten
- 5ml/1 tsp natural vanilla essence (extract)

1 Wash the currants, raisins, prunes and mixed peel, then drain and pat dry. Place in a food processor and process until roughly chopped. Transfer to a large bowl and add the the mixed spice, rum and sherry. Stir in 115g/4oz/½ cup of sugar. Mix well, then cover with a lid and set aside for anything from 2 weeks to 3 months – the longer it is left, the better the flavour will be.

2 Stir the fruit mixture occasionally, adding more alcohol, if you like, before replacing the cover.

3 Preheat the oven to 160°C/325°F/ Gas 3. Grease a 25cm/10in round cake tin (pan) and line with a double layer of greaseproof (waxed) paper or baking parchment.

4 Sift the flour into a bowl, and set it aside. In a large mixing bowl, cream the butter with the remaining sugar. Beat in the eggs until the mixture is smooth and creamy, adding a little of the flour if the mixture starts to curdle.

5 Add the fruit mixture, then gradually stir in the remaining flour and the vanilla essence. Mix well, adding 15–30ml/1–2 tbsp more sherry if the mixture is too stiff; it should just fall off the back of the spoon, but should not be too runny.

6 Spoon the mixture into the prepared pan, cover loosely with foil and bake for about 2½ hours, until the cake is firm and springy. Leave to cool in the pan overnight. Unless serving immediately, sprinkle the cake with more rum and wrap in greaseproof paper and foil to keep it moist.

COOK'S TIP

Although it is usual to roughly chop the dried fruits, they can be marinated whole if you prefer. If there is no time to marinate the fruit, simmer it gently in the alcohol mixture for about 30 minutes, and leave overnight.

APPLE AND CINNAMON CRUMBLE CAKE

THIS SCRUMPTIOUS CAKE, POPULAR IN THE CARIBBEAN, HAS LAYERS OF SPICY FRUIT AND CRUMBLE AND IS QUITE DELICIOUS WHEN SERVED WARM WITH FRESH CREAM.

MAKES ONE CAKE

INGREDIENTS

- 250g/9oz/1 cup plus 30ml/2 tbsp butter, softened
- 250g/9oz/1¼ cups caster (superfine) sugar
- 4 eggs
- 450g/1lb/4 cups self-raising (self-rising) flour
- 3 large cooking apples
- 2.5ml/½ tsp ground cinnamon

For the crumble topping

- 175g/6oz/¾ cup demerara (raw) sugar
- 125g/4¼oz/generous 1 cup plain (all-purpose) flour
- 5ml/1 tsp ground cinnamon
- 65g/2½oz/scant 1 cup desiccated (dry unsweetened shredded) coconut
- 115g/4oz/½ cup butter

1 Preheat the oven to 180°C/350°F/Gas 4. Grease and base-line a 25cm/10in round cake tin (pan). To make the crumble topping, mix the sugar, flour, cinnamon and coconut in a bowl, then rub in the butter with your fingertips until the mixture resembles breadcrumbs. Set aside.

2 Put the butter and sugar in a bowl and cream with an electric mixer until light and fluffy. Beat in the eggs, one at a time, beating well after each addition, and adding a little of the flour if the mixture starts to curdle.

3 Sift in half the remaining flour, mix well, then add the rest of the flour and stir until smooth.

4 Peel and core the apples, then grate them coarsely. Place the grated apples in a bowl and sprinkle with the cinnamon and set aside.

5 Spread half the cake mixture evenly over the base of the prepared tin. Spoon the apples on top and sprinkle over half the crumble topping.

6 Spread the remaining cake mixture over the crumble and finally top with the remaining crumble topping.

7 Bake for 1 hour 10 minutes–1 hour 20 minutes, covering the cake with foil if it browns too quickly. Leave in the pan for about 5 minutes before turning out on to a wire rack. Serve when cool.

BANANA AND PECAN BREAD

Bananas and pecans just seem to belong together. This is a really moist and delicious tea bread. Spread it with cream cheese or jam, or serve as a dessert with whipped cream.

MAKES ONE LOAF

INGREDIENTS
- 115g/4oz/½ cup butter, softened
- 175g/6oz/1 cup light muscovado (brown) sugar
- 2 large eggs, beaten
- 3 ripe bananas
- 75g/3oz/¾ cup pecan nuts, chopped
- 225g/8oz/2 cups self-raising (self-rising) flour
- 2.5ml/½ tsp mixed (apple-pie) spice

1 Preheat the oven to 180°C/350°F/Gas 4. Generously grease a 900g/2lb loaf tin (pan) and line it with non-stick baking parchment. Cream the butter and muscovado sugar in a large mixing bowl until the mixture is light and fluffy. Gradually add the eggs, beating after each addition, until well combined.

2 Peel and then mash the bananas with a fork. Add them to the creamed mixture with the chopped pecan nuts. Beat until well combined.

COOK'S TIP

If the mixture shows signs of curdling when you add the eggs, stir in a little of the flour to stabilize it.

3 Sift the flour and mixed spice together and fold into the banana mixture. Spoon into the tin, level the surface and bake for 1–1¼ hours or until a skewer inserted into the middle of the loaf comes out clean. Cool for 10 minutes in the tin, then invert the tin on a wire rack. Lift off the tin, peel off the lining paper and cool completely.

PUMPKIN AND WALNUT BREAD

PUMPKIN, NUTMEG AND WALNUTS COMBINE TO YIELD A MOIST, TANGY AND SLIGHTLY SWEET BREAD WITH A GOOD FLAVOUR. SERVE PARTNERED WITH MEATS OR CHEESE, OR SIMPLY LIGHTLY BUTTERED.

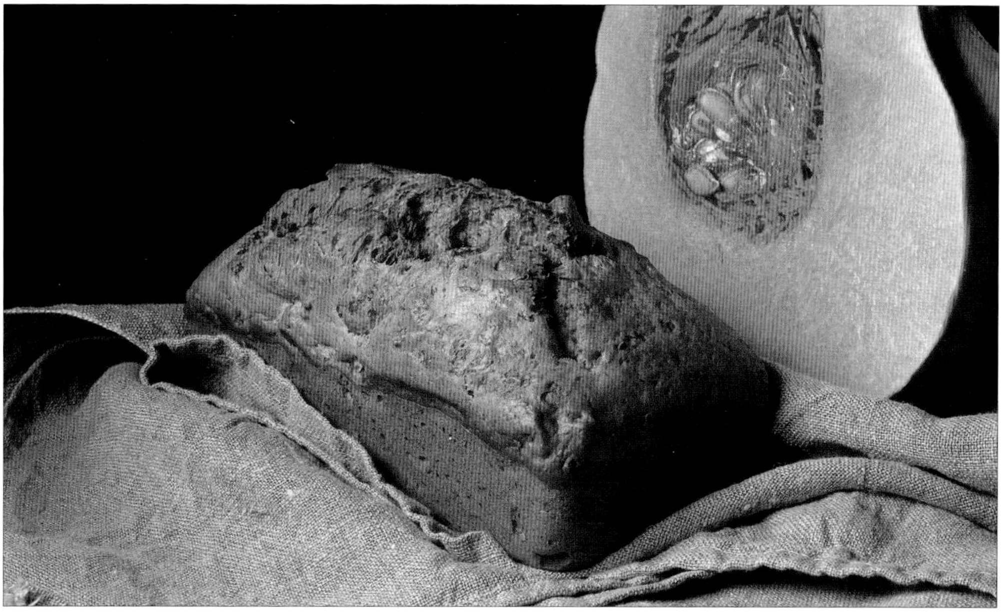

MAKES ONE LOAF

INGREDIENTS
- 600g/1¼lb pumpkin, peeled, seeded and cut into chunks
- 75g/3oz/6 tbsp caster (superfine) sugar
- 5ml/1 tsp grated nutmeg
- 50g/2oz/¼ cup butter, melted
- 3 eggs, lightly beaten
- 350g/12oz/3 cups unbleached white bread flour
- 10ml/2 tsp baking powder
- 2.5ml/½ tsp salt
- 75g/3oz/¾ cup walnuts, chopped

1 Grease and base line a loaf tin (pan) measuring 21.5 x 11cm/8½ x 4½in. Preheat the oven to 180°C/350°F/Gas 4.

2 Place the pumpkin in a pan, add water to cover by about 5cm/2in, then bring to the boil. Cover, lower the heat and simmer for 20 minutes, or until the pumpkin is very tender. Drain well, then purée in a food processor or blender. Leave to cool.

COOK'S TIP

You may have slightly more pumpkin purée than you actually need – use the remainder in soup.

3 Place 275g/10oz/1¼ cups of the purée in a large bowl. Add the sugar, nutmeg, melted butter and eggs to the purée and mix together. Sift the flour, baking powder and salt together into a large bowl and make a well in the centre.

4 Add the pumpkin mixture to the centre of the flour and stir until smooth. Mix in the walnuts. Transfer to the prepared tin and bake for 1 hour, or until golden and starting to shrink from the sides of the tin. Turn out on to a wire rack to cool.

NUTTY CHOCOLATE SQUARES

PECANS AND CHOCOLATE ARE AN IRRESISTIBLE COMBINATION IN THESE NUTTY SQUARES.

MAKES 16

INGREDIENTS
- 2 eggs
- 10ml/2 tsp vanilla essence (extract)
- pinch of salt
- 170g/6oz pecan nuts, chopped
- 50g/2oz/2 tbsp plain (all-purpose) flour
- 50g/2oz caster (superfine) sugar
- 124ml/4fl oz golden (light corn) syrup
- 85g/3oz plain (semisweet) chocolate, finely chopped
- 45g/1½oz/3 tbsp butter
- 16 pecan halves, for decorating

1 Preheat an oven to 170°C/325°F/ Gas 3. Line the bottom and sides of a 20cm/8in square baking tin (pan) with baking parchment and grease.

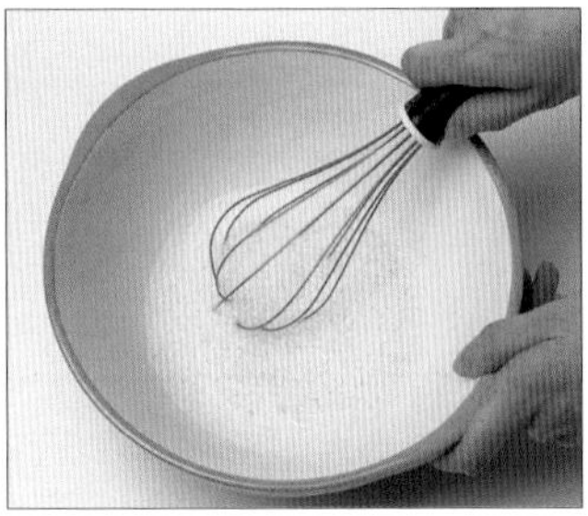

2 Whisk the eggs, vanilla and salt.

3 In another bowl, mix together the pecans and flour. Set both aside.

4 In a pan, bring the sugar and golden syrup to a boil. Remove from the heat and stir in the chocolate and butter.

5 Mix in the beaten eggs, then fold in the pecan mixture.

6 Pour into the tin and bake until set, for about 35 minutes. Leave in the tin for 10 minutes before unmoulding. Cut into 5cm (2in) squares and press pecan halves into the tops while warm.

PECAN SQUARES

THESE TEATIME TREATS HAVE A SCRUMPTIOUS NUTTY TOPPING ON A PASTRY CRUST.

MAKES 36

INGREDIENTS
- 225g/8oz/2 cups plain (all-purpose) flour
- pinch of salt
- 115g/4oz/½ cup granulated sugar
- 225g/8oz/1 cup cold butter or margarine, chopped
- 1 egg
- finely grated rind of 1 lemon

For the topping
- 175g/6oz/¾ cup butter
- 75g/3oz honey
- 50g/2oz/¼ granulated sugar
- 115g/4oz/½ cup dark brown sugar
- 75ml/5 tbsp whipping cream
- 450g/1lb/4 cups pecan halves

1 Preheat the oven to 190°C/375°F Gas 5. Lightly grease a 37 x 27 x 2.5cm/15½ x 10½ x 1in Swiss roll tin (jelly roll pan).

2 Sift the flour and salt into a large mixing bowl. Stir in the sugar. Cut and rub in the butter or margarine until the mixture resembles coarse breadcrumbs. Add the egg and lemon rind and blend with a fork until the mixture just holds together.

COOK'S TIP
To cut baked items neatly into squares or bars, use a sharp knife dipped into very hot water.

3 Spoon the mixture into the prepared tin. With floured fingertips, press into an even layer right up into the corners of the tin. Prick the pastry all over with a fork and chill in the refrigerator for 10 minutes.

4 Bake the pastry crust for 15 minutes. Remove the tin from the oven, but keep the oven on while making the topping.

5 To make the topping, melt the butter, honey and both sugars. Bring to the boil. Boil, without stirring, for 2 minutes. Off the heat, stir in the cream and pecans. Pour over the crust, return to the oven and bake for 25 minutes.

6 When cool, run a knife around the edge. Invert on to a baking sheet, place another sheet on top and invert again.

Barbadian Coconut Sweet Bread

Often made at Christmas time in Barbados, this delicious coconut bread is most enjoyable with a cup of hot chocolate or a glass of fruit punch.

MAKES TWO SMALL LOAVES

INGREDIENTS
- 175g/6oz/¾ cup butter or margarine
- 115g/4oz/½ cup demerara (raw) sugar
- 225g/8oz/2 cups self-raising (self-rising) flour
- 200g/7oz/scant 2 cups plain (all-purpose) flour
- 115g/4oz desiccated (dry unsweetened shredded) coconut
- 5ml/1 tsp mixed spice (pumpkin pie spice)
- 10ml/2 tsp vanilla essence (extract)
- 15ml/1 tbsp rum (optional)
- 2 eggs
- about 150ml/¼ pint/⅔ cup milk
- 15ml/1 tbsp caster (superfine) sugar, blended with 30ml/2 tbsp water, to glaze

1 Preheat the oven to 180°C/350°F/Gas 4. Grease two 450g/1lb loaf tins (pans) or one 900g/2lb tin.

2 Place the butter or margarine and sugar in a large mixing bowl and sift in all of the flour. Rub the ingredients together with your fingertips until the mixture begins to resemble fine breadcrumbs.

3 Add the coconut, mixed spice, vanilla essence, rum, if using, eggs and milk. Mix together well with your hands. If the mixture is too dry, add more milk. Knead on a floured board until firm and pliable.

4 Halve the mixture and place in the loaf tins. Glaze with sugared water and bake for about 1 hour, or until a skewer inserted into the loaf comes out clean.

DUCKANOO

THIS TASTY CARIBBEAN CAKE, WHICH HAS ITS ORIGINS IN WEST AFRICA, IS STEAMED IN FOIL PARCELS TO RETAIN MOISTURE. IT CONSISTS MAINLY OF CORN MEAL AND COCONUT AND IS DELICIOUS WITH FRESH CREAM.

MAKES SIX

INGREDIENTS

- 450g/1lb/3 cups fine corn meal
- 350g/12oz fresh coconut, chopped
- 600ml/1 pint/2½ cups fresh milk
- 115g/4oz currants or raisins
- 50g/2oz/¼ cup butter or margarine, melted
- 115g/4oz/½ cup demerara (raw) sugar
- 60ml/4 tbsp water
- 1.5ml/¼ tsp freshly grated nutmeg
- 2.5ml/½ tsp ground cinnamon
- 5ml/1 tsp vanilla essence (extract)

1 Place the corn meal in a large bowl. Blend the coconut and the milk in a blender or food processor until smooth. Stir the coconut mixture into the corn meal, then add all of the remaining ingredients and stir well.

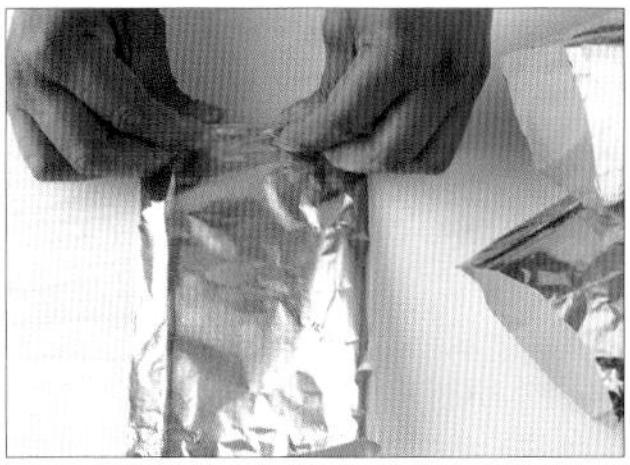

2 Take 6 pieces of foil and fold into 13 x 15cm/5 x 6in pockets leaving an opening on one short side. Fold over the edges of the remaining sides tightly to ensure that they are well sealed. This will prevent liquid seeping in.

3 Put one or two spoonfuls of the corn meal mixture into each foil pocket and fold over the final edge of foil to seal tightly.

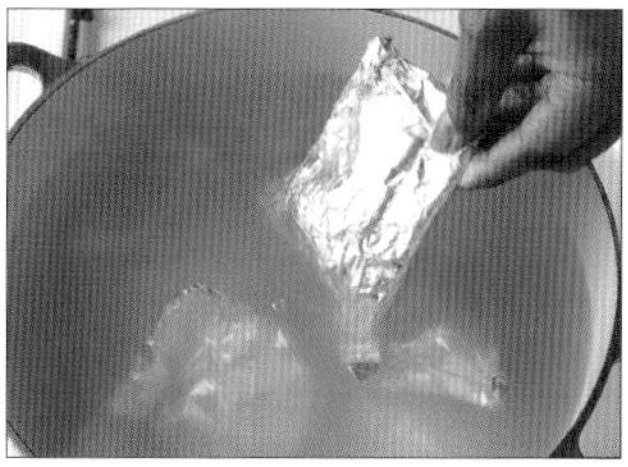

4 Place the foil pockets in a large pan of boiling water. Cover and simmer for about 45–60 minutes. Lift the pockets out of the water and carefully remove the foil. Serve the duckanoo alone or with fresh cream.

Cornmeal and Fennel Seed Cake

Being a staple food, cornmeal is often used in baking. Here it makes a delicious tea cake or after-school snack for the children.

MAKES ONE LOAF

INGREDIENTS
- 40g/1½oz/3 tbsp unsalted (sweet) butter, softened
- 200g/7oz/1 cup caster (superfine) sugar
- 200g/7oz/1⅓ cups coarse cornmeal
- 200g/7oz/1¾ cups plain (all-purpose) flour
- 350ml/12fl oz/1½ cups full-fat (whole) milk
- 10ml/2 tsp baking powder
- 5ml/1 tsp salt
- 4 eggs
- 5ml/1 tsp fennel seeds

COOK'S TIP
The cake batter will seem very runny before baking. Don't let this worry you; the result will be a well-risen, moist cake.

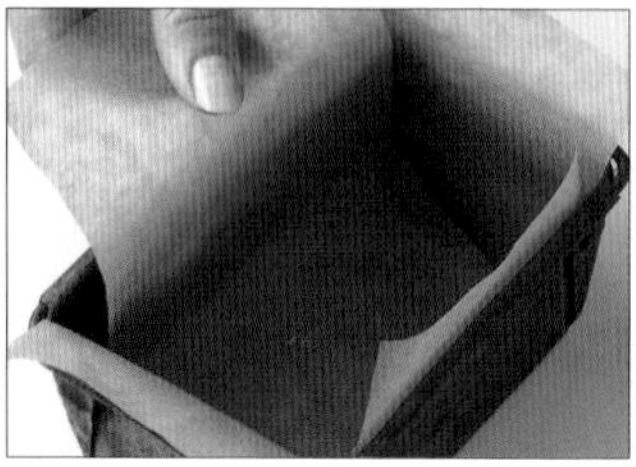

1 Preheat the oven to 180°C/350°F/Gas 4. Grease a 23 x 13cm/9 x 5in loaf tin (pan) and line with baking parchment.

VARIATION
A popular version of this cake is made with the addition of grated fresh white cheese. Stir 150g/5oz into the cake batter before baking. The result will be much creamier and even more moist.

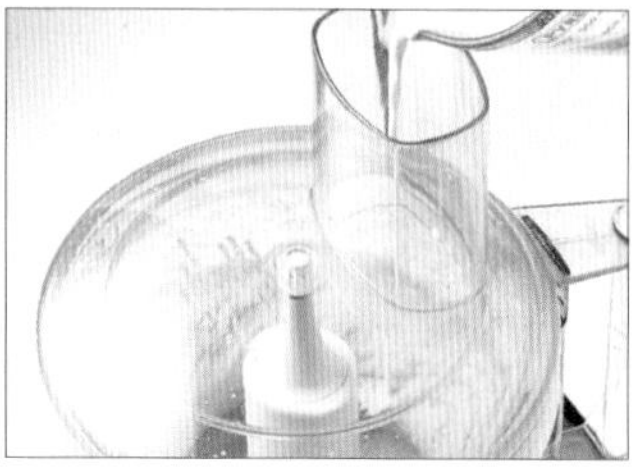

2 Cream the butter and sugar in a food processor until thoroughly combined. Add the remaining ingredients to the food processor and blend again to make a thin cake batter.

3 Pour the batter into the prepared loaf tin and bake for 40–45 minutes, or until a skewer inserted in the centre of the cake comes out clean. Allow to cool slightly, then transfer to a wire rack. Serve at room temperature.

Banana Bread

This is more of a cake than a bread, and is delicious eaten on its own for breakfast or as an afternoon snack. It also makes an impressive informal dessert when toasted, buttered and served with lashings of brandy cream.

MAKES ONE LOAF

INGREDIENTS
- 2 ripe bananas
- 115g/4oz/½ cup butter, softened, plus extra for greasing
- 75g/3oz/6 tbsp light brown sugar
- 2.5ml/½ tsp ground cinnamon
- 2.5ml/½ tsp ground ginger
- large pinch of ground cloves
- 2 eggs, lightly beaten
- 175g/6oz/1½ cups self-raising (self-rising) flour
- 15ml/1 tbsp milk (optional)
- 50g/2oz/½ cup walnut pieces

1 Preheat the oven to 180°C/350°F/Gas 4. Grease a 23 x 13cm/9 x 5in loaf tin (pan) and line with baking parchment. Mash the bananas with a fork and set them aside.

2 Cream the butter with the sugar by hand or in a food processor until light and creamy. Add the spices, eggs and flour and blend again until thoroughly combined. The mixture should be thin enough to fall reluctantly off a spoon. If it is too thick, stir in the milk.

COOK'S TIP
Do not blend the banana in a food processor – it will become too runny.

3 Fold the mashed bananas and walnut pieces into the mixture, then tip it into the prepared loaf tin. Bake the banana bread for about 1 hour, or until a skewer inserted in the centre comes out clean. Transfer to a wire rack to cool.

KINGS' DAY BREAD

ON TWELFTH NIGHT, JANUARY 6TH, MEXICAN CHILDREN RECEIVE GIFTS TO MARK THE DAY THE THREE KINGS BROUGHT GIFTS TO THE INFANT JESUS. THIS SWEETENED RICH BREAD, DECORATED WITH CANDIED FRUIT, IS AN IMPORTANT PART OF THE CELEBRATIONS. A DOLL AND A BEAN ARE HIDDEN INSIDE THE CAKE, AND THE PERSON WHO GETS THE DOLL HAS TO HOST A PARTY ON FEBRUARY 2ND, ANOTHER FEAST DAY. THE PERSON WHO FINDS THE BEAN BRINGS THE DRINKS.

SERVES EIGHT

INGREDIENTS
- 120ml/4fl oz/½ cup lukewarm water
- 6 eggs
- 10ml/2 tsp active dried yeast
- 275g/10oz/2½ cups plain (all-purpose) flour
- 2.5ml/½ tsp salt
- 50g/2oz/¼ cup granulated sugar
- 115g/4oz/½ cup butter, plus 25g/1oz/2 tbsp melted butter, for glazing
- 225g/8oz/1½ cups crystallized (candied) fruit and peel
- 175g/6oz/1½ cups icing (confectioners') sugar, plus extra, for dusting
- 30ml/2 tbsp single (light) cream
- crystallized fruit and glacé (candied) cherries, to decorate

1 Pour the water into a small bowl, stir in the dried yeast and leave in a warm place until frothy.

2 Crack four of the eggs and divide the yolks from the whites. Place the yolks in a small bowl and discard the whites.

3 Put 150g/5oz/1¼ cups of the flour in a mixing bowl. Add the salt and sugar. Break the remaining two eggs into the bowl, then add the four egg yolks.

4 Add 115g/4oz/½ cup of the butter to the bowl together with the yeast and water mixture. Mix all the ingredients together well.

5 Put the crystallized fruit and peel into a separate bowl. Add 50g/2oz/½ cup of the remaining flour and toss the fruit with the flour to coat it.

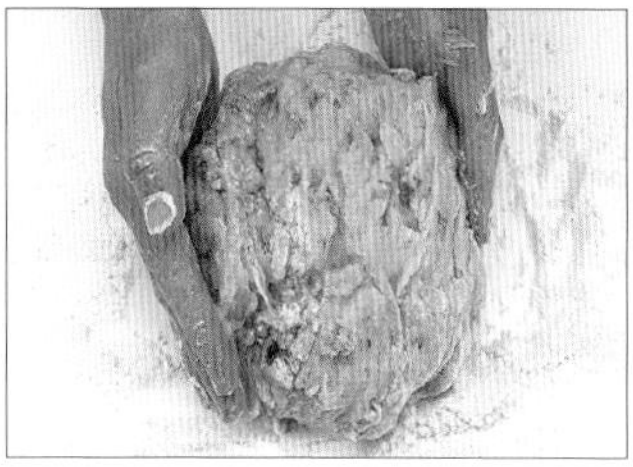

6 Add the floured fruit to the egg mixture, with the rest of the flour. Mix to a soft, non-sticky dough. Knead the dough on a lightly floured surface for about 10 minutes, until smooth.

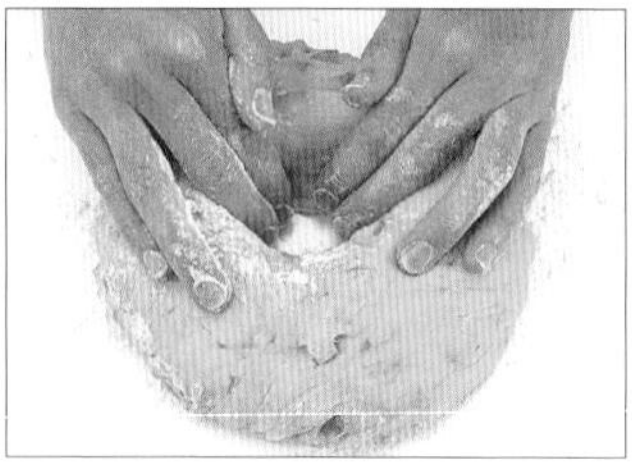

7 Shape the dough into a ball. Using the floured handle of a wooden spoon, make a hole in the centre, and enlarge.

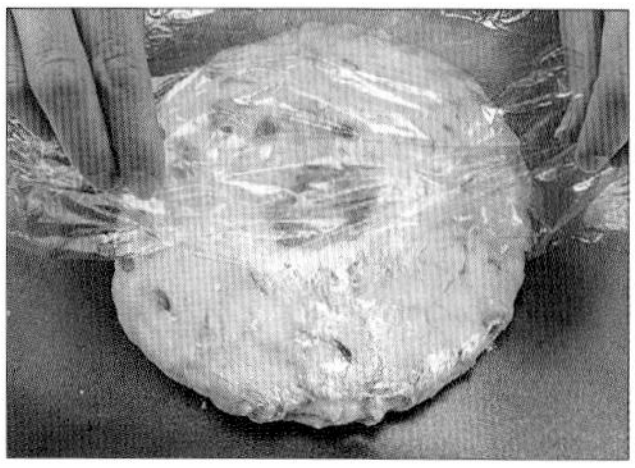

8 Put the dough ring onto a greased baking sheet and cover with oiled clear film (plastic wrap). Leave in a warm place for 2 hours, until doubled in bulk.

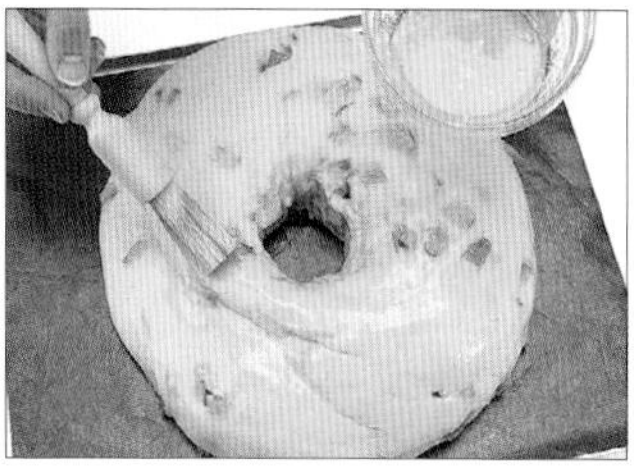

9 Preheat the oven to 180°C/350°F/Gas 4. Brush the dough with the melted butter and bake for about 30 minutes or until it has risen well and is cooked through and springy.

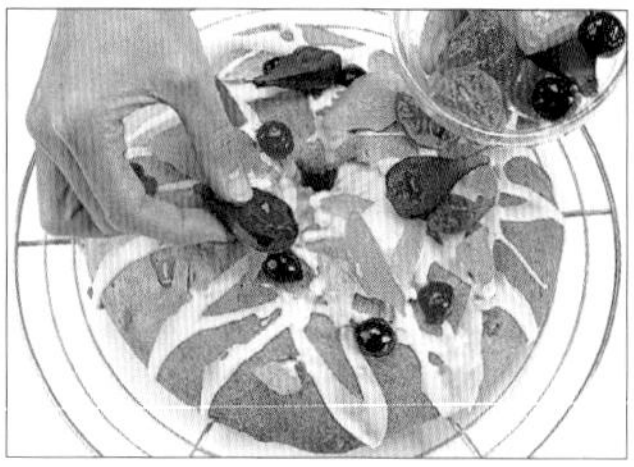

10 Mix the icing sugar and cream in a bowl. Drizzle the mixture over the bread when it is cool and decorate it with the crystallized fruit and glacé cherries. Dust with icing sugar.

Pan Dulce

These "sweet breads" of various shapes are made throughout Mexico, and are eaten as a snack or with jam or marmalade for breakfast.

MAKES 12

INGREDIENTS

- 120ml/4fl oz/½ cup lukewarm milk
- 10ml/2 tsp active dried yeast
- 450g/1lb/4 cups strong bread flour
- 75g/3oz/6 tbsp caster (superfine) sugar
- 25g/1oz/2 tbsp butter, softened
- 4 large (US extra large) eggs, beaten
- oil, for greasing

For the topping

- 75g/3oz/6 tbsp butter, softened
- 115g/4oz/½ cup granulated sugar
- 1 egg yolk
- 5ml/1 tsp ground cinnamon
- 115g/4oz/1 cup plain (all-purpose) flour

1 Pour the milk into a small bowl, stir in the dried yeast and leave in a warm place until frothy.

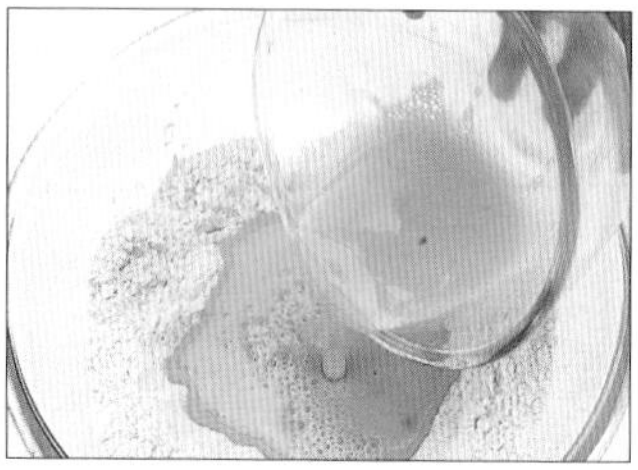

2 Put the flour and sugar in a mixing bowl, add the butter and beaten eggs and mix to a soft, sticky dough.

3 Place the dough on a lightly floured surface and dredge it with more flour. Using floured hands, turn the dough over and over until it is completely covered in a light coating of flour. Cover it with lightly oiled clear film (plastic wrap) and leave to rest for 20 minutes.

4 Meanwhile, make the topping. Cream the butter and sugar in a bowl, then mix in the egg yolk, cinnamon and flour. The mixture should have a slightly crumbly texture.

5 Divide the dough into 12 equal pieces and shape each of them into a round. Space well apart on greased baking sheets. Sprinkle the topping over the breads, dividing it more or less equally among them, then press it lightly into the surface.

6 Leave the rolls in a warm place to stand for about 30 minutes until they are about one and a half times their previous size. Preheat the oven to 200°C/400°F/Gas 6 and bake the breads for about 15 minutes. Allow to cool slightly before serving.

ALMOND BISCUITS

ICING SUGAR AND BUTTER COMBINE TO GIVE THESE BISCUITS A LIGHT, DELICATE TEXTURE. THEY CAN BE MADE DAYS AHEAD, AND ARE DELICIOUS WITH DESSERTS OR COFFEE.

MAKES ABOUT 24

INGREDIENTS
- 115g/4oz/1 cup plain (all-purpose) flour
- 175g/6oz/1½ cups icing (confectioners') sugar
- pinch of salt
- 50g/2oz/½ cup chopped almonds
- 2.5ml/½ tsp almond essence (extract)
- 115g/4oz/½ cup unsalted butter, softened
- icing sugar, for dusting
- halved almonds, to decorate

1 Preheat the oven to 180°C/350°F/Gas 4. Combine the flour, icing sugar, salt and chopped almonds in a bowl. Add the almond essence.

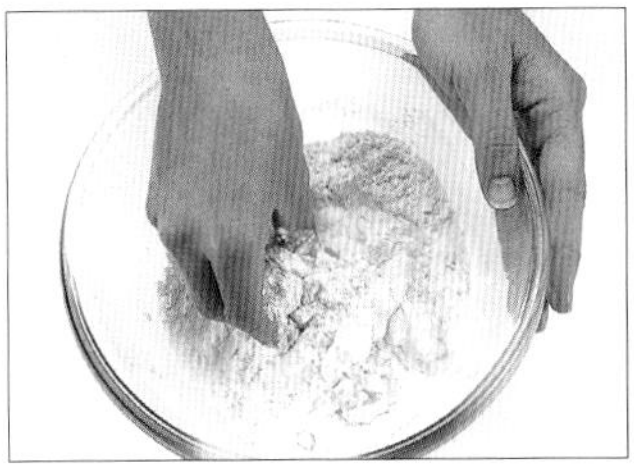

2 Put the softened butter in the centre of the flour mixture and use a knife or your fingertips to draw the dry ingredients into the butter until a dough is formed. Shape the dough into a ball.

COOK'S TIPS
Use fancy or themed cutters for celebrations and special occasions.

3 Place the dough on a lightly floured surface and roll it out to a thickness of about 3mm/⅛in. Using a 7.5cm/3in biscuit cutter, cut out about 24 rounds, re-rolling the dough as necessary. Place the rounds on baking sheets. Bake for 25–30 minutes until pale golden.

4 Leave for 10 minutes, then transfer to wire racks to cool. Dust thickly with icing sugar before serving, decorated with halved almonds.

DESSERTS

The abundant supply of sweet and juicy tropical fruit available in Latin America and the Caribbean means that dessert usually consists of fresh fruit. Otherwise, desserts tend to be rice dishes based on eggs and sugar and are usually of Spanish or Portuguese origin, where rich custard tarts and crème caramels have always been popular.

FRUITS OF THE TROPICS SALAD

CANNED GUAVAS DO NOT HAVE QUITE THE SAME FLAVOUR AS FRESH ONES, BUT ARE AN EXCELLENT INGREDIENT IN THEIR OWN RIGHT – DELICIOUS IN THIS CARIBBEAN FRUIT SALAD.

SERVES SIX

INGREDIENTS

- 1 medium pineapple
- 400g/14oz can guava halves in syrup
- 2 bananas, sliced
- 1 large mango, peeled, stoned (pitted) and diced
- 115g/4oz preserved stem ginger plus 30ml/2 tbsp of the syrup from the jar
- 60ml/4 tbsp thick coconut milk
- 10ml/2 tsp sugar
- 2.5ml/½ tsp freshly grated nutmeg
- 2.5ml/½ tsp ground cinnamon
- strips of coconut, to decorate

1 Remove the leafy top of the pineapple, saving it to decorate the serving platter if you like. Cut the pineapple lengthways into quarters, then remove the peel and core from each piece. Cube the pineapple, and place in a serving bowl. Drain the guavas, reserving the syrup, and chop. Add the guavas to the bowl with half the bananas and all the mango.

2 Chop the stem ginger and add it to the pineapple mixture.

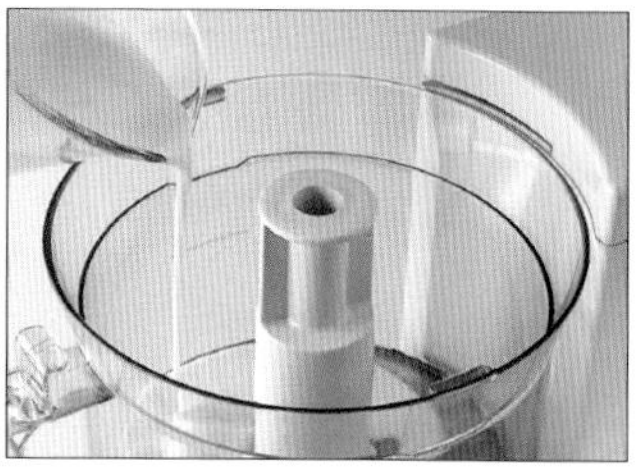

3 Pour the ginger syrup into a blender or food processor. Add the remaining banana, the coconut milk and the sugar. Pour in the reserved guava syrup and blend to a smooth creamy purée.

4 Pour the banana and coconut dressing over the fruit, add a little grated nutmeg and a sprinkling of cinnamon. Cover and chill.

5 Serve the salad chilled, decorated with fresh strips of coconut. If you are serving the mixture on a large platter, the pineapple top can be placed in the centre as a decoration.

COCONUT ICE CREAM

THIS HEAVENLY ICE CREAM, POPULAR THROUGHOUT THE CARIBBEAN, IS EASY TO MAKE AND USES STORECUPBOARD INGREDIENTS, SO IS PERFECT FOR EASY ENTERTAINING.

SERVES EIGHT

INGREDIENTS
- 400g/14oz can evaporated (unsweetened condensed) milk
- 400g/14oz can condensed milk
- 400g/14oz can coconut milk
- freshly grated nutmeg
- 5ml/1 tsp almond essence (extract)
- fresh lemon balm sprigs, lime slices and shredded coconut, to decorate

COOK'S TIP
If using an ice-cream maker, mix the ingredients in a jug (pitcher), chill in the freezer for 30 minutes. Pour into the ice-cream maker and churn as directed.

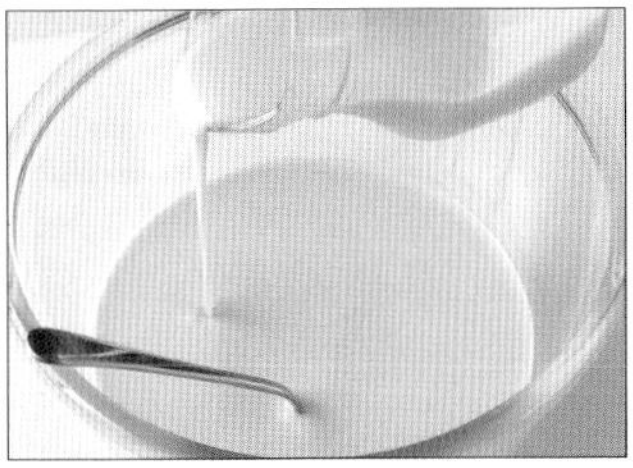

1 Mix the evaporated, condensed and coconut milk in a large freezerproof bowl until thoroughly combined.

2 Stir in the grated nutmeg and almond essence. Place the bowl in the freezer and chill the mixture for about 1–2 hours or until semi-frozen.

3 Remove the bowl from the freezer and whisk the mixture vigorously until it is light and fluffy and has almost doubled in volume.

4 Pour into a freezer container, then cover and freeze. Soften slightly before serving, decorated with lemon balm, lime slices and shredded coconut.

Mango Sorbet

This foolproof recipe is incredibly easy to make without an ice-cream maker. A smooth texture and fruity, concentrated flavour is guaranteed.

SERVES SIX

INGREDIENTS

- 200g/7oz/1 cup caster (superfine) sugar
- 150ml/¼ pint/⅔ cup water
- 3 large ripe mangoes
- juice of 1 lime
- 1 egg white

COOK'S TIP

Home-made sorbets (sherbets) tend to set more solidly than bought versions, so always transfer them to the refrigerator to thaw slightly before serving.

VARIATION

The sorbet can be made with ripe papayas instead of mangoes. Add the grated rind of the lime as well as the juice.

1 Dissolve the sugar in the water in a small pan over a low heat. Allow to cool.

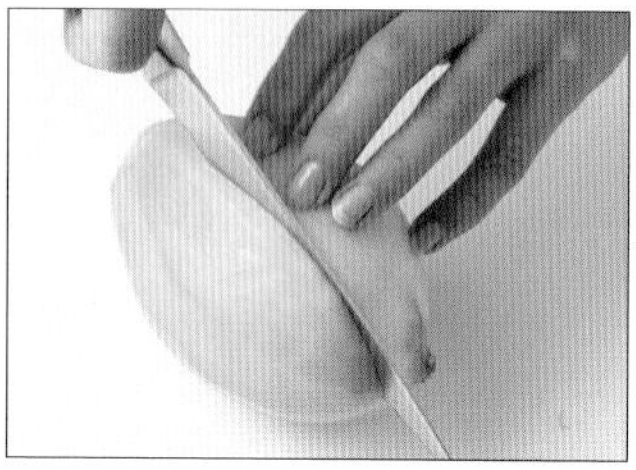

2 Cut off a thick lengthways slice from either side of each mango. Cut off any flesh, peel and chop it roughly. Put the mango flesh in a food processor or blender and process until smooth.

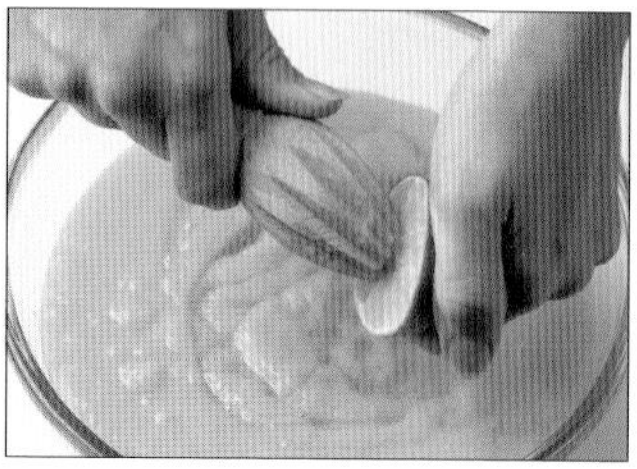

3 Scrape into a freezerproof bowl and stir in the syrup and lime juice. Freeze for 2–4 hours until almost solid.

4 Scoop into a food processor and blend until soft. Pour in the egg white and blend until combined. Return to the bowl, cover and freeze until firm.

Colombian Pineapple Custard

These pineapple crème caramels are the perfect dinner party dessert. They are very easy to make, especially if you buy prepared fresh pineapple from the supermarket.

MAKES SIX

INGREDIENTS
- 350g/12oz peeled fresh pineapple, chopped
- 150g/5oz/⅔ cup caster (superfine) sugar
- 4 eggs, lightly beaten

For the caramel
- 60ml/4 tbsp granulated sugar
- juice of 1 lime

1 Put the pineapple in a blender or food processor and process until smooth. Scrape the purée into a pan and add the sugar. Cook for 5 minutes or until reduced by one-third. The mixture should be thick but not jam-like, so add a little water if it is too thick. Transfer to a bowl and leave to cool.

COOK'S TIP

Avoid over-whisking the eggs. Gently stir them into the pineapple mixture without incorporating air.

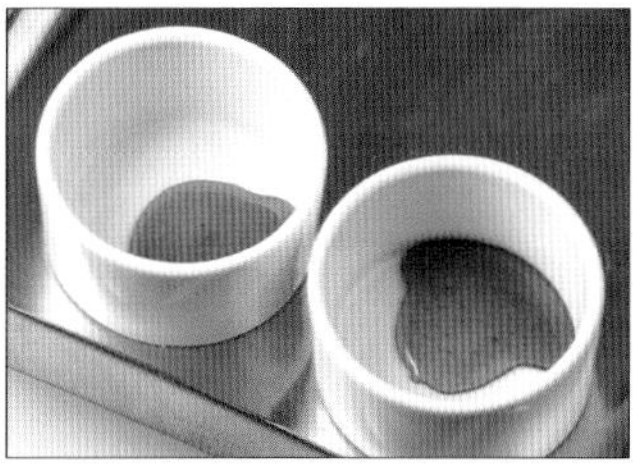

2 Meanwhile make the caramel. Place the granulated sugar in a heavy pan over a medium heat. As the sugar starts to caramelize around the edges, shake the pan to mix the sugar, but do not stir. Remove the pan from the heat as soon as all the sugar has dissolved and the caramel has become golden brown. Immediately stir in the lime juice taking care not to burn yourself. The hot caramel will spit when the lime juice is added, but this will stop. Divide the caramel among six ramekins and turn them so that they are coated evenly.

3 Preheat the oven to 180°C/350°F/Gas 4. Stir the eggs into the cool pineapple mixture. Divide the mixture equally among the ramekins. Place the moulds in a roasting pan and pour in warm water to come halfway up their sides. Cover with foil and bake for 45 minutes, until set. Allow to cool.

4 Just before serving, unmould the custards directly on to dessert plates. Loosen the edges with a knife, invert a dessert plate on top of each mould and turn both over.

CHURROS

These delectable treats are traditionally made by forcing dough through a churrera, which is a utensil fitted with a wooden plunger. An icing bag fitted with a large star nozzle makes a good substitute. Churros are usually served with Cafe de Olla or Mexican Hot Chocolate and are perfect for dipping.

MAKES ABOUT 24

INGREDIENTS
- 350g/12oz/3 cups plain (all-purpose) flour
- 5ml/1 tsp baking powder
- 600ml/1 pint/2½ cups water
- 2.5ml/½ tsp salt
- 25g/1oz/3 tbsp soft dark brown sugar
- 2 egg yolks
- oil, for deep frying
- 2 limes, cut in wedges
- caster (superfine) sugar, for dusting

1 Sift the flour and baking powder into a bowl and set aside. Bring the measured water to the boil in a pan, add the salt and brown sugar, stirring all the time until both have dissolved. Remove from the heat, tip in all the flour and baking powder and beat the mixture continuously until smooth.

2 Beat in the egg yolks, one at a time, until the mixture is smooth and glossy. Set the batter aside to cool. Have ready a piping bag fitted with a large star nozzle which will give the *churros* their traditional shape.

3 Pour oil into a deep fryer or suitable saucepan to a depth of about 5cm/2in. Heat to 190°C/375°F, or until a cube of dried bread, added to the oil, floats and turns golden after 1 minute.

4 Spoon the batter into the piping bag. Pipe five or six 10cm/4in lengths of the mixture into the hot oil, using a knife to slice off each length as it emerges from the nozzle. Fry for 3–4 minutes or until they are golden brown. Drain the *churros* on kitchen paper while cooking successive batches, then arrange on a plate with the lime wedges, dust them with caster sugar and serve warm.

SOPAIPILLAS

These golden pillows of puff pastry can be served as a dessert, with honey, or plain with soups. They are also ideal for finger buffets.

MAKES ABOUT 30

INGREDIENTS
- 225g/8oz/2 cups plain (all-purpose) flour
- 15ml/1 tsp baking powder
- 5ml/1 tsp salt
- 25g/1oz/2 tbsp white cooking fat or margarine
- 175ml/6fl oz/¾ cup warm water
- oil, for deep frying
- clear honey, for drizzling
- ground cinnamon for sprinkling
- crème fraîche or thick double (heavy) cream, to serve

VARIATION

Instead of drizzling honey over the *sopaipillas*, use a mixture of 50g/2oz/ ¼ cup caster (superfine) sugar and 10ml/2 tsp ground cinnamon.

1 Sift the flour, baking powder and salt into a bowl. Rub in the cooking fat or margarine until the mixture resembles fine breadcrumbs. Gradually add enough of the water to form a dough. Wrap the dough in clear film (plastic wrap) and leave for 1 hour.

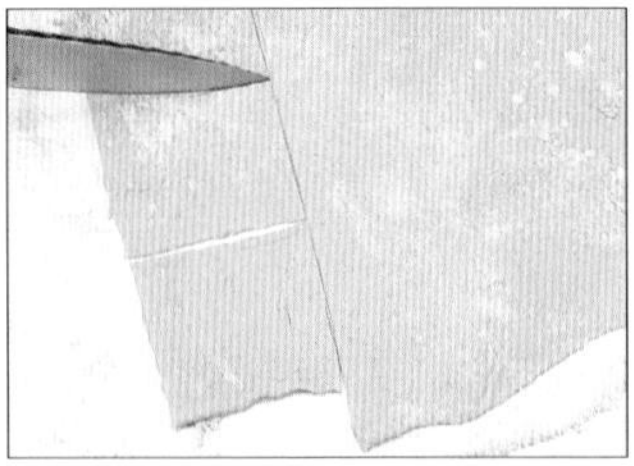

2 Working with half the dough at a time, roll it out to a square, keeping it as even and as thin as possible. Cut into 7.5cm/ 3in squares. When both pieces of the dough have been rolled and cut, set the squares aside.

3 Heat the oil for deep frying to 190°C/ 375°F, or until a cube of dried bread, added to the oil, floats and turns golden after 1 minute. Add a few pastry squares, using tongs to push them down into the oil. Cook in batches until golden on both sides, turning them once, and drain on kitchen paper.

4 When all the *sopaipillas* have been cooked, arrange on a large serving plate, drizzle with honey and sprinkle with ground cinnamon Serve warm, with crème fraîche or thick double cream.

Coconut Cream Tart

The ultimate in Caribbean desserts, this creamy pie provides a wonderful treat.

SERVES EIGHT

INGREDIENTS

- 175g/6oz desiccated (dry unsweetened shredded) coconut
- 200g/7oz/1 cup caster (superfine) sugar
- 60ml/4 tbsp cornflour (cornstarch)
- 1/8 tsp salt
- 600ml/1 pint/2½ cups milk
- 60ml/4 tbsp whipping cream
- 2 egg yolks
- 25g/1oz/2 tbsp unsalted (sweet) butter
- 10ml/2 tsp vanilla essence (extract)

For the pastry

- 140g/5oz/1¼ cups plain (all-purpose) flour
- ¼ tsp salt
- 45g/1½oz/3 tbsp butter, chopped
- 30g/1oz/2 tbsp vegetable fat or lard
- 30–45ml/2–3 tbsp iced water

1 For the pastry, sift the flour and salt into a bowl. Add the butter and fat and cut in with a pastry blender until the mixture resembles coarse breadcrumbs.

2 With a fork, stir in just enough water to bind the pastry. Gather into a ball, wrap in baking parchment and refrigerate for 20 minutes.

3 Preheat the oven to 220°C/425°F/Gas 7 oven. Roll out the pastry to 3mm (1/8in) thick. Line a 23cm (9in) pie dish. Trim and flute the edges. Prick the bottom. Line with baking parchment and fill with baking beans. Bake for 10 minutes. Remove the paper and beans, reduce the heat to 180°C/350°F/Gas 4 and bake until brown, 10–15 minutes.

4 Spread half the coconut on a baking sheet and toast in the oven for 6–8 minutes until golden, stirring often. Set aside.

5 Put the sugar, cornflour and salt in a pan. In a bowl, whisk the milk, cream and egg yolks. Add to the pan.

6 Cook over a low heat, stirring, and bring to the boil. Boil for 1 minute, then remove from the heat. Add the butter, vanilla and remaining coconut.

7 Pour into the pastry case. When cool, sprinkle over the toasted coconut.

Lemon Coconut Layer Cake

Lemon juice gives the coconut topping a lovely tangy flavour, balancing the sweetness.

SERVES EIGHT TO TEN

INGREDIENTS

- 140g/5oz/1¼ cups plain (all-purpose) flour
- pinch of salt
- 8 eggs
- 350g/12oz/3 cups caster (superfine) sugar
- 15ml/1 tbsp grated orange rind
- grated rind of 2 lemons
- juice of 1 lemon
- 75g/2½oz desiccated (dry unsweetened shredded) coconut
- 30ml/2 tbsp cornflour (cornstarch)
- 250ml/8fl oz/1 cup water
- 75g/3oz/⅓ cup butter

For the frosting

- 115g/4oz/½ cup unsalted (sweet) butter
- 115g/4oz/1 cup icing (confectioners') sugar
- grated rind of 1 lemon
- 6–8 tablespoons lemon juice
- 115g/4oz desiccated (dry unsweetened shredded) coconut

1 Preheat the oven to 350°F/180°C/ Gas 4 oven. Line three 20cm (8in) cake tins with baking parchment and grease. In a bowl, sift together the flour and salt and set aside.

2 Place six of the eggs in a bowl set over hot water. With an electric mixer, beat until frothy. Beat in half the caster sugar until the mixture doubles in volume and leaves a ribbon trail when the beaters are lifted, about 10 minutes.

3 Remove the bowl from the hot water. Fold in the orange rind, half the grated lemon rind and 1 tbsp lemon juice until blended. Fold in the coconut.

4 Sift over the flour mixture in three batches, folding in after each addition.

5 Divide the mixture between the prepared tins. Bake until the cakes pull away from the sides of the tins, 25–30 minutes. Let stand for 3–5 minutes, then turn out to cool on a rack.

6 In a bowl, blend the cornflour with a little cold water to dissolve. Whisk in the remaining eggs just until blended.

7 In a pan, combine the remaining lemon rind and juice, the water, remaining sugar and butter.

8 Over a moderate heat, bring the mixture to the boil. Whisk in the eggs and cornflour mixture, and return to the boil. Whisk continuously until thick, about 5 minutes. Remove from the heat. Cover with clear film (plastic wrap) to stop a skin forming, and set aside.

9 For the frosting, cream the butter and icing sugar until smooth. Stir in the lemon rind and enough lemon juice to obtain a thick, spreadable consistency.

10 Sandwich the three cake layers with the lemon custard mixture. Spread the frosting over the top and sides. Cover the cake with the desiccated coconut, pressing it in gently.

Caramel Custard

If you order "Flan" from the menu in Mexico you might be disconcerted if you were expecting a sponge case filled with fruit. This hugely popular pudding is actually a caramel custard, and has its origins in Spain, where the same name is used. It is similar to the French crème caramel.

SERVES SIX

INGREDIENTS
- 1 litre/1¾ pints/4 cups milk
- 1 vanilla pod (bean), split
- 6 eggs
- 115g/4oz/½ cup sugar
- 5ml/1 tsp vanilla essence (extract)

For the caramel
- 175g/6oz/¾ cup caster (superfine) sugar

1 Put six ramekins or dariole moulds in a sink of hot water. Make the caramel. Spread out the caster sugar evenly on the bottom of a large pan. Heat it slowly, without stirring, tilting the pan backwards and forwards on the heat until the sugar melts.

2 Lift the heated ramekins or moulds out of the water and dry them quickly. Watch the melted sugar closely, and when it turns a rich golden colour, pour the mixture into the dishes and simply turn until they are coated, or brush the caramel over the insides of the dishes. Set them aside.

3 Preheat the oven to 180°C/350°F/Gas 4. Pour the milk into a pan, add the vanilla pod and bring the milk to just below boiling point. Pour it into a jug (pitcher) and set it aside to cool.

4 Put the eggs in a bowl, beat them lightly, then gradually beat in the sugar. Remove the vanilla from the milk, then gradually mix the milk into the egg.

5 Strain the egg mixture into the caramel-lined ramekins or moulds and stand them in a roasting tin. Pour boiling water into the roasting tin until it comes halfway up the sides of the dishes, then carefully put the tin in the oven.

6 Bake the caramel custards for about 40 minutes. The custards are done when a slender knife blade, inserted in one of them, comes out clean.

7 Lift the dishes out of the water, let them cool, then chill them for several hours in the refrigerator.

8 To serve, run a round-bladed knife around the edge of each custard, place a dessert plate upside down on top of the dish and turn the dish and plate over together. Lift off the dish. Some of the caramel will settle in a puddle around the custard, so it is important not to choose dessert dishes that are too shallow. Try serving these custards with fresh fruit.

VARIATIONS

Flavour the custard with cinnamon, cocoa or rum instead of vanilla. In the Tabasco region, where chestnuts grow, chestnut purée is sometimes added.

Cold Mango Soufflés Topped with Toasted Coconut

Fragrant, fresh mango is one of the most delicious exotic fruits around, whether it is simply served in slices or used as the basis for an ice cream or soufflé.

MAKES FOUR

INGREDIENTS

- 4 small mangoes, peeled, stoned and chopped
- 30ml/2 tbsp water
- 15ml/1 tbsp powdered gelatine
- 2 egg yolks
- 115g/4oz/½ cup caster (superfine) sugar
- 120ml/4fl oz/½ cup milk
- grated rind of 1 orange
- 300ml/½ pint/1¼ cups double (heavy) cream
- toasted flaked or coarsely shredded coconut, to decorate

1 Place a few pieces of mango in the base of each of four 150ml/¼ pint/⅔ cup ramekins. Wrap a greased collar of non-stick baking parchment around the outside of each dish, extending well above the rim. Secure with adhesive tape, then tie tightly with string.

2 Pour the water into a small heatproof bowl and sprinkle the gelatine over the surface. Leave for 5 minutes or until spongy. Place the bowl in a pan of hot water, stirring occasionally, until the gelatine has dissolved.

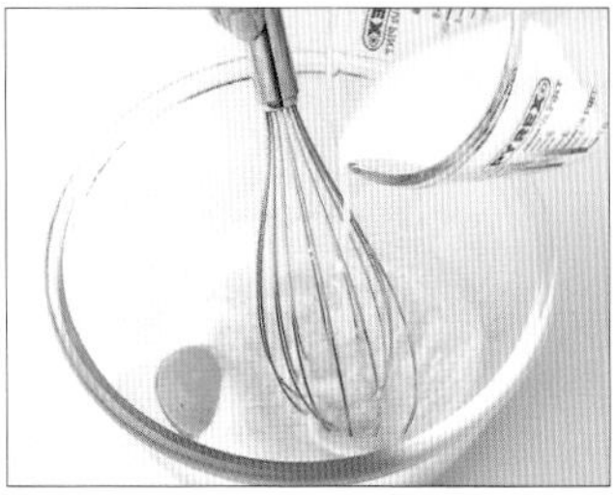

3 Meanwhile, whisk the egg yolks with the caster sugar and milk in another heatproof bowl. Place the bowl over a pan of simmering water and continue to whisk until the mixture is thick and frothy. Remove from the heat and continue whisking until the mixture cools. Whisk in the liquid gelatine.

4 Purée the remaining mango pieces in a food processor or blender, then fold the purée into the egg yolk mixture with the orange rind. Set the mixture aside until starting to thicken.

5 Whip the double cream to soft peaks. Reserve 60ml/4 tbsp and fold the rest into the mango mixture. Spoon into the ramekins until the mixture is 2.5cm/1in above the rim of each dish. Chill for 3–4 hours or until set.

6 Carefully remove the paper collars from the soufflés. Spoon a little of the reserved cream on top of each soufflé and decorate with some toasted flaked or coarsely shredded coconut.

ALMOND PUDDING WITH CUSTARD

This dish may well date from the time of the French occupation of Mexico, for it bears a close resemblance to Île flottante – floating islands – although in that recipe the meringues are actually poached in the custard. Delicious and very light, it makes the perfect dessert to follow a substantial main course.

SERVES SIX

INGREDIENTS
- 250ml/8fl oz/1 cup water
- 15g/½oz sachet powdered gelatine
- 275g/10oz/1¼ cups sugar
- 2.5ml/½ tsp almond essence (extract)
- 6 eggs, separated
- pinch of salt
- 475ml/16fl oz/2 cups single (light) cream
- 2.5ml/½ tsp vanilla essence (extract)
- ground cinnamon, for dusting

1 Pour the water into a saucepan and sprinkle the gelatine over the surface. When it has softened, add 225g/8oz/1 cup of the sugar and place the pan over a low heat. Stir until both the gelatine and the sugar have dissolved, then stir in the almond essence. Pour the mixture into a bowl and chill in the fridge until it starts to thicken.

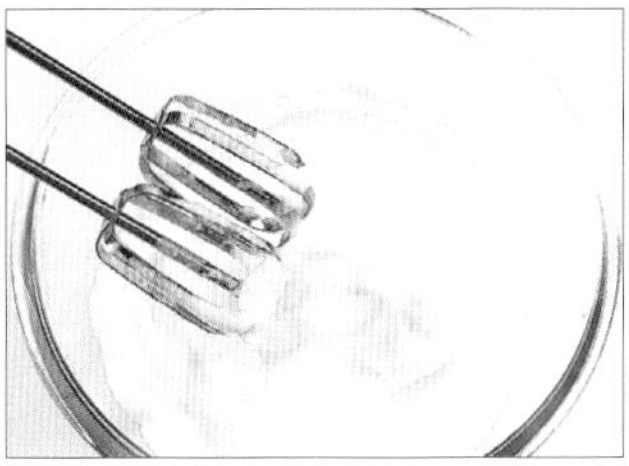

2 Whisk the egg whites until they are stiff. Whisk the gelatine mixture until is frothy, then fold in the egg whites carefully. Chill until firm.

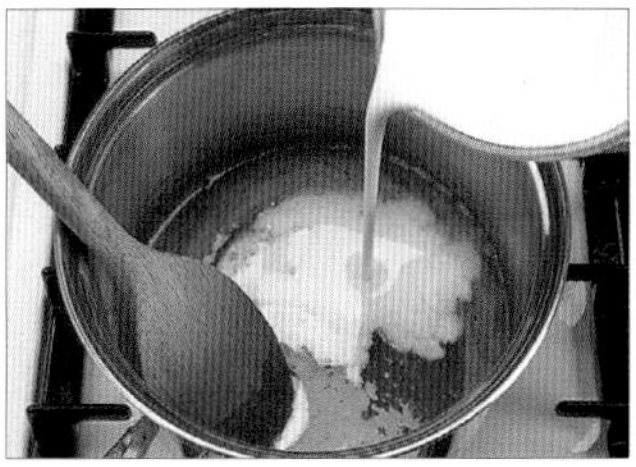

3 Meanwhile, make the custard. Put the egg yolks, remaining sugar and salt in a heavy pan. Stir in the cream and vanilla essence. Cook over a very low heat, stirring constantly until the custard thickens to a soft dropping consistency, enough to coat the back of a wooden spoon.

4 Pour the custard into dessert bowls. Cover each with a piece of dampened greaseproof paper until ready to serve to prevent the formation of a skin.

5 Serve each custard topped with a few spoonfuls of the meringue mixture and a sprinkle of ground cinnamon.

Tapioca Pudding

This is one of those desserts that provokes strong reactions. Most people either love it or loathe it, but it is very popular throughout Latin America. For its many fans, there is nothing nicer than this creamy dessert strewn with crunchy cashews.

SERVES SIX

INGREDIENTS

- 90g/3½oz/generous ½ cup tapioca
- 750ml/1¼ pints/3 cups full-fat (whole) milk
- 1 cinnamon stick, bruised
- 45ml/3 tbsp caster (superfine) sugar
- 30ml/2 tbsp chopped cashew nuts

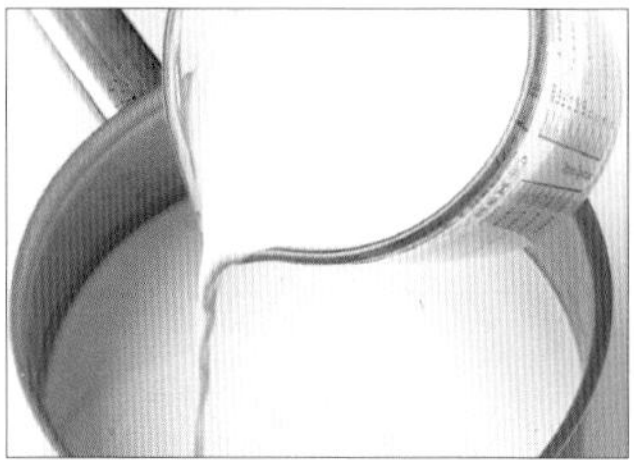

1 Put the tapioca in a strainer and rinse under cold running water. Drain and tip into a heavy pan.

VARIATION

For coconut-flavoured tapioca pudding, simply replace the milk with the same quantity of coconut milk.

2 Pour in the milk and soak for 30 minutes. Place the pan over a medium heat and bring to the boil. Add the bruised cinnamon stick, then lower the heat and simmer gently for 30 minutes, or until most of the milk has been absorbed. Stir occasionally to prevent the tapioca from sticking.

3 Stir in the sugar and gently simmer for a further 10 minutes. Carefully remove the cinnamon stick and spoon the pudding into individual dessert bowls. Lightly toast the cashew nuts in a dry frying pan, taking care not to burn them, and scatter over the puddings. Serve warm rather than hot or cold.

FRIED BANANAS WITH SUGAR AND RUM

CHILDREN LOVE FRIED BANANAS, BUT THIS CARIBBEAN VERSION WITH RUM DELIVERS AN EXTRA KICK AND IS STRICTLY FOR GROWN-UPS. FRIED BANANAS CAN BE INCREDIBLY SWEET, BUT THE LIME JUICE CUTS THROUGH THE SWEETNESS WITH DELICIOUS RESULTS.

SERVES FOUR

INGREDIENTS
- 50g/2oz/¼ cup caster (superfine) sugar
- 45ml/3 tbsp rum
- 65g/2½oz/5 tbsp unsalted (sweet) butter
- grated rind and juice of 1 lime
- 4 bananas, peeled
- vanilla ice cream, to serve

1 Place the sugar, rum, butter, grated lime rind and lime juice in a large heavy frying pan over a low heat. Cook for a few minutes, stirring occasionally, until the sugar has completely dissolved.

COOK'S TIP
Avoid using bananas that are too ripe, otherwise they may break apart in the pan before they get a chance to colour.

2 Add the bananas to the pan, turning to coat them in the sauce. Cook over a medium heat for 5 minutes on each side, or until the bananas are golden.

3 Remove from the heat and cut the bananas in half. Serve two pieces of banana per person with a scoop of vanilla ice cream and a generous drizzle of the hot sauce.

Coconut and Pumpkin Compote

Latin Americans love whole preserved fruits in syrup. Also popular are compotes like this one, traditionally served with fresh cheese.

SERVES SIX

INGREDIENTS
- 800g/1¾lb pumpkin, peeled and seeded
- 450g/1lb/2¼ cups caster (superfine) sugar
- 4 cloves
- 350ml/12fl oz/1½ cups water
- 115g/4oz/1⅓ cups desiccated (dry unsweetened shredded) coconut
- ricotta cheese, to serve

VARIATION
This preserve is more traditionally made without coconut. For pure pumpkin compote, leave out the coconut and double the quantity of pumpkin.

1 Cut the pumpkin into even-size pieces and place in a heavy pan. Add the sugar, cloves and water. Heat gently, without bringing to the boil, until the sugar has dissolved.

2 Increase the heat to medium. Simmer the mixture for 30–35 minutes, until the pumpkin is soft. Using a fork mash the cooked pumpkin until it is reduced to a rough purée.

3 Stir in the coconut and simmer for a further 15 minutes. The mixture should be thick but still liquid, so add more water if necessary. Leave to cool, then transfer to an airtight container and store in the refrigerator for up to 2 weeks.

4 Spoon the compote into a serving bowl and allow it to come to room temperature before serving with a fresh white cheese, such as ricotta.

Dulce de Leche

Spanish in origin, this toffee-like dessert is a children's favourite throughout Latin America. Literally translated as "caramelized milk", it is traditionally made with milk and sugar, but this version is much quicker and just as delicious.

SERVES SIX

INGREDIENTS
- 400g/14oz can condensed milk
- 400g/14oz can evaporated (unsweetened condensed) milk

VARIATION
A classic trick to making low-maintenance *dulce de leche* is to cook a whole, closed can of condensed milk in a pan of boiling water for 30 minutes, but this must be done with care as the can could explode if not continuously immersed in water. South American cooks often add a can of condensed milk to the pan when cooking beans, so side dish and dessert cook together.

1 Combine the condensed and evaporated milk in a heavy pan. Place over a medium heat and bring to the boil. Reduce the heat slightly and cook, stirring constantly, for 30–35 minutes until thickened and toffee-coloured. Use a relatively large pan, as the milk has a tendency to boil over.

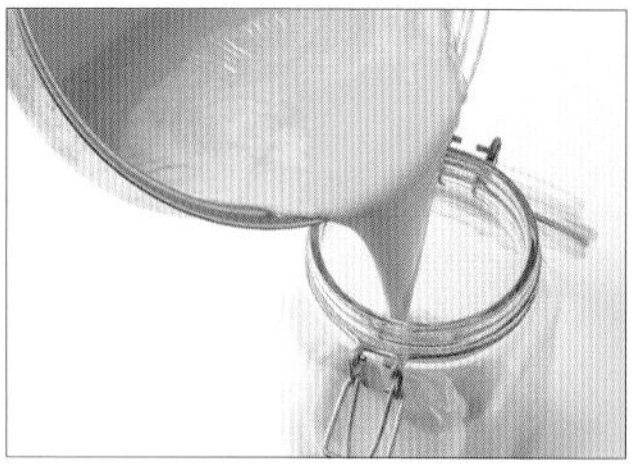

2 Pour into a sterilized jar and seal. *Dulce de leche* will keep for months, but with time, the texture will alter and won't be as smooth.

3 Serve with ice cream, as a filling for pancakes or cakes, or even with a white cheese, such as ricotta.

PUMPKIN IN BROWN SUGAR

RICH, STICKY AND SWEET, THIS WARMING DESSERT LOOKS VERY ATTRACTIVE AND IS NOT AT ALL DIFFICULT TO PREPARE.

SERVES SIX

INGREDIENTS

- 1 small pumpkin, about 800g/1¾lb
- 350g/12oz/1½ cups soft dark brown sugar
- 120ml/4fl oz/½ cup water
- 5ml/1 tsp ground cloves
- 12 cinnamon sticks, each about 10cm/4in in length
- fresh mint sprigs, to decorate
- thick yogurt or crème fraîche, to serve

1 Halve the pumpkin, remove the seeds and fibres and cut into wedges. Arrange in a single layer in a shallow, flameproof casserole or heavy-based pan. Fill the hollows with the sugar.

2 Pour the water carefully into the pan, taking care not to wash all the sugar to the bottom. Make sure that some of the water trickles down to the bottom to prevent the pumpkin from burning. Sprinkle on the ground cloves and add two of the cinnamon sticks.

3 Cover the pan tightly and cook over a low heat for about 30 minutes, or until the pumpkin is tender and the sugar and water have formed a syrup. Check the casserole or pan occasionally to make sure that the pumpkin does not dry out or catch on the bottom.

4 Transfer the pumpkin to a platter and pour the hot syrup over. Decorate each portion with mint and cinnamon sticks and serve with thick yogurt or crème fraîche.

COOK'S TIP

Pumpkin cooked in this way can be used to fill sweet empanadas, so cook all of it and use the rest as filling.

COCONUT CUSTARD

LIGHT AND CREAMY, THIS IS THE PERFECT PUDDING FOR SERVING AFTER A SPICY MAIN COURSE. CHILDREN LIKE IT, AND IT IS IDEAL FOR ENTERTAINING AS IT CAN BE MADE AHEAD OF TIME AND KEPT IN THE FRIDGE OVERNIGHT.

SERVES SIX

INGREDIENTS
- 225g/8oz/1 cup sugar
- 250ml/8fl oz/1 cup water
- 1 cinnamon stick, about 7.5cm/3in in length
- 175g/6oz/2 cups desiccated (dry unsweetened shredded) coconut
- 750ml/1¼ pints/3 cups milk
- 4 eggs
- 175ml/6fl oz/¾ cup whipping cream
- 50g/2oz/½ cup chopped almonds, toasted
- strips of orange rind, to decorate

VARIATION
Use about 115g/4oz/1 cup fresh coconut, and grate it in a food processor.

1 To make the cinnamon syrup, place the sugar and water in a very large pan, add the cinnamon stick and bring to the boil. Lower the heat and simmer, uncovered, for 5 minutes.

2 Add the coconut and cook over a low heat, stirring occasionally, for 5 minutes. Stir in the milk until the mixture has thickened slightly. Remove the cinnamon stick. Remove from the heat.

3 Whisk the eggs until light and fluffy. Gradually incorporate the coconut mixture, then scrape into a clean pan.

4 Cook over a low heat, stirring constantly, until the mixture becomes a thick custard. Cool, then chill. Just before serving, whip the cream. Transfer to individual bowls, top with the cream, chopped almonds and orange rind and serve. Toasted flaked almonds also go well with this.

Fruit Platter

Mexicans like to eat fruit with chilli and lime as a starter or hors d'oeuvre, but the combination also makes a refreshing end to a meal. The selection of fruit below is just a suggestion; use any fruit in season, bearing in mind that the aim is to produce a colourful platter with plenty of flavour.

SERVES SIX

INGREDIENTS
- ½ small watermelon
- 2 mangoes
- 2 papayas
- 1 small pineapple
- 1 fresh coconut
- 1 *jicama*
- juice of 2 limes, plus lime wedges, to serve
- sea salt
- mild red chilli powder

1 Slice the watermelon thinly, then cut each slice into bite-size triangles, removing as many of the seeds as possible. Take a large slice off the stone on either side of each mango, then cross-hatch the mango flesh on each slice. Turn the slices inside out so that the cubes of mango flesh stand proud. Slice these off and put them in a bowl.

2 Cut the payayas in half, scoop out the seeds, then cut each half into wedges, leaving the skin on. Cut the leafy green top off the pineapple, then slice off the base. With a sharp knife, remove the skin, using a spiral action and cutting deeply enough to remove most of the "eyes". Use a small knife to take out any remaining "eyes". Cut the pineapple lengthways in quarters and remove the core from the centre of each piece. Slice each of the pieces into bite-size wedges.

3 Make a hole in two of the "eyes" at the top of the coconut, using a nail and hammer. Pour out the liquid. Tap the coconut with a hammer until it breaks into pieces. Remove the hard outer shell, then use a potato peeler to remove the thin brown layer. Cut the coconut into neat pieces.

4 Peel and slice the *jicama*. Arrange all the fruits on a platter, sprinkle them with lime juice and serve with lime wedges and small bowls of sea salt and chilli powder for sprinkling.

COOK'S TIP
Cut all the fruit into bite-size pieces, so that it can be speared on cocktail sticks (toothpicks) and eaten.

Ice Cream with Mexican Chocolate

This rich, creamy ice cream has a wonderfully complex flavour, thanks to the cinnamon and almonds in the Mexican chocolate.

SERVES FOUR

INGREDIENTS
- 2 large (US extra large) eggs
- 115g/4oz/½ cup caster (superfine) sugar
- 2 bars Mexican chocolate, total weight about 115g/4oz
- 400ml/14fl oz/1⅔ cups double (heavy) cream
- 200ml/7fl oz/scant 1 cup milk
- chocolate curls, to decorate

1 Put the eggs in a bowl and whisk them with an electric whisk until they are thick, pale and fluffy. Gradually whisk in the sugar.

2 Melt the chocolate in a heavy-based pan over a low heat, then add it to the egg mixture and mix thoroughly. Whisk in the cream, then stir in the milk, a little at a time. Cool the mixture, then chill. Pour the mixture into an ice cream maker and churn until thick.

3 Alternatively freeze it in a shallow plastic box in the fast-freeze section of the freezer for several hours, until ice crystals have begun to form around the edges. Process to break up the ice crystals, then freeze again. To serve, decorate with chocolate curls.

Capirotada

Mexican cooks believe in making good use of everything available to them. This pudding was invented as a way of using up food before the Lenten fast, but is now eaten at other times too.

SERVES SIX

INGREDIENTS
- 1 small French stick, a few days old
- 75–115g/3–4oz/⅓–½ cup butter, softened, plus extra for greasing
- 200g/7oz/scant 1 cup soft dark brown sugar
- 1 cinnamon stick, about 15cm/6in long
- 400ml/14fl oz/1⅔ cups water
- 45ml/3 tbsp dry sherry
- 75g/3oz/¾ cup flaked almonds, plus extra, to decorate
- 75g/3oz/½ cup raisins
- 115g/4oz/1 cup grated Monterey Jack or mild Cheddar cheese
- single (light) cream, for pouring

1 Slice the bread into about 30 rounds, each 1cm/½in thick. Lightly butter on both sides. Cook in batches in a warm frying pan until browned, turning over once. Set the slices aside.

2 Place the sugar, cinnamon stick and water in a pan. Heat gently, stirring all the time, until the sugar has dissolved. Bring to the boil, then lower the heat and simmer for 15 minutes without stirring. Remove the cinnamon stick, then stir in the sherry.

COOK'S TIP

This recipe works well with older bread that is quite dry. If you only have fresh bread, slice it and dry it out for a few minutes in a low oven.

3 Preheat the oven to 180°C/350°F/Gas 4. Grease a 20cm/8in square baking dish with butter. Layer the bread rounds, almonds, raisins and cheese in the dish, pour the syrup over, letting it soak into the bread. Bake the pudding for about 30 minutes until golden brown.

4 Remove from the oven, leave to stand for 5 minutes, then cut into squares. Serve cold, with single cream poured over, decorated with the extra flaked almonds.

Drunken Plantain

Mexicans enjoy their native fruits and until their cuisine was influenced by the Spanish and the French, they had no pastries or cakes, preferring to end their meals with fruit, which was abundant. This dessert is quick and easy to prepare, and tastes delicious.

SERVES SIX

INGREDIENTS
- 3 ripe plantains
- 50g/2oz/¼ cup butter, diced
- 45ml/3 tbsp rum
- grated rind and juice of 1 small orange
- 5ml/1 tsp ground cinnamon
- 50g/2oz/¼ cup soft dark brown sugar
- 50g/2oz/½ cup whole almonds, in their skins
- fresh mint sprigs, to decorate
- crème fraîche or thick double (heavy) cream, to serve

1 Preheat the oven to 180°C/350°F/Gas 4. Peel the plantains and cut them in half lengthways. Put the pieces in a shallow baking dish, dot them all over with butter, then spoon over the rum and orange juice.

2 Mix the orange rind, cinnamon and brown sugar in a bowl. Sprinkle the mixture over the plantains.

3 Bake for 25–30 minutes, until the plantains are soft and the sugar has melted into the rum and orange juice to form a sauce.

4 Meanwhile, slice the almonds and dry fry them in a heavy-based frying pan until the cut sides are golden. Serve the plantains in individual bowls, with some of the sauce spooned over. Sprinkle the almonds on top, decorate with the fresh mint sprigs and offer crème fraîche or double cream separately.

Caribbean Spiced Rice Pudding

Some recipes from the Caribbean can be extremely sweet, particularly desserts. If this rice pudding is a little too sweet for your taste, simply reduce the sugar quantity and rely upon the natural sweetness of the fruit.

SERVES SIX

INGREDIENTS

- 25g/1oz/2 tbsp butter
- 1 cinnamon stick
- 115g/4oz/½ cup soft brown sugar
- 115g/4oz/⅔ cup ground rice
- 1.2 litres/2 pints/5 cups milk
- 2.5ml/½ tsp allspice
- 50g/2oz/⅓ cup sultanas (golden raisins)
- 75g/3oz mandarin oranges, chopped
- 75g/3oz pineapple, chopped

1 Melt the butter in a non-stick pan. Add the cinnamon stick and sugar. Heat over a medium heat until the sugar just begins to caramelize. Remove from the heat.

2 Carefully stir in the rice and three-quarters of the milk. Slowly bring to the boil, stirring all the time, being careful not to let the milk burn. Reduce the heat and simmer gently for about 10 minutes, or until the rice is cooked, stirring constantly.

3 Add the remaining milk, the allspice and the sultanas. Leave to simmer for 5 minutes, stirring occasionally.

4 When the rice is thick and creamy, allow to cool slightly, then stir in the mandarin and pineapple pieces.

JAMAICAN FRUIT TRIFLE

THIS TRIFLE IS ACTUALLY BASED ON A CARIBBEAN FOOL THAT CONSISTS OF FRUIT STIRRED INTO THICK VANILLA-FLAVOURED CREAM. THIS VERSION IS MUCH LESS RICH, REDRESSING THE BALANCE WITH PLENTY OF FRUIT, AND WITH CRÈME FRAÎCHE REPLACING SOME OF THE CREAM.

SERVES EIGHT

INGREDIENTS

- 1 large pineapple, peeled and cored
- 300ml/½ pint/1¼ cups double (heavy) cream
- 200ml/7fl oz/scant 1 cup crème fraîche
- 60ml/4 tbsp icing (confectioners') sugar, sifted
- 10ml/2 tsp pure vanilla essence (extract)
- 30ml/2 tbsp white or coconut rum
- 3 papayas, peeled, seeded and chopped
- 3 mangoes, peeled, stoned (pitted) and chopped
- thinly pared rind and juice of 1 lime
- 25g/1oz/⅓ cup coarsely shredded or flaked coconut, toasted

1 Cut the pineapple into large chunks, place in a food processor or blender and process briefly until chopped. Tip into a sieve placed over a bowl and leave for 5 minutes so that most of the juice drains from the fruit.

2 Whip the double cream to soft peaks, then fold in the crème fraîche, sifted icing sugar, vanilla extract and rum.

3 Fold the drained chopped pineapple into the cream mixture. Place the chopped papayas and mangoes in a large bowl and pour over the lime juice. Gently stir the fruit mixture to combine. Shred the pared lime rind.

4 Divide the fruit mixture and the pineapple cream among eight dessert plates. Decorate with the lime shreds, toasted coconut and a few small pineapple leaves, if you like, and serve at once.

COOK'S TIP

It is important to let the pineapple purée drain thoroughly, otherwise, the pineapple cream will be watery. Don't throw away the drained pineapple juice – mix it with fizzy mineral water for a refreshing drink.

Brazilian Coconut Flan

This is a somewhat unconventional but very successful recipe for quindao, a classic Brazilian dessert made with no fewer than 18 egg yolks. It is available as a packet mix throughout Latin America, but it is much more delicious if you make your own.

SERVES 12

INGREDIENTS

- 150g/5oz/1⅔ cups desiccated (dry unsweetened shredded) coconut
- 200ml/7fl oz/scant 1 cup full-fat (whole) milk
- 40g/1½oz/3 tbsp unsalted (sweet) butter, softened
- 400g/14oz/2 cups caster (superfine) sugar, plus extra for dusting
- 18 egg yolks

1 Put the desiccated coconut in a bowl. Pour over the milk and leave to stand for about 15 minutes, or until all the milk has been absorbed.

2 Meanwhile, grease a 23cm/9in ring mould with some of the butter and then lightly dust with a sprinkling of caster sugar.

3 Put the remaining butter in a large bowl. Add the sugar and soaked coconut, and mix vigorously until thoroughly combined.

4 Using a wooden spoon, gently stir in the egg yolks, one at a time. When the ingredients are thoroughly combined, cover the bowl with a clean dishtowel and leave the mixture to stand in a cool place for about 1 hour.

5 Tip the coconut mixture into the prepared ring mould and place this in the centre of a large, deep roasting pan. Pour in enough warm water to come halfway up the outside of the mould. Place this bain marie and its pudding in a cold oven.

6 Heat the oven to 220°C/425°F/Gas 7 and bake the flan for about 1 hour, or until the surface is a dark golden, caramelized brown. Remove from the oven and leave to cool in the water in the roasting pan.

COOK'S TIP

You can use the extra egg whites to make a special fluffy tortilla or omlette. Whisk two or three of the whites up and fold them into the eggs before cooking.

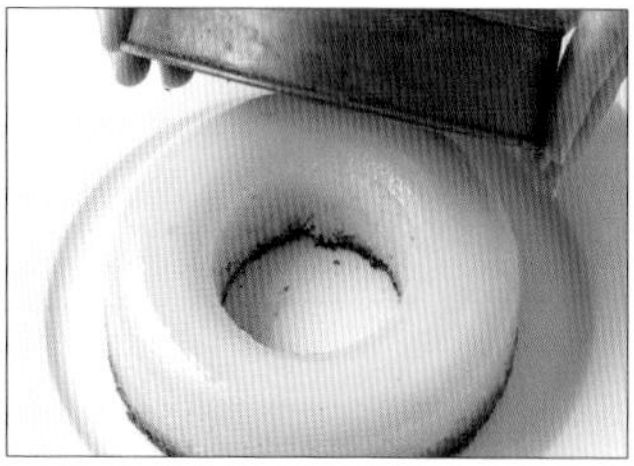

7 When the flan is cold, loosen the edges carefully with a palette knife. Cover with an upturned serving platter and turn the ring mould gently upside down. Gently lift off the ring mould, being careful not to let it touch the top of the flan. Serve cut in thick slices.

VARIATIONS

When available, use finely grated fresh coconut instead of desiccated. There is no need to soak the fresh coconut in the milk; just add both ingredients to the butter and sugar. For a more fragrant, even sweeter flan, try adding a whole vanilla pod to the egg and coconut mixture before it is left to stand. Make sure you remove it before cooking.

MEXICAN WEDDING COOKIES

ALMOST HIDDEN BENEATH THEIR VEIL OF ICING SUGAR, THESE LITTLE SHORTBREAD BISCUITS ARE TRADITIONALLY SERVED AT WEDDINGS, AND ARE ABSOLUTELY DELICIOUS. SERVE THEM AFTER DINNER WITH COFFEE AND PERHAPS A GLASS OF THE MEXICAN COFFEE LIQUEUR – KAHLÚA.

MAKES 30

INGREDIENTS

- 225g/8oz/1 cup butter, softened
- 175g/6oz/1½ cups icing (confectioners') sugar
- 5ml/1 tsp vanilla essence (extract)
- 300g/11oz/2¾ cups plain (all-purpose) flour
- pinch of salt
- 150g/5oz/1¼ cups pecan nuts, chopped

1 Preheat the oven to 190°C/375°F/ Gas 5. Beat the butter until light and fluffy, then beat in 115g/4oz/1 cup icing sugar, with the vanilla essence.

2 Gradually add the flour and salt to the creamed mixture until it starts to form a dough. Add the finely chopped pecans with the remaining flour. Knead the dough lightly.

3 Divide the dough into 30 equal pieces and roll them into balls. Space about 5mm/¼in apart on baking sheets. Press each ball lightly with your thumb, to flatten it slightly.

4 Bake the biscuits for 10–15 minutes until they are starting to brown. Cool on the baking sheets for 10 minutes, then transfer to wire racks to cool completely.

5 Put the remaining icing sugar in a bowl. Add a few biscuits at a time, shaking them in the icing sugar until they are heavily coated. Serve straight-away or store in an airtight tin.

ALMOND ORANGE BISCUITS

THE COMBINATION OF LARD AND ALMONDS GIVES THESE BISCUITS A LOVELY SHORT TEXTURE, SO THAT THEY MELT IN THE MOUTH. THEY ARE PERFECT WITH COFFEE OR HOT CHOCOLATE.

MAKES 36

INGREDIENTS

- 250g/9oz/generous 1 cup lard
- 125g/4½oz/generous ½ cup caster (superfine) sugar
- 2 eggs, beaten
- grated rind and juice of 1 small orange
- 300g/11oz/1¾ cups plain (all-purpose) flour, sifted with 5ml/1 tsp baking powder
- 200g/7oz/1¾ cups ground almonds

For dusting

- 50g/2oz/½ cup icing (confectioners') sugar
- 5ml/1 tsp ground cinnamon

COOK'S TIP

If you can't be bothered to roll out the dough, just divide it into 36 pieces and roll each one into a ball. Place these on baking sheets and flatten each one into a biscuit shape with a fork.

1 Preheat the oven to 200°C/400°F/ Gas 6. Place the lard in a large bowl and beat with an electric whisk until light and aerated. Gradually beat in the caster sugar.

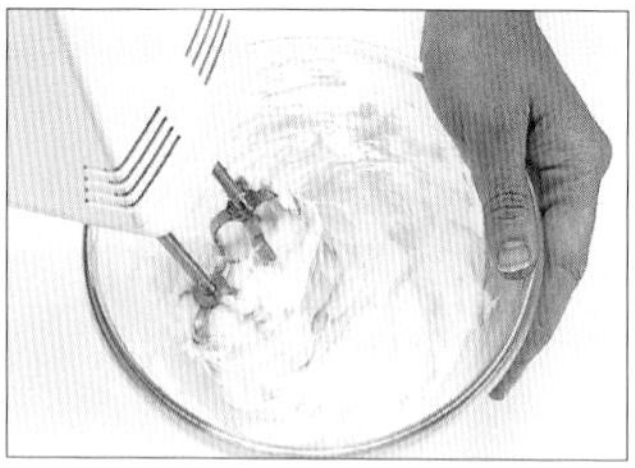

2 Continue to whisk the mixture while you add the eggs, orange rind and juice. Whisk for 3–4 minutes more, then stir in the flour mixture and ground almonds to form a dough.

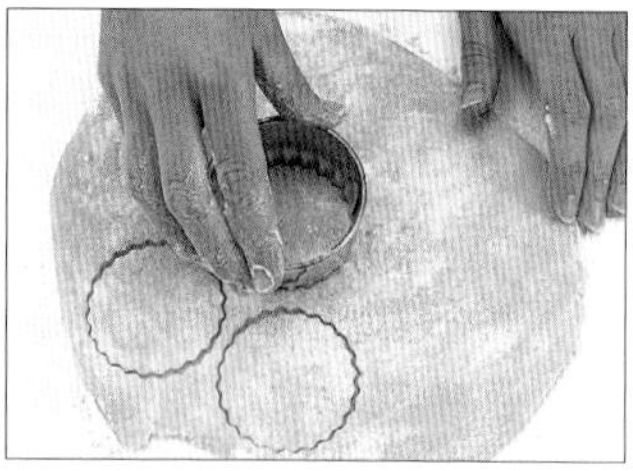

3 Roll out the dough on a lightly floured surface until it is about 1cm/½in thick. Using biscuit cutters, cut out 36 rounds, re-rolling the dough if necessary. Gently lift the rounds on to baking sheets.

4 Bake for about 10 minutes, or until the biscuits are golden. Leave to stand on the baking sheets for 10 minutes to cool and firm slightly.

5 Mix together the icing sugar and cinnamon. Put the mixture in a small sieve or tea strainer and dust the biscuits well. Leave to cool completely.

Rum and Banana Waffles

To save time, these scrumptious dessert waffles can be made in advance, wrapped tightly, frozen, and then warmed through in the oven just before serving.

SERVES FOUR

INGREDIENTS
- 225g/8oz/2 cups plain (all-purpose) flour
- 10ml/2 tsp baking powder
- 5ml/1 tsp bicarbonate of soda (baking soda)
- 15ml/1 tbsp caster (superfine) sugar
- 2 eggs
- 50g/2oz/¼ cup butter, melted
- 175ml/6fl oz/¾ cup milk
- 300ml/½ pint/1¼ cups buttermilk
- 5ml/1 tsp vanilla essence (extract)
- single (light) cream, to serve

For the bananas
- 6 bananas, thickly sliced
- 115g/4oz/1 cup chopped pecan nuts
- 50g/2oz/⅓ cup demerara sugar
- 75ml/5 tbsp maple syrup
- 45ml/3 tbsp dark rum

1 Sift the dry ingredients into a large mixing bowl. Make a well in the centre. Add the eggs, melted butter and milk. Whisk together, gradually incorporating the flour mixture, until smooth.

COOK'S TIP
If you don't own a waffle iron, prepare the batter as directed, but make small pancakes in a heavy-based frying pan. Alternatively, use ready-made waffles, which are available from large supermarkets, and reheat as directed on the packet before serving with the hot banana topping.

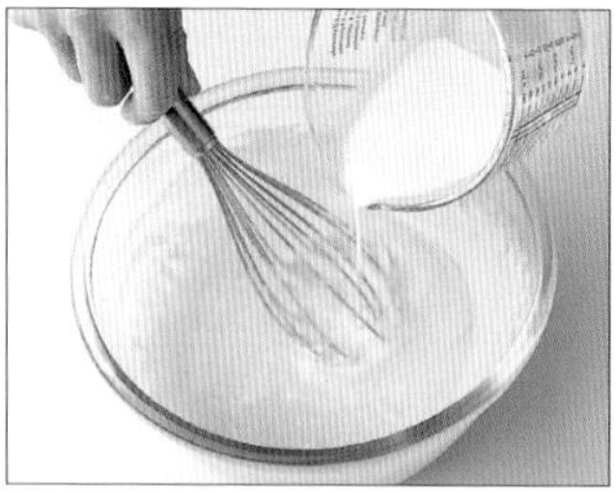

2 Add the buttermilk and vanilla to the batter and whisk well. Cover and leave to stand for 30 minutes. Preheat the oven to 150°C/300°F/Gas 2.

3 Heat a hand-held waffle iron over the heat. Stir the batter and add more milk if required (the consistency should be quite thick). Open the waffle iron and pour some batter over two thirds of the surface. Close it and wipe off any excess batter.

4 Cook for 3–4 minutes, carefully turning the waffle iron over once during cooking. If using an electric waffle maker, follow the manufacturer's instructions for cooking.

VARIATIONS
Use other fruits for the waffle topping, if you like. Small chunks of fresh or drained, canned pineapple, thin wedges of peaches or nectarines or even orange slices would be delicious alternatives to the banana.

5 When the batter stops steaming, open the iron and lift out the waffle with a fork. Put it on a heatproof plate and keep it hot in the oven. Repeat with the remaining batter to make eight waffles in all. Preheat the grill (broiler).

6 Cook the bananas: spread them out on a large shallow baking tin and top with the nuts. Scatter over the demerara sugar. Mix the maple syrup and rum together and spoon over.

7 Grill (broil) for 3–4 minutes or until the sugar begins to bubble. Serve on top of the waffles with single cream.

FRUIT-FILLED EMPANADAS

IMAGINE BITING THROUGH CRISP BUTTERY PASTRY TO DISCOVER A RICH FRUITY FILLING FLAVOURED WITH ORANGES AND CINNAMON. THIS IS THE STUFF THAT DREAMS ARE MADE OF.

MAKES 12

INGREDIENTS
- 275g/10oz/2½ cups plain (all-purpose) flour
- 25g/1oz/2 tbsp granulated sugar
- 90g/3½oz/scant ½ cup chilled butter, cubed
- 1 egg yolk
- iced water
- milk, to glaze
- caster (superfine) sugar, for sprinkling
- whole almonds and orange wedges

For the filling
- 25g/1oz/2 tbsp butter
- 3 ripe plantains, peeled and mashed
- 2.5ml/½ tsp ground cloves
- 5ml/1 tsp ground cinnamon
- 225g/8oz/1⅓ cups raisins
- grated rind and juice of 2 oranges

1 Combine the flour and sugar in a mixing bowl. Rub in the chilled cubes of butter until the mixture resembles fine breadcrumbs.

2 Beat the egg yolk and add to the flour mixture. Add iced water to make a smooth dough. Shape it into a ball.

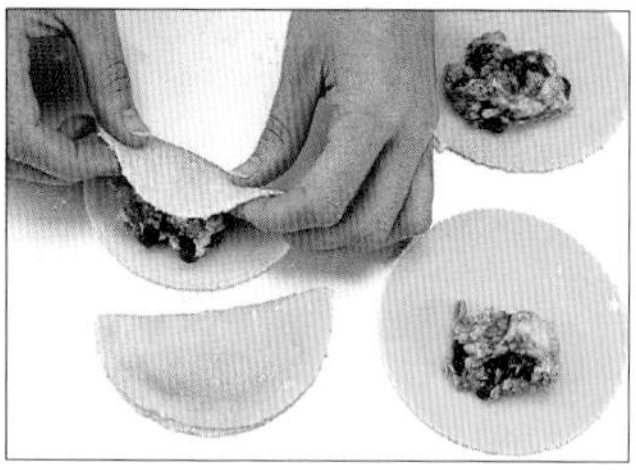

3 Melt the butter for the filling in a pan. Add the plantains, cloves and cinnamon and cook over a moderate heat for 2–3 minutes. Stir in the raisins, with the orange rind and juice. Lower the heat so that the mixture barely simmers. Cook for about 15 minutes, until the raisins are plump and the juice has evaporated. Set the mixture aside to cool.

4 Preheat the oven to 200°C/400°F/Gas 6. Roll out the pastry on a lightly floured surface. Cut it into 10cm/4in rounds. Place the rounds on a baking sheet and spoon on a little of the filling. Dampen the rim of the pastry rounds with water, fold the pastry over the filling and crimp the edges to seal.

5 Brush the empanadas with milk. Bake them, in batches if necessary, for about 15 minutes or until they are golden. Allow to cool a little, sprinkle with caster sugar and serve warm, with whole almonds and orange wedges.

COOK'S TIP

Use a little of the leftover egg white instead of milk for glazing, if you like.

CHRISTMAS COOKIES WITH WALNUTS

AT CHRISTMAS TIME, THESE ARE INDIVIDUALLY WRAPPED IN SMALL SQUARES OF BRIGHTLY COLOURED TISSUE PAPER AND ARRANGED IN LARGE BOWLS, OFTEN TRANSFORMED INTO GIFTS.

MAKES 24

INGREDIENTS

- 115g/4oz/½ cup lard, softened
- 75g/3oz/¾ cup icing (confectioners') sugar
- 5ml/1 tsp vanilla essence (extract)
- 150g/5oz/1¼ cups unbleached plain (all-purpose) flour
- 75g/3oz/¾ cup broken walnuts, finely chopped
- 50g/2oz/½ cup icing (confectioners') sugar, for dusting
- 10ml/2 tsp ground cinnamon

COOK'S TIP

Pecan nuts can be used instead of the walnuts, if you like.

1 Preheat the oven to 190°C/375°F/ Gas 5. Place the lard in a large bowl and beat with an electric whisk until light and aerated.

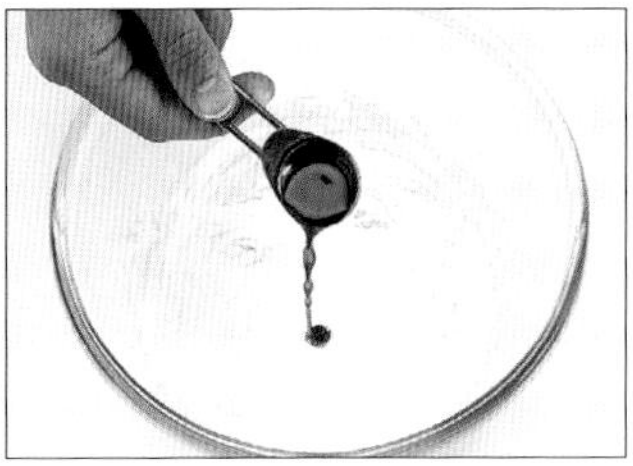

2 Gradually beat in 25g/1oz/¼ cup of the icing sugar, then add the vanilla essence and beat well.

3 Add the flour by hand, working it gently into the mixture. Do not be tempted to use a spoon or the mixture will be too sticky. Add the walnuts and mix carefully.

4 Divide the dough evenly into 24 small pieces, roll each to a ball, and space well apart on baking sheets. Bake for 10–15 minutes, until golden, switching the baking sheets around halfway through, to ensure even baking. Cool the biscuits on wire racks.

5 Put the remaining icing sugar in a bowl and stir in the cinnamon. Add a few biscuits at a time, shaking them in the icing sugar until they are heavily coated. Shake off the excess sugar. Serve wrapped in coloured paper.

NUT BRITTLE

NUTS ARE VERY POPULAR IN SOUTH AMERICA AND VARIATIONS OF THIS SNACK ARE TO BE FOUND THROUGHOUT THE CONTINENT. IN BRAZIL IT'S CALLED PE-DE-MOLEQUE *(KID'S FEET).*

MAKES ABOUT TEN

INGREDIENTS
- vegetable oil, for greasing
- 250g/9oz/2¼ cups unsalted peanuts
- 250g/9oz/generous 1 cup granulated sugar

COOK'S TIP
Act quickly once the sugar has reached the ideal colour, otherwise the caramel could burn and become bitter. Don't worry if the pieces of brittle don't snap evenly when cooled – they'll be just as delicious if irregular.

1 Using vegetable oil, grease a shallow 30 x 20cm/12 x 8in baking tin (pan). Tip the sugar and peanuts into a heavy pan and place over a low heat.

2 As the sugar begins to melt, start stirring the nuts with a wooden spoon, bringing the sugar that is beginning to caramelize around the edges of the pan into the centre.

3 When all the mixture has caramelized and has taken on a deep brown colour, remove the pan from the heat and quickly pour the mixture into the prepared baking tin. Leave it to cool.

4 When the brittle has almost set, use a knife to mark it into regular squares or rectangles. This will make it easier to snap the cold brittle into pieces.

COCONUT SWEETS

THESE CHEWY SWEETS (CANDIES) ARE A FAVOURITE WITH CHILDREN. THEY CAN BE MADE PLAIN, BUT THE LIME JUICE AND CLOVES ADD AN INTERESTING TWIST THAT ADULTS CANNOT RESIST EITHER.

MAKES 25

INGREDIENTS
- 50g/2oz/⅔ cup desiccated (dry unsweetened shredded) coconut
- 105ml/7 tbsp water
- 175g/6oz/¾ cup light muscovado (brown) sugar
- large pinch ground cloves
- juice of ½ lime

COOK'S TIP
Store the coconut sweets in an airtight container in a cool place and they will last for a few weeks or more. If you use fresh ingredients, such as grated fresh coconut or pumpkin, they should be kept chilled and consumed within a week.

1 Line a baking tray with baking parchment. Place the coconut in a pan with the water and sugar. Heat gently until the sugar dissolves.

2 Stir in the ground cloves and lime juice and increase the heat. Cook, stirring with a wooden spoon, until the mixture has thickened and become dark golden brown.

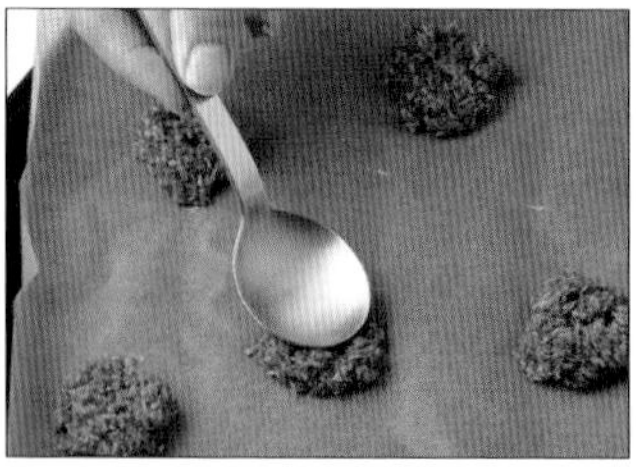

3 Drop spoonfuls of the mixture on to the lined tray, pressing the mixture down with the back of the spoon to flatten it lightly into chunky, irregular pieces. Leave to cool before eating.

VARIATION
Equal quantities of grated fresh coconut and grated raw pumpkin can be used instead of the desiccated coconut.

DRINKS

Nothing is more refreshing or nutritious than freshly squeezed fruit juice or coconut juice straight from the shell. Fruit bars serving these juices are found throughout the Caribbean and Latin America. The region is also famous for its cocktails, and every country has its favourite spirit – there's Brazilian cachaça, Peruvian pisco, Caribbean rum and Mexican tequila.

MANGO SHAKE

CHILDREN LOVE FRESH FRUIT SHAKES, AND WITH THE VARIETY OF TROPICAL FRUIT AVAILABLE THROUGHOUT THE REGION, THEY ARE SPOILT FOR CHOICE.

MAKES 1 LITRE/1¾ PINTS/4 CUPS

INGREDIENTS
- 2 large ripe mangoes
- 750ml/1¼ pints/3 cups full-fat (whole) milk
- juice of ½ lime
- caster (superfine) sugar, to taste

VARIATION

In Brazil, a similar drink is made with avocados. Simply use 2 ripe avocados in place of the mangoes. Until recently, Brazilians viewed avocados as fruit and would not have dreamed of eating them in savoury dishes. Once you have tasted this unusual, delicious variation, you will understand why.

1 Place each mango in turn on a board with the narrow side down. Cut off a thick lengthways slice, keeping as close to the stone (pit) as possible. Turn the mango around and repeat on the other side. Cut off the flesh that is still attached to the stone. Remove the peel and chop the flesh roughly.

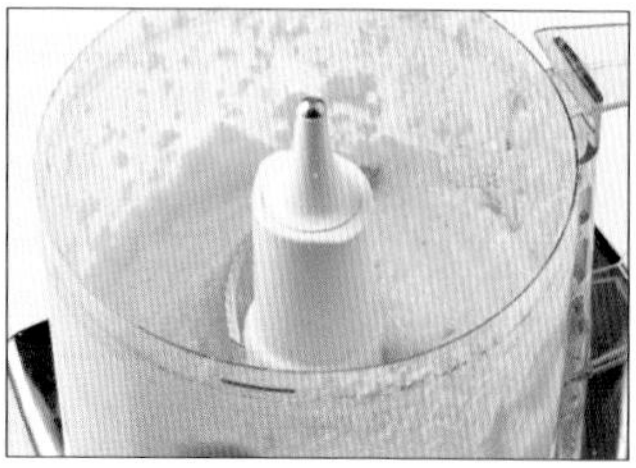

2 Put the chopped mango in a blender or food processor and add the milk and lime juice. Process until smooth.

3 Pour the mango shake into a jug (pitcher), stir in sugar to taste and chill in the refrigerator. Serve in tall glasses with ice cubes.

PINEAPPLE AND MINT JUICE

THIS DRINK IS PERFECTLY REFRESHING ON A SUNNY DAY – THE MINT REALLY BRINGS OUT THE SWEETNESS OF THE FRUIT, AND ADDED SUGAR IS RARELY REQUIRED. IT IS A FAVOURITE FOR ENJOYING ON THE BEACH OR RELAXING OUTSIDE A STREET CAFE THROUGHOUT SOUTH AND CENTRAL AMERICA AND ACROSS THE CARIBBEAN, OFTEN WITH SMALL AMOUNTS OF OTHER FRUITS ADDED.

MAKES 1 LITRE/1¾ PINTS/4 CUPS

INGREDIENTS
- 1kg/2¼lb pineapples
- 10 fresh mint leaves
- crushed ice
- caster (superfine) sugar, to taste

VARIATION

To make a pineapple and mint granita, pour the juice into a shallow metal container and place in the freezer until almost firm. Break up the mixture using a fork and return it to the freezer. Repeat this procedure two or three times, until the mixture is semi-frozen, then serve.

1 Cut the top and base off each pineapple, then cut off the skin, being careful to remove all the "eyes". Discard the skin and cut the pineapple, including the core, into large chunks.

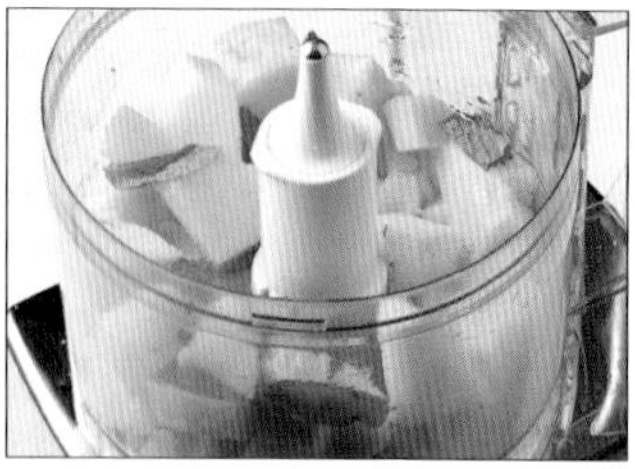

2 Blend the pineapple chunks with the mint leaves in a blender or food processor until smooth. Pour into a jug (pitcher) and stir in the crushed ice. Stir until the ice has dissolved slightly.

Cashew Nut Milk

In mainland Spain and Mexico a similar drink – horchata – is made with almonds, but this Cuban variation with cashews is even more delicious. The result is rich and creamy. It is great for kids and even better for adults who need a hangover cure.

1 Finely grind the cashews in a food processor. Add the sugar and cinnamon and grind the mixture again to make a smooth paste.

2 With the motor still running, gradually pour in 900ml/1½ pints/3¾ cups of boiling water, until the drink becomes smooth and frothy. Scrape down the mixture occasionally, if necessary.

3 Pour the cashew nut milk into a jug (pitcher). Cover and chill in the refrigerator. Stir well before serving in tall glasses. Float ice cubes in each glass. As the ice melts, it will dilute the drink, giving it a lighter texture.

MAKES 1.2 LITRES/2 PINTS/5 CUPS

INGREDIENTS

- 400g/14oz/3½ cups blanched cashews
- 225g/8oz/generous 1 cup caster (superfine) sugar
- 1.5ml/¼ tsp ground cinnamon

COOK'S TIP

For a smooth drink, make this the night before, allow it to stand in the refrigerator overnight, and strain before serving.

Passion Fruit Batida

Brazilian BATIDAS *can be made with a variety of juices, such as lime or coconut milk. Do not be fooled by the fruity sweetness: a small glass of* BATIDA, *sipped slowly, is more than enough to get the party started.*

MAKES TWO

INGREDIENTS
- 8 passion fruit
- 200ml/7fl oz/scant 1 cup *cachaça*
- 30ml/2 tbsp caster (superfine) sugar
- 3 ice cubes

1 Cut the passion fruit in half and scoop the flesh and seeds into a cocktail shaker or mixing jug (pitcher).

2 Add the remaining ingredients, including the ice cubes, and shake vigorously or stir thoroughly.

3 Strain into two cocktail glasses and serve the *batida* immediately.

VARIATIONS
- Two other flavours of *batida* that are also very popular are lime and coconut. Simply replace the passion fruit with 60ml/4 tbsp lime juice or coconut milk.
- If you are unable to find *cachaça*, replace with equal quantities of vodka.

CITRUS AGUA FRESCA

THESE REFRESHING FRUIT JUICES ARE SOLD FROM STREET STALLS IN TOWNS ALL OVER MEXICO. THE VARIETIES OF FRUIT USED CHANGE WITH THE SEASONS.

SERVES FOUR

INGREDIENTS
- 12 limes
- 3 oranges
- 2 grapefruit
- 600ml/1 pint/2½ cups water
- 75g/3oz/6 tbsp caster (superfine) sugar
- extra fruit wedges, to decorate

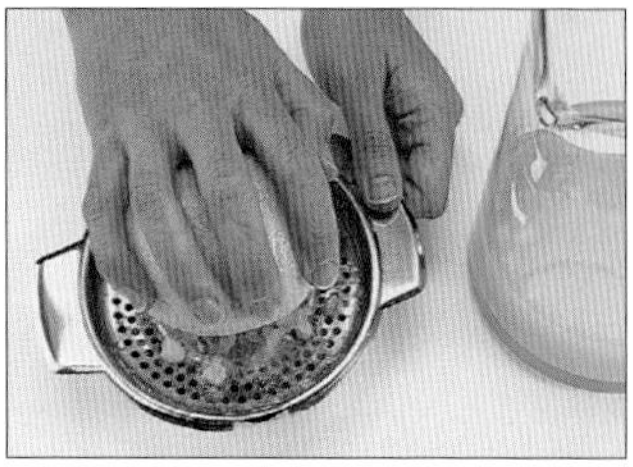

1 Squeeze the juice from the limes, oranges and grapefruit. Some fruit pulp may collect along with the juice. This should also be used, once any seeds have been discarded. Pour the mixture into a large jug (pitcher).

2 Add the water and sugar and stir until all the sugar has dissolved.

3 Chill for at least 1 hour before serving with ice and fruit wedges. The drink will keep for up to 1 week in a covered container in the refrigerator.

VARIATION
Use pink or ruby red grapefruit instead of white for a slightly sweeter drink with a deeper colour.

TAMARIND AGUA FRESCA

TAMARIND, SOMETIMES REFERRED TO AS THE INDIAN DATE, IS NATIVE TO ASIA AND NORTH AFRICA. SEEDS CAME TO MEXICO VIA INDIA. IT IS USED MEDICINALLY AND AS AN ANTISEPTIC. THE FRUIT HAS A SWEET-SOUR TASTE AND MAKES A DRINK SIMILAR TO LEMONADE.

SERVES FOUR

INGREDIENTS

- 1 litre/1¾ pints/4 cups water
- 225g/8oz tamarind pods
- 25g/1oz/2 tbsp caster (superfine) sugar

1 Pour the water into a pan and heat until warm. Remove from the heat and pour into a bowl. Peel the tamarind pods and add the pulp to the warm water. Soak for at least 4 hours.

2 Place a sieve (strainer) over a clean bowl. Pour the tamarind pulp and water into the sieve, then press the pulp through the sieve with the back of a wooden spoon, leaving the black seeds behind. Discard the seeds.

3 Add the sugar to the tamarind mixture and stir well until dissolved. Allow to cool for a few minutes. Pour into a jug (pitcher) and chill thoroughly – the mixture will keep fresh if covered and chilled for at least one day. Serve in tumblers filled with ice.

COOK'S TIP

Jars of tamarind pulp or paste are sold at Indian food shops and Oriental stores. The dried pulp is also sold in solid blocks. All these products need soaking and sieving, but you will be spared the time-consuming task of peeling the pods.

Pineapple and Lime Agua Fresca

The vivid colours of this fresh fruit drink give some indication of its wonderful flavour. It makes a delicious midday refresher, mid-afternoon break, or chilled pick-me-up at the end of a hard day.

SERVES FOUR

INGREDIENTS

- 2 pineapples
- juice of 2 limes
- 475ml/16fl oz/2 cups still mineral water
- 50g/2oz/¼ cup caster (superfine) sugar

COOK'S TIP

When peeling a pineapple cut off the top and bottom and remove the skin with a spiral action, cutting deeply enough to remove most of the "eyes". Any remaining "eyes" can be cut out using a small knife.

1 Peel the pineapples and chop the flesh, removing the core and "eyes". You should have about 450g/1lb flesh. Put this in a food processor or blender and add the lime juice and half the mineral water. Purée to a smooth pulp. Stop the machine and scrape the mixture from the side of the goblet once or twice during processing.

2 Place a sieve (strainer) over a large bowl. Tip the pineapple pulp into the sieve and press it through with a wooden spoon. Pour the sieved mixture into a large jug, cover and chill in the fridge for about 1 hour.

3 Stir in the remaining mineral water and sugar to taste. Serve with ice.

Lime Agua Fresca

This is the lime version of real English lemonade. Traditionally, lime peel would have been ground in a molcajete *to extract the oil. Mexican limes –* limones *– are harder and more tart than the smooth-skinned varieties most often sold in Western supermarkets.*

SERVES SIX

INGREDIENTS
- 1.75 litres/3 pints/7½ cups water
- 75g/3oz/6 tbsp caster (superfine) sugar
- 10 limes, plus slices, to decorate

1 Pour the water into a jug (pitcher), add the sugar and stir until all the sugar has dissolved. Chill for at least 1 hour.

2 Using a zester or grater, remove the rind from the limes, taking care to take only the coloured zest, not the pith. Squeeze the juice from the limes and add this to the chilled sugar water, with the lime rind. Stir well and chill again until required. Serve with ice in tall glasses, decorated with lime slices.

COOK'S TIP
To extract the maximum amount of juice from the limes, roll firmly between your palms for a few moments, or pierce with a skewer, put in a bowl, and microwave on maximum power for 10–15 seconds before juicing. This works with all citrus fruits.

Pisco Sour

This cocktail, enjoyed in Peru, Bolivia, Ecuador and Chile, gets its name from the Peruvian brandy with which it is made. Give the cocktail a good shake to encourage the egg whites to foam up, and finish with the bitter, spicy taste of Angostura.

MAKES TWO

INGREDIENTS
- 105ml/7 tbsp *pisco*
- 10ml/2 tsp egg white
- 30ml/2 tbsp caster (superfine) sugar
- juice of 1 lime
- 6 ice cubes
- Angostura bitters

COOK'S TIPS
- Don't stir the cocktail after adding the Angostura bitters, so each sip tastes slightly different.
- If you prefer not to eat raw egg white, the drink can be made without it.

1 Chill two tumblers in the freezer for 10 minutes, until they are frosty white.

2 Combine all the ingredients, except for the Angostura bitters, in a cocktail shaker and shake vigorously for about 30 seconds.

3 Strain into the chilled glasses. If you like you can fill the tumblers with ice first, which will dilute the cocktail slightly. Shake 2–3 drops of the bitters on top, without stirring them into the cocktail. Serve immediately.

Caipirinha

This Brazilian drink can be enjoyed at any time of day – on the beach while snacking on seafood, as an aperitif before a meal and even with steak at a barbecue. It is a very popular drink in the cities, especially at Mardi Gras festivities. As any tourist to Brazil will know, once you have tasted it, you are hooked for life!

MAKES TWO

INGREDIENTS
- 2 limes
- 30ml/2 tbsp caster (superfine) sugar
- 105ml/7 tbsp *cachaça*
- crushed ice

1 Wash the limes thoroughly, scrubbing the rind to remove any artifical wax coating that may have been applied. You can buy limes that do not have this wax coating, which will make it easier to crush out the juice from the rind. Cut each scrubbed lime into eight large chunks.

2 Place the lime chunks in two tall glasses and divide the sugar equally between them. Pound the sugar and lime together with a pestle. The skill lies in being vigorous enough to extract the juice and oil from the rind, yet delicate enough not to break the glass.

3 Top with the crushed ice and divide the *cachaça* equally between the glasses. Stir vigorously and serve.

VARIATION
Use the same recipe to make *caipiroska*, with vodka replacing the *cachaça*. You could also try making a *caipirissima*, using white rum instead of *cachaça*.

TEQUILA

THERE ARE SEVERAL DIFFERENT TYPES OF TEQUILA, MEXICO'S NATIONAL SPIRIT. EACH TYPE OF TEQUILA IS AVAILABLE IN A NUMBER OF DIFFERENT BRANDS, EACH WITH A DISTINCTIVE FLAVOUR INFLUENCED BY THE SOIL TYPE, THE SUGAR CONTENT AND FLAVOUR OF THE AGAVE PLANTS, THE LOCAL CLIMATE, AND THE COOKING AND FERMENTING PROCESSES.

There are many different ways of serving tequila. Perhaps the best known of these is the slammer, when shots of chilled tequila are drunk with salt and lime. *Joven* (young) or *reposada* (rested) tequila is often served at room temperature in small shot glasses called *caballitos*, and sipped slowly so that all the flavours can be savoured. *Anejo* (aged) tequila should be served in a small balloon glass (a large glass would allow too much of the aroma to escape). It can be diluted with a little water, but ice should not be added.

TEQUILA SLAMMERS

Mexicans have long enjoyed the taste of lime and salt with their food and drink. Beer is also taken with lime and salt.

INGREDIENTS

- chilled tequila
- salt
- wedges of lime

HOW TO SERVE TEQUILA

Pour a shot glass of tequila. Lick the space between the thumb and the index finger on your left hand, then sprinkle this area with salt. Taking care not to spill the salt, hold a lime wedge in the same hand. Pick up the shot glass in your right hand. Lick the salt, down the tequila in one, suck the lime, then slam down your empty glass. Some drinkers manage salt, lime and tequila in the same hand, but this takes practice.

TEQUILA SUNRISE

THIS DRINK TAKES ITS NAME FROM THE WAY THE GRENADINE – A BRIGHT RED CORDIAL MADE FROM POMEGRANATE JUICE – FIRST SINKS IN THE GLASS OF ORANGE JUICE AND THEN RISES TO THE SURFACE. IT BECAME POPULAR IN THE TWENTIES AND THIRTIES WHEN COCKTAILS WERE ALL THE RAGE IN THE CARIBBEAN AND IN MEXICO.

SERVES ONE

INGREDIENTS
- 25ml/1½ tbsp golden tequila
- 60ml/4 tbsp freshly squeezed orange juice
- juice of 1 lime
- 5ml/1 tsp grenadine

VARIATION
To make a Pink Cadillac, use Grand Marnier instead of orange juice. This will provide a lovely two-tone effect from the red grenadine on the bottom covered by a layer of deep orange-brown Grand Marnier. It has a delicious tangy orange flavour from the liqueur.

1 Half fill a cocktail glass with crushed ice. Pour in the tequila, then the orange and lime juices, which should be freshly squeezed. Don't be tempted to use concentrated orange juice from a carton or bottled lime juice, or the flavour of the finished drink will be spoiled.

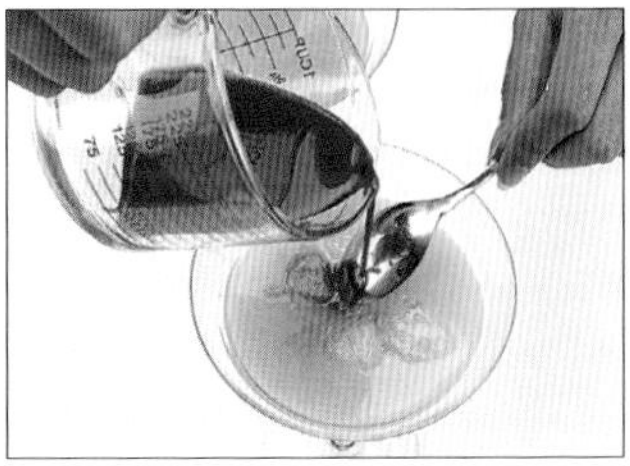

2 Quickly add the grenadine, pouring it down the back of a teaspoon held in the glass so that it sinks to the bottom of the drink. This will give the drink its characteristic two-tone colouring. Serve immediately.

Pineapple Tequila

Flavours such as almonds or quince have been added to blanco or reposada tequila for some time. Many bars have developed unique flavours by combining ingredients such as chillies with blanco tequila and leaving them for a period of time. The method below will make a smooth fruity drink.

SERVES SIX

INGREDIENTS
- 1 large pineapple
- 50g/2oz soft dark brown sugar
- 1 litre blanco tequila
- 1 vanilla pod (bean)

1 Rinse a large (about 2 litre/3½ pint) wide-necked bottle or demijohn and sterilize by placing it in an oven and then turning on the oven and setting it at 110°C/225°F/Gas ¼. After 20 minutes remove the bottle from the oven with oven gloves and allow to cool.

2 Cut the top off the pineapple and then cut away the skin, being careful to get rid of all the scales. Cut in half, remove the hard centre core and discard it. Chop the rest of the pineapple into chunks, ensuring they are small enough to fit in the bottle neck.

3 When the bottle is completely cold, put the pineapple into the bottle. Mix the sugar and tequila together in a jug until the sugar dissolves and then pour into the bottle. Split the vanilla pod and add it to the rest of the ingredients.

4 Gently agitate the bottle a few times each day to stir the contents. Allow the tequila to stand for at least 1 week before drinking. When all the tequila has been drunk the pineapple can be used in desserts such as ice cream or warmed with butter and cinnamon and served with cream.

VARIATION
If you like, add a piece of fresh pineapple and some ice to each glass before serving.

MARGARITA

THE MOST RENOWNED TEQUILA COCKTAIL, THIS CAN BE SERVED OVER ICE CUBES OR "FROZEN" – MIXED WITH CRUSHED ICE IN A COCKTAIL SHAKER TO CREATE A LIQUID SORBET EFFECT, THEN POURED INTO THE GLASS. THE SHARP BITTERNESS OF THE TEQUILA IS OFFSET BY THE TARTNESS OF THE LIME AND THE SALT ON TH LIP OF THE GLASS.

SERVES ONE

INGREDIENTS
- 45ml/3 tbsp tequila
- 25ml/1½ tbsp triple sec
- 25ml/1½ tbsp freshly squeezed lime juice
- crushed ice or ice cubes
- lime wedge and salt, for frosting glass

COOK'S TIP
White tequila is the traditional spirit to use, but today many people prefer to make margaritas with reposada tequila, which gives a more rounded flavour.

1 Frost a cocktail glass by rubbing the outer rim with the wedge of lime. Dip the glass in a saucer of salt so that it is evenly coated. It is important that there is no salt inside the glass, so take care that lime juice is only applied to the outer rim.

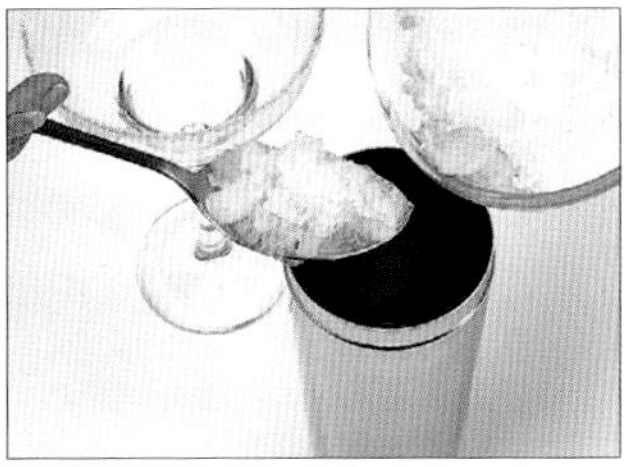

2 Combine the tequila, triple sec and lime juice in a cocktail shaker, add crushed ice, if using, and shake to mix. Carefully pour into the frosted glasses. If crushed ice is not used, place ice cubes in the glass and then pour the mixture over.

MANGO AND PEACH MARGARITA

ADDING PURÉED FRUIT TO THE CLASSIC TEQUILA MIXTURE ALTERS THE CONSISTENCY AND MAKES FOR A GLORIOUS DRINK WHICH RESEMBLES A MILKSHAKE BUT PACKS CONSIDERABLY MORE PUNCH.

SERVES FOUR

INGREDIENTS

- 2 mangoes, peeled and sliced
- 3 peaches, peeled and sliced
- 120ml/4fl oz/½ cup tequila
- 60ml/4 tbsp triple sec
- 60ml/4 tbsp freshly squeezed lime juice
- 10 ice cubes, crushed, if necessary (see Cook's Tip)
- mango slices, skin on, to decorate

COOK'S TIP

Check that your processor or blender can be used for crushing ice. If you are not sure, break ice cubes into smaller pieces by putting them in a strong plastic bag and pounding them with a meat mallet.

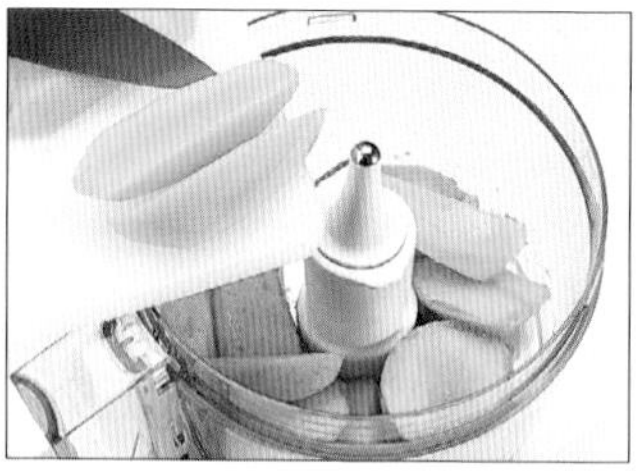

1 Place the mango and peach slices in a food processor or blender. Process or blend until all the fruit is finely chopped, scrape down the sides of the goblet, then blend again until the purée is perfectly smooth.

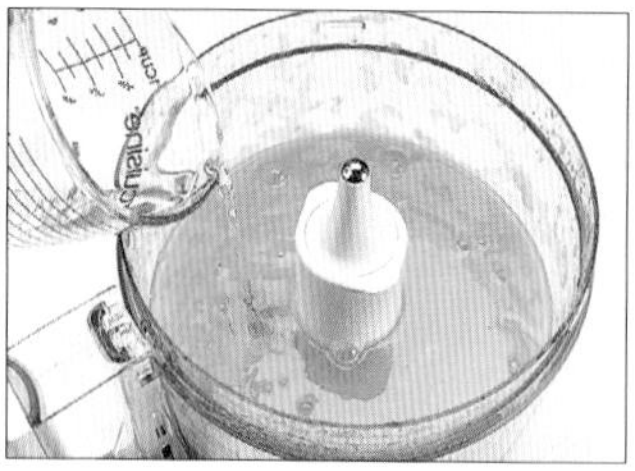

2 Add the tequila, triple sec and lime juice, process or blend for a few seconds, then add the ice. Process or blend again until the drink has the consistency of a milkshake.

3 Pour into cocktail glasses, decorate with the mango slices and serve.

LICUADO DE MELON

AMONG THE MOST REFRESHING DRINKS MEXICANS MAKE ARE FRUIT EXTRACTS MIXED WITH HONEY AND CHILLED WATER. PILE SOME ICE INTO A GLASS AND POUR OVER THE SUCCULENT LIQUID.

SERVES FOUR

INGREDIENTS
- 1 watermelon
- 1 litre/1¾ pints/4 cups chilled water
- juice of 2 limes
- honey

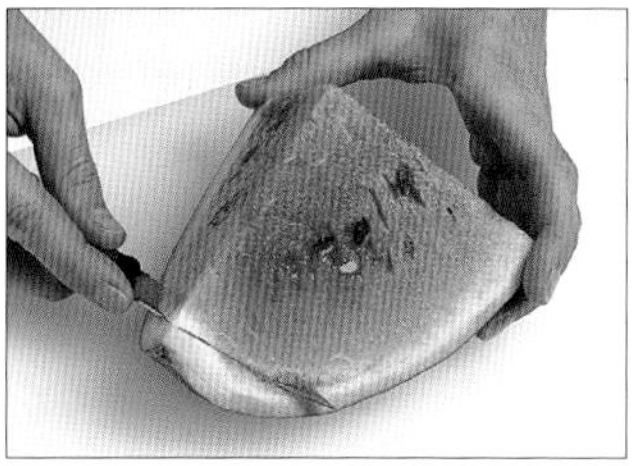

1 Cut the watermelon flesh into chunks, cutting away the skin and discarding the shiny black seeds.

2 Place the chunks in a large bowl, pour over the chilled water and leave to stand for 10 minutes.

COOK'S TIP
It can be hard to extract the juice from a lime; often they have little juice and it is firmly compacted within their flesh. Pressing machines are excellent for juicing citrus fruits, although the small hand squeezers can make for hard work. Using a fork to crush the insides can be very useful if you are having trouble getting the last drips out – and you may get some juicy bits of flesh too.

3 Tip the mixture into a large sieve (strainer) set over a bowl. Using the back of a wooden spoon, press gently on the fruit to extract all the liquid.

4 Squeeze the limes by cutting each lime in half and pressing the flesh with a fork. Stir in the lime juice and sweeten to taste with honey.

Mojito

A refreshing Cuban cocktail, this incorporates rum, mint and lime. Take your time drinking it and the flavour of the mint will gradually intensify.

MAKES ONE

INGREDIENTS

- juice of 1 lime
- 15ml/1 tbsp caster (superfine) sugar
- 4 fresh mint sprigs
- 75ml/5 tbsp white rum
- crushed ice
- 90ml/6 tbsp soda water (club soda)

COOK'S TIPS

- If you don't have a refrigerator that delivers crushed ice or a blender with sufficiently tough blades, put the ice in a freezer bag, wrap it in a dishtowel and beat it with a rolling pin. Alternatively, process the ice in a blender or food processor briefly.
- Shaking the cocktail bruises the mint leaves, releasing their flavour. If you do not have a cocktail shaker, bruise the mint leaves by hand before adding them.

1 Mix the lime juice and sugar in a cocktail shaker and shake until the sugar has dissolved. If necessary, add a few drops of the soda water to provide a little more moisture.

VARIATION

If you like, use cane sugar syrup instead of the caster sugar to provide a more authentic West Indian experience.

2 Add three of the mint sprigs, the rum and some crushed ice and shake vigorously. Pour into a tall glass, top with the soda water and decorate with the remaining mint. You can make a larger quantity and keep it chilled in an airtight bottle, although you should drink it quickly as it will only keep for a few hours.

Cuba Libre

This simple cocktail has always been very popular, the heady concoction of white or golden rum and cola refreshed with ice and the sting of lime makes it a great favourite throughout the Caribbean. However, in its Cuban homeland the name has become politically incorrect since Castro took power in 1959. Cuban exiles have sarcastically renamed it MENTIRITA, *meaning "little lie".*

MAKES ONE

INGREDIENTS

- crushed ice
- 45ml/3 tbsp white rum
- 75ml/5 tbsp cola
- 1 lime wedge, optional

COOK'S TIPS

Rum is made by fermenting and distilling the thick brown liquid (molasses) that is left behind after extracting sugar from sugar cane.

1 Spoon the crushed ice into a tall glass and top with the white rum.

2 Pour in the cola and decorate with a wedge of lime. Serve immediately.

STRAWBERRY AND BANANA PREPARADO

SIMILAR TO A SMOOTHIE, THIS IS A THICK, CREAMY FRUIT DRINK. LEAVE OUT THE ALCOHOL FOR CHILDREN OR IF YOU WOULD PREFER A LONG, REFRESHING DAYTIME DRINK.

SERVES FOUR

INGREDIENTS
- 200g/7oz/2 cups strawberries, plus extra, to decorate
- 2 bananas
- 115g/4oz block of creamed coconut
- 120ml/4fl oz/½ cup water
- 175ml/6fl oz/¾ cup white rum
- 60ml/4 tbsp grenadine
- 10 ice cubes

1 Hull the strawberries and chop them in halves or quarters if they are large fruits. Peel the bananas and chop them into rough chunks.

2 Put the fruit in a food processor or blender, crumble in the coconut and add the water. Process until smooth, scraping down the sides of the goblet as necessary.

3 Add the rum, grenadine, and ice cubes, crushing the ice first unless you have a heavy-duty processor. Blend until smooth and thick. Serve at once, decorated with the extra strawberries.

Bloody Maria

This simple cocktail consists of tequila and tomato juice mixed together and served in the same glass. The Tabasco sauce provides a spicy kick.

SERVES TWO

INGREDIENTS

- 250ml/8fl oz/1 cup tomato juice, chilled
- 5ml/1 tsp Worcestershire sauce
- 60ml/4 tbsp tequila
- few drops of Tabasco sauce
- juice of ½ lemon
- pinch of celery salt
- salt and ground black pepper
- 2 celery sticks, cut into batons, to serve

1 Pour the chilled tomato juice into a large jug (pitcher) and stir in the tequila. Add the Worcestershire sauce and stir the mixture well.

2 Add a few drops of Tabasco sauce and the lemon juice. Taste and season with celery salt, salt and pepper. Serve over ice cubes, with celery batons.

SANGRITA

Sipping sangrita and tequila alternately is a taste sensation not to be missed, the warm flavours of the first balancing the harshness of the second. The drinks are often served with ANTOJITOS *(nibbles) as an appetizer.*

SERVES EIGHT

INGREDIENTS
- 450g/1lb ripe tomatoes
- 1 small onion, finely chopped
- 2 small fresh green fresno chillies, seeded and chopped
- 120ml/4fl oz/½ cup juice from freshly squeezed oranges
- juice of 3 limes
- 2.5ml/½ tsp caster (superfine) sugar
- pinch of salt
- 1 small shot glass of golden or aged tequila per person

1 Cut a cross in the base of each tomato. Place the tomatoes in a heatproof bowl and pour over boiling water to cover. Leave for 3 minutes.

2 Lift the tomatoes out on a slotted spoon and plunge them into a second bowl of cold water. The skins will have begun to peel back from the crosses. Remove the skins, then cut the tomatoes in half and scoop out the seeds with a teaspoon.

3 Chop the tomato flesh and put in a food processor. Add the onion, chillies, orange juice, lime juice, sugar and salt.

4 Process until all the mixture is very smooth, then pour into a jug (pitcher) and chill for at least 1 hour before serving. Offer each drinker a separate shot glass of tequila as well. The drinks are sipped alternately.

COOK'S TIP
This drink can be made with a 400g/14oz can of chopped tomatoes and tastes almost as good as when made with fresh tomatoes.

SANGRIA

Testament to the Spanish influence on Mexican cooking, this popular thirst-quencher is often served in large jugs, with ice and citrus fruit slices floating on top.

SERVES SIX

INGREDIENTS
- 750ml/1¼ pints/3 cups dry red wine
- juice of 2 limes
- 120ml/4fl oz/½ cup freshly squeezed orange juice
- 120ml/4fl oz/½ cup brandy
- 50g/2oz/¼ cup caster (superfine) sugar
- 1 lime, sliced, to decorate

VARIATION
In some parts of Mexico a less potent but equally refreshing version of sangria is served. Fill tall glasses with ice. Fill each glass two-thirds full with fresh lime juice diluted with water and sweetened with sugar. Top up with red wine. Tequila is sometimes added to the lime mixture.

1 Combine the wine, lime juice, orange juice and brandy in a large jug (pitcher).

COOK'S TIP
If no caster (superfine) sugar is available, use sugar syrup. Heat 50g/2oz/¼ cup granulated sugar in 50ml/2fl oz/¼ cup water. Boil for 3 minutes, chill and store in a tightly sealed jar.

2 Stir in the sugar until it has dissolved completely.

3 Serve in tall glasses with ice. Decorate each glass with a slice of lime.

Demerara Rum Punch

The inspiration for this punch came from the rum distillery at Plantation Diamond Estate in Guyana, where some of the finest rum in the world is made, and the tantalizing aromas of sugar cane and rum pervade the air.

SERVES FOUR

INGREDIENTS

- 150ml/¼ pint/⅔ cup orange juice
- 150ml/¼ pint/⅔ cup pineapple juice
- 150ml/¼ pint/⅔ cup mango juice
- 120ml/4fl oz/½ cup water
- 250ml/8fl oz/1 cup dark rum
- a shake of angostura bitters
- freshly grated nutmeg
- 25g/1oz/2 tbsp demerara (raw) sugar
- 1 small banana
- 1 large orange

1 Pour the orange, pineapple and mango juices into a large punch bowl. Stir in the water.

2 Add the rum, angostura bitters, nutmeg and sugar. Stir gently for a few minutes until the sugar has dissolved.

3 Slice the banana thinly and stir the slices gently into the punch.

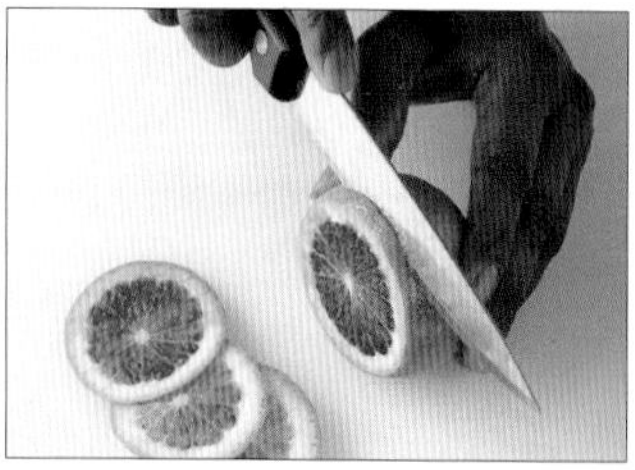

4 Slice the orange and add to the punch. Chill and serve in tumblers with ice.

VARIATIONS

You can use white rum instead of dark, if you prefer. To make a stronger punch, simply add more rum.

Caribbean Cream Stout Punch

This fairly unusual punch, made using stout, condensed milk and sherry, is a well-known "pick-me-up" that is popular all over the Caribbean. With a sweet, heady aroma of vanilla, it soothes and revives tired minds and bodies.

SERVES TWO

INGREDIENTS

- 475ml/16fl oz/2 cups stout
- 300ml/½ pint/1¼ cups evaporated (unsweetened condensed) milk
- 75ml/5 tbsp condensed milk
- 75ml/5 tbsp sherry
- 2 or 3 drops vanilla essence (extract)
- freshly grated nutmeg

1 Mix together the stout, evaporated and condensed milks, sherry and vanilla essence in a blender or food processor, or whisk together in a large mixing bowl, until creamy.

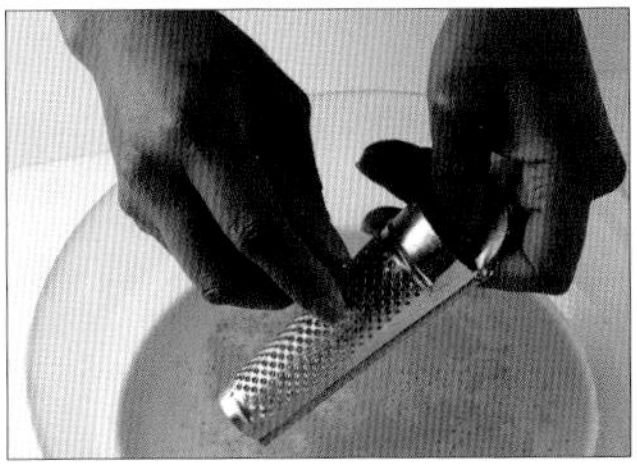

2 Add a little grated nutmeg to the stout mixture and blend or whisk thoroughly again for a few minutes.

3 Chill for at least 45 minutes, or until really cold, before ladling into small glasses to serve.

Cafe con Leche

Many Mexicans start the day with this spiced milky coffee, and those who have enjoyed a hearty midday meal will often opt for a cup of it with a sweet pastry as the afternoon merienda. *It is also popular throughout the Caribbean and Central and South America, where it is sometimes flavoured with cocoa or chocolate either with or instead of the traditional cinnamon sticks.*

SERVES FOUR

INGREDIENTS
- 50g/2oz/⅔ cup ground coffee
- 475ml/16fl oz/2 cups boiling water
- 475ml/16fl oz/2 cups milk
- 4 cinnamon sticks, each about 10cm/4in long
- sugar, to taste

1 Put the coffee in a cafetière (press pot) or jug (pitcher), pour on the boiling water and leave for a few minutes until the coffee grounds settle at the bottom.

2 Push down the plunger of the cafetière or strain the jug of coffee to separate the liquid from the grounds. Pour the strained coffee into a clean jug.

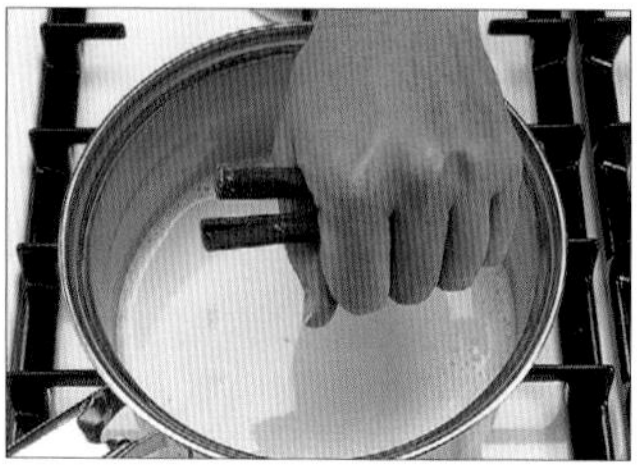

3 Pour the milk into a heavy-based pan, add the cinnamon sticks and bring to the boil, stirring occasionally.

4 Using a slotted spoon, lift out the cinnamon sticks and use a smaller spoon to press down on them to release any liquid they have absorbed. Set the cinnamon sticks aside for serving.

5 Add the coffee to the hot milk, then pour into cups. Add a cinnamon stick to each cup. Drinkers should add sugar to taste.

Horchata

This delicious, aromatic rice drink tastes wonderfully creamy, yet does not contain a drop of milk. Mexicans swear by it as a means of settling stomach upsets or curing hangovers, and it is often served at breakfast.

SERVES FOUR

INGREDIENTS
- 450g/1lb/2¼ cups long grain rice
- 750ml/1¼ pints/3 cups water
- 150g/5oz/1¼ cups blanched whole almonds
- 10ml/2 tsp ground cinnamon
- finely grated rind of 1 lime, plus strips of rind, to decorate
- 50g/2oz/¼ cup sugar

1 Tip the rice into a sieve and rinse thoroughly under cold running water. Drain, tip into a large bowl and pour over the water. Cover and soak for at least 2 hours, preferably overnight.

2 Drain the rice, reserving 600ml/1 pint/ 2½ cups of the soaking liquid. Spoon the rice into a food processor or blender and grind as finely as possible.

3 Add the almonds to the processor or blender and continue to grind in the same way until finely ground.

4 Add the cinnamon, grated lime rind and sugar to the ground rice and ground almonds. Add the reserved soaking water from the rice and mix until all the sugar has dissolved.

5 Serve in tall glasses with ice cubes. Decorate with strips of lime rind.

CAFE DE OLLA

THIS IS ONE OF THE MOST POPULAR DRINKS IN MEXICO. THE NAME MEANS "OUT OF THE POT", WHICH REFERS TO THE CONTAINER IN WHICH THE COFFEE IS MADE. TRADITIONALLY, THE SWEETENER IS PILONCILLO, *THE LOCAL UNREFINED BROWN SUGAR, BUT ANY SOFT DARK BROWN SUGAR CAN BE USED. THIS COFFEE IS ALWAYS DRUNK BLACK.*

SERVES FOUR

INGREDIENTS

- 1 litre/1¾ pints/4 cups water
- 115g/4oz/½ cup *piloncillo* or soft dark brown sugar
- 4 cinnamon sticks, each about 15cm/6in long
- 50g/2oz/⅔ cup freshly ground coffee, from dark-roast coffee beans

COOK'S TIP

If you do not have a fine sieve (strainer), improvise with a regular one lined with coffee filter paper. For a special occasion serve the coffee with chocolate-dipped cinnamon sticks which can be used to stir with.

1 Place the water, sugar and cinnamon sticks in a pan. Heat gently, stirring occasionally to make sure that the sugar dissolves, then bring to the boil. Boil rapidly for about 20 minutes until the syrup has reduced by a quarter.

2 Add the ground coffee to the syrup and stir well, then bring the liquid back to the boil. Remove from the heat, cover the pan and leave to stand for around 5 minutes.

3 Strain the coffee through a fine sieve (strainer), pour into cups and serve immediately.

ATOLE

THIS DRINK, WHICH IS MADE FROM WHITE CORN MASA, *IS TRADITIONALLY FLAVOURED WITH* PILONCILLO *(MEXICAN UNREFINED BROWN SUGAR) AND GROUND CINNAMON. IT HAS THE CONSISTENCY OF A THICK MILKSHAKE. FRESH FRUIT PURÉES ARE OFTEN ADDED BEFORE SERVING AND SOME RECIPES INTRODUCE GROUND ALMONDS OR MILK.*

SERVES SIX

INGREDIENTS

- 200g/7oz/1¾ cups white *masa harina*
- 1.2 litres/2 pints/5 cups water
- 1 vanilla pod (bean)
- 50g/2oz/¼ cup *piloncillo* or soft dark brown sugar
- 2.5ml/½ tsp ground cinnamon
- 115g/4oz/1 cup fresh strawberries, chopped pineapple or orange segments (optional)

1 Put the *masa harina* in a heavy-based pan, without appying any heat. Gradually stir in the water. Beat it to make a smooth paste.

2 Place the pan over a moderate heat add the vanilla pod and bring the mixture to the boil, stirring constantly until it thickens. Beat in the sugar and ground cinnamon and continue to beat until the sugar has dissolved. Remove from the heat.

3 If adding the fruit, purée it in a food processor or blender until smooth, then press through a sieve (strainer).

4 Stir the purée into the corn mixture and return to the heat until warmed through. Remove the vanilla pod. Serve.

CHAMPURRADA

This popular version of atole is made with Mexican chocolate. A special wooden whisk called a molinollo is traditionally used when making this frothy drink.

SERVES SIX

INGREDIENTS
- 115g/4oz Mexican chocolate, about 2 discs
- 1.2 litres/2 pints/5 cups water or milk, or a mixture
- 200g/7oz white *masa harina*
- 30ml/2 tbsp soft dark brown sugar

COOK'S TIP
If you can't locate Mexican chocolate, improvise by mixing 115g/4oz dark bitter chocolate (minimum 70 per cent cocoa solids) with 25g/1oz/¼ cup ground almonds, 50g/2oz/¼ cup caster (superfine) sugar and 10ml/2 tsp ground cinnamon in a food processor. Process until a fine powder is obtained.

1 Put the chocolate in a mortar and grind with a pestle until it becomes a fine powder. Alternatively, grind the chocolate in a food processor.

2 Put the liquid in a heavy-based pan and gradually stir in all the *masa harina* until a smooth paste is formed. Use a traditional wooden *molinollo*, if you have one, or a wire whisk for a frothier drink.

3 Place the pan over a moderate heat and bring the mixture to the boil, stirring all the time until the frothy drink thickens.

4 Stir in the ground chocolate, then add the sugar. Serve immediately.

MEXICAN HOT CHOCOLATE

Mexican chocolate is flavoured with almonds, cinnamon and vanilla, and is sweetened with sugar. All the ingredients are crushed together in a special mortar, and heated over coals. The powdered mixture is then shaped into discs. Making the chocolate is quite a fiddly business, but fortunately the discs can be bought in specialist stores.

SERVES FOUR

INGREDIENTS
- 1 litre/1¾ pints/4 cups milk
- 50–115g/2–4oz Mexican chocolate (1–2 discs)
- 1 vanilla pod (bean)

VARIATION
If you prefer, you can use dark bitter chocolate instead of Mexican chocolate. You will need slightly less, as the flavour will be more intense.

1 Pour the milk into a pan and add the chocolate. Precisely how much to use will depend on personal taste. Start with one disc and use more next time if necessary.

2 Split the vanilla pod lengthways using a sharp knife, and add it to the milk.

3 Heat the chocolate milk gently, stirring until all the chocolate has dissolved, then whisking with a wire whisk or a *molinollo* until the mixture boils. Remove the vanilla pod and divide the drink among four mugs or heatproof glasses. Serve at once.

Nutritional Information

The nutritional analysis below is per portion, unless otherwise stated.

p84 Cassava Chips Energy 453Kcal/1,900kJ; Protein 3g; Carbohydrate 56.4g, of which sugars 1.4g; Fat 25.6g, of which saturates 3.8g; Cholesterol 0mg; Calcium 30mg; Fibre 2.6g; Sodium 4mg.
p85 Cheese Tamales Energy 197Kcal/825kJ; Protein 3.3g; Carbohydrate 21.2g, of which sugars 0.3g; Fat 11.6g, of which saturates 5.8g; Cholesterol 21mg; Calcium 80mg; Fibre 0g; Sodium 560mg.
p86 Tortilla Chips Energy 172Kcal/723kJ; Protein 2.9g; Carbohydrate 22.6g, of which sugars 0.5g; Fat 8.5g, of which saturates 1.5g; Cholesterol 0mg; Calcium 56mg; Fibre 2.3g; Sodium 323mg.
p86 Pepitas Energy 193Kcal/800kJ; Protein 6.5g; Carbohydrate 7.1g, of which sugars 1.6g; Fat 15.5g, of which saturates 1.5g; Cholesterol 0mg; Calcium 36mg; Fibre 2g; Sodium 1mg.
p88 Tamales de Picadillo Energy 188Kcal/785kJ; Protein 7.8g; Carbohydrate 14.7g, of which sugars 3.0g; Fat 11.3g, of which saturates 4.4g; Cholesterol 26mg; Calcium 13mg; Fibre 0.4g; Sodium 175mg.
p89 Mixed Tostadas Energy 253Kcal/1,068kJ; Protein 14.7g; Carbohydrate 32.8g, of which sugars 3.4g; Fat 7.9g, of which saturates 2.8g; Cholesterol 25mg; Calcium 192mg; Fibre 3.0g; Sodium 424mg.
p90 Chillies Rellenos Energy 498Kcal/2,072kJ; Protein 14.9g; Carbohydrate 27.8g, of which sugars 3.2g; Fat 36.5g, of which saturates 18.6g; Cholesterol 127mg; Calcium 322mg; Fibre 1.8g; Sodium 374mg.
p92 Tortas Energy 638Kcal/2,683kJ; Protein 48.6g; Carbohydrate 53.4g, of which sugars 5.3g; Fat 25.9g, of which saturates 14.6g; Cholesterol 138mg; Calcium 566mg; Fibre 5.7g; Sodium 1,164mg.
p93 Taquitos with Beef Energy 120Kcal/500kJ; Protein 10.6g; Carbohydrate 9.4g, of which sugars 0.2g; Fat 4.3g, of which saturates 1.6g; Cholesterol 24mg; Calcium 3mg; Fibre 0.3g; Sodium 27mg.
p94 Plantain and Sweet Potato Chips

Energy 396Kcal/1,658kJ; Protein 1.7g; Carbohydrate 51.5g, of which sugars 12.6g; Fat 21.7g, of which saturates 2.5g; Cholesterol 0mg; Calcium 11mg; Fibre 2.8g; Sodium 11mg.
p94 Coconut King Prawns Energy 186Kcal/774kJ; Protein 11.2g; Carbohydrate 3.1g, of which sugars 2.6g; Fat 14.5g, of which saturates 8.4g; Cholesterol 182mg; Calcium 111mg; Fibre 1.7g; Sodium 443mg.
p96 Butterflied Prawns in Chilli Chocolate Energy 133Kcal/554kJ; Protein 9.5g; Carbohydrate 7.4g, of which sugars 3.6g; Fat 6.9g, of which saturates 1.5g; Cholesterol 98mg; Calcium 49mg; Fibre 0.3g; Sodium 97mg.
p97 Desert Nachos (per batch) Energy 1,534Kcal/6,413kJ; Protein 47g; Carbohydrate 135.6g, of which sugars 3.1g; Fat 90.6g, of which saturates 33.8g; Cholesterol 109mg; Calcium 1,196mg; Fibre 14.2g; Sodium 3,314mg.
p98 Empanadas with Ropas Viejas Energy 208Kcal/867kJ; Protein 3.4g; Carbohydrate 25.6g, of which sugars 2g; Fat 10.2g, of which saturates 1.1g; Cholesterol 0mg; Calcium 16mg; Fibre 1.3g; Sodium 4mg.
p100 Cheesy Eggs Energy 167Kcal/693kJ; Protein 9.9g; Carbohydrate 0.1g, of which sugars 0.1g; Fat 14.2g, of which saturates 4.7g; Cholesterol 240mg; Calcium 108mg; Fibre 0g; Sodium 179mg.
p101 Red Enchiladas Energy 283Kcal/1,178kJ; Protein 9.5g; Carbohydrate 18.6g, of which sugars 5.3g; Fat 19.5g, of which saturates 10.3g; Cholesterol 47mg; Calcium 181mg; Fibre 1.5g; Sodium 432mg.
p102 Tostadas with Tomato Salsa Energy 360Kcal/1,511kJ; Protein 11.8g; Carbohydrate 46.6g, of which sugars 7.3g; Fat 15.2g, of which saturates 4.5g; Cholesterol 14mg; Calcium 201mg; Fibre 6.9g; Sodium 481mg.
p103 Enchiladas with Hot Tomato and Green Chilli Sauce Energy 774Kcal/3,243kJ; Protein 44.1g; Carbohydrate 68.1g, of which sugars 8.8g; Fat 37g, of which saturates 20.3g; Cholesterol 154mg; Calcium 526mg; Fibre 3.8g; Sodium 716mg.
p104 Chicken Flautas Energy 156Kcal/656kJ; Protein 10.3g; Carbohydrate 16.6g, of which sugars 1.7g; Fat 5.8g, of which saturates 1.6g; Cholesterol 26mg; Calcium 60mg; Fibre 1g; Sodium 198mg.
p106 Black-eyed Bean and Shrimp Fritters Energy 136Kcal/570kJ; Protein 7.7g; Carbohydrate 14.7g, of which sugars 1.6g; Fat 5.5g, of which saturates 0.7g; Cholesterol 10mg; Calcium 33mg; Fibre 2.3g; Sodium 83mg
p107 Beef Empanadas Energy 138Kcal/579kJ; Protein 6.6g; Carbohydrate 12.7g, of which sugars 0.8g; Fat 7.1g, of which saturates 3.1g; Cholesterol 23mg; Calcium 20mg; Fibre 0.7g; Sodium 102mg.
p108 Sopes with Picadillo Energy 299Kcal/1,244kJ; Protein 5.2g; Carbohydrate 35.6g, of which sugars 5g; Fat 13.9g, of which saturates 3.8g; Cholesterol 8mg; Calcium 16mg; Fibre 1.8g; Sodium 5mg.
p109 Panuchos Energy 249Kcal/1,038kJ; Protein 18.6g; Carbohydrate 19.1g, of which sugars 0.8g; Fat 10.7g, of which saturates 1.6g; Cholesterol 104mg; Calcium 15mg; Fibre 0.8g; Sodium 61mg.
p110 Quesadillas Energy 260Kcal/1,091kJ; Protein 12.9g; Carbohydrate 29.9g, of which sugars 0.6g; Fat 10.7g, of which saturates 6.9g; Cholesterol 29mg; Calcium 236mg; Fibre 1.2g; Sodium 338mg.
p111 Mexican Rice Energy 162Kcal/676kJ; Protein 2.8g; Carbohydrate 28.4g, of which sugars 1.6g; Fat 4g, of which saturates 0.5g; Cholesterol 0mg; Calcium 11mg; Fibre 0.5g; Sodium 167mg.
p112 Pan-fried Squid Energy 250Kcal/1,043kJ; Protein 32.8g; Carbohydrate 2.6g, of which sugars 0.1g; Fat 9.2g, of which saturates 1.5g; Cholesterol 500mg; Calcium 33mg; Fibre 0g; Sodium 475mg.
p112 Fried Whitebait with Cayenne Pepper Energy 328Kcal/1,359kJ; Protein 12.2g; Carbohydrate 3.3g, of which sugars 0.1g; Fat 29.7g, of which saturates 5.9g; Cholesterol 0mg; Calcium 538mg; Fibre 0.1g; Sodium 144mg.
p114 Eggs with Chorizo Energy 402Kcal/1674kJ; Protein 34.3g; Carbohydrate 2.9g, of which sugars 2.5g; Fat 27g, of which saturates 9.5g; Cholesterol 375mg; Calcium 76mg; Fibre 0.5g; Sodium 198mg.
p114 Chillies in Cheese Sauce Energy 774Kcal/3,202kJ; Protein 33.6g; Carbohydrate 3.1g, of which sugars 2.7g; Fat 67g, of which saturates 42g; Cholesterol 181mg; Calcium 960mg; Fibre 0.5g; Sodium 918mg.
p116 Molettes Energy 450Kcal/1,886kJ; Protein 19.2g; Carbohydrate 39.9g, of which sugars 4.2g; Fat 24.1g, of which saturates 15g; Cholesterol 63mg; Calcium 392mg; Fibre 4.5g; Sodium 889mg.
p116 Eggs Motulenos Energy 524Kcal/2,208kJ; Protein 34.7g; Carbohydrate 60.3g, of which sugars 4.6g; Fat 17.8g, of which saturates 5.4g; Cholesterol 225mg; Calcium 239mg; Fibre 12.5g; Sodium 978mg.
p118 Eggs Rancheros Energy 294Kcal/1,227kJ; Protein 16g; Carbohydrate 17.2g, of which sugars 2.6g; Fat 18.7g, of which saturates 7.7g; Cholesterol 401mg; Calcium 125mg; Fibre 1.1g; Sodium 225mg.
p120 Mexican Tortilla Parcels Energy 576Kcal/2,422kJ; Protein 17.3g; Carbohydrate 79.5g, of which sugars 12g; Fat 22.5g, of which saturates 7.8g; Cholesterol 28mg; Calcium 340mg; Fibre 5g; Sodium 639mg.
p121 Caribbean Crab Cakes Energy 70Kcal/290kJ; Protein 3.5g; Carbohydrate 2.9g, of which sugars 0.7g; Fat 5g, of which saturates 1.1g; Cholesterol 26mg; Calcium 24mg; Fibre 0.3g; Sodium 95mg.
p122 Spiced Plantain Chips Energy 232Kcal/962kJ; Protein 0.6g; Carbohydrate 14.7g, of which sugars 2.9g; Fat 19.4g, of which saturates 2.3g; Cholesterol 0mg; Calcium 5mg;

Fibre 0.7g; Sodium 2mg.
p123 Popcorn with Lime and Chilli (per batch) Energy 1,334Kcal/5,553kJ; Protein 13.9g; Carbohydrate 109.6g, of which sugars 2.5g; Fat 96.3g, of which saturates 9.7g; Cholesterol 0mg; Calcium 23mg; Fibre 0g; Sodium 9mg.
p126 Vermicelli Soup Energy 128Kcal/537kJ; Protein 4.4g; Carbohydrate 10.5g, of which sugars 5.7g; Fat 8.0g, of which saturates 2.1g; Cholesterol 6mg; Calcium 86mg; Fibre 1.9g; Sodium 101mg.
p126 Tomato Soup Energy 78Kcal/327kJ; Protein 2.1g; Carbohydrate 10.0g, of which sugars 9.0g; Fat 3.6g, of which saturates 0.6g; Cholesterol 0mg; Calcium 26mg; Fibre 2.8g; Sodium 103mg.
p128 Creamy Heart of Palm Soup Energy 441Kcal/1,824kJ; Protein 4.9g; Carbohydrate 13.1g, of which sugars 7.1g; Fat 41.4g, of which saturates 24.5g; Cholesterol 99mg; Calcium 91mg; Fibre 4.5g; Sodium 219mg.
p129 Peanut and Potato Soup with Coriander Energy 259Kcal/1,076kJ; Protein 8.1g; Carbohydrate 14.5g, of which sugars 6.1g; Fat 19.2g, of which saturates 3.7g; Cholesterol 0mg; Calcium 30mg; Fibre 3.0g; Sodium 141mg.
p130 Tlalpeño-Style Soup Energy 225Kcal/946kJ; Protein 22.7g; Carbohydrate 11.3g, of which sugars 0.6g; Fat 10g, of which saturates 3.8g; Cholesterol 53mg; Calcium 131mg; Fibre 3.4g; Sodium 274mg.
p130 Corn Soup Energy 205Kcal/861kJ; Protein 4g; Carbohydrate 27.2g, of which sugars 12.7g; Fat 9.7g, of which saturates 3.7g; Cholesterol 14mg; Calcium 33mg; Fibre 2.2g; Sodium 235mg.
p132 Chilled Coconut Soup Energy 485Kcal/2,009kJ; Protein 8.5g; Carbohydrate 14.4g, of which sugars 14.4g; Fat 44.2g, of which saturates 33.1g; Cholesterol 56mg; Calcium 245mg; Fibre 5.1g; Sodium 163mg.
p133 Avocado Soup Energy 382Kcal/1,573kJ; Protein 2.9g; Carbohydrate 3g, of which sugars 2.1g; Fat 39.8g, of which saturates 22.4g; Cholesterol 85mg; Calcium 69mg; Fibre 2.2g; Sodium 514mg.
p134 Fish and Sweet Potato Soup Energy 125Kcal/528kJ; Protein 11.6g; Carbohydrate 16.7g, of which sugars 5.0g; Fat 1.7g, of which saturates 0.3g; Cholesterol 20mg; Calcium 44mg; Fibre 8.4g; Sodium 223mg.
p134 Caribbean Vegetable Soup Energy 195Kcal/820kJ; Protein 3.8g; Carbohydrate 33.7g, of which sugars 16.0g; Fat 5.9g, of which saturates 3.4g; Cholesterol 13mg; Calcium 52mg; Fibre 3.4g; Sodium 62mg
p136 Mexican Bean Chilli with Nachos Energy 787Kcal/3,291kJ; Protein 50.4g; Carbohydrate 52.9g, of which sugars 9.5g; Fat 41.7g, of which saturates 17.9g; Cholesterol 105mg; Calcium 606mg; Fibre 14.3g; Sodium 1,476mg.
p137 Roasted Pumpkin Soup with Pumpkin Crisps Energy 212Kcal/877kJ; Protein 2.2g; Carbohydrate 5.5g, of which sugars 4.3g; Fat 20.3g, of which saturates 3.1g; Cholesterol 0mg; Calcium 89mg; Fibre 2.7g; Sodium 1mg.
p138 South American Red Bean Soup Energy 254Kcal/1,064kJ; Protein 10.8g; Carbohydrate 29.2g, of which sugars 9.1g; Fat 11.2g, of which saturates 2.1g; Cholesterol 0mg; Calcium 111mg; Fibre 10.6g; Sodium 535mg.
p139 Corn and Red Chilli Chowder Energy 632Kcal/2,632kJ; Protein 9.6g; Carbohydrate 49.1g, of which sugars 21.3g; Fat 45.5g, of which saturates 26.7g; Cholesterol 109mg; Calcium 175mg; Fibre 3.5g; Sodium 332mg.
p140 Tortilla Soup Energy 172Kcal/723kJ; Protein 2.9g; Carbohydrate 22.6g, of which sugars 0.5g; Fat 8.5g, of which saturates 1.5g; Cholesterol 0mg; Calcium 56mg; Fibre 2.3g; Sodium 323mg.
p142 Jamaican Rice and Bean Soup Energy 435Kcal/1,819kJ; Protein 23.7g; Carbohydrate 47.8g, of which sugars 5.1g; Fat 16.8g, of which saturates 8.3g; Cholesterol 64mg; Calcium 101mg; Fibre 3.1g; Sodium 524mg.
p143 Avocado and Lime Soup Energy 282Kcal/1,169kJ; Protein 6.6g; Carbohydrate 10.4g, of which sugars 9.4g; Fat 23.9g, of which saturates 8.9g; Cholesterol 28mg; Calcium 171mg; Fibre 3.5g; Sodium 71mg.
p144 Crab, Coconut and Coriander Soup Energy 232Kcal/972kJ; Protein 23.8g; Carbohydrate 7.4g, of which sugars 6.5g; Fat 12.2g, of which saturates 3.7g; Cholesterol 90mg; Calcium 188mg; Fibre 1.0g; Sodium 937mg.
p145 Chilli Clam Broth Energy 141Kcal/595kJ; Protein 8.8g; Carbohydrate 11.0g, of which sugars 4.1g; Fat 4.3g, of which saturates 0.7g; Cholesterol 31mg; Calcium 74mg; Fibre 1.2g; Sodium 403mg.
p146 Chunky Prawn Chupe Energy 259Kcal/1,089kJ; Protein 23.2g; Carbohydrate 26.8g, of which sugars 7.3g; Fat 7.3g, of which saturates 1.1g; Cholesterol 233mg; Calcium 125mg; Fibre 3.7g; Sodium 1.4g.
p147 Caribbean Salt Cod Soup Energy 323Kcal/1,358kJ; Protein 10.7g; Carbohydrate 37g, of which sugars 5.6g; Fat 12.9g, of which saturates 6.7g; Cholesterol 40mg; Calcium 159mg; Fibre 4.6g; Sodium 138mg.
p148 Spiced Lamb Soup Energy 469Kcal/1,974kJ; Protein 41.1g; Carbohydrate 34.2g, of which sugars 6.9g; Fat 19.7g, of which saturates 9.1g; Cholesterol 128mg; Calcium 66mg; Fibre 4.2g; Sodium 157mg.
p149 Plantain Soup with Corn and Chilli Energy 191Kcal/808kJ; Protein 2.5g; Carbohydrate 33.9g, of which sugars 9.8g; Fat 6.1g, of which saturates 3.4g; Cholesterol 13mg; Calcium 15mg; Fibre 2g; Sodium 243mg.
p150 Kale, Chorizo and Potato Soup Energy 414Kcal/1,750kJ; Protein 14g; Carbohydrate 67.9g, of which sugars 4.9g; Fat 11.5g, of which saturates 4.2g; Cholesterol 15mg; Calcium 170mg; Fibre 4.4g; Sodium 825mg.

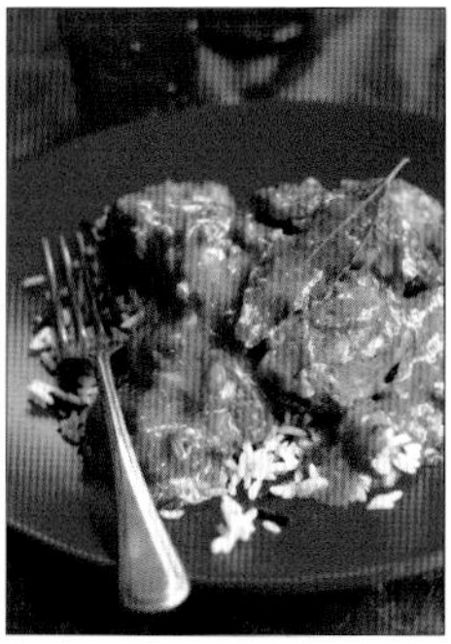

p151 Corn and Sweet Potato Soup Energy 131Kcal/555kJ; Protein 2.7g; Carbohydrate 25.3g, of which sugars 9.7g; Fat 2.9g, of which saturates 0.5g; Cholesterol 0mg; Calcium 11mg; Fibre 1.9g; Sodium 210mg.
p152 Beef and Cassava Soup Energy 332Kcal/1,400kJ; Protein 27.3g; Carbohydrate 28.6g, of which sugars 8.7g; Fat 7.8g, of which saturates 3.1g; Cholesterol 78mg; Calcium 62mg; Fibre 2.4g; Sodium 295mg.
p153 Lamb and Lentil Soup Energy 530Kcal/2,225kJ; Protein 57.0g; Carbohydrate 35.2g, of which sugars 2.8g; Fat 18.8g, of which saturates 8.0g; Cholesterol 167mg; Calcium 57mg; Fibre 3.0g; Sodium 180mg.
p156 Baked Sea Bass with Coconut Energy 227Kcal/961kJ; Protein 38.2g; Carbohydrate 5.4g, of which sugars 4.6g; Fat 6.1g, of which saturates 0.9g; Cholesterol 95mg; Calcium 125mg; Fibre 0.5g; Sodium 326mg.
p156 Pan-Fried Sea Bream with Lime and Tomato Salsa Energy 208Kcal/870kJ; Protein 28.1g; Carbohydrate 2.5g, of which sugars 2.5g; Fat 9.5g, of which saturates 1.4g; Cholesterol 69mg; Calcium 21mg; Fibre 0.8g; Sodium 97mg.
p158 Halibut with Peppers and Coconut Milk Energy 279Kcal/1,175kJ; Protein 23.8g; Carbohydrate 19.9g, of which sugars 7.5g; Fat 12.3g, of which saturates 5.6g; Cholesterol 41mg; Calcium 48mg; Fibre 2.3g; Sodium 122mg.
p159 Caribbean Fish Steaks Energy 176Kcal/735kJ; Protein 17.1g; Carbohydrate 6.5g, of which sugars 5.8g; Fat 9.2g, of which saturates 1.2g; Cholesterol 40mg; Calcium 23mg; Fibre 1.4g; Sodium 63mg.
p160 Salmon in Mango and Ginger Sauce Energy 718Kcal/2,999kJ; Protein 56.8g; Carbohydrate 32.6g, of which sugars 32.3g; Fat 40.9g, of which saturates 11.9g; Cholesterol 164mg; Calcium 79mg; Fibre 2.5g; Sodium 359mg.
p160 Fried Snapper with Avocado Energy 294Kcal/1,223kJ; Protein 27.0g; Carbohydrate 0.9g, of which sugars 0.3g; Fat 20.2g, of which saturates 3.5g; Cholesterol 90mg; Calcium 31mg; Fibre 1.7g; Sodium 146mg.

p162 Salt Cod for Christmas Eve Energy 301Kcal/1,249kJ; Protein 17.8g; Carbohydrate 6g, of which sugars 5.4g; Fat 23g, of which saturates 2.6g; Cholesterol 35mg; Calcium 77mg; Fibre 3.4g; Sodium 493mg.
p164 Ceviche with Red Onion, Avocado and Sweet Potato Energy 309Kcal/1,292kJ; Protein 24.7g; Carbohydrate 17.9g, of which sugars 5.4g; Fat 15.8g, of which saturates 2.6g; Cholesterol 111mg; Calcium 78mg; Fibre 3.2g; Sodium 155mg.
p165 Seared Tuna Steaks with Red Onion Salsa Energy 405Kcal/1,697kJ; Protein 49.1g; Carbohydrate 7.7g, of which sugars 6.9g; Fat 20g, of which saturates 4.3g; Cholesterol 56mg; Calcium 70mg; Fibre 2.6g; Sodium 105mg.
p166 Red Snapper with Coriander and Almonds Energy 482Kcal/2,011kJ; Protein 35.6g; Carbohydrate 16.3g, of which sugars 1.5g; Fat 31g, of which saturates 11.4g; Cholesterol 95mg; Calcium 160mg; Fibre 2.6g; Sodium 237mg.
p167 Veracruz-style Red Snapper Energy 468Kcal/1,955kJ; Protein 41.3g; Carbohydrate 11.8g, of which sugars 10.3g; Fat 28.8g, of which saturates 4.5g; Cholesterol 74mg; Calcium 125mg; Fibre 3.3g; Sodium 1,070mg.
p168 Pickled Fish Energy 383Kcal/1,594kJ; Protein 41.4g; Carbohydrate 1.2g, of which sugars 0.9g; Fat 23.6g, of which saturates 3.4g; Cholesterol 104mg; Calcium 24mg; Fibre 0.2g; Sodium 136mg.
p169 Citrus Fish with Chillies Energy 253Kcal/1,056kJ; Protein 32.5g; Carbohydrate 3.2g, of which sugars 0.9g; Fat 12.3g, of which saturates 1.8g; Cholesterol 81mg; Calcium 23mg; Fibre 0.3g; Sodium 106mg.
p170 Mexican Spicy Fish Energy 217Kcal/911kJ; Protein 39.5g; Carbohydrate 2.6g, of which sugars 2.4g; Fat 5.4g, of which saturates 0.8g; Cholesterol 115mg; Calcium 34mg; Fibre 0.7g; Sodium 176mg.
p171 Salt Cod in Mild Chilli Sauce Energy 178Kcal/743kJ; Protein 27.8g; Carbohydrate 1.6g, of which sugars 1.2g; Fat 6.6g, of which saturates 1g; Cholesterol 69mg; Calcium 20mg; Fibre 0.3g; Sodium 91mg.
p172 Red Snapper Burritos Energy 519Kcal/2,177kJ; Protein 30g; Carbohydrate 54.5g, of which sugars 2.9g; Fat 20.7g, of which saturates 6.7g; Cholesterol 52mg; Calcium 326mg; Fibre 3g; Sodium 430mg.
p173 Sea Bass with Orange Chilli Salsa Energy 178Kcal/749kJ; Protein 30.2g; Carbohydrate 5.6g, of which sugars 5.2g; Fat 4g, of which saturates 0.6g; Cholesterol 120mg; Calcium 228mg; Fibre 1.1g; Sodium 108mg.
p174 Fried Sole with Lime Energy 287Kcal/1,205kJ; Protein 27.9g; Carbohydrate 14.6g, of which sugars 0.3g; Fat 13.5g, of which saturates 1.6g; Cholesterol 90mg; Calcium 52mg; Fibre 0.6g; Sodium 143mg.
p174 Baked Salmon with Guava Sauce Energy 389Kcal/1,621kJ; Protein 31.7g; Carbohydrate 8.7g, of which sugars 8.2g; Fat 25.5g, of which saturates 3.8g; Cholesterol 75mg; Calcium 55mg; Fibre 5.8g; Sodium 76mg.
p176 Trout in Wine Sauce with Plantain Energy 324Kcal/1,353kJ; Protein 22.0g; Carbohydrate 17.6g, of which sugars 6.1g; Fat 16.2g, of which saturates 5.2g; Cholesterol 83g; Calcium 28mg; Fibre 0.6g; Sodium 139mg.
p177 Eschovished Fish Energy 210Kcal/879kJ; Protein 28.0g; Carbohydrate 5.4g, of which sugars 4.7g; Fat 8.5g, of which saturates 1.1g; Cholesterol 69mg; Calcium 28mg; Fibre 0.8g; Sodium 91mg.
p178 Chargrilled Tuna with Fiery Pepper Purée Energy 411Kcal/1,718kJ; Protein 43.1g; Carbohydrate 10.1g, of which sugars 6.4g; Fat 22.3g, of which saturates 4.2g; Cholesterol 49mg; Calcium 46mg; Fibre 1.7g; Sodium 121mg.
p179 Mackerel Escabeche Energy 576Kcal/2,393kJ; Protein 38.5g; Carbohydrate 8.4g, of which sugars 1.5g; Fat 43.3g, of which saturates 8.2g; Cholesterol 108mg; Calcium 40mg; Fibre 0.6g; Sodium 127mg
p180 Salmon with Tequila Cream Sauce Energy 490Kcal/2,032kJ; Protein 32.7g; Carbohydrate 2.6g, of which sugars 1.9g; Fat 36.9g, of which saturates 9.6g; Cholesterol 96mg; Calcium 77mg; Fibre 1.1g; Sodium 82mg.
p181 Yucatan-style Shark Steak Energy 265Kcal/1,117kJ; Protein 46.1g; Carbohydrate 1.2g, of which sugars 1.2g; Fat 7.7g, of which saturates 1.2g; Cholesterol 88mg; Calcium 38mg; Fibre 0g; Sodium 282mg.
p182 Chargrilled Swordfish with Chilli and Lime Sauce Energy 470Kcal/1,957kJ; Protein 37.5g; Carbohydrate 3.4g, of which sugars 3.3g; Fat 34.2g, of which saturates 14.9g; Cholesterol 131mg; Calcium 39mg; Fibre 0.8g; Sodium 522mg.
p182 Swordfish Tacos Energy 246Kcal/1,036kJ; Protein 21.1g; Carbohydrate 22.8g, of which sugars 3.1g; Fat 8.4g, of which saturates 1.4g; Cholesterol 41mg; Calcium 56mg; Fibre 1.7g; Sodium 229mg.
p184 Marinated Red Mullet Energy 338Kcal/1,408kJ; Protein 29.9g; Carbohydrate 12.3g, of which sugars 7.2g; Fat 19.1g, of which saturates 2.8g; Cholesterol 69mg; Calcium 60mg; Fibre 3.9g; Sodium 636mg.
p185 Cod Caramba Energy 307Kcal/1,286kJ; Protein 20.6g; Carbohydrate 18.5g, of which sugars 7.1g; Fat 14.1g, of which saturates 6.9g; Cholesterol 78mg; Calcium 119mg; Fibre 2.7g; Sodium 720mg.
p186 Creole Fish Stew Energy 172Kcal/724kJ; Protein 17.8g; Carbohydrate 5.8g, of which sugars 5.1g; Fat 8.7g, of which saturates 1.9g; Cholesterol 45.8mg; Calcium 59mg; Fibre 1.8g; Sodium 222mg.
p187 Salt Fish and Ackee Energy 292Kcal/1,225kJ; Protein 38.4g; Carbohydrate 7.7g, of which sugars 6.2g; Fat 12.2g, of which saturates 4.3g; Cholesterol 80mg; Calcium 78mg; Fibre 2.4g; Sodium 494mg.
p188 Escabeche Energy 372Kcal/1,549kJ; Protein 41.7g; Carbohydrate 1.2g, of which sugars 0.9g; Fat 22.2g, of which saturates 3.2g; Cholesterol 104mg; Calcium 47mg; Fibre 1.3g; Sodium 979mg.
p189 Chilean Squid Casserole Energy 260Kcal/1,089kJ; Protein 19.9g; Carbohydrate 17.2g, of which sugars 3.5g; Fat 8.1g, of which saturates 1.3g; Cholesterol 267mg; Calcium 42mg; Fibre 1.5g; Sodium 333mg.
p190 Jamaican Fish Curry Energy 695Kcal/2,921kJ; Protein 39.5g; Carbohydrate 69.7g, of which sugars 11.2g; Fat 30.7g, of which saturates 19.3g; Cholesterol 51mg; Calcium 112mg; Fibre 3.3g; Sodium 216mg.
p192 Pueblo Fish Bake Energy 257Kcal/1,077kJ; Protein 31.1g; Carbohydrate 1.5g, of which sugars 1.1g; Fat 14.1g, of which saturates 2g; Cholesterol 92mg; Calcium 59mg; Fibre 1.3g; Sodium 75mg.
p196 Chilean Seafood Platter Energy 205Kcal/863kJ; Protein 32.7g; Carbohydrate 3.5g, of which sugars 0.5g; Fat 6.8g, of which saturates 1.1g; Cholesterol 267mg; Calcium 146mg; Fibre 0.4g; Sodium 1.6g.
p197 Prawn and Scallop Ceviche Energy 137Kcal/576kJ; Protein 19.6g; Carbohydrate 4.5g, of which sugars 2.5g; Fat 4.6g, of which saturates 1g; Cholesterol 156mg; Calcium 49mg; Fibre 1.2g; Sodium 166mg.
p198 Prawns with Almond Sauce Energy 457Kcal/1,903kJ; Protein 39.9g; Carbohydrate 6.1g, of which sugars 5.2g; Fat 30.4g, of which saturates 10g; Cholesterol 154mg; Calcium 304mg; Fibre 2.8g; Sodium 2.4g.
p200 Prawns in Garlic Butter Energy 223Kcal/924kJ; Protein 13.3g; Carbohydrate 0.3g, of which sugars 0.3g; Fat 18.8g, of which saturates 10.5g; Cholesterol 87mg; Calcium 103mg; Fibre 0.4g; Sodium 1,034mg.
p201 Prawn Salad Energy 419Kcal/1,734kJ; Protein 25g; Carbohydrate 4.8g, of which sugars 4.4g; Fat 33.4g, of which saturates 7.6g; Cholesterol 380mg; Calcium 165mg; Fibre 1.5g; Sodium 1,591mg.
p202 Crab with Green Rice Energy 422Kcal/1,769kJ; Protein 28.6g; Carbohydrate 52.2g, of which sugars 6.5g; Fat 9.8g, of which saturates 1.5g; Cholesterol 90mg; Calcium

205mg; Fibre 2.7g; Sodium 706mg.
p203 Scallops with Garlic and Coriander Energy 291Kcal/1,213kJ; Protein 24.2g; Carbohydrate 4.4g, of which sugars 1g; Fat 19.8g, of which saturates 10.6g; Cholesterol 87mg; Calcium 45mg; Fibre 0.5g; Sodium 294mg.
p204 King Prawns in a Coconut and Nut Cream Energy 496Kcal/2,072kJ; Protein 46.5g; Carbohydrate 18.1g, of which sugars 6.4g; Fat 26.8g, of which saturates 12.5g; Cholesterol 448mg; Calcium 254mg; Fibre 2.3g; Sodium 2.8g.
p205 Stuffed Crab Energy 162Kcal/680kJ; Protein 15.9g; Carbohydrate 8.7g, of which sugars 3.5g; Fat 7.3g, of which saturates 3.7g; Cholesterol 129mg; Calcium 162mg; Fibre 0.9g; Sodium 475mg.
p206 Crab and Corn Gumbo Energy 274Kcal/1,144kJ; Protein 9.8g; Carbohydrate 24.2g, of which sugars 6.8g; Fat 11.4g, of which saturates 4.1g; Cholesterol 31mg; Calcium 77mg; Fibre 3.4g; Sodium 349mg.
p208 Cuban Seafood Rice Energy 326Kcal/1,379kJ; Protein 28.4g; Carbohydrate 40.9g, of which sugars 1.1g; Fat 6.6g, of which saturates 1.2g; Cholesterol 286mg; Calcium 112mg; Fibre 0.5g; Sodium 1.2g.
p210 Pumpkin and Prawns with Dried Shrimp Energy 210Kcal/877kJ; Protein 17.5g; Carbohydrate 8.7g, of which sugars 6.9g; Fat 11.9g, of which saturates 4.3g; Cholesterol 187mg; Calcium 147mg; Fibre 3.0g; Sodium 1g.
p211 Spicy Prawns with Cormeal Energy 378Kcal/1,582kJ; Protein 42.5g; Carbohydrate 21.2g, of which sugars 0.2g; Fat 13.4g, of which

saturates 1.5g; Cholesterol 439mg; Calcium 194mg; Fibre 1g; Sodium 430mg.
p212 Fisherman's Stew Energy 487Kcal/2,032kJ; Protein 40.9g; Carbohydrate 17.6g, of which sugars 8.7g; Fat 26.8g, of which saturates 15g; Cholesterol 215mg; Calcium 208mg; Fibre 2.2g; Sodium 393mg.
p216 The Gaucho Barbecue Energy 839Kcal/3,501kJ; Protein 88.1g; Carbohydrate 3.8g, of which sugars 1.1g; Fat 52.5g, of which saturates 22.5g; Cholesterol 249mg; Calcium 63mg; Fibre 0.4g; Sodium 1.2g.
p217 Beef Stuffed with Eggs and Spinach Energy 318Kcal/1,328kJ; Protein 39.0g; Carbohydrate 3.4g, of which sugars 2.8g; Fat 16.7g, of which saturates 4.6g; Cholesterol 161mg; Calcium 103mg; Fibre 1.6g; Sodium 299mg.
p218 Carbonada Criolla Energy 505Kcal/2,124kJ; Protein 46.1g; Carbohydrate 33.6g, of which sugars 11.4g; Fat 18.3g, of which saturates 6.1g; Cholesterol 125mg; Calcium 44mg; Fibre 3.6g; Sodium 175mg.
p220 Garlic and Chilli Marinated Beef with Corn-Crusted Onion Rings Energy 428Kcal/1,787kJ; Protein 44.2g; Carbohydrate 17.4g, of which sugars 3g; Fat 20g, of which saturates 5.4g; Cholesterol 91mg; Calcium 51mg; Fibre 0.8g; Sodium 136mg.
p221 Mexican Spicy Beef Tortilla Energy 595Kcal/2,516kJ; Protein 30.3g; Carbohydrate 91.2g, of which sugars 11.5g; Fat 14.7g, of which saturates 4.7g; Cholesterol 53mg; Calcium 153mg; Fibre 4.0g; Sodium 379mg.
p222 Tacos with Shredded Beef Energy 222Kcal/930kJ; Protein 19g; Carbohydrate 19.1g, of which sugars 0.6g; Fat 7.6g, of which saturates 1.8g; Cholesterol 44mg; Calcium 6mg; Fibre 0.7g; Sodium 209mg.
p223 Beef Enchiladas with Red Sauce Energy 503Kcal/2,121kJ; Protein 43g; Carbohydrate 51.9g, of which sugars 2.9g; Fat 15.1g, of which saturates 3.7g; Cholesterol 98mg; Calcium 101mg; Fibre 2.5g; Sodium 335mg.
p224 Black Bean Chilli con Carne Energy 374Kcal/1,575kJ; Protein 39.0g; Carbohydrate 27.9g, of which sugars 7.4g; Fat 12.6g, of which saturates 4.1g; Cholesterol 83mg; Calcium 60mg; Fibre 4.7g; Sodium 111mg.
p225 Spicy Meatballs with Tomato Sauce Energy 552Kcal/2,296kJ; Protein 29.9g; Carbohydrate 21.8g, of which sugars 6.0g; Fat 39.0g, of which saturates 11.6g; Cholesterol 132mg; Calcium 75mg; Fibre 2.0g; Sodium 268mg.
p226 Feijoada Energy 779Kcal/3,262kJ; Protein 58.0g; Carbohydrate 49.9g, of which sugars 3.8g; Fat 39.9g, of which saturates 13.5g; Cholesterol 142mg; Calcium 135mg; Fibre 7.3g; Sodium 1.5g.
p228 Stuffed Butterfly of Beef with Cheese and Chilli Sauce Energy 554Kcal/2,300kJ; Protein 45.6g; Carbohydrate 1.2g, of which sugars 0.9g; Fat 37.9g, of which saturates 19.9g; Cholesterol 160mg; Calcium 365mg; Fibre 0.2g; Sodium 723mg.
p230 Hearty Beef Stew Energy 515Kcal/2,158kJ; Protein 62.6g; Carbohydrate 13.0g, of which sugars 6.7g; Fat 22.9g, of which saturates 10.9g; Cholesterol 186mg; Calcium 70mg; Fibre 1.5g; Sodium 245mg.
p231 Oxtail and Butter Beans Energy 773Kcal/3,240kJ; Protein 88.0g; Carbohydrate 29.6g, of which sugars 6.2g; Fat 34.4g, of which saturates 0.2g; Cholesterol 275mg; Calcium 92mg; Fibre 4.8g; Sodium 522mg.
p232 "Seasoned-up" Lamb in Spinach Sauce Energy 331Kcal/1,380kJ; Protein 35.6g; Carbohydrate 4.0g, of which sugars 3.1g; Fat 19.4g, of which saturates 6.7g; Cholesterol 125mg; Calcium 80mg; Fibre 1.2g; Sodium 241mg.
p232 Lamb Pelau Energy 652Kcal/2,726kJ; Protein 32.1g; Carbohydrate 96.3g, of which sugars 5.7g; Fat 15.0g, of which saturates 7.3g; Cholesterol 97mg; Calcium 51mg; Fibre 1.0g; Sodium 231mg.
p234 Lamb Stew with Chilli Sauce Energy 367Kcal/1536kJ; Protein 34g; Carbohydrate 11.8g, of which sugars 1.9g; Fat 20.8g, of which saturates 9g; Cholesterol 127mg; Calcium 19mg; Fibre 0.9g; Sodium 151mg.
p235 Albondigas Energy 412Kcal/1,717kJ; Protein 26.2g; Carbohydrate 16g, of which sugars 5.9g; Fat 27.6g, of which saturates 7.7g; Cholesterol 118mg; Calcium 50mg; Fibre 1.9g; Sodium 265mg.
p236 Spiced Roast Leg of Lamb Energy 470Kcal/1,962kJ; Protein 37.2g; Carbohydrate 22.6g, of which sugars 6.5g; Fat 24.9g, of which saturates 9.1g; Cholesterol 117mg; Calcium 38mg; Fibre 7.4g; Sodium 651mg.
p237 Rabbit in Coconut Milk Energy 301Kcal/1,260kJ; Protein 29.9g; Carbohydrate 10.8g, of which sugars 9.2g; Fat 15.7g, of which saturates 4.0g; Cholesterol 68mg; Calcium 73mg; Fibre 1.5g; Sodium 236mg.
p238 Caribbean Lamb Curry Energy 338Kcal/1,409kJ; Protein 30.8g; Carbohydrate 3.2g, of which sugars 2.3g; Fat 22.6g, of which saturates 10.1g; Cholesterol 128mg; Calcium 29mg; Fibre 0.5g; Sodium 229mg.
p239 Pork with Pineapple Energy 492Kcal/2,041kJ; Protein 28.7g; Carbohydrate 12.9g, of which sugars 12.2g; Fat 36.4g, of which saturates 12.6g; Cholesterol 92g; Calcium 30mg; Fibre 1.2g; Sodium 136mg.
p240 Stuffed Loin of Pork Energy 554Kcal/2,318kJ; Protein 71.8g; Carbohydrate 8.2g, of which sugars 7.7g; Fat 24.7g, of which saturates 7.1g; Cholesterol 213mg; Calcium 54mg; Fibre 1.2g; Sodium 240mg.
p242 Enchiladas with Pork and Green Sauce Energy 613Kcal/2,574kJ; Protein 48.9g; Carbohydrate 53.5g, of which sugars 6.2g; Fat 23.4g, of which saturates 8.9g; Cholesterol 129mg; Calcium 299mg; Fibre 3.5g; Sodium 534mg.
p243 Pork in Green Sauce with Cactus Energy 225Kcal/943kJ; Protein 27.8g; Carbohydrate 4.2g, of which sugars 3.9g; Fat 10.9g, of which saturates 2.5g; Cholesterol 79mg; Calcium 49mg; Fibre 1.8g; Sodium 140mg.
p244 Tamales filled with Spiced Pork Energy 490Kcal/2,050kJ; Protein 27.4g; Carbohydrate 73.9g, of which sugars 0.6g; Fat 8.5g, of which saturates 1.4g; Cholesterol 53mg; Calcium 11mg; Fibre 2.3g; Sodium 59mg.
p246 Pork Roasted wtih Herbs, Spices and Rum Energy 410Kcal/1,712kJ; Protein 42.4g; Carbohydrate 3.9g, of which sugars 3.8g; Fat 21.4g, of which saturates 8.2g; Cholesterol 132mg; Calcium 16mg; Fibre 0.1g; Sodium 577mg.
p247 Tostadas with Shredded Pork and Spices Energy 334Kcal/1,397kJ;

Protein 25.5g; Carbohydrate 22.9g, of which sugars 3.8g; Fat 16.1g, of which saturates 6.7g; Cholesterol 75mg; Calcium 152mg; Fibre 3.8g; Sodium 836mg.
p248 Pork in Milk Energy 472Kcal/1,957kJ; Protein 27.2g; Carbohydrate 7.5g, of which sugars 7.5g; Fat 37.1g, of which saturates 15.9g; Cholesterol 103g; Calcium 209mg; Fibre 0g; Sodium 159mg.
p248 Baked Ham with Orange and Lime Energy 348Kcal/1,448kJ; Protein 43.8g; Carbohydrate 0.6g, of which sugars 0.6g; Fat 18.8g, of which saturates 6.3g; Cholesterol 58g; Calcium 18mg; Fibre 0g; Sodium 2.2g.
p250 Carnitas Energy 465Kcal/1,931kJ; Protein 40.5g; Carbohydrate 3g, of which sugars 2.6g; Fat 32.3g, of which saturates 12.7g; Cholesterol 141mg; Calcium 25mg; Fibre 0.5g; Sodium 256mg.
p252 Pork Casserole with Onions, Chilli and Dried Fruit Energy 491Kcal/2,053kJ; Protein 39g; Carbohydrate 18.3g, of which sugars 15.3g; Fat 22.5g, of which saturates 4.3g; Cholesterol 105mg; Calcium 62mg; Fibre 3.1g; Sodium 127mg.
p254 Tortilla Pie with Chorizo Energy 740Kcal/3,070kJ; Protein 34.1g; Carbohydrate 14.4g, of which sugars 4.4g; Fat 59.2g, of which saturates 34.1g; Cholesterol 184mg; Calcium 514mg; Fibre 1.5g; Sodium 644mg.
p255 Scrambled Eggs with Chorizo Energy 322Kcal/1,335kJ; Protein 20.3g; Carbohydrate 5.7g, of which sugars 0.6g; Fat 24.3g, of which saturates 7.6g; Cholesterol 472mg; Calcium 101mg; Fibre 0.3g; Sodium 687mg.
p258 Cuban Chicken Pie Energy 521Kcal/2,814kJ; Protein 39.8g; Carbohydrate 35.2g, of which sugars 20.1g; Fat 25.6g, of which saturates 10.8g; Cholesterol 324g; Calcium 62mg; Fibre 2.5g; Sodium 190mg.
p259 Chicken with Okra Energy 122Kcal/511kJ; Protein 10.8g; Carbohydrate 9.7g, of which sugars 7.9g; Fat 4.8g, of which saturates 1.0g; Cholesterol 32g; Calcium 162mg; Fibre 5.1g; Sodium 40mg.
p260 Burritos with Chicken and Rice Energy 552Kcal/2,318kJ; Protein 35.1g; Carbohydrate 65.5g, of which sugars 3.3g; Fat 16.9g, of which saturates 8.7g; Cholesterol 89mg; Calcium 375mg; Fibre 2.5g; Sodium 531mg.
p262 Chicken and Tomatillo Chimichangas Energy 468Kcal/1,968kJ; Protein 27.5g; Carbohydrate 51.1g, of which sugars 6g; Fat 18.5g, of which saturates 2.3g; Cholesterol 61mg; Calcium 105mg; Fibre 3.3g; Sodium 271mg.
p263 Drunken Chicken Energy 752Kcal/3,148kJ; Protein 25.9g; Carbohydrate 62.4g, of which sugars 33.4g; Fat 27.1g, of which saturates 2.9g; Cholesterol 79mg; Calcium 141mg; Fibre 4.9g; Sodium 346mg.
p264 Colombian Chicken Hot-pot Energy 368Kcal/1,559kJ; Protein 29.2g; Carbohydrate 49.6g, of which sugars 6.5g; Fat 7.2g, of which saturates 1.8g; Cholesterol 107mg; Calcium 29mg; Fibre 3.7g; Sodium 190mg.
p266 Chicken with Chipotle Sauce Energy 229Kcal/963kJ; Protein 36.7g; Carbohydrate 4.5g, of which sugars 3.3g; Fat 7.3g, of which saturates 1.1g; Cholesterol 105mg; Calcium 21mg; Fibre 0.8g; Sodium 92mg.
p268 Spinach and Potato Stuffed Chicken Breasts Energy 212Kcal/888kJ; Protein 26.6g; Carbohydrate 5.7g, of which sugars 2.8g; Fat 9.4g, of which saturates 5g; Cholesterol 119mg; Calcium 60mg; Fibre 1.5g; Sodium 159mg.
p269 Mole Poblano de Guajolote Energy 732Kcal/3,061kJ; Protein 76.4g; Carbohydrate 19.3g, of which sugars 14.7g; Fat 39.3g, of which saturates 8.5g; Cholesterol 252mg; Calcium 139mg; Fibre 3.6g; Sodium 263mg.

p270 Peanut Chicken Energy 326Kcal/1,374kJ; Protein 55.5g; Carbohydrate 4.2g, of which sugars 3.1g; Fat 9.8g, of which saturates 4.5g; Cholesterol 171mg; Calcium 25mg; Fibre 0.9g; Sodium 190mg.
p270 Breast of Turkey with Mango and Wine Energy 351Kcal/1,476kJ; Protein 49.9g; Carbohydrate 9.0g, of which sugars 6.4g; Fat 10.4g, of which saturates 6.0g; Cholesterol 135mg; Calcium 29mg; Fibre 1.5g; Sodium 190mg.
p272 Chicken Fajitas Energy 398Kcal/1,670kJ; Protein 23g; Carbohydrate 44.3g, of which sugars 11.8g; Fat 15.5g, of which saturates 4.4g; Cholesterol 60mg; Calcium 76mg; Fibre 2.8g; Sodium 51mg.
p274 Barbecued Jerk Chicken Energy 460Kcal/1,924kJ; Protein 59.7g; Carbohydrate 2.2g, of which sugars 2.2g; Fat 23.6g, of which saturates 6.4g; Cholesterol 254g; Calcium 26mg; Fibre 0g; Sodium 210mg.
p275 Thyme and Lime Chicken Energy 495Kcal/2,053kJ; Protein 31.6g; Carbohydrate 0.4g, of which sugars 0.4g; Fat 40.8g, of which saturates 16.7g; Cholesterol 212g; Calcium 24mg; Fibre 0.1g; Sodium 250mg.
p276 Chicken, Pork and Potatoes in Peanut Sauce Energy 405Kcal/1,697kJ; Protein 41.1g; Carbohydrate 18.2g, of which sugars 4.1g; Fat 19.0g, of which saturates 3.8g; Cholesterol 105g; Calcium 40mg; Fibre 2.5g; Sodium 440mg.
p278 Spicy Fried Chicken Energy 345Kcal/1,442kJ; Protein 35.5g; Carbohydrate 6.7g, of which sugars 1.0g; Fat 19.8g, of which saturates 4.5g; Cholesterol 177g; Calcium 54mg; Fibre 0.2g; Sodium 170mg.
p279 Sunday Roast Chicken Energy 348Kcal/1,455kJ; Protein 37.5g; Carbohydrate 7.8g, of which sugars 7.8g; Fat 18.8g, of which saturates 8.8g; Cholesterol 155mg; Calcium 18mg; Fibre 0g; Sodium 200mg.
p280 Turkey Mole Energy 700Kcal/2,920kJ; Protein 50.6g; Carbohydrate 27.7g, of which sugars 19.1g; Fat 43.8g, of which saturates 6.9g; Cholesterol 86mg; Calcium 267mg; Fibre 7g; Sodium 178mg.
p282 Peruvian Duck with Rice Energy 527Kcal/2,207kJ; Protein 17.6g; Carbohydrate 55.2g, of which sugars 2.8g; Fat 24.6g, of which saturates 7.2g; Cholesterol 58mg; Calcium 62mg; Fibre 1.8g; Sodium 100mg.
p282 Drunken Duck Energy 693Kcal/2,895kJ; Protein 24.7g; Carbohydrate 45.5g, of which sugars 14.9g; Fat 41.7g, of which saturates 12.5g; Cholesterol 106mg; Calcium 91mg; Fibre 5.6g; Sodium 220mg.
p286 Corn Soufflé Energy 385Kcal/1,605kJ; Protein 15.2g; Carbohydrate 25.3g, of which sugars 8.7g; Fat 25.5g, of which saturates 13.7g; Cholesterol 246mg; Calcium 246mg; Fibre 2.5g; Sodium 480mg.
p287 Layered Potato Bake with Cheese Energy 442Kcal/1,831kJ; Protein 12.2g; Carbohydrate 16.3g, of which sugars 4.1g; Fat 36.9g, of which saturates 7.2g; Cholesterol 132mg; Calcium 137mg; Fibre 2.4g; Sodium 610mg.
p288 Frijoles Energy 201Kcal/851kJ; Protein 13.4g; Carbohydrate 28.3g, of which sugars 3.6g; Fat 4.6g, of which saturates 0.7g; Cholesterol 0mg; Calcium 66mg; Fibre 9.8g; Sodium 14mg.
p289 Black Bean Burritos Energy 586Kcal/2,460kJ; Protein 29.8g; Carbohydrate 59.8g, of which sugars 7.7g; Fat 25.7g, of which saturates 13.4g; Cholesterol 55mg; Calcium 546mg; Fibre 7.1g; Sodium 1g.
p290 Chilli Cheese Tortilla with Fresh Tomato Salsa Energy 375Kcal/1,562kJ; Protein 19.3g; Carbohydrate 13.5g, of which sugars 5.7g; Fat 27.1g, of which saturates 10g; Cholesterol 314mg; Calcium 305mg; Fibre 2.6g; Sodium 589mg.
p291 Potato and Onion Tortilla Energy 512Kcal/2,132kJ; Protein 15g; Carbohydrate 40g, of which sugars 5g; Fat 34g, of which saturates 6g; Cholesterol 285mg; Calcium 73mg; Fibre 3.7g; Sodium 100mg.
p292 Heart of Palm Pie Energy 566Kcal/2,361kJ; Protein 10.8g; Carbohydrate 57.1g, of which sugars 6.3g; Fat 34.2g, of which saturates 18.2g; Cholesterol 139mg; Calcium 164mg; Fibre 4.4g; Sodium 430mg.
p294 Macaroni Cheese Pie Energy 609Kcal/2,553kJ; Protein 25.1g; Carbohydrate 60.0g, of which sugars 9.9g; Fat 31.6g, of which saturates 18.6g; Cholesterol 135mg; Calcium 494mg; Fibre 2.4g; Sodium 560mg.
p295 Red Bean Chilli Energy 291Kcal/1,224kJ; Protein 12.7g;

Carbohydrate 35.7g, of which sugars 11.0g; Fat 6.5g, of which saturates 0.8g; Cholesterol 0mg; Calcium 86mg; Fibre 6.1g; Sodium 1.2g.

p296 Peppers Stuffed with Beans Energy 528Kcal/2,201kJ; Protein 26.1g; Carbohydrate 32.3g, of which sugars 6.8g; Fat 33.6g, of which saturates 12.1g; Cholesterol 118mg; Calcium 286mg; Fibre 10.1g; Sodium 360mg.

p297 Black-Eyed Bean Stew with Spicy Pumpkin Energy 412Kcal/1,734kJ; Protein 20.8g; Carbohydrate 57.1g, of which sugars 16.2g; Fat 12.7g, of which saturates 6.8g; Cholesterol 18mg; Calcium 156mg; Fibre 11.3g; Sodium 80mg.

p298 Spicy Vegetable Chow Mein Energy 414Kcal/1,740kJ; Protein 12.4g; Carbohydrate 62.5g, of which sugars 8.5g; Fat 14.4g, of which saturates 2.7g; Cholesterol 23mg; Calcium 74mg; Fibre 4.7g; Sodium 266mg.

p298 Aubergines Stuffed with Sweet Potato Energy 249Kcal/1,013kJ; Protein 8.1g; Carbohydrate 24.6g, of which sugars 7.9g; Fat 13.1g, of which saturates 5.1g; Cholesterol 15mg; Calcium 186mg; Fibre 5.0g; Sodium 170mg.

p300 Tomato Rice and Beans with Avocado Salsa Energy 530Kcal/2,236kJ; Protein 12g; Carbohydrate 90.1g, of which sugars 10.2g; Fat 16g, of which saturates 2.8g; Cholesterol 0mg; Calcium 120mg; Fibre 7.9g; Sodium 168mg.

p301 Leek, Squash and Tomato Gratin Energy 317Kcal/1,316kJ; Protein 6.7g; Carbohydrate 13g, of which sugars 11.6g; Fat 26.8g, of which saturates 11.1g; Cholesterol 41mg; Calcium 168mg; Fibre 6g; Sodium 44mg.

p302 Bean and Tomato Casserole Energy 263Kcal/1,111kJ; Protein 11.7g; Carbohydrate 34.3g, of which sugars 10.3g; Fat 9.8g, of which saturates 1.5g; Cholesterol 0mg; Calcium 91mg; Fibre 10g; Sodium 104mg.

p302 Mixed Vegetable Casserole Energy 573Kcal/2,416kJ; Protein 32.5g; Carbohydrate 81.5g, of which sugars 19.5g; Fat 15.3g, of which saturates 2.5g; Cholesterol 0mg; Calcium 250mg; Fibre 25.7g; Sodium 60mg.

p304 Spinach Plantain Rounds Energy 266Kcal/1,113kJ; Protein 5.9g; Carbohydrate 30.8g, of which sugars 7.6g; Fat 14.1g, of which saturates 3.6g; Cholesterol 65mg; Calcium 207mg; Fibre 3.6g; Sodium 205mg.

p305 Peppery Bean Salad Energy 248Kcal/1,046kJ; Protein 14.0g; Carbohydrate 35.4g, of which sugars 6.5g; Fat 6.5g, of which saturates 0.9g; Cholesterol 0mg; Calcium 122mg; Fibre 11.0g; Sodium 660mg.

p306 Avocado and Grapefruit Salad Energy 351Kcal/1,448kJ; Protein 2.5g; Carbohydrate 5.4g, of which sugars 4.0g; Fat 35.7g, of which saturates 6.4g; Cholesterol 0mg; Calcium 28mg; Fibre 4.1g; Sodium 80mg.

p307 Quinoa Salad with Citrus Dressing Energy 225Kcal/938kJ; Protein 4.1g; Carbohydrate 22.1g, of which sugars 3.1g; Fat 13.9g, of which saturates 2.1g; Cholesterol 0mg; Calcium 40mg; Fibre 3.0g; Sodium 10mg.

p308 Okra and Tomato Salad Energy 154Kcal/639kJ; Protein 3.7g; Carbohydrate 7.9g, of which sugars 6.6g; Fat 12.3g, of which saturates 1.9g; Cholesterol 0mg; Calcium 174mg; Fibre 5.2g; Sodium 15mg.

p308 Tomato, Heart of Palm and Onion Salad Energy 152Kcal/632kJ; Protein 2.8g; Carbohydrate 8.7g, of which sugars 7.7g; Fat 12.0g, of which saturates 1.8g; Cholesterol 0mg; Calcium 38mg; Fibre 3.9g; Sodium 16mg.

p310 Chayotes with Corn and Chillies Energy 324Kcal/1,345kJ; Protein 6.6g; Carbohydrate 27.5g, of which sugars 16.2g; Fat 21.6g, of which saturates 9.3g; Cholesterol 28mg; Calcium 159mg; Fibre 4.4g; Sodium 227mg.

p311 Spinach Salad Energy 181Kcal/748kJ; Protein 4.7g; Carbohydrate 4.2g, of which sugars 4.1g; Fat 16.3g, of which saturates 5.7g; Cholesterol 18mg; Calcium 209mg; Fibre 3.4g; Sodium 177mg.

p312 Baked Sweet Potato Energy 263Kcal/1,122kJ; Protein 6g; Carbohydrate 60.6g, of which sugars 21g; Fat 1.5g, of which saturates 0.5g; Cholesterol 1mg; Calcium 170mg; Fibre 7.7g; Sodium 151mg.

p313 Warm Hazelnut and Pistachio Salad Energy 380Kcal/1,587kJ; Protein 6.9g; Carbohydrate 37.4g, of which sugars 3.8g; Fat 23.6g, of which saturates 2.7g; Cholesterol 0mg; Calcium 36mg; Fibre 3.3g; Sodium 65mg.

p314 Jalapeño and Prawn Salad Energy 419Kcal/1,734kJ; Protein 25g; Carbohydrate 4.8g, of which sugars 4.4g; Fat 33.4g, of which saturates 7.6g; Cholesterol 380mg; Calcium 165mg; Fibre 1.5g; Sodium 1,591mg.

p315 Broad Bean, Mushroom and Chorizo Salad Energy 287Kcal/1,192kJ; Protein 10.7g; Carbohydrate 11g, of which sugars 2.1g; Fat 22.6g, of which saturates 5.7g; Cholesterol 26mg; Calcium 80mg; Fibre 4.7g; Sodium 384mg.

p316 Nopalitos Salad Energy 78Kcal/325kJ; Protein 1.4g; Carbohydrate 5g, of which sugars 4.5g; Fat 6g, of which saturates 0.8g; Cholesterol 0mg; Calcium 63mg; Fibre 2.4g; Sodium 51mg.

p317 Jicama, Chilli and Lime Salad Energy 24Kcal/100kJ; Protein 0.9g; Carbohydrate 4.8g, of which sugars 4.6g; Fat 0.3g, of which saturates 0g; Cholesterol 0mg; Calcium 49mg; Fibre 2.4g; Sodium 261mg.

p318 Chayote Salad Energy 126Kcal/521kJ; Protein 1.2g; Carbohydrate 4.9g, of which sugars 4.1g; Fat 11.4g, of which saturates 1.7g; Cholesterol 0mg; Calcium 36mg; Fibre 1.7g; Sodium 5mg.

p319 Caesar Salad Energy 279Kcal/1,159kJ; Protein 8.3g; Carbohydrate 14g, of which sugars 1.4g; Fat 21.5g, of which saturates 4.4g; Cholesterol 58mg; Calcium 152mg; Fibre 0.8g; Sodium 418mg.

p320 Green Bean and Chilli Pepper Salad Energy 280Kcal/1,153kJ; Protein 3.1g; Carbohydrate 9.4g, of which sugars 8.4g; Fat 25.8g, of which saturates 3.8g; Cholesterol 0mg; Calcium 55mg; Fibre 3.9g; Sodium 5mg.

p321 Mango, Tomato and Red Onion Salad Energy 93Kcal/390kJ; Protein 1.0g; Carbohydrate 10.1g, of which sugars 9.5g; Fat 5.8g, of which saturates 0.7g; Cholesterol 0mg; Calcium 17mg; Fibre 2.1g; Sodium 6mg.

p322 Peruvian Salad Energy 226Kcal/945kJ; Protein 6.2g; Carbohydrate 23.1g, of which sugars 4.6g; Fat 12.7g, of which saturates

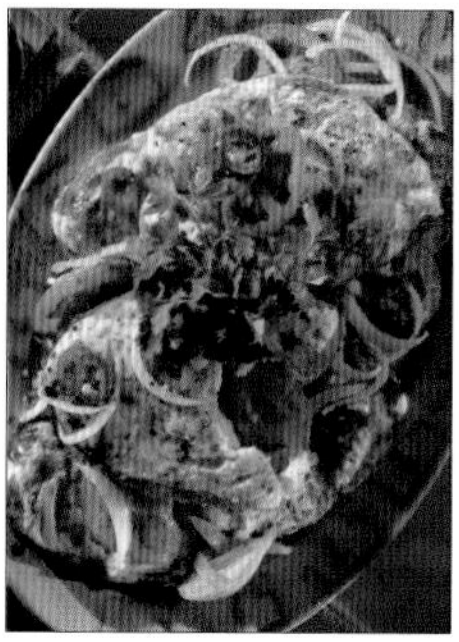

2.6g; Cholesterol 78mg; Calcium 59mg; Fibre 3.3g; Sodium 570mg.

p323 Pumpkin Salad Energy 384Kcal/1,583kJ; Protein 2.2g; Carbohydrate 8.7g, of which sugars 6.5g; Fat 38.1g, of which saturates 5.5g; Cholesterol 0mg; Calcium 84mg; Fibre 3.0g; Sodium 10mg.

p326 Plain Rice Energy 241Kcal/1,018kJ; Protein 3.7g; Carbohydrate 42.9g, of which sugars 0g; Fat 7.3g, of which saturates 1.1g; Cholesterol 0mg; Calcium 26mg; Fibre 0.2g; Sodium 0mg.

p326 Black Beans Energy 319Kcal/1,347kJ; Protein 20.7g; Carbohydrate 40.6g, of which sugars 2.2g; Fat 9.4g, of which saturates 2.4g; Cholesterol 12mg; Calcium 62mg; Fibre 6.2g; Sodium 250mg.

p328 Coconut Rice Energy 337Kcal/1,435kJ; Protein 5.5g; Carbohydrate 69.4g, of which sugars 15.8g; Fat 6.2g, of which saturates 3.1g; Cholesterol 8mg; Calcium 120mg; Fibre 0.3g; Sodium 400mg.

p329 Toasted Cassava Flour with Egg and Bacon Energy 218Kcal/918kJ; Protein 8.4g; Carbohydrate 29.2g, of which sugars 0.6g; Fat 8.3g, of which saturates 3.2g; Cholesterol 93mg; Calcium 67mg; Fibre 1.2g; Sodium 230mg.

p330 Green Rice Energy 255Kcal/1,064kJ; Protein 4.8g; Carbohydrate 44.6g, of which sugars 4.5g; Fat 6.2g, of which saturates 0.7g; Cholesterol 0mg; Calcium 40mg; Fibre 1.7g; Sodium 7mg.

p330 Yellow Rice Energy 159Kcal/662kJ; Protein 2.7g; Carbohydrate 27.9g, of which sugars 1.1g; Fat 3.9g, of which saturates 0.4g; Cholesterol 0mg; Calcium 10mg; Fibre 0.3g; Sodium 1mg.

p332 Rice and Peas Energy 449Kcal/1,903kJ; Protein 13.9g; Carbohydrate 83.3g, of which sugars 4.4g; Fat 9.1g, of which saturates 5.7g; Cholesterol 0mg; Calcium 82mg; Fibre 6.3g; Sodium 10mg.
p333 Cou-Cou Energy 264Kcal/1,115kJ; Protein 1.2g; Carbohydrate 52.7g, of which sugars 0.8g; Fat 6.8g, of which saturates 4.1g; Cholesterol 16mg; Calcium 56mg; Fibre 1.2g; Sodium 80mg.
p334 Buttered Spinach and Rice Energy 520Kcal/2,169kJ; Protein 11.5g; Carbohydrate 95.4g, of which sugars 4.6g; Fat 9.7g, of which saturates 5.3g; Cholesterol 21mg; Calcium 184mg; Fibre 2.7g; Sodium 190mg.
p334 Creamed Sweet Potatoes Energy 313Kcal/1,321kJ; Protein 4.4g; Carbohydrate 51.1g, of which sugars 13.4g; Fat 11.6g, of which saturates 6.8g; Cholesterol 27mg; Calcium 74mg; Fibre 9.6g; Sodium 170mg.
p336 Colombian Cheesy Potatoes Energy 448Kcal/1,882kJ; Protein 11.5g; Carbohydrate 55.8g, of which sugars 6.5g; Fat 21.4g, of which saturates 13g; Cholesterol 52mg; Calcium 166mg; Fibre 3.8g; Sodium 150mg.
p337 Caribbean Potato Salad Energy 167Kcal/705kJ; Protein 3.7g; Carbohydrate 30.2g, of which sugars 7.1g; Fat 4.3g, of which saturates 0.7g; Cholesterol 4mg; Calcium 24mg; Fibre 3.5g; Sodium 90mg.
p338 Potatoes with Chorizo and Green Chillies Energy 542Kcal/2,267kJ; Protein 20.9g; Carbohydrate 45.7g, of which sugars 4.9g; Fat 31.1g, of which saturates 15.9g; Cholesterol 66mg; Calcium 332mg; Fibre 3g; Sodium 905mg.
p339 Red Cauliflower Energy 63Kcal/262kJ; Protein 4.2g; Carbohydrate 4.5g, of which sugars 4g; Fat 3.2g, of which saturates 1.9g; Cholesterol 9mg; Calcium 74mg; Fibre 1.9g; Sodium 192mg.
p340 Green Lima Beans in Tomato Sauce Energy 170Kcal/714kJ; Protein 10.1g; Carbohydrate 18.7g, of which sugars 6.3g; Fat 6.6g, of which saturates 1g; Cholesterol 0mg; Calcium 80mg; Fibre 8.7g; Sodium 19mg.
p340 Green Beans with Eggs Energy 120Kcal/497kJ; Protein 6.3g;

Carbohydrate 2.4g, of which sugars 1.7g; Fat 9.4g, of which saturates 3.1g; Cholesterol 103mg; Calcium 96mg; Fibre 1.2g; Sodium 96mg.
p342 Courgettes with Cheese and Green Chillies Energy 143Kcal/587kJ; Protein 2.7g; Carbohydrate 3.3g, of which sugars 3g; Fat 13.3g, of which saturates 6.2g; Cholesterol 18mg; Calcium 47mg; Fibre 1.2g; Sodium 62mg.
p343 Courgette Torte Energy 421Kcal/1,747kJ; Protein 18.8g; Carbohydrate 13.2g, of which sugars 3.2g; Fat 32g, of which saturates 12.9g; Cholesterol 216mg; Calcium 356mg; Fibre 1.7g; Sodium 359mg.
p344 Pumpkin with Spices Energy 84Kcal/347kJ; Protein 1.2g; Carbohydrate 3.7g, of which sugars 2.9g; Fat 7.2g, of which saturates 4.5g; Cholesterol 18mg; Calcium 50mg; Fibre 1.7g; Sodium 214mg.
p345 Potato Cakes Energy 149Kcal/621kJ; Protein 4.8g; Carbohydrate 9.8g, of which sugars 0.9g; Fat 10.1g, of which saturates 3.4g; Cholesterol 30mg; Calcium 101mg; Fibre 0.8g; Sodium 197mg.
p346 Fried Plantain Energy 205Kcal/861kJ; Protein 1.2g; Carbohydrate 29.5g, of which sugars 5.8g; Fat 10g, of which saturates 5.5g; Cholesterol 21mg; Calcium 11mg; Fibre 1.3g; Sodium 65mg.
p346 Fried Potatoes Energy 186Kcal/775kJ; Protein 2.5g; Carbohydrate 19.4g, of which sugars 2.4g; Fat 11.4g, of which saturates 1.4g; Cholesterol 0mg; Calcium 14mg; Fibre 1.3g; Sodium 14mg.
P348 Potato and Onion Tortilla with Broad Beans Energy 755Kcal/3,151kJ; Protein 41.2g; Carbohydrate 59.2g, of which sugars 18.2g; Fat 40.7g, of which saturates 9g; Cholesterol 761mg; Calcium 306mg; Fibre 14.4g; Sodium 716mg.
p349 Bean Feast with Tomato and Avocado Salsa Energy 436Kcal/1,837kJ; Protein 22.8g; Carbohydrate 67.6g, of which sugars 23.7g; Fat 10g, of which saturates 1.9g; Cholesterol 0mg; Calcium 236mg; Fibre 21.8g; Sodium 1,181mg.
p350 Corn with Cream Energy 258Kcal/1,077kJ; Protein 6.7g; Carbohydrate 23.1g, of which sugars 8.8g; Fat 16.1g, of which saturates 9.6g; Cholesterol 41mg; Calcium 87mg; Fibre 1.3g; Sodium 394mg.
p351 Frijoles de Olla Energy 259Kcal/1,094kJ; Protein 17.6g; Carbohydrate 34.1g, of which sugars 6.9g; Fat 6.8g, of which saturates 3.8g; Cholesterol 18mg; Calcium 166mg; Fibre 11.7g; Sodium 207mg.
p352 Potatoes with Red Chillies Energy 101Kcal/421kJ; Protein 1.4g; Carbohydrate 11.4g, of which sugars 1.8g; Fat 5.8g, of which saturates 0.7g; Cholesterol 0mg; Calcium 20mg; Fibre 1.2g; Sodium 501mg.
p353 Corn with a Garlic Butter Crust Energy 543Kcal/2,267kJ; Protein 6.4g; Carbohydrate 50.6g, of which sugars 13.6g; Fat 36.5g, of which saturates 20.3g; Cholesterol 80mg; Calcium 42mg; Fibre 2.4g; Sodium 734mg.
p354 Vegetables in Peanut and Chilli Sauce Energy 157Kcal/656kJ; Protein 5.5g; Carbohydrate 13g, of which sugars 11.4g; Fat 9.6g, of which saturates 2.1g; Cholesterol 0mg; Calcium 110mg; Fibre 5.5g; Sodium 65mg.
p355 Chilli Courgettes Energy 97Kcal/402kJ; Protein 3.2g; Carbohydrate 6.9g, of which sugars 6.4g; Fat 6.4g, of which saturates 1g; Cholesterol 0mg; Calcium 55mg; Fibre 2.7g; Sodium 14mg.
p356 Refried Beans Energy 279Kcal/1,174kJ; Protein 16.9g; Carbohydrate 32.8g, of which sugars 5.4g; Fat 9.9g, of which saturates 4.4g; Cholesterol 15mg; Calcium 148mg; Fibre 11.3g; Sodium 197mg.
p357 Frijoles Charros Energy 504Kcal/2,098kJ; Protein 15g; Carbohydrate 33.9g, of which sugars 14.7g; Fat 34.7g, of which saturates 13.7g; Cholesterol 43mg; Calcium 112mg; Fibre 8.7g; Sodium 976mg.
p358 Okra Fried Rice Energy 305Kcal/1,286kJ; Protein 4.7g; Carbohydrate 50.6g, of which sugars 1.9g; Fat 10.7g, of which saturates 3.1g; Cholesterol 8mg; Calcium 35mg; Fibre 0.5g; Sodium 65mg.
p358 Aubergines with Garlic and Spring Onions Energy 132Kcal/551kJ; Protein 3.2g; Carbohydrate 9.3g, of which sugars 8.7g; Fat 9.5g, of which saturates 1.3g; Cholesterol 0mg; Calcium 36mg; Fibre 5.7g; Sodium 550mg.
p360 Cassava with a Citrus Salsa Energy 305Kcal/1,294kJ; Protein 3g; Carbohydrate 57.2g, of which sugars 2.2g; Fat 8.9g, of which saturates 1.4g; Cholesterol 0mg; Calcium 31mg; Fibre 2.6g; Sodium 0mg.
p361 Stir-fried Spring Greens Energy 111Kcal/459kJ; Protein 6.3g; Carbohydrate 2.5g, of which sugars 2g; Fat 8.5g, of which saturates 2.3g; Cholesterol 16mg; Calcium 159mg; Fibre 2.6g; Sodium 330mg.
p362 Corn Sticks Energy 64Kcal/272kJ; Protein 1.4g; Carbohydrate 11.7g, of which sugars 1.9g; Fat 1.7g, of which saturates 0.9g; Cholesterol 15mg; Calcium 36mg; Fibre 0.2g; Sodium 160mg.
p363 Mushrooms with Chipotle Chillies Energy 84Kcal/346kJ; Protein 1.7g; Carbohydrate 1.9g, of which sugars 1.4g; Fat 7.8g, of which saturates 1.2g; Cholesterol 0mg; Calcium 9mg; Fibre 1.4g; Sodium 5mg.
p366 Argentinian Barbecue Salsa Energy 132Kcal/543kJ; Protein 0.7g; Carbohydrate 3.2g, of which sugars 2.6g; Fat 13g, of which saturates 1.9g; Cholesterol 0mg; Calcium 10mg; Fibre 0.8g; Sodium 0mg.
p366 Hot Chilli Salsa Energy 441Kcal/1,820kJ; Protein 3.8g; Carbohydrate 5.8g, of which sugars 5.8g; Fat 45g, of which saturates 6.4g; Cholesterol 0mg; Calcium 40mg; Fibre 1.5g; Sodium 20mg.
p368 Green Tomatillo Sauce Energy 42Kcal/174kJ; Protein 0.9g; Carbohydrate 2.7g, of which sugars 2.6g; Fat 3.1g, of which saturates 0.4g; Cholesterol 0mg; Calcium 30mg; Fibre 1.4g; Sodium 11mg.
p369 Guacamole Energy 262Kcal/1,083kJ; Protein 3.2g; Carbohydrate 5g, of which sugars 3g;

Fat 25.4g, of which saturates 5.4g; Cholesterol 0mg; Calcium 37mg; Fibre 5.5g; Sodium 15mg.
p370 Pinto Bean Salsa Energy 103Kcal/438kJ; Protein 8.1g; Carbohydrate 17.2g, of which sugars 3.3g; Fat 0.7g, of which saturates 0.1g; Cholesterol 0mg; Calcium 44mg; Fibre 5.8g; Sodium 12mg.
p371 Black Bean Salsa Energy 129Kcal/544kJ; Protein 8g; Carbohydrate 17.6g, of which sugars 3.2g; Fat 3.5g, of which saturates 0.5g; Cholesterol 0mg; Calcium 67mg; Fibre 6.3g; Sodium 11mg.
p372 Chipotle Sauce Energy 63Kcal/265kJ; Protein 1g; Carbohydrate 10.4g, of which sugars 10.4g; Fat 0.3g, of which saturates 0.1g; Cholesterol 0mg; Calcium 12mg; Fibre 0.8g; Sodium 11mg.
p372 Guajillo Chilli Sauce Energy 43Kcal/181kJ; Protein 1.6g; Carbohydrate 8.3g, of which sugars 8g; Fat 0.6g, of which saturates 0.2g; Cholesterol 0mg; Calcium 15mg; Fibre 1.9g; Sodium 9mg.
p374 Roasted Tomato Salsa Energy 54Kcal/226kJ; Protein 0.8g; Carbohydrate 4.2g, of which sugars 3.7g; Fat 4g, of which saturates 0.6g; Cholesterol 0mg; Calcium 11mg; Fibre 1.1g; Sodium 8mg.
p376 Tamarillo Sauce Energy 112Kcal/468kJ; Protein 0.7g; Carbohydrate 15.5g, of which sugars 15.2g; Fat 5.7g, of which saturates 0.8g; Cholesterol 0mg; Calcium 9mg; Fibre 2.2g; Sodium 0mg.
p377 Avocado Salsa Energy 190Kcal/786kJ; Protein 1.9g; Carbohydrate 5.6g, of which sugars 4g; Fat 18g, of which saturates 3.2g; Cholesterol 0mg; Calcium 20mg; Fibre 3g; Sodium 10mg.
p378 Jicama Salsa Energy 69Kcal/291kJ; Protein 2.4g; Carbohydrate 14.9g, of which sugars 14.3g; Fat 0.5g, of which saturates 0g; Cholesterol 0mg; Calcium 106mg; Fibre 4.7g; Sodium 23mg.
p379 Sweet Potato Salsa Energy 154Kcal/657kJ; Protein 2.3g; Carbohydrate 37.4g, of which sugars 11g; Fat 0.6g, of which saturates 0.2g; Cholesterol 0mg; Calcium 46mg; Fibre 4.2g; Sodium 70mg.
p380 Nopales Salsa Energy 16Kcal/67kJ; Protein 0.8g; Carbohydrate 2.8g, of which sugars 2.4g; Fat 0.3g, of which saturates 0g; Cholesterol 0mg; Calcium 34mg; Fibre 1.3g; Sodium 286mg.
p382 Chilli Bean Dip Energy 240Kcal/1,002kJ; Protein 12.3g; Carbohydrate 20.3g, of which sugars 5.4g; Fat 12.3g, of which saturates 4.8g; Cholesterol 18mg; Calcium 219mg; Fibre 6.6g; Sodium 527mg.
p383 Piquant Pineapple Relish Energy 81Kcal/343kJ; Protein 0.7g; Carbohydrate 20.5g, of which sugars 20.4g; Fat 0.1g, of which saturates 0g; Cholesterol 0mg; Calcium 26mg; Fibre 0.9g; Sodium 4mg.
p384 Mango Salsa Energy 56Kcal/239kJ; Protein 1.2g; Carbohydrate 12.9g, of which sugars 12g; Fat 0.4g, of which saturates 0.1g; Cholesterol 0mg; Calcium 40mg; Fibre 2.9g; Sodium 7mg.
p384 Roasted Tomato and Coriander Salsa Energy 21Kcal/88kJ; Protein 1g; Carbohydrate 3.6g, of which sugars 3.3g; Fat 0.4g, of which saturates 0.1g; Cholesterol 0mg; Calcium 25mg; Fibre 1.4g; Sodium 11mg.
p386 Chayote Salsa Energy 25Kcal/107kJ; Protein 0.6g; Carbohydrate 5.6g, of which sugars 5.4g; Fat 0.2g, of which saturates 0g; Cholesterol 0mg; Calcium 21mg; Fibre 0.7g; Sodium 188mg.
p387 Pumpkin Seed Sauce Energy 237Kcal/986kJ; Protein 7.6g; Carbohydrate 10g, of which sugars 4.5g; Fat 18.6g, of which saturates 1.9g; Cholesterol 0mg; Calcium 48mg; Fibre 3.2g; Sodium 13mg.
p388 Fiery Citrus Salsa Energy 18Kcal/75kJ; Protein 0.4g; Carbohydrate 4.1g, of which sugars 4.1g; Fat 0.1g, of which saturates 0g;

Cholesterol 0mg; Calcium 18mg; Fibre 0.8g; Sodium 2mg.
p389 Grilled Corn-on-the-Cob Salsa Energy 224Kcal/945kJ; Protein 4.7g; Carbohydrate 37g, of which sugars 15.7g; Fat 7.4g, of which saturates 1.2g; Cholesterol 0mg; Calcium 20mg; Fibre 3.1g; Sodium 348mg.
p390 Orange, Tomato and Chive Salsa Energy 101Kcal/423kJ; Protein 1.9g; Carbohydrate 10.8g, of which sugars 10.8g; Fat 5.9g, of which saturates 0.8g; Cholesterol 0mg; Calcium 78mg; Fibre 2.9g; Sodium 14mg.
p391 Sour Cream Dip Energy 202Kcal/838kJ; Protein 4.1g; Carbohydrate 11.8g, of which sugars 11.5g; Fat 15.7g, of which saturates 9.6g; Cholesterol 45mg; Calcium 104mg; Fibre 2.9g; Sodium 47mg.
p392 Chilli Strips with Lime Energy 45Kcal/189kJ; Protein 3.8g; Carbohydrate 6.2g, of which sugars 4.9g; Fat 0.7g, of which saturates 0g; Cholesterol 0mg; Calcium 49mg; Fibre 0.9g; Sodium 9mg.
p393 Onion Relish Energy 151Kcal/629kJ; Protein 5.8g; Carbohydrate 31.8g, of which sugars 22.6g; Fat 1g, of which saturates 0g; Cholesterol 0mg; Calcium 111mg; Fibre 5.6g; Sodium 14mg.
p394 Habeñero Salsa Energy 62Kcal/259kJ; Protein 5.3g; Carbohydrate 7.4g, of which sugars 7.1g; Fat 1.5g, of which saturates 0g; Cholesterol 0mg; Calcium 147mg; Fibre 3g; Sodium 31mg.
p395 Adobo Seasoning Energy 10Kcal/41kJ; Protein 0.9g; Carbohydrate 1.4g, of which sugars 0.2g; Fat 0.1g, of which saturates 0g; Cholesterol 0mg; Calcium 4mg; Fibre 0.3g; Sodium 165mg.
p396 Red Rub Energy 11Kcal/48kJ; Protein 0.3g; Carbohydrate 2.6g, of which sugars 2.6g; Fat 0g, of which saturates 0g; Cholesterol 0mg; Calcium 14mg; Fibre 0.5g; Sodium 2mg.
p396 Red Salsa Energy 195Kcal/818kJ; Protein 2.6g; Carbohydrate 20.6g, of which sugars 20.6g; Fat 12g, of which saturates 1.9g; Cholesterol 0mg; Calcium 35mg; Fibre 3.3g; Sodium 29mg.
p400 Corn Tortillas Energy 70Kcal/296kJ; Protein 0.1g; Carbohydrate 18.1g, of which sugars 0g; Fat 0.1g, of which saturates 0g; Cholesterol 0mg; Calcium 3mg; Fibre 0g; Sodium 10mg.
p401 Flour Tortillas Energy 64Kcal/272kJ; Protein 1.5g; Carbohydrate 12.5g, of which sugars 0.2g; Fat 1.3g, of which saturates 0.5g; Cholesterol 1mg; Calcium 23mg; Fibre 0.5g; Sodium 140mg.
p402 Dhal Puri Energy 237Kcal/1,004kJ; Protein 9.2g; Carbohydrate 40.8g, of which sugars 1.1g; Fat 5.2g, of which saturates 0.6g; Cholesterol 0mg; Calcium 120mg; Fibre 2.8g; Sodium 120mg.
p403 Fried Dumplins Energy 205Kcal/868kJ; Protein 5g; Carbohydrate 36.3g, of which sugars 2.8g; Fat 5.4g, of which saturates 0.9g; Cholesterol 2mg; Calcium 194mg; Fibre 1.4g; Sodium 270mg.
p404 Corn Griddle Cakes Energy 87Kcal/366kJ; Protein 2.2g; Carbohydrate 12.5g, of which sugars 0.2g; Fat 3.5g, of which saturates 1.9g; Cholesterol 9mg; Calcium 50mg; Fibre 0g; Sodium 260mg.
p406 Paraguayan Corn Bread Energy 232Kcal/971kJ; Protein 6.0g; Carbohydrate 24.7g, of which sugars 3.4g; Fat 12.8g, of which saturates 7.6g; Cholesterol 80mg; Calcium 128mg; Fibre 0.3g; Sodium 340mg.
p407 Mexican "Bread of the Dead" (per loaf) Energy 4,071Kcal/1,7154kJ; Protein 86.6g; Carbohydrate 660.6g, of which sugars 146.2g; Fat 123.5g, of which saturates 67g; Cholesterol 949mg; Calcium 1,080mg; Fibre 20.9g; Sodium 2.9g
p408 Mango Tea Bread (per loaf) Energy 2,109Kcal/8,815kJ; Protein 27.1g; Carbohydrate 227.4g, of which sugars 118.6g; Fat 127.8g, of which saturates 31.7g; Cholesterol 285mg; Calcium 320mg; Fibre 13.3g; Sodium 1,100mg.
p408 Courgette Tea Bread (per loaf) Energy 5,232Kcal/21,854kJ; Protein 68g; Carbohydrate 543.4g, of which sugars 324.5g; Fat 325g, of which saturates 61.5g; Cholesterol 688mg; Calcium 813mg; Fibre 14.7g; Sodium 1,562mg.
p410 Buñuelos Energy 203Kcal/848kJ; Protein 2.8g; Carbohydrate 25.1g, of which sugars 10.8g; Fat 10.8g, of which saturates 3.2g; Cholesterol 29mg; Calcium 47mg; Fibre 0.6g; Sodium 38mg.
p412 Garbanzo Cake Energy

277Kcal/1,172kJ; Protein 9.2g; Carbohydrate 50.7g, of which sugars 40.2g; Fat 5.7g, of which saturates 1.2g; Cholesterol 127mg; Calcium 68mg; Fibre 2.7g; Sodium 197mg.

p413 Pecan Cake Energy 421Kcal/1,755kJ; Protein 5.6g; Carbohydrate 34.7g, of which sugars 27.4g; Fat 29.9g, of which saturates 12.4g; Cholesterol 139mg; Calcium 48mg; Fibre 1g; Sodium 163mg.

p414 Caribbean Fruit and Rum Cake (per cake) Energy 10,871Kcal/45,678kJ; Protein 146.1g; Carbohydrate 1,526.5g, of which sugars 1,192.2g; Fat 448g, of which saturates 254.6g; Cholesterol 3.3g; Calcium 2,987mg; Fibre 49.8g; Sodium 5.92g.

p415 Apple and Cinnamon Crumble Cake (per cake) Energy 7,217Kcal/30,269kJ; Protein 89.9g; Carbohydrate 929.9g, of which sugars 500.3g; Fat 374.7g, of which saturates 233.7g; Cholesterol 1.7g; Calcium 2,062mg; Fibre 34.1g; Sodium 4.22g.

p416 Banana and Pecan Bread (per loaf) Energy 3,277Kcal/13,745kJ; Protein 52.8g; Carbohydrate 413.7g, of which sugars 239.9g; Fat 168.2g, of which saturates 69.2g; Cholesterol 1,263mg; Calcium 1,056mg; Fibre 13.1g; Sodium 1,701mg.

p417 Pumpkin and Walnut Bread (per loaf) Energy 2,663Kcal/11,186kJ; Protein 66.8g; Carbohydrate 364.1g, of which sugars 94.4g; Fat 114.7g, of which saturates 36.1g; Cholesterol 677mg; Calcium 840mg; Fibre 18.5g; Sodium 1,516mg.

p418 Nutty Chocolate Squares Energy 180Kcal/749kJ; Protein 2.6g; Carbohydrate 16.1g, of which sugars 13.3g; Fat 12.1g, of which saturates 3.2g; Cholesterol 31mg; Calcium 30mg; Fibre 0.7g; Sodium 52mg.

p419 Pecan Squares Energy 245Kcal/1,016kJ; Protein 2.1g; Carbohydrate 15.5g, of which sugars 10.5g; Fat 19.8g, of which saturates 7.6g; Cholesterol 33mg; Calcium 26mg; Fibre 0.8g; Sodium 71mg.

p420 Barbadian Coconut Sweet Bread (per cake) Energy 4,078Kcal/17,076kJ; Protein 59.2g; Carbohydrate 473.7g, of which sugars 154.2g; Fat 229.5g, of which saturates 156.9g; Cholesterol 609mg; Calcium 1,373mg; Fibre 28.9g; Sodium 2.06g.

p421 Duckanoo Energy 827Kcal/3,499kJ; Protein 7.3g; Carbohydrate 161.4g, of which sugars 57.9g; Fat 21.5g, of which saturates 15g; Cholesterol 36mg; Calcium 224mg; Fibre 2.4g; Sodium 220mg.

p422 Cornmeal and Fennel Seed Cake Energy 514Kcal/2,170kJ; Protein 10.4g; Carbohydrate 94.7g, of which sugars 38.2g; Fat 12.9g, of which saturates 6.3g; Cholesterol 179mg; Calcium 163mg; Fibre 1.1g; Sodium 630mg.

p422 Banana Bread (per loaf) Energy 2,444Kcal/10,218kJ; Protein 41.4g; Carbohydrate 259.4g, of which sugars 124.4g; Fat 144.9g, of which saturates 67.1g; Cholesterol 714mg; Calcium 782mg; Fibre 9.4g; Sodium 1.5g.

p424 Kings' Day Bread Energy 444Kcal/1,868kJ; Protein 8.3g; Carbohydrate 65g, of which sugars 38.8g; Fat 18.7g, of which saturates 10g; Cholesterol 178mg; Calcium 122mg; Fibre 2.4g; Sodium 344mg.

p426 Pan Dulce Energy 366Kcal/1,538kJ; Protein 7.3g; Carbohydrate 53.7g, of which sugars 17.8g; Fat 15.1g, of which saturates 8.4g; Cholesterol 112mg; Calcium 100mg; Fibre 1.5g; Sodium 119mg.

p427 Almond Biscuits Energy 93Kcal/391kJ; Protein 1g; Carbohydrate 11.5g, of which sugars 7.8g; Fat 5.2g, of which saturates 2.6g; Cholesterol 10mg; Calcium 16mg; Fibre 0.3g; Sodium 30mg.

p430 Fruits of the Tropics Salad Energy 154Kcal/658kJ; Protein 1.3g; Carbohydrate 39.0g, of which sugars 38.1g; Fat 0.4g, of which saturates 0.1g; Cholesterol 0mg; Calcium 31mg; Fibre 4.1g; Sodium 40mg.

p431 Coconut Ice Cream Energy 253Kcal/1,065kJ; Protein 8.6g; Carbohydrate 34.5g, of which sugars 34.5g; Fat 9.9g, of which saturates 6.2g; Cholesterol 35mg; Calcium 305mg; Fibre 0g; Sodium 220mg.

p432 Mango Sorbet Energy 176Kcal/753kJ; Protein 1g; Carbohydrate 45.6g, of which sugars 45.4g; Fat 0.2g, of which saturates 0.1g; Cholesterol 0mg; Calcium 13mg; Fibre 2g; Sodium 10mg.

p433 Colombian Pineapple Custard Energy 214Kcal/908kJ; Protein 5.3g; Carbohydrate 40.5g, of which sugars 40.5g; Fat 4.6g, of which saturates 1.3g; Cholesterol 156mg; Calcium 38mg; Fibre 0.7g; Sodium 60mg.

p434 Churros Energy 101Kcal/421kJ; Protein 1.6g; Carbohydrate 12.4g, of which sugars 1.3g; Fat 5.3g, of which saturates 0.7g; Cholesterol 17mg; Calcium 23mg; Fibre 0.5g; Sodium 42mg.

p434 Sopaipillas Energy 77Kcal/319kJ; Protein 0.7g; Carbohydrate 5.8g, of which sugars 0.1g; Fat 5.8g, of which saturates 0.6g; Cholesterol 0mg; Calcium 11mg; Fibre 0.2g; Sodium 72mg.

p436 Coconut Cream Tart Energy 420Kcal/1,751kJ; Protein 6.3g; Carbohydrate 37g, of which sugars 23.6g; Fat 28.5g, of which saturates 19.1g; Cholesterol 87mg; Calcium 144mg; Fibre 2.9g; Sodium 101mg.

p437 Lemon Coconut Layer Cake Energy 727Kcal/3,044kJ; Protein 9.7g; Carbohydrate 86.1g, of which sugars 65.9g; Fat 40.7g, of which saturates 27g; Cholesterol 244mg; Calcium 96mg; Fibre 3.7g; Sodium 236mg.

p438 Caramel Custard Energy 341Kcal/1,444kJ; Protein 12.2g; Carbohydrate 58.4g, of which sugars 58.4g; Fat 8.4g, of which saturates 3.3g; Cholesterol 200mg; Calcium 254mg; Fibre 0g; Sodium 145mg.

p440 Cold Mango Soufflé Topped with Toasted Coconut Energy 615Kcal/2,566kJ; Protein 4.9g; Carbohydrate 53.9g, of which sugars 53.4g; Fat 43.8g, of which saturates 26.3g; Cholesterol 205mg; Calcium 118mg; Fibre 3.9g; Sodium 39mg.

p441 Almond Pudding with Custard Energy 407Kcal/1,708kJ; Protein 9.1g; Carbohydrate 49.6g, of which sugars 49.6g; Fat 20.7g, of which saturates 11.2g; Cholesterol 234mg; Calcium 123mg; Fibre 0g; Sodium 96mg.

p442 Tapioca Pudding Energy 190Kcal/799kJ; Protein 6.1g; Carbohydrate 25.2g, of which sugars 13.8g; Fat 7.9g, of which saturates 3.7g; Cholesterol 18mg; Calcium 156mg; Fibre 0.2g; Sodium 70mg.

p443 Fried Bananas with Sugar and Rum Energy 290Kcal/1,213kJ; Protein 1.3g; Carbohydrate 36.4g, of which sugars 34.1g; Fat 13.7g, of which saturates 8.6g; Cholesterol 35mg; Calcium 10mg; Fibre 1.1g; Sodium 100mg.

p444 Coconut and Pumpkin Compote Energy 429Kcal/1,811kJ; Protein 2g; Carbohydrate 82.9g, of which sugars 82.2g; Fat 12.2g, of which saturates 10.4g; Cholesterol 0mg; Calcium 51mg; Fibre 4g; Sodium 100mg.

p444 Dulce de Leche Energy 323Kcal/1,357kJ; Protein 11.3g; Carbohydrate 42.7g, of which sugars 42.7g; Fat 13g, of which saturates 8.1g; Cholesterol 47mg; Calcium 387mg; Fibre 0g; Sodium 210mg.

p446 Pumpkin in Brown Sugar Energy 247Kcal/1,054kJ; Protein 1.2g; Carbohydrate 63.9g, of which sugars 63.2g; Fat 0.3g, of which saturates 0.1g; Cholesterol 0mg; Calcium 70mg; Fibre 1.3g; Sodium 4mg.

p447 Coconut Custard Energy 593Kcal/2,474kJ; Protein 12.6g; Carbohydrate 48.3g, of which sugars 48.1g; Fat 40.3g, of which saturates 25.7g; Cholesterol 165mg; Calcium 233mg; Fibre 4.6g; Sodium 119mg.

p448 Fruit Platter Energy 235Kcal/999kJ; Protein 3.3g; Carbohydrate 47.8g, of which sugars 42.8g; Fat 4.8g, of which saturates 0.2g; Cholesterol 0mg; Calcium 84mg; Fibre 6.5g; Sodium 90mg.

p448 Ice Cream with Mexican Chocolate Energy 823Kcal/3,420kJ; Protein 8.6g; Carbohydrate 52.4g, of which sugars 52.1g; Fat 65.9g, of which saturates 39.7g; Cholesterol 256mg; Calcium 151mg; Fibre 0.7g; Sodium 89mg.

p450 Capirotada Energy 555Kcal/2,332kJ; Protein 12.5g; Carbohydrate 72.6g, of which sugars 45.6g; Fat 24.5g, of which saturates 11.4g; Cholesterol 45mg; Calcium 258mg; Fibre 2.4g; Sodium 534mg.

p450 Drunken Plantain Energy 244Kcal/1,021kJ; Protein 2.6g; Carbohydrate 29.7g, of which sugars 13.6g; Fat 11.7g, of which saturates 4.8g; Cholesterol 18mg; Calcium 33mg; Fibre 1.5g; Sodium 56mg.

p452 Caribbean Spiced Rice Pudding Energy 304Kcal/1,288kJ; Protein 8.6g; Carbohydrate 53.9g, of which sugars 37.4g; Fat 7.6g, of which saturates 4.5g; Cholesterol 20mg; Calcium 266mg; Fibre 0.4g; Sodium

110mg.
p453 Jamaican Fruit Trifle Energy 400Kcal/1,664kJ; Protein 2.2g; Carbohydrate 29.1g, of which sugars 28.9g; Fat 30.4g, of which saturates 19.4g; Cholesterol 80mg; Calcium 70mg; Fibre 3.9g; Sodium 20mg.
p454 Brazilian Coconut Flan Energy 334Kcal/1,398kJ; Protein 5.6g; Carbohydrate 36.6g, of which sugars 36.6g; Fat 19.4g, of which saturates 11.2g; Cholesterol 312mg; Calcium 62mg; Fibre 1.7g; Sodium 50mg.
p456 Mexican Wedding Cookies Energy 147Kcal/615kJ; Protein 1.5g; Carbohydrate 14.2g, of which sugars 6.5g; Fat 9.8g, of which saturates 4.2g; Cholesterol 16mg; Calcium 22mg; Fibre 0.5g; Sodium 46mg.
p456 Almond Orange Biscuits Energy 148Kcal/617kJ; Protein 2.3g; Carbohydrate 12.1g, of which sugars 5.6g; Fat 10.4g, of which saturates 3.1g; Cholesterol 17mg; Calcium 29mg; Fibre 0.7g; Sodium 6mg.
p458 Rum and Banana Waffles Energy 826Kcal/3,466kJ; Protein 17.4g; Carbohydrate 106.8g, of which sugars 60.7g; Fat 36.9g, of which saturates 10.6g; Cholesterol 148mg; Calcium 275mg; Fibre 4.4g; Sodium 223mg.
p460 Fruit-filled Empanadas Energy 256Kcal/1,078kJ; Protein 3.3g; Carbohydrate 43.6g, of which sugars 18.2g; Fat 8.8g, of which saturates 5.2g; Cholesterol 37mg; Calcium 49mg; Fibre 1.5g; Sodium 73mg.
P461 Christmas Cookies with Walnuts Energy 148Kcal/617kJ; Protein 2.3g; Carbohydrate 12.1g, of which sugars 5.6g; Fat 10.4g, of which saturates 3.1g; Cholesterol 17mg; Calcium 29mg; Fibre 0.7g; Sodium 6mg.
p462 Nut Brittle Energy 239Kcal/1,005kJ; Protein 6.5g; Carbohydrate 29.3g, of which sugars 27.2g; Fat 11.5g, of which saturates 2.2g; Cholesterol 00mg; Calcium 22mg; Fibre 1.5g; Sodium 2mg.
p462 Coconut Sweets Energy 40Kcal/168kJ; Protein 0.1g; Carbohydrate 7.4g, of which sugars 7.4g; Fat 1.2g, of which saturates 1.1g; Cholesterol 0mg; Calcium 3mg; Fibre 0.3g; Sodium 1mg.
p466 Mango Shake Energy 667Kcal/2,793kJ; Protein 26.9g; Carbohydrate 76.2g, of which sugars 75.3g; Fat 29.9g, of which saturates 19.1g; Cholesterol 105mg; Calcium 922mg; Fibre 7.8g; Sodium 330mg.
p466 Pineapple and Mint Juice Energy 113Kcal/485kJ; Protein 2g; Carbohydrate 26.6g, of which sugars 25.3g; Fat 0.7g, of which saturates 0g; Cholesterol 0mg; Calcium 98mg; Fibre 3g; Sodium 10mg.
p468 Cashew Nut Milk Energy 805Kcal/3,397kJ; Protein 29.4g; Carbohydrate 136.6g, of which sugars 133g; Fat 19.2g, of which saturates 2.4g; Cholesterol 0mg; Calcium 192mg; Fibre 2.4g; Sodium 390mg.
p469 Passion Fruit Batida Energy 151Kcal/631kJ; Protein 0.8g; Carbohydrate 9.6g, of which sugars 9.6g; Fat 0.1g, of which saturates 0g; Cholesterol 0mg; Calcium 4mg; Fibre 1g; Sodium 10mg.
p470 Citrus Agua Fresca Energy 106Kcal/452kJ; Protein 0.6g; Carbohydrate 27.5g, of which sugars 27.5g; Fat 0.1g, of which saturates 0g; Cholesterol 0mg; Calcium 23mg; Fibre 0.1g; Sodium 9mg.
p471 Tamarind Agua Fresca Energy 68Kcal/287kJ; Protein 2.9g; Carbohydrate 14.5g, of which sugars 14.5g; Fat 0.2g, of which saturates 0g; Cholesterol 0mg; Calcium 23mg; Fibre 1.6g; Sodium 136mg.
p472 Pineapple and Lime Agua Fresca Energy 131Kcal/564kJ; Protein 0.7g; Carbohydrate 34.1g, of which sugars 34.1g; Fat 0.2g, of which saturates 0g; Cholesterol 0mg; Calcium 23mg; Fibre 0g; Sodium 17mg.
p473 Lime Agua Fresca Energy 52Kcal/221kJ; Protein 0.2g; Carbohydrate 13.6g, of which sugars 13.6g; Fat 0g, of which saturates 0g; Cholesterol 0mg; Calcium 9mg; Fibre 0g; Sodium 1mg.
p474 Pisco Sour Energy 187Kcal/783kJ; Protein 2.9g; Carbohydrate 15.8g, of which sugars 15.8g; Fat 0g, of which saturates 0g; Cholesterol 0mg; Calcium 3mg; Fibre 0g; Sodium 60mg.
p474 Caipirinha Energy 176Kcal/736kJ; Protein 0g; Carbohydrate 15.8g, of which sugars 15.8g; Fat 0g, of which saturates 0g; Cholesterol 0mg; Calcium 2mg; Fibre 0g; Sodium 0mg.
p476 Tequila Energy 111Kcal/460kJ; Protein 0g; Carbohydrate 2g, of which sugars 1.5g; Fat 0g, of which saturates 0g; Cholesterol 0mg; Calcium 0mg; Fibre 0g; Sodium 0mg.
p477 Tequila Sunrise Energy 90Kcal/377kJ; Protein 0.3g; Carbohydrate 6.9g, of which sugars 6.9g; Fat 0.1g, of which saturates 0g; Cholesterol 0mg; Calcium 6mg; Fibre 0.1g; Sodium 7mg.

p478 Pineapple Tequila Energy 403Kcal/1,672kJ; Protein 0.1g; Carbohydrate 8.7g, of which sugars 8.7g; Fat 0g, of which saturates 0g; Cholesterol 0mg; Calcium 5mg; Fibre 0g; Sodium 1mg.
p479 Margarita Energy 167Kcal/696kJ; Protein 0.1g; Carbohydrate 8.6g, of which sugars 8.6g; Fat 0g, of which saturates 0g; Cholesterol 0mg; Calcium 3mg; Fibre 0g; Sodium 3mg.
p480 Mango and Peach Margarita Energy 167Kcal/704kJ; Protein 1.1g; Carbohydrate 19.7g, of which sugars 19.5g; Fat 0.2g, of which saturates 0.1g; Cholesterol 0mg; Calcium 15mg; Fibre 2.8g; Sodium 4mg.
p481 Licuado de Melon Energy 37Kcal/157kJ; Protein 0.2g; Carbohydrate 9.5g, of which sugars 9.5g; Fat 0.1g, of which saturates 0g; Cholesterol 0mg; Calcium 3mg; Fibre 0g; Sodium 2mg.
p482 Mojito Energy 226Kcal/941kJ; Protein 0g; Carbohydrate 15.8g, of which sugars 15.8g; Fat 0g, of which saturates 0g; Cholesterol 0mg; Calcium 2mg; Fibre 0g; Sodium 0mg.
p482 Cubra Libre Energy 130Kcal/542kJ; Protein 0g; Carbohydrate 8.1g, of which sugars 8.1g; Fat 0g, of which saturates 0g; Cholesterol 0mg; Calcium 4mg; Fibre 0g; Sodium 0mg.
p484 Strawberry and Banana Prepado Energy 341Kcal/1,413kJ; Protein 2.6g; Carbohydrate 14.3g, of which sugars 13.4g; Fat 20g, of which saturates 17.1g; Cholesterol 0mg; Calcium 17mg; Fibre 1g; Sodium 12mg.
p485 Bloody Maria Energy 84Kcal/353kJ; Protein 1g; Carbohydrate 3.8g, of which sugars 3.8g; Fat 0g, of which saturates 0g; Cholesterol 0mg; Calcium 13mg; Fibre 0.8g; Sodium 288mg.
p486 Sangrita Energy 73Kcal/305kJ; Protein 0.6g; Carbohydrate 3.7g, of which sugars 3.5g; Fat 0.2g, of which saturates 0.1g; Cholesterol 0mg; Calcium 7mg; Fibre 0.7g; Sodium 7mg.
p487 Sangria Energy 170Kcal/708kJ; Protein 0.3g; Carbohydrate 10.7g, of which sugars 10.7g; Fat 0g, of which saturates 0g; Cholesterol 0mg; Calcium 15mg; Fibre 0g; Sodium 11mg.
p488 Demerara Rum Punch Energy 237Kcal/993kJ; Protein 1.4g; Carbohydrate 24.1g, of which sugars 24.1g; Fat 0.3g, of which saturates 0g; Cholesterol 0g; Calcium 20mg; Fibre 0mg; Sodium 10mg.
p489 Caribbean Cream Stout Punch Energy 466Kcal/1,950kJ; Protein 16.8g; Carbohydrate 37.7g, of which sugars 37.7g; Fat 17.9g, of which saturates 11.2g; Cholesterol 65mg; Calcium 556mg; Fibre 0g; Sodium 340mg.
p490 Cafe con Leche Energy 79Kcal/337kJ; Protein 4.1g; Carbohydrate 12.1g, of which sugars 12.1g; Fat 2g, of which saturates 1.3g; Cholesterol 7mg; Calcium 146mg; Fibre 0g; Sodium 52mg.
p490 Horchata Energy 683Kcal/2,850kJ; Protein 16.3g; Carbohydrate 105.4g, of which sugars 14.6g; Fat 21.5g, of which saturates 1.7g; Cholesterol 0mg; Calcium 118mg; Fibre 2.8g; Sodium 6mg.
p492 Cafe de Olla Energy 118Kcal/503kJ; Protein 1.1g; Carbohydrate 30.3g, of which sugars 30.1g; Fat 0g, of which saturates 0g; Cholesterol 0mg; Calcium 24mg; Fibre 0g; Sodium 7mg.
p492 Atole Energy 161Kcal/675kJ; Protein 3.3g; Carbohydrate 34.2g, of which sugars 9.9g; Fat 1.1g, of which saturates 0g; Cholesterol 0mg; Calcium 9mg; Fibre 1g; Sodium 2mg.
p494 Champurrada Energy 240Kcal/1,007kJ; Protein 4.1g; Carbohydrate 41.8g, of which sugars 17.2g; Fat 6.5g, of which saturates 3.2g; Cholesterol 1mg; Calcium 10mg; Fibre 1.2g; Sodium 2mg.
p495 Mexican Hot Chocolate Energy 179Kcal/755kJ; Protein 9.1g; Carbohydrate 19.7g, of which sugars 19.6g; Fat 7.8g, of which saturates 4.8g; Cholesterol 16mg; Calcium 304mg; Fibre 0.3g; Sodium 108mg.

INDEX

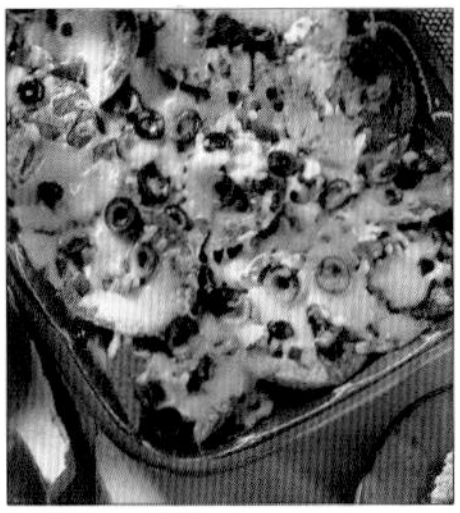

N

O

P

T

U

V

W

Y